THE LONDON MARATHON

Chris Brasher

portrait by
Snowdon

THE LONDON MARATHON

Foreword by
Lord Snowdon

Queen Anne Press

with the support of the makers of NutraSweet[®]
and in aid of the Snowdon Award Scheme

First published in 1993 by
Queen Anne Press
a division of Lennard Associates Ltd
Mackerye End
Harpenden
Herts AL5 5DR

© Lennard Associates Ltd 1993

ISBN 1 85291 529 3

British Library Cataloguing in Publication Data
is available

Design by COOPER-WILSON

Printed and bound in Great Britain by
Butler & Tanner Ltd, Frome and London

NutraSweet and the NutraSweet symbol
are registered trademarks of The NutraSweet Company

CONTENTS

Foreword by Lord Snowdon   7

The Story of the London Marathon   9
by Patrick Collins

The 1993 NutraSweet London Marathon   37
captions by Nigel Dempster

The Finishers and their Times   121

SNOWDON AWARD SCHEME

The Snowdon Award Scheme was created in 1981 by Lord Snowdon, who contributed the initial £14,000 out of fees received from photographs of the Royal Family, which he had accumulated in a trust fund. The aim of the Scheme is to help physically disabled students to meet the additional costs of studying in further education or training.

So far 400 students have received awards of up to £1,500 per year for electrical wheelchairs, computers, Braille machines, readers or sign language interpreters, travel costs and many other forms of help, totalling £380,000.

The 1993 NutraSweet London Marathon gave the Snowdon Award Scheme the opportunity to raise a significant amount more capital, which will enable the Scheme to provide help for a greater number of students in the future.

FOREWORD

Thanks to Christopher Brasher and his team of enthusiastic supporters, the London Marathon has captivated the imagination of the entire country.

Coincidentally, the first race was in 1981, the International Year of Disabled People (of which I had the honour to be President for England). So it gave me particular pleasure to be asked by NutraSweet, the sponsor of the l993 NutraSweet London Marathon, to start the wheelchair race, where the ability and stoic determination of every entrant was universally admired. NutraSweet also nominated my Award Scheme, which benefits further education for physically disabled students, as their charity for the 1993 race.

The scale of the event is gigantic, and I have seldom experienced such patriotism and enjoyment shown by competitors and onlookers alike.

This book, *The London Marathon*, with over 150 photographs resulting from the competition sponsored by Olympus Cameras and those provided by Allsport, is a record of all the various aspects of the race – from the starts at Greenwich and Blackheath to the finish on Westminster Bridge.

I was filled with admiration for all the competitors, from the serious professionals at one end of the scale, to all those who entered just for the fun of it and who raised substantial monies for charity.

I hope that this book will be enjoyed by all the competitors who are photographed in it, by the photographers both amateur and professional who contributed to the record and to all those who enjoy this great sporting event. I further hope that the London Marathon will continue to grow yearly from strength to strength and will raise even more money for the many worthwhile charities it supports.

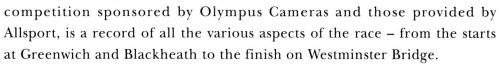

Many talented and creative people have
contributed to the publication of
The London Marathon.
The makers of NutraSweet pay special thanks to
the Earl of Snowdon, Christopher Brasher,
Patrick Collins, Nigel Dempster,
Adrian Stephenson, Ian Dickens, Simon Deverell
and, above all, the people of Britain and their
visitors who have made this book possible.

THE STORY OF THE LONDON MARATHON

by Patrick Collins

The cannon boomed across Greenwich at nine o'clock, and five minutes later the first of the runners arrived at the top of our road. We were a thin crowd, some sportingly keen but most simply curious, as we turned our collars against the soft drizzle and peered at the helicopter humming through the sulky grey clouds.

But it wasn't the size of the audience which lingers in the memory. It was the reaction. We were unused to having marathons pass the top of our road on a Sunday morning, so our response was embarrassingly uncertain. To the leaders, swift and purposeful, we offered formal, fatuous nods. For athletes of the second rank, we mustered a smattering of handclaps. They seemed faintly disappointed.

And then came the cavalcade, the magical mystery tourists, the poor bloody infantry; one mile gone and twenty-five to go. How should we greet them? What

The London Marathon gets off to a wet start in 1981.

9

were they expecting? The answer came from a middle-aged man, padding and portly and alarmingly puce of face. He wore a sweat-stained rugby jersey and ancient sneakers, and he paused to address his public. "Give us a cheer," he pleaded. "For God's sake, give us a bloody cheer."

That single, simple exhortation lit the blue touch-paper. The cheers of approval and admiration exploded through the sombre morning. They crackled along the course, igniting a chain reaction which swept through Charlton and Woolwich, royal and ancient Greenwich and the old docklands of Rotherhithe and Bermondsey. Across Tower Bridge and into the East End. Around the endless loop of the Isle of Dogs and through the new docklands, where wall-eyed towers of chrome and glass were rising haughtily from the rubble.

Despite the weather the crowds packed the route to cheer on the runners in the first London Marathon.

Cheering, cheering all the way. Clattering around the Conqueror's fortress, ruffling the skirts of the City, surging along the Embankment, passing through Trafalgar Square, past the big house at the end of the Mall, rising to a dizzy, deafening crescendo on Constitution Hill.

Londoners were discovering the pain and the joy, the agony and the ultimate ecstasy of the finest foot race that man has devised. London was welcoming the birth of its marathon.

On October 26, 1979, readers of the *Observer* newspaper found its distinguished athletics correspondent in unusually euphoric mood. "Last Sunday," wrote Christopher Brasher, "millions of us saw a vision of the human race, happy and united, willing their fellow human beings to a pointless but wonderful victory over mental doubt and bodily frailty." He had encountered this vision in New York

City, a metropolis in which mental doubt and bodily frailty are in plentiful supply.

For all its troubles, it inspires fierce loyalty and raging pride. It is, we have been told, "the town where everybody mutinies and nobody deserts". And on that autumn Sunday, Brasher found New York City decked in its finest colours, with half a million people taking to the sidewalks to cheer on 11,532 marathon runners.

There was music and there was dancing. There was beer in the Bronx and cocktails on Fifth Avenue. At the front, there was a new women's world record of 2 hours 27 minutes 29 seconds for Grete Waitz. Behind her, far behind in most cases, more than 10,000 finishers were winning their own personal victories. Brasher trotted through the twenty-six miles, entranced by the seething carnival. The seed of the idea had been planted, and when he came to write his account, his thoughts were taking shape. "I wonder," he wrote, "whether London could stage such a festival...do we have the heart and hospitality to welcome the world?"

In fact, London had welcomed the world a time or two before. Indeed, the 1908 Olympic marathon, staged on the western fringes of the capital, was the race which first established the distance in the public imagination.

History tells its tale of Dorando Pietri, the Italian pastry chef, who ran from Windsor through the Middlesex suburbs of Ruislip and Pinner, Harrow, Sudbury and Willesden before arriving at the old White City Stadium at Shepherd's Bush. He reached the stadium at the head of the field but in an exhausted state, and he tottered away in the wrong direction upon entering the arena. His suffering was intense and he fell five times. Doctors attended him and he revived, but eventually he had to be helped across the line by willing hands. He collapsed once more and for two and a half hours lay close to death, while the race he had tried so desperately to win was taken from him and awarded to the American John Joseph Hayes, in a time of 2 hours 55 minutes 18 seconds. Dorando's consolation came in the form of immortal celebrity, a song written in his honour by Irving Berlin and a huge gold cup, presented by Queen Alexandra.

Yet, in truth, the gallant Dorando had precious little reason to be grateful to the British Royal family. At that time, the generally accepted distance for the race was twenty-five miles or forty kilometres, and each of the three preceding Olympic

Competitors for the 1908 Olympic marathon gather on the lawns of Windsor Castle.

marathons had obeyed that convention. London, too, had prepared for a twenty-five-mile marathon in a number of trials carried out by members of the South London Harriers. But as the race drew near and interest increased, the Queen made it known that the younger members of her family would dearly like to watch the start. Accordingly, the existing plans were abandoned and it was decided that the Olympic marathon should start in front of Windsor Castle, on the East Lawn.

The runners gathered, having changed in the station-master's office at Windsor railway station. Princess Mary gave a signal to a peer of the realm, who sat in his open Bentley. The said peer then rose to his feet, fired his pistol and, watched by four princes and two princesses, the field set off. The entire performance added a full mile to the race, and the necessity of finishing in front of the Royal Box at the White City added a further 385 yards, which was to become the classic distance. Had the original plan been observed, then Dorando would probably have become Olympic champion; briefly fêted, lavishly praised...and long since forgotten.

Nothing could approach the drama and significance of Dorando's marathon but, in 1948, London played host to another memorable Olympic contest. Once

Dorando Pietri leads the Olympic marathon through the streets of west London. Inset: (top) Dorando is helped across the line, (bottom) Hayes finishes in second place.

again, the race yielded a victim, and on this occasion that role fell to Etienne Gailly, a twenty-one-year-old Belgian paratrooper. Gailly led the race from six to eighteen miles, and with just one mile remaining he was within five seconds of the new leader, Delfo Cabrera of Argentina. He regained the lead 200 yards from the entrance to Wembley Stadium, but the effort had destroyed him. Lurching through the final lap, he was overhauled first by the victorious Cabrera and then by Britain's Tom Richards. It is perhaps worthy of note that the winner's time of 2:34:51 was almost five minutes slower than that of the leading woman in the marathon which London was to stage forty-one years later. It is also worth noting that Cabrera's preparations never extended beyond thirty-six training miles per week. By 1981, there would be legions of fun-runners who would consider such mileage woefully inadequate.

Delfo Cabrera overtakes the exhausted Etienne Gailly on the final lap of the 1948 Olympic marathon.

It began over lunch in 1980. The lunch was hosted by Donald Trelford, Editor of the *Observer*, and the relevant authorities were invited. There was Sir Horace Cutler, leader of the Greater London Council and a man well-intentioned towards the project: "Providing, always providing, that the rate-payers are never asked to bail you out." There were representatives of the British Amateur Athletics Board, the Amateur Athletic Association, the Women's AAA and the Metropolitan Police. Crucially, there was no opposition. A London marathon was, they agreed, A Good Idea. Whether that Good Idea could ever be cajoled from the drawing board, well, that was quite another matter.

Brasher was despatched to America, to study at the feet of the acknowledged masters. He went to Boston, home of the oldest of the major city marathons. More importantly, he returned to New York, to the source of his inspiration. The New York Marathon was born into poverty in 1970, and its midwife was a Romanian immigrant named Fred Lebow. The first race attracted 127 starters and delivered just 55 finishers at the close of four laps around Central Park. But Lebow kept

The GLC "Working for London" and supporting the London Marathon.

faith with his dream, and in 1976 he persuaded the authorities to agree to a route which took in the five boroughs of his adopted city. The town closed down for half a day, and the numbers of entries began to match the occasion. In 1980, there were 14,012 starters and 12,512 finishers. The numbers were extraordinary, yet this was the standard to which London must aspire.

A second lunch was arranged on Brasher's return. He had prepared a budget showing expected total expenditure of £75,000. He has also, through agents, found a sponsor, Gillette coming up with £50,000. With the cautionary words of Sir Horace ringing in his ears - "not a penny from the ratepayers" – Brasher was authorised to turn A Good Idea into brave reality.

In company with his old Olympic colleague John Disley, Brasher then set out the following objectives:

■   To improve the overall standard and status of British marathon running by providing a fast course and strong international competition. (The standard was then at a dismal level. All six British competitors had failed to finish in the Olympic marathons of Montreal in 1976 and Moscow in 1980.)

■   To show to mankind that, on occasions, the Family of Man can be united. (An extravagant ambition, but the New York Marathon had offered an encouraging example).

■   To raise money for the provision of much-needed recreational facilities in London.

■   To help London tourism.

■   To prove that when it comes to organising major events "Britain is best". (Another lofty ambition, since the chronic absence of facilities had denied Britain the chance to stage such events.)

■   To have fun and provide some happiness and sense of achievement in a troubled world. (This, perhaps, was the loftiest aim of all. Strangely, it proved to be the ambition which was most gloriously realised.)

Madge Sharples, a great character of the early London Marathons who embodied many of the event's objectives, completes the course in 1984.

Pantomime frequently attended the initial attempts at organisation. An early plan had the race finishing on Constitution Hill, but this raised certain problems. There would be a vast amount of scaffolding at the finish, and a logistical survey indicated that this would be likely to sever the heads of countless soldiers when they rode off to Change the Guard. The GOC London Command was consulted. Could he possibly agree to alter the route of that ancient ceremony on Marathon Sunday? At first, he was shocked. Why, they hadn't changed the route in centuries. But then, perhaps that was because nobody had ever asked them to. The Constitution Hill plan was discarded after 1981, but in this first year the

Queen's Guard subsequently agreed to petition Her Majesty for permission to Change the Guard one hour earlier on Marathon Sunday to ensure that horsemen and runners did not clash. This admirable compromise had unforeseen consequences. A few years later, a Japanese tour company threatened to sue the Guard because their tour group turned up an hour too late for the ceremony. But no matter. The military did everything in their power to assist, probably because they, too, could recognise A Good Idea when they saw it.

Resources were on the slender side of Spartan. The Marathon office consisted of a desk and two chairs in the GLC Recreation Office. The problems were vast and complex, but one by one they were attacked and one by one they succumbed. "Our policy was never risk the answer No," recalls Brasher. "If you looked like getting a refusal, then you backed off, worked around the obstacle, manoeuvred your way to the top man and persuaded him to say Yes."

Meanwhile, Disley had come up with a course. "We spent a year trying to design a route which would not paralyse London", he said. "The Met Police had firm ideas, and we respected them. If we disrupted traffic throughout the capital, it would not only make their job a hell of a sight harder, it would make the Marathon pretty unpopular too. The only way they would be happy was if the route went through two of the most remote areas close to central London; Surrey Docks and the Isle of Dogs. In the early years, that part of the course was pretty hard going. The loneliness used to get to some of the runners because they wouldn't see a soul for ages. Fortunately, those areas came alive as the docklands were developed and now there's no real problem.

Chris Brasher, the driving force behind a great idea.

"When we first saw the New York Marathon, with the Manhattan skyline and Central Park, we realised that our route had to be visually exciting as well. I think we achieved that from the Naval College and the Cutty Sark at Greenwich, right through to Cleopatra's Needle on the Embankment, Buckingham Palace and the finish close by Parliament, using the Thames as a kind of hand-rail all the way. Perhaps it's not for me to say,

The Cutty Sark in Greenwich provides one of the early landmarks.

but I honestly believe we've got a magnificent course, one of the finest in the world. Given all the restrictions of a major city, I really don't think we can better it."

And so, after five months of high endeavour and low cunning; of pulling strings, twisting arms, tearing hair and racking brains, they were almost ready. With two weeks remaining, the doughty Lebow flew the Atlantic to offer expertise and reassurance. He had spent more than a decade organising New York, so there wasn't a problem he hadn't met and solved. Everything would be just fine. And he sounded almost convincing.

At the beginning of the eighties, running was considered a faintly eccentric pastime. Of course there were real runners, and they trained on tracks or over the country, and they were lean and fast and fit and nobody mocked their preparations. But the fun runners, the men or – far less likely – the women who pounded city pavements in a simple effort to get fit, lose weight and rejuvenate a flabby, listless body, well, they were exposing themselves to the mockery of the populace.

The wiser joggers ignored the abuse. The more intense, determined and, frankly, half-baked plodders devised defensive measures. A representative of this curious breed told the readers of *Running* magazine how he and his regular running companion coped with the canine menace. "We found that the best way with dogs is to face them as they charge up," he wrote, "and snarl and bark and shout at them very loudly. This disconcerts them. Sometimes, like this morning, the owner takes the counter-attack personally; the next move, I suppose, is to bite the owner's leg."

Barking, indeed. And yet there was evidence that this kind of demented zealotry was becoming prevalent. A couple of weeks before the first London Marathon, I encountered an ample-waisted, Adidas-shod gentleman moving slowly and painfully through Greenwich Park. Upon his tee-shirt, he carried the motto: "I Jog". It was, I realised, his statement of faith: "I Jog, therefore I Am". Had his chest been larger, then the message would surely have been amplified: "I am not as other men. I am not a slothful, sedentary, swilling sluggard. Because I Jog...and, what's more to the point, You Don't".

This hair-shirted, sweatier-than-thou attitude was calculated to antagonise not only the general public, but also the hedonistic sports writers of Fleet Street. One celebrated columnist seized the chance to hire a chauffeured Rolls-Royce and take Brasher on a drinking man's tour of the marathon course. They stopped at practically every pub and wine bar en route, drinking vast quantities of champagne washed down with vintage port. When they reached Westminster Bridge, the journalist staggered off to his office in a stumbling haze. For his part, Brasher changed into tracksuit and trainers and ran home to Richmond. "It was then," recalled the columnist, "that I knew there must be something in this running lark."

Yet, in truth, Brasher himself did little to dispel the fun-runner's reputation for eccentricity. On the eve of the first London Marathon, he offered the following guidance to competitors: "Vaseline all moving parts; toes, ball of foot, heel, groin and where your arm meets your back." Excellent advice, of course, yet he made it sound like a 10,000-mile service. Indeed, if every runner were to take his hints to heart, then you would fear that the start of the race would resemble an oil-slick.

He also offered advice on appropriate clothing. If the weather turned cold, then he had decided to wear a long-sleeved polypropylene vest and long johns, a tee-shirt, an extra top, old gloves and a hat. "I should check that Worzel Gummidge has not submitted a late entry before you offer the race director a cheer," wrote one sceptical hack. And I fear that Brasher was slow to forgive my jest.

Yet the real fears were far more serious. We had all seen Olympic marathons, with their attendant suffering. We had watched British events like the traditional Windsor to Chiswick race, and had seen highly trained, utterly competent club runners fall shattered by the wayside. For all the marvellous spirit which the London had provoked, and for all the soaring ambitions that would soon be tested, some of us believed that there would be casualties. Ordinary joggers, indifferently prepared and with no distance background, could have no concept of what was involved in running twenty-six miles. Many, surely, would over-estimate their capacity and over-stretch their resources. And the results, we suspected, might prove devastating.

At five minutes to ten on the morning of Sunday March 29, 1981, Mrs Maggie Osborne set out to attend Mass at Holy Trinity Church, Dockhead. An elderly lady of regular habits, she crossed Jamaica Road in her usual manner; raising her walking stick, striding out purposefully and leaving the traffic to make its own arrangements.

There was a good deal of shouting as Mrs Osborne found herself surrounded by young men in running vests, moving swiftly and swerving desperately to avoid the good lady. She walked on, stick aloft and eyes ahead, just as she had done for decades past. The rest of London might be bending over backwards to accommodate its marathon, but Mrs Osborne's priorities were of a rather higher order. The lady, indeed, was not for turning.

Ten o'clock Mass was thinly attended that morning, which was understandable in its way. After all, the streets were full of cheering people, a Dixieland jazz band was blowing its heart out fifty yards down the road and around 7,000 runners were variously striding, shuffling and staggering past the front door. So the parish priest of Holy Trinity took a decision: from here on, Mass on Marathon Sunday would be brought forward to nine-thirty. The move met with the general approval of his parishioners, although it is said that Mrs Osborne needed a good deal of convincing.

In truth, a lot of entrenched customs were broken that day. The idea that Londoners were too reserved, too smart and too world-weary to be impressed by such a festival did not survive the morning. After the initial uncertainty, they leaped aboard the careering bandwagon and claimed it gleefully for their own.

The notion that London could not organise an event of such magnitude was similarly dispelled. The mass start worked with swift efficiency, the drink stations were superbly manned by adroit volunteers, the Metropolitan Police supervised enthusiastic crowds with maximum tact and minimum trouble, while the route that John Disley had devised was proving an unqualified success.

More importantly, and most mercifully, the fears of those who had believed that there might be serious casualties were proved groundless. Around half of the runners were attempting their first marathon, and they heeded experienced advice: start slowly, do not be carried away by the occasion, take plenty of fluid, walk when you have to, endure it but enjoy it.

Up at the front, in a quite different world, more earnest issues were being debated. The organisers had tried to strike a balance between carnival and solid competition, between those who hoped merely to finish and those who intended to finish ahead of the rest.

The race developed into a duel between the American Dick Beardsley and Inge

Simonsen of Norway. They broke early, imposed a gap of more than a minute between themselves and their pursuers and as they sped up Constitution Hill they made a gesture which perfectly matched the spirit of the day; linking hands and loping home in 2 hours 22 minutes 48 seconds. Encouragingly, the rest of the top ten male runners were exclusively British, led by the splendid veteran Trevor Wright in 2:12:53.

The women's race quickly became a procession, and few complained about that, since the lady at its head was Joyce Smith; forty-three years old, the mother of two children and an athlete whose courage was matched only by her talent. Her 2:29:57 was a new British record and saw her finish precisely nine minutes ahead of the New Zealander Gillian Drake, with another Briton, Gillian Adams, almost two minutes behind in third place. Times would improve still further as the race attracted fields of deeper quality, but already London had proved that its course was fast and true. Given the right day and the right conditions – along with the active encouragement of tens of thousands of screaming citizens – somebody was destined to deliver a quite extraordinary performance along this route.

And yet, for the ordinary, enchanted Londoner, the appeal of the day did not lie in events at the head of the field. This fact did not please the purists. Indeed, one athletics writer haughtily declined his invitation to attend on the grounds that "I am employed to cover marathons, not circuses". It was a judgement he was later to regret for, in the space of a single morning, the London Marathon had engendered more interest and more public involvement than the event had ever known.

On occasion, the involvement was wonderfully misplaced. A back-marker, suffering grievously and hauling his bulk across Tower Bridge, was brutally cut down by a lady bystander: "They've finished, love," she said helpfully. "I've just seen it on the telly. Lovely race, it was. Still, ne'mind, not far to go now." He considered the twelve miles he had just covered and contemplated the fourteen which lay ahead. And he sank to his knees, weeping silently.

But everybody was rewarded with a cheer: the freaks and the downright foolhardy, the exhibitionists who waved at helicopters on the off-chance that they might contain a camera, and Jimmy Savile, arrayed in gold lamé, surrounded by panting acolytes and reeling off twenty-six miles with the ease of a Sunday morning stroll. A few boxers, legs and lungs conditioned by a lifetime of road-work, trotted past at a nifty pace, while a rugby man named

Jimmy Savile in more traditional kit, but still running in 1987.

Dick Beardsley (left) and Inge Simonsen joined hands to cross the finishing line on Constitution Hill and shared victory in the inaugural race.

Williams, who enjoys the most famous initials in the whole world of sports, trundled by at prop-forward pace. It was the first time that an English audience had found reason to sympathise with J.P.R.

In that famous article which set the ball rolling, Brasher had mentioned overtaking a dinner-jacketed waiter in the New York Marathon: "He was carrying a tray with a bottle of Perrier water, steady as a rock," he wrote. "He can't be running the whole distance, I thought. But he was, and he did." The "waiter", one Roger Bourban, arrived for the London, complete with bottle, glass and tray. He finished in a shade under three hours and poured himself a drink. Two years later,

I met him in Los Angeles, close by the restaurant on Sunset Boulevard where he served at table. He had reduced his personal best with bottle and tray to an incredible 2 hours 47 minutes. Manufacturers of mineral waters were paying large sums to set their bottles on his tray. He now employed two agents and a manager and marathon promoters were scuffling for his services. So prosperous had he become that he was hoping to open his own restaurant. An engaging extrovert, he was proud of his popularity. "Me, I make friends everywhere, like a dog in a bowling alley," he said. "But London was friendly beyond belief. London was the big one. In fact, you could say that it was the place where my legend was created."

And when it was all over, when the last weary stride had been completed and the last legend had been created, the statistics told an amazing tale. Not only had the event made a surplus of £12,857, but more than 80 per cent of the accepted entries had managed to finish the race, a total of 6,255. No fewer than 144 runners had completed the course in less than 2

Roger Bourban, with bottle, glass and tray in 1982.

hours 30 minutes, 1,294 in under three hours and 4,881 in under four hours. The marathon was no longer the exclusive preserve of supermen and superwomen. On that morning in March, it had become an event for ordinary, fallible, weary, footsore and sublimely determined people.

After reading the ecstatic reviews and revelling in the reception of their initial effort, the creators of the London Marathon began to wonder just what they had started. The running boom, frequently promised, had become reality, legitimised by the scope and success of the event. No longer were the pavement-pounders derided; for one thing, they had proved themselves from Greenwich Park to Westminster, and for another, well, there were just too many of them. The sales of shoes, vests, tracksuits, running magazines and even that dubious invention called the pedometer all soared to unprecedented heights. Running was suddenly revealed as healthy, sensible, socially acceptable and even chic. And the chic were about to inherit the earth.

In 1981, the London organisers had been surprised and delighted to receive more than 20,000 applications for a place in their race, and they accepted 7,747 candidates. In 1982, the UK and world-wide applications exceeded 90,000, of which 18,059 were successful. Gillette responded in practical terms to this surge of interest, doubling their sponsorship to £100,000, while the GLC allocated an office which was rather larger than a desk and two chairs.

Bob Wilson checks on the condition of BBC rugby league commentator Harry Gration during the 1987 marathon.

Much of that interest undoubtedly could be traced to the excellence of the television presentation. Over the years, the BBC had earned an unrivalled reputation for the quality of their athletics coverage, but the London Marathon offered them a quite different challenge. It was that old question of balance, reaching an accommodation between the swift and capable athletes at the sharp end and the heart-warming, occasionally hilarious strivers at the rear. In fact, they brought it off with a flourish, thanks to perceptive direction, the eternal professionalism of David Coleman and the marvellously informed enthusiasm of the late and quite irreplaceable Ron Pickering. And, as a totally unexpected bonus, they also devised an item which achieved a kind of cult status; I refer, of course, to the extraordinary interviews which a tracksuited Bob Wilson conducted with an array of celebrities, eccentrics and honest, flagging plodders upon Tower Bridge. They were brief to the point of brusqueness. Wilson: "How d'you feel?" Honest flagging plodder: "Knackered." Wilson: "Thanks very much." And the nation cackled fit to burst.

The sheer weight of numbers involved in 1982 provoked logistical problems of a quite different dimension to those encountered in the inaugural year, but invaluable lessons had been learned at every level of organisation and once again the occasion passed off without serious hitch. Indeed, its appeal was strengthened by the happy coincidence of two British successes. Joyce Smith once again brought home the women virtually unchallenged in 2:29:43, while Hugh Jones discovered irresistible form in the men's event. Jones ran an enormously impressive 2:09:24 to finish almost three minutes ahead of the Norwegian Oyvind Dahl, with Mike Gratton from Kent in third place.

Once again, the statistics were startling. More than 83 per cent of the accepted entries, or 15,116 runners, actually made it to the finish. And of that number, no fewer than 9,759 came home in under four hours.

Two British winners in 1982. Hugh Jones and Joyce Smith are flanked on the victory rostrum by (left) Mike Gratton (GB) and Judith Hine (NZ) and (right) Lorraine Moller (NZ) and Oyvind Dahl (Norway).

ABOVE AND BELOW   Encouragement from all ages.

It became a much-abused cliché to declare that every one of those finishers was a winner, and yet, like so many clichés, it happened to be true. I recall standing close to the finishing line that year as the four-hour brigade came trudging home. One unremarkable character, plump and fortyish, tottered through and murmured a private prayer as his ordeal ended. Then he began an agitated search for a familiar figure. His face suddenly cracked into a smile as he spotted a small girl, skipping frantically by the parapet of the bridge and waving a placard which bore the message: "Well Done Dad". He hurried across, swept her into his arms and the two of them stood there weeping tears of joy and relief as the rest of us looked away, blinking furiously. I last saw them shuffling off in the general direction of County Hall; the child still waving her placard, still clutching her father's hand.

I thought again of the words which had been used to describe the marathon phenomenon: healthy, sensible, even chic. All true, of course. But I knew that they didn't even begin to tell the story.

The wheelchair athletes arrived in 1983, their presence immeasurably enhancing the appeal of the marathon. When the definitive history of disabled

sport comes to be written, it may be seen that their arrival marked the beginning of a change in public attitudes towards the disabled athlete. They were welcomed, it must be said, with a mixture of curiosity and instinctive sympathy. "Brave people," you heard. "Battling through twenty-six miles in a wheelchair. It's hard enough for men and women without disabilities. How on earth do they do it?" A decade later, curiosity had disappeared and the faintly patronising sympathy had yielded to outright admiration.

In truth, there were initial problems. The massed runners averaged no more than seven miles per hour, while wheelchair competitors can exceed 30 mph on downhill sections. In hindsight, the potential for damaging collisions was obvious, and in that first year, when twenty-one wheelchairs started at the back of the field, there were three accidents with foot runners.

But the problems were resolved by the simple expedient of starting the

The start of the BSAD Wheelchair London Marathon in 1991.

wheelchairs fifteen minutes ahead of the field, thus giving them a clear run and allowing many of them to finish before the first of the foot runners. As a further, well-earned bonus, the early start brought them enormous television exposure and

Peter Hull during the 1989 wheelchair marathon – an inspiration to all fellow athletes.

thus helped to alter attitudes not only on the streets of London but also across the living rooms of the nation.

As so often happens in all sports, increased attention prompted improved standards. Once again, the statistics tell a convincing story. In that first year of 1983, and starting from the rear of the field, the men's wheelchair marathon was won in 3 hours 20 minutes 7 seconds and the women's race in 4:29:03. In 1990, for instance, when there were sixty-seven wheelchair starters, the leading man came home in 1:57:12, while the leading woman returned an amazing 2:10:25.

In time, the London would incorporate a mini-wheelchair race for children to set alongside the age group races for young runners, which attract a total field of more than 2,300 from the London boroughs. The children in wheelchairs proved

Chris Hallam, a pioneer of the wheelchair marathon, wins in 1987.

every bit as keen and as capable as their seniors; their potential untapped, their promise apparently unlimited.

Disabled, or as some would have it, "differently abled", it no longer seemed relevant. They were now simply athletes, and marvellously talented ones at that.

Roger Gibbs was a man of singular determination. Having experienced the scourge of cancer, he was resolved to strike a few retaliatory blows at that vilest of enemies. And so he ran in the 1982 London Marathon. Now, as chairman of one of the City's great financial houses, Mr Gibbs was in an excellent position to exert a degree of influence where sponsorship was concerned. And he used that position quite shamelessly. His friends were harangued, his business associates were canvassed and, it is whispered, a number of his employees were made aware of the importance their chairman placed upon this splendid cause.

Whatever his methods, they were brilliantly effective. When the cash was finally counted, it was discovered that Roger Gibbs had raised the mind-boggling total of £440,000. It was, by common consent, a world record for a charitable enterprise of this nature, and he used the money to purchase a body scanner for Guy's Hospital in London. As retaliatory blows go, it was quite devastating. Incidentally, he had also accepted a side bet of £10,000 that he would break five hours for the course. For a man of such singular determination, collection was no more than a piece of cake.

Brian 'The Hop' Cleaver, completes another marathon in 1990.

Now most marathon aspirants cherish rather more modest ambitions. Theirs is a round of offices, factory floors, football clubs, school common rooms, church halls, saloon bars and shopping centres; hustling forms and seeking pledges. And when the race is over and the mission successfully completed, they must make that same onerous pilgrimage to redeem those pledges. It is a wearisome and

Liverpool and Everton supporters run in the 1989 London Marathon to raise money for the relatives of those who died in the Hillsborough disaster a few weeks earlier.

frequently thankless task, yet they see it as part of the marathon experience, and a part which is every bit as important as the training miles or the high-carbo diet.

From time to time, a kind of coup is effected: not so dazzling as that brought off by the remarkable Roger Gibbs, perhaps, but a coup nonetheless. Inevitably, the most dramatic examples have City affiliations. In 1987, Christopher Castleman and Kate Brasher of the merchant bankers Hill Samuel devised a scheme by which fifty marathon places were awarded to those who had made major contributions to British sport. The names ranged from Fred Perry, winner of three Wimbledon singles titles, to Ian Rush, who scores goals on a regular basis for Liverpool. Runners were nominated to compete in the place of these distinguished names, and the "substitute" athletes raised £145,000 for Great Ormond Street Children's Hospital, an average of £2,900 per competitor.

This served as the prototype for the 1988 Great Ormond Street Wishing Well Appeal, for which 300 places were allocated. City institutions and other industries were asked to underwrite three members of their staff to run in aid of the appeal. The scheme raised more than a million pounds in little more than a day. In addition, the Wishing Well was one of the two charities recommended that year by the organisers and sponsor. Around 600 accepted runners responded, and raised a further half a million pounds.

The list of successes is formidable. In a single year, 1990, ten members of Lloyd's raised £70,000 for the London Hospital Children's Wards, one runner raised £5,575 for Children With Special Needs, 120 runners raised £160,000 for Action on Addiction, 200 competitors raised £225,000 for the Community Action Trust and twenty-seven runners, all from the property and construction business, raised £159,000 for the Propcon Appeal for mentally handicapped children, an average of £5,889 per runner.

One of the many runners in the 1985 London Marathon raising money for hospital appeals.

In truth, it is impossible to attempt an accurate calculation of the amount by which charities have benefited during the London Marathon's twelve-year span. But the most conservative estimate, based upon surveys and simple observation, suggests that individuals – quite apart from money generated by the London Marathon Charitable Trust itself – have raised a total which comfortably exceeds fifty million pounds.

If the event should ever need to justify its existence, then those figures alone would constitute an eloquent case.

The London Marathon was scarcely more than a year old when athletics turned professional. Of course, the sport didn't come right out and say: "We're all pros now, chaps, just turn up and fill your pockets", since the International Amateur Athletics Federation doesn't do things that way. But when you burrowed through masses of clauses, sub-clauses and arcane conditions emerging from the IAAF Congress, you realised that the game was up; shamateurism had died its inevitable death.

Athletes would now demand fees for participating, and if London were to maintain its place in the forefront of world marathons, then it needed more money to attract the finest performers. The Gillette sponsorship was retained for the 1983 race, which saw another British victory in the men's event, Mike Gratton overcoming his compatriot Gerry Helme in 2:09:43. It also saw the arrival of one of history's greatest woman athletes. Blonde, serene and utterly remorseless, Grete Waitz reduced the course to 2:25:29, a world-best time which took more than four minutes off the London record and saw her finish almost three minutes ahead of Mary O'Connor of New Zealand and Britain's Glynis Penny.

A new sponsor was found later that year, Mars agreeing to pay £150,000 for the 1984 race, rising to £217,000 for 1985. In fact, the Mars sponsorship endured for five years, a fruitful collaboration which ensured that the best in the world would come to the capital.

Grete Waitz passes Tower Bridge on her way to victory in 1983.

Amongst the public at large, there was a hint of resentment at the kind of fees which the top people could now, legitimately, attract. The common perception was that athletes were people who ran for fun. Lavish money upon them – as if they were golfers, tennis players or boxers – and you would remove that endearing element of altruism. That reasoning ignored the fact that the dedication, time and effort which a major marathon demanded was certainly no less than that required to play a round of championship golf.

It also ignored the reality that the world was suddenly full of marathons: New York, Boston, Rotterdam, Los Angeles, Berlin, Tokyo, Fukuoka, Paris, Hamburg and Vienna. Most enjoyed the lucrative assistance of corporate sponsors and each was committed to attracting the finest available athletes. Prize money in itself was not sufficient, since any marathon is full of hazards for even the most talented runners. They needed a form of insurance against accident, and participation fees offered them that guarantee.

Basically, it was a question of survival. And the equation was stark and simple. The sponsor needed television to ensure maximum exposure for his product. Television needed a large field of runners to create a sense of equation, plus a real

race between the top men and women at the sharp end. And the marathon, any marathon, needed television coverage to sustain public interest and preserve a high rate of entries. To remove just one of those ingredients was to invite oblivion.

Glasgow provided the terrible, definitive example. In 1985, the Glasgow Marathon attracted 20,062 entries. Yet it failed to attract sufficient high-profile competitors and paid the price of diminishing media interest. By 1988, it was dead.

London continued to seek the balance between high quality and mass participation. Accepted entries broke all the significant barriers: 20,000-plus in 1984, 25,000 in 1986, 30,000-plus in 1989. Yet the front of the race maintained its own formidable standards. Gateshead's Charlie Spedding came home in 2:09:57 in 1984 to ensure selection for the Los Angeles Olympics, at which he went on to win the bronze medal, while the women's race featured the London debut of that other massively talented Norwegian Ingrid Kristiansen, who returned a new London record of 2:24:26.

Chris Brasher, in his customary position on Westminster Bridge, encourages Ingrid Kristiansen to one final surge in 1988.

If '84 was encouraging, then '85 may be seen as the vintage year in terms of performance. Kristiansen was operating at the peak of her powers and she had set herself to lower the world-best performance. In the event, she completely demolished it, attacking all the way from Greenwich and stripping more than a minute and a half from the previous world mark with an incredible 2:21:06. In a normal year, that run would have commanded every headline, yet this was not a normal year, nor a normal marathon. For the men's race developed into a genuine epic, Spedding and Steve Jones battling stride for stride at unnerving pace before Jones found

Steve Jones (2), the 1985 winner, shares the lead with Charlie Spedding (1), winner the previous year, and Christoph Herle of Germany. Behind are two future winners, Allister Hutton (1990) and Henrik Jorgensen (1988).

improbable resources in the final mile to win by seventeen seconds in 2:08:16, the fastest time ever recorded in the United Kingdom.

The worldwide status of the London Marathon was confirmed in '86 and '87, when the Japanese came and comfortably conquered the men's field; first Toshihiko Seko, then Hiromi Taniguchi. But the women's event remained relentlessly Norwegian, Waitz winning again in 1986, then Kristiansen taking her third and fourth victories in '87 and '88, in which year the men were brought home by the talented Dane Henrik Jorgensen.

Toshihiko Seko celebrates victory in 1986.

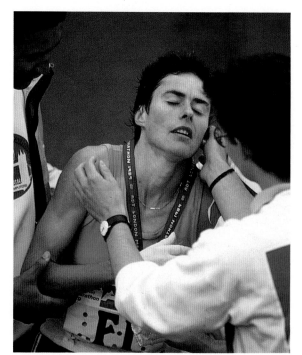

Veronique Marot, an exhausted winner in 1989.

In 1989 a new sponsor, the security systems and vehicle auction group ADT, agreed to back the race to the tune of at least £2 million over three years. In fact, they extended their term to four years, invested several millions on sponsorship and promotion, transformed a little-known company into a household name and declared that the whole enterprise had represented money well spent.

That same year of 1989 brought a welcome success and a British best performance in the women's race for the persistent Veronique Marot, the first British winner since Joyce Smith. It also produced another classic contest among the men. As they moved past Parliament, a mere handful of strides separated Steve Moneghetti of Australia, Ahmed Salah of

Left to right: Steve Moneghetti, Ahmed Salah and Douglas Wakiihuri within sight of the finish in 1989.

Djibouti and Douglas Wakiihuri of Kenya. Yet the Kenyan, who is surely one of the great masters of the event, had calculated his effort with disturbing precision. He simply lifted a gear and eased home by three seconds from Moneghetti with Salah three more seconds adrift of the Australian. Six seconds covered three men at the end of twenty-six miles, with the winner returning 2:09:03. It was quite breathtaking and utterly memorable.

Allister Hutton, a well-deserved success in 1990.

In 1990 came a welcome British victory from Allister Hutton in 2:10:10, fine reward for a man who had toiled long and hard to win a London, while Wanda Panfil from Poland took the women's race with some ease. In the

Hugh Jones, Steve Brace and Dave Long of Great Britain, winners of the World Team Championship in 1991.

following year, the London Marathon gained the ultimate seal of international approval by becoming the World

Marathon Cup, a mark of prestige which may well have been lost on most of the record 26,500 starters but was of immense significance to the Russian Yakov Tolstikov, who took the title in 2:09:17. The brilliant Rosa Mota of Portugal led the women home by more than a minute in 2:26:14. And the standard was maintained in 1992, when Antonio Pinto of Portugal won the men's race in 2:10:02. Sadly, not a single Briton found a place in the men's top ten, although Andrea Wallace gave notice of a promising marathon career when she finished third among the women in a race won by Katrin Dorre of Germany.

And that, dear reader, is where the matter rests for the moment. London has entered a new era under the sponsorship of NutraSweet who, in September 1992, signed a £2million, two-year deal with an option to

Rosa Mota, winner in 1991, leads the field in 1992 from Nan Doak-Davis (USA) and eventual winner Katrin Dorre (Germany). Andrea Wallace, who finished third is at the back of the group.

renew the contract for 1995 and 1996. Chris Brasher was enthusiastic about this new partnership: "The lifestyle of the 1990s is a healthy lifestyle – good eating, good drinking and some exercise. With NutraSweet and the London Marathon, you get all three together." The involvement of NutraSweet will enable the continuing recruitment of world-class fields and will enable London to maintain its place among the great marathons of the world.

David Bedford, former world-record holder at 10,000 metres and International Co-ordinator of the London Marathon, at the press conference announcing the NutraSweet sponsorship – in the words of Chris Brasher "a natural fit".

It is a pity that so many of the achievements of the London Marathon should have to be expressed in cash terms, but once again, the hard figures tell an impressive story. More than fifty million pounds raised for charities by vast armies of foot-soldiers. More than £1,400,000 distributed in grants by the London Marathon Charitable Trust to a wide range of recreational schemes in the capital, from disabled children in Greenwich to walkers in Hillingdon. And an economic impact on London, through trade and tourism, of more than fifteen million pounds every year since 1981.

They are extraordinary figures, yet they only hint at the true merit of one of the largest sports participation events in the world. For the enduring value of London's great race may be found on marathon day itself.

It lies in the laughter and the cheers, the sweat and the suffering. It lies in all the private battles, fearfully undertaken and tenaciously won. It lies in the tens of thousands of dreams, patiently nourished and gloriously delivered. And, for some of us, it lies most poignantly in the exhausted tears of a father and the face of a small girl, dancing triumphantly upon Westminster Bridge and clutching a placard which bears the message "Well Done Dad".

Ah yes, the London Marathon was not just A Good Idea. It was, quite simply, the best idea that British sport has ever known.

THE 1993 NutraSweet LONDON MARATHON

Photographs by Allsport UK
and entrants to the Olympus Cameras
'Essence of the Marathon'
photographic competition

Captions by
Nigel Dempster
who completed the London Marathon
in 1981, 1982 and 1987

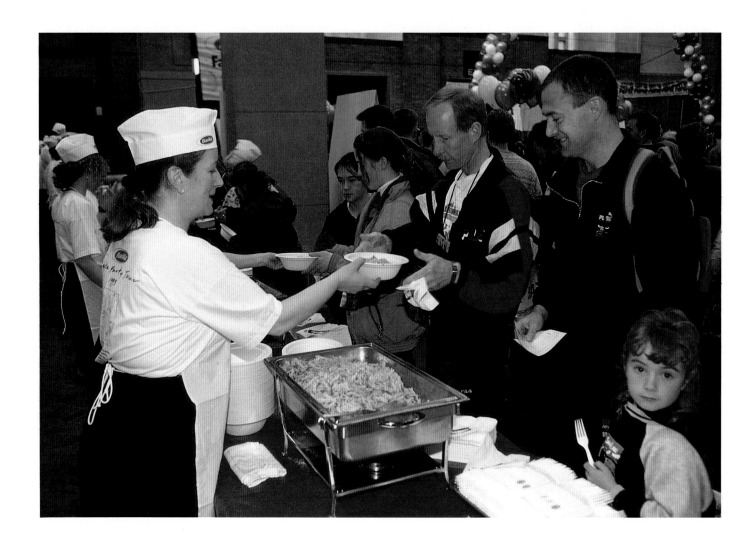

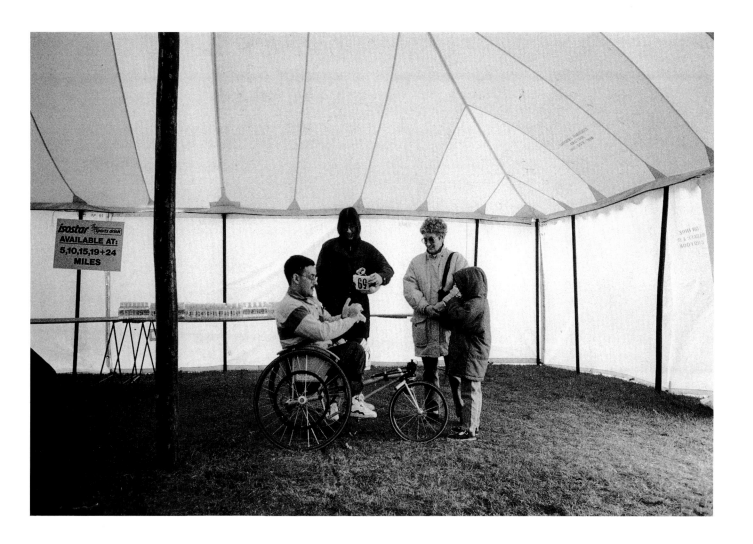

LEFT The last chance for carbohydrate loading!
Runners at the pasta party on the eve of the
Marathon enjoying the hospitality at the Royal
Horticultural Hall – the first pasta party in 1981 took
place at the Royal Lancaster Hotel with Sir Horace
Cutler, leader of the Greater London Council,
greeting those of the 7,000 competitors in the first
London Marathon who turned up for loading.

ABOVE This year Lord Snowdon, whose Award
Scheme was NutraSweet's nominated charity,
started the wheelchair race which had sixty-five
entrants, including five women and three
quadraplegics. Sadly, Chris Hallam, who had won
the event twice and had tried on several other
occasions to become the first athlete to win three
times in London, did not make the start – he was
recovering from a broken leg.

LEFT Minutes before the start in Greenwich and only 26 miles and 385 yards to go! Final preparations for three of the of the 25,500 runners who started, out of an entry of 35,750. When I ran the first London Marathon, the best advice I had came from Chris Brasher who told me: "Grease all moving parts."

BELOW Taking direction: a marshal with a megaphone attempting to assert authority over the good natured scene at the mass start.

RIGHT Does Hugh M. Hefner know about this?
While the founder of the Bunny empire's principal
exertions might be in the realms of horizontal
jogging, this cotton-tail is preparing to hop it.
Hefner's lasting legacy to culture is the 'Bunny Dip',
the manoeuvre his girls had to perform when serving
drinks to seated male customers from a tray whereby
they managed to bend without exposing any
cleavage, which may explain why some of these
marshals are looking on the sombre side. Costumes
add to the levity of the Marathon but my worst
experience one year was being overtaken by both
parts of a circus horse around the 16 mile area. It
takes time to recover from such a humiliation.

ABOVE They're off! A rather more successful start than that of the Grand National fifteen days earlier. While those at the front can set off running, the mass behind start at a shuffle and, eventually, break into a jog. It takes up to ten minutes for those at the back to reach the starting line, a factor to be taken into consideration when working out personal times. I was once accused by *The Times* of enhancing my time after writing about how long the race had taken me. They checked with the official finishing times but the journalist in question did not realise about the staggered start. An apology quickly followed.

RIGHT The historic Cutty Sark in its Greenwich dry dock is the first scenic point of the race, 6.5 miles from the start and reached by the leaders in around 32 minutes.

Built in 1869, the tea clipper brought cargoes from China to Britain and the name means 'short chemise'. It comes from the witch in Robert Burns's poem 'Tam O'Shanter'. Runners are less appreciative of this fine sight – it is the first U-turn in the race and uncomfortable to negotiate, but there are lighter diversions ahead, including a local jazz band.

LEFT   Not quite halfway but Tower Bridge is where runners begin to feel they are 'cracking it'. No such problems for these three rhinos – if they were on show at Regent's Park Zoo, the crowds would flock in.

RIGHT   The wheelchair marathons for men and women started a minute apart at 9.20 and 9.21 and this aerial shot at Tower Bridge, twelve miles into the race, shows how close it still is. Rose Hill of England, a veteran with a best time of 1:50:13, is piggy in the middle here. London is a notoriously slow course because of its numerous turns and a road surface which does not favour wheels. The oldest competitor this year was Jean Goessens, a 54-year-old butcher from Maastricht – a town few people had heard of before 1992! – while the youngest was Karl Nicholson, an 18-year-old student from Manchester whose ambition was to break the two-hour barrier.

OVERLEAF   Heading for the magic half way mark – a welcome boost as this is where the race loops away from the finishing post with a tour of Docklands. You have a frustrating view of the faster runners on their way home as you look down to the parallel road in the Cable Street area, bringing the realisation that you are eight and a half miles behind them – with 'the wall' to come on the Isle of Dogs.

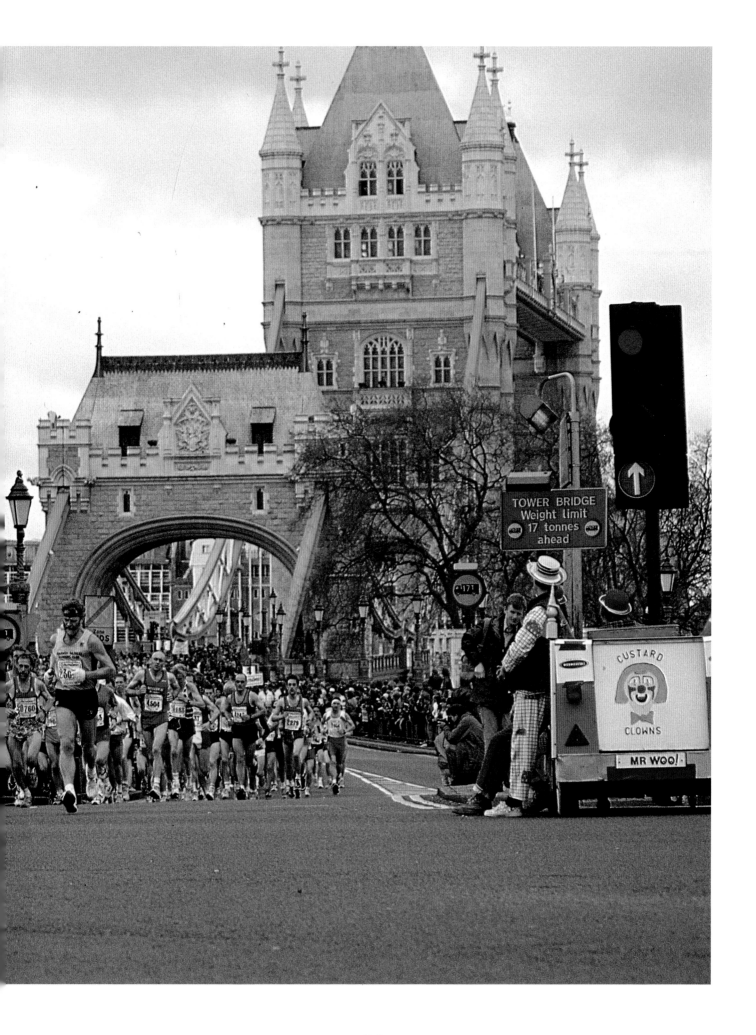

ABOVE   Has Celia Greenwood, a 47-year-old from Great Western Runners with a best time of 3:14:36, seen a friend or is she rehearsing for the cameras ahead?

The video teams capturing as many of the runners as possible are a recent innovation and a must for those making their debut who need to have evidence of the memorable day. The universal initial reaction of a runner completing the marathon for the first time is: 'Never again.' But with a rerun of the video, you can see how much you enjoyed it, especially if you are Celia.

ABOVE RIGHT   The winner in the 'Support' category of the unique photo competition, sponsored by Olympus. The boxer looks marginally more enthusiastic than his master whose Tartan tipple has had its effect.

RIGHT   Nothing so strong in the Docklands water station where this fine figure of a man is to be found hardly endorsing the cola of his sweatshirt. What will the advertisers say?

ABOVE How to get involved as a spectator: a line of half a dozen kids reaching out to receive a hand rattle, obligingly delivered by 34-year-old Sandra Thornton who has taken a slight detour from the centre of the road to press the flesh on the way to raising money for the Anthony Nolan fund.

RIGHT White Elephant or landmark for the 21st Century? Canary Wharf, until the Government agrees funding for the extension of the Jubilee Line underground, will always be more accessible to those on foot but we should thank the Canadian Reichman brothers for producing another focal point for the London race.

ABOVE The Docklands loop contains some of the dreariest environs and now some of the most majestic, part of the changing panorama of London's once desolate acres, but clearly runners are so intent in getting through – 'the wall' can hit you at any time down this area – that this water station is treated like a pub with no beer, that is to say ignored.....

RIGHT Clearly, James McGuire (9593) hasn't heard the fireman's siren. The six-strong brigade are about to embark on an overtaking manoeuvre, while the four stretcher-bearers are making light of their load and the colour coordinates of the third group are a focal point.

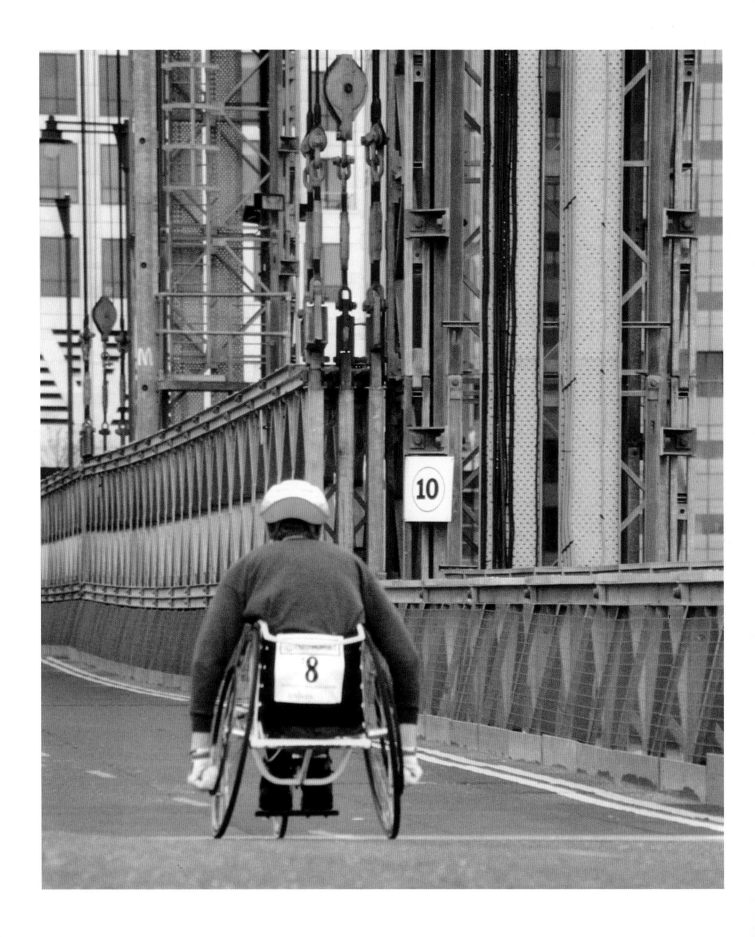

LEFT Ploughing a lonely furrow: Ian Lea of England who started the race with a best time of 1:41:00.

ABOVE Another winner, this time in the 'Pain' category of the photo competition. This shot captures the expressions of runners coming to the end of their tether, summoning deep reserves and wondering whether it has all been worth it. After fifteen miles or so, the race becomes quieter, the confident chatter of the early stages giving way to silent concentration on finishing, as runners strive to achieve their personal goals. The secret is never to stop, just keep moving and walk fast if you can't jog or run. Once you come to a halt, the difficulty is getting started again, not only mentally but physically.

Out of the 25,500 starters this year, 1,050 did not
make it to the finishing line, and those who did owe
much of their courageous effort to the enthusiasm of
the spectators and supporters along the route.

The courage of the blind runners and their 'eyes' is
one of the more humbling experiences of the
Marathon. Here Michael Pickin (32189) is deep in
thought, relying on his partner to keep in step and
out of trouble – and able to ignore the temptations of
the City Pride tavern in West Ferry Road, reflected in
the mirrored cladding of the Britannia International
Hotel.

LEFT   Where's 'the wall'? The invisible barrier which runners can hit somewhere in the Isle of Dogs is seen in some of these faces, noticeably, 49 -year-old Peter Maisel (5702), who according to the official programme was also given shirt numbers 5709 and 5711 – so let's hope this is the real Peter Maisel! While the Isle of Dogs is, perhaps, not the most photogenic stretch in the marathon, it has always been one of the most friendly and if you feel like stopping off for a while and having a chat, here's your chance. Interludes in the hospitable wine bars and pubs en route are not part of the recommended method of marathon running, inviting though they may be.

LEFT Better to keep going, take in the atmosphere and be serenaded by a band.

ABOVE Civilisation again: St Katharine's Dock heralds the final stages of the Marathon – runners are now facing west again and heading straight towards Westminster Bridge and, if they cannot see it, they are able to sense it. Ahead lies the Tower of London and, above, Tower Bridge over which you pounded ten long miles ago, by now seeming almost a lifetime.

The St John's Ambulance brigade is on hand,
literally, to ease the aches and pains as 24-year-old
Mark Higgins (17743) experiences the cobbles by
the Tower. For the very tired this is an irritating
section: although a carpet is placed over the
cobbles, any deviation rankles and there is a nasty
turn past the Tower which tends to grate, especially
with those who are looking for any excuse to pack it
in! Sadly the history of this original centre of London
makes little impact on the tired eyes and minds and
even the encouragement of the Beefeaters en route
tends to be ignored.

Relief for a wheelchair competitor shows during this brief downhill run as a happy smile breaks out, but for runner 26426, Robert Tooze, who is 46, it is not such a happy time. Decisions now have to be made – whether to walk the rest of the way, less than four miles, or run to each water station, walk through them, and then run on again.

Blackfriars underground station, with the promise of free transport home, looks mightily inviting. But with around two and half miles left, perseverance is the name of the game. Even for those who have trained diligently for upwards of six months, it's the legs that go first, not the lungs surprisingly.

RIGHT Clark Kent he ain't but no one is about to spoil the fun of Laurence Wynter as the 27-year-old runner mugs for the camera as he passes Cleopatra's Needle on Victoria Embankment with the end in sight, albeit reached via a slight detour up Northumberland Avenue and through The Mall.

ABOVE The secret of taking water is to drink little and often, and regularly from the second or third mile mark. Dehydration is the enemy of the marathoner and on the whole it's more advisable to put it down your throat than on your head.

RIGHT Almost there. Once you have passed Queen Boadicea you can almost start the celebrations and these clowns will soon have something to laugh about themselves, having made people smile for the previous twnety-four miles.

LEFT Earlier in the morning it was the turn of the girls in the Mini Marathon, but now the ladies race has come down to Katrin Dorre of Germany (101), Lisa Ondieki, the Australian (102), and Britain's heroine Liz McColgan (104). Katrin was competing in her 26th marathon, having won fifteen of them. Would this be number sixteen?

ABOVE After signing to run the NutraSweet London Marathon is 1993/4/5, there was to be no fairytale for Liz McColgan. Katrin Dorre, with the obscured figure of Lisa Ondieki right behind her, turns off the Embankment by Charing Cross up Northumberland Avenue, with Liz trailing more than half a minute behind and less than two miles to run. The green light is a sign that everything's going Katrin's way.

If you've reached Admiralty Arch, sitting at the opposite end of The Mall to Buckingham Palace, you feel it's over – but there's still a mile and a quarter to go and the crowd won't let you stop. The slightest attempt to slow to a walk and they shout: "Keep running. Don't stop now". And it is good advice.

Stop and your muscles stiffen and the will to start again recedes. By now, no runners are talking to each other and the sound of the soles of running shoes on the red tarmac of The Mall is all that the competitors hear. Even a smile at jokes like this one carried on a hat takes an effort.

The fancy dress runners may grin for the cameras but must be wishing they had worn something more sensible. Whatever happened to the waiter who used to run in well under three hours balancing a tray with a full bottle of mineral water on it and two glasses? That was a staggering athletic feat and not a little disconcerting to those who couldn't break 200 minutes without any encumbrance.

ABOVE Here's one policeman whose girth denotes
he is happier directing the runners than joining
them. Perhaps this St Trinian's figure could give the
officer a ride?

ABOVE Few bother to look up and see whether the Queen's Standard is flying, denoting that HM is at home. But as it's a Sunday, she is at Windsor for the weekend which is just as well. The first London Marathon finished not on Westminster Bridge but on Constitution Hill, just about opposite her private apartments on the second floor of the north side of the Palace. The only runner in the Royal family is Prince Charles, who used to train hard in the '70s when he was an amateur National Hunt jockey, but the security element would have been a nightmare had he ever taken up an invitation to compete in the London Marathon.

LEFT Terry Hall (26951) seems happy with the clarinet playing of 53-year-old Eric 'Busker' Newton but is Eric equally happy with Terry's designer kit?

ABOVE Studies in valour: 30-year-old Bruce Lee (18687), who competes on crutches and still beats many home, and 22-year-old Vivien Mullett, the recipient of a Snowdon Award, being 'chauffeured' in the final stages.

No sporting event, not least the London Marathon, could even be contemplated without the fantastic support of the St John's Ambulance Brigade and their tireless team of workers. While everyone hopes they will not need their assistance, many receive it and within sight of the finish this competitor is being exhorted on by a marshal, as an ambulanceman comes over to see what he can do to help – perhaps a fireman's lift over the finish line? I once saw someone crawl the last fifty yards or so and the agony of watching him was almost as intense as the pain he was experiencing.

RIGHT   Harmony for Joanna, Cynthia, Sue and Jean who started together and finished together, in step for the final yards as they had been throughout the race. And not a bow out of place!

BELOW A moment shared, memories of which will remain with 36-year-old Margaret Cefferty (36132) and 42 -year-old Janice Kennedy forever (especially if they purchase this book) – holding hands as they reach Westminster Bridge and a sight of the finish.

ABOVE LEFT Frank McKenna (14108) lending a shoulder to an exhausted Stuart Crosscombe (11062) as they meet the bridge while (above right)

68-year-old David Hornady (16693), a veteran of the New York Marathon, shows not a sign of distress as he reaches the finish.

RIGHT A winner of a more personal battle and recovering from chemotherapy, escorted by Kevin 'Kev' Rattle (14254) and David Smith (34927).

ABOVE One of the most impressive sights of a former London Marathon was the squad of Gurkhas who competed in full kit, a feat emulated this year by the Royal Marines, who just failed to beat the team record.

RIGHT The moment Eamonn Martin, who was making his marathon debut at the age of 34, proved he was neither too old nor too big for the event – as he demonstrates the speed which took him to the British 10,000 metres record and powers away from Mexican Isidro Rico meeting the rise to the bridge opposite the Houses of Parliament.

ABOVE Someone's missing here: 34-year-old Linda Shelton (33666) and Alison Leslie (33664) appear to have lost Carol Dunne, who was supposed to be wearing 33665.

RIGHT Philip Thornalley (7142), aged 33, shows commendable joy as he realises he's done it. The time doesn't matter, the camaraderie of the occasion has made it all worthwhile.

As the massed start of the marathon takes place in Greenwich, nearer the finish along the Embankment the Mini Marathon is set in motion – a four-mile diversion for spectators and proud parents and relations alike, followed forty-five minutes later by the Wheelchair Mini Marathon in Lower Thames Street, won this year by Graham Burns (top right) who made it look easy! Like the competitors in all the other sections of the marathon, there is a reward: a treasured medal which these two young ladies were taking back to their homes in Brent.

OVERLEAF Georges Vandammo of Belgium salutes victory as he breaks the tape to win the Wheelchair Marathon in a time of 1:44:10.

![NutraSweet London Marathon Citizen 2:10:50 Unisys Computer NutraSweet - male runner #59 breaking the tape](finish-line-photo)

ABOVE LEFT   Three days after his wife Julie gave birth to their first son Eamonn Jnr, who weighed in at 9lbs 10oz, Eamonn Martin wins $55,000 as he breaks the tape in his first marathon. The couple have two daughters, Lydia, six, and four-year-old Rosie, so young Eamonn was just what the stork ordered.

ABOVE RIGHT   For the women's victor, Katrin Dorre, every race is a bonus. Twelve years ago following major knee surgery it seemed unlikely that she would ever compete again but the East German authorities persevered and in 1982 Katrin returned to their elite squad.

RIGHT   For every runner, finishing is a personal victory, whatever the time and around here, the 3:43 mark, is where I would have come in – although before my last London Marathon I slipped on a ball my dog Tulip had carefully left on the stairs and fell fifteen feet just two nights before the race. I hobbled round with an injured knee in just under four hours – my worst time ever, but valiant in the circumstances!

LEFT Computerised timing at the finish gives everyone the figure from which they will deduct the exact time that it took them to cross the official start line.

BELOW For Lord Snowdon, his first association with the London Marathon was a tremendous bonus for the Award Scheme which he set up in 1981, with £14,000 earned from reproduction fees of his photographs of the Royal Family. Since then £380,000 has been awarded to around 400 disabled students to help them pursue further education. Lord Snowdon was disabled himself as a teenager when he spent more than a year in bed with polio but recovered enough to cox the Cambridge Eight to victory in the 1950 Varsity Boatrace.

RIGHT Every one a winner!

LEFT To the victors the spoils while (below) Liz McColgan is 'chaperoned' by one of the officials whose role is to supervise the dope-testing of the elite runners, a now customary procedure after all big races.

ABOVE The advertisement on the back of the programme encourages one weary runner through the recovery period.

Reflections of successful completion of this greatest of races which dates back to Pheidippides, the Greek soldier who ran the distance of approximately twenty-four miles (thirty-nine kilometres) from the battlefield of Marathon to Athens with the news of the Greek victory over the Persians in 490BC. It was first included in the Olympic Games in Athens in 1896. Although of little intrinsic value, the badges are much prized. When I flew back on British Airways after running in the New York Marathon, most of the passengers had also competed and wore their badges throughout the flight around their necks – the cabin staff ignored them at their peril!

Among the statistics of the 1993 London Marathon is that of the 35,570 original entries – 25,500 started and 24,450 finished – 48 were clergymen. No mention however of the two Sikhs who added an exotic touch to the competitors and were the centre of attention after they finished – and who could resist the happy smiles (right) of 62-year-old Amrik Singh (27082) and his running partner. For the record there were also 500 bankers, 64 beauticians, 15 film-makers, 28 gamekeepers, 24 airline pilots, 792 students, and 1,406 unemployed. The oldest runner was Alfred W. Gibson, aged 85, the oldest woman runner Jenny Allen, aged 81, and the youngest 18-year-olds Daniel Bailey and Jennie Lewis.

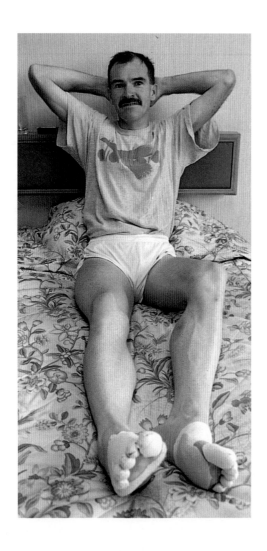

LEFT The party's over for the legendary Rob de Castello, resting after the race back at the Tower Hotel. Known as 'Deke', he won the inaugural world championship marathon back in 1983 but was not able to bow out on a victorious note, sadly – and with toes like that who can blame him! After fifteen years of marathoning, London was to have been his swansong, but after a disappointing race he has said he may try to go out on a happier note.

BELOW AND RIGHT For all runners, whether champions like Deke or ordinary folk who want, perhaps even just once, to prove themselves in the greatest personal test, the end of the race is a time for reflection. In the morning the aches and pains, especially for those who did not 'educate' their legs by putting in the miles of training, will be a temporary reminder of a unique moment.

The months of sacrifice are behind, the long hours of
training, the personal battle finally won and
exhaustion allows few positive thoughts, other than a
sense of accomplishment.

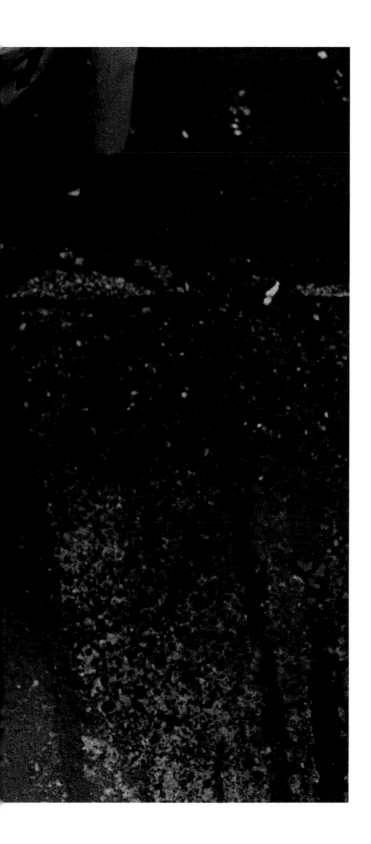

For all there is one lasting, beautiful memory:
'I ran the Marathon'

THE FINISHERS
AND
THEIR TIMES

The 1993 NutraSweet London Marathon

	1-100		101-200		201-300		301-400		401-500	
1	E MARTIN	2:10:50	A GEEN	2:29:11	A RUBEN	2:34:41	C FINILL	2:38:54	O PHIPPS	2:42:01
2	I RICO	2:10:53	S DAVIES	2:29:15	R LEMETTINEN	2:34:44	S DOYLE	2:39:00	K JUERGEN	2:42:04
3	G GAJDUS	2:11:07	P LOWERY	2:29:17	P WATKINS	2:34:45	J SKOSANA	2:39:04	J PRICE	2:42:06
4	S BETTIOL	2:11:55	R MURUGIAH	2:29:18	M SUMMERS	2:34:48	N RUSSELL	2:39:07	S LOUNDES	2:42:08
5	F BJORKLI	2:12:23	S TRUMP	2:29:20	B SIMPSON	2:34:52	J REES	2:39:11	J HOOD	2:42:10
6	D BUZZA	2:12:24	W MCTAGGART	2:29:21	B HUGHES	2:34:54	S GAIR	2:39:16	K ALLEN	2:42:12
7	S BAEK	2:12:34	R BELL	2:29:23	G GREEN	2:34:56	G TAYLOR	2:39:18	J HESELTON	2:42:13
8	A SALAH	2:12:40	N MOORE	2:29:28	J VERITY	2:35:00	P LOCKETT	2:39:18	L CORMIER	2:42:13
9	J TORRES	2:13:44	G WATERSON	2:29:33	P ROONEY	2:35:03	E VERMEIREN	2:39:20	J HUNTER	2:42:14
10	S BRACE	2:14:00	L MCCOLGAN	2:29:37	M PACKER	2:35:05	M CROOK	2:39:21	G HOROVITZ	2:42:14
11	T MOQHALI	2:14:40	P BLAKE	2:29:39	S SMITH	2:35:05	J DONNELLY	2:39:21	R WATT	2:42:16
12	T BEKELE	2:15:43	K WILKINSON	2:29:40	S MARLAND	2:35:17	T CRADDOCK	2:39:22	P HIRST	2:42:16
13	O OBDILLAHI	2:16:00	M GORMLEY	2:29:41	S MEEK	2:35:24	I CARDEN	2:39:23	R WHITTAKER	2:42:18
14	V BUKHANOU	2:16:16	A BROWN	2:29:42	M LEE	2:35:27	P SIMPSON	2:39:25	S INGALL	2:42:19
15	H JONES	2:16:35	B JONES	2:29:43	M TENERYD	2:35:35	D PAGET	2:39:26	T JOHANSSON	2:42:19
16	E TLHOBO	2:16:53	B BROWN	2:29:49	J WALLIS	2:35:39	C WOODWARD	2:39:28	K DAVIES	2:42:21
17	V SILVA	2:17:00	P HALL	2:29:49	R STANIER	2:35:48	T MAGUIRE	2:39:30	R HATFIELD	2:42:21
18	M MCLOUGHLIN	2:17:27	A CASTRO	2:29:56	P O'BRIEN	2:35:50	P VUORINEN	2:39:40	D CHALFEN	2:42:22
19	J SILVA	2:17:30	V NEW	2:29:59	P ALLEN	2:35:55	S ALMOND	2:39:40	R ROTTIGNI	2:42:24
20	C BUCKLEY	2:17:42	A LONG	2:29:59	P BRUNNING	2:35:57	W BROWN	2:39:40	B EVANS	2:42:26
21	T SATO	2:17:46	M HOEY	2:30:00	L PASINI	2:35:57	G TRIMBLE	2:39:40	A JONES	2:42:26
22	T NAESS	2:17:50	R ROBINSON	2:30:12	I BARNES	2:36:05	T RICHARDSON	2:39:41	P MULLER	2:42:30
23	G BORKA	2:18:52	S MOORE	2:30:19	D JONES	2:36:08	D MOULD	2:39:42	M WALKER	2:42:31
24	J RIBEIRO	2:18:56	A KEAN	2:30:24	P JOHNSON	2:36:09	G GRAVES	2:39:43	R PITT	2:42:34
25	P WHITEHEAD	2:18:57	E BROWN	2:30:24	N ODDY	2:36:17	M GREEN	2:39:43	D SANDERSON	2:42:37
26	D RATHBONE	2:18:58	C WOODD	2:30:29	D SMITH	2:36:18	M WALFORD	2:39:45	A LINES	2:42:42
27	P CARPENITO	2:18:59	A SIMPSON	2:30:33	M WOLSEY	2:36:22	R FERRIS-KAAN	2:39:45	S HOME	2:42:42
28	S ROZNAN	2:19:00	M GOATLEY	2:30:35	C BAILEY	2:36:23	D MCKENNA	2:39:46	M FRENCH	2:42:43
29	R PIERCE	2:19:07	G STEIERT	2:30:39	M HAWKINS	2:36:27	J BARKER	2:39:46	P SIBBETT	2:42:45
30	A VARLET	2:19:10	M FERGUSON	2:30:43	K MEARDON	2:36:28	I GREENHALGH	2:39:48	A LEFEVRE	2:42:51
31	P DAVIES-HALE	2:19:35	B MCNULTY	2:30:43	G BARNES	2:36:29	C OWENS	2:39:49	B HOWIE	2:42:51
32	N FILHO	2:19:44	N BERRILL	2:31:12	D BOX	2:36:29	S HARRISON	2:39:55	J HUSBANDS	2:42:52
33	R DE CASTELLA	2:19:44	J COOPER	2:31:17	E COOK	2:36:29	M BOWERING	2:39:55	J MARTIN	2:42:54
34	R BJORKLI	2:20:02	M BUMSTEAD	2:31:25	C MCLOUGHLIN	2:36:30	S THRAVES	2:39:55	N LIPSCOMBE	2:42:54
35	G DAVIES	2:20:43	P ROGERS	2:31:29	T O'FLYNN	2:36:36	P GREEN	2:39:58	R MARCHANT	2:42:55
36	D MCGRATH	2:21:02	J BENNETT	2:31:34	R JONES	2:36:39	J STAPLES	2:39:59	E HAMREN	2:42:56
37	M COWMAN	2:21:13	D ROBERTSON	2:31:43	M ASPINALL	2:36:39	F SAVRE	2:40:02	G GLOVER	2:42:57
38	D DE REUCK	2:21:41	Y ADEN	2:31:50	R GARDNER	2:36:41	I MONTE	2:40:02	R FRANCIS	2:42:57
39	S GARCIA	2:22:25	M HENDERSON	2:31:50	H MATTISSON	2:36:44	H DOBSON	2:40:06	G PENHALIGON	2:42:59
40	P CATERINO	2:22:43	L MERCER	2:31:50	F PLIESTER	2:36:46	N MILLS	2:40:07	C BAKER	2:43:03
41	A GUILDER	2:23:08	L JONSSON	2:31:52	L GOWLAND	2:36:47	S SWANSTON	2:40:08	D CHAPLIN	2:43:05
42	P DESRUMAUX	2:23:28	S NORMANDALE	2:31:57	A HEMMINGS	2:36:50	G HOBDEN	2:40:09	J CUMMINS	2:43:05
43	L MOSCHINI	2:23:29	J BELL	2:32:03	R RETTER	2:36:53	W ADAMS	2:40:10	P COLLING	2:43:09
44	C BLOMME	2:23:34	J MERRYFIELD	2:32:10	P BATES	2:36:58	P DEPINOY	2:40:11	K DAVIS	2:43:11
45	A SHAHANGA	2:23:50	I PATTEN	2:32:13	H SCHWUERZINGER	2:36:58	J IVORY	2:40:11	D SIMON	2:43:11
46	J STEPHENS	2:24:03	A ROGERS	2:32:15	T COUSINS	2:37:01	I TACK	2:40:15	A HORSEY	2:43:12
47	R NASH	2:24:10	R DE SCHACHT	2:32:22	M KLEANTHOUS	2:37:02	S HANCOCK	2:40:17	D WILKES	2:43:12
48	D HILL	2:24:18	B GAFFNEY	2:32:29	K COOK	2:37:04	A NICKSON	2:40:19	F TERZONI	2:43:13
49	A HOLT	2:24:26	R KOKOWSKA	2:32:30	G CUNLIFFE	2:37:05	Y JEHANNO	2:40:20	P HOUGHTON	2:43:15
50	P PFEIFENBERGER	2:24:27	J DINGWALL	2:32:34	N CAMP	2:37:07	C THOMPSON	2:40:24	N HUSBAND	2:43:17
51	W FOSTER	2:24:35	M LAVENDER	2:32:42	N DRAKE	2:37:08	E THOMAS	2:40:25	D BYRNE	2:43:20
52	G WIGHTMAN	2:25:14	N CLARK	2:32:45	D WOOD	2:37:09	D CLARK	2:40:29	R HOWARTH	2:43:21
53	E WILLIAMS	2:25:16	S PASCOE	2:32:46	P DAWS	2:37:10	G MATTHEWS	2:40:37	B VOLLENTINE	2:43:23
54	P FROUD	2:25:18	C DRYDEN	2:32:49	R HANCOCK	2:37:11	M WILCOX	2:40:38	P ROUND	2:43:24
55	P PLANCKE	2:25:25	S WATTS	2:32:50	C YOUNGSON	2:37:14	J WEST	2:40:42	D HAMLING	2:43:25
56	S VERMEULEN	2:25:27	L MOLLER	2:32:56	R LATHAM	2:37:15	B SWEENY	2:40:49	A CRONIN	2:43:30
57	D KNIGHT	2:25:29	P FRAZER	2:33:00	T HARRIS	2:37:16	G KNIGHT	2:40:50	M CLARKE	2:43:30
58	M CADMAN	2:25:34	A BROUX	2:33:03	B BLACKWELL	2:37:17	M JACKETT	2:40:52	G SALMI	2:43:31
59	T HOLE	2:25:36	D WUST	2:33:04	G DENNIS	2:37:17	D SWEENEY	2:40:53	J LUMSDEN	2:43:33
60	E TWOHIG	2:25:39	A JONES	2:33:10	A IVANOVA	2:37:21	T PARKINSON	2:40:57	H KONIETZKO	2:43:35
61	P PETERSEN	2:25:40	D MILLER	2:33:14	C CASSIDY	2:37:24	I CARSWELL	2:40:58	T POTTER	2:43:36
62	J HOOPER	2:25:48	J STEPHENSON	2:33:15	M WHITELOCK	2:37:24	D RITCHIE	2:40:58	I MORRIS	2:43:41
63	A MASON	2:25:51	S MC ANANEY	2:33:17	W CHANCE	2:37:25	K BENNETT	2:41:04	G BELL	2:43:42
64	D GREEN	2:25:55	D LACY	2:33:20	M EDDY	2:37:27	Z VEGVARI	2:41:06	P CHAPMAN	2:43:43
65	J COLLINS	2:25:59	A POOLEY	2:33:22	J BARKER	2:37:31	A CARRUTHERS	2:41:06	J LUMB	2:43:44
66	W SNELGROVE	2:25:59	D COX	2:33:23	R BEAUMONT	2:37:32	D EMERY	2:41:07	D HARTWELL	2:43:45
67	M MINN	2:26:02	S BEATTIE	2:33:29	M PARKER	2:37:34	K COURTNEY	2:41:10	R PARSONS	2:43:45
68	V SHTYRTS	2:26:06	C WEBB	2:33:29	D PHILPOT	2:37:36	D SPEAKE	2:41:11	C BAILEY	2:43:46
69	P BETTRIDGE	2:26:17	A PAUNONEN	2:33:32	M ROUSE	2:37:37	A GRAY	2:41:11	W SCOTT	2:43:47
70	T SAUTIERE	2:26:29	C HIBBERD	2:33:33	M LEE	2:37:39	R BAMSEY	2:41:20	D JONES	2:43:48
71	C TALL	2:26:36	D MOUTHON	2:33:33	A MCNEILL	2:37:40	C LOIZOU	2:41:21	W GRAHAM	2:43:48
72	A CHILTON	2:26:47	C HUGHES	2:33:35	R EVANS	2:37:45	S FLOHIC	2:41:22	A STENNING	2:43:48
73	K DORRE	2:27:09	J MCNEILL	2:33:37	F FIOLET	2:37:52	R COCHRANE	2:41:23	R LAWRENCE	2:43:49
74	T CHARLES	2:27:13	J MADDISON	2:33:41	B TICKNER	2:37:54	J REILLY	2:41:23	J ALLEN	2:43:51
75	M MILES	2:27:20	C SMALE	2:33:41	G ASTILL	2:37:54	M EARTHY	2:41:25	P FLETCHER	2:43:52
76	A WILTON	2:27:27	W OXBOROUGH	2:33:42	S SHEARD	2:38:02	R RATHJEN	2:41:26	T JOHNSON	2:43:52
77	L ONDIEKI	2:27:27	S JONES	2:33:43	N BATESON	2:38:04	D TRUEPENNY	2:41:27	M STOLL	2:43:53
78	C NOYON	2:27:31	D LONG	2:33:45	M COLLINS	2:38:05	P HURCOMBE	2:41:30	A MOULD	2:43:55
79	D ELLIS	2:27:38	I HAMER	2:33:45	P VESEY	2:38:07	A GASKELL	2:41:30	D BASTABLE	2:43:55
80	G RAWLINSON	2:27:50	C WILLIAMS	2:33:45	M WITTERING	2:38:08	A EMMITT	2:41:30	Z MARCHANT	2:43:59
81	K MCLELLAN	2:27:57	D NAGEL	2:33:49	D HURDWELL	2:38:09	G HALL	2:41:34	R SIMPSON	2:44:00
82	W GRISTWOOD	2:27:57	D LEE	2:33:50	J COLLINS	2:38:20	A MAZZEO	2:41:34	W SICHEL	2:44:02
83	A AMRAOUI	2:27:59	J CARSWELL	2:33:51	J STEVENS	2:38:22	P WHITEHEAD	2:41:39	M PEACE	2:44:05
84	R CEDARO	2:27:59	J SHAW	2:33:51	J BROWN	2:38:22	M CLEMENTS	2:41:40	J ABEL	2:44:07
85	M RILEY	2:28:03	M AIREY	2:33:55	K PERKKIO	2:38:27	P RICHARDSON	2:41:43	K FOTHERBY	2:44:07
86	J WIECZOREK	2:28:07	C GIULIANO	2:34:01	D ALEXANDER	2:38:28	M FRANCIS	2:41:43	P ARNOUX	2:44:07
87	S WHEELER	2:28:18	E WILSON	2:34:05	S BADGERY	2:38:28	S ABBEY	2:41:44	G WHITCHURCH	2:44:09
88	G DELL	2:28:23	N DOYLE	2:34:09	M EDE	2:38:30	P PEREIRA	2:41:46	G KUFFNER	2:44:10
89	J JARVIS	2:28:37	R MCLEARY	2:34:18	T KARPINSKI	2:38:31	P BROWN	2:41:50	D HOLLEY	2:44:10
90	A WARD	2:28:39	T ANDERSON	2:34:19	M KEATING	2:38:33	J MASON	2:41:50	B COURTNEY	2:44:11
91	J ESTALL	2:28:44	A RYBICKA	2:34:21	A MAKOVEC	2:38:33	G ZHULIEVA	2:41:50	R PLATTS	2:44:11
92	R HIGGINS	2:28:45	N NICHOLSON	2:34:21	P MARSHALL	2:38:35	C STEPTOE	2:41:51	B WEBB	2:44:12
93	D MANSBRIDGE	2:28:47	A BOTTOMLEY	2:34:24	R ELSTONE	2:38:39	L GODIER	2:41:52	F ROYLE	2:44:18
94	M MCGEOCH	2:28:49	P STURTRIDGE	2:34:28	P DUNN	2:38:41	G COULAM	2:41:52	S SKINNER	2:44:18
95	S KEYWOOD	2:28:50	A RIDGWAY	2:34:31	F DAY	2:38:48	P DOVE	2:41:53	D CHAPMAN-JONES	2:44:20
96	W TWEED	2:28:51	D NANKIVELL	2:34:34	B LAWS	2:38:50	C MASON	2:41:54	P WIDDISON	2:44:21
97	R WYLIE	2:28:55	G MACFADYEN	2:34:34	P KINSELLA	2:38:51	S BRADY	2:41:56	S COURTNEY	2:44:21
98	R CALLISTER	2:28:59	L AUZOU	2:34:35	J BATEMAN	2:38:52	A HARRAN	2:41:56	C SKAIFE	2:44:21
99	P BARR	2:29:04	P PAPE	2:34:37	B HALL	2:38:53	D MELLOR	2:41:58	S DOXEY	2:44:21
100	D YAKIMISHYN	2:29:07	R SHUM	2:34:38	A PEAD	2:38:53	C HAIRS	2:41:58	S BRIGNALI	2:44:22

	501-600		601-700		701-800		801-900		901-1000	
1	A SCALFE	2:44:23	R MORRELL	2:46:35	M STUART	2:48:18	R GARLAND	2:49:53	A EADIE	2:51:25
2	M HACKERAY	2:44:24	P WATERS	2:46:36	I RUSSELL	2:48:20	A ROSS	2:49:54	A DICKENSON	2:51:26
3	K WALFORD	2:44:24	D KITCHING	2:46:37	D ROWLAND	2:48:20	S AMORANITIS	2:49:54	C YOUNG	2:51:26
4	S COMBE	2:44:24	M MATTISON	2:46:37	L TURNER	2:48:20	M GATENS	2:49:54	A MOORE	2:51:26
5	R WILLIAMS	2:44:26	S ANDREW	2:46:38	B BARRETT	2:48:23	M MCMAINS	2:49:54	M HAYLEY	2:51:27
6	K WILSON	2:44:27	M SMITH	2:46:41	K ALBINSON	2:48:24	A CHELL	2:49:54	B HAGE	2:51:27
7	F HUGHES	2:44:29	S SMYTHE	2:46:41	D O'TOOLE	2:48:25	A MURPHY	2:49:55	R KELLY	2:51:28
8	M HARRISON	2:44:32	T WATT	2:46:43	S PARTINGTON	2:48:27	A CRUMP	2:49:55	K WOULFE	2:51:28
9	W CROOK	2:44:33	K JONES	2:46:43	M MCKENZIE	2:48:28	B GORE	2:49:56	M DEVINE	2:51:28
10	P KING	2:44:35	J BUICK	2:46:51	A FARMER	2:48:29	L PRATT	2:49:56	R PRITCHARD	2:51:29
11	P JACKSON	2:44:37	P MOTTRAM	2:46:52	G TREGENZA	2:48:29	M PICKARD	2:49:57	D FRANCIS	2:51:32
12	P MANN	2:44:38	H BELL	2:46:57	R DAVIS	2:48:30	E ROBINSON	2:49:59	A CHUTTER	2:51:36
13	R WOOD	2:44:40	J BRADY	2:46:57	W CAMERON	2:48:31	N HOLLIER	2:50:02	R HYLAND	2:51:37
14	G RUBEY	2:44:40	J BEARDSWORTH	2:46:58	M GODERSKI	2:48:31	S COLEMAN	2:50:02	M JONES	2:51:38
15	K WADELEY	2:44:42	A LANAHAN	2:46:58	D PLATT	2:48:32	J PLUMRIDGE	2:50:02	K SCUDAMORE	2:51:39
16	J PRIEST	2:44:46	B MEON	2:46:59	R DOBSON	2:48:35	Z LOWE	2:50:05	S STRETCH	2:51:40
17	S VINES	2:44:47	T GOULDING	2:47:00	P GOODYEAR	2:48:36	T HAIR	2:50:06	D MULLINGS	2:51:41
18	G KNOTT	2:44:48	R JOHNSTON	2:47:01	S COOPER	2:48:38	A HUDSON	2:50:06	R NOVIS	2:51:42
19	G STEWART	2:44:49	C ABBOTT	2:47:02	P PALMER	2:48:38	S MCHUGH	2:50:07	R HUNTLEY	2:51:43
20	J BOADA	2:44:50	F DUGUID	2:47:02	R DOMAN	2:48:40	G STYAN	2:50:07	R GARDENER	2:51:44
21	T SIMMONS	2:44:51	A PEACOCK	2:47:06	R SANDSTRAK	2:48:40	D CAVE	2:50:09	C BIRCH	2:51:45
22	A COOK	2:44:51	M SLEATH	2:47:08	S WESTHEAD	2:48:40	T LOUTON	2:50:10	P TARRIER	2:51:45
23	B DAVIES	2:44:52	S THOMAS	2:47:09	B OSBORNE	2:48:43	A FORREST	2:50:12	G FUBL	2:51:45
24	M HOLLIDAY	2:44:52	K FRANKLIN	2:47:09	C LEROY	2:48:44	J YATES	2:50:12	R CLEVERLEY	2:51:46
25	P MESSENGER	2:44:53	P LEE	2:47:10	G SYKES	2:48:45	S THIRSK	2:50:12	D SMITH	2:51:47
26	C MORGAN	2:44:55	G ARMSTRONG	2:47:11	V YUBERO	2:48:46	B CARRINGTON	2:50:13	A KURSE	2:51:47
27	K HEWINGS	2:44:56	G HANNAFORD	2:47:13	S BOYES	2:48:47	D BOWDEN	2:50:13	M FLEMING	2:51:49
28	W GARDNER	2:44:57	S PORTER	2:47:13	A DAWSON	2:48:48	T CHALMERS	2:50:14	J CROCKFORD	2:51:50
29	S BURTHEM	2:44:57	L HEAP	2:47:14	A KEEN	2:48:48	E TICKNER	2:50:14	F GONZALEZ	2:51:51
30	M KAESER	2:44:58	A BROWN	2:47:16	R FOWLER	2:48:48	D GARNER	2:50:15	C DAVIES	2:51:54
31	J HARRIMAN	2:44:58	M SYMONS	2:47:17	J FRAZER	2:48:49	T SJOSTROM	2:50:15	B COURTNEY	2:51:56
32	C HUNTER-ROWE	2:44:59	M BAGGOTT	2:47:17	C MORRIS	2:48:53	M DOYLE	2:50:16	S FLETCHER	2:51:58
33	D MOSELEY	2:45:00	R BOON	2:47:18	B SMALL	2:48:54	T KNIGHTLEY	2:50:16	A AUSTIN	2:51:59
34	G DE KESEL	2:45:01	G LOCK	2:47:18	P MURRELL	2:48:54	C PRICE	2:50:17	A STEWART	2:52:03
35	A MORRISON	2:45:05	D NIXON	2:47:19	A EVANS	2:48:55	R WILD	2:50:19	H CARPENTER	2:52:06
36	J WHITE	2:45:06	M BOSTOCK	2:47:20	M FLOWER	2:48:56	I PETFIELD	2:50:22	P LEADER	2:52:06
37	A DUMPER	2:45:06	I BRIDGETT	2:47:21	J LAMMAS	2:48:56	I HAETTA	2:50:23	A HAWKINS	2:52:07
38	E FRANCIS	2:45:07	C JACKSON	2:47:22	P CHRISTMAS	2:48:56	G CASTELLO CONEJO	2:50:23	J REEVES	2:52:07
39	L WILLIAMS	2:45:12	J HEYWOOD	2:47:23	R NEENAN	2:48:57	C HEVEY	2:50:23	P MADDISON	2:52:07
40	T SCREEN	2:45:12	G SLIGHT	2:47:23	D MARSHALL	2:48:57	J SAYNOR	2:50:24	S OWEN	2:52:08
41	R HEDGES	2:45:12	D PERCY	2:47:23	E WATSON	2:48:58	G SCHOLEFIELD	2:50:25	A ALLEN	2:52:08
42	S MARTIN	2:45:13	T MERRINGTON	2:47:23	A PETON	2:48:58	A PATERSON	2:50:26	D SMITH	2:52:09
43	D WALKER	2:45:13	L CARR	2:47:23	T TEMPLE	2:48:59	G LYALL	2:50:26	A MARSH	2:52:10
44	J CROSS	2:45:16	N MPOFU	2:47:26	G LAVENDER	2:49:00	I STEMP	2:50:27	M ANDERSON	2:52:11
45	M FARRELL	2:45:21	R BOWYER	2:47:26	F SAETHRE	2:49:01	G SCOTT	2:50:28	A BADHAM	2:52:15
46	D GREEN	2:45:23	M STENNING	2:47:26	R BENNETT	2:49:02	D VERITY	2:50:29	T SMITH	2:52:15
47	E HALL	2:45:23	P BOUVET	2:47:28	C MORRISON	2:49:04	M WIGGINS	2:50:30	P DOBBS	2:52:16
48	M MURPHY	2:45:27	S BENTLEY	2:47:33	D DENMAN	2:49:04	M O'BRIEN	2:50:34	A RUSSELL	2:52:17
49	H HOEGEN	2:45:27	T DAVIES	2:47:33	M NAHVI	2:49:05	T KEELING	2:50:34	T WATSON	2:52:17
50	J DRYDEN	2:45:28	B KALAND	2:47:33	N MACGREGOR	2:49:08	R ALLEN	2:50:35	B LENNOR	2:52:18
51	M DIAS	2:45:28	M LAMBERT	2:47:34	M DE GRANDE	2:49:08	J COUNSELL	2:50:36	J DOHERTY	2:52:19
52	P KEMP	2:45:29	C SHEA	2:47:36	D LITTLEWOOD	2:49:09	P LEWIN	2:50:37	A POVER	2:52:19
53	J TYLER	2:45:31	D ALLAWAY	2:47:36	S BALL	2:49:09	J RENE	2:50:38	A CAVANAGH	2:52:19
54	G HINES	2:45:32	J CROSLAND	2:47:37	N JONES	2:49:09	R BLANDFORD	2:50:39	S BLACKBURN	2:52:20
55	P ALLEN	2:45:34	A WOOD	2:47:39	D PRUDHOMME	2:49:09	W FITZPATRICK	2:50:39	C MABOGE	2:52:20
56	A GILL	2:45:38	G FRAYNE	2:47:41	C SCOBEY	2:49:10	I STAINTHORPE	2:50:40	J HUMPHRIES	2:52:21
57	P QUINE	2:45:40	D MILLER	2:47:42	C KIRBY	2:49:11	D VIEILLE	2:50:41	G TODD	2:52:22
58	S BECKETT	2:45:41	M NEALE	2:47:42	N SAUNDERS	2:49:17	P REDDEN	2:50:41	R WILSON	2:52:22
59	D WOODLEY	2:45:42	G DOULMAN	2:47:43	J BOSTOCK	2:49:17	J RICHARDSON	2:50:42	J HUDSPITH	2:52:22
60	P HURD	2:45:48	K GRAHAM	2:47:44	D GROOM	2:49:18	L DUFFY	2:50:42	M BLACK	2:52:24
61	S HICKSON	2:45:49	K MARLEY	2:47:46	R DICKINSON	2:49:19	B LONG	2:50:43	M FERLEIRA	2:52:25
62	R POLLEY	2:45:50	K HART	2:47:47	D HAGAN	2:49:21	E SHOESMITH	2:50:45	S CONNELLY	2:52:25
63	A PAYNE	2:45:53	S PERRY	2:47:47	M DILAVER	2:49:22	M BLEASOALE	2:50:47	R REYNOLDS	2:52:25
64	J MADDISON	2:45:53	R BRETT	2:47:47	B GWYTHER	2:49:24	R DAVISON	2:50:48	R AB-ELWYN	2:52:25
65	F JUDSON	2:45:54	K COOK	2:47:48	G KAY	2:49:25	A STOREY	2:50:48	R ALLARD	2:52:29
66	C MERRIOTT	2:45:54	J GROGAN	2:47:49	N HOLMES	2:49:25	M GAUGHAN	2:50:49	M TAYLOR	2:52:29
67	C PRICE	2:45:54	C LEEMAN	2:47:50	P CRUTCHLEY	2:49:26	E DUNCAN	2:50:49	R RADCLIFFE	2:52:31
68	C CONNOR	2:45:54	C BALDWIN	2:47:50	R HARRISON	2:49:26	L RAMWELL	2:50:50	M WALKER	2:52:32
69	G COX	2:45:55	A COOPER	2:47:51	C BROWN	2:49:29	G HALSEY	2:50:51	J FOWLER	2:52:32
70	D WHITE	2:45:56	A FIELDING	2:47:53	P MARSH	2:49:29	G MACDONALD	2:50:52	S COX	2:52:32
71	D BURKE	2:45:56	I DENT	2:47:54	P DAVISON	2:49:29	G CANFIELD	2:50:52	C MOODY	2:52:33
72	P GOODING	2:45:56	A WATSON	2:47:55	P JUGAN	2:49:30	C TORDOFF	2:50:53	M STARR	2:52:33
73	W WILLMITT	2:45:57	J SPROSON	2:47:56	P SHIRLEY	2:49:30	J DAUGIRAS	2:50:53	J HOLLOWAY	2:52:35
74	R HANNA	2:46:00	J WILLIS	2:47:58	F LE GOFF	2:49:31	P HURLEY	2:50:54	B BURLINGHAM	2:52:36
75	V TINDLE	2:46:01	T SINAR	2:47:58	D NEEDHAM	2:49:32	E CLEMENTS	2:50:55	C JOHNSON	2:52:37
76	K CURTIS	2:46:02	G MARSDEN	2:47:59	G HERRON	2:49:32	A KINGLEY	2:50:55	E EVANS	2:52:38
77	M FLOYMO	2:46:05	D BONNINGTON	2:47:59	B MOWSSAY	2:49:34	M JOHNSON	2:50:57	G VANHOUDENHOVEN	2:52:38
78	A BROCKLEHURST	2:46:05	I MITCHELL	2:48:01	M CONNOR	2:49:35	G DAVIES	2:50:57	D CUMPSTY	2:52:39
79	V PETURHOV	2:46:06	W MURPHY	2:48:01	F HOLMES	2:49:35	C WALTON	2:50:59	C BLOOMFIELD	2:52:40
80	S MCINTOSH	2:46:08	J WIGLEY	2:48:02	M OGLESBY	2:49:35	R KINGSTON	2:50:59	R PHIPPS	2:52:40
81	G COLUMBERG	2:46:10	M VANZULLI	2:48:02	M VANZULLI	2:49:38	A JACOBSSON	2:51:02	D HOPKINS	2:52:40
82	C LITSON	2:46:12	M ARMITAGE	2:48:05	W PAGE	2:49:39	D ANTHONY	2:51:04	M HYDER	2:52:40
83	K CLARKE	2:46:13	P BOWKER	2:48:05	M ELDRED	2:49:39	R SELDON	2:51:06	J CLARKSON	2:52:41
84	R RUSTON	2:46:15	D WILDE	2:48:07	G BRENNAN	2:49:40	I GILES	2:51:06	M BYFORD	2:52:41
85	L GOLDER	2:46:16	C DORAN	2:48:08	A STEDMAN	2:49:41	S CLAYTON	2:51:06	D WATERS	2:52:42
86	M POWELL	2:46:17	D HARGRAVE	2:48:08	A AUSTIN	2:49:43	P ILOTT	2:51:09	P ASHBY	2:52:43
87	M WOODS	2:46:18	B CAIN	2:48:09	M WARD	2:49:43	M TAYLOR	2:51:09	R SEWELL	2:52:43
88	N WHITE	2:46:19	A SHEDDEN	2:48:09	M LURY	2:49:43	D THOMPSON	2:51:09	A ABBOTT	2:52:43
89	I MCDOUGALL	2:46:20	D TATE	2:48:10	S PENNINGTON	2:49:44	I FISHER	2:51:09	D WOOLLEY	2:52:44
90	I PRICE	2:46:21	J GROUT	2:48:10	L COLLINS	2:49:44	D KIRK	2:51:10	B ANDRIAMASOANDRO	2:52:45
91	W JOHNSON	2:46:21	D HENRY	2:48:12	T ALLEN	2:49:45	S VEAL	2:51:11	C DULSON	2:52:45
92	S BRICKER	2:46:23	G HUGHES	2:48:14	I MITCHELL	2:49:47	T WILSON	2:51:12	P GOULD	2:52:46
93	M TINSLEY	2:46:24	J GALLAGHER	2:48:14	T NORTON	2:49:47	K OBRIEN	2:51:14	G OLIVER	2:52:46
94	K BANYARD	2:46:24	M ORMROD	2:48:15	S POWELL	2:49:48	D DOWDLE	2:51:16	E TOMLINSON	2:52:46
95	P JOHNSON	2:46:27	K EVANS	2:48:15	P SUGDEN	2:49:49	R HERNANDEZ	2:51:16	D MYATT	2:52:47
96	L YOUNG	2:46:28	D OGDEN	2:48:15	M PASK	2:49:50	T LYTHE	2:51:17	S LATHWELL	2:52:47
97	G BEZZI	2:46:29	D HUBAND	2:48:15	M MORGAN	2:49:50	A MACLACHLAN	2:51:20	D PETTIFER	2:52:49
98	P FREEMAN	2:46:32	T CUMMINGS	2:48:17	T MC CLENAGHAN	2:49:52	G ANDERSON	2:51:21	G PRATT	2:52:49
99	H GUARDIOLA	2:46:33	G SMITH	2:48:17	I GRINDLEY	2:49:52	J COOMBES	2:51:24	I NYE	2:52:49
100	C GAYNOR	2:46:34	B DAVIS	2:48:18	S JONES	2:49:53	J BURCHAM	2:51:25	P OULD	2:52:50

#	1001-1100		1101-1200		1201-1300		1301-1400		1401-1500	
1	B BROWN	2:52:50	S LAPPAGE	2:54:13	S THOMAS	2:55:10	R PAWSON	2:56:31	A COOPER	2:57:19
2	A DUNN	2:52:51	P JENKINS	2:54:17	P MORAN	2:55:10	B MITCHELL	2:56:32	D FAZACKERLEY	2:57:19
3	D GRITTON	2:52:53	S BARRATT	2:54:17	D LEE	2:55:11	D SYMONDS	2:56:32	D HYDE	2:57:20
4	A LAMBOURNE	2:52:54	A PINFIELD	2:54:17	J MONTEIRO	2:55:11	M CARNE	2:56:32	J BUNERT	2:57:20
5	R GURNEY	2:52:54	R WILLIAMS	2:54:17	C GOEDHALS	2:55:12	S SHINOHARA	2:56:32	T BROWNING	2:57:21
6	M CLACK	2:52:55	B MYERS	2:54:17	G STANLEY	2:55:13	M HOFMANN	2:56:32	R COCKS	2:57:21
7	J MOORE	2:52:55	A WILLIAMS	2:54:17	D ORR	2:55:16	G HILL	2:56:32	J PARDINILLA	2:57:21
8	I RANKINE	2:52:55	G BOOTH	2:54:18	J LUSARDI	2:55:16	A CLARKE	2:56:33	J FELGENTRAEGER	2:57:22
9	T KOCKELBERGH	2:52:56	B HARDY	2:54:18	A LUCK	2:55:16	D MACDONALD	2:56:33	S THOMAS	2:57:22
10	J STEVENSON	2:52:57	H CAILLAUD	2:54:18	P DAVIDSON	2:55:22	J POWER	2:56:34	W WOODS	2:57:22
11	S BOYNTON	2:53:00	J BRAIDE	2:54:19	C ROUTLEDGE	2:55:23	A GLEN	2:56:34	J DAVIES	2:57:22
12	J CHARTER	2:53:01	A CARTWRIGHT	2:54:22	G CUMBER	2:55:23	R PICKERING	2:56:35	P WEEKS	2:57:23
13	J GREY	2:53:02	T ROGERS	2:54:23	M LANGMAN	2:55:28	S STYLES	2:56:36	K MASLEN	2:57:24
14	D COLCLOUGH	2:53:03	K ROBERTS	2:54:23	J LECLERC	2:55:31	R TITCHMARSH	2:56:37	C ANGOVE	2:57:24
15	G ALEXANDER	2:53:03	I EKROL	2:54:24	J NEEDHAM	2:55:33	F WATT	2:56:37	C BINKS	2:57:26
16	C KENNARD	2:53:04	P BUXTON	2:54:26	K REAY	2:55:37	E HAMILTON	2:56:38	M STATHAM	2:57:27
17	A BEXON	2:53:05	N CLEMENT	2:54:26	C REID	2:55:37	A MARQUES E MARQUES	2:56:38	P MACQUAID	2:57:27
18	A MANSI	2:53:05	D GILPIN	2:54:26	I DALRYMPLE	2:55:38	M SMITH	2:56:38	E CAIRNS	2:57:28
19	A MATSON	2:53:05	A MITCHELL	2:54:27	A SWANTON	2:55:39	D COOPER	2:56:39	B PASCOE	2:57:29
20	I BARBER	2:53:06	M FOXON	2:54:28	E DICKENS	2:55:39	P EMBLETON	2:56:40	W EINSEL	2:57:30
21	F GOLDING	2:53:07	A CULSHAW	2:54:28	A WHIDDETT	2:55:41	S COUSINS	2:56:40	J HUNT	2:57:31
22	F BRIFFAUT	2:53:08	B PARADISE	2:54:28	P HUCK	2:55:42	K HATTER	2:56:40	J HOGAN	2:57:31
23	M CHORLEY	2:53:09	D BUTCHER	2:54:29	C ANGUS	2:55:43	H WATSON	2:56:40	E FLATHER	2:57:32
24	J NISBET	2:53:09	P WRIGHT	2:54:29	P BEAL	2:55:45	B LORCY	2:56:40	S KEATING	2:57:32
25	D GRANDIN	2:53:10	A JACOB	2:54:30	F SUBACCHI	2:55:45	D WILLIAMS	2:56:40	R AUERBACK	2:57:32
26	S GEE	2:53:12	A KELLY	2:54:30	P CLIFFORD	2:55:45	K DONKIN	2:56:40	P EVANS	2:57:34
27	L CARR	2:53:14	S GALE	2:54:31	D COX	2:55:45	S VAN HAUWE	2:56:40	E JONES	2:57:35
28	M MANN	2:53:14	D ROSE	2:54:31	G WALKER	2:55:45	J GARVEY	2:56:41	K BESSANT	2:57:35
29	S SCHNEIDERS	2:53:17	L SCHAFER	2:54:34	P LOFTUS	2:55:46	J RUST	2:56:41	S PAGE	2:57:37
30	C THOMAS	2:53:18	D WARREN	2:54:34	J NORTON	2:55:46	P LALOY	2:56:42	P DOVEY	2:57:38
31	A MC KIE	2:53:18	S MANNIX	2:54:35	K OAKLEY	2:55:46	P WILLIAMSON	2:56:43	S HAMPSON	2:57:38
32	L PEETERS	2:53:18	K MORREY	2:54:36	A JOHNSON	2:55:47	B MCGRATH	2:56:43	B CAMERON	2:57:40
33	M GELLION	2:53:19	J PRUDHAM	2:54:36	S KELLY	2:55:48	K MILNE	2:56:44	J PEREZ LUIS	2:57:40
34	B VIRONDEAU	2:53:19	K STOREY	2:54:36	J THOMAS	2:55:49	D LEAVY	2:56:47	I GODDEN	2:57:40
35	P WALKER	2:53:20	H BETHKE	2:54:38	A FALKSON	2:55:49	N YOUNG	2:56:48	W LEANEY	2:57:40
36	D HALL	2:53:20	P DOWLES	2:54:38	A NICHOLL	2:55:49	M TOWNSEND	2:56:48	M JOHNSTON	2:57:42
37	K KNOX	2:53:22	D STEVENS	2:54:38	M BURROWS	2:55:50	D OSTINS	2:56:48	C DENNIS	2:57:43
38	S TURVEY	2:53:23	J HUGHES	2:54:39	P GAME	2:55:50	P SIMPSON	2:56:49	A VERDIE	2:57:43
39	K PENALUNA	2:53:24	D GILLETT	2:54:39	R LAWRENCE	2:55:51	P ROBERTS	2:56:50	B READ	2:57:43
40	P DELAHAYE	2:53:25	N KENCHINGTON	2:54:39	J MULLIS	2:55:51	J EDWARDS	2:56:51	A ADAMS	2:57:43
41	P COURTNEY	2:53:27	P HARTLEY	2:54:40	B STREET	2:55:51	L VANDE VELDE	2:56:51	P HASSALL	2:57:46
42	L ARNOTT	2:53:28	D KLINKNER	2:54:40	C FARMER	2:55:54	S SCHEUBER	2:56:51	M ATKINSON	2:57:46
43	R EVANS	2:53:29	R HURLEY	2:54:40	J GOURLEY	2:55:54	N BAINES	2:56:53	J NOLAN	2:57:46
44	N ORRELLS	2:53:29	F JONES	2:54:41	M SMITH	2:55:54	P JONES	2:56:53	D SCHIFF	2:57:48
45	D GRANT	2:53:30	P ROWLANDS	2:54:42	M HUGHES	2:55:54	M LEGGETT	2:56:54	D MORTON	2:57:48
46	K THIERSTEIN	2:53:30	S COOK	2:54:43	F SANUDO	2:55:55	G DAVIES	2:56:55	M POWELL	2:57:48
47	J ROBERTS	2:53:30	K MACDONALD	2:54:44	E MORGAN	2:55:56	M PYMM	2:56:55	M HORNER	2:57:49
48	J MOOREKITE	2:53:30	D FENTON	2:54:44	P JACKSON	2:55:56	J ROBERTSON	2:56:55	L SKINNER	2:57:49
49	C STOREY	2:53:31	H PINKNEY	2:54:45	A BAIN	2:55:58	T AKIENS	2:56:55	P HOOSON	2:57:50
50	S KELLEHER	2:53:32	A OBRIEN	2:54:46	T MCKENZIE	2:55:58	J PENNINCK	2:56:56	K KETTRIDGE	2:57:50
51	E CHRISTIE	2:53:32	D MACDIARMID	2:54:48	M MOULD	2:55:59	G ANDERSON	2:56:57	P JARVIS	2:57:50
52	J ASTON	2:53:32	R CURWEN	2:54:49	J WINDER	2:55:59	M MANN	2:56:58	S BUTCHER	2:57:50
53	S ASKHAM	2:53:33	B WILKS	2:54:49	M LEVY	2:56:00	D ROE	2:56:59	J KLUFT	2:57:50
54	R FEENEY	2:53:33	A BASS	2:54:50	A DUMBRECK	2:56:00	G ORCHARD	2:56:59	R NICHOLLS	2:57:50
55	J HARANT	2:53:34	J BUTTERWORTH	2:54:50	P WOODMAN	2:56:00	A ECCLES	2:56:59	O THOMPSON	2:57:52
56	D POTTS	2:53:38	M GRIFFITH	2:54:50	D HEPPLEWHITE	2:56:02	M ALMROTH	2:56:59	B O'SHEA	2:57:53
57	E ABRAHAM	2:53:41	C EARL	2:54:52	J RALPH	2:56:02	K SMITH	2:56:59	D COOPER	2:57:53
58	J TYMUKAS	2:53:42	D THOMAS	2:54:52	J GRISTWOOD	2:56:02	P DAVIES	2:57:00	R WEBSTER	2:57:54
59	S INGLIS	2:53:42	L WRIGHT	2:54:53	K HOWE	2:56:02	E MCALYNN	2:57:00	D ROSEN	2:57:54
60	S WALKER	2:53:42	D WILSON	2:54:54	T HEDGE	2:56:03	A STODDART	2:57:00	P MALO	2:57:56
61	M DAVIS	2:53:43	J BONE	2:54:56	J THOMAS	2:56:03	G DINGLEY	2:57:01	D ALSOP	2:57:56
62	P MARRIOTT	2:53:44	J CRAMP	2:54:57	P PELLECCHIA	2:56:05	E DUFFY	2:57:01	G MORGAN	2:57:56
63	A SHIPP	2:53:44	P MOTYER	2:54:57	C STEPHENS	2:56:07	A KERR	2:57:01	M FAUGHNAN	2:57:56
64	R RENWICK	2:53:45	D SLEATH	2:54:57	R ROWE	2:56:07	N HUKE	2:57:01	P CLAYDON	2:57:57
65	S ALLEN	2:53:45	S FITZPATRICK	2:54:59	D CLARKE	2:56:08	P DIBBEN	2:57:02	M HYDE	2:57:57
66	J PIGNARD	2:53:46	J WESTERN	2:54:59	M BRANSON	2:56:09	W LEARMONTH	2:57:02	L CAFFIER	2:57:57
67	D HALA	2:53:47	R LONG	2:54:59	D BRYSON	2:56:09	J PORRITT	2:57:02	D AGNEW	2:57:57
68	N ROBERTS	2:53:47	E GRAY	2:54:59	J FLATLEY	2:56:09	D COLES	2:57:03	G JACKSON	2:57:59
69	B STUBBINS	2:53:47	D KENWORTHY	2:55:00	T HAUXWELL	2:56:10	S MANN	2:57:04	G EZAN	2:57:59
70	M THURGOOD	2:53:48	E KING	2:55:01	M CRONIN	2:56:11	D LACROIX	2:57:04	J LORYMAN	2:58:00
71	K BURNITT	2:53:48	A STEWART	2:55:02	N THORNBORROW	2:56:12	B BROWN	2:57:04	A LEVERTON	2:58:01
72	R MCDONALD	2:53:49	B MOODY	2:55:05	M WHITE	2:56:12	N KENNEDY	2:57:04	D MADDISON	2:58:02
73	P GATELY	2:53:49	P RAMSDEN	2:55:06	J HARKNESS	2:56:12	A BRADBURY	2:57:05	M DOBSON	2:58:04
74	C RUSTON	2:53:50	J FERNANDES	2:55:06	S PIERCE	2:56:12	J BRADLEY	2:57:05	R MORRIS	2:58:04
75	P BAMSEY	2:53:50	H GRANHOLT	2:55:06	D SMITH	2:56:13	K HOLMES	2:57:06	R PORTER	2:58:05
76	D PEDLEY	2:53:51	J MCMORROW	2:55:06	D HARRIS	2:56:13	J HOWELL	2:57:07	L EVANS	2:58:06
77	R THOMAS	2:53:53	W KERR	2:55:06	R LINES	2:56:14	C BROUGHTON	2:57:08	M STOKER	2:58:07
78	A BROOKS	2:53:54	D LIVESEY	2:55:06	C RANKIN	2:56:14	P LUSTY	2:57:08	J HARKNESS	2:58:07
79	E LOCKE	2:53:54	D DRAPER	2:55:06	C GILLESPIE	2:56:14	B VINE	2:57:08	P RAMPLEY	2:58:08
80	I MANNERS	2:53:55	A JURIC	2:55:06	R LOW	2:56:15	J GODDARD	2:57:10	A O'NEILL	2:58:08
81	M ANGLIM	2:53:57	J GONZALEZ	2:55:06	S TINDALE	2:56:16	J GALLEY	2:57:11	M KESTLE	2:58:08
82	D HARRIS	2:53:57	R HOLMES	2:55:06	M WILKIE	2:56:16	P BUCKMASTER	2:57:11	P SARGENT	2:58:09
83	A EAKINS	2:53:58	G RON	2:55:06	D HILL	2:56:17	J GAUGHAN	2:57:11	A SMITH	2:58:09
84	M BAILIE	2:53:59	F CHARLES	2:55:06	K CLARKE	2:56:18	A SYKES	2:57:12	S BOWLES	2:58:10
85	K BUE	2:53:59	N WHITBY	2:55:06	M PAGE	2:56:19	C HESS	2:57:13	L PARROTT	2:58:10
86	A POLLARD	2:54:00	R SHORT	2:55:06	K MAHON	2:56:20	M RYFFEL	2:57:13	D TINCELIN	2:58:11
87	J D'ARCY	2:54:03	G FINE	2:55:06	S INNES	2:56:20	M BUCCOLI	2:57:13	J KELLY	2:58:11
88	M GALLE	2:54:05	M MITCHELL	2:55:06	R STEVENS	2:56:21	B EMMERSON	2:57:14	J TOWSEY	2:58:11
89	C ARNOLD	2:54:05	J CHANDLER	2:55:06	D SELBY	2:56:21	R HORTON	2:57:15	S HILL	2:58:11
90	P FOLEY	2:54:06	P WALSH	2:55:06	W BROWNING	2:56:21	P BUTLER	2:57:15	R MAWER	2:58:11
91	J FRANCE	2:54:07	S MCALLISTER	2:55:06	D PARKIN	2:56:21	P ALDERSLEY	2:57:16	P JAMES	2:58:11
92	M BELSHAW	2:54:07	A HONORATO	2:55:06	J CUNHA	2:56:22	J WHITE	2:57:17	B RIVERS	2:58:11
93	A PENLOUP	2:54:08	R GIBBON	2:55:06	A BOWKER	2:56:22	D DENYER	2:57:17	P FOLEY	2:58:13
94	R JACOBS	2:54:08	D DUNCAN	2:55:06	A FRASER HARRIS	2:56:23	P LAFFEY	2:57:17	P MOHN	2:58:13
95	M CAHILL	2:54:10	A ROBERTS	2:55:06	A WEBSTER	2:56:24	D SAUNDERS	2:57:18	S BANKS	2:58:13
96	N HOLDING	2:54:10	D WARNES	2:55:06	O CANDELA	2:56:26	C BENNETT	2:57:18	S GILLSON	2:58:14
97	P LINCOLN	2:54:11	N PEARS	2:55:07	K WOODCOCK	2:56:26	S DUDDELL	2:57:19	R GREEN	2:58:15
98	J ASSER	2:54:11	B MACKEY	2:55:07	S CORDING	2:56:28	W O'CONNOR	2:57:19	C TATIBOUET	2:58:15
99	D TOWNSEND	2:54:12	K GRIFFITHS	2:55:08	A BARRY	2:56:29	D ATKINS	2:57:19	T TITTERTON	2:58:15
100	C NORRIS	2:54:12	P ROBERTSON	2:55:10	R HOWE	2:56:29	R MCANDREW	2:57:19	C SINNOTT	2:58:16

#	1501-1600		1601-1700		1701-1800		1801-1900		1901-2000	
1	R BALLANTYNE	2:58:16	V HILLS	2:59:01	M SKINNER	2:59:51	J PARE	3:00:43	G HOBDEN	3:01:42
2	C KILPATRICK	2:58:17	G GITTINGS	2:59:01	O BALDOMERO	2:59:52	M BEARDSMORE	3:00:44	N WALSH	3:01:44
3	D FOUDRAIN	2:58:17	G JONES	2:59:01	A READ	2:59:52	J DONNEKY	3:00:44	C DAUNCEY	3:01:44
4	B HENRY	2:58:18	M WITTS	2:59:02	A MCKAY	2:59:52	D HOWARTH	3:00:44	H ELHOUSSEINI	3:01:44
5	A THOMAS	2:58:18	D MCGILVRAY	2:59:02	R CLIFTON	2:59:52	J ROBINSON	3:00:45	J CONWAY	3:01:46
6	M O'HALLORAN	2:58:18	J WILLIAMS	2:59:03	D BENSTEAD	2:59:53	J HOWE	3:00:45	F MACFARLANE	3:01:46
7	P MILES	2:58:19	R MORENO LOPEZ	2:59:03	R SARGENT	2:59:54	D WOODWARD	3:00:45	E BLAIR	3:01:47
8	P SPENCER	2:58:19	D CAMPBELL	2:59:03	A BUS	2:59:54	S MCKENZIE	3:00:46	J CUTMORE	3:01:49
9	A FLETCHER	2:58:19	J CAUNT	2:59:05	N VAUGHAN	2:59:54	A BROWN	3:00:47	A VOWLES	3:01:49
10	F GASKELL	2:58:20	P COOK	2:59:06	M FLAHERTY	2:59:55	A HILLIER	3:00:48	W LEMOR	3:01:49
11	K WILLIS	2:58:21	K CHRISTMAS	2:59:07	A CARD	2:59:56	M CARTWRIGHT	3:00:48	D SLATER	3:01:50
12	A WIGMORE	2:58:21	W WILSON	2:59:07	L CALVER	2:59:56	J BARKER	3:00:49	J PRINCE	3:01:50
13	J KNIGHTS	2:58:22	S GUZMAN	2:59:08	P RATHGEB	2:59:56	T THOMPSON	3:00:49	G CAMPBELL	3:01:51
14	A FLYNN	2:58:22	W REILLY	2:59:08	A SUTHERLAND	2:59:56	P METCALFE	3:00:50	C NAISH	3:01:51
15	A GREEN	2:58:23	L NILSSON	2:59:09	M GATHERCOLE	2:59:57	B CULLEN	3:00:51	N WONFOR	3:01:52
16	M MILLER	2:58:23	G COE	2:59:10	J MCGLYNN	2:59:57	B COLEMAN	3:00:51	M REID	3:01:53
17	C MARKS	2:58:23	D LHOMME	2:59:10	P WEBSTER	2:59:58	T PHILLIPS	3:00:52	P SWABY	3:01:53
18	K PRATT	2:58:24	J LILLEY	2:59:10	H BILLINGS	2:59:58	I ANDERSON	3:00:53	B BOOTH	3:01:54
19	I STEPHEN	2:58:24	J SOWRAY	2:59:11	P AIRD	2:59:58	J MCSKIMMING	3:00:53	L BRANCH	3:01:54
20	R HAGUE	2:58:24	M LEHMANN	2:59:11	S SCHOFIELD	2:59:58	T PRESTHAUG	3:00:53	S DELLWING	3:01:56
21	M GIROLAMI	2:58:24	P ETHERIDGE	2:59:11	F HO	3:00:00	E WEAVER	3:00:53	M MCGUINNESS	3:01:57
22	R BOND	2:58:25	M COLE	2:59:13	D TOWNEND	3:00:01	D JONES	3:00:53	G JENSEN	3:01:58
23	A GOODWIN	2:58:25	K JACKSON	2:59:13	C GORLIER	3:00:01	J COX	3:00:54	G AVERY	3:01:58
24	K LEE	2:58:25	G MICHAEL	2:59:13	A DODD	3:00:01	J GUILLEN	3:00:54	A DOYLE	3:01:59
25	A MURRAY	2:58:26	I PERCIVAL	2:59:14	B HOBBS	3:00:01	P BARRETT	3:00:54	I COLTON	3:01:59
26	W COLLINS	2:58:26	B BAKER	2:59:14	J BOCHET	3:00:01	S MURRAY	3:00:55	A LOWE	3:02:00
27	C MORGAN	2:58:27	D BOULDSTRIDGE	2:59:14	A ELLIOTT	3:00:01	A BARNARD	3:00:55	H GRUBER	3:02:00
28	I THOMAS	2:58:28	G COPP	2:59:14	Z KARCZENSKI	3:00:01	M GLUNING	3:00:56	R PENLINGTON	3:02:00
29	N GREGORY	2:58:28	J LINGARD	2:59:14	A GOLD	3:00:02	S MURGATROYD	3:00:56	H THOMAS	3:02:00
30	P CARROLL	2:58:28	P HOWARD	2:59:14	I FERNANDEZ DE LA HOZ	3:00:02	B HAIGHTON	3:00:57	T SWINDELL	3:02:00
31	G WALKER	2:58:28	A FARQUHARSON	2:59:15	G JOHN	3:00:02	K NISBET	3:00:57	G LIVSEY	3:02:01
32	R KABISCH	2:58:30	N SALMON	2:59:15	B APPLEBY	3:00:03	R WILLIAMS	3:00:59	S MILTON	3:02:01
33	A FERNANDEZ	2:58:30	J POPIOLEK	2:59:16	D ENGLISH	3:00:03	R TRINDER	3:00:59	K WINCHURCH	3:02:01
34	T WHITE	2:58:30	D BIRD	2:59:16	S CHAPMAN	3:00:04	G BUISAN	3:01:01	C POOLE	3:02:01
35	H FOWLER	2:58:31	M HEATON	2:59:16	G MASTERS	3:00:06	I HILL	3:01:01	A VERNON	3:02:01
36	R TYSON	2:58:31	B GROTE	2:59:17	J TEIXEIRA	3:00:07	P HYLAND	3:01:01	R JOHNSON	3:02:06
37	S REYNOLDS	2:58:31	T HAMER	2:59:17	P DEARING	3:00:07	R ARNOLD	3:01:04	D ROLLINS	3:02:06
38	P CHADWICK	2:58:31	S FRASER	2:59:18	T SAUNDERS	3:00:09	P PLOWMAN	3:01:05	M WARD	3:02:06
39	B KENNEDY	2:58:31	P HELLIWELL	2:59:18	R BELL	3:00:10	R BARTLETT	3:01:06	M THORNTON	3:02:08
40	D PARKES	2:58:32	P MAISEL	2:59:18	M NUTBURN	3:00:11	T GARDNER	3:01:07	D BROWN	3:02:08
41	A JENNINGS	2:58:32	A AUKIM	2:59:19	D ROBERTS	3:00:11	S CRISP	3:01:07	J BENOIT	3:02:09
42	J HARRAP	2:58:32	C SMITH	2:59:19	P NORTH	3:00:11	M BEVERLY	3:01:08	J LACIRE	3:02:10
43	D WINDER	2:58:34	C JONES	2:59:20	J LEE	3:00:11	V LEMMIS	3:01:10	H EVANS	3:02:11
44	B ANDERSSON	2:58:34	D MICHAEL	2:59:20	S ENDERSBY	3:00:12	B ROTH	3:01:10	A TRAVE	3:02:12
45	T BLOOMER	2:58:35	A POINTET	2:59:21	D RAINBIRD	3:00:12	H LIECHTI	3:01:10	P REDDAWAY	3:02:13
46	M TYSON	2:58:36	S OWEN	2:59:21	D THORNTON	3:00:12	A BOVIJN	3:01:10	O CARTWRIGHT	3:02:15
47	M DUFOUR	2:58:36	C VASSIE	2:59:21	P MARTINEAU	3:00:13	E MAMET	3:01:11	D DAVID	3:02:16
48	G WATKIN	2:58:37	H PLETINCK	2:59:22	I SHARPE	3:00:13	A FINCH	3:01:11	M MCDEVITT	3:02:16
49	R BEARDSWORTH	2:58:37	K RAINFORD	2:59:22	K WARDELL	3:00:14	D THURLOW	3:01:13	T MURRAY	3:02:17
50	P JENKINS	2:58:37	M MINETT	2:59:23	D MOOREKITE	3:00:15	J OSBORNE	3:01:14	T BRIGHTWELL	3:02:17
51	J GIBSON	2:58:37	M COATES	2:59:23	D MINDEN	3:00:15	J PONCHELLE	3:01:14	D CATTERMOLE	3:02:18
52	G ROMAIN	2:58:38	B KARLSSON	2:59:24	C HARWOOD	3:00:15	S BUTLER	3:01:15	M EDWARDS	3:02:18
53	G THRESH	2:58:38	D LAWLESS	2:59:25	P MCNULTY	3:00:15	C WHITEHAND	3:01:15	S MACKAY	3:02:18
54	L DERN	2:58:38	M SPEAKE	2:59:26	T BROOKS	3:00:15	D TAYLOR	3:01:15	G FALLON	3:02:19
55	R LINDSAY	2:58:39	A LAVERICK	2:59:26	I WHITMORE	3:00:15	J ROWE	3:01:17	G TILL	3:02:20
56	J STELFOX	2:58:39	S WARD	2:59:27	J GLENNIE	3:00:15	N TAYLOR	3:01:18	B NOEL	3:02:21
57	D MILLAR	2:58:39	A ROPER	2:59:27	G SIBERIL	3:00:15	A COTTAM	3:01:20	J HODSON	3:02:21
58	C BRETT	2:58:40	A COTTON	2:59:28	D HUGHES	3:00:16	A PERSSON	3:01:20	B LUCK	3:02:21
59	L JONES	2:58:40	G HUDSON	2:59:31	T MADGWICK	3:00:17	E HUNTER	3:01:20	W LITTLE	3:02:21
60	M STACEY	2:58:40	J TASKER	2:59:34	S FORTUNE	3:00:17	J FALVO	3:01:20	J DRYMMOND	3:02:22
61	N WATKIN	2:58:41	D DOE	2:59:35	J SEGAERT	3:00:17	P CHANEL	3:01:21	S HUTCHINSON	3:02:22
62	J JOYNER	2:58:42	G HYATT	2:59:35	S SMITH	3:00:19	D ORMISTON	3:01:22	T BUXTON	3:02:22
63	J DELANY	2:58:42	J KOUACS	2:59:36	P BROOK	3:00:19	E HILLS	3:01:22	K GREY	3:02:23
64	P MARTIN	2:58:43	S HOLLOWAY	2:59:36	R PETTITT	3:00:19	J MCPARLAND	3:01:23	J CASTLE	3:02:24
65	A RABINEL	2:58:43	B CHAPUY	2:59:37	W WALSH	3:00:20	A BAGLEY	3:01:23	G JONES	3:02:26
66	D UTTERIDGE	2:58:43	M CONLON	2:59:37	A RATHBONE	3:00:21	G EVERITT	3:01:23	U KERRN	3:02:26
67	A WILLIAMS	2:58:43	M BINGHAM	2:59:37	J SWINDEN	3:00:21	N MOON	3:01:23	A CONWAY	3:02:27
68	R BARONOWSKI	2:58:43	K ROYLE	2:59:38	I GARDNER	3:00:22	E MUSGROVE	3:01:23	R COX	3:02:27
69	P FORTE	2:58:44	M LO	2:59:38	P LYDON	3:00:24	J PIEDNOIR	3:01:23	S SATO	3:02:29
70	R THOMAS	2:58:44	M BENNETT	2:59:39	J STANNERS	3:00:25	E WALLACE	3:01:25	P ROBINSON	3:02:30
71	N BOUCHEBIA	2:58:45	R FRANSSEN	2:59:39	M BROWN	3:00:25	S WITT	3:01:25	E DELCOUR	3:02:32
72	J COOKE	2:58:45	A OLIVER	2:59:39	R BRAITHWAITE	3:00:26	C LUNN	3:01:25	J KINGDOM	3:02:33
73	J STAMMERS	2:58:45	H TUMMERS	2:59:40	R GASPERI	3:00:26	M PERSSON	3:01:26	R GREEN	3:02:34
74	R POUNTNEY	2:58:46	M OSBORNE	2:59:40	R SHIPWAY	3:00:27	P BENDER	3:01:27	M SILVEY	3:02:35
75	B PRICE	2:58:46	J WOODFORD	2:59:41	M PERRYMAN	3:00:29	R HEMMINGS	3:01:27	P MORRIS	3:02:36
76	E CHICO	2:58:46	G JEFFERIES	2:59:42	N JONES	3:00:29	G JONES	3:01:28	B MIDDLETON	3:02:37
77	T ROBINSON	2:58:46	N ANTHONY	2:59:43	P HAWKINS	3:00:30	S JONES	3:01:28	P VIVEASH	3:02:38
78	P NICHOLLS	2:58:47	B FINDEL-HAWKINS	2:59:44	S GILLESPIE	3:00:30	V VANZETTA	3:01:28	B LEWIS	3:02:38
79	H BENEDIK	2:58:47	K JENNINGS	2:59:44	D BUCKINGHAM	3:00:30	B BLADH	3:01:29	J BENDALL	3:02:38
80	G ANGOUIN	2:58:48	S REES	2:59:44	K WAKERLEY	3:00:30	K ENDRES	3:01:29	T HOERLER	3:02:39
81	M WALTER	2:58:48	B EDEN	2:59:44	R WHEELER	3:00:31	L FIOLET	3:01:30	I DAVISON	3:02:39
82	D LATTER	2:58:48	J WINGROVE	2:59:45	G PARRY	3:00:33	G ADNITT	3:01:30	H WARREN	3:02:39
83	W RABANEK	2:58:49	C KNOX	2:59:45	D LOVERIDGE	3:00:33	K MEDJERAL	3:01:30	A DAVIS	3:02:39
84	D STOCK	2:58:49	S BIELBY	2:59:46	M MORTON	3:00:34	B NEAVES	3:01:30	J JOKIPII	3:02:40
85	S WATTS	2:58:49	R NOKE	2:59:47	D JONES	3:00:34	E TURNER	3:01:31	R ARLISS	3:02:40
86	J WHITFIELD	2:58:50	M SWEENEY	2:59:47	S NOBLE	3:00:36	D RAMSAY	3:01:31	S LUFF	3:02:40
87	A OUGH	2:58:51	J HINCHLIFFE	2:59:48	T PEDERSEN	3:00:37	M HOBBS	3:01:31	J PASK	3:02:41
88	M SANDFORD	2:58:51	S THIRKELL	2:59:48	M WALLIS	3:00:38	M BURGOYNE	3:01:33	F WYCHERLEY	3:02:41
89	M ANDRE	2:58:52	S BARR	2:59:49	D HUMPHREY	3:00:39	C GRIFFIN	3:01:35	I HILL	3:02:42
90	A BERRY	2:58:52	B MCKAY	2:59:49	A KENDRA	3:00:39	M OTERD	3:01:36	J WITHEY	3:02:42
91	D MCCUNE	2:58:54	M BULGER	2:59:50	P BURTON	3:00:40	N STANLEY	3:01:37	M ROBERTS	3:02:42
92	N WILSON	2:58:55	M SEDGE	2:59:50	N GOTTS	3:00:40	R DAVIES	3:01:38	G BROWNHILL	3:02:44
93	O INGVARSEN	2:58:56	D SCOTT	2:59:50	U ALBRECHT	3:00:41	L BIBBY	3:01:38	T MCCARTHY	3:02:44
94	M MISKIN	2:58:57	J MC CONVILLE	2:59:50	J HOUOT	3:00:42	R SLOWE	3:01:39	J ACKERMAN-MARTIN	3:02:45
95	S HARRIS	2:58:59	E BUCKLE	2:59:50	J PIERSON	3:00:42	S POGGETTI	3:01:40	V ROMERO-COLAS	3:02:46
96	P BOWDEN	2:58:59	S WHITTLE	2:59:50	C SIMPSON	3:00:42	D THORNTON	3:01:40	C HWHEDDON	3:02:47
97	S SINCLAIR	2:58:59	P JARVIS	2:59:50	D HUGHES	3:00:42	A SPELLING	3:01:41	M SIMM	3:02:47
98	J CROSSAN	2:59:00	S BAILEY	2:59:50	T O'NEILL	3:00:43	M SADLER	3:01:41	M MONAGHAN	3:02:47
99	M OTTLEY	2:59:00	R LILLICO	2:59:51	S POLAK	3:00:43	F FOX	3:01:42	M GEE	3:02:47
100	R WILKES	2:59:00	M NADAL BUADES	2:59:51					K OEISETH	3:02:48

#	2001-2100		2101-2200		2201-2300		2301-2400		2401-2500	
1	B O'HAGAN	3:02:48	P MCQUILLEN	3:03:44	P BAILEY	3:04:38	M GRIGG	3:05:42	S PAYNE	3:06:30
2	M SMITH	3:02:51	M O'CONNOR	3:03:44	A HORTON	3:04:39	G HAMMOND	3:05:42	M BRYANT	3:06:31
3	M COSTA RIERA	3:02:51	P MORRISON	3:03:44	C JARVIS	3:04:39	J HORNSBY	3:05:42	A HUNT	3:06:31
4	D ROOTS	3:02:52	M GOSS	3:03:44	R EIKENES	3:04:40	D BELLINGHAM	3:05:43	A PALMER	3:06:32
5	R MAIDEN	3:02:53	A STAINSBY	3:03:44	B GUSTARD	3:04:40	T COE	3:05:43	S CLAYTON	3:06:32
6	G JENKINS	3:02:53	P HUDDLESTONE	3:03:44	J BROWN	3:04:41	M JELLEY	3:05:43	G BROWN	3:06:32
7	V GIANNI	3:02:54	W MARSH	3:03:44	J GARDINER	3:04:42	D CHAPMAN	3:05:46	K STENMARK	3:06:32
8	P COOK	3:02:54	J CLIFF	3:03:44	J HISCOX	3:04:42	F CAIRNS	3:05:46	T BRANNAN	3:06:33
9	P HAMILTON	3:02:54	P GIBBS	3:03:44	D BURNS	3:04:42	A THOMAS	3:05:46	P BARRETT	3:06:33
10	P OWEN	3:02:54	J KING	3:03:44	B MILLS	3:04:43	A RAWLINSON	3:05:46	A SUTER	3:06:35
11	J MCCAFFERTY	3:02:54	K SHIMIZU	3:03:45	P HAIG	3:04:43	A DAVIS	3:05:47	B CRADDEN	3:06:35
12	J WILLIAMS	3:02:54	T PRESTON	3:03:45	J MC LOUGHLIN	3:04:44	C VERNON	3:05:47	P COPELAND	3:06:35
13	J ANTENTAS	3:02:55	S DE VRIES	3:03:47	D HOLDEN	3:04:44	J FREEMAN	3:05:48	K WILKINSON	3:06:35
14	P MATTHEWS	3:02:57	S WATSON	3:03:47	G COX	3:04:45	V GROSS	3:05:49	J WORTHINGTON	3:06:35
15	M TILLER	3:02:57	P CHARLTON	3:03:47	R YEAMAN	3:04:46	S HEATH	3:05:49	S HURST	3:06:36
16	F MORTIER	3:02:57	F STRAND	3:03:48	C SNOOK	3:04:47	A BUCKLEY	3:05:49	S NYMAN	3:06:36
17	C SVEDING	3:02:59	M COLE	3:03:48	C MERRIEN	3:04:47	E HANSEN	3:05:50	L BALL	3:06:36
18	C FORREST	3:02:59	H SENN	3:03:48	J LLOBET	3:04:50	R HARRIS	3:05:50	T TIMPSON	3:06:37
19	G GAUTHIER	3:02:59	S NUTLAND	3:03:49	J COLQUHOUN	3:04:50	L PICHON	3:05:50	S HAUG	3:06:37
20	C REID	3:03:00	P SMITH	3:03:49	J GIROUD	3:04:51	J MIDDLETON	3:05:52	A HOOPER	3:06:38
21	P FOSTER	3:03:00	M TREES	3:03:50	M BENT	3:04:51	M EVANS	3:05:52	P JIOLLENT	3:06:38
22	I WYLIE	3:03:01	S DEVEREUX	3:03:50	M MOWLE	3:04:51	R STEVENS	3:05:53	P LOVER	3:06:41
23	A MCDONALD	3:03:01	M RALPH	3:03:51	P KENNEDY	3:04:52	V AISTHORPE	3:05:53	S KARL	3:06:41
24	D TURNER	3:03:01	P NEILAN	3:03:51	A BLADEN	3:04:52	G DUNBAR	3:05:53	K DAWSON	3:06:42
25	J READ	3:03:01	K BISHOP	3:03:52	P DEAVILLE	3:04:52	C VAN LANDUYT	3:05:53	N TURNER	3:06:43
26	L LAINE	3:03:02	P WITTICH	3:03:52	A SIMMONDS	3:04:53	T DOMAN	3:05:54	R COLLISON	3:06:43
27	R SMYTH	3:03:05	S LE POIDEVIN	3:03:53	P WAGHORN	3:04:53	C SIMPSON	3:05:54	L HOGENBOOM	3:06:43
28	B BERRY	3:03:06	D GRANT	3:03:54	J BORN	3:04:54	S JACKSON	3:05:54	P CAPRIOLI	3:06:44
29	M HYDES	3:03:06	S HODGES	3:03:55	K CROSSLAND-PAGE	3:04:56	E FALCK-THERKELSEN	3:05:55	R HORN	3:06:45
30	H NITSCHE	3:03:06	R EDWARDS	3:03:55	M WRIGHT	3:04:59	H NUTTALL	3:05:55	A WATSON	3:06:47
31	P HOWARD	3:03:06	J BRESLIN	3:03:55	D READ	3:04:59	L GODDING	3:05:55	M AMES	3:06:48
32	A COURT	3:03:06	R TWOMEY	3:03:57	G TUCKER	3:04:59	M LEATHERDALE	3:05:56	A SFACTERIA	3:06:48
33	S HORN	3:03:09	P BEAL	3:03:57	A NEWMAN	3:05:01	B HUGHES	3:05:56	M GLEAVE	3:06:50
34	C STOKES	3:03:09	P HALL	3:03:57	G UWINS	3:05:02	A HUTTON	3:05:57	P OGDEN	3:06:50
35	W WOLEDGE	3:03:11	L TAYLOR	3:03:58	R LLOYD	3:05:03	B DUNN	3:05:57	A BEDFORD	3:06:51
36	I THEAKSTONE	3:03:13	N HAMPTON	3:03:58	G LEWIS	3:05:03	G DUNCAN	3:05:57	M MACKAY	3:06:52
37	D OLIVER	3:03:13	C KERIN	3:03:59	L NIELSEN	3:05:03	T THOMSON	3:05:58	M LAVINE	3:06:54
38	D HERD	3:03:14	K BRIDGE	3:03:59	A MERRETT	3:05:05	M TROMAS	3:05:58	H VAN DER JEUGHT	3:06:54
39	P BECK	3:03:15	G PUCCI	3:03:59	G CRILL	3:05:06	J HARVEY	3:05:59	P STAVELEY	3:06:54
40	M MCCALLUM	3:03:15	R RUSSELL	3:04:00	T HOUGHTON	3:05:06	S HOLLINGDALE	3:05:59	J MCCORMICK	3:06:54
41	P FINNEGAN	3:03:15	K KOESTER	3:04:00	C ROBINSON	3:05:06	M GRIMWOOD	3:05:59	A HORNE	3:06:55
42	J MONTERO	3:03:16	M REES	3:04:01	J MAGNUS	3:05:06	M ROBERTS	3:06:00	D GRIFFITHS	3:06:55
43	A CORNELL	3:03:16	C RUIZ	3:04:01	P COUCH	3:05:06	T MEADE	3:06:00	T RICHARDSON	3:06:56
44	A CODLIN	3:03:16	D DREW	3:04:02	A BURNS	3:05:06	A CORONAS	3:06:00	P MCMASTER	3:06:56
45	P SHAW	3:03:16	A ANDERSON	3:04:03	V POLLARD	3:05:08	M CHARLTON	3:06:01	M REDMAN	3:06:56
46	A HEGARTY	3:03:16	L TINCELIN	3:04:03	P COMBES	3:05:08	D DAWSON	3:06:02	K RAINS	3:06:57
47	K BAILEY	3:03:17	R BAKER	3:04:04	S LOVKVIST	3:05:09	J FEE	3:06:05	C HARGRAVE	3:06:57
48	J PETERS	3:03:17	R SCOONES	3:04:06	N ASKER	3:05:09	P SKIPP	3:06:06	N WALES	3:06:58
49	K STREET	3:03:20	P ROBINSON	3:04:08	D JACQUES	3:05:10	C HOLLEWORTH	3:06:06	J MUSSELWHITE	3:06:59
50	P WOOD	3:03:20	A POWELL	3:04:08	W POWNALL	3:05:11	S GOULD	3:06:07	K TIFFIN	3:06:59
51	G PRIGENT	3:03:20	T DABLE	3:04:09	M SUMPTER	3:05:11	C HORECZY	3:06:10	D LITTLEFIELD	3:06:59
52	P STEEN	3:03:22	P COOK	3:04:09	R GRAHAM	3:05:11	C WILLIAMS	3:06:10	P SLAVIN	3:06:59
53	M BARKER	3:03:22	H ROSTAD	3:04:09	M BURRIDGE	3:05:11	P THOMPSON	3:06:10	D DIXON	3:07:00
54	I MCCOID	3:03:22	M DYER	3:04:09	J KJELDSEN	3:05:11	J ARKLIE	3:06:10	M PICKSLEY	3:07:00
55	B SPENCE	3:03:24	D ROCKALL	3:04:09	D JACKSON	3:05:11	A MALINGS	3:06:11	T PARTON	3:07:01
56	M TYLER	3:03:26	B MCKEEVER	3:04:09	T WILLIAMS	3:05:12	S DOBBS	3:06:11	R MARSTON	3:07:01
57	S SAGERER	3:03:28	T MALMGREN	3:04:10	S ASHLEY	3:05:12	E HILL	3:06:11	A GENOVESE	3:07:01
58	A CALLAGHAN	3:03:29	G COTTINGTON	3:04:10	A HEMINGWAY	3:05:12	M VENTE	3:06:12	N CHARMAN	3:07:01
59	J LUNT	3:03:29	D WHITEHEAD	3:04:13	H EDER	3:05:12	M KEENAN	3:06:12	A HOOD	3:07:03
60	C BOWEN	3:03:30	R COOMBES	3:04:14	B ALDRICH	3:05:12	C RYAN	3:06:12	D HERNE	3:07:03
61	M WARNER	3:03:31	J COWLEY	3:04:15	R DOGANA	3:05:12	M TURNER	3:06:12	P COPPENS	3:07:03
62	J SEARS	3:03:31	M POCOCK	3:04:15	A GARDINER	3:05:13	B BURATTI	3:06:13	D ADDISS	3:07:03
63	A MATTHEWS	3:03:32	J HORTON	3:04:16	P SMITH	3:05:13	G LLOYD	3:06:13	D PICKUP	3:07:04
64	E BARTLETT	3:03:32	J SHEPHERD	3:04:17	D HOPKINS	3:05:13	T HEBERT	3:06:13	M CHRISTIE	3:07:05
65	R TAYLOR	3:03:32	L LEE	3:04:17	T PARKE-DAVIS	3:05:15	C ESTRUP	3:06:15	R DUNN	3:07:05
66	J MOHIKI	3:03:32	K DUTTON	3:04:18	P NEWMAN	3:05:17	F KAMAN	3:06:15	M VAN DEN BERGH	3:07:05
67	L TURNER	3:03:33	J GUBBINS	3:04:18	S HUMPHRIES	3:05:19	L CALDER	3:06:16	J CHAPMAN	3:07:07
68	M RICE	3:03:33	O SAAF	3:04:19	E RANDON	3:05:19	H MALOONADO	3:06:18	M PEEL	3:07:08
69	L CLARK	3:03:33	R PERRY	3:04:19	M DAVIS	3:05:20	C MIDDLETON	3:06:19	S THEW	3:07:08
70	G ZITELLI	3:03:33	C REDVERS	3:04:20	P MCDONALD	3:05:20	H CHADWICK	3:06:19	A JACOBS	3:07:09
71	I CHARLES	3:03:33	J SMITH	3:04:21	S NEE	3:05:20	G HOEDTKE	3:06:19	R ORMESHER	3:07:09
72	R GEORGE	3:03:33	A PEARCE	3:04:22	W MARTIN	3:05:20	B PHILP	3:06:19	C MYCOCK	3:07:09
73	N MC GUINNESS	3:03:34	P BATEY	3:04:23	M ROGERS	3:05:21	M POYSER	3:06:21	P COWLING	3:07:10
74	D MARTINSON	3:03:34	P LIST	3:04:24	T TILLBROOKE	3:05:22	L MEAD	3:06:21	H LLEWELYN	3:07:11
75	N GRIMLEY	3:03:34	A HIND	3:04:25	F SHEARERRIACH	3:05:22	S AKSLAND	3:06:21	G HALES	3:07:11
76	J FUNNELL	3:03:34	C CRONK	3:04:25	E FRENCH	3:05:22	T LARSEN	3:06:21	S MAZZI	3:07:11
77	J HOBBS	3:03:34	D SWIFT	3:04:26	A BATTY	3:05:23	R PECK	3:06:21	A GRIFFITHS	3:07:11
78	M DURCAN	3:03:35	I JAMES	3:04:26	M LITTLE	3:05:23	G WEBSTER	3:06:22	D LINDSAY	3:07:11
79	C COOKSEY	3:03:36	P STEPHENS	3:04:27	A PEDLEY	3:05:23	B NAYLOR	3:06:23	J DODSON	3:07:11
80	A STEWART	3:03:36	G JONES	3:04:28	S MOHAN	3:05:24	A WILSMORE	3:06:23	C SIMPSON	3:07:11
81	K SMITH	3:03:36	B HEALEY	3:04:29	S ANNETT	3:05:25	N FARROW	3:06:23	R FENTUM	3:07:12
82	S SICA	3:03:36	T COPE	3:04:30	O HAUGLAND	3:05:25	W SCHILLER	3:06:24	P LEACH	3:07:12
83	B SHORT	3:03:36	D POTTER	3:04:30	S MACKLIN	3:05:26	D CHAPMAN	3:06:24	A CONSTANTINE	3:07:13
84	R ALVARADO	3:03:37	S BROADFOOT	3:04:30	G HOWELLS	3:05:26	Y DIEN	3:06:25	A PAGE	3:07:14
85	J WARRINGTON	3:03:38	P SHARP	3:04:30	C BROWN	3:05:30	T MUNDAL	3:06:25	P EMERY	3:07:14
86	P COVENTRY	3:03:38	S EASBY	3:04:31	D OWEN	3:05:31	I BRITTEN	3:06:25	D SIFFORD	3:07:16
87	P TAYLOR	3:03:40	C HODGES	3:04:32	H HINDERLING	3:05:32	H SIEKMANN	3:06:26	G FENLON	3:07:16
88	N LLOYD	3:03:40	P SHEPHEARD	3:04:32	L FERRIDAY	3:05:32	R SINCLAIR	3:06:26	D SHETLAR	3:07:16
89	J STOKOE	3:03:40	J GILBERT	3:04:32	I HARDSTAFF	3:05:32	P MATHON	3:06:26	J GRANT	3:07:16
90	C FINNEY	3:03:40	D ARCHER	3:04:32	D PARRY	3:05:33	S HOWELL	3:06:27	M HOOKER	3:07:16
91	R GIGANDET	3:03:41	S CLARK	3:04:33	P MAXWELL	3:05:34	B BROOKS	3:06:27	R WOOD	3:07:17
92	J LOPEZ	3:03:41	S HADLEY	3:04:34	J SINGLETON	3:05:34	C ESSON	3:06:27	G MCGREGOR	3:07:18
93	P MCCANN	3:03:42	A RUSSELL	3:04:34	G CARLIN	3:05:34	D ROBSON	3:06:28	K PHILLIPS	3:07:18
94	R JANSSEN	3:03:42	J MCGINTY	3:04:35	M BENN	3:05:35	S EARNSHAW	3:06:28	J MAZURKIEVIC	3:07:18
95	R BRERETON	3:03:42	A PARKER	3:04:35	C EVAR	3:05:36	A BEARDS	3:06:29	D ALCOCK	3:07:19
96	R LANSDELL	3:03:43	J MILLS	3:04:35	M LEE	3:05:36	T JOSEPH	3:06:29	G MORGAN	3:07:19
97	R MARTIN	3:03:43	C BROWN	3:04:35	W BRANTJES	3:05:36	M ELLIOTT	3:06:29	M GAMBRILL	3:07:20
98	T TOWNSEND	3:03:43	A SPALDING	3:04:36	M RUSSELL	3:05:38	T NORTH	3:06:29	N MOCKRIDGE	3:07:20
99	R CRESSWELL	3:03:44	K DAVIES	3:04:36	M REEVES	3:05:40	N LAWRENCE	3:06:30	C BENSON	3:07:23
100	T GRAVINA	3:03:44	S ANDREWS	3:04:37	M THOMPSON	3:05:41	P CASBEARD	3:06:30	C SMYTH	3:07:23

	2501-2600		2601-2700		2701-2800		2801-2900		2901-3000	
1	S SMITH	3:07:24	J ROOK	3:08:20	A MARSHALL	3:09:05	R WILKINSON	3:10:05	A BUTTURINI	3:10:50
2	P LOCK	3:07:25	I HORNER	3:08:20	C IWAHASHI	3:09:06	J HOOK	3:10:06	K FELLOWS	3:10:50
3	T THACKWRAY	3:07:25	A REYNOLDS	3:08:20	R KAMAL	3:09:06	R REEVES	3:10:06	P WEBER	3:10:51
4	J COKER	3:07:25	A DOMINEY	3:08:20	B HOPWOOD	3:09:06	C BRANDON-TRYE	3:10:06	A CLEMENTS	3:10:51
5	P SCHORCH	3:07:25	R EGAN	3:08:20	C ANDERSON	3:09:08	J JEWELL	3:10:07	E FOGARTY	3:10:52
6	R SAUNDERS	3:07:26	E ACKE	3:08:20	D SMITH	3:09:08	A LOUGHNEY	3:10:07	M HAWTHORNE	3:10:53
7	D MURRAY	3:07:26	B WOODWARD	3:08:20	A PRINGLE	3:09:08	Y DAVID	3:10:07	R GURD	3:10:54
8	A WOODROW	3:07:27	J JOHNSON	3:08:21	C HORNE	3:09:09	B ONESIME	3:10:07	C LECOMTE	3:10:54
9	T SMITH	3:07:27	T WITTS	3:08:21	P IRVING	3:09:09	D MADDISON	3:10:07	M LECK	3:10:55
10	D EDWARDS	3:07:27	N BULLEN	3:08:21	K REED	3:09:09	B SMITH	3:10:08	P HAWKER	3:10:55
11	M CHRESTA	3:07:28	N DALBY	3:08:23	M MCINERNEY	3:09:10	K HAYNES	3:10:08	R MURDOCH	3:10:57
12	J KERSHAW	3:07:28	E WINSTONE	3:08:23	S SMYTHE	3:09:10	G MORRIS	3:10:08	R GONZALEZ	3:10:57
13	C HUGHES	3:07:30	M COCHEN	3:08:24	S JERRAM	3:09:10	R CHARLES	3:10:08	S CONNOLLY	3:10:58
14	J WOODWARD	3:07:30	G FORRESTER	3:08:24	C RELTON	3:09:11	B COATES	3:10:08	D BANKS	3:10:58
15	D HAYE	3:07:30	D TAYLOR	3:08:24	R SCOTT	3:09:11	T OWENS	3:10:08	B WILSON	3:10:58
16	A LAIDLOW	3:07:30	P SWAIN	3:08:25	A JONES	3:09:11	T SENGIER	3:10:09	M FLOOD	3:10:58
17	C TAYLOR	3:07:30	C JENKINS	3:08:25	G PORTER	3:09:11	C KERMISCH	3:10:09	C KENCHINGTON	3:10:58
18	B HASTINGS	3:07:30	A JANSSON	3:08:26	G MERFIELD	3:09:12	R DONALDSON	3:10:09	J BLACKBURN	3:10:58
19	A CORNISH	3:07:30	C DAVIES	3:08:26	J JOHANSSON	3:09:13	M HARVEY	3:10:09	S EDWARDS	3:10:59
20	K BARNES	3:07:32	P ROBINSON	3:08:26	A MOORE	3:09:13	D CANNON	3:10:09	J PRICE	3:10:59
21	P JACKSON	3:07:33	J BRIGHT	3:08:27	B MOUNTJOY-ROW	3:09:13	J OWEN	3:10:10	S MORRISON	3:10:59
22	D BENNETT	3:07:34	M BURGE	3:08:27	P WISDOM	3:09:14	A SMITH	3:10:11	B MUIR	3:11:01
23	C COHEN	3:07:34	J APPLETON	3:08:27	M NEWEY	3:09:15	G DAVIES	3:10:11	G COLLINS	3:11:03
24	D WARD	3:07:34	E STENDER	3:08:27	C LAWES	3:09:15	C NEVIN	3:10:12	D ANDERSON	3:11:03
25	P HEMINGWAY	3:07:34	J CAVANAGH	3:08:27	A GRINDLEY	3:09:15	G PALSER	3:10:12	D SMITH	3:11:03
26	D SWAN	3:07:34	R SHARP	3:08:29	D WALKER	3:09:16	L MELLOR	3:10:13	P ECKLOFF	3:11:04
27	A YOUNG	3:07:35	K WILLIAMS	3:08:29	I HOPE	3:09:16	A HULME	3:10:14	T ELKINGTON	3:11:05
28	M POPE	3:07:36	A FORSTER	3:08:30	G BROWN	3:09:16	G JOHNSON	3:10:14	P HAMILTON	3:11:05
29	M CLARKE	3:07:37	J CURRY	3:08:30	A DENNISON	3:09:17	J OCALLAGHAN	3:10:15	C LANGLEY	3:11:05
30	D LEVENS	3:07:37	B RICHARDS	3:08:31	S HONEY	3:09:17	J MOLLOY	3:10:16	W ROBSHAW	3:11:06
31	M WOLFENDEN	3:07:37	C LINDSAY-GUNN	3:08:31	P THOMAS	3:09:18	M PHILLIPS	3:10:17	R MOORE	3:11:06
32	L GREEN	3:07:38	N HAZELL	3:08:32	D WILON	3:09:18	A MCKNIGHT	3:10:18	P MACKMAN	3:11:06
33	A FOX	3:07:38	K JACKSON	3:08:33	J HICKS	3:09:18	A HAINES	3:10:18	L WATSON	3:11:06
34	P MCDADE	3:07:38	C OBORNE	3:08:34	R HAWKINS	3:09:19	M FOGARTY	3:10:18	H RENNEN	3:11:07
35	S PHILLIPS	3:07:38	D PICKERING	3:08:34	F LITTLER	3:09:19	I WILKINSON	3:10:19	C HOWARD	3:11:07
36	A FLAHERTY	3:07:38	N KNIGHTS	3:08:34	M MELLORS	3:09:19	B HATCHER	3:10:19	D MATTHEWS	3:11:07
37	M LODWIG	3:07:39	S JONES	3:08:35	J EVANS	3:09:19	J ROBERTS	3:10:19	M KELLY	3:11:07
38	P WHITE	3:07:39	M AGATE	3:08:35	R SHEPHERD	3:09:21	W BONSALL	3:10:19	B SWINDELLS	3:11:08
39	L HAANSTRA	3:07:39	C GEE	3:08:36	I WILLIAMS	3:09:21	G PALLISTER	3:10:19	S JONES	3:11:08
40	R HOUGHTON	3:07:39	M BATENS	3:08:36	R PECK	3:09:21	M MACNAUGHTAN	3:10:19	J LAWRENE	3:11:08
41	R AWCOCK	3:07:39	B BENNETT	3:08:36	R PYE	3:09:21	M COX	3:10:21	V MILLARD	3:11:08
42	N FRENCH	3:07:39	B WARD	3:08:36	N THOMAS	3:09:24	P WALMSLEY	3:10:21	C EVERETT	3:11:09
43	A JOHNSON	3:07:40	O SIDDU	3:08:37	P SMITH	3:09:24	P SMITH	3:10:21	S MATHIAS	3:11:09
44	A STARKEY	3:07:40	J JAMES	3:08:37	G MURDOCH	3:09:24	A GOUGH	3:10:21	R TOONE	3:11:10
45	S PHILLIPS	3:07:40	M JORDAN	3:08:38	D BRINDLEY	3:09:24	K PALMER	3:10:23	P JARROSSAY	3:11:11
46	D KINGSNORTH	3:07:41	R ROITHER	3:08:38	D LITTLE	3:09:25	D KELLY	3:10:23	P JOHNSON	3:11:11
47	N STARKEY	3:07:42	K BATTY	3:08:38	S CUDDIHY	3:09:26	C LEE	3:10:24	B SEMELET	3:11:11
48	S GOULDING	3:07:42	A DUFFY	3:08:39	G LIVOTI	3:09:27	J MAZURKIEVIC	3:10:25	B DOWNS	3:11:11
49	D HAYES	3:07:43	P BARTLETT	3:08:39	K CALDER	3:09:27	P JONES	3:10:25	W SLACK	3:11:12
50	M THOMPSON	3:07:43	R MILLER	3:08:39	D QUINLIVAN	3:09:27	R TAYLOR	3:10:26	M OSBORN	3:11:12
51	S REYNOLDS	3:07:44	A PRATT	3:08:40	J SHERWOOD	3:09:29	B HARDMAN	3:10:27	M FRANKLIN	3:11:12
52	W JAMESON	3:07:44	B LLOYD	3:08:40	T DODD	3:09:30	J LOVICK	3:10:28	M BRESLIN	3:11:12
53	P CHAPLIN	3:07:48	R PLEAVIN	3:08:41	R EBBERLEY	3:09:30	J DYER	3:10:28	F WILLIAMS	3:11:13
54	F STRIDE	3:07:49	M ANTONETTI	3:08:41	I CHRISTIE	3:09:31	A POLLINTINE	3:10:28	M ZAHN	3:11:13
55	A FAUCIE	3:07:51	P DYER	3:08:41	R WALSH	3:09:32	T BERG	3:10:28	J JONES	3:11:14
56	S BARNABY	3:07:52	E HIGNETT	3:08:41	H PATTINSON	3:09:33	J KEANEY	3:10:29	G MEAKINS	3:11:15
57	M LEYENDA	3:07:52	C UNGARI	3:08:41	D MAUD	3:09:33	J HOLMAN	3:10:30	D GREEN	3:11:16
58	P JAEDERFELDT	3:07:53	D SWIFT	3:08:43	M MUIR	3:09:33	J COFFEY	3:10:30	R WOOD	3:11:16
59	J KING	3:07:54	D ELLIS	3:08:46	I COATES	3:09:34	L EDWARDS	3:10:30	R JONES	3:11:17
60	B SHACKLETON	3:07:54	J BROGAN	3:08:46	J ADAMS	3:09:34	A HEMMINGS	3:10:31	J RISLEY	3:11:17
61	J LE JEUNE	3:07:55	A CLEGG	3:08:47	J HARDWICK	3:09:35	J RIVAUD	3:10:32	J REA	3:11:18
62	A COMBES	3:07:55	M LAFLIN	3:08:47	T BIRD	3:09:35	P STUBBINGTON	3:10:32	D MOORE	3:11:18
63	B MCEVOY	3:07:55	S NEMEZAWA	3:08:48	S DIBABA	3:09:36	C NAYLOR	3:10:32	R GEORGE	3:11:19
64	M SMITH	3:07:56	M RADFORD	3:08:48	J LEE	3:09:36	T ROBSON	3:10:32	N FISHER	3:11:19
65	G PRINCE	3:07:57	G WHITE	3:08:49	A SCHULTZ	3:09:37	D KEAR	3:10:33	S WORTHINGTON	3:11:19
66	G JONES	3:07:58	A DYER	3:08:49	A CHARTERS	3:09:38	D PRYCE	3:10:33	M GAUNT	3:11:21
67	S OLIVER	3:08:00	J GOODE	3:08:50	J DAVIES	3:09:39	K FOX	3:10:34	T SMITH	3:11:21
68	P ALDERSON	3:08:00	D BROWN	3:08:52	J ATTRIDGE	3:09:40	M HOWARD	3:10:34	S ROWLINGS	3:11:22
69	C BELDON	3:08:00	J WOODS	3:08:52	D MAHER	3:09:41	I RAMSEY	3:10:34	R RUDDICK	3:11:23
70	S BELLAL	3:08:01	C GIBLIN	3:08:53	H LINDELL	3:09:42	P MARTIN	3:10:34	F MIDDLETON	3:11:23
71	M NEWELL	3:08:01	K KEANE	3:08:53	T WEST	3:09:42	C RAGUEL	3:10:35	C LACROIX	3:11:23
72	J LEWIS	3:08:01	P LAUBE	3:08:53	J JAINES	3:09:45	J HEALD	3:10:35	M THOMPSON	3:11:24
73	J TURNER	3:08:03	K ROSS	3:08:53	A RENSHAW	3:09:46	J TEAGUE	3:10:35	A BROBYN	3:11:24
74	N GRIFFITHS	3:08:03	P WALKDEN	3:08:54	M LEARY	3:09:46	K WAKELEN	3:10:36	P LANGLEY	3:11:24
75	F WHITFORD	3:08:05	B STEVENS	3:08:54	R GIBBS	3:09:47	M WILLIAMS	3:10:37	L SERVOTTE	3:11:25
76	E REUTER	3:08:05	G CHESTER	3:08:54	I PARKER	3:09:47	G CRAVEN	3:10:38	M DALY	3:11:25
77	D HARVEY	3:08:06	J WILMSHURST	3:08:54	M BENNETT	3:09:48	G RINGER	3:10:38	A BOLTON	3:11:26
78	J SIEGERTSZ	3:08:06	R THORN	3:08:54	G BISHOP	3:09:49	P BROWN	3:10:38	J SIMM	3:11:26
79	R FELLINGHAM	3:08:06	J DUCHON	3:08:55	B LUCAS	3:09:49	R WILLIAMS	3:10:38	D FORDHAM	3:11:26
80	N BOULET	3:08:06	J MURPHY	3:08:56	J THOMPSON	3:09:51	J MOORE	3:10:39	P STUDD	3:11:26
81	K EYKYN	3:08:07	D STEWART	3:08:57	S HALE	3:09:51	A STEWART	3:10:39	P CLARKE	3:11:27
82	J WYNNE JONES	3:08:09	P FLINT	3:08:58	A ROWLANDS	3:09:52	G OGDEN	3:10:40	S DUROSE	3:11:28
83	I STONE	3:08:09	D WOLLACOTT	3:08:58	L WOODLEY	3:09:53	D TANTOT	3:10:41	G MILLS	3:11:28
84	R FESSEL	3:08:10	J GRICE	3:08:59	J WHITTAKER	3:09:53	I GRANT	3:10:42	M BROOKS	3:11:29
85	S PROCTOR	3:08:11	P CROSBY	3:08:59	P BOYDEN	3:09:55	G ADDISON	3:10:42	P GANIVET	3:11:29
86	R LUNGMUSS	3:08:13	D POPPLE	3:08:59	T HYNAM	3:09:55	E KIRKMAN	3:10:42	C CHILD	3:11:29
87	C AWDE	3:08:13	J HUMBLE	3:09:00	J ASHTON	3:09:55	J WHITE	3:10:42	J JEHANNO	3:11:29
88	W ROBERTS	3:08:13	D CARR	3:09:00	P MAHIQUES	3:09:56	J GUTIERREZ	3:10:42	K MINOGUE	3:11:29
89	M JARVIS	3:08:14	P HOWELL	3:09:01	O LENNOX	3:09:57	S HART	3:10:42	D ST CROIX	3:11:30
90	S TAIT	3:08:14	W KELLENS	3:09:01	S HARBUT	3:09:57	J COUDRAIS	3:10:43	A OLNEY	3:11:30
91	M CRAWSHAW	3:08:15	S EVANS	3:09:02	D ROBERTS	3:09:58	J NEVIN	3:10:43	M HARDING	3:11:30
92	I JAMES	3:08:16	K HARRIS	3:09:02	K BURNETT	3:09:58	S NEAL	3:10:43	M MATTHEWS	3:11:30
93	C MAWER	3:08:16	D MILLS	3:09:02	E PALUDAN	3:09:58	E KING	3:10:45	S FOSTER	3:11:30
94	L AUSTIN	3:08:16	M FAIRCLOUGH	3:09:03	T FRENCH	3:10:00	T BURKE	3:10:45	M JONES	3:11:31
95	V CUFF	3:08:17	C SERVANT	3:09:03	W HENDRY	3:10:00	P MCLAUGHLIN	3:10:45	M HODBEN	3:11:31
96	L SHAW	3:08:18	A MATTHEWS	3:09:03	O WILLIAMS	3:10:02	I COOPER	3:10:46	G EARLEY	3:11:31
97	H WALKER	3:08:18	N CLARKE	3:09:04	J RUSSELL	3:10:03	W ORTON	3:10:47	P NORTON	3:11:32
98	L WANSTROM	3:08:19	A KIRK	3:09:04	J RAEMAN	3:10:03	R PAYNE	3:10:48	M STACEY	3:11:33
99	W SOUTHGATE	3:08:20	P ARMBRUSTER	3:09:04	A BEASTY	3:10:05	R HOWE	3:10:48	S MATTHEWS	3:11:35
100	T BELLIS	3:08:20	R KENNEDY	3:09:05	B CLARKE	3:10:05	H HUNTER	3:10:49	I JONES	3:11:35

#	3001-3100		3101-3200		3201-3300		3301-3400		3401-3500	
1	M FOUNTAINE	3:11:36	A PAYS	3:12:17	F LARDERET	3:13:07	I MCILWEE	3:13:55	J ATKINSON	3:14:40
2	D SKINNER	3:11:36	I KEARY	3:12:18	M GOODSON	3:13:08	C UPTON	3:13:56	A GOODRICH	3:14:40
3	S JOHNSON	3:11:36	A HAUGHTON	3:12:18	C PITMAN	3:13:09	D CHARLES	3:13:56	C CLARKE	3:14:41
4	C SCHMIDT	3:11:38	W MITTEN	3:12:18	N SINGH	3:13:10	G COWLING	3:13:57	M YEATES	3:14:42
5	G HOFMANN	3:11:38	B TROMANS	3:12:19	M MCDOUGALL	3:13:11	M DAVIES	3:13:57	S DANDO	3:14:43
6	M BARKER	3:11:38	D WICKS	3:12:19	D GIBON	3:13:11	M DE FEYTER	3:13:58	A HERBERT	3:14:43
7	I MACDONALD	3:11:39	M PITTOCK	3:12:19	D GRANT	3:13:11	D HEALY	3:13:58	S FACCENDA	3:14:43
8	M HOPKINSON	3:11:39	G MARTIN	3:12:19	R WOOD	3:13:11	F CAPRA	3:13:58	F POUSSEUR	3:14:44
9	D MUNDAY	3:11:40	R JOHNSON	3:12:20	D MAYLOTTE	3:13:11	P FOSTER	3:13:58	M PURSE	3:14:44
10	H FAURE	3:11:40	D FEINTUCK	3:12:21	R WADE	3:13:11	K DAVIS	3:13:59	P DAVIES	3:14:45
11	N JONES	3:11:41	K WILLIAMS	3:12:22	P LUPI	3:13:12	A THOMPSON	3:14:00	G GUILLAUME	3:14:46
12	D WALLIS	3:11:41	P DAVIES	3:12:24	P PATTERSON	3:13:14	P QUINN	3:14:00	G KENNEDY	3:14:46
13	H MAIER	3:11:42	A DI CAVIO	3:12:24	G LAMB	3:13:15	D THOMPSON	3:14:00	I LAWLEY	3:14:46
14	I CHELL	3:11:42	J SHILLING	3:12:24	G CULVERHOUSE	3:13:15	C CORRANCE	3:14:02	I WILLIAMS	3:14:47
15	E POULSSON	3:11:42	A CURATOLO	3:12:25	S ROBB	3:13:15	A BOULTON	3:14:02	A STRANZINGER	3:14:47
16	R HODGES	3:11:42	M LAWRENCE	3:12:26	R FISH	3:13:16	B HOMER	3:14:02	H LAPPALAINEN	3:14:47
17	M MAUNDERS	3:11:43	G CARBUTT	3:12:27	J MATHIEU	3:13:17	J THORN	3:14:02	J HAMLYN	3:14:48
18	J LEDERER	3:11:43	A WILMOT	3:12:27	D BRAVERMAN	3:13:18	A FLYNN	3:14:02	P HOLLAS	3:14:48
19	M MARULLO	3:11:44	D TUCKER	3:12:28	D HAFFENDEN	3:13:18	S JAMES	3:14:02	L ELLIOTT	3:14:48
20	E ILIFFE	3:11:44	G WEST	3:12:29	A KELLY	3:13:19	R SMITH	3:14:03	G DELAHUNTY	3:14:48
21	F WATINE	3:11:44	M SVENDSEN	3:12:31	A BROWN	3:13:19	J PERRY	3:14:03	C FITZGERALD	3:14:48
22	M HORSEY	3:11:44	D BUTTON	3:12:31	A STOPHER	3:13:19	N ALFORD	3:14:03	J MITCHELL	3:14:49
23	T NEILD	3:11:44	A JORDAN	3:12:31	P BONGERS	3:13:19	N KLEJMAN	3:14:03	P LAING	3:14:50
24	S HINDLEY	3:11:44	P GOSSELIN	3:12:31	M COLE	3:13:19	J WARBURTON	3:14:03	R TIPSON	3:14:50
25	M COPE	3:11:44	L FORREST	3:12:32	R BRAYBROOKS	3:13:20	J HARPER	3:14:04	P FRANCIS	3:14:50
26	R HUCKS	3:11:44	A BRENNAN	3:12:33	D BESTON	3:13:20	T BEAVAN	3:14:05	H SLIMON	3:14:50
27	J HIGGON	3:11:44	G WILSON	3:12:33	N FOX	3:13:21	J MCNULTY	3:14:05	T HODGE	3:14:50
28	B GRIERSON	3:11:44	G MOYSE	3:12:33	I HAWKINS	3:13:21	M FARNHAM	3:14:06	G DAVIDSON	3:14:51
29	P MARILLY	3:11:44	J VICENTE	3:12:33	A DEACON	3:13:21	C WOOLLEY	3:14:07	D LOVELL	3:14:51
30	S FOWLES	3:11:44	C MARSH	3:12:34	G DAVIES	3:13:21	B DALTON	3:14:08	K HAYWOOD	3:14:52
31	G WHITE	3:11:45	J BLOMME	3:12:34	D ALVAREZ	3:13:22	A SMITH	3:14:08	K GOLDING	3:14:52
32	J GREGORY	3:11:45	N MCCULLOUGH	3:12:34	D CLARK	3:13:22	P JONES	3:14:08	B CLAPSON	3:14:52
33	S CROFT	3:11:45	T NIGHTINGALE	3:12:36	P MC CONVILLE	3:13:22	P ETOURNEAU	3:14:08	M HALES	3:14:52
34	Y PERRIN	3:11:45	P ZYWITH	3:12:37	M VRBANCIC	3:13:23	R MAY	3:14:08	P DALE	3:14:52
35	J ALLEN	3:11:47	A INNOCENZI	3:12:37	D STEVENS	3:13:23	C REDMAN	3:14:08	S CURRY	3:14:52
36	U ALEANDRI	3:11:48	G ASHBY	3:12:38	C CABRAL	3:13:24	G DEACON	3:14:08	B PARRY	3:14:52
37	G THOMAS	3:11:48	B COOK	3:12:38	R SHORT	3:13:24	A MORRISON	3:14:08	D WALLACE	3:14:53
38	R MEREDITH	3:11:48	N ELDRED	3:12:38	J HOLTON	3:13:25	C HEWINS	3:14:08	A ABBOTT	3:14:53
39	R WILLIAMS	3:11:48	J BIRD	3:12:39	D HANKINS	3:13:25	S WAGSTAFF	3:14:08	A CRISP	3:14:53
40	A MAZZUCA	3:11:49	G WILLIAMS	3:12:39	M WILCOX	3:13:25	M FRICKER	3:14:08	R MINETT	3:14:53
41	T COCKING	3:11:50	G COX	3:12:40	I YOUNG	3:13:25	D PETERS	3:14:09	A PODDA	3:14:53
42	H COSTE	3:11:50	P CLEMENT	3:12:40	A HITZL	3:13:26	P WARING	3:14:09	L SKINNER	3:14:53
43	C SYNNOTT	3:11:50	C WILKINSON	3:12:40	D POLLARD	3:13:27	I WATERS	3:14:11	R STUART	3:14:53
44	R MORRELL	3:11:51	G ONNERBY	3:12:41	A DAMPS	3:13:27	C SARNEL	3:14:11	R SEXTON	3:14:54
45	A WELCH	3:11:51	M BERGH	3:12:41	D BOWERS	3:13:28	M SELL	3:14:11	S PERRIN	3:14:54
46	J WISHART	3:11:52	C BOSTOCK	3:12:41	B HICKEY	3:13:28	D PLESSIER	3:14:11	M RAZAQ	3:14:54
47	D STREADER	3:11:52	A ROCKLIFFE	3:12:42	R COPE	3:13:29	C AUSTIN	3:14:13	A BROWN	3:14:54
48	M BLACKBURN	3:11:53	A BREWER	3:12:42	J JONES	3:13:29	D RUGMAN	3:14:13	R CARTER	3:14:55
49	R BROOM	3:11:53	C POWELL	3:12:42	C MCLEAN	3:13:30	J WICKS	3:14:14	P COTTON	3:14:55
50	P POULSEN	3:11:55	A MITCHELL	3:12:42	B HOLMES	3:13:30	M ILOTT	3:14:14	R BURCHETT	3:14:56
51	J LATTE	3:11:56	L MCCABE	3:12:42	R LILLIE	3:13:30	W SCOTT	3:14:15	B JEWELS	3:14:56
52	M HOOPER	3:11:56	S STONEBRIDGE	3:12:42	L MEEK	3:13:30	T MARSHALL	3:14:15	K PATEL	3:14:56
53	J MOUAT	3:11:58	L PAYS	3:12:43	J HENNESSY	3:13:30	R EDGAR	3:14:16	R ROGERS	3:14:57
54	J GORDON	3:11:58	N ANDERSON	3:12:44	N MCKNIGHT	3:13:31	K GLOMSAKER	3:14:16	G STRAFFI	3:14:57
55	M ROBINS	3:12:01	C CARRARA	3:12:44	S DRAPER	3:13:31	Y THOMAS	3:14:17	P SMITH	3:14:57
56	S HARDMAN	3:12:01	A FERREIRA	3:12:45	W FAIRFIELD	3:13:31	P MARTIN	3:14:17	B WHITTELL	3:14:58
57	M APPLEBY	3:12:01	D ROSA	3:12:46	P DOYLE	3:13:32	D TILLEY	3:14:18	K DWYER	3:14:58
58	F BROOKS	3:12:02	F GOUGH	3:12:46	S MILNE	3:13:32	S GARVEY	3:14:18	J PERKINS	3:14:59
59	N SKIDMORE	3:12:02	T SLADE	3:12:46	P KIRBY	3:13:33	P BJELLAND	3:14:19	A MARSH	3:14:59
60	J ALLSOP	3:12:03	C TEZIER	3:12:46	S OWEN	3:13:33	D RANDLE	3:14:19	C WESTON	3:15:00
61	M LEGGOTT	3:12:03	R LYNES	3:12:47	T ROBINSON	3:13:34	S COX	3:14:20	J SHEPHERD	3:15:00
62	K HAWKINS	3:12:03	D FRASER	3:12:48	D CERANIC	3:13:35	T CAULTON	3:14:21	A PONTIFEX	3:15:00
63	A THOMAS	3:12:04	D DEAN	3:12:48	J BORJES	3:13:36	T KELLY	3:14:22	M REYNOLDS	3:15:00
64	J SKELSEY	3:12:04	J FOSTER	3:12:48	J DAVIES	3:13:37	A OWEN	3:14:24	R DERWENT	3:15:01
65	M HOLMAN	3:12:04	G BARNES	3:12:49	C MANN	3:13:37	B JONES	3:14:25	P HUNT	3:15:01
66	S SMITH	3:12:04	D BRACEY	3:12:49	E KEVILLE	3:13:37	J GADEIX	3:14:25	N MCCONOCHIE	3:15:01
67	D FRANCIS	3:12:05	S ELKINS	3:12:49	G SAGE	3:13:37	J PRATT	3:14:25	R HEAP	3:15:03
68	R HANDLEY	3:12:05	M BRADBURN	3:12:49	S SCOTT	3:13:37	G CLEMENTS	3:14:25	F MCCONOCHIE	3:15:03
69	S SMITH	3:12:05	A WILLIAMS	3:12:50	B PIKE	3:13:37	J CRANE	3:14:25	K REMNANT	3:15:03
70	M SIMMONS	3:12:05	H HELLWEG	3:12:50	C WILD	3:13:38	E CARPINTERO	3:14:26	P SHERLOCK	3:15:04
71	M SEQUEIRA	3:12:06	R DUTOIT	3:12:50	T GLEADEN	3:13:38	R WILLIAMS	3:14:26	A STEVENSON	3:15:04
72	S LEE	3:12:06	J NOLTE	3:12:50	A POTTER	3:13:39	M JORDAN	3:14:27	G ADAMS	3:15:05
73	D ROBINSON	3:12:06	I BLAIR	3:12:51	M CRAIG	3:13:39	P TUCKER	3:14:28	S NENDICK	3:15:05
74	P CORVEE	3:12:06	S BRADSHAW	3:12:51	D GILLARD	3:13:40	G BLAKE	3:14:28	G HAIRE	3:15:09
75	A COX	3:12:07	I SLATER	3:12:51	W JOHNSON	3:13:40	P HARRIS	3:14:28	R HILLS	3:15:10
76	I GIBBON	3:12:07	D THOMPSON	3:12:51	M O'ROURKE	3:13:41	D MCELHENNY	3:14:28	D WYNN-WILLIAMS	3:15:10
77	M MCLAREN	3:12:07	J JARVIS	3:12:52	G DAVIES	3:13:41	R BALDWIN	3:14:28	V SOLOMON	3:15:10
78	R BOWLING	3:12:07	G CHARLES	3:12:53	P EVANS	3:13:42	B FRENCH	3:14:30	R WOLD	3:15:11
79	H HOLTEN	3:12:07	S BROUGHTON	3:12:54	S CHILD	3:13:42	D HOWARD	3:14:31	J GUESS	3:15:11
80	J BOURNE	3:12:07	M STROUD	3:12:55	C KIRBY	3:13:44	W LIMBERT	3:14:32	T MC MANAMON	3:15:11
81	A JENKINS	3:12:08	S BATHGATE	3:12:56	W KING	3:13:44	G DUCKETT	3:14:32	J WHIBLEY	3:15:11
82	J BARKER	3:12:09	K SARGEANT	3:12:56	I PRICE	3:13:45	D MISELL	3:14:32	P CAPDEUILA	3:15:11
83	G MOSSMAN	3:12:10	H VAN LENNEP	3:12:57	R PORTER	3:13:45	A POPE	3:14:32	N READ	3:15:12
84	J PROSSER	3:12:10	M WALLER	3:12:57	B FELDMAN	3:13:45	P QUIBELL	3:14:32	M SALTER	3:15:14
85	K POLLARD	3:12:11	C WESCOMB	3:12:58	A CARTER	3:13:46	D BARNBY	3:14:32	R MOUZER	3:15:14
86	G STAPLEY	3:12:11	P LYNSDALE	3:12:58	G LOWE	3:13:46	L VOONG	3:14:33	S SYMONDS	3:15:16
87	T HYLAND	3:12:12	M MOSES	3:12:58	J HANSON	3:13:47	M HILLYER	3:14:33	S KELLY	3:15:16
88	N HOUSTON	3:12:12	C GREEN	3:12:59	S MATTHEWS	3:13:48	P PHILLIPS	3:14:34	D PREECE	3:15:16
89	D STEWART	3:12:12	D BARRETT	3:12:59	L MOSS	3:13:49	J BUTLER	3:14:34	D PUGH	3:15:17
90	D OWENS	3:12:12	R ROBERTS	3:12:59	J MITCHELL	3:13:49	S HEWITT	3:14:35	J JENSEN	3:15:17
91	R GRIMLEY	3:12:12	A VAUGHAN	3:12:59	J JAMES	3:13:49	D KING	3:14:36	B COLLIS	3:15:17
92	M EVANS	3:12:12	B JOHNSON	3:13:00	A YOUNG	3:13:51	K CAMPBELL	3:14:36	M EMM	3:15:17
93	D ORBACH	3:12:13	D KUKAINIS	3:13:00	J CUVIER	3:13:51	T FAIRHURST	3:14:36	J KEMP	3:15:17
94	G CORCOLAN	3:12:13	P DIMMOCK	3:13:00	P GILLESPIE	3:13:51	M BARKWAY	3:14:37	D WHITE	3:15:18
95	G JOHNSON	3:12:13	S GARNHAM	3:13:01	D RILEY	3:13:52	A TAYLOR	3:14:37	S PETRUSO	3:15:19
96	L TUHEY	3:12:15	M DURAND	3:13:02	D MOORE	3:13:52	J LEGGETT	3:14:37	M PETERS	3:15:20
97	D LAMB	3:12:15	D JACKSON	3:13:02	M MURRAY	3:13:53	R TOMPKINS	3:14:37	N WELLS	3:15:21
98	M STEADMAN	3:12:16	R MENZIES	3:13:02	I TINMOUTH	3:13:53	M YAHIAOUI	3:14:38	D KNIGHT	3:15:22
99	S REASON	3:12:16	W INSKIP	3:13:03	K STONE	3:13:54	B MATTHEWS	3:14:39	D NORRIS-ROSS	3:15:22
100	K JUNGE	3:12:17	K COLEMAN	3:13:05	A THOMAS	3:13:55	P HARPER	3:14:39	A PEERS	3:15:23

#	3501-3600		3601-3700		3701-3800		3801-3900		3901-4000	
1	G CAMPBELL	3:15:23	P JONES	3:16:04	M MONDELLO	3:16:53	D FOLEY	3:17:36	G TEBBENHAM	3:18:14
2	T BASS	3:15:23	S SILBERSTON	3:16:04	R DAY	3:16:53	W TURNER	3:17:36	R SWEENEY	3:18:15
3	T WALTON	3:15:23	S HOPKINS	3:16:04	I GUILD	3:16:53	R TOWNSHEND	3:17:37	M CIVITANI	3:18:15
4	J WETZEL	3:15:24	W REUSCHEL	3:16:04	G CHAPMAN	3:16:53	W MCALISTER	3:17:37	T LANDER	3:18:15
5	J MURRAY	3:15:25	P BURCHER	3:16:05	E SCHNEIDER	3:16:54	H MOLYNEUX	3:17:37	D FISHER	3:18:16
6	D HAMILTON	3:15:25	D WRIGHT	3:16:06	J LINDLEY	3:16:54	A WEAVER	3:17:38	C WADFORTH	3:18:16
7	D SCOTT	3:15:25	M JONES	3:16:06	F CROCE	3:16:54	R DURANCE	3:17:39	J THOMSON	3:18:16
8	D GRAVES	3:15:25	V WITHEY	3:16:06	S POOLE	3:16:54	F CUNNINGHAM	3:17:39	P KEYTE	3:18:17
9	P BAXTER	3:15:25	D FINN	3:16:07	J GERKEN	3:16:55	I BUTLER	3:17:39	P SNELL	3:18:17
10	S GALLAGHER	3:15:25	N SMITH	3:16:09	D ROBINSON	3:16:55	C HAYWOOD	3:17:40	A IRVINE	3:18:17
11	S LAMBERT	3:15:26	P CORRIGAN	3:16:10	R BARNES	3:16:55	N GREEN	3:17:40	A CROWTHER	3:18:17
12	K COOPER	3:15:27	J MURRAY	3:16:11	M WILLMOTT	3:16:55	B PEMBRIDGE	3:17:41	N FAURE	3:18:18
13	A SUMNER	3:15:28	G SMITH	3:16:12	J COOK	3:16:55	C BENNETT	3:17:41	J DAVISON	3:18:18
14	M ATKINS	3:15:28	D ROBERTS	3:16:13	D SKILTON	3:16:56	B WINN	3:17:42	T WELSH	3:18:18
15	A WILLIAMS	3:15:29	S MCHIGGINS	3:16:13	M FARMER	3:16:56	C WROTH	3:17:43	L MATEUS	3:18:18
16	M VILLANI	3:15:30	M NEWBITT	3:16:14	S EDWARDS	3:16:57	C EASON	3:17:43	A MOORE	3:18:18
17	M HAIGNERE	3:15:30	P SINGLE	3:16:14	E RODGER	3:16:59	C DAVID	3:17:43	A JALABERT	3:18:19
18	C CALLAGHAN	3:15:31	P LAWRENCE	3:16:15	G KING	3:16:59	I WRIGHT	3:17:43	A PEPPER	3:18:19
19	T SLATER	3:15:33	W FORD	3:16:15	E CRAIG	3:17:00	G DAVIS	3:17:44	B SAINSBURY	3:18:20
20	T AVEY	3:15:33	L NICHOLLS	3:16:15	G LEDWITH	3:17:00	J HOPKINS	3:17:44	A ROBERTS	3:18:20
21	A BLACKER	3:15:33	M KERSHAW	3:16:16	D THOMSON	3:17:00	J CLARKE	3:17:45	H VIBE	3:18:21
22	J CABRITA	3:15:34	E BROWN	3:16:16	M BOYLE	3:17:00	M RENDER	3:17:45	M GALLAGHER	3:18:21
23	F MCSLOY	3:15:34	M MCCARTHY	3:16:16	S MARTIN	3:17:02	A SIMPSON	3:17:46	P WEBB	3:18:21
24	W PURSER	3:15:34	R BECKER	3:16:17	R THOMSON	3:17:03	C DAVIES	3:17:46	R HAWKEN	3:18:21
25	D NALDER	3:15:34	D WILDMAN	3:16:17	P STACK	3:17:03	P EDWARDS	3:17:46	P ERIKSEN	3:18:21
26	P MATTHEWS	3:15:35	M STACEY	3:16:18	G LAWRENCE	3:17:05	S FARRIS	3:17:47	M ANDERSON	3:18:23
27	D HATTON	3:15:36	G BELL	3:16:18	D WHILLIS	3:17:05	R CRILLY	3:17:47	M BARKER	3:18:24
28	R HUSHER	3:15:36	P MICHEL	3:16:19	K WALKER	3:17:05	J HOLLIDAY	3:17:47	K HOCKNEY	3:18:24
29	T HARNDEN	3:15:36	E BJARNASON	3:16:19	M BLACKMAN	3:17:05	G PARIS	3:17:48	J NEALES	3:18:25
30	J BRADBURY	3:15:37	A SCOTT	3:16:19	B NORTON	3:17:05	N CHAMBERLAIN	3:17:49	T DAY	3:18:25
31	J LUND	3:15:38	J MENNEN	3:16:20	E WALKER	3:17:06	H BRENTNALL	3:17:49	M CRAMER	3:18:25
32	A YOUNG	3:15:38	K GRONINGER	3:16:20	G PYE	3:17:06	M GALLAGHER	3:17:50	J CUNNINGHAM	3:18:26
33	C CLARKE	3:15:39	M BARLOW	3:16:20	J BOZON	3:17:07	J QUANTRILL	3:17:50	A CLARKE	3:18:27
34	G MAUCHER	3:15:39	J PORTER	3:16:20	C GOODWIN	3:17:08	K VAN DEYNSE	3:17:50	S CHAPMAN	3:18:27
35	B FROST	3:15:40	J BIBBY	3:16:20	D FLUDE	3:17:08	P ADOLFSSON	3:17:51	N WRIGHT	3:18:27
36	J STEWARD	3:15:42	J DILLAMORE	3:16:20	T MUNDAL	3:17:09	N HOGAN	3:17:51	J PADBURY	3:18:27
37	P WEBB	3:15:42	T CHARLES	3:16:21	C MORRISON	3:17:09	C GRAPY	3:17:51	P DAVIDSON	3:18:29
38	W GUY	3:15:43	J DONOHOE	3:16:22	H LACHLAN	3:17:09	R NISTL	3:17:51	P FALLOON	3:18:29
39	R COUPE	3:15:43	M ROBERTS	3:16:23	E VAN DE VEIRE	3:17:11	I BLACKBURN	3:17:51	B GRIEVES	3:18:30
40	J BASSON	3:15:43	I HEPWORTH	3:16:23	F BOLTON	3:17:11	I GUNN	3:17:51	N BARRY	3:18:30
41	R GETLIFFE	3:15:44	C MCDONALD	3:16:23	L MOREAU	3:17:12	P WOOD	3:17:52	S PHILLIPS	3:18:31
42	A FULLER	3:15:45	E PARKER	3:16:24	L WARMAN	3:17:13	T HUCKLESBY	3:17:53	C DEARDS	3:18:31
43	G JERVIS	3:15:45	A PIKE	3:16:24	I JORGENSEN	3:17:14	I HOWARD	3:17:53	J WILTSHIRE	3:18:32
44	P BARLOW	3:15:45	C MARTIN	3:16:24	R KEMP	3:17:14	R BURKE	3:17:54	N WRITER	3:18:32
45	R SMITH	3:15:45	L SHILLINGFORD	3:16:25	M CURLEY	3:17:15	M DEAN	3:17:54	L LAMPMANN	3:18:33
46	J MERRICK	3:15:46	E JUDGE	3:16:25	D THOMAS	3:17:15	R GENTRY	3:17:54	J LACEY	3:18:33
47	J FAUSCH	3:15:46	M JESSERMINO	3:16:26	S PARRETT	3:17:16	T HALEY	3:17:54	N BROCKWELL	3:18:33
48	P KELLY	3:15:47	C COPUS	3:16:27	W VAN AMERONGEN	3:17:16	K LAWRENCE	3:17:55	C BREDA	3:18:33
49	B RICHARDSON	3:15:47	P KING	3:16:27	E SHERWOOD	3:17:17	A TURNER	3:17:55	K DAY	3:18:34
50	K COUSINS	3:15:47	J COMRIE	3:16:28	P PRIESTLEY	3:17:18	U KETELSEN	3:17:55	J CALTHROP	3:18:34
51	S WINTER	3:15:48	M QUINCEY	3:16:28	B SMITH	3:17:18	T BRANIGAN	3:17:56	L MENGHINI	3:18:34
52	D PEARSON	3:15:48	D RAWSON	3:16:31	P MORTON	3:17:19	G DUDLEY	3:17:56	A DA SILVA	3:18:34
53	C STURGESS	3:15:49	G DONALDSON	3:16:32	L GREENWOOD	3:17:19	J TAYLOR	3:17:57	A JONES	3:18:35
54	D SWANBROW	3:15:49	B SMITH	3:16:32	M HAFFENDEN	3:17:19	M WHITE	3:17:57	P BEAVER	3:18:35
55	D HILL	3:15:50	S HAYES	3:16:32	D LIDDLE	3:17:20	D JUKES	3:17:58	B PLASMANS	3:18:35
56	A DAWSON	3:15:50	M JONES	3:16:33	N LUNN	3:17:20	I THOMAS	3:17:59	J MACGREGOR	3:18:35
57	J WHALLEY	3:15:50	D DUPOUY	3:16:33	T KELLY	3:17:20	J DUNNE	3:17:59	A BURGHALL	3:18:35
58	S MULLEN	3:15:50	J ROWE	3:16:34	D HAYNES	3:17:21	P LOVICK	3:17:59	S BARKER	3:18:36
59	R TOWELL	3:15:50	C STARNES	3:16:35	K VICKERY	3:17:22	D HOLLIDAY	3:17:59	C GOSS	3:18:36
60	D HUISH	3:15:51	G PETTENGELL	3:16:35	R YOUNG	3:17:22	P HERBERT	3:18:00	V MILLER	3:18:36
61	J STRATFORD	3:15:51	P ARCHMAN	3:16:36	J JACKSON	3:17:22	H PHILPOTT	3:18:01	R CARVELL	3:18:37
62	P ROBINSON	3:15:52	C DOE	3:16:36	P BAALHAM	3:17:23	S BUCHAN	3:18:01	D STANLEY	3:18:37
63	M POOLEY	3:15:52	J LEROUSSEAU	3:16:37	N SHARP	3:17:23	V HAMLET	3:18:01	W CLARKE	3:18:37
64	I SWIFT	3:15:52	G BAINBRIDGE	3:16:37	G FRYER	3:17:23	D HOOD	3:18:02	A ISERN	3:18:37
65	R WEBBER	3:15:52	C DEVOY	3:16:38	J STAATS	3:17:24	M VASSEUR	3:18:04	D MITCHELL	3:18:37
66	G WORMALD	3:15:52	J SQUIRE	3:16:38	M EPSON	3:17:24	M KAVANAGH	3:18:04	R JONES	3:18:38
67	G HOLMES	3:15:53	D MURPHY	3:16:39	G BALFOUR	3:17:24	I KENDRICK	3:18:04	J PICTON	3:18:38
68	B MONK	3:15:53	S WEBBER	3:16:39	L DOBIE	3:17:25	W WILSHER	3:18:04	C ADDISON	3:18:38
69	D PENNEY	3:15:53	R OESTERLUND	3:16:39	B MILLER	3:17:25	D SCOTT	3:18:04	D DOWNES	3:18:39
70	R SHARPE	3:15:53	I EDWARDS	3:16:40	A HAINES	3:17:25	P THYS	3:18:04	D BARKER	3:18:39
71	D GROSS	3:15:53	M WILLCOX	3:16:40	C MARCOL	3:17:26	S WINSON	3:18:04	K LOCKYEAR	3:18:39
72	C GUNBY	3:15:54	D BROWN	3:16:41	D BROOKE	3:17:26	W VORBECK	3:18:05	H CHALMERS	3:18:39
73	L TITTERTON	3:15:54	D BRAME	3:16:41	D MCEVOY	3:17:26	P HANDLEY	3:18:05	R PAYNE	3:18:39
74	D RICHARDS	3:15:54	L BRUCE	3:16:41	T MITCHESON	3:17:27	D WILLIAMS	3:18:05	M MCCARTHY	3:18:39
75	D YORK	3:15:54	S LOVELESS	3:16:41	P KIRBY	3:17:27	R HOWARD	3:18:06	C LEE	3:18:39
76	D WALTON	3:15:54	C HALL	3:16:41	R LAAN	3:17:27	M BACH	3:18:06	L JAMES	3:18:40
77	P HAYCOCK	3:15:54	E MARZLOFF	3:16:42	P REEVE	3:17:28	G CRQADDOCK	3:18:06	D MCKENZIE	3:18:40
78	A EVANS	3:15:54	M CALDWELL	3:16:43	F REINECKE	3:17:28	P BOWDEN	3:18:06	B ANDREWS	3:18:40
79	I MCLACHLAN	3:15:54	I MCVEIGH	3:16:43	R DUNBAR	3:17:28	M LUCAS	3:18:07	M CULLEN	3:18:41
80	A WHEELER	3:15:54	C AITCHISON	3:16:45	S TANDY	3:17:29	C CUTNER	3:18:08	R STIBBARDS	3:18:41
81	F DOHERTY	3:15:54	J THOMAS	3:16:45	C WISBEY	3:17:29	D LONG	3:18:08	R WHITEHEAD	3:18:41
82	F SPRENGHERS	3:15:54	S SKIAKER	3:16:46	S ISHII	3:17:29	W LUETHY	3:18:08	M ROBERTSON	3:18:41
83	N WARNER	3:15:55	A SMEDHAUGEN	3:16:46	M POUNDER	3:17:30	D EARTHROLL	3:18:08	K HAGELQVIST PETERSEN	3:18:41
84	M JOHNSON	3:15:55	A MEARLEIN	3:16:46	D REYMOND	3:17:30	W BALMER	3:18:08	A SIDI-MOUSSA	3:18:42
85	P NIKKILA	3:15:56	D DAY	3:16:46	B MCSHANE	3:17:30	P SMITH	3:18:09	P EVERETT	3:18:42
86	S TURNER	3:15:57	A HANSEN	3:16:47	P WOODCOCK	3:17:31	A SMART	3:18:09	R LEE	3:18:43
87	F BARRETT	3:15:58	B FURHOFF	3:16:48	R PROIETTI	3:17:31	D BROSNAN	3:18:10	K FRY	3:18:43
88	A BIRD	3:16:00	D FOXLEY	3:16:49	M ROWBOTHAM	3:17:32	D RAPP	3:18:10	V BATTEN	3:18:43
89	M BOCHARDT	3:16:00	K MCCORD	3:16:49	D TROTTER	3:17:32	J GROVER	3:18:10	K ROBSON	3:18:43
90	B JONSSON	3:16:01	R NEWMAN	3:16:51	M DICKINSON	3:17:32	K CARTER	3:18:11	P EDWARDS	3:18:44
91	G STEVENS	3:16:01	A FLEMING	3:16:51	K BAILEY	3:17:33	I KING	3:18:12	E DAVIES	3:18:44
92	P WHALAN	3:16:01	A RANGER	3:16:51	D HAW	3:17:33	L HORTON	3:18:12	P ALDERSON	3:18:44
93	D RUSSELL	3:16:02	A WILSON	3:16:51	R VALOGNES	3:17:33	R PRITCHARD	3:18:12	C WHITESIDE	3:18:44
94	W BAKKER	3:16:02	K KELLEY	3:16:52	E MALAGISI	3:17:33	S PARKER	3:18:12	J MACDONALD	3:18:44
95	R ROSS	3:16:02	L MEADOWS	3:16:52	J LARTER	3:17:34	D KEMSLEY	3:18:13	S SALTER	3:18:45
96	L HOUGHTON	3:16:03	L MEADOWS	3:16:52	P BAILEY	3:17:34	A BYE	3:18:13	D HILEY	3:18:46
97	R MASON	3:16:03	K DOOLAN	3:16:53	D HUYGHEBAERT	3:17:35	J PARK	3:18:14	S MITCHELL	3:18:46
98	B PEACOCK	3:16:03	G CRACK	3:16:53	K O'NEILL	3:17:36	A ROFTS	3:18:14	S BROADBENT	3:18:47
99	P GARGIN	3:16:03	M LAMB	3:16:53	L HICKEY	3:17:36	K O'ROURKE	3:18:14	M SMITH	3:18:47
100	P OGDEN	3:16:04	F VANSCHAIK	3:16:53	B WORTHINGTON	3:17:36	S ARNOLD	3:18:14	J WEAVER	3:18:47

	4001-4100		4101-4200		4201-4300		4301-4400		4401-4500	
1	R EADE	3:18:48	M PHILLIPS	3:19:27	P IRESON	3:20:02	J WATSON	3:20:43	J MCQUILLIN	3:21:19
2	J COOKE	3:18:48	R WEBSTER	3:19:28	V MCLACHLAN	3:20:02	M MANNUCARI	3:20:44	Y JOYCE	3:21:19
3	K SUMMERS	3:18:49	N GEEAR	3:19:28	K JONES	3:20:02	G WILLIAMS	3:20:44	C PHILLIPS	3:21:19
4	J GOURGEOT	3:18:49	J GRIFFITHS	3:19:29	M BARNES	3:20:02	S LIVETT	3:20:44	G ROSE	3:21:21
5	G KRIER	3:18:50	A VOORTMAN	3:19:30	D CROWDER	3:20:03	A ROBINSON	3:20:45	J KARTZ	3:21:21
6	M WESTERBERG	3:18:51	R TITTENSOR	3:19:31	P SWANN	3:20:03	A MCBARNET	3:20:45	S NERDLING	3:21:21
7	C NAUGHTON	3:18:51	L BROWN	3:19:31	V MEYERS	3:20:04	J RICE	3:20:46	K HURLEY	3:21:21
8	C FARRAR-BELL	3:18:51	D BAILEY	3:19:32	E SIMPSON	3:20:04	M REILLY	3:20:46	O MCTEGGART	3:21:22
9	P MONK	3:18:52	W KNIGHT	3:19:32	J PURICELLI	3:20:05	J CUNLIFFE	3:20:46	P MACE	3:21:23
10	B FARRELL	3:18:52	R COOK	3:19:32	T RAYNER	3:20:05	A PRITCHARD	3:20:46	C SCOTT	3:21:24
11	P O'BRIEN	3:18:54	G PARKER	3:19:32	R WHITTLE	3:20:06	N SHAW	3:20:47	R JOLLYE	3:21:25
12	C ASTON	3:18:54	D JACKSON	3:19:32	R FRAMPTON	3:20:06	P SCHNEIDER	3:20:47	B SMULDERS	3:21:25
13	M CLARKE	3:18:54	A READ	3:19:32	C STARR	3:20:06	J HEATHER	3:20:47	W HARLEY	3:21:26
14	M BRICE	3:18:55	W HANNAM	3:19:33	K CARTER	3:20:07	R HITT	3:20:48	M BATES	3:21:26
15	C WHITE	3:18:55	E WALLS	3:19:33	P TONKS	3:20:07	D LITCHFIELD	3:20:48	B YOUNG	3:21:27
16	J HARRISON	3:18:55	L MARTENSSON	3:19:35	G HARRIS	3:20:07	M BIGNELL	3:20:48	W HALES	3:21:27
17	S PRIEST	3:18:55	S BAKER	3:19:35	I COOK	3:20:07	P MANLEY	3:20:48	M PANTLING	3:21:27
18	M ZAFFARONI	3:18:56	J WILSON	3:19:35	S NOLAN	3:20:08	J WINTER	3:20:48	S WAKEHAM	3:21:27
19	K ROBINSON	3:18:56	R BALL	3:19:36	J SHAW	3:20:08	G WRIGHT	3:20:48	S LENKIEWICZ	3:21:28
20	P GUSTAVSSON	3:18:56	J BOULTON	3:19:37	D PLANT	3:20:08	D VARLEY	3:20:49	R WILSON	3:21:28
21	K RISBERG	3:18:57	C RACCA	3:19:37	P BOWDEN	3:20:08	H SVEDIN	3:20:49	G CONWAY	3:21:28
22	K HILLGREN	3:18:57	L COUSENS	3:19:37	D UTTON	3:20:09	M HOWARTH	3:20:49	P TOWNSHEND	3:21:28
23	D CONNOR	3:18:58	B DUDDING	3:19:38	J DOWSON	3:20:10	S GIDDINGS	3:20:49	C HARRIS	3:21:29
24	S CHAPMAN	3:18:58	I GILL	3:19:38	B BOOTH	3:20:11	J CHEETHAM	3:20:50	S HUG	3:21:29
25	R MORGAN	3:18:58	F PETRY	3:19:38	D BATEMAN	3:20:11	T HOWES	3:20:50	B GRIFFITHS	3:21:30
26	S JOHNSON	3:18:58	D VIVIAN	3:19:39	M BLAKE	3:20:12	L ERICSSON	3:20:50	D WILLIAMS	3:21:30
27	D MILNER	3:18:59	M LYONS	3:19:39	N STREET	3:20:12	S ROBERTS	3:20:50	R BEST	3:21:30
28	C OSMOND	3:18:59	J BEANGE	3:19:40	M SMITH	3:20:13	P DOWD	3:20:50	P BAKX	3:21:30
29	J ADAIR	3:18:59	M BOLTON	3:19:40	S O'DEA	3:20:14	P STEPHENS	3:20:50	G MOULINET	3:21:30
30	L ADAMS	3:19:00	J MILLS	3:19:40	S BAERT	3:20:15	G ALOY	3:20:50	K HARRISON	3:21:31
31	S PRICE	3:19:01	A FLYNN	3:19:40	C GATLEY	3:20:15	G WHITER	3:20:50	M WARRICK	3:21:31
32	R WALSTROM	3:19:02	F MC HARG	3:19:41	K RUNESSON	3:20:16	D ALLEBONE	3:20:51	D BENNETT	3:21:32
33	M EDWARDS	3:19:02	J DE CONINCK	3:19:41	R FREEMAN	3:20:16	C BENNETT	3:20:51	G PULLEN	3:21:33
34	S CAPELLETTI	3:19:02	J MAYOR	3:19:41	N KIRKBY	3:20:17	A LOURENCO	3:20:51	C PARKER	3:21:33
35	W DRIESSEN	3:19:02	D CHANDLER	3:19:41	C BOOTH	3:20:17	F PICHAL	3:20:51	P HOLE	3:21:33
36	D WELLS	3:19:02	R SIMPSON	3:19:42	M ROGERS	3:20:17	G THORLEY	3:20:51	J CHAMPOUX	3:21:33
37	R BRIDGES	3:19:03	D STOPP	3:19:42	M MCGOWAN	3:20:18	J CLARKE	3:20:51	R WILD	3:21:33
38	A POELS	3:19:03	B WHITEHILL	3:19:42	S ROBERTSON	3:20:19	G GINN	3:20:51	M MCDONOUGH	3:21:34
39	D WRIGGLESWORTH	3:19:03	R GRIFFIN	3:19:42	E COLON	3:20:19	N PEARCE	3:20:52	C PILLAR	3:21:34
40	D TRICKEY	3:19:04	I CHAPMAN	3:19:43	M GOULD	3:20:19	T JOLLEY	3:20:52	M BURNINGHAM	3:21:34
41	T SHARKEY	3:19:04	P MC GILL	3:19:43	S SUGDEN	3:20:20	J PERRY	3:20:52	D TOPPING	3:21:35
42	P LAWTON	3:19:04	M MORROW	3:19:45	V MAROT	3:20:21	D SMITH	3:20:52	D WILLIAMS	3:21:35
43	F OWEN	3:19:04	J AYLMER	3:19:45	A OVENS	3:20:21	T KEATINGS	3:20:52	J PEDLEY	3:21:36
44	G TAYLOR	3:19:04	M INGRAM	3:19:45	K CORNELIUS	3:20:22	B VAUGHAN	3:20:52	K PEARSON	3:21:37
45	R BRAND	3:19:04	M YAMADA	3:19:46	V COX	3:20:24	K WATERS	3:20:52	J RAWLINGS	3:21:40
46	P ROGERS	3:19:05	J HARRAN	3:19:46	J MILLER	3:20:24	M STANCLIFFE	3:20:53	M FORDE	3:21:40
47	B WARD	3:19:05	M VELAYOUDON	3:19:47	J GREGORY	3:20:25	A FRANCO	3:20:53	C MAHER	3:21:41
48	K FLOOR	3:19:05	P CHALLIS	3:19:47	H SCHNEIDER	3:20:25	A PEEL	3:20:53	S EDWARDS	3:21:41
49	L MOONEY	3:19:06	A MEADES	3:19:47	D WATMORE	3:20:25	C MILLS	3:20:53	D WALLER	3:21:42
50	J AZIZA	3:19:06	S LONGHORN	3:19:47	R BROWN	3:20:25	E BIDDLE	3:20:54	G LORHO	3:21:42
51	R WALSH	3:19:07	J GILLATT	3:19:48	P HAYWARD	3:20:26	R ALLEN	3:20:55	K EDEL	3:21:42
52	K FISCHER	3:19:07	J CARMICHAEL	3:19:48	G CRUICKSHANK	3:20:26	T KINGHAM	3:20:55	W KEMPER	3:21:42
53	B WALKER	3:19:07	R HEYWOOD	3:19:48	K MAGEE	3:20:26	A MEIKLEJOHN	3:20:55	C MANDEMAKERS	3:21:42
54	T CARTWRIGHT	3:19:08	J COOKE	3:19:48	A BARR	3:20:27	I ARMSTRONG	3:20:55	M PAUTARD	3:21:43
55	P LANGLEY	3:19:09	K HUGHES	3:19:48	F FERRERE	3:20:27	A NIXON	3:20:56	N BARBER	3:21:43
56	R WILDMAN	3:19:09	M BROWN	3:19:48	C PENZHOLZ	3:20:27	C HEDLEY	3:20:57	D ELLIS	3:21:44
57	B CHAMBON	3:19:10	S PRICE	3:19:49	D RICHTER	3:20:28	M JAKEMAN	3:20:58	J WATKIN	3:21:44
58	R PRESTON	3:19:10	R VENABLES	3:19:50	S DUNNE	3:20:28	P SCARFF	3:20:59	G HORNE	3:21:45
59	W SARTAIN	3:19:11	I BLACKMORE	3:19:50	D JENNESS	3:20:28	S PROSSER	3:21:00	F RISBY	3:21:45
60	B EVANS	3:19:11	J BARNFIELD	3:19:51	G SHAW	3:20:28	B PETTERSEN	3:21:00	D NAPPER	3:21:45
61	P HARTSHORN	3:19:11	C PARKER	3:19:53	K BOOTH	3:20:29	A WHITTLE	3:21:00	I CAMPBELL	3:21:46
62	S BRUNGER	3:19:11	B TREVETTE	3:19:53	D MOSS	3:20:29	C MURRAY	3:21:00	D STEEL	3:21:46
63	J FLETCHER	3:19:11	E BARTLETT	3:19:53	C FLORENCIO	3:20:29	D CARR	3:21:01	R FORREST	3:21:46
64	R HANDSCOMBE	3:19:12	A BASS	3:19:53	S MCCLENNON	3:20:29	J GANNON	3:21:03	A GRIFFITH	3:21:46
65	R TINKLER	3:19:12	D JACKSON	3:19:54	J TURNER	3:20:30	P BURNS	3:21:03	S HERITAGE	3:21:46
66	S THOMAS	3:19:12	T DEWINTON-PULLAR	3:19:54	O BLACK	3:20:30	J WEEKS	3:21:03	R PARSONS	3:21:46
67	D MENZIES	3:19:13	H DAVIES	3:19:54	S OLIVER	3:20:30	A HOOKE	3:21:06	J MARRIOTT	3:21:46
68	L MANNION	3:19:13	F THOMSON	3:19:54	M QUINN	3:20:30	S HANSFORD	3:21:06	D RAYFIELD	3:21:47
69	B LANGHAM	3:19:14	W CLARKE	3:19:54	T OWEN	3:20:31	J FLYNN	3:21:06	I LIDDEL	3:21:48
70	A EWBANK	3:19:15	M FREWER	3:19:55	V GREENBERG	3:20:31	S MC CUDDEN	3:21:06	B JONES	3:21:48
71	M COTTRELL	3:19:15	P KIMBER	3:19:55	I ROBINSON	3:20:32	C DAY	3:21:06	N NAVILLE	3:21:48
72	D HILTON	3:19:16	P ANGELL	3:19:55	G LIVESEY	3:20:32	R ANDERSON	3:21:07	R O'BRIEN	3:21:49
73	B SPICER	3:19:16	A LAWRENCE	3:19:56	R ASUAJE	3:20:32	V CATANZARO	3:21:07	J GIGGAL	3:21:49
74	C COUSSONS	3:19:16	D WILSON	3:19:56	J MCGHEE	3:20:33	F HUDSON	3:21:07	K MITCHELL	3:21:50
75	W BASKERVILLE	3:19:17	S CLARKSON	3:19:56	A NASSETTI	3:20:33	C BEEDEN	3:21:08	D HOWELL	3:21:50
76	C MAXWELL	3:19:17	A BENT	3:19:56	E COVER	3:20:33	G SCULLY	3:21:08	D SCHINDLER	3:21:50
77	D PARSONS	3:19:17	C LANDER	3:19:57	I JONES	3:20:33	A NORRIS	3:21:08	A MCKEEMAN	3:21:50
78	P ALDAG	3:19:18	B STEVENS	3:19:57	G STIMSON	3:20:33	K DELLA PENNA	3:21:08	C GREEN	3:21:50
79	P NUTTALL	3:19:18	A PURDY	3:19:57	G STIMSON	3:20:33	T KORTBEEK	3:21:10	A WESTON	3:21:51
80	G GETULI	3:19:18	R MELLOR	3:19:57	W NEUWIRTH	3:20:34	R FORD	3:21:10	T HARRISON	3:21:51
81	M JONES	3:19:20	V KUBLER	3:19:58	R WOOLFORD	3:20:34	D STETSON	3:21:11	R DAVIDSON	3:21:51
82	M BAILEY	3:19:20	M WILSON	3:19:58	B TAYLOR	3:20:34	O GUDMESTAD	3:21:11	K SANDERS	3:21:51
83	D BOWMAN	3:19:20	K BRAITHWAITE	3:19:58	A HANSSON	3:20:35	L REUHL	3:21:11	J STEPHAN	3:21:51
84	J PARDON	3:19:21	J ROBINSON	3:19:58	N BUNNAGE	3:20:35	T BONDS	3:21:11	C GILES	3:21:52
85	T HEARD	3:19:21	P DUFFY	3:19:58	P GALLOWAY	3:20:35	I JABARINE	3:21:12	D HALLSON	3:21:52
86	P DE VITA	3:19:22	J GUITTET	3:19:58	R GUILLERMO	3:20:36	J PAGE	3:21:12	D LEWIS	3:21:52
87	T KILCULLEN	3:19:22	M LOUWERS	3:19:58	F BERRY	3:20:36	B CRAIGIE	3:21:12	A COPE	3:21:53
88	L LEE	3:19:22	G ARMSTRONG	3:19:59	K HENDRIKS	3:20:37	J TRACEY	3:21:12	W ATKINSON	3:21:54
89	P WOOD	3:19:22	A LYNE	3:19:59	K RAYSON	3:20:37	G SHEPPARD	3:21:13	A ROCHE	3:21:54
90	R LAUGHTON-ZIMMERMAN	3:19:22	J STOREY	3:19:59	P SMITH	3:20:38	M MCCARTHY	3:21:13	K DAY	3:21:55
91	A FAURE	3:19:23	D HARPER	3:20:00	S CATTELL	3:20:38	D MOSCA	3:21:13	A RASPAUD	3:21:55
92	K DRYLAND	3:19:24	A HOLT	3:20:00	S OWEN	3:20:38	E LATTO	3:21:14	G DECOURCY	3:21:55
93	D BASSETT	3:19:24	N MURRAY	3:20:00	C HARDY	3:20:39	S LOY	3:21:14	A PROSSER	3:21:55
94	A WRIGHT	3:19:24	M HARPER	3:20:00	V PREMA	3:20:39	P MCGROARTY	3:21:15	B SMITH	3:21:56
95	G COOK	3:19:24	A SALMON	3:20:01	K BARTON	3:20:40	A GARRETT	3:21:15	B BOOLE	3:21:56
96	L EGERTON	3:19:25	B ECCLES	3:20:01	P MOODY	3:20:41	L ROBINSON	3:21:15	W ARCHMENT	3:21:56
97	D WALKER	3:19:25	M GOVENDER	3:20:01	H RIEDEL-BROOS	3:20:41	M WELLS	3:21:17	W CURRY	3:21:57
98	R ARMIST	3:19:26	R MCROBBIE	3:20:01	F VANVLASSELAER	3:20:41	G RIMMER	3:21:18	P MATTHEWS	3:21:57
99	R MAES	3:19:26	P DUFFY	3:20:01	B MATTHEWS	3:20:41	S LEWIS	3:21:18	P HART	3:21:57
100	T TRAUB	3:19:27	D GREGORY	3:20:02	R SMALE	3:20:43	J NICHOLS	3:21:18	T MC ARTNEY	3:21:57

	4501-4600		4601-4700		4701-4800		4801-4900		4901-5000	
1	M HUTTON	3:21:57	J EMBLEN	3:22:38	P CARROLL	3:23:14	R TROTMAN	3:23:45	A EVANS	3:24:21
2	A REESE	3:21:57	N NICHOLAS	3:22:39	P STERRY	3:23:14	S JACKSON	3:23:46	G FRANCIS	3:24:21
3	M BRAKE	3:21:58	E MORALES LEON	3:22:39	C HARTLETT	3:23:14	P BREST	3:23:46	J DAVIES	3:24:21
4	B PORTER	3:21:58	W GLASGOW	3:22:39	I BENSTEAD	3:23:14	R GUNNING	3:23:48	R NICOLL	3:24:23
5	E HOLMQUIST	3:21:58	D LAWMAN	3:22:40	J CONLON	3:23:16	C BESSON	3:23:48	R TOON	3:24:23
6	R CLEPPERTON	3:21:58	K GOURNAY	3:22:41	P LAMBERT	3:23:16	A BLAND	3:23:48	D ELLIOTT	3:24:23
7	P LENNON	3:21:58	D WALTERS	3:22:41	R BANNISTER	3:23:16	A JENKINS	3:23:49	R GIBBY	3:24:23
8	J DONNELLY	3:21:58	M WHITE	3:22:41	C HARCASTLE	3:23:17	T LUNDH	3:23:49	K BATES	3:24:23
9	G URRON	3:21:59	T KRAEMER	3:22:41	R WASHBOURNE	3:23:18	H MURRAY	3:23:50	J ASPINALL	3:24:24
10	A STANHOFF	3:21:59	J GRAVELLS	3:22:42	P GANDER	3:23:18	R NEWMAN	3:23:50	Q BRITTAIN	3:24:25
11	J WALTERS	3:21:59	N LIONNET	3:22:42	M SULLIVAN	3:23:18	B KOHBERGER	3:23:50	S MURPHY	3:24:25
12	R SAULET	3:21:59	P BURTON	3:22:42	J CONVILLE	3:23:18	M HEARE	3:23:50	G PENN	3:24:25
13	A DEARLING	3:22:00	M LIONNET	3:22:42	D HICKEY	3:23:18	J FINCH	3:23:51	H FIDDAMENT-HARRIS	3:24:26
14	P MORRIS	3:22:02	G FAHERTY	3:22:42	P RYLANCE	3:23:19	T ROBBENS	3:23:51	P SVENSSON	3:24:27
15	M THOMAS	3:22:02	C BRIGHTON	3:22:42	R COWLING	3:23:19	M TAYLOR	3:23:52	L SUTHERLAND	3:24:27
16	K DACK	3:22:03	J PIERSON	3:22:43	J KNOTT	3:23:19	S SMITH	3:23:52	T CAVENEY	3:24:28
17	M WOOD	3:22:03	D DERUSSY	3:22:43	S WARNER	3:23:19	B HARVEY	3:23:53	R VAN NUFFEL	3:24:28
18	J JOHNSTONE	3:22:03	G STEPHENSON	3:22:43	J KERR	3:23:19	J ANDREWS	3:23:53	H HOMANS	3:24:28
19	W ROLFE	3:22:03	P CARON	3:22:45	K RITCHIE	3:23:19	J TURNER	3:23:53	T HEALY	3:24:29
20	T PANZERI	3:22:03	R BURKE	3:22:46	M LEEMING	3:23:20	B BARTON	3:23:53	R GREEN	3:24:29
21	G HEWSON	3:22:03	P WOODALL	3:22:47	M WATSON	3:23:20	R THELEN	3:23:53	M PAGE	3:24:30
22	J BOWIE	3:22:03	J CLOSE	3:22:47	C MELTON	3:23:22	M BAKER	3:23:54	M LYNCH	3:24:30
23	C SPINNER	3:22:04	D HEWITT	3:22:47	I SWANSON	3:23:22	K GALLAGHER	3:23:54	T MCELHERON	3:24:30
24	E AUSTIN	3:22:05	G MICHALOWICZ	3:22:48	D KERRIGAN	3:23:23	S POUND	3:23:54	D WEATHERLEY	3:24:31
25	R DAVIES	3:22:06	G HOEIEM	3:22:48	J BROWN	3:23:23	P CRAGG	3:23:54	C CLAIR	3:24:31
26	R LEE	3:22:07	C MCINTOSH	3:22:48	P SMITH	3:23:23	J HOLMGREN	3:23:55	J STRANGE	3:24:32
27	C FRY	3:22:08	K WRIGHT	3:22:49	S CORD	3:23:24	A GENDLER	3:23:55	J GREGORY	3:24:32
28	G SMITH	3:22:08	H LUEHR	3:22:49	G LAZELL	3:23:24	M ROWLAND	3:23:55	J COUTANCHE	3:24:33
29	N SIMPSON	3:22:08	M BRIGGS	3:22:49	T RYLANCE	3:23:24	D FRANCHINI	3:23:56	R PARRY	3:24:34
30	G LEA	3:22:08	A VOJTICKO	3:22:49	K HYDE	3:23:24	J OVERBEEK	3:23:57	P STOLL	3:24:34
31	G SMITH	3:22:08	J OLIVER	3:22:50	K MCMANUS	3:23:25	P FORD	3:23:57	M BOOTH	3:24:35
32	F SMITH	3:22:09	C CLARKE	3:22:50	G LEARY	3:23:25	E COLLIER	3:23:57	M THOMAS	3:24:35
33	P DREIFUSS	3:22:09	G DI CARLO	3:22:50	S GREENER	3:23:25	R HANNA	3:23:57	D GOLDEN	3:24:36
34	J FORDHAM	3:22:10	S WHITE	3:22:51	G YOUNG	3:23:25	R COPPING	3:23:58	D OKSENIUK	3:24:36
35	M CURRAN	3:22:10	S FERRARO	3:22:51	P KJELDSEN	3:23:26	J BEADLE	3:23:58	J WIGHTMAN	3:24:36
36	D TANSER	3:22:12	D FLOOD	3:22:52	D HILL	3:23:26	P FORD	3:23:59	R DAVIS	3:24:36
37	T LID	3:22:13	P DURSLEY	3:22:52	N HURLSTONE	3:23:26	S CASSELTON	3:23:59	K CHAPMAN	3:24:37
38	P DANEL	3:22:13	F DI GENNARO	3:22:52	S PIZZICANNELLA	3:23:26	J OLEY	3:23:59	M HAWKRIDGE	3:24:38
39	B REYNOLDS	3:22:14	A PATON	3:22:52	S COONEY	3:23:26	D FULLER	3:23:59	N CARPENTER	3:24:38
40	J DAVIES	3:22:15	T KELLY	3:22:53	A BLACKFORD	3:23:26	R THOMAS	3:24:00	K PEARSON	3:24:38
41	P ROSSITER	3:22:15	T KING	3:22:53	P ROSE	3:23:27	D GRANT	3:24:00	F OUTERINO	3:24:38
42	J WILLIAMS	3:22:15	B STANFORD	3:22:53	J TAYLOR	3:23:27	M COOK	3:24:00	R PUGH	3:24:39
43	J NYE	3:22:15	G SHEFFIELD	3:22:53	V ROGERS	3:23:27	W BRADLEY	3:24:01	P SHEPPARD	3:24:39
44	T OCKWELL	3:22:16	P PHEBY	3:22:54	P WISCOMBE	3:23:27	C LETOUBLON	3:24:01	A MAYA	3:24:39
45	M HEAP	3:22:16	S CRAGG	3:22:54	E TURNER	3:23:28	D THOMAS	3:24:01	R HILL	3:24:40
46	G CLARK	3:22:16	D SHEPHERD	3:22:54	V SHADBOLT	3:23:28	S PENDLEBURY	3:24:01	C FORD	3:24:40
47	C OLSON	3:22:16	L THURSTON	3:22:54	P HOPKINS	3:23:28	F WOOD	3:24:03	P BEALES	3:24:41
48	J SHACKLEFORD	3:22:17	M MCATEER	3:22:55	D BRAIN	3:23:29	D CULLEN	3:24:03	M POTTS	3:24:41
49	J BROWNE	3:22:18	P STAUFFENBERG	3:22:55	J SMITH	3:23:29	S OWENS	3:24:03	B EDWARDS	3:24:41
50	A AITKEN	3:22:19	S BRADLEY	3:22:55	S WILBY	3:23:29	D COUPE	3:24:03	J TEDFORS	3:24:41
51	R HOLMES	3:22:19	R BARTLETT	3:22:56	M ROWE	3:23:30	D LEWIS	3:24:04	R SISSON	3:24:41
52	M HUBBARD	3:22:20	D BOYD	3:22:57	T HLAVACEL	3:23:30	B CLARKE	3:24:04	J RIGLIN	3:24:42
53	D CROSS	3:22:20	J HINE	3:22:57	D BAUDRY	3:23:30	B BURR	3:24:04	R BOULAIRE	3:24:42
54	W LAUWERS	3:22:21	P GRANTHAM	3:22:57	D HEARN	3:23:30	A COX	3:24:04	I PIERCY	3:24:42
55	A BRUNEAU	3:22:21	G CLIFFORD	3:22:57	D PHILLIPS	3:23:31	M CLARK	3:24:05	D DRISCOLL	3:24:42
56	J SHIPP	3:22:21	I WATERSON	3:22:57	A SWEETE	3:23:31	D CAIRD	3:24:05	D PACEY	3:24:43
57	M RENWICK	3:22:21	D STAMMERS	3:22:58	T MACEY	3:23:32	D JONES	3:24:06	K ALLEN	3:24:44
58	C HARPER	3:22:21	G PAYNE	3:22:58	S HARRISON	3:23:32	C KNIGHT	3:24:06	O LE BIHAN	3:24:45
59	J CRAYFORD	3:22:23	A GILES	3:22:58	K MORRIS	3:23:32	H SOUTHWORTH	3:24:06	C EGAN	3:24:45
60	C PAVIOUR	3:22:23	C CHAMBERLAIN	3:22:58	E GAUTHIER	3:23:33	L PINDER	3:24:06	B MATTISSON	3:24:45
61	G DANCE	3:22:23	R THOMAS	3:22:59	P ROBSON	3:23:33	P WORTHY	3:24:07	P WARD	3:24:46
62	P GREENWOOD	3:22:24	M THOMAS	3:22:59	A MOSS	3:23:33	R MCBEAN	3:24:07	I CLARKE	3:24:46
63	M MC SORLEY	3:22:24	G BAGGULEY	3:22:59	M BIONDINI	3:23:34	R BOILEAU	3:24:07	N GILL	3:24:46
64	D VAN DEN HENDE	3:22:25	R BROWNBRIDGE	3:23:00	D ALLEN	3:23:35	A CHESTERFIELD	3:24:08	M KLINGENSPOR	3:24:47
65	H KLASSMANN	3:22:25	M HOLT	3:23:01	A KEELER	3:23:36	S ROBERTS	3:24:09	C JACKSON	3:24:47
66	D WOOD	3:22:25	P SMITH	3:23:01	C STITT	3:23:36	E ENRIGHT	3:24:09	R BLACKMAN	3:24:47
67	J MC NEILL	3:22:25	M WILSON	3:23:02	J TILBROOK	3:23:37	S CURD	3:24:09	F WEBB	3:24:48
68	I THOMAS	3:22:26	M WARWICK	3:23:02	S CLAMP	3:23:38	P MARSHALL	3:24:09	C HALL	3:24:48
69	D FEREDAY	3:22:26	G RUSSANT	3:23:03	M CORNWALL	3:23:38	C READMAN	3:24:10	B SHELDON	3:24:48
70	I SMITH	3:22:26	A HOLMES	3:23:03	K KILMURRAY	3:23:38	D EATON	3:24:11	B KITCHENER	3:24:48
71	D RICHARD	3:22:26	J BESNARD	3:23:03	L UNSWORTH	3:23:39	M CRACKNELL	3:24:11	R YOUNG	3:24:48
72	S SMITH	3:22:26	A MUCKLE	3:23:03	A JOHNSON	3:23:39	G CORSO	3:24:11	D RATA	3:24:49
73	C PATTISON	3:22:27	R WHILE	3:23:03	H PARRY	3:23:39	T CUISIN	3:24:11	J RHODES	3:24:49
74	M SCHROEDER	3:22:27	A LUPTON	3:23:04	R SCHOLES	3:23:39	L MOLE	3:24:12	D FOSTER	3:24:50
75	D COLLIER	3:22:27	S HAMMERTON	3:23:04	A MACHADO	3:23:40	N ALLAOUI	3:24:12	A CARVER	3:24:50
76	M DUTHIE	3:22:27	H MOULAM	3:23:05	D HUNT	3:23:41	A EDKINS	3:24:12	I MARTINDALE	3:24:51
77	R KING	3:22:27	A CADELL	3:23:05	D SOUTHGATE	3:23:41	D HOLDSWORTH	3:24:14	I RICCI	3:24:51
78	E GUSHLOW	3:22:28	S WILLIAMS	3:23:07	P DEWBERRY	3:23:41	J SHEPHERD	3:24:14	D LARKMAN	3:24:51
79	M BERTHOUD	3:22:29	J CHORLEY	3:23:07	A CASBURN	3:23:42	G MITCHELL	3:24:15	C GOODYEAR	3:24:51
80	J MURPHY	3:22:30	A DI MARINO	3:23:07	R LONSDALE	3:23:42	M JOHNSON	3:24:15	W UIJMEKE	3:24:51
81	P THORPE	3:22:30	A SKATES	3:23:08	J PEREZ FERNANDEZ	3:23:42	R WITHNALL	3:24:15	R BAECHTOLD	3:24:52
82	D HICKEY	3:22:30	T SANDERSON	3:23:08	R HAARUP	3:23:42	S BRAZIL	3:24:16	S CURTIS	3:24:52
83	A CAUZARD	3:22:30	P CROSS	3:23:08	M BUGLIONE	3:23:42	R LE HAZIF	3:24:16	J WOODLEY	3:24:53
84	B ARTHUR	3:22:30	P FINN	3:23:09	J SCHATTE	3:23:42	M WIDDOP	3:24:16	R ARNOLD	3:24:53
85	A SCORAH	3:22:31	R COPP	3:23:09	J ELLIOTT	3:23:42	P POWELL	3:24:16	E EVANS	3:24:54
86	S WHEELTON	3:22:31	J AMOURETTE	3:23:09	R BEACHAM	3:23:42	E AVERY	3:24:16	W GRAY	3:24:54
87	L WATSON	3:22:31	S LORAINE	3:23:10	S BIENKOWSKI	3:23:42	M MCGONGALE	3:24:17	I PEAK	3:24:56
88	M LEYLAND	3:22:31	D LADD	3:23:10	E STEPHENSON	3:23:43	K HALE	3:24:17	M SILK	3:24:56
89	R BARTRAM	3:22:31	J SERRA	3:23:10	D WILSON	3:23:43	C MARTIN	3:24:17	W KREUTNER	3:24:56
90	P DIXON	3:22:32	E FRY	3:23:11	G REED	3:23:43	F GALVEZ	3:24:17	R FARRELLY	3:24:57
91	J WOOTTON	3:22:33	T HEDGES	3:23:11	P FENAROLI	3:23:43	C SMITH	3:24:17	D MAGNAT	3:24:58
92	B GREEN	3:22:33	M PUOTI	3:23:11	M RUTHERFORD	3:23:44	M CROWDER	3:24:17	D BROWNLEE	3:24:58
93	A SMITH	3:22:33	H SCOTT	3:23:11	J ARCHER	3:23:44	A MORRIS	3:24:18	D WEEKS	3:24:58
94	J JOLY	3:22:34	K HEDGES	3:23:11	H STEPHENS	3:23:44	C HEATH	3:24:18	T DELL	3:24:58
95	J HATTERSLEY	3:22:34	G GAUDIN	3:23:12	S EJSING	3:23:44	D COWE	3:24:19	M SACCO	3:24:58
96	C EGERTON	3:22:34	D JOHNSON	3:23:12	D GARNETT	3:23:45	P GOTTLIEB	3:24:19	R FOSTER	3:24:59
97	S KARLSSON	3:22:35	L CHAMPION	3:23:12	T FIELD	3:23:45	M ALLEN	3:24:19	A MCGURK	3:24:59
98	C GARRIGAN	3:22:36	M SIVITER	3:23:13	P HARDS	3:23:45	T DEPUMIET DE PARRY	3:24:20	M SITCH	3:24:59
99	M HOLMES	3:22:36	M O'SULLIVAN	3:23:13	M MADELIN	3:23:45	T LEAHY	3:24:20	G BLOGG	3:24:59
100	P WILSON	3:22:37	M BLACKMORE	3:23:13	D GUTHRIE	3:23:45	D COX	3:24:21	P BURROWS	3:24:59

#	5001-5100		5101-5200		5201-5300		5301-5400		5401-5500	
1	J SMITH	3:25:00	J BRIGGS	3:25:35	D HARRISON	3:26:06	J UPHAM	3:26:45	P INGLEBY	3:27:25
2	R SWINSTEAD	3:25:00	J COCK	3:25:36	P KJENSLI	3:26:06	P SOUTHWELL	3:26:46	B WORTHINGTON	3:27:26
3	G HEIDEN	3:25:00	D MILLS	3:25:36	N THOMAS	3:26:06	J RIPOLL	3:26:46	W MOSSMAN	3:27:26
4	A ZUHDERT	3:25:00	T STONE	3:25:36	R VARNHAM	3:26:06	O FERLAY	3:26:46	D WAINHOUSE	3:27:26
5	M LOCKEY	3:25:01	N VERDE	3:25:37	M HENRY	3:26:07	A MARTIN	3:26:46	A HOLMES	3:27:27
6	D CALLISTER	3:25:01	K HAITH	3:25:37	M VALLIS	3:26:07	M LEWIS	3:26:47	M LAYZELL	3:27:27
7	P BLUNDELL	3:25:01	D DURAND	3:25:37	E AIRSON	3:26:08	D WARLEY	3:26:47	R BAUCKHAM	3:27:28
8	D HOBIN	3:25:01	S BICKERTON	3:25:37	D JONES	3:26:08	D DOBLE	3:26:50	W ELKINGTON	3:27:28
9	S BLEWETT	3:25:02	J DAVIES	3:25:37	D ENRIGHT	3:26:08	A LOADER	3:26:51	P BELLIS	3:27:28
10	F HARDING	3:25:03	K KIRBY	3:25:38	P MANDER	3:26:09	P KEAREY	3:26:51	M JAMES	3:27:28
11	M BENT	3:25:03	K CHAPMAN	3:25:38	M LOWBRIDGE	3:26:10	A BENTLEY	3:26:51	M HARSUM	3:27:29
12	M LAUGHTON	3:25:04	G GENTLE	3:25:38	L JEHANNIN	3:26:10	D LINDSAY	3:26:52	M OLIVER	3:27:29
13	M GRAHAM	3:25:04	M MARTINEAU	3:25:39	E THOMPSON	3:26:10	M PARKER	3:26:52	G BAILYES	3:27:29
14	H BRODIE	3:25:05	P NOKE	3:25:40	R TROTTER	3:26:11	S MYLLYPERKIO	3:26:53	M NAVIN	3:27:29
15	S SAMUELS	3:25:06	S HAWKINS	3:25:40	D DURNIN	3:26:11	M HEXTALL	3:26:53	D PERRIER	3:27:30
16	J HUNTER	3:25:06	C KINGSLEY	3:25:41	K TUSON	3:26:11	F DEACON	3:26:54	B LOURME	3:27:30
17	R SMITH	3:25:06	V MARTIN	3:25:41	P MILLS	3:26:11	J BRIAN	3:26:54	D COSSEN	3:27:30
18	R SUDDENS	3:25:06	R DAVIES	3:25:41	M GORDON	3:26:13	D LEE	3:26:54	R OSBORN	3:27:30
19	P HARBIDGE	3:25:08	F COMINI	3:25:42	P MULHOLLAND	3:26:13	T ADAMS	3:26:55	R GOODWIN	3:27:30
20	J TAYLOR	3:25:08	T SIMS	3:25:42	J LEGGE	3:26:14	M JENKINS	3:26:55	S HOLGATE	3:27:30
21	M MACDONALD	3:25:09	R LEE	3:25:43	J DAVIES	3:26:14	O BLAKKISRUD	3:26:56	S BLACKMORE	3:27:31
22	A AHMED	3:25:10	M DAVY	3:25:43	B WREAVES	3:26:14	T KEENAN	3:26:56	C FORD	3:27:31
23	S TURTON	3:25:10	J NEWPORT	3:25:43	S GOWANS	3:26:14	D HUDSON	3:26:57	G HOPKINS	3:27:31
24	D CLARKE	3:25:10	G WILLIAMS	3:25:44	R FORD	3:26:17	K BAYLEY	3:26:57	R OWEN	3:27:31
25	C CIEROCKI	3:25:10	K DEARMAN	3:25:44	B MILLAR	3:26:18	P HEY	3:26:57	J DAVIES	3:27:32
26	S RUDD	3:25:11	D FORSHAW	3:25:45	J GAUTRON	3:26:18	F BOEHNKE	3:26:57	S TAGUE	3:27:32
27	D VAUGHAN	3:25:11	I FENWICK	3:25:45	K HELIN	3:26:18	J LINGARD	3:26:58	J DAILY	3:27:32
28	R AIRTH	3:25:12	P EVISON	3:25:46	H BELL	3:26:18	P OATHAM	3:26:59	B PORTER	3:27:33
29	P CABBAN	3:25:12	M GHIJSEN	3:25:46	C ANDREWS	3:26:18	M HAMILTON	3:26:59	G KIRK	3:27:33
30	J HALL	3:25:12	N RICHARDS	3:25:46	R STONE	3:26:19	K THOMPSON	3:27:00	D PRATT	3:27:34
31	P LE GALL	3:25:14	S DONEGAN	3:25:47	B SMITH	3:26:19	A KENYON	3:27:00	J HAIN	3:27:34
32	T HAMMOND	3:25:14	B ENGLISH	3:25:47	G MONAGHAN	3:26:19	J WALKER	3:27:01	R RODDY	3:27:34
33	R SHAW	3:25:14	N BEARDSLEY	3:25:48	M COLBY	3:26:20	A DESBOROUGH	3:27:01	T SAILL	3:27:34
34	R RIGGALL	3:25:14	R STEWART	3:25:48	G SAUNDERS	3:26:20	J SOUTHERN	3:27:01	D PHILPOTT	3:27:34
35	K NEWBY	3:25:15	N MANNING	3:25:48	K WILDMAN	3:26:21	K PERRY	3:27:01	K TATE	3:27:35
36	R MILLS	3:25:15	D EARLEY	3:25:48	R MCGONNELL	3:26:21	M DAVIES	3:27:03	D SMITH	3:27:35
37	V MC CLOUD	3:25:16	O SAHAR	3:25:49	G TELFORD	3:26:21	M DUFFY	3:27:03	M CLAVERN	3:27:35
38	C BOSSA	3:25:16	D STOCKMAN	3:25:49	R ANNECCHINI	3:26:21	W BROWN	3:27:04	P SODERSTROM	3:27:35
39	D INNES	3:25:16	R DIXON	3:25:49	R SOUTHGATE	3:26:21	M CAPSTAFF	3:27:04	R SMITH	3:27:35
40	J KARAKULA	3:25:16	L GIFFARD	3:25:49	G DUESTER	3:26:22	C SCHULTE	3:27:04	J BARRETT-LENNARD	3:27:36
41	M ROMERIL	3:25:16	W FENLON	3:25:50	P HESLOP	3:26:22	K JONES	3:27:05	P AARONSON	3:27:36
42	C GILBERT	3:25:16	J GILBERT	3:25:50	R WHITTACKER	3:26:22	D NEWMAN	3:27:06	R WOLLERTON	3:27:36
43	N PETO	3:25:16	J WILDIN	3:25:50	M HAY	3:26:22	F IZOLDI	3:27:06	C BROOKS	3:27:36
44	H DODD	3:25:16	R BROWN	3:25:51	P HILL	3:26:22	E TIIRA	3:27:06	T FRIEDMANN	3:27:37
45	M COX	3:25:16	T BIDDLE	3:25:51	D GUITE	3:26:23	J MILLAR	3:27:06	C CRAWFORD	3:27:37
46	J FULLER	3:25:16	R RAMOS	3:25:51	J BEER	3:26:23	C GRAY	3:27:07	J INGRAM	3:27:37
47	C BOWLER	3:25:17	B WAREING	3:25:51	G PHILLIPS	3:26:23	L YALLUP	3:27:07	C BLISS	3:27:37
48	G DELAFOSSE	3:25:17	K MEDCRAFT	3:25:51	E IEMALI	3:26:24	D SIMPSON	3:27:08	B DOUARD	3:27:37
49	B CHAMBERLAIN	3:25:17	R GRAF	3:25:51	M SALTER	3:26:24	J REGIS	3:27:09	T COOPER	3:27:38
50	G PARROTT	3:25:17	P RODGERS	3:25:52	L SHUTTLEWORTH	3:26:25	S HOLMES-BROWN	3:27:09	J BEDFORD	3:27:38
51	J BURGESS	3:25:18	J CHAMPION	3:25:53	S LIGHT	3:26:25	P STARR	3:27:10	G EVANS	3:27:38
52	R STAFFORD	3:25:18	P PERKINS	3:25:53	C ADAMS	3:26:25	D SEWELL	3:27:11	K PRITCHARD	3:27:38
53	R HAMILTON	3:25:18	B GUNSTON	3:25:53	M WALLER	3:26:25	E HUDSON	3:27:11	B BOUCHE	3:27:38
54	K CLARKE	3:25:19	M GREENFIELD	3:25:53	P VAN GILSE	3:26:25	D STEVENS	3:27:12	A ROWE	3:27:38
55	K WARDLE	3:25:20	J LOGIE	3:25:54	R HOLTE	3:26:25	G SIEWERTSEN	3:27:12	M KNIGHT	3:27:38
56	J ORBELL	3:25:20	R HAMMERSON	3:25:54	M MC ERLANE	3:26:25	J GREGORY	3:27:12	M JARAS	3:27:39
57	A EVANS	3:25:20	C JONES	3:25:55	K PEART	3:26:26	N BROOKES	3:27:12	·J MC CARTHY	3:27:39
58	P JOHNSON	3:25:20	P CORRIGAN	3:25:56	H KAMPE	3:26:26	K BROWNING	3:27:12	S HEROD	3:27:39
59	K TAYLOR	3:25:20	D ROBINSON	3:25:56	P FERME	3:26:27	M REYNOLDS	3:27:12	T BURN	3:27:39
60	R HOUGHTON	3:25:21	D DORMER	3:25:56	M SIMPSON	3:26:27	C GIBBS	3:27:12	J WILLIAMS	3:27:40
61	J HULATT	3:25:21	G RICHARDS	3:25:56	M SWEETLOVE	3:26:27	P MANGOLD	3:27:12	M AUSTIN	3:27:41
62	C BULLOCK	3:25:21	M FERGUSON	3:25:56	S FIELD	3:26:28	D PEDRAZA	3:27:12	D CYGAN	3:27:42
63	L MENS	3:25:21	M HICKMAN	3:25:57	M VIVIAN	3:26:29	J ARNAUD	3:27:13	D SACKETT	3:27:42
64	J JENNER	3:25:22	D DUGMORE	3:25:57	G READ	3:26:29	A DISLEY	3:27:13	J WYNSTANLY	3:27:42
65	B GORCE	3:25:22	F OTERO GARCIA	3:25:57	R BICKERSTUFF	3:26:29	L EARL	3:27:14	D JONES	3:27:43
66	P BOUVAT	3:25:22	E HYHOLT	3:25:57	J KIRK	3:26:30	N BLEWETT	3:27:14	D ANDREWS	3:27:43
67	D PHILLIPS	3:25:22	C HALL	3:25:57	L CLAMPETT	3:26:30	A HOLLIMAN	3:27:14	R GRIFFITHS	3:27:45
68	T PETTIFER	3:25:23	B LEACH	3:25:57	F MURPHY	3:26:30	J PAUL	3:27:14	G GARLAND	3:27:45
69	B WRIGHT	3:25:23	M ROBINSON	3:25:57	R LETHABY	3:26:31	K BARLOW	3:27:15	T GALLOIS	3:27:46
70	I BOND	3:25:23	C HUBER	3:25:57	J THOMAS	3:26:31	T FLOETHMANN	3:27:15	A MAIN	3:27:46
71	K WALKER	3:25:24	R SOWERBY	3:25:57	W WINZER	3:26:31	R KORBALSKI	3:27:15	N LOCHHEAD	3:27:47
72	K MONTGOMERY	3:25:25	P BELCHER	3:25:58	S BOWERS	3:26:31	D BAIN	3:27:15	M MAHON	3:27:47
73	A MARTIN	3:25:25	M DIBLEY	3:25:59	C GOMEZ	3:26:32	P MAY	3:27:17	P MINSHULL	3:27:47
74	K RYDER	3:25:25	S WHITE	3:25:59	J ELLIOTT	3:26:32	A WILLIAMS	3:27:17	M BURCH	3:27:48
75	S SUTHERLAND	3:25:25	R SPINKS	3:25:59	B READ	3:26:32	A BANSAIS	3:27:18	C JEAL	3:27:48
76	J WATERS	3:25:25	E GABBOTT	3:25:59	I MADDIESON	3:26:33	K BOOTH	3:27:18	R MARSH	3:27:48
77	I KING	3:25:26	A SCARFE	3:25:59	D WHARAM	3:26:33	R COX	3:27:19	A MILSOM	3:27:48
78	N TOMKINSON	3:25:27	T WEARNE	3:26:00	C NIXON	3:26:33	P DUQUENNE	3:27:19	J MATTHEWS	3:27:49
79	R PORTER	3:25:27	J REEVELL	3:26:00	C TURNBULL	3:26:34	J EVANS	3:27:19	G RANFORD	3:27:49
80	M DOLEMAN	3:25:28	N SHEA	3:26:00	P JOHNSON	3:26:34	G BROWN	3:27:19	S WEHRLE	3:27:49
81	R MCLAREN	3:25:29	R HULBERT	3:26:00	N CAMP	3:26:35	S EVANS	3:27:19	G LOWE	3:27:49
82	S HUGHES	3:25:29	A BONCHRISTIANO	3:26:00	C BRITTLE	3:26:37	M MILLS	3:27:20	T REA	3:27:49
83	D HEATH	3:25:30	A HOPKINS	3:26:01	C FORDE	3:26:37	R PRUESSNER	3:27:20	M CONROY	3:27:49
84	T DYER	3:25:30	R NEWTON	3:26:01	A CROUCHER	3:26:37	A KUNZEL	3:27:21	L HESTER	3:27:49
85	G TWIGG	3:25:30	P MALONE	3:26:02	P ROSS	3:26:38	B WILTON	3:27:22	P DAVIES	3:27:49
86	J STOUT	3:25:30	S DAVIES	3:26:02	N ADAMS	3:26:38	D WATERMAN	3:27:23	D LOCK	3:27:50
87	M WOODING	3:25:31	N BETTS	3:26:02	R BEATSON	3:26:38	M STREETING	3:27:23	R DAVIS	3:27:50
88	J KILBANE	3:25:32	L NORLEY	3:26:02	J JAMES	3:26:38	M NUNN	3:27:23	C BUTTLE	3:27:50
89	S BAUCHOP	3:25:32	C PATENDEN	3:26:02	R SONTROP	3:26:40	D HOWELLS	3:27:23	S PAUL	3:27:50
90	G HEARN	3:25:32	R ADAMS	3:26:03	M STUART	3:26:40	M STUART	3:27:23	C KNOWLES	3:27:50
91	J LANDMAN	3:25:32	N HALE	3:26:04	R YOUNG	3:26:40	L JONES	3:27:23	V PRICE	3:27:51
92	C BAVERSTOCK	3:25:32	T ROSE	3:26:04	A MAIR	3:26:41	G CATLIN	3:27:23	I MACQUEEN	3:27:51
93	V GOMES	3:25:33	P NOBLE	3:26:04	G CALDWELL	3:26:41	J BARRY	3:27:23	D RIVETT	3:27:52
94	J STILLMAN	3:25:33	N HAVERCROFT	3:26:05	D ELLIS	3:26:41	H MCCLAFFERTY	3:27:24	J RAMSBOTTOM	3:27:52
95	J FITZGERALD	3:25:33	N JAMES	3:26:05	E THORNHILL	3:26:42	D MOYNIHAN	3:27:24	C KITCHEN	3:27:52
96	M HAMPSHIRE	3:25:34	M SUTHERLAND	3:26:05	D SPILLINGS	3:26:43	T HOBBS	3:27:24	K PEARSON	3:27:52
97	D ROBINSON	3:25:34	K FLOOD	3:26:05	J WILDE	3:26:43	G COUSINS	3:27:24	S DOUGAL	3:27:52
98	G HOLT	3:25:34	P BATTERBURY	3:26:05	M LONGSTAFF	3:26:43	W WADDELL	3:27:24	D RAMSEY SMITH	3:27:53
99	M BARKER	3:25:35	P CHANDLER	3:26:05	J HIPKIN	3:26:45	L BURROUGHS	3:27:25	J BAILEY	3:27:53
100	C MUTTON	3:25:35	J RICHARDSON	3:26:05	G EARLE	3:26:45	D HARLING	3:27:25	I MINETT	3:27:53

	5501-5600		5601-5700		5701-5800		5801-5900		5901-6000	
1	J FRANKLIN	3:27:54	B SLEEMAN	3:28:29	P DURRANT	3:29:02	K FOTHERBY	3:29:23	S CARISS	3:29:55
2	D JONES	3:27:54	A JONES	3:28:29	E CAMPBELL	3:29:02	B FRY	3:29:23	K MATHER	3:29:55
3	M MASLEN	3:27:54	K ROBINSON	3:28:30	B LAMBERT	3:29:03	L WISE	3:29:23	A FOSTER	3:29:55
4	I COLEMAN	3:27:55	A KING	3:28:30	D WAREING	3:29:03	G WATSON	3:29:24	A EVANS	3:29:55
5	C ILLSLEY	3:27:55	R MENEAR	3:28:30	S CAMPBELL	3:29:03	J BESSA DA SILVA	3:29:24	M MATTHEWS	3:29:55
6	F SMITH	3:27:56	M SMYTH	3:28:30	G SHAW	3:29:04	P BUTTON	3:29:24	B SMITH	3:29:55
7	F COX	3:27:56	H MCGOVERN	3:28:30	T MCARDLE	3:29:04	J CLANET	3:29:24	P WIRTZFELD	3:29:55
8	P HARDY	3:27:56	S GODWIN	3:28:31	I COOKSON	3:29:04	S SHEPPARD	3:29:25	P SHARPE	3:29:56
9	G LEWIS	3:27:57	S WHILEY	3:28:31	A JEPSON	3:29:04	J CUSHION	3:29:25	L KOSTER	3:29:56
10	S MOLYNEUX	3:27:57	V GAMMON	3:28:32	M LOMAX	3:29:04	J WOODALL	3:29:25	J ADAMS	3:29:56
11	J PAYNE	3:27:58	W HANSCOMB	3:28:32	P GRIFFITHS	3:29:04	M ANSTEY	3:29:25	A INGLES	3:29:56
12	C NESBITT	3:27:58	J CUMMINGS	3:28:33	P CHANDLER	3:29:04	F SOUSA-PIMENTEL	3:29:25	J HALLIWELL	3:29:56
13	S DALEY	3:27:58	M MAJOR	3:28:33	D ROBERTSON	3:29:04	G OLLERHEAD	3:29:26	K THOMSON	3:29:56
14	H HUGHES	3:27:58	P WEYELL	3:28:33	L BARLEY	3:29:04	M BLOWFIELD	3:29:26	D BAILEY	3:29:57
15	A ECKBRETH	3:27:59	J GALLAGHER	3:28:33	A CROFT	3:29:04	F MILLS	3:29:26	T MITCHELL	3:29:57
16	M POTTER	3:27:59	P LUCCARDI	3:28:34	T HARTIGAN	3:29:04	A ABOUSSERHANE	3:29:27	M DAVENPORT	3:29:57
17	A HARDING	3:27:59	B FLETCHER	3:28:35	J DUESTER	3:29:04	R TAYLOR	3:29:27	S PRITCHARD	3:29:57
18	C WILLIAMS	3:27:59	M SMITH	3:28:35	S PORTER	3:29:05	N GREEN	3:29:28	J CHAPMAN	3:29:57
19	F BROUSSE	3:28:00	K PIKE	3:28:36	B ALLEN	3:29:05	I GANOT	3:29:29	G SHONE	3:29:57
20	A HERNANDEZ	3:28:00	J WILSON	3:28:36	G MACKERNESS	3:29:05	M KABBAJ	3:29:29	K NILSSON	3:29:57
21	D FIELON	3:28:00	M HENDERSON	3:28:36	J BROWN	3:29:05	C DOWDALL	3:29:29	R BAYLISS	3:29:58
22	S CAPEY	3:28:00	S MARSHALL	3:28:37	T SCHMUCKI	3:29:06	C VERRALL	3:29:30	D CLATWORTHY	3:29:58
23	D EDGAR	3:28:00	B BERING	3:28:37	R JARVIS	3:29:06	A EL MOUADDEN	3:29:30	P KINGSFORD	3:29:58
24	M CALLOW	3:28:01	R FELTER	3:28:38	M RYAN	3:29:07	R TILLETT	3:29:31	D BRIATTE	3:29:58
25	D CHRISTIAUSEN	3:28:01	P VAILLANT	3:28:38	D ADAMS	3:29:07	R DOYLE	3:29:31	D MULLEN	3:29:58
26	P CHADWICK	3:28:01	R WALTON	3:28:38	D ARMES	3:29:07	J THOMAS	3:29:32	I RATCLIFFE	3:29:58
27	J FREEMAN	3:28:02	R GILBERT	3:28:38	S JAMES	3:29:07	D PRITCHARD	3:29:32	H SEDDON	3:29:59
28	K THOMASSEN	3:28:02	S FLEMING	3:28:39	J KNOWLTON	3:29:08	G DE SANTIS	3:29:33	M SHERVINGTON	3:29:59
29	E COLEMAN	3:28:02	J CHIPPERFIELD	3:28:39	A PATES	3:29:08	W RAINE	3:29:33	H NEUMANN	3:29:59
30	T PAGRAM	3:28:02	S BOWLEY	3:28:39	C MOSS	3:29:08	J TURNER	3:29:33	P WINGFIELD	3:29:59
31	J MACCARFRAE	3:28:03	N WHITE	3:28:39	D PHILLIPS	3:29:08	E PEZZINI	3:29:33	A STANILAND	3:29:59
32	A APTE	3:28:03	M DUNMORE	3:28:39	C LENSING	3:29:08	P BARKWORTH	3:29:34	M PEMBERTON	3:29:59
33	J EVANS	3:28:03	K MASON	3:28:40	D KEATING	3:29:09	M BROOKES	3:29:34	A DUDLEY	3:29:59
34	S BLAKEY	3:28:03	F BUTCHER	3:28:40	C FROST	3:29:09	E COLGIN	3:29:34	R WEBSTER	3:30:00
35	K FEAKES	3:28:03	S CLARK	3:28:40	J SMALL	3:29:10	C PAVERI	3:29:34	R TOZER	3:30:00
36	I BLISS	3:28:03	B EVANS	3:28:40	R POULTON	3:29:10	M DUNN	3:29:35	P WATSON	3:30:00
37	G WHITEHEAD	3:28:04	M HOGAN	3:28:40	O KNIGHT	3:29:10	A DAVIDSON	3:29:36	E ATKINS	3:30:00
38	A FOSTER	3:28:04	G PATERSON	3:28:40	J GIBSON	3:29:10	A WHITE	3:29:36	J SPAGNOL	3:30:00
39	C ANDREW	3:28:04	K HADLEY	3:28:40	M PHILLIPS	3:29:11	D CONOLLY	3:29:37	P HALFORD	3:30:00
40	J FUCHS	3:28:04	W WILLIAMS	3:28:41	T HAYES	3:29:11	J MARSHALL	3:29:37	P SPARKS	3:30:00
41	J LAMB	3:28:05	N MORRIS	3:28:41	J EID	3:29:11	J SIMPSON	3:29:37	B BROCKALL	3:30:01
42	S BLUNT	3:28:05	I MCKENZIE	3:28:41	J ROSKRUGE	3:29:11	G BEARDSLEY	3:29:37	M THORNTON	3:30:01
43	P WOOD	3:28:05	C HURT	3:28:41	T MILLINGS	3:29:11	R VICKERS	3:29:37	B ROBERTS	3:30:01
44	J RICHARDS	3:28:06	D JERDAN	3:28:41	R BELLAMY	3:29:12	G DENIS	3:29:37	N GRAY	3:30:01
45	M ROBINS	3:28:06	R WILSON	3:28:42	G TOWNSEND	3:29:12	J VERNON	3:29:38	N MARTIN	3:30:02
46	S KING	3:28:06	C PARSI	3:28:42	E STAGG	3:29:12	G JOHN	3:29:38	A RINK	3:30:02
47	A WINTERTON	3:28:06	A HAY	3:28:43	R GAUNT	3:29:12	M WHEATLEY	3:29:39	R BLYTH	3:30:02
48	T GOMERSALL	3:28:06	T SCHUMACHER	3:28:43	K PIKO	3:29:12	L USHER	3:29:39	J CLAUSEN	3:30:02
49	P STICKINGS	3:28:06	D KING	3:28:43	C KING	3:29:12	G NORTHWOOD	3:29:40	B LEAHY	3:30:03
50	C CROFTS	3:28:06	A TRENDER	3:28:43	K SARGENT	3:29:13	N MORRIS	3:29:40	A RENTON	3:30:03
51	C BRAMWELL	3:28:06	P COLES	3:28:43	D BENEZET	3:29:13	S PAULL	3:29:41	S PATE	3:30:03
52	R FESTA	3:28:06	E NORTH	3:28:43	D THOMPSON	3:29:13	B ENGELMANN	3:29:42	E JONES	3:30:06
53	M TAYLOR	3:28:06	J TAYLOR	3:28:43	B QUINN	3:29:13	W SAYER	3:29:42	G DE LEEUW	3:30:07
54	D WILLIS	3:28:06	C BRIGHT	3:28:45	A O'RIORDAN	3:29:13	R MADDISON	3:29:42	D WATKINSON	3:30:07
55	M MARSH	3:28:06	R WARD	3:28:46	E FALQUERO	3:29:13	I JEFFERY	3:29:42	Y RIOT	3:30:08
56	P MCLAUGHLIN	3:28:07	L VARESCO	3:28:46	A BEARDSHALL	3:29:13	G KEENAN	3:29:42	C GREENWOOD	3:30:08
57	B WILSON	3:28:08	J WRIGHT	3:28:47	J FONTVIEILLE	3:29:13	M COURT-BORAN	3:29:42	K ADAMS	3:30:08
58	A WILLIAMS	3:28:08	S HOBBS	3:28:47	G BOOTH	3:29:14	N BROAD	3:29:42	N CROOK	3:30:08
59	C MCGRATH	3:28:08	I BIELBY	3:28:49	G SMITH	3:29:14	R HOWIE	3:29:43	R COMPTON	3:30:08
60	D WILKINSON	3:28:08	W COULSON	3:28:49	P CHATER	3:29:14	A MCAULIFFE	3:29:43	D WALSH	3:30:10
61	R OAK	3:28:09	D LEAMAN	3:28:49	N TEAGUE	3:29:15	P FRANKLIN	3:29:43	D ROSCH	3:30:10
62	V LODER	3:28:09	V GOULTER	3:28:49	I WHITENSTALL	3:29:15	S MCREYNOLDS	3:29:43	G SPROTT	3:30:10
63	N BALDOCK	3:28:10	D TAYLOR	3:28:50	A DOLFE	3:29:15	G MARSHALL	3:29:44	M WHEELER	3:30:10
64	G OCONNELL	3:28:10	K MILLICAN	3:28:51	V SEWELL	3:29:15	S THELMARK	3:29:44	W ELLIS	3:30:12
65	D POCOCK	3:28:11	J MARTIN	3:28:51	P GALATOIRE	3:29:15	M SHEEHAN	3:29:44	E REYNOLDS	3:30:12
66	A LOWTHIAN	3:28:11	R HILL	3:28:51	L BAYS	3:29:16	D RAWCLIFFE	3:29:44	M WADE	3:30:13
67	P EUSTACE	3:28:11	M PREISEL	3:28:52	C JONES	3:29:16	H LINDLEY	3:29:44	J POPPLE	3:30:13
68	J SCOTT	3:28:12	R PLATT	3:28:52	R KELEHAR	3:29:17	N MUNRO	3:29:45	P WAKEMAN	3:30:14
69	I CRESSWELL	3:28:12	J BENNETT	3:28:52	D OWENS	3:29:17	H LARSEN	3:29:45	D POND	3:30:15
70	M HECQUET	3:28:14	P MCHUGH	3:28:52	N FITZGERALD	3:29:17	M COATES	3:29:45	S HAND	3:30:15
71	A VANSTONE	3:28:16	M COX	3:28:52	H JOHNSON	3:29:17	C ACREY	3:29:45	G KELLY	3:30:16
72	T MULCAHY	3:28:16	R UNHJEM	3:28:53	J MCBRIDE	3:29:18	G MCVEY	3:29:46	J ARMSTRONG	3:30:16
73	G LITTLE	3:28:17	M COOPER	3:28:53	N GOVIER	3:29:18	B FRIEND	3:29:46	P MERRITT	3:30:17
74	S MCCABE	3:28:18	J STARRITT	3:28:53	M ATKINSON	3:29:18	W THORPE	3:29:46	K WAINE	3:30:17
75	D FLINTSTONE	3:28:20	B BOWYER	3:28:53	W STOECKER	3:29:18	A SIMMONDS	3:29:46	M GILL	3:30:18
76	B MORGAN	3:28:20	F LAWRENCE	3:28:54	J GOMEZ	3:29:18	A NUTTALL	3:29:47	E CULSHAW	3:30:18
77	K HORNSEY	3:28:20	J STOTT	3:28:55	A SAYERS	3:29:18	J BOND	3:29:47	P BREWSTER	3:30:19
78	D TICHENER	3:28:20	J SAWBRIDGE	3:28:56	J GRAY	3:29:18	P SILVI	3:29:47	S WILLISON	3:30:19
79	J DANIELS	3:28:20	N TIBBLE	3:28:57	C HOO TAN	3:29:18	G NORCOTT	3:29:48	G CRABTREE	3:30:19
80	G DANIELS	3:28:20	K NEVITT	3:28:58	J WORZENCRAFT	3:29:18	M HARDING	3:29:48	T GOLDER	3:30:20
81	W WILLEMS	3:28:20	G MCKENNA	3:28:58	K BUSBY	3:29:18	L HORNSEY	3:29:48	R WHISTLECROFT	3:30:20
82	P COULMAN	3:28:21	R FUELLE	3:28:59	G RIPPIN	3:29:19	C SHORT	3:29:49	G MAGUIRE	3:30:20
83	G PARKER	3:28:21	R HENSSER	3:28:59	C NABAVI	3:29:19	S RUDD	3:29:49	J SULLIVAN	3:30:21
84	K BARNES	3:28:22	K NEWTON	3:28:59	S GASLARD	3:29:19	B EKE	3:29:49	R PHIPPS	3:30:21
85	J TAIT	3:28:22	R PRIDAY	3:29:00	K OTTLEY	3:29:19	J COURTNEY	3:29:49	T SIMPSON	3:30:22
86	A TAYLOR	3:28:22	K CLARKE	3:29:00	C SENTANCE	3:29:19	P ROSS	3:29:49	S HOLT	3:30:22
87	W BARKER	3:28:23	B HELM	3:29:00	M CRICKETT	3:29:19	P MCPAUL	3:29:50	J CAHILL	3:30:22
88	J MCDERMOTT	3:28:23	M COLLINS	3:29:01	J HARRISON	3:29:20	J FULCHER	3:29:50	A SINGH	3:30:22
89	P CRUDDINGTON	3:28:23	M SECKINGTON	3:29:01	L SMALLBONE	3:29:20	A PAYNE	3:29:50	M ELLIOTT	3:30:22
90	M GIBSON	3:28:23	J JOHNSON	3:29:01	R TWEDDLE	3:29:20	J HUNTER	3:29:50	D SMITH	3:30:23
91	T MERMAGEN	3:28:24	M COULSTON	3:29:01	J BUTLER	3:29:20	J JUDGE	3:29:50	A SCOTT	3:30:23
92	C AMIGUES	3:28:25	M BIDDULPH	3:29:01	B BEDFORD	3:29:21	B WESTON	3:29:50	A MOTHERSILL	3:30:23
93	C TURNER	3:28:27	J SCHNEIDER	3:29:01	D RICHARDSON	3:29:21	M WEIR	3:29:51	S CORNELL	3:30:23
94	R THOMSON	3:28:27	E BOUVAT	3:29:01	S MURRAY	3:29:21	M DAWSON	3:29:52	J HITZL	3:30:23
95	P KAPADIA	3:28:28	P GIBSON	3:29:01	S CLIFFORD	3:29:21	G WOODMAN	3:29:52	C HORSLEY	3:30:23
96	J COBBETT	3:28:28	M KITANO	3:29:01	K MIAH	3:29:21	W DUFF	3:29:53	A GOODMAN	3:30:23
97	M FENN	3:28:28	T JEAVONS-FELLOWS	3:29:02	M JEWKES	3:29:21	J HANSEN	3:29:54	T MARU	3:30:23
98	I MCGREGOR	3:28:28	P PHELAN	3:29:02	A HOLMES	3:29:22	J DANSKIN	3:29:54	T EGAN	3:30:23
99	R TERRY	3:28:28	S ELLIOTT	3:29:02	H WOODWARD	3:29:22	D NORTHERN	3:29:54	A DAVIES	3:30:24
100	D WOOD	3:28:29	J WINTER	3:29:02	G SWAN	3:29:23	D WHADCOCK	3:29:54	J BESSEAU	3:30:24

	6001-6100		6101-6200		6201-6300		6301-6400		6401-6500	
1	A WAGHORN	3:30:24	D WATSON	3:30:58	J IZABEL	3:31:35	M CLINTON	3:32:17	R WILGOSS	3:32:54
2	F DIPROSE	3:30:25	J HARDY	3:30:59	P SAXON	3:31:36	A MCCARTHY	3:32:17	W BLAISDALE	3:32:54
3	A DE PEREIRA	3:30:25	D SEARS	3:31:00	J FILLON	3:31:36	R STARTIN	3:32:17	S CHILLINGWORTH	3:32:54
4	J SOHL	3:30:25	E CUDMORE	3:31:00	D SAY	3:31:37	G BAYLIS	3:32:18	J BRAILSFORD	3:32:54
5	P DOBSON	3:30:25	C CARKETT	3:31:00	D ELSLEY	3:31:38	R TOGNETTI	3:32:18	J JOHNSON	3:32:55
6	D GIMBERT	3:30:25	H CRAVEN	3:31:00	G WRIGHT	3:31:38	SCARROTT	3:32:18	P HORAN	3:32:55
7	M O'NEILL	3:30:25	G BRYAN	3:31:00	D CAMPIN	3:31:39	B MAETZ	3:32:19	S SHERWOOD	3:32:55
8	G BUCHAN	3:30:25	J GEURTS	3:31:00	J HOPKINS	3:31:39	M BOISSONNET	3:32:20	P MARSHALL	3:32:56
9	S ONEILL	3:30:25	H GERSEN	3:31:00	A NICHOLSON	3:31:39	T BRAME	3:32:20	K KANT	3:32:56
10	J SHARPE	3:30:26	C WOODWISS	3:31:01	S KITCHENER	3:31:39	R TURNER	3:32:20	M SHEPHARD	3:32:57
11	P ALLEN	3:30:26	T THORNDYKE	3:31:02	J HARGREAVES	3:31:39	S WISE	3:32:20	J HINES	3:32:57
12	A TAVERNER	3:30:26	D QUICKENDEN	3:31:02	D MAURICE	3:31:39	D HOYER	3:32:20	A ADAMS	3:32:58
13	P PULLMAN	3:30:26	K LOWTHER	3:31:03	P ATKINS	3:31:39	B WIBBERLEY	3:32:21	J LIPPE	3:32:59
14	R LANGER	3:30:28	J MARTIN	3:31:03	A SHUTTER	3:31:40	J SPENCER	3:32:21	S LOWDEN	3:32:59
15	A EVANS	3:30:28	J WAITE	3:31:03	N WHEELER	3:31:41	B EVANS	3:32:21	A RAVEN	3:32:59
16	E WILLIAMS	3:30:28	N SIMPSON	3:31:04	A STENTIFORD	3:31:41	L GIROLI	3:32:22	E MANSFIELD	3:32:59
17	J MCBURNEY	3:30:28	P LAUJAC	3:31:04	D FORGET	3:31:42	S BIESIADA	3:32:22	K BARRY	3:32:59
18	J BILLAC	3:30:29	G GILLIVER	3:31:05	C JENKINS	3:31:42	M ASHTON	3:32:22	S ROBERTS	3:32:59
19	C MALLOY	3:30:29	W NIESSEN	3:31:05	M LOWRY	3:31:42	H GERBER	3:32:24	C BRUN	3:32:59
20	T LE SERVOISIER	3:30:30	V BOWLES	3:31:06	H STOCKS	3:31:43	J FORREST	3:32:24	J LAIDLAW	3:32:59
21	A FENNELL	3:30:30	D JONES	3:31:07	R SCOTT	3:31:43	S COLE	3:32:25	J COOPER	3:33:00
22	A MCILVAIN	3:30:30	K RUSSELL	3:31:07	A LOWE	3:31:43	G WEST	3:32:25	A MERARD	3:33:00
23	J DIPPLE	3:30:31	A LAMMAS	3:31:07	M JONES	3:31:43	I RUSSELL	3:32:25	T SLANEY	3:33:00
24	D HATTERSLEY	3:30:31	J COOPER	3:31:07	G WATKINS	3:31:44	J CUMMING	3:32:25	M HARROLD	3:33:01
25	A REED	3:30:31	T NEWELL	3:31:07	D DUGGAL	3:31:44	D BLOXIDGE	3:32:26	C PARNELL	3:33:01
26	D HIGGINBOTHAM	3:30:32	W TOMLINSON	3:31:07	J GALLAGHER	3:31:45	K WOONTON	3:32:27	J COURIVAUD	3:33:01
27	M JONES	3:30:32	A MOORE	3:31:08	F EVANS	3:31:46	D LOVEJOY	3:32:27	J HOLMES	3:33:01
28	R DIXON	3:30:32	K WINTER	3:31:08	J INKSTER	3:31:47	J ROE	3:32:27	R HARRIS	3:33:02
29	A CROCK	3:30:32	P GIBSON	3:31:09	W EVANS	3:31:48	D CLARKE	3:32:27	M HORFORD	3:33:02
30	M CLARKE	3:30:33	M SANDERSON	3:31:09	R MARSHALL	3:31:48	W MAIN	3:32:27	D KEEBLE	3:33:02
31	J HELMORE	3:30:33	T BURKE	3:31:10	D GHANI	3:31:49	C SKUSE	3:32:27	S GORE	3:33:02
32	R CARLONI	3:30:34	A HEDGES	3:31:11	S GAZE	3:31:49	B DREW	3:32:28	I ANSON	3:33:02
33	K GLASBY	3:30:35	M GIBSON	3:31:11	C BROADHURST	3:31:49	K VAN ROY	3:32:28	B PAYNE	3:33:03
34	W MUCCIOLI	3:30:35	R CHADWICK	3:31:11	S BARNSHAW	3:31:50	K SAMBROOK	3:32:28	C CASPER	3:33:03
35	I DAVIES	3:30:35	R CLEMENT	3:31:12	R FLOU	3:31:50	A ENGLISH	3:32:28	R PICKERING	3:33:03
36	M MINNETTI	3:30:35	A JOY	3:31:12	F BOND	3:31:51	J WONG	3:32:28	A DURKIN	3:33:04
37	M CLARK	3:30:35	F GRANT	3:31:12	T MORRI	3:31:51	J YUDKIN	3:32:28	W SMITH	3:33:05
38	P MAISEL	3:30:35	K MADDOX	3:31:12	P MASON	3:31:51	M AISTHORPE	3:32:28	P BOLTON	3:33:05
39	A BANHAM	3:30:36	G SWANN	3:31:12	J EDGLEY	3:31:52	B MORGAN	3:32:28	M KIRBY	3:33:05
40	J SIDAWAY	3:30:36	P CLARK	3:31:12	M SEERS	3:31:52	C GIBBS	3:32:28	M SAMESHIMA	3:33:05
41	P MCCARTNEY	3:30:36	J WILSON	3:31:13	N RICHARDS	3:31:53	J ALLEN	3:32:28	R HOARE	3:33:05
42	C DESMOND	3:30:37	J LEWIS	3:31:13	M FIELD	3:31:54	R BRIGHT	3:32:29	W BANNERMAN	3:33:06
43	A BOYLE	3:30:37	J SEXTON	3:31:13	R PARRY	3:31:54	M LEONARD	3:32:29	A LEMON	3:33:06
44	G HENDERSON	3:30:38	B KNAPMAN	3:31:14	S ILES	3:31:54	I GRUNDY	3:32:29	R KIBBLE	3:33:06
45	P WARNER	3:30:38	B JANSSEN	3:31:14	T URANO	3:31:54	R WESTLUND	3:32:29	T ROLLS	3:33:06
46	B CULLEN	3:30:39	J THOMAS	3:31:14	D THOMAS	3:31:54	P JUPP	3:32:29	P FRINDLE	3:33:07
47	R WRIGHT	3:30:39	D SHERWOOD	3:31:14	V DOSANJH	3:31:55	T KENNEDY	3:32:29	M SHEPHERD	3:33:07
48	K STEIN	3:30:39	L CEDIEL	3:31:15	W MARTIN	3:31:55	G JACKSON	3:32:30	D EDGAR	3:33:07
49	T STUBBS	3:30:39	M SOUTHWELL	3:31:15	J LUCAS	3:31:55	A NICHOLSON	3:32:31	K PREDDY	3:33:07
50	K DYER	3:30:39	H NOEL	3:31:15	WHITMORE	3:31:56	J BARRETT	3:32:31	N COLLINGWOOD	3:33:07
51	J POWER	3:30:40	J TOWERSEY	3:31:16	C HIPWELL	3:31:56	D MCDERMOTT	3:32:31	M COOPER	3:33:07
52	D BLOUNT	3:30:41	M CASE	3:31:17	P AMOS	3:31:57	J NAGORSKI	3:32:31	C EVANS	3:33:08
53	D GUDGION	3:30:41	J FOLAN	3:31:17	A EDWARDS	3:31:57	P TUCKER	3:32:32	C CLARK	3:33:08
54	L BOWERS	3:30:42	R HAYES	3:31:17	R LANE	3:31:58	R REID	3:32:32	A MARSH	3:33:08
55	S BONEWELL	3:30:42	L WARD	3:31:17	D NICHOL	3:31:58	A SWALEHEEN	3:32:32	J OLEARY	3:33:08
56	D BOULTON	3:30:42	D CONNOP	3:31:17	G BEASLEY	3:31:58	J HAMPSON	3:32:32	S BASSNETT	3:33:08
57	C BRADISH	3:30:42	H KOCH	3:31:17	K DILLON	3:31:59	P COSGROVE	3:32:33	R WILSON	3:33:08
58	R FRYER	3:30:42	C MARSHALL	3:31:17	C THOMPSON	3:31:59	B FALOMI	3:32:33	J TYSZKIEWICZ	3:33:09
59	M CAILLOUX	3:30:43	R WEBBER	3:31:17	J ALLISTON	3:31:59	D PRIOR	3:32:33	N WOODWARD	3:33:09
60	C HAYMAN	3:30:44	D HARPER	3:31:18	T ALDEN	3:32:01	G BROWN	3:32:33	J THORPE	3:33:09
61	G CORPART	3:30:44	J KAEHLER	3:31:18	R MACKENZIE	3:32:01	P PICKERING	3:32:34	D KIDD	3:33:09
62	D GARDNER	3:30:45	M RUSSELL	3:31:19	E TRENDELL	3:32:01	G BROOK	3:32:34	S O'HARA	3:33:10
63	T RODGERS	3:30:45	S CLARIDGE	3:31:19	J ELLIOTT	3:32:02	J BOOT	3:32:34	I HORSFALL-TURNER	3:33:10
64	A MULLINS	3:30:45	G LUCIDI	3:31:19	C PUTLEY	3:32:02	E SWAILES	3:32:34	C PARDOE	3:33:10
65	P WRIGHT	3:30:46	N POWIS	3:31:20	R DICKSON	3:32:03	C TREACHER	3:32:34	G AGOSTEO	3:33:10
66	G MCCORMICK	3:30:46	D CARRUTHERS	3:31:20	M BERTRAND	3:32:03	B WEATHERILL	3:32:35	R FIRTH	3:33:11
67	D CLARKE	3:30:46	A CLARK	3:31:20	M DANIELS	3:32:03	N HUNT	3:32:35	F AIELLO	3:33:11
68	J MCSHARRY	3:30:46	A GREEN	3:31:20	G BOX	3:32:03	S WAKE	3:32:35	A KIRKHAM	3:33:11
69	B HALSALL	3:30:46	A CREIGHTON	3:31:21	P RIGHELATO	3:32:03	M DANBY	3:32:36	D MURRAY	3:33:11
70	J MOLLOY	3:30:47	G WAGG	3:31:21	J LENAGHAN	3:32:03	C EDMONDSON	3:32:36	R MENEAR	3:33:12
71	V COTTON	3:30:47	D JOLLY	3:31:21	G CARDNELL	3:32:03	B BAXTER	3:32:37	P TAYLOR	3:33:12
72	B CHISHOLM	3:30:47	P STRATTON	3:31:21	N WEBB	3:32:04	K STINEMETZ	3:32:37	P LYTHGOE	3:33:12
73	A BIRCKNELL	3:30:47	D FORTUNE	3:31:22	K KANE	3:32:04	M FLECK	3:32:38	P MONK	3:33:12
74	P HODGKINS	3:30:47	K BROWN	3:31:22	J JONES	3:32:04	J MCGREGOR	3:32:38	D ELLIOTT	3:33:12
75	M DOYLE	3:30:48	A MERCER	3:31:22	J BEATON	3:32:04	L MAULT	3:32:38	R WILLIS	3:33:12
76	S FRAMPTON	3:30:48	J MOORE	3:31:23	G SWANSON	3:32:04	J BELL	3:32:39	M QUEVAL	3:33:12
77	M AMBLER	3:30:48	G HERD	3:31:23	A WRIGHT	3:32:04	B LOVELL	3:32:39	C EWIN	3:33:12
78	A SMITH	3:30:48	A LITTLE	3:31:24	J CONAGHAN	3:32:06	J SHAW	3:32:40	S BOUND	3:33:12
79	A AUDAS	3:30:48	G WREGHITT	3:31:26	N BAKER	3:32:06	S MAYES	3:32:40	P TAYLOR	3:33:13
80	B WOJCIK	3:30:48	C BARRON	3:31:27	K MOOG	3:32:07	B RAVEL	3:32:40	D NICHOLLS	3:33:13
81	R ROBSON	3:30:48	C WIPF	3:31:27	J DAVID	3:32:07	P CARLOTTI	3:32:41	P HOWARTH	3:33:13
82	D COOK	3:30:49	J GUILBOT	3:31:27	M WHITE	3:32:07	T BAVERSTOCK	3:32:41	A RAGGETT	3:33:13
83	D CLAUS	3:30:49	C HAMILTON	3:31:28	J MASON	3:32:08	M BROWNE	3:32:42	J JOHNSON	3:33:14
84	G HAYLES	3:30:50	C TOOKEY	3:31:28	A MALLON	3:32:08	K GOODBY	3:32:42	D BEMBRIDGE	3:33:14
85	R STRAND	3:30:50	B WOOD	3:31:28	M HENSEY	3:32:09	P BECKETT	3:32:46	D CANDEY	3:33:14
86	A DUNN	3:30:51	M HARRIS	3:31:30	M BUTLER	3:32:10	C ANSELL	3:32:47	T VERSTEGEN	3:33:15
87	I TAYLOR	3:30:51	M SIPPLI	3:31:30	R BROOKS	3:32:11	N CLAWSON	3:32:47	D HAVERCROFT	3:33:15
88	G CRISCOLL	3:30:51	D WHITTY	3:31:31	V GUERRI	3:32:12	R STEUEH	3:32:47	M ROWE	3:33:17
89	G DEOT	3:30:52	J RINK	3:31:31	D MACLEAN	3:32:13	L WALKER	3:32:48	D WOOLLEY	3:33:17
90	P OSBORNE	3:30:52	D LEIGH	3:31:32	E SAKANO	3:32:14	R OLIVER	3:32:48	I COX	3:33:17
91	D GRANT	3:30:52	M DOBSON	3:31:32	N CLOTHIER	3:32:14	B COLES	3:32:49	W MORGAN	3:33:18
92	R COOKSEY	3:30:53	I DAVIS	3:31:32	J GAILLARD	3:32:14	M BARRATT	3:32:49	M BUCKLEY	3:33:18
93	C BURNETT	3:30:53	D HARDCASTLE	3:31:32	M MAREK	3:32:14	P SYMINGTON	3:32:50	J GRAHAM	3:33:18
94	I GOW	3:30:54	P SMITHURST	3:31:32	M CASHMAN	3:32:15	N CROASDELL	3:32:51	M ROWE	3:33:18
95	B MELING	3:30:54	M GREENE	3:31:33	D LINDSAY	3:32:15	J RODRIGUES	3:32:51	D BAKER	3:33:18
96	J MCGUINNESS	3:30:55	J SMITH	3:31:33	M CHAPMAN	3:32:15	Y PERRIN	3:32:52	N WRIGLEY	3:33:19
97	J GARDET	3:30:55	S FARESTVEDT	3:31:34	G HOGLUND	3:32:15	M HAGAN	3:32:53	R HERZIG	3:33:19
98	B BAGGOTT	3:30:55	E SPOONER	3:31:35	N WATTS	3:32:15	J MALLET	3:32:53	A KINAL	3:33:19
99	M LILL	3:30:56	R HADDOW	3:31:35	D BIRD	3:32:16	S SALT	3:32:53	J EVANS	3:33:19
100	M BOWE	3:30:56	G FALCONER	3:31:35	D BEAULIEU	3:32:17	R VICKERS	3:32:53	R ROTHFARB	3:33:19

#	6501-6600	6601-6700	6701-6800	6801-6900	6901-7000
1	A THOMPSON 3:33:20	J SORLIE 3:33:49	A PRATT 3:34:30	M WILES 3:35:06	G SEILEA 3:35:41
2	J SHARPE 3:33:20	T JEE 3:33:50	G USHER 3:34:31	A AVY 3:35:06	S ROBINSON 3:35:41
3	P EVANS 3:33:20	K WALSH 3:33:50	Y YKRELEF 3:34:31	D GLYNN 3:35:06	W FREEBURN 3:35:41
4	T NELDER 3:33:20	R ELLIOTT 3:33:50	D COATES 3:34:31	J PRENTOUT 3:35:07	J HOBBS 3:35:41
5	D RYAN 3:33:21	C BARRETT 3:33:52	G JEFFREY 3:34:32	M DOMINGUEZ 3:35:07	A MHANNI 3:35:42
6	K BEATON 3:33:21	S PATTEN 3:33:52	R LANGLEY 3:34:33	K BENCH 3:35:08	G CAMPBELL 3:35:42
7	T STABLES 3:33:21	C LOREY 3:33:52	D MROSS 3:34:33	D EDWARDSON 3:35:08	S ALLARD 3:35:42
8	J CONWAY 3:33:21	E KETTERICK 3:33:53	G FLEMING 3:34:33	J STEPHENS 3:35:08	J FOSTER 3:35:42
9	S KENNEDY 3:33:22	G BARNETT 3:33:54	W COURTHARD 3:34:34	C ELLIOTT 3:35:08	P WEBB 3:35:43
10	P KENT 3:33:22	K EDWARDS 3:33:54	F LEVY 3:34:34	C SLOAN 3:35:09	M ALSEY 3:35:43
11	P MARCHANT 3:33:22	J MELVILLE 3:33:54	R LEAHY 3:34:34	R KELLY 3:35:09	G BROCKING 3:35:44
12	D LINDSAY 3:33:23	H MACKLER 3:33:55	L THOMPSON 3:34:34	G STAPLETON 3:35:10	S EDYE 3:35:44
13	R CRAIG 3:33:23	J OLLEY 3:33:55	F MEABY 3:34:34	T CADOGAN 3:35:11	T HENNION 3:35:44
14	P GALLAGHER 3:33:23	A MOUNTER 3:33:55	H HANSEN 3:34:34	T MYERS 3:35:12	P JONES 3:35:44
15	G CHAMBERS 3:33:24	H VARLEY 3:33:55	C PRITCHARD 3:34:34	B LANE 3:35:12	F SCHLUETER 3:35:45
16	D EVANS 3:33:24	C PULLEN 3:33:55	A HARBY 3:34:34	D ROSSOUW 3:35:13	M WEST 3:35:46
17	J PERRY 3:33:24	J DHELLEMME 3:33:56	J HETT 3:34:34	M HEMMS 3:35:13	G QUINLAN 3:35:46
18	M OWEN 3:33:25	D JAMES 3:33:56	I WALLHEAD 3:34:36	P FAIR 3:35:13	D ACHESON 3:35:47
19	C FOSKER 3:33:25	A HUGHES 3:33:56	C WARDELL 3:34:37	B MURPHY 3:35:14	I ROWSON 3:35:47
20	J LODGE 3:33:25	T AVELING 3:33:57	T CALDER 3:34:37	C GRANT 3:35:14	B AVELING 3:35:47
21	G BETSORTH 3:33:26	H LIAGRE 3:33:57	L EYERMANN 3:34:38	J HIBBERT 3:35:14	A GUY 3:35:47
22	J BUCHANAN 3:33:26	S DEAR 3:33:57	E SCANLON 3:34:38	B BAILEY 3:35:15	D FUNNELL 3:35:48
23	P LESTER 3:33:26	D WILLIAMS 3:33:57	W RITCHIE 3:34:38	R BLADE 3:35:16	N BUTLER 3:35:48
24	S PARKER 3:33:26	G ATKINSON 3:33:57	D BUSKIN 3:34:39	H HEMPEL 3:35:16	C BROWN 3:35:49
25	M COLE 3:33:26	P THOM 3:33:57	H HAYNES 3:34:39	J DILLON 3:35:16	R COWDRY 3:35:50
26	P ALLEN 3:33:27	J CARTWRIGHT 3:33:57	C STIMSON 3:34:39	J CROW 3:35:16	A BRACHER 3:35:50
27	P SMITH 3:33:27	T MCHUGH 3:33:58	T DAVIES 3:34:39	S PERRY 3:35:16	T WOOTTON 3:35:51
28	D GARDNER 3:33:27	S PAILOR 3:33:58	M DANGER 3:34:39	P DAVIES 3:35:16	O SUGINO 3:35:51
29	R KENT 3:33:27	R MCPAUL 3:33:59	J CONDON 3:34:40	D PURVIS 3:35:17	J MEREDITH 3:35:52
30	W HOED 3:33:28	S APPLETON 3:33:59	V RAWAT 3:34:40	D BROWN 3:35:17	S BELL 3:35:53
31	J CHAPMAN 3:33:28	K DYER 3:33:59	M QUINLIVAN 3:34:40	P BIERTON 3:35:17	J MARIEZCURRENA 3:35:53
32	P NICHOLSON 3:33:28	W MORRIS 3:33:59	J HUIN 3:34:40	R COOLS 3:35:17	A POWELL 3:35:53
33	D KELNER 3:33:28	M PASSINI 3:34:00	S ANSTISS 3:34:41	K BWYE 3:35:17	D HARRISON 3:35:54
34	M SHARP 3:33:28	W ROSS 3:34:01	N TURK 3:34:41	V SPITERI 3:35:18	S TISI 3:35:56
35	D GOLDING 3:33:29	R BERGER 3:34:02	J WATSON 3:34:42	F MAURIAT 3:35:18	L VAN DER SPEK 3:35:57
36	J HAYES 3:33:30	A RINGWOOD 3:34:04	L DUNHAM 3:34:42	S BLIGHT 3:35:18	S COUSINS 3:35:58
37	R GOULD 3:33:31	K CRUTCHLEY 3:34:04	N GOSBEE 3:34:42	M JEULIN 3:35:19	S HARLEY 3:35:58
38	N WHITFIELD 3:33:31	M NELMES 3:34:05	B MIATT 3:34:43	A COX 3:35:20	M DYER 3:35:58
39	M COOPER 3:33:31	M DINKELDEIN 3:34:05	A WATT 3:34:43	P ROSS 3:35:20	I HOLT 3:35:59
40	C PATTERSON 3:33:32	G PEARSON 3:34:05	K PRIEST 3:34:43	M MCDERMOTT 3:35:21	E GILMARTIN 3:35:59
41	M DAY 3:33:32	C COUSENS 3:34:05	A RADCLIFFE 3:34:43	A GITTINGS 3:35:21	A THOMSON 3:35:59
42	I CHIVERS 3:33:32	R WEEDEN 3:34:06	A ROBSON 3:34:44	D EDELSTEN 3:35:22	J WROE 3:35:59
43	A PINSART 3:33:33	J ROBSON 3:34:06	M ROWLEY 3:34:44	D COLES 3:35:24	W CASELY 3:36:00
44	A CURTIS 3:33:33	D HUMPLEBY 3:34:06	J ASPREY 3:34:44	L WELLS 3:35:24	R VIGAR 3:36:00
45	P GLAZE 3:33:34	M CLARKE 3:34:06	J SENIOR 3:34:44	L COMINI 3:35:25	J POTTS 3:36:00
46	B RAPALI 3:33:35	D HENDERSON 3:34:07	V SOLLAS 3:34:45	E CAMPBELL 3:35:25	M CHINAZZO 3:36:00
47	N BLAKE 3:33:35	D TOWERS 3:34:07	M CARPENTER 3:34:45	W LEE 3:35:25	W BLACKBURN 3:36:01
48	A HANCOCK 3:33:36	D NURSE 3:34:09	J COOK 3:34:46	F WILCKE 3:35:25	M WORRALL 3:36:01
49	J ROBINSON 3:33:36	A SMITH 3:34:09	C LACEY 3:34:47	F HAWKES 3:35:25	D GOWANS 3:36:01
50	J CRANHAM 3:33:36	J KING 3:34:09	A PRESLY 3:34:47	L DAVAUX 3:35:25	I GREENWOOD 3:36:02
51	E HEWITT 3:33:36	J CROCKFORD 3:34:09	B GRIDLEY 3:34:48	J MCDONALD 3:35:26	P CONNELL 3:36:03
52	D ROSEWELL 3:33:36	T TORNABONI 3:34:09	K DAVEY 3:34:48	E BELLERBY 3:35:27	S FORRESTER 3:36:03
53	N SCOTT 3:33:37	C CLOSE 3:34:09	D BEASLEY 3:34:48	J MILLAN 3:35:27	W PORTERFIELD 3:36:03
54	K POTTER 3:33:37	P HERMAN 3:34:10	A ANTHONY 3:34:49	A BREMNER 3:35:28	R HARRIS 3:36:04
55	W PATTEN 3:33:38	C RAYMOND 3:34:10	A FROST 3:34:49	U PASQUINI 3:35:28	J LOWE 3:36:04
56	G SHIPP 3:33:38	T ROBERTS 3:34:10	G ION 3:34:49	A SILMAN 3:35:28	R THOMAS 3:36:04
57	R CLAYTON 3:33:39	D CHILCOTT 3:34:10	S PITTS 3:34:49	M PAINTER 3:35:29	W WHITWORTH 3:36:05
58	R READ 3:33:39	A DICKMAN 3:34:11	M BEASLEY 3:34:50	A CLEMENT 3:35:30	F MOSS 3:36:05
59	P THOMAS 3:33:39	A OLIVER 3:34:11	R ROGERS 3:34:50	H TURNER 3:35:31	P CRADDOCK 3:36:06
60	D LAWTON 3:33:40	M WINSTANLEY 3:34:12	G WEBB 3:34:51	D STAINER 3:35:32	P CHANTON 3:36:06
61	K WRIGHT 3:33:40	A SMITH 3:34:13	C EARL 3:34:51	S FOWLER 3:35:32	J CARNELL 3:36:07
62	J SEARS 3:33:41	S BLOY 3:34:13	J JONES 3:34:51	T MOORE 3:35:32	K SMITH 3:36:08
63	M TONINI 3:33:41	N WATSON 3:34:13	W HART 3:34:51	P LUDDINGTON 3:35:32	P BIELBY 3:36:08
64	J HURLEY 3:33:42	K NORMAN 3:34:14	E GEORGE 3:34:52	D DOWNES 3:35:32	C EKE 3:36:08
65	K MCKIE 3:33:42	T PORTER 3:34:14	J EIEIZAIDE 3:34:53	N RUMSEY 3:35:33	J PURVES 3:36:08
66	D HAND 3:33:42	P AVENELL 3:34:14	A CAPP 3:34:53	B ADAMSON 3:35:34	J BUXTON 3:36:08
67	S FERRY 3:33:42	T WIDDOWS 3:34:14	S PATEY 3:34:53	K HAYWOOD 3:35:34	J MAXIM 3:36:09
68	E MOSES 3:33:42	G CHAPLIN 3:34:15	D HISLOP 3:34:53	M CHEW 3:35:34	G DOUILLARD 3:36:10
69	J FERRY 3:33:43	J WILKINSON 3:34:15	E TYSON 3:34:54	D COPE 3:35:34	P RIDLEY 3:36:10
70	B KING 3:33:43	M BEARD 3:34:15	J WILDEN 3:34:54	M TAYLOR 3:35:34	B KRISHNAKUMAR 3:36:10
71	A POTE 3:33:43	W SCHAAF 3:34:15	R HOGG 3:34:56	S BIRCH 3:35:35	M FABRY 3:36:10
72	L WHITE 3:33:43	M CROWTHER 3:34:17	P JANSSENS 3:34:56	G THOMPSON 3:35:35	R KIRKBRIDE 3:36:11
73	O DELTA 3:33:43	S HOWE 3:34:19	M ANDREY 3:34:56	A DIPPLE 3:35:35	R TANNER 3:36:11
74	R LINDSAY 3:33:44	I QUANT 3:34:19	R SANKEY 3:34:56	L VERNON 3:35:35	R THORPE 3:36:11
75	S REEDER 3:33:44	P SNOWDON 3:34:19	J DENMAN 3:34:56	M GARRETT 3:35:36	L STEVENSON 3:36:11
76	M SHELDON 3:33:44	B HEREDGE 3:34:19	J TILLEY 3:34:56	J DALTON 3:35:36	S BARHAM 3:36:11
77	J LOPEZ 3:33:44	A CLARK 3:34:19	P BEARD 3:34:57	B CAREY 3:35:36	K BERRY 3:36:11
78	P RICHARDSON 3:33:44	T FITZALAN HOWARD 3:34:19	A POUSSIER 3:34:58	T DEAN 3:35:36	P COLLINS 3:36:11
79	L STEELE 3:33:44	K JANSEN 3:34:19	C PARISE 3:34:58	S BROWN 3:35:37	D BUCKE 3:36:11
80	M SLEETH 3:33:44	C BROOM 3:34:19	D EBBAGE 3:34:58	D FAWCETT 3:35:37	G FIUMANO 3:36:11
81	J GILLIES 3:33:45	A BISHOP 3:34:19	R GOWLING 3:34:59	M SARGEANT 3:35:37	J MCCOURT 3:36:11
82	J SPALDING 3:33:46	A ROBERTS 3:34:20	T WOOLF 3:35:00	R PEGG 3:35:37	D DUVAL 3:36:11
83	D MOORE 3:33:46	M BONARD 3:34:20	C FENN 3:35:00	K CALLOW 3:35:37	S CHARLESTON 3:36:11
84	R COLLINS 3:33:46	K BOND 3:34:20	P TRICKER 3:35:00	J WITTERICK 3:35:38	A MONTANARI 3:36:11
85	M DAMS 3:33:47	D DIMMOCK 3:34:20	F DUMAS 3:35:01	R NEAL 3:35:38	L OLIVA 3:36:11
86	J KEIRS 3:33:47	P JONES 3:34:20	P ROBERTS 3:35:01	J JOHNSON 3:35:38	P DENNY 3:36:12
87	N CONEY 3:33:47	G DE ANNA 3:34:21	I SANGSTER 3:35:02	K BENT 3:35:39	S FALCHETTI 3:36:12
88	C JORDAN 3:33:47	G FLETCHER 3:34:21	R CLAY 3:35:02	D PAGET 3:35:39	C RAYMOND 3:36:12
89	J WOODHEAD 3:33:47	J STANDRING 3:34:22	N GWYNNE 3:35:02	M BURROWES 3:35:39	K HAYES 3:36:13
90	J NEUT 3:33:47	J MELLON 3:34:22	A SPRATT 3:35:02	P GOUW 3:35:39	P CROUDACE 3:36:13
91	M HARMENING 3:33:47	A ARNOLD 3:34:22	N EMBLEM-ENGLISH 3:35:02	W DODDS 3:35:40	A HIGHLANDS 3:36:13
92	N BATES 3:33:47	R ROBERTS 3:34:23	J BARKER 3:35:02	M WILKINSON 3:35:40	S MENNELL 3:36:13
93	T BAKER 3:33:47	M CROFT 3:34:24	G TURNBULL 3:35:05	D CHILDERHOUSE 3:35:40	C BRAY 3:36:13
94	H MANTE 3:33:48	P MCCABE 3:34:24	D HALKYARD 3:35:05	N COULTER 3:35:40	D BRAILSFORD 3:36:13
95	J AINSLEY 3:33:49	D HOLDEN 3:34:25	A BRUNDLE 3:35:05	G SIMONELLI 3:35:40	G ANDERSON 3:36:14
96	W WITHERS 3:33:49	B TITLEY 3:34:26	C TACK 3:35:05	T JARVIS 3:35:40	M DAVEY 3:36:14
97	G TOTTERDELL 3:33:49	J DUSTON 3:34:27	D CRIPS 3:35:06	J GODFREY 3:35:40	R COLES 3:36:14
98	M MOAKES 3:33:49	P WOOLLFORD 3:34:28	C SUMMERS 3:35:06	A VERRALL 3:35:40	D STEATON 3:36:14
99	C MUNNS 3:33:49	P RUSSELL 3:34:29	M JONES 3:35:06	R SLATER 3:35:40	J FOSTER 3:36:15
100	L RICHARDSON 3:33:49	C DARNILL 3:34:30		C ADAMS 3:35:41	H BOENNINGHAUSEN 3:36:15

#	7001-7100		7101-7200		7201-7300		7301-7400		7401-7500	
1	A WATTS	3:36:15	A HEWETT	3:36:47	B FUESSER	3:37:14	G PLUMPTON	3:37:40	O FRYER	3:38:14
2	A DURSTON	3:36:15	B PETTERSSON	3:36:47	P CLEGG	3:37:15	B KIRTLEY	3:37:41	J COULTER	3:38:14
3	M MORTAZAVI	3:36:15	A FARNIE	3:36:47	J IGUCHI	3:37:15	M WILLIAMS	3:37:41	M SHAW	3:38:15
4	A CIRILLO	3:36:15	J HOUTBY	3:36:48	D BOOTH	3:37:15	S SMITH	3:37:41	C HAWKSHAW-BURN	3:38:15
5	A IMESON	3:36:15	A HOLLINSHEAD	3:36:48	J PANTER	3:37:15	J GASKIN	3:37:41	H SMYTH	3:38:15
6	I WALKER	3:36:15	P MESNEY	3:36:48	M LAWRENCE	3:37:15	N COLE	3:37:42	C SUMMERS	3:38:15
7	B MOORE	3:36:16	B WORTHINGTON	3:36:48	P WOODGATE	3:37:16	G SHAW	3:37:42	S CANHAM	3:38:16
8	P LAWLER	3:36:16	D METCALFE	3:36:49	K DAVIS	3:37:16	D HARRATT	3:37:42	P NICHOLS	3:38:16
9	M WARD	3:36:17	L CROSS	3:36:49	S GIBBONS	3:37:16	T MEE	3:37:42	B SANSOM	3:38:16
10	J HORN	3:36:17	I VOLANS	3:36:49	S WOOD	3:37:17	P DIXON	3:37:42	P HILL	3:38:17
11	J RHODES	3:36:17	G CAMERON	3:36:49	B WALKER	3:37:17	A MOORE	3:37:43	M BALLARD	3:38:17
12	J DOVEY	3:36:18	A LEA GERRARD	3:36:49	G CREBER	3:37:17	M THOMAS	3:37:43	R GRIEF	3:38:17
13	A HOLLIS	3:36:18	S EGGAR	3:36:49	B ALLSOBROOK	3:37:18	T MCDONALD	3:37:43	G QUINLIVAN	3:38:18
14	D MUNDY	3:36:19	R SHERWOOD	3:36:50	I HALL	3:37:18	T JARDINE	3:37:43	J NELSON	3:38:18
15	S ELLIS	3:36:19	G RAVEN	3:36:50	T HORNE	3:37:18	K OTTOSSON	3:37:43	J MARSH	3:38:18
16	D KINNIER	3:36:19	P HAINSWORTH	3:36:50	K BRETAG	3:37:18	I FARQUHAR	3:37:44	R ELLIS	3:38:19
17	G STOCKER	3:36:19	P SKEGGS	3:36:50	T HARVEY	3:37:18	J MILNER	3:37:44	G BODA	3:38:19
18	D HINDE	3:36:19	G RIDLEY	3:36:50	B FREDRIC	3:37:19	M BURNS	3:37:44	R KEYLOCK	3:38:20
19	G BLYTHE	3:36:19	T TAYLOR	3:36:50	H HARDING	3:37:19	T MURRAY	3:37:45	R CARRICK	3:38:20
20	M HALL	3:36:20	R CURRIE	3:36:50	J GILL	3:37:19	P DABLE	3:37:45	N DEACON	3:38:21
21	K TIDMARSH	3:36:20	R FOREMAN	3:36:50	R ALLET	3:37:19	J MCLEVY	3:37:45	D CARSON	3:38:21
22	J INGRAM	3:36:21	P SPICER	3:36:50	C CASTELIJNS	3:37:20	M WILSON	3:37:45	S SUMMERS	3:38:22
23	J HORTON	3:36:21	K BUTLER	3:36:50	N MYLAND	3:37:20	M COLE	3:37:45	A DYBDAHL	3:38:22
24	M MCQUILLAN	3:36:21	V CARTER	3:36:51	J LEWIN	3:37:20	R LAWES	3:37:46	O LANZILLOTTA	3:38:22
25	D KEELING	3:36:22	W LEE	3:36:51	K POPE	3:37:20	P BLANDE	3:37:46	P PORTER	3:38:23
26	L LOGAN	3:36:22	J HALLS	3:36:52	C LEATHLEY	3:37:20	P MOUNTFORD	3:37:47	A CARBONARI	3:38:23
27	P BURTON	3:36:22	B ARMSTRONG	3:36:52	J MAYNE	3:37:21	N JONES	3:37:47	R SARTIN	3:38:24
28	C POOLE	3:36:23	D HARGREAVES	3:36:52	L MANN	3:37:21	E MCPHERSON	3:37:48	J LINCOLN	3:38:24
29	K BINGLEY	3:36:23	A WEBSTER	3:36:52	J TUCKER	3:37:21	R KAJALA	3:37:48	D FISH	3:38:24
30	T LAWSON-CRUTTENDEN	3:36:23	F CLARKE	3:36:52	M RYAN	3:37:21	W FLINT	3:37:49	C ROSENBERG	3:38:24
31	W HAMERTON	3:36:23	S CORBOUKD	3:36:53	S KEYES	3:37:22	A SHEPHERD	3:37:49	M MILBURN	3:38:25
32	P LEWIS	3:36:23	N JAKOBSEN	3:36:53	K LAWLOR	3:37:23	W MARSDEN	3:37:49	D BUCKERFIELD	3:38:25
33	D LEGATE	3:36:24	M SANDERSON	3:36:53	A KENNEDY	3:37:23	J NIEWIAROWSKI	3:37:49	D TRANTER	3:38:25
34	C JONES	3:36:24	C SPONG	3:36:53	I GROCOTT	3:37:23	A MACFARLANE	3:37:49	J STOKES	3:38:26
35	D MANSON	3:36:24	A BOOTH	3:36:54	K FRANCIS	3:37:23	D WHITAKER	3:37:49	C HELYER	3:38:26
36	J MURDOCK	3:36:25	C JONES	3:36:54	S NELSON	3:37:23	R TRIBICK	3:37:50	P HUNT	3:38:27
37	S BRAYSHAW	3:36:25	P GILLHAM	3:36:54	J ROSS	3:37:24	C EVERED	3:37:50	J COUBROUGH	3:38:27
38	R LEWIS	3:36:25	M HUMPHRIS	3:36:54	B CRANE	3:37:24	S FORDHAM	3:37:51	J WILLIAMS	3:38:27
39	S MICHAEL	3:36:25	R COTTERILL	3:36:54	M BURRIDGE	3:37:24	J SLAYMAKER	3:37:51	K JONES	3:38:28
40	N COOPER	3:36:25	G WOODS	3:36:55	J BALL	3:37:25	M POLLARD	3:37:51	L PERSSON	3:38:28
41	T STOCKS	3:36:25	G JONES	3:36:55	J COLEMAN	3:37:25	C JOHN	3:37:51	I ATKINSON	3:38:28
42	G HOARE	3:36:26	J HORNY	3:36:55	M ARMSTRONG	3:37:26	R PULFORD	3:37:51	S DENNIS	3:38:28
43	P HINTON	3:36:26	A HAMILTON	3:36:55	A GREENHOUGH	3:37:27	W LAURIE	3:37:52	D JONES	3:38:29
44	K CAMPION	3:36:27	C BLACK	3:36:56	J FIELD	3:37:27	V COLLINS	3:37:53	G NICHOLSON	3:38:29
45	E MARTIN	3:36:27	D FOWLER	3:36:56	D POCKNELL	3:37:27	R BERGEOT	3:37:53	S BARCLAY	3:38:29
46	C WAYNE	3:36:27	T BALL	3:36:56	G LIDDLE	3:37:28	C CAMPBELL	3:37:53	S LEVETT	3:38:29
47	C RICHES	3:36:28	K GJUECK	3:36:56	S TODD	3:37:28	J WEST	3:37:54	B OTTE	3:38:30
48	A BECK	3:36:28	J FOSTER	3:36:57	D HIGH	3:37:28	K JANISZEWSKI	3:37:54	J MURRAY	3:38:30
49	D COXHEAD	3:36:29	G HOUGH	3:36:57	H REMBLANCE	3:37:28	J MORRISROE	3:37:54	J HART	3:38:30
50	S CHANDLER	3:36:29	A MASON	3:36:57	R CLARK	3:37:29	N STAMMERS	3:37:55	J ISAACS	3:38:30
51	D BLOFIELD	3:36:30	V BRUNI	3:36:57	S HENDRY	3:37:29	E TIPPING	3:37:55	D KING	3:38:30
52	C WARD	3:36:30	N PAINTER	3:36:58	P BUSH	3:37:29	D BOULD	3:37:56	T PATIENT	3:38:30
53	A DEARMAN	3:36:30	A BROUGHTON	3:36:58	R OLDALE	3:37:29	R BELL	3:37:56	J HOEZ	3:38:30
54	P POLLARD	3:36:30	I NUNN	3:36:58	D JOHNS	3:37:30	S WOOLHAM	3:37:57	J PEEPALL	3:38:31
55	J ASHMAN	3:36:30	N KHAN	3:36:58	D TOMLINSON	3:37:30	G HARRIS	3:37:57	K FAINT	3:38:31
56	J OLIVER	3:36:30	A MILLS	3:36:58	P LEAVER	3:37:30	D RAMSEY	3:37:57	N WOLDEN	3:38:31
57	J BARON	3:36:30	M TEROL	3:36:58	S GRONGSTAD	3:37:31	D CAUVIN	3:37:57	S TAYLOR	3:38:32
58	P AKERBOOM	3:36:30	P WILLIAMSON	3:36:59	J DINE	3:37:31	V LUNN	3:37:58	M HAINSBY	3:38:32
59	K GRENDON	3:36:30	K JOHNSON	3:36:59	T SHILLING	3:37:31	C SMITH	3:37:58	B PHIPPS	3:38:32
60	L MASON	3:36:30	R NOURSE	3:36:59	I BANDEIRA	3:37:31	M HUTCHINSON	3:37:59	J TURNER	3:38:32
61	E CZERNUSZKA	3:36:30	T ELSE	3:37:00	K KNIGHT	3:37:31	K DAHLQVIST	3:37:59	I BEATTIE	3:38:32
62	D OLEARY	3:36:30	M ROGERS	3:37:00	B JONES	3:37:32	D FISHBURN	3:37:59	E BARLOW	3:38:32
63	G EVANS	3:36:30	P MCBAIN	3:37:00	D CLEARY	3:37:32	D BRETT	3:38:00	R BARLOW	3:38:32
64	L DE SMET	3:36:30	M SEALEY	3:37:00	J GAGNEUR	3:37:32	S CAREY	3:38:00	H MARCHAL	3:38:32
65	A HUDSON	3:36:30	G LANGTON	3:37:00	J WALKER	3:37:33	R NEWTON	3:38:00	C WEAVER	3:38:33
66	H LUNDESTAD	3:36:30	J HAINSBY	3:37:00	M VIGNI	3:37:33	G BARKS	3:38:00	R BEST	3:38:33
67	M HOPKINS	3:36:30	B BROMBLEY	3:37:00	A DREW	3:37:34	R COLLOM	3:38:01	K ASHMAN	3:38:33
68	P EDWARDS	3:36:30	J DOUGLAS	3:37:00	R PIERSON	3:37:34	D STEVENS	3:38:01	J TERVIT	3:38:34
69	G TAYLOR	3:36:31	S REVILL	3:37:01	T WALBY	3:37:35	K ROBBINS	3:38:01	P BROOKS	3:38:34
70	I MAHONEY	3:36:31	T STEELE	3:37:02	A BOSCOMTWE	3:37:35	D GIBBS	3:38:02	A DEACON	3:38:34
71	F MARR	3:36:31	G JOHNSON	3:37:02	D BOWERMAN	3:37:35	M BAYLISS	3:38:02	P WRIGHT	3:38:36
72	K MCCARTHY	3:36:31	L GERMAIN	3:37:02	P COLEMAN	3:37:35	A COLTMAN	3:38:03	E SHAWSMITH	3:38:36
73	J LEPOIVRE	3:36:32	J ROSS	3:37:02	P BULL	3:37:35	J HENNESSEY	3:38:04	N BALL	3:38:37
74	C HAWKSHAW	3:36:32	T PHILLIPS	3:37:03	D SIMPSON	3:37:35	K BADACSONYI	3:38:05	A HARRINGTON	3:38:37
75	J URENA	3:36:33	J CHAPMAN	3:37:04	J LERIVRAY	3:37:36	N STEWARD	3:38:05	J OXBOROUGH	3:38:37
76	J MCDONALD	3:36:33	P NEWMAN	3:37:04	D MCCARTHY	3:37:36	D LEVAN	3:38:05	M RANKIN	3:38:38
77	R SHAPLAND	3:36:33	P BOCKLER	3:37:04	T ROBSON	3:37:36	D CLIFTON	3:38:06	A DAVIES	3:38:38
78	S HOOTON	3:36:33	P MAY	3:37:04	J LANDON	3:37:36	P ORR	3:38:07	M STUART	3:38:38
79	A TOMAZ	3:36:33	A THORNLEY	3:37:05	T STAMP	3:37:36	N GRANT	3:38:07	P IANTOSCA	3:38:38
80	M BEULAH	3:36:34	D BUSH	3:37:05	G HAIDER	3:37:36	D MCNAMARA	3:38:07	N HART	3:38:39
81	R POOLEY	3:36:34	W HORNAL	3:37:05	R SAUNDERS	3:37:36	M DAVIS	3:38:07	P HOLLAND	3:38:39
82	R FORD	3:36:34	B DEBESSON	3:37:06	T BOYLE	3:37:36	M DOWDESWELL	3:38:09	J ATKINSON	3:38:40
83	S MANNING	3:36:39	J PITT	3:37:06	R RIEDEL	3:37:36	M MURPHY	3:38:10	D WEDDELL	3:38:40
84	D JACKSON	3:36:40	F HEISSAT	3:37:08	T PAIGE	3:37:36	M MEALING	3:38:10	P SAVAGE	3:38:40
85	G GODFREY	3:36:40	C BUTLER	3:37:08	M SWINDON	3:37:37	C GROUTAGE	3:38:11	D MCMILLAN	3:38:41
86	S GREEN	3:36:40	L NUTTON	3:37:09	J HUMPHRIES	3:37:37	M DUVERNOIS	3:38:11	R MILLER	3:38:42
87	A JONES	3:36:41	M HAYCOCK	3:37:09	S LEMOINE	3:37:37	S CURNEEN	3:38:11	M HOLMES	3:38:42
88	R BROUGHTON	3:36:41	L PASSERI	3:37:09	L LANNERDAHL	3:37:38	P POWELL	3:38:11	M FONTVIEILLE	3:38:43
89	N WALTON	3:36:43	N SHAW	3:37:09	D TAYLOR	3:37:38	C RILEY	3:38:11	A AAS	3:38:43
90	M BAILEY	3:36:43	K TURNER	3:37:09	K DAVIES	3:37:38	M DEMPSEY	3:38:12	C BARRACLOUGH	3:38:44
91	D HILL	3:36:44	P FRENCH	3:37:10	R BENNETT	3:37:38	S GOODWIN	3:38:12	P HADGRAFT	3:38:44
92	J TYNAN	3:36:44	J HAWORTH	3:37:11	A KASOULIS	3:37:38	R BELSOM	3:38:12	A HORN	3:38:44
93	R BREAM	3:36:44	P LANE	3:37:12	N HOLTBY	3:37:38	M TURNER	3:38:12	T TSUCHIYA	3:38:45
94	R PINKNEY	3:36:45	S BRIGGS	3:37:12	I DEIRO	3:37:39	C ROBINSON	3:38:12	G JONES	3:38:46
95	J COLE	3:36:45	N LAMBERT	3:37:12	M GODSALVE	3:37:39	M PEEL	3:38:13	P LIPSETT	3:38:46
96	L YACAMINI	3:36:45	T BASEN	3:37:12	A TAYLOR	3:37:39	M GEORGE	3:38:13	N OBRIEN	3:38:47
97	T WOODS	3:36:45	J BARROWCLOUGH	3:37:13	C DIMMOCK	3:37:39	G COOK	3:38:13	K SMITH	3:38:47
98	H HASELEY	3:36:46	P AUDAS	3:37:13	C MULHALL	3:37:40	R COLLEDGE	3:38:14	S ARMITAGE	3:38:48
99	R GIBSON	3:36:46	K CLARK	3:37:13	E NAISBY	3:37:40	D STEAD	3:38:14	R FRANKL	3:38:48
100	P TROTMAN	3:36:46	A BAINBRIDGE	3:37:14	P MATHER	3:37:40	A BRAY	3:38:14	E ROBAYNA	3:38:48

	7501-7600		7601-7700		7701-7800		7801-7900		7901-8000	
1	M NORTHEY	3:38:48	S MCCRIRRICK	3:39:21	J HAGANS	3:39:49	B BROOKES	3:40:15	G CROSBY	3:40:46
2	J NASLUND	3:38:48	P HOLDSWORTH	3:39:23	H MORGAN	3:39:50	R SWAN	3:40:15	T RIVERS	3:40:46
3	N MICHAEL	3:38:49	G SINGH	3:39:23	B TRIBE	3:39:50	L CHAMBERS	3:40:16	B DOVELL	3:40:47
4	P TONKS	3:38:49	C BURGESS	3:39:23	I ORCHARD	3:39:50	S STOFFELL	3:40:16	N RUTTER	3:40:47
5	A DAKIN	3:38:49	H HOOGEBOOM	3:39:23	T WARD	3:39:50	K MOLYNEUX	3:40:17	A BELL	3:40:47
6	C EARL	3:38:49	S TUCKER	3:39:23	T HYLAND	3:39:50	J DALY	3:40:17	J ROULSTONE	3:40:47
7	D CAPSTICK	3:38:49	J OBLING	3:39:23	M WHITNEY	3:39:51	D BIRKIN	3:40:17	M MCCORMICK	3:40:48
8	M JONES	3:38:50	C JONES	3:39:23	B STEELE	3:39:51	R KYTE	3:40:17	D QUARANTA	3:40:48
9	S BUXTON	3:38:50	I KILSHAW	3:39:24	J GILLON	3:39:51	S NATALICIO CANDIDO	3:40:17	M BENSON-SMITH	3:40:48
10	D JENKINS	3:38:50	P GREGORY	3:39:24	J OSULLIVAN	3:39:51	R SAUNDERS	3:40:17	S SMITH	3:40:49
11	P GALE	3:38:51	D MOORES	3:39:24	J COWAN	3:39:52	U SCHUEMICHEN	3:40:17	M BORGNE	3:40:49
12	M WENGENROTH	3:38:51	B JOHNSTON	3:39:25	G FREEBORN	3:39:52	I SANDERSON	3:40:17	T SAWFORD	3:40:49
13	D HOLLETT	3:38:52	D DREWITT	3:39:25	W EYLES	3:39:52	S MUSSELLE	3:40:17	T SVENSSON	3:40:49
14	R OXLEY	3:38:52	C HALL	3:39:25	R GILLIAT	3:39:52	D MAYES	3:40:17	V CRAWFORD	3:40:49
15	C THACKWELL	3:38:52	J RALPHS	3:39:25	D ALDCROFT	3:39:52	N BUCHANAN	3:40:18	D BAXTER	3:40:50
16	E SUNDERLAND	3:38:53	R ARCHBOLD	3:39:25	A PERRY	3:39:53	M METCALFE	3:40:18	T ATHERTON	3:40:50
17	D WHITEHOUSE	3:38:54	G FERGUSON	3:39:26	K SEWELL	3:39:53	O ST JOHN	3:40:18	C FLYNN	3:40:50
18	A BRIXTON	3:38:54	E RENDELL	3:39:26	J SMITH	3:39:53	M MAYNARD	3:40:19	R CROUZILHAC	3:40:50
19	B KING	3:38:55	I MONK	3:39:26	D BELL	3:39:53	D RAYNOR	3:40:19	S RIVERS	3:40:51
20	A BLISS	3:38:55	T MELERO	3:39:26	J BARLOW	3:39:53	K MCCLOY	3:40:19	H FOORD	3:40:51
21	P TRUSCOTT	3:38:55	A LEE	3:39:26	J TAYLOR	3:39:54	G EVANS	3:40:20	J RABBETTS	3:40:51
22	J EVERETT	3:38:55	J HOSKYN	3:39:26	J BRIMACOMBE	3:39:55	M THORN	3:40:20	B FINNIE	3:40:51
23	B CAMMELL	3:38:56	J SEYMOUR	3:39:26	G CRAMP	3:39:55	G HUGHES	3:40:20	K MACKESSACK	3:40:51
24	T WHITLOCK	3:38:56	I DEL AMO	3:39:27	D RATCLIFFE	3:39:56	A WILLIAMS	3:40:20	A POWELL	3:40:51
25	P ROLLENHAGEN	3:38:56	J FIDGE	3:39:27	J DAWSON	3:39:56	D JACKSON	3:40:21	N RUSSELL	3:40:51
26	R PICKLES	3:38:56	C DENLEY	3:39:27	C ELLIOTT	3:39:56	H MAINWARING	3:40:21	M WILLIAMSON	3:40:51
27	S KIBERD	3:38:56	T KING	3:39:27	T ROBERTSON	3:39:56	R DAVIES	3:40:21	R CARRIE	3:40:52
28	P FOLEY	3:38:56	G FINDLAY	3:39:28	P VICENTE PEREZ	3:39:56	M MCMASTER	3:40:21	R STONE	3:40:52
29	S CLUTTON	3:38:56	A BARLOW	3:39:28	J CHEVAS FERNANDO	3:39:57	A LANDAIS	3:40:22	A THYNNE	3:40:52
30	L ANELLI	3:38:57	S HUTCHINGS	3:39:28	I HAYES	3:39:57	G SMITHERS	3:40:22	M REID	3:40:52
31	S WALL	3:38:57	F JURASCHEK	3:39:28	S BISHOP	3:39:57	B WILLIAMS	3:40:22	S HILL	3:40:52
32	A HILDERLY	3:38:57	S FURK	3:39:28	R HORROCKS	3:39:57	J CLARKE	3:40:22	J ADLAM	3:40:53
33	K HAHN	3:38:57	K CORBETT	3:39:29	P SMITH	3:39:57	M LANE	3:40:22	A JOHNSON	3:40:53
34	K WELLS	3:38:58	F SENLECQ	3:39:29	J GREENLEES	3:39:57	P KEETLEY	3:40:25	J BOWDEN	3:40:55
35	M MCKEEVER	3:38:58	J LYNCH	3:39:30	I BEESLEY	3:39:57	G BRAZIER	3:40:25	R DURHAM	3:40:56
36	D BERGIN	3:38:59	J BANGS	3:39:30	I NICHOLSON	3:39:57	P COSTELLO	3:40:25	A PARSONS	3:40:56
37	G GARDNER	3:38:59	S ALLWOOD	3:39:31	M ENRIQUE	3:39:57	P VINEY	3:40:26	A ROWE	3:40:56
38	K RATCLIFFE	3:39:00	E ENGDAHLWRIGHT	3:39:31	T KIGGINS	3:39:57	P SMOOTHY	3:40:26	D DIXON	3:40:56
39	H KRESSLER	3:39:00	J EKSTROM	3:39:31	K GUNN	3:39:57	R MANN	3:40:26	C CRESSWELL	3:40:57
40	A HOWE	3:39:00	L QUIGLEY	3:39:32	R PICOT	3:39:57	C MULDOON	3:40:27	R SAMMONS	3:40:57
41	J BURCHFIELD	3:39:00	D JACOBS	3:39:32	J FLATT	3:39:57	R GOMPERTZ	3:40:27	N THOMPSON	3:40:57
42	A PAGE	3:39:03	M ROBSON	3:39:32	M HUYGHEBAERT	3:39:57	S ROWLANDS	3:40:27	L WATSON	3:40:58
43	K TIMPSON	3:39:03	K OLDING	3:39:32	E UBEL	3:39:58	D PHILLIPS	3:40:27	M HOBSON	3:40:58
44	R BARWELL	3:39:03	P FLYNN	3:39:32	S HEAD	3:39:58	V KILGOUR	3:40:27	M SPENCER	3:40:59
45	G SMITH	3:39:06	R WADDINGHAM	3:39:32	E DEVINE	3:39:58	M CLARKE	3:40:28	M BOSWELL	3:40:59
46	F SCHOEFFL	3:39:06	I CAMPBELL	3:39:34	I CAMPBELL	3:39:58	A CAST	3:40:28	R COOPER	3:41:00
47	G AUGUST	3:39:06	I KIMURA	3:39:34	C O'HEA	3:39:59	J MAPLES	3:40:28	S FLOWERS	3:41:00
48	G CASSARO	3:39:06	W SIKKENS	3:39:35	B WEMME	3:39:59	J GAADE	3:40:29	D WALKER	3:41:00
49	A ROCCO	3:39:06	J MARTIN	3:39:35	M COLOMBO	3:39:59	B SHEPHERD	3:40:29	R MATTHEWS	3:41:00
50	C HAMBLIN	3:39:06	T NADE	3:39:35	J FLINT	3:39:59	P MOIR	3:40:29	M HOBSON	3:41:00
51	G BARCLAY	3:39:06	A IRVIN	3:39:35	J WOOD	3:39:59	A PARKER	3:40:30	J WELSH	3:41:00
52	P BREYDIN	3:39:07	M GOODWIN	3:39:35	A UNDERWOO	3:39:59	W STRINGER	3:40:30	D ROWDEN	3:41:00
53	G CAMPBELL	3:39:07	L LANDUCCI	3:39:35	J COOPER	3:40:00	M GUEVEL	3:40:30	J LIMA	3:41:01
54	P RICHARDSON	3:39:07	T COXON	3:39:36	T MELLBYE	3:40:00	R WAGNER	3:40:30	P SLATER	3:41:01
55	A PICCHIONE	3:39:08	A LONG	3:39:36	N HOWELLS	3:40:00	J AMELL	3:40:30	N MATTHEWS	3:41:01
56	P WATKINS	3:39:08	A OLIVER	3:39:37	P HARRIS	3:40:00	D WARMAN	3:40:30	M WRIGHT	3:41:01
57	M INCE	3:39:08	R THOMPSON	3:39:37	T BALE	3:40:00	D STEVENS	3:40:31	S CRUICKSHANK	3:41:01
58	B HURWITZ	3:39:09	A RING	3:39:38	D LINDLEY	3:40:02	R HOGAN	3:40:31	D PALFREY	3:41:01
59	K GORDON	3:39:09	C DIEGO	3:39:38	T GUILBERT	3:40:02	A BAKER	3:40:31	I WILSON	3:41:01
60	T MOFFAT	3:39:09	I BROWN	3:39:38	A THOMAS	3:40:02	J MCVEAN	3:40:31	M PINNEY	3:41:02
61	N COURAGIER	3:39:10	R PALMER	3:39:39	R WILLOCK	3:40:03	P SLATER	3:40:32	T LEBER	3:41:03
62	S SATCHELL	3:39:10	X DELPLANQUE	3:39:39	S LISTER	3:40:03	P AUSTIN	3:40:32	R WARNE	3:41:03
63	M CAMPBELL	3:39:10	R CLARK	3:39:39	J ROBERTS	3:40:04	I STRANGE	3:40:32	M HART	3:41:04
64	M MACGIBBON	3:39:10	C MCDONALD	3:39:39	G BATTY	3:40:04	J STEVENS	3:40:32	R STUBBS	3:41:04
65	S KEVAN	3:39:11	D BUCKNALL	3:39:39	A PHELPS	3:40:04	D MARTIN	3:40:33	H BREITSPRECHER	3:41:04
66	D GREEN	3:39:11	D DURIE	3:39:40	S HOSKINS	3:40:04	P HARDING	3:40:33	D TRAYNOR	3:41:04
67	R LITTLE	3:39:12	J TOTH	3:39:40	P LUCAS	3:40:05	C MCKEAN	3:40:33	D DUDDEN	3:41:05
68	J CRAWFORD	3:39:12	P TANSWELL	3:39:41	J MELLOR	3:40:05	O O'DONOGHUE	3:40:34	S DUNN	3:41:05
69	G SIMMONDS	3:39:12	F PICCO	3:39:41	C FRITZBOEGER	3:40:05	M SMALE	3:40:34	N THURSTON	3:41:05
70	S VANSTONE	3:39:13	P MORRIS	3:39:41	C DAY	3:40:05	P PEDDER	3:40:34	D FLYNN	3:41:06
71	M WRIGHT	3:39:13	A HAUGHTON	3:39:42	F WAIN	3:40:06	C HOPE	3:40:35	P GREEN	3:41:06
72	N CLEMENTS	3:39:14	C MOEGLIN	3:39:43	S MONCRIEF	3:40:06	C PARKER	3:40:35	G THOMPSON	3:41:06
73	J HART	3:39:14	J HALLETT	3:39:43	J HEADING	3:40:06	A RAY	3:40:35	T CLIFFE	3:41:07
74	J VINCE	3:39:14	D BOWMAN	3:39:43	B HANSEN	3:40:06	D ROBERTS	3:40:36	T FITZGERALD	3:41:07
75	N KARIM	3:39:14	P GIBBINS	3:39:43	A SMITH	3:40:06	J SELS	3:40:36	S RITCHIE	3:41:07
76	S GRANDFIELD	3:39:14	S GEORGE	3:39:44	J LUNA	3:40:06	R PRICE	3:40:36	A FITZGERALD	3:41:08
77	E WEEDON	3:39:14	N BAILEY	3:39:44	M PITTMAN	3:40:07	R SIMPSON	3:40:36	P CLARKE	3:41:08
78	I ELLISON	3:39:14	A SEARLE	3:39:44	A GREGGS	3:40:07	P HIRSCHBERGER	3:40:36	G STONE	3:41:08
79	T TAKANO	3:39:15	L LAURENT	3:39:44	S POLES	3:40:07	W TOMLINSON	3:40:36	M BRIDGMAN	3:41:08
80	L BERNEY	3:39:15	D WOODCOCK	3:39:44	M MOSS	3:40:07	E COOK	3:40:37	F VAN ALDERWEGEN	3:41:09
81	J COX	3:39:15	J FARMER	3:39:45	J BENNETT	3:40:07	P AUTRUSSEAU	3:40:38	P JAGGS	3:41:10
82	S WILKIN	3:39:15	W CROWLEY	3:39:45	J HUNT	3:40:07	H WALLIS	3:40:38	S LUNT	3:41:11
83	D SWEENEY	3:39:16	J SHERLOCK	3:39:46	M HALL	3:40:08	S GETTINGS	3:40:38	M WRIGHT	3:41:11
84	C CLARKE	3:39:16	M WILSON	3:39:46	N SORENSEN	3:40:08	R BALLINGER	3:40:39	J HILDRETH	3:41:11
85	M STONE	3:39:16	V PHILLIPS	3:39:47	B POGORZELSKI	3:40:09	S PALISSE	3:40:39	F DRIES	3:41:11
86	P ROGERS	3:39:17	P ACKROYD	3:39:47	A MEECHAN	3:40:11	D WHORLOW	3:40:39	D O'HARA	3:41:11
87	G MITCHELL	3:39:17	D HOGARTH	3:39:47	S WEST	3:40:11	N ROGERS	3:40:39	C DOWD	3:41:13
88	G FERGUSON	3:39:18	J THOMPSON	3:39:47	D INETT	3:40:11	W LEWIS	3:40:40	P SLATER	3:41:13
89	P TACCONI	3:39:18	A MARSHALL	3:39:48	D GRUENEBERG	3:40:11	M UPTON	3:40:40	B DIXON	3:41:13
90	S BOSWELL	3:39:18	G GIAMPAOLI	3:39:48	M VINANTE	3:40:11	S TURNER	3:40:40	G COLLINS	3:41:13
91	T DARKE	3:39:19	R PICK	3:39:48	F FIELD	3:40:11	P ASLETT	3:40:41	A WATKINS	3:41:13
92	I DAVIS	3:39:19	G KATKOV	3:39:48	R BILLINGHURST	3:40:12	D AMOR	3:40:42	A DICKSON	3:41:13
93	J DICKENS	3:39:19	N WARD	3:39:49	A KEEN	3:40:12	J HORWOOD	3:40:43	B HALE	3:41:13
94	H GOLDSMITH	3:39:19	R ROBINSON	3:39:49	J LENTON	3:40:12	A SWAIN	3:40:43	S REYNOLDS	3:41:13
95	R GOULD	3:39:20	F BARFOOT	3:39:49	D COX	3:40:13	A GENT	3:40:43	C LARAMAN	3:41:14
96	R ADCOCK	3:39:20	R WOOD	3:39:49	M SMALL	3:40:13	A MORIS	3:40:44	R WARLEY	3:41:14
97	J READ	3:39:20	D MARDLE	3:39:49	I MATHEW	3:40:13	G HOOD	3:40:44	B COOK	3:41:14
98	J BRETHERTON	3:39:21	B ROBERTSON	3:39:49	W CABA	3:40:14	D JOHNSTON	3:40:45	D SHILLING	3:41:15
99	C BAKKER	3:39:21	M ORBAN	3:39:49	M TAGLIAVIA	3:40:14	A WIGHTMAN	3:40:46	I PUTMAN	3:41:16
100	G LOUVEL	3:39:21	M MASON	3:39:49	R JONES	3:40:14	A ORAM	3:40:46	E JOYCE	3:41:17

	8001-8100			8101-8200			8201-8300			8301-8400			8401-8500	
1	D WATSON	3:41:17	S BARNETT	3:41:43	S GRIFFITHS	3:42:16	J GOULDTHORPE	3:42:46	P STEVENS	3:43:13
2	K QUALMANN	3:41:17	A ESCOTT	3:41:43	M TANNER	3:42:16	D ARNOLD	3:42:46	B MANSELL	3:43:13
3	D BESSEAU	3:41:17	R MARTIN	3:41:43	B DAVIES	3:42:16	R BRITTON	3:42:46	H GUNDLACH	3:43:13
4	C BATES	3:41:18	E MC CREADIE	3:41:44	B LEONARD	3:42:17	M GADD	3:42:46	T OWEN	3:43:14
5	G GARSIDE	3:41:18	A LEGGETT	3:41:44	O RUDIG	3:42:17	J PIGGINS	3:42:47	V UWAERTS	3:43:14
6	J CAIRNS	3:41:18	P MAIN	3:41:45	B COSTIGAN	3:42:18	M LANDER	3:42:47	J SOUSTELLE	3:43:14
7	J DUNNAGE	3:41:18	P SMITH	3:41:46	J CURLEY	3:42:18	T COOPER	3:42:47	N JACKSON	3:43:14
8	A DAVIS	3:41:19	R BRAND	3:41:46	M RIDLEY	3:42:18	A ANDREWS	3:42:48	P HOUGH	3:43:14
9	H HOPWOOD	3:41:20	G TAYLOR	3:41:46	C REEVES	3:42:19	D HEATHFIELD	3:42:48	A WOODROW	3:43:15
10	D SCOTT	3:41:20	N BROOM	3:41:46	B REILHAC	3:42:19	C EDWARDS	3:42:48	M WEBSTER	3:43:15
11	P MCGOVERN	3:41:20	R PHILLIPS	3:41:46	A BUNTING	3:42:19	R WHEELER	3:42:48	P RYAN	3:43:15
12	D SHEPHERD	3:41:20	P MAIER	3:41:46	C WATSON	3:42:19	C TAYLOR	3:42:48	A ROLLINGS	3:43:15
13	G TIMMINS	3:41:20	R LUTOSCHKA	3:41:47	A SHIPMAN	3:42:20	D WALLER	3:42:49	K SMITH	3:43:15
14	G DAY	3:41:20	R HOLMES	3:41:47	M HOFFMAN	3:42:20	D SHOESMITH	3:42:49	C MAGEE	3:43:15
15	R GREZES	3:41:20	D KELLY	3:41:49	I TRUESDALE	3:42:20	R ASHCROFT	3:42:49	J PEACEY	3:43:15
16	R LOVER	3:41:20	P HOPGOOD	3:41:49	D THOMSON	3:42:20	D WOODHOUSE	3:42:50	A GRAHAM	3:43:15
17	I MALLEN	3:41:20	N EALAND	3:41:49	P LYON	3:42:20	T QUINN	3:42:50	P MARKHAM	3:43:16
18	R WILLIAMS	3:41:21	M CARRUTHERS	3:41:49	A PHILLIPS	3:42:20	F MULDOON	3:42:50	I MCKEE	3:43:16
19	J WILSON	3:41:21	R WOODRUFF	3:41:50	A ARCHER	3:42:20	N GIBBONS	3:42:50	A TEAGUE	3:43:16
20	B LAVAL-CHESTERTON	3:41:21	M FEENEY	3:41:50	D SEWELL	3:42:20	N MISON	3:42:52	W FIRESTONE	3:43:16
21	W BARTLETT	3:41:21	D DINGWALL	3:41:50	A HODGETTS	3:42:20	R SCOTT	3:42:52	G ELLIS	3:43:16
22	A WHITEHEAD	3:41:22	S FARMER	3:41:51	N WILLCOCKS	3:42:20	I MUNCASTER	3:42:52	A VALDES	3:43:17
23	T CHARLTON	3:41:22	K HULME	3:41:51	A CHANDLER	3:42:21	C HUME	3:42:53	G GOODWIN	3:43:17
24	A THOMAS	3:41:22	I WATSON	3:41:52	D DUFF	3:42:21	A THORNE	3:42:53	B HIGGINS	3:43:17
25	D HORSEMAN	3:41:22	G DAVIES	3:41:52	J JACKSON	3:42:21	N WESTROPE	3:42:54	S LYON	3:43:17
26	S MCGOWAN	3:41:22	K LISTER	3:41:52	A MUSSIL	3:42:22	M WHITE	3:42:54	L GRIFFITHS	3:43:18
27	J COOPER	3:41:22	J GRAHAM	3:41:53	M SOULAIMANI	3:42:22	K NEWNHAM	3:42:54	J JOYCE	3:43:18
28	J MARQUARDT	3:41:23	R CLOWES	3:41:54	C O'HANLON	3:42:23	M BODDY	3:42:54	G BURGIN	3:43:18
29	N JAMES	3:41:23	S QURESHI	3:41:54	S TAZI	3:42:23	W ZIEGLER	3:42:55	R REICHENBACH	3:43:18
30	M GAEHWILER	3:41:23	G ALTON	3:41:54	J CRAMPHORN	3:42:23	K FISKVIK	3:42:55	M GLENISTER	3:43:18
31	A NENO	3:41:23	G JOSEY	3:41:54	J DIAPER	3:42:24	J RICE	3:42:55	L THOMPSON	3:43:18
32	J BOLAND	3:41:23	A MCVEY	3:41:55	P BROWN	3:42:24	S AHLT	3:42:55	P STANBRIDGE	3:43:18
33	P JENNINGS	3:41:23	A PALLETT	3:41:55	M BROWN	3:42:24	J TAIT	3:42:56	S MURPHY	3:43:18
34	A CLARK	3:41:23	T EDWARDS	3:41:55	R BLENCOWE	3:42:25	R BLENCOWE	3:42:56	B ABBEY	3:43:19
35	P BECKWITH	3:41:24	G ROSS	3:41:56	J GABARRA	3:42:25	K ROBSON	3:42:57	J DORAN	3:43:19
36	K SHEIBANI	3:41:24	P STEWART	3:41:56	P BAKER	3:42:25	M SNORTUM	3:42:58	M TOMASSINI	3:43:20
37	D GOY	3:41:25	A ROWLAND	3:41:56	B HAFERBURG	3:42:26	G HICKEY	3:42:58	P DILLOW	3:43:20
38	R CLEMENTS	3:41:25	D SHAW	3:41:56	I POTTERTON	3:42:26	J EXLEY	3:42:58	M POULTON	3:43:20
39	H SCHRANK	3:41:25	H SAGE	3:41:56	A SHEPHERD	3:42:27	D LISTER	3:42:58	F LASSERRE	3:43:21
40	D PROCTOR	3:41:25	G VAN BEEK	3:41:59	S NORRIS	3:42:27	J PETTERSEN	3:42:58	S SNOOK	3:43:21
41	G PHILLIPS	3:41:25	I HOWELL	3:41:59	S SAVAGE	3:42:27	J HERRON	3:42:59	T PREUVENEERS	3:43:21
42	M RHODES	3:41:25	R STUART	3:41:59	C LIVINGSTONE	3:42:28	S FORTUNE	3:42:59	D HASTINGS	3:43:22
43	C GREGSON	3:41:26	S CLULEY	3:42:00	A STEELE	3:42:28	C JUDD	3:42:59	K HAZLETON	3:43:22
44	D WELFARE	3:41:26	A PRESS	3:42:01	R MAGUIRE	3:42:28	J BRIER	3:42:59	B ANDERSON	3:43:22
45	S ROBERTS	3:41:26	M BERRY	3:42:02	T WHYTE	3:42:28	D CHURCH	3:42:59	R CHUDLEY	3:43:22
46	R CLEGG	3:41:27	A BROOK	3:42:03	F DICKENSON	3:42:29	A STONEMAN	3:43:00	A WALLACE	3:43:23
47	D SCHONENBERG	3:41:28	P LOVICK	3:42:04	M HAMMOND	3:42:29	P WELBOURN	3:43:00	C TAN	3:43:23
48	L SCHULTE	3:41:28	G CESAREI	3:42:04	H ARMENGOD	3:42:29	R GARMAN	3:43:00	R GRAHAM	3:43:23
49	B WROE	3:41:29	A HOLDER	3:42:05	A SOLOMON	3:42:29	A CHALMERS	3:43:00	J SCARROTT	3:43:23
50	N HUGHES	3:41:29	N DOMINEY	3:42:05	H LIDDELL	3:42:29	J CHILDS	3:43:01	A WATKINSON	3:43:23
51	D WARDLE	3:41:29	D SNOW	3:42:05	P GRAFF	3:42:29	M WRIGHT	3:43:01	P BARKWAY	3:43:23
52	G SJOBERG	3:41:30	G ALLDAY	3:42:06	R KARIM	3:42:29	R KIRBY	3:43:01	P ABRAMI	3:43:24
53	K GYPPS	3:41:30	C HARRIS	3:42:06	P BROWNE	3:42:29	P NESBITT	3:43:01	N PONTING	3:43:24
54	A MARKUS	3:41:30	G BRADLEY	3:42:06	M PYE	3:42:30	T CALLALY	3:43:01	S KAPLAN	3:43:24
55	A TREVETT	3:41:30	S CROFTS	3:42:06	N HOWARD	3:42:30	F HALL	3:43:02	R WINE	3:43:24
56	D SCHOFIELD	3:41:30	B HATCH	3:42:06	M SMITH	3:42:30	S COOPER	3:43:02	P SUTTON	3:43:24
57	M WOODASON	3:41:30	S HOWELL	3:42:06	D COATES	3:42:31	A HILL	3:43:02	M STORRIE	3:43:24
58	D EARLY	3:41:31	J BROWN	3:42:06	A SANVOISIN	3:42:31	T MARTIN	3:43:03	R THOMPSON	3:43:24
59	P LAWSON	3:41:31	M JABERG	3:42:06	A WINN	3:42:31	K BENNETT	3:43:03	D WILLMOTT	3:43:25
60	P WALLACE	3:41:31	P PALMER	3:42:06	N MARCHANT	3:42:32	R GIRVAN	3:43:03	M MORDI	3:43:25
61	J BEST	3:41:31	R MEESON	3:42:07	P DEE-SHAPLAND	3:42:32	C SCOTT	3:43:03	M EATON	3:43:26
62	R VENN	3:41:32	J TAYLOR	3:42:07	W MCLELLAN	3:42:34	A STEWART	3:43:05	S MOLLOY	3:43:26
63	M WILSON	3:41:32	M NEVILLE	3:42:07	M WATSON	3:42:34	C ELLIOTT	3:43:05	S BETTS	3:43:26
64	R BACON	3:41:32	D WILLS	3:42:07	D RUSSELL	3:42:34	J HILLS	3:43:06	M BATTISTESSA	3:43:26
65	P SWINDELL	3:41:32	M WILLIAMSON	3:42:07	E COLON-RODRIQUEZ	3:42:35	A JONES	3:43:06	M KIRBY	3:43:26
66	E LEWIN	3:41:32	R HALL	3:42:07	A FORRESTER	3:42:35	S BUTCHER	3:43:06	S SALHA	3:43:27
67	G SIMMONDS	3:41:32	C ADCOCK	3:42:08	T HAINSBY	3:42:36	W WARD	3:43:07	J FLEMING	3:43:28
68	K GRONGSTAD	3:41:32	M CONNOLLY	3:42:08	R MCLACHLAN	3:42:36	A PHILLIPS	3:43:07	R FELTHAM	3:43:28
69	P NASH	3:41:33	B CRAMPHORN	3:42:08	R CARPENTER	3:42:36	M LARKIN	3:43:07	A HARKER	3:43:28
70	J FULBROOK	3:41:33	K RAO	3:42:08	P ANTONETTI	3:42:36	J PHIPPS	3:43:08	B BATHGATE	3:43:29
71	P JONES	3:41:33	M TODD	3:42:08	J MELIS	3:42:36	S HOSKIN	3:43:08	D TAYLOR	3:43:29
72	S WHITE	3:41:33	N NEWMAN	3:42:09	C WOODS	3:42:36	B JONES	3:43:08	T BROWN	3:43:30
73	J TEIXEIRA	3:41:33	E HOLLEY	3:42:09	M HUTTON	3:42:37	G ROBERTS	3:43:09	J COLLINS	3:43:32
74	I FERGUSON	3:41:33	R VETTER	3:42:09	G HOLMES	3:42:37	J MCCLURE	3:43:10	T HARKER	3:43:32
75	D MCROBB	3:41:33	N BEER	3:42:09	G ERIKSON	3:42:37	P TWYMAN	3:43:10	M SHEPPERSON	3:43:33
76	G DUNNE	3:41:33	A SPANGSGAARD	3:42:09	J LUZURIAGA YRIZAR	3:42:38	A WOOD	3:43:10	E HOLLIGER	3:43:33
77	H RUTTER	3:41:33	M PALLISGAARD	3:42:09	N CAUGHEY	3:42:38	S WHITWAM	3:43:10	M WARE	3:43:34
78	P SMYTH	3:41:34	A BELL	3:42:09	C ELLIS	3:42:38	D HANSON	3:43:10	J YUSUF	3:43:34
79	K TAYLOR	3:41:34	J NEAL	3:42:09	E CLIFFORD	3:42:39	D BENNET	3:43:10	J MORRIS	3:43:35
80	A TAYLOR	3:41:35	F ARNOTT	3:42:09	J JANSEM	3:42:39	K SIMPSON	3:43:10	P ADAMS	3:43:35
81	R GALLEY	3:41:35	S PRICE	3:42:09	J FORD	3:42:40	I SEWELL	3:43:10	R HILL	3:43:36
82	A ROBINSON	3:41:36	B HAMILTON	3:42:09	J O'DEA	3:42:40	O EIDE	3:43:10	P OAKLEY	3:43:37
83	M MCMAHON	3:41:36	J ROURKE	3:42:09	J ROBERTSON	3:42:40	D THOMAS	3:43:10	A NICHOLLS	3:43:37
84	S JEHU	3:41:36	I BRUCE	3:42:09	T GUY	3:42:40	P HUGHES-D'AETH	3:43:10	P FORDHAM	3:43:37
85	O STOPFORTH	3:41:36	K JONES	3:42:10	A EVANS	3:42:41	P DIGBY	3:43:10	R STRAPP	3:43:38
86	J HEIKES	3:41:37	A RICHARDSON	3:42:10	G MCCLURE	3:42:41	W ALLEN	3:43:10	J HARTEVELDT	3:43:38
87	W CROSSLAND	3:41:37	R WALDOCK	3:42:10	G BAYES	3:42:41	M HUSHER	3:43:10	C MUEHLHUBER	3:43:38
88	C DREW	3:41:37	J CLARKE	3:42:11	A CLAPOT	3:42:42	A HUGHES	3:43:10	D ROFFEY	3:43:39
89	P BURKE	3:41:37	D FRIEN	3:42:12	F WOODS	3:42:42	S MADELEY	3:43:11	M MACHIRAN	3:43:39
90	D KEYS	3:41:38	A ALCOCK	3:42:12	M CRAIG	3:42:43	N EVANS	3:43:11	D WITTICH	3:43:39
91	P JENKINS	3:41:39	C WHITE	3:42:13	A LLOYD	3:42:43	P COX	3:43:12	E BARNFATHER	3:43:39
92	K WRIGHT	3:41:39	S DODD	3:42:13	N GRAINGER	3:42:44	L LINDBJERG	3:43:12	B LEATHLEY	3:43:40
93	P HAMMOND	3:41:39	B JONES	3:42:13	M PADLEY	3:42:44	K OAKLEY	3:43:12	T LINGENS	3:43:40
94	M BENNETT	3:41:40	M ALLISON	3:42:14	M HARGADON	3:42:45	K BARNARD	3:43:13	H PAPACHRISTOS	3:43:40
95	J MCAUSLAN	3:41:40	C HOLDER	3:42:15	A DI BERNARDO	3:42:45	T WRAFTER	3:43:13	I HILL	3:43:40
96	J WILLARD	3:41:40	R GARRARD	3:42:15	A WOODWARD	3:42:45	D CULLEN	3:43:13	E FREIJSEN	3:43:40
97	R ANDERSSON	3:41:41	J MACGREGOR	3:42:15	S HULM	3:42:45	S HULCOOP	3:43:13	R EDDE	3:43:40
98	F HARRINGTON	3:41:42	S LITTLECOTT	3:42:15	W CUNNINGHAM	3:42:45	R CRITTENDEN	3:43:13	H UNGER	3:43:41
99	I ROSE	3:41:42	M BRAZIER	3:42:15	D RAYNES	3:42:46	W MCLEAN	3:43:13	K HARRIS	3:43:41
100	F BURGER	3:41:43	A COUSINS	3:42:16	J WRIGHT	3:42:46	M AHNIEN	3:43:13	T MILLS	3:43:42

#	8501-8600		8601-8700		8701-8800		8801-8900		8901-9000	
1	S KHAN	3:43:42	N FOLBIGG	3:44:05	D HODGSON	3:44:29	D MERRITT	3:44:56	E NORTH	3:45:23
2	C COX	3:43:42	N WOLLISCROFT	3:44:06	J BROOK	3:44:30	I BARNETT	3:44:56	J MARTIN	3:45:24
3	W BURNS III	3:43:43	L LEWIS	3:44:07	K MARKEY	3:44:30	J GARCIA	3:44:56	J COLLINS	3:45:24
4	C DEANE	3:43:43	P FENCOTT	3:44:07	G CASEY	3:44:30	J PETTITT	3:44:57	B FLANNERY	3:45:24
5	G HALL	3:43:43	C PHILLIPS	3:44:07	A CURTET	3:44:30	A COLE	3:44:57	G BINNEY	3:45:25
6	F BENTHEM	3:43:43	S PRICE	3:44:07	J CHILDS	3:44:31	K COOKE	3:44:57	H VIK-MO	3:45:25
7	I SMITH	3:43:44	R WHEATLAND	3:44:09	P WHARTON	3:44:31	A MARSDEN	3:44:57	J RAINS	3:45:25
8	F INGRAM	3:43:44	A GIBB	3:44:09	P BESWICK	3:44:32	M LEDDEN	3:44:57	J CALLAWAY	3:45:26
9	J DUCAT	3:43:44	W BRIERLY	3:44:10	S BECKWITH	3:44:32	R METCALF	3:44:58	A EVANS	3:45:26
10	R MCFADDEN	3:43:45	A VECCHIE	3:44:10	R BAKER	3:44:33	G HUGHES	3:44:58	D ANDERSON	3:45:27
11	G LLOYD	3:43:45	J PICKSTONE	3:44:10	H HARRIS	3:44:33	T TESCH	3:44:59	L MILLS	3:45:27
12	C WILLIAMS	3:43:45	P WILSON	3:44:10	C SMITH	3:44:33	K LOTHAR	3:44:59	A JONES	3:45:27
13	F LAMERTON	3:43:46	T JONES	3:44:11	F HELAS	3:44:34	T BROOKS	3:44:59	J MIRFIN	3:45:27
14	D STATON	3:43:46	R BROWN	3:44:11	E RATHBONE	3:44:34	G ODONNELL	3:45:00	S AGUILAR	3:45:28
15	D RAESIDE	3:43:46	J PATAKY	3:44:11	D LEVERETT	3:44:34	C BOULTER	3:45:00	E BOLTON	3:45:28
16	N GORMAN	3:43:47	N MEEHAN	3:44:11	R GIBBS	3:44:34	A SMYTH	3:45:00	S SALMON	3:45:29
17	A BLACKMORE	3:43:47	K DIPLCOK	3:44:12	R STONE	3:44:35	V TESTER	3:45:01	H KHAIHRA	3:45:29
18	A LANGLET	3:43:47	A SMITH	3:44:13	P STANSBY	3:44:35	S FARROW	3:45:01	A BOGGIS	3:45:30
19	R ALLEN	3:43:47	K BEGGS	3:44:14	M DONNELLY-GODWIN	3:44:35	G PRICE	3:45:02	C HARWOOD	3:45:30
20	R HAMMERSLEY	3:43:47	A COOK	3:44:14	I FREEMAN	3:44:35	J WAKELY	3:45:02	D CHURCHUS	3:45:30
21	A MOUSSI	3:43:47	J SENAUD	3:44:15	J DRURY	3:44:36	A MERRITT	3:45:03	E BUGBY	3:45:31
22	D CARR	3:43:47	M KENNEDY	3:44:16	M RANSLEY	3:44:36	R SUBDEN	3:45:04	N CRITCHELL	3:45:31
23	A JONES	3:43:48	H COATES	3:44:16	T EDMONDS	3:44:37	C ANDREW	3:45:05	G WILLIAMS	3:45:31
24	J ANTOS	3:43:48	S BRICE	3:44:16	T WEBB	3:44:37	J HIBBERD	3:45:05	G LOVELL	3:45:31
25	R GILLESPIE	3:43:49	J MAGET	3:44:16	J COOKSLEY	3:44:37	P SHARPE	3:45:05	V GOODWIN	3:45:33
26	G WATTON	3:43:49	J WARRY	3:44:16	A MARTIN	3:44:38	T BRISLEY	3:45:05	P SAMPSON	3:45:33
27	S WILLIAMS	3:43:49	M DE-ATM	3:44:16	J MATTHEWS	3:44:38	P ALDRIDGE	3:45:06	A AFONSO	3:45:34
28	R MEHRA	3:43:49	D SHARPE	3:44:16	G BARNES	3:44:38	A ALSOP	3:45:06	W SNELL	3:45:34
29	N HESEY	3:43:50	S NICOL	3:44:16	M COOK	3:44:38	L JAMES	3:45:06	A OGDEN	3:45:34
30	I BUSSELL	3:43:50	R REYNOLDS	3:44:17	S COATES	3:44:39	I MARTIN	3:45:07	I SHORT	3:45:34
31	A TRAVIS	3:43:50	M TROY	3:44:17	L PARTON	3:44:39	M TROUGHTON	3:45:09	C PARKER	3:45:35
32	C COOMBER	3:43:50	M FAWCETT	3:44:17	L VOICE	3:44:39	A BANKS	3:45:09	A RIMMER	3:45:36
33	E ASHTON	3:43:50	R REINERT	3:44:17	K COLVER	3:44:39	C WARD	3:45:09	H MATHESON	3:45:36
34	P WHITEHEAD	3:43:50	C WILSON	3:44:17	M CLEARY	3:44:41	C CULLEY	3:45:10	J HOLDWAY	3:45:36
35	J PENHALIGON	3:43:50	L BREITFELD	3:44:17	R BELBIN	3:44:41	G SYMONS	3:45:10	D SAYER	3:45:36
36	P SOLOMONS	3:43:51	E YANO	3:44:17	L BROWN	3:44:41	D MINDEN	3:45:10	G HOLLAND	3:45:36
37	M FREEMAN	3:43:51	M CLOLUS	3:44:17	P OSBORNE	3:44:42	J INGLEDEW	3:45:11	J MCINTYRE	3:45:36
38	M UTULAHTI	3:43:51	B ARKELL	3:44:18	M FIDDIMORE	3:44:42	C DYER	3:45:11	S FREEMAN	3:45:36
39	A WALDRON	3:43:51	N BRAMALL	3:44:18	C SMITH	3:44:42	M HALLIDAY	3:45:11	J WELLS	3:45:36
40	M BEHR	3:43:51	K MCNAMEE	3:44:18	J PLOMMER	3:44:42	M BIRRELL	3:45:11	D SIMMONS	3:45:36
41	K STEEN	3:43:51	W LAWLEY	3:44:19	K DAVIES	3:44:43	P CATTERALL	3:45:11	O DENIAUX	3:45:36
42	J MCDONNELL	3:43:51	H HAUMANN	3:44:19	A MOFFAT	3:44:43	D SHARPE	3:45:12	R WHALEY	3:45:36
43	P SARNEY	3:43:52	D TOSELAND	3:44:19	S HINKS	3:44:43	P ACKERS	3:45:12	J MORELL	3:45:36
44	J MORENO-SANCHEZ	3:43:53	P FOLTETE	3:44:19	R PECK	3:44:44	C PAOLILLO	3:45:12	C SWEEPER	3:45:36
45	D LAMPARAS	3:43:53	G SOMLO	3:44:19	J LITTLE	3:44:44	J FERGUSON	3:45:13	C HIRST	3:45:37
46	R GOSS	3:43:54	S MOORE	3:44:20	C HUTCHESON	3:44:44	J DUMAS	3:45:13	P HAYWARD	3:45:37
47	E MAY	3:43:55	R LEE	3:44:20	R WALWYN	3:44:44	R BARNES	3:45:13	S WAKEMAN	3:45:38
48	J DAHLGREN	3:43:55	A LEVER	3:44:20	P GARLICK	3:44:45	C LEPREUX	3:45:14	R STUBBINGS	3:45:38
49	C BOWRING	3:43:55	M HAIGH	3:44:20	J WRIGHT	3:44:45	D JONKERS	3:45:14	R WATKINS	3:45:38
50	K WURM	3:43:55	E MARJORAM	3:44:20	J MACMILLAN	3:44:45	D GOULD	3:45:14	R HEATON	3:45:39
51	P FORD	3:43:56	M PEARCE	3:44:20	R ECKERSLEY	3:44:45	S EASON	3:45:15	P WHITE	3:45:39
52	M PARKIN	3:43:56	H CATLING	3:44:21	M MATTHIAS	3:44:45	M ROGERS	3:45:15	E HUDSON	3:45:41
53	T KEELEY	3:43:56	J ABBEY	3:44:21	C VOSPER	3:44:46	L FONTANGE	3:45:15	B NORRIS	3:45:41
54	M DELAHAYE	3:43:56	L NOKE	3:44:21	D HAYNES	3:44:46	S HULL	3:45:15	J BUDIRO	3:45:42
55	D DOWLING	3:43:56	J OGG	3:44:21	J ENSING	3:44:46	S RADFORD	3:45:15	D MARSTON	3:45:42
56	P TETSTALL	3:43:56	S WOOD	3:44:21	K GOOCH	3:44:47	P SWINDALE	3:45:15	J DAVIES	3:45:42
57	T KOTSCH	3:43:56	D INGRAM	3:44:21	S GRANT	3:44:47	J HILLIARD	3:45:15	E JOERGENSEN	3:45:44
58	A CIOLKOVITCH	3:43:57	J CAIN	3:44:21	P BEDFORD	3:44:47	J GREENFIELD	3:45:15	W BOWERS	3:45:44
59	W DINEEN	3:43:57	C FIRMIN	3:44:21	R REEVES	3:44:47	B PRISSMAN	3:45:15	B SMITH	3:45:44
60	G DAVIES	3:43:57	J OSBORNE	3:44:21	N SMITH	3:44:47	C CALCATELLI	3:45:15	D BURY	3:45:45
61	M SHINER	3:43:57	R HEDDERMAN	3:44:21	S MAINS	3:44:48	E PORCILE	3:45:15	G CRISTILLI	3:45:46
62	J DRAPER	3:43:58	C SYKES	3:44:21	G STANFORD	3:44:48	A MACKNESS	3:45:15	M POWELL	3:45:46
63	S PHILLIPS	3:43:58	D PUGH	3:44:21	C ECCLESTONE	3:44:49	M SALTER	3:45:15	M KJORUM	3:45:46
64	K HOARE	3:43:58	M SALIH	3:44:21	C WILLIAMS	3:44:49	M POAD	3:45:15	M FORNASARI	3:45:46
65	K TAYLOR	3:43:58	J JACKSON	3:44:22	A MORRIS	3:44:49	H MORRISON	3:45:15	M KNIGHT	3:45:46
66	M DIXON	3:43:59	S ROBINSON	3:44:22	J YOUNG	3:44:49	H RAYNHAM	3:45:15	E LOPEZ	3:45:46
67	T WINFIELD	3:43:59	D PATEL	3:44:22	S BODARE	3:44:49	E BRADSHAW	3:45:15	M MILLIES	3:45:47
68	R WISDOM	3:43:59	G HILTON	3:44:22	G BARLAFANTE	3:44:50	D MANNING	3:45:15	K CRAMPTON	3:45:47
69	R HARDY	3:43:59	A ADDRISON	3:44:22	M DEVONSHIRE	3:44:50	A MCEVOY	3:45:16	A LEE	3:45:47
70	A STOREY	3:43:59	J HAMILTON	3:44:23	K BRUSHETT	3:44:50	T BEEDLE	3:45:16	R IVESON	3:45:48
71	D IRILLI	3:43:59	M HOOK	3:44:23	P PRICE	3:44:51	G ARNOLD	3:45:17	S WHITEHEAD	3:45:48
72	J DAVIDSON	3:44:00	J TEE	3:44:23	D DIMSEY	3:44:51	C GREENWOOD	3:45:17	I CAMPBELL	3:45:48
73	J GWATKIN	3:44:00	M CORBETT	3:44:23	H HIELDS	3:44:51	A LEHMANN	3:45:17	J WILKINSON	3:45:48
74	J JOHNSON	3:44:00	J HALLIDAY	3:44:23	L HILL	3:44:51	F TAMLYN	3:45:17	C LINDSEY	3:45:49
75	B MUELLER	3:44:00	A BOWMAN	3:44:23	M WISDOM	3:44:51	M SADLER	3:45:17	D WHITELEY	3:45:49
76	T BOOKER	3:44:00	R GRAHAM	3:44:23	M BAILEY	3:44:51	E WOODRUFF	3:45:17	M PAUL	3:45:49
77	B NORRIS	3:44:01	R SHARP	3:44:24	A BECKER	3:44:52	E MCCALL	3:45:17	K TAKKINEN	3:45:50
78	D NELSON	3:44:01	A ELIAS	3:44:24	A GEE	3:44:52	C DARKIN	3:45:17	S BAYNE	3:45:50
79	W BEWG	3:44:01	I BROWN	3:44:24	L HAYLES	3:44:52	J BEER	3:45:17	J HAMILTON	3:45:50
80	R MOIR	3:44:01	S BERESFORD-WEBB	3:44:25	Y GARRIGUE	3:44:52	G THOMSON	3:45:17	K RILEY	3:45:50
81	L WHITE	3:44:01	E JANSEN	3:44:25	L SHORT	3:44:52	S VERSCHOOR	3:45:18	C DELEDGAR ST CLAIRE	3:45:50
82	J MUSGROVE	3:44:01	R THOMAS	3:44:25	M HEAL	3:44:52	B CHAMPNESS	3:45:18	L CAZZATA	3:45:51
83	G FORP	3:44:01	D LEE	3:44:25	D JONES	3:44:52	D PARSONS	3:45:18	P CORRINGHAM	3:45:51
84	D PAY	3:44:02	N BALES	3:44:26	M WADDELL	3:44:52	J O'LEARY	3:45:19	C THOMAS	3:45:51
85	R MCPHILLIPS	3:44:02	M PASCUZZI	3:44:26	R MITCHELL	3:44:52	M CHAPMAN	3:45:19	P THOMAS	3:45:52
86	P BAILEY	3:44:02	J CARLEY	3:44:27	J KIPPS	3:44:52	S PIMM	3:45:19	B HALSEY	3:45:52
87	P AINSLEY	3:44:02	M CLAY	3:44:27	S BARRY	3:44:53	J SMITH	3:45:19	B WHORLOW	3:45:52
88	J ROSSI	3:44:02	B HUMBLE	3:44:27	B CLAYSON	3:44:53	G MILLS	3:45:19	N CASS	3:45:52
89	J LAVERY	3:44:02	P CHAMPKEN	3:44:27	P COONEY	3:44:53	R CHAPMAN	3:45:20	G PAGE	3:45:52
90	J RAUNSBAEK	3:44:02	D SCOTT	3:44:28	P JONES	3:44:53	W ROUTLEDGE	3:45:20	H CASALLAS	3:45:53
91	S WRIGHT	3:44:02	G SHARMAN	3:44:28	Y DUBOT	3:44:53	J MOESTERMANS	3:45:21	P YORE	3:45:53
92	M LOVE	3:44:03	J MOORE	3:44:28	C COVE	3:44:54	P ROCHE	3:45:21	J SINGLEHURST	3:45:54
93	R GRAY	3:44:03	C CAWTHORN	3:44:29	J RYDER-JONES	3:44:54	S SLATER	3:45:22	K MATTHEWS	3:45:54
94	G LOCKTON	3:44:03	S RAWLINGS	3:44:29	T LASTRA	3:44:54	H MORRIS	3:45:22	G ALMOND	3:45:55
95	D TOOTH	3:44:04	S SWIFT	3:44:29	G HIRSCH	3:44:54	J FENTON	3:45:22	W BLAIN	3:45:56
96	J FOULDS	3:44:04	C MILLER	3:44:29	S WHITMORE	3:44:54	S HOWELL	3:45:22	D BAILEY	3:45:56
97	G LANE FOX	3:44:04	A CAMPBELL	3:44:29	J ROBINSON	3:44:54	G STAMMERS	3:45:23	K MOEN	3:45:56
98	R MICHIE	3:44:05	G HAMILTON	3:44:29	C STANLEY	3:44:55	P STUBBS	3:45:23	H PARR	3:45:57
99	S PERRY	3:44:05	P LEWSEY	3:44:29	A MEEK	3:44:56	T EDMONDSON	3:45:23	A HALLICHE	3:45:57
100	G NUNN	3:44:05	C WRIGLEY	3:44:29	D HAMBLY	3:44:56	S ASHLEY	3:45:23	E FOXLEY	3:45:58

#	9001-9100		9101-9200		9201-9300		9301-9400		9401-9500	
1	P CHILDS	3:45:59	C BLACHERE	3:46:24	P CRITCHLEY	3:46:47	A COLE	3:47:19	P HALL	3:47:40
2	K CALCUTT	3:46:00	J TERRY	3:46:24	N COPPING	3:46:47	S NARDI	3:47:19	S DANIELS	3:47:40
3	J KNOWLES	3:46:00	S DOYLE	3:46:24	E OSBORNE	3:46:48	P DUFTON	3:47:19	B BALDWIN	3:47:40
4	R BEALES	3:46:00	J SCOTT	3:46:24	D LUPTON	3:46:48	A EATON	3:47:19	D BALL	3:47:40
5	Q HOWES	3:46:00	J LARSSON	3:46:24	K MEISTER	3:46:49	M DANGEUL	3:47:19	P COTTERELL	3:47:41
6	N MILNE HOME	3:46:01	G BERRY	3:46:24	C CHURCHER	3:46:49	S FORAN	3:47:20	S BOWD	3:47:41
7	D SINGER	3:46:01	E PARKER	3:46:24	H PETERS	3:46:49	J STOELKER	3:47:20	K VEJDANI	3:47:41
8	L CARTER	3:46:01	L BROWN	3:46:24	D MUTTER	3:46:49	N SMITH	3:47:20	P PASSELEGUE	3:47:41
9	I GOULDING	3:46:02	M RIDLEY	3:46:24	J PARKINSON	3:46:50	C HUGHES	3:47:20	K JONES	3:47:41
10	D MARGETTS	3:46:03	C LAURENT	3:46:24	G ERMISZ	3:46:51	P RENAUD	3:47:20	T NIELSEN	3:47:41
11	K FULKER	3:46:03	J MICALLEF	3:46:24	J MARK	3:46:51	S FYFFE	3:47:20	J GRIFFITH	3:47:42
12	C EDWARDS	3:46:03	S GRANHOLM	3:46:24	P BOYNES	3:46:52	P HAMER	3:47:20	W ROFFEY	3:47:42
13	G CASTELEIRO	3:46:03	P MURRAY	3:46:24	J PARKER	3:46:52	M MULLIER	3:47:20	A TAYLOR	3:47:42
14	C GIBBONS	3:46:03	R UNSWORTH	3:46:24	K MOLINEUX	3:46:53	P ALMOND	3:47:21	A CALERWOOD	3:47:43
15	C OTTERPOHL	3:46:03	C HALLIDAY	3:46:25	S LLOYD	3:46:54	A KERR	3:47:21	M OUTRAM	3:47:43
16	S YATES	3:46:03	A POZONIO	3:46:25	G ERICSSON	3:46:54	J HARLEY	3:47:21	A ORLANDO	3:47:43
17	C HARDING	3:46:04	M AFIA	3:46:25	M BRACE	3:46:54	I MACFARLANE	3:47:21	C STEPHENSON	3:47:43
18	D DANIEL	3:46:04	J CLAUSEN	3:46:25	K MILLS	3:46:55	T KING	3:47:22	D SAUNDERS	3:47:44
19	J HAMON	3:46:04	B O'FLYNN	3:46:25	P MCGROTTY	3:46:55	P LONGMORE	3:47:22	N TAYLOR	3:47:44
20	P HAMMOND	3:46:04	L MURRAY	3:46:25	M HEMMING	3:46:57	A RUSSELL	3:47:22	J LERICHE	3:47:44
21	O LONG	3:46:04	R GOODACRE	3:46:26	M DALEY	3:46:57	A STACKIEWICZ	3:47:22	B FUGISTIER	3:47:45
22	S WEBSTER	3:46:04	L SUNDGREN	3:46:26	S DAWE	3:46:57	N THOMAS	3:47:23	M ASSORATI	3:47:46
23	J TOPPING	3:46:04	P DE JONGHE	3:46:26	P CUNNIFFE	3:46:58	S ALLEN	3:47:23	P SAMPEY	3:47:47
24	D GOURLEY	3:46:04	N STODDART	3:46:27	A BENGTSON	3:46:59	C MARKHAM	3:47:23	B SHOULER	3:47:47
25	M BRADY	3:46:04	K SCRIVENER	3:46:28	C HAXBY	3:46:59	N MAIDMENT	3:47:23	C JONES	3:47:47
26	B CZEPULKOWSKI	3:46:04	A NORMAN	3:46:28	H OAKES	3:46:59	N BEST	3:47:24	K ROBINSON	3:47:48
27	G O'HANLON	3:46:04	C DODD	3:46:28	M BARROWMAN	3:46:59	M RIMMER	3:47:24	R MOAT	3:47:48
28	R SMITH	3:46:05	S CROFT	3:46:29	G JONES	3:47:00	C HOARE	3:47:24	P ROSE	3:47:48
29	P WESTLAND	3:46:05	P KELLY	3:46:29	J SPEAKMAN	3:47:00	V ROBINSON	3:47:24	D STOREY	3:47:49
30	A BARTON	3:46:05	S PLUMB	3:46:29	J HOLLAND	3:47:00	M TRACEY	3:47:25	J HAMMOND	3:47:49
31	R BROWN	3:46:05	S SMITH	3:46:30	F BARCELLONA	3:47:00	L HATTON-RADFORD	3:47:25	A JONES	3:47:49
32	K FROST	3:46:05	M MANFREDONIA	3:46:30	M TOVO	3:47:00	L TURPIN	3:47:25	C HIZETTE	3:47:49
33	M LINLEY	3:46:05	S MANES	3:46:30	M SADLER	3:47:00	D MINIHANE	3:47:25	G HUNTER	3:47:49
34	D SANDERSON	3:46:06	R GORMAN	3:46:31	S GARRY	3:47:00	J BOSTOCK	3:47:27	K MASON	3:47:50
35	P COZZI	3:46:06	R WILBERT	3:46:31	B HOWES	3:47:01	M SWARBRICK	3:47:27	G PARTRIDGE	3:47:50
36	D RAWLINGS	3:46:06	R GARVIN	3:46:31	S BARTON	3:47:01	L CULLEN	3:47:28	R LAMBERT	3:47:50
37	P TORRE	3:46:06	J AYSHFORD	3:46:32	A JEAL	3:47:01	C HALL	3:47:28	P DE'ATH	3:47:50
38	P BRUINENBERG	3:46:07	S CALVERT	3:46:32	P WHITE	3:47:01	D BERRY	3:47:28	T TOMLIN	3:47:51
39	P BENNETT	3:46:07	R BORDINI	3:46:32	D BAER	3:47:01	M NEWLAND	3:47:29	N CHISHOLM	3:47:51
40	A HARRISON	3:46:07	N AMES	3:46:32	J CHAPPELL	3:47:01	G BROOKS	3:47:30	A SORDI	3:47:51
41	T RYAN	3:46:07	N COLVERSON	3:46:32	A SELDEN	3:47:01	S SKELTON	3:47:30	D EVANS	3:47:51
42	M BOND	3:46:07	J BEAL	3:46:33	M CORBETT	3:47:02	G VESTEY	3:47:30	P MAXWELL	3:47:52
43	A LINTERN	3:46:07	I RAYNER	3:46:33	P BLAND	3:47:02	M WILKINS	3:47:30	K COLLIER BAKER	3:47:52
44	H VINCENT	3:46:07	D MASTERS	3:46:33	I MIDDLETON	3:47:02	P RODWELL	3:47:31	C RICHARDSON	3:47:52
45	R ATTI	3:46:07	J TODD	3:46:33	M MCHUGH	3:47:02	D CHAPMAN	3:47:31	P MARKS	3:47:52
46	D AUSTIN	3:46:07	D COLE	3:46:33	M REGAN	3:47:03	T STEWART	3:47:32	D JOHNS	3:47:52
47	D FISHER	3:46:07	T GILMOUR	3:46:33	G ROBERTS	3:47:03	J STREETER	3:47:32	S DOHERTY	3:47:52
48	S HARMAN	3:46:07	P VAUGHAN	3:46:33	A BROWN	3:47:03	G BRIAULT	3:47:32	G BEAUMONT	3:47:52
49	M BROWN	3:46:07	M MANN-HEATLEY	3:46:33	B MCCREADIE	3:47:04	M LONGSTAFF	3:47:32	C TALLENT	3:47:53
50	S FACCHINI	3:46:07	N ROSS	3:46:33	S FOGELSTROM	3:47:04	L GARROD	3:47:32	K WILLIAMS	3:47:53
51	S WELLS	3:46:07	T MCKAY	3:46:33	S MOORE	3:47:04	K LOWDE	3:47:32	R GEORGE	3:47:53
52	A JONES	3:46:08	D MILNER	3:46:34	B BROWN	3:47:04	D TINGLE	3:47:32	T APPS	3:47:53
53	J PRINGLE	3:46:08	R HINKLY	3:46:34	E STAUNTON	3:47:05	S WHITESIDE	3:47:33	B QUANT	3:47:53
54	I MOORE	3:46:08	T PEREGO	3:46:34	T RAVEN	3:47:06	P LEESON	3:47:33	S ALLEN	3:47:53
55	P WEBB	3:46:08	D BOYDEN	3:46:34	T MOCKRIDGE	3:47:08	A PRINCE	3:47:33	R SISK	3:47:53
56	R TAYLOR	3:46:09	C EMBERSON	3:46:34	P PORTLOCK	3:47:09	R CAPE	3:47:33	G GWYTHER	3:47:53
57	D WILLOUGHBY	3:46:09	S HEDLEY	3:46:34	S EVERED	3:47:09	A MCGROARTY	3:47:34	P SUTTON	3:47:53
58	V GIBBONS	3:46:09	P GUIHEN	3:46:34	M KALISCH	3:47:10	T GERAGHTY	3:47:34	S DUNN	3:47:53
59	P BIRD	3:46:10	T HASSAN-HICKS	3:46:34	R LEDGER	3:47:10	P HARLEY	3:47:34	J COUSINS	3:47:53
60	Y CHARPIOT	3:46:10	E RENTON	3:46:35	J EVANS	3:47:10	W LUTHER	3:47:34	M CHANTLER	3:47:54
61	A CHIRKOV	3:46:10	S HOUSDEN	3:46:35	P LECAVALIER	3:47:11	C DURY	3:47:35	D MILLGATE	3:47:55
62	G CATLIN	3:46:10	N GRONGSTAD	3:46:35	M PRICE	3:47:11	T THOMPSON	3:47:35	H MEYER	3:47:55
63	P HARVEY	3:46:11	K KANKARE	3:46:35	E CHANTREL	3:47:11	K DU MAIRE	3:47:35	D NASH	3:47:56
64	J GILLIES	3:46:11	P GARDINER	3:46:35	K SMITH	3:47:11	A CHURCH	3:47:35	R HODGE	3:47:56
65	T TIMS	3:46:11	K MAHONEY	3:46:35	S ROGERS	3:47:12	W DUTSCHKE	3:47:35	P WICKMAN	3:47:56
66	B FINCH	3:46:12	S ROBERTS	3:46:36	A HUWS	3:47:12	M BEST	3:47:35	E WOODS	3:47:57
67	I AYRES	3:46:12	D MACKLIN	3:46:36	T HAGAN	3:47:12	L IRWIN	3:47:35	T STEELE	3:47:57
68	B WHITHAM	3:46:12	P NICHOLS	3:46:36	C BROWN	3:47:12	A EDWARDS	3:47:35	M WATSON	3:47:57
69	G LLOYD	3:46:12	A CHALLACOMBE	3:46:36	D TAYLOR	3:47:12	M RAIMBAULT	3:47:35	A COLLINS	3:47:57
70	D CONDON	3:46:12	D BURNS	3:46:37	J BULL	3:47:12	E POOLE	3:47:36	S COOPER	3:47:58
71	M WAKERELL	3:46:13	T STEVENS	3:46:37	L DANIELSSON	3:47:12	R LEVY	3:47:37	D TURLAND	3:47:58
72	D GRIFFITHS	3:46:13	K SHANKS	3:46:37	N CHAPMAN	3:47:12	G WHITE	3:47:38	E MASON	3:47:58
73	D SCHOLAERT	3:46:14	C GURNEY	3:46:38	L STEINPRESS	3:47:12	J CLARKE	3:47:38	A HODD	3:47:59
74	R MILNE	3:46:14	M BADALE	3:46:38	J RIDCUN	3:47:12	P HARDMAN	3:47:38	G HODGSON	3:47:59
75	R HORTON	3:46:15	R CROUCH	3:46:38	A ELBOURNE	3:47:13	P PORTER	3:47:38	T PROBETS	3:47:59
76	D MOEGLIN	3:46:15	C EDGE	3:46:38	B HUDSON	3:47:13	S HANNAN	3:47:38	K FROSTICK	3:47:59
77	G HOYLAND	3:46:16	P MOORE	3:46:39	G ARTINO	3:47:13	J HUSTWAIT	3:47:38	D FLAHEY	3:47:59
78	K MUREZ	3:46:17	L DONKIN	3:46:39	L MAYO	3:47:13	M ATKINSON	3:47:38	J HAYTREE	3:47:59
79	E OLESEN	3:46:17	T PEARCE	3:46:39	G WEST	3:47:14	S SZAPPANOS	3:47:38	W HUTCHINSON	3:48:00
80	C SCOTT	3:46:17	T SKRETTING	3:46:40	M ROBERTS	3:47:14	J AINDOW	3:47:38	D ORMAN	3:48:00
81	M DELPY	3:46:17	B GRAY	3:46:40	K WALLIS	3:47:14	S CHENG	3:47:38	P GAEHWILER	3:48:00
82	H WILLIAMS	3:46:18	H MITCHELL	3:46:41	R DYER	3:47:14	S BARKER	3:47:38	P REILLY	3:48:01
83	M REGAN	3:46:18	S VAN SCHUERBEEK	3:46:41	M MISSELBROOK	3:47:14	R ALLISON	3:47:38	D HEPWORTH	3:48:01
84	T HARRISON	3:46:19	G REDHABER	3:46:42	R GILBERT	3:47:15	T CUDMORE	3:47:38	D PETERS	3:48:01
85	C AUSTIN	3:46:19	D LUDBROOK	3:46:42	C CHATWIN	3:47:16	K READ	3:47:38	C BAILEY-HAGUE	3:48:02
86	D WALTERS	3:46:21	H BORGMANN	3:46:43	E WILSON	3:47:16	R MCDONALD	3:47:38	D HAMMOND	3:48:02
87	N GROVER	3:46:21	S BURTON	3:46:43	M BROWN	3:47:16	K CHANTER	3:47:38	A JOMES	3:48:04
88	L BLACKBURN	3:46:22	R ARMSTRONG	3:46:43	E WILSON	3:47:17	B SMITH	3:47:38	C NORMAN	3:48:04
89	B ROBERTS	3:46:23	G PRATT	3:46:43	A FOWLIE	3:47:17	J MILLER	3:47:38	R JONES	3:48:04
90	A BARNETT	3:46:23	C RAWLINS	3:46:43	W NEILL	3:47:17	F RASMUSSEN	3:47:38	A TAYLOR	3:48:05
91	R DOYLE	3:46:23	R JAMES	3:46:44	M BETTS	3:47:17	C JORGENSEN	3:47:38	A GAULD-CLARK	3:48:05
92	M CARNEY	3:46:24	T GABRIELLI	3:46:44	A PENDROUS	3:47:18	A PALMER	3:47:38	N MOLYNEUX	3:48:06
93	J HALL	3:46:24	S HAINES	3:46:44	R STAPLETON	3:47:18	M MURPHY	3:47:38	K WRIGHT	3:48:07
94	D GREEN	3:46:24	D GUNNER	3:46:45	C LANE	3:47:18	P CLARKE	3:47:38	D EDWARDS	3:48:07
95	R DAVIS	3:46:24	S LYNCH	3:46:45	P RUCK	3:47:18	D CARTER	3:47:38	G OCCHIOBELLO	3:48:08
96	P BUGDEN	3:46:24	A GLAISTER	3:46:46	A REEVE	3:47:18	T MAGUIRE	3:47:38	S WEEDEN	3:48:08
97	R MONEY-WYRLE	3:46:24	H KARLSSON	3:46:46	B RUSSE	3:47:19	I TANIUCHI	3:47:39	P O DONOHUE	3:48:08
98	S LEE	3:46:24	D MARTELL	3:46:46	A SHERWIN	3:47:19	R GROOM	3:47:39	P THORNTON	3:48:09
99	B VAN DER HELM	3:46:24	S POPE	3:46:46	A REDMOND	3:47:19	S GREER	3:47:39	R WOODALL	3:48:09
100	S MCGRATH	3:46:24	G MIFSUD	3:46:47	A REDMOND	3:47:19	J DUPRAS	3:47:40	M ATKINSON	3:48:09

#	Name	Time	Name	Time	Name	Time	Name	Time	Name	Time
1	J DAVIES	3:48:10	L OWEN	3:48:42	P DUNPHY	3:49:12	A DE FAZI	3:49:46	S OSMAN	3:50:13
2	R OLHS	3:48:11	J SNYMAN	3:48:43	K DUFFY	3:49:12	N DEANS	3:49:46	A LAGER	3:50:14
3	M COOKE	3:48:11	G NEAL	3:48:44	A WILSON	3:49:12	P HATFIELD	3:49:47	D CURTIS	3:50:14
4	P CROSS	3:48:12	R BYRON	3:48:44	P HINGLEY	3:49:12	P NEZAN	3:49:47	J ROCHAT	3:50:14
5	N HOOPER	3:48:13	A VATLAND	3:48:45	L SKINNER	3:49:12	M LAZENBY	3:49:47	P JOHNSTONE	3:50:14
6	T TIFFT	3:48:13	H DODDS	3:48:45	J ALLISON	3:49:12	G DAVIES	3:49:47	J MISERAY	3:50:14
7	E ODELL	3:48:14	K CADEY	3:48:45	R MISTRY	3:49:12	A EADY	3:49:48	P WILKINSON	3:50:15
8	I CHITTY	3:48:15	R HARVEY	3:48:46	N BONHAM	3:49:12	R PIERSON	3:49:48	A TREMAIN	3:50:15
9	J DESTOUBES	3:48:15	T WOOD	3:48:46	D KAY	3:49:12	L KELLY	3:49:49	A CHEMINGUI	3:50:15
10	H HOUBAER	3:48:15	N RATHBONE	3:48:46	J CLIFF	3:49:12	D NEWBERRY	3:49:49	K PRITCHARD	3:50:15
11	S TWEEDY	3:48:16	S STRACHAN	3:48:48	B PETIT	3:49:12	M CARPENTER	3:49:49	A YOUNG	3:50:15
12	H JAMES	3:48:16	J PICKARD	3:48:48	J BURRELL	3:49:12	I BUNTON	3:49:49	K WILLIAMS	3:50:15
13	W BROWN	3:48:16	J NAPIER	3:48:48	R WHITTAKER	3:49:13	I SLEE	3:49:49	L ALUJA	3:50:15
14	E ADAMSON	3:48:17	R ROBERTS	3:48:48	M NONGBRI	3:49:13	R VRIES	3:49:49	P ALDERMAN	3:50:16
15	J URIBE	3:48:17	S HICKEY	3:48:50	S HENLY	3:49:13	E CRANNEY	3:49:49	D CHARLTON	3:50:16
16	K HOBBS	3:48:17	A BLACK	3:48:50	P COTTAM	3:49:13	G CLEMETT	3:49:50	B XAVIER	3:50:16
17	S BENNETT	3:48:17	V CONNOR	3:48:51	S SLACK	3:49:13	A GEERING	3:49:50	L GRACE	3:50:16
18	M HOLLAND	3:48:17	E YATES	3:48:51	J ANNAN	3:49:13	M PEACOCK	3:49:51	D MANNING	3:50:16
19	A WILKINSON	3:48:17	R HOWE	3:48:51	N HALL	3:49:13	T MCCARNEY	3:49:51	R COTTON	3:50:16
20	S KENDALL	3:48:18	A GARDINER	3:48:51	C CLARKE	3:49:13	L CLEAVER	3:49:51	P LOPES	3:50:17
21	J RHODES	3:48:18	G GOODE	3:48:52	R HOGWOOD	3:49:14	A MURDOCK	3:49:51	N BELL	3:50:17
22	H SPENCE	3:48:18	C CONNOLLY	3:48:52	F CADDICK	3:49:14	B TUNVEY	3:49:51	I HARKER	3:50:18
23	S BROOKS	3:48:18	S PEPLOW	3:48:53	I CHAMPION	3:49:14	H MARSHALL	3:49:52	G ROBERTSON	3:50:18
24	P LEANE	3:48:19	J SOGAARD	3:48:53	P FORDER	3:49:14	D LAWRIE	3:49:52	E GIANNERINI	3:50:19
25	T STOKES	3:48:20	J PRESIO	3:48:53	M SMITH	3:49:15	G NUTTER	3:49:52	C ADAMS	3:50:19
26	R READ	3:48:20	S HARRISON	3:48:53	P MCQUEEN	3:49:15	C SMYTH	3:49:52	S COLLIN	3:50:21
27	T BOND	3:48:20	R THORLEY	3:48:53	J GREENWOOD	3:49:16	T TUPLING	3:49:53	W SCHLADITZ	3:50:22
28	M BOOTH	3:48:20	C MASON	3:48:53	G JEPHCOTT	3:49:16	C ELLIOTT	3:49:53	F FOLLEGATTI	3:50:22
29	B FITZSIMMONS	3:48:21	M ALLEN	3:48:53	A CHAPMAN	3:49:17	B BARLOW	3:49:53	W JONES	3:50:22
30	N WATSON	3:48:22	P PEPLOW	3:48:53	M LAUKO	3:49:17	C LEWIS	3:49:54	G EVERSON	3:50:22
31	J HEAP	3:48:22	D ODRISCOLL	3:48:54	D BURTON	3:49:17	J GREET	3:49:54	S WALTHO	3:50:22
32	T JORGENSEN	3:48:22	S JOHN	3:48:54	A URWIN	3:49:18	L HAWKINS	3:49:54	A MCLEAN	3:50:22
33	J LAY	3:48:22	K MATHER	3:48:55	M DRAPER	3:49:19	A DALTON	3:49:54	M SULLIVAN	3:50:22
34	C LAWRENCE	3:48:22	J TRIM	3:48:55	R MANLY	3:49:19	A EMONS	3:49:54	M SINCLAIR	3:50:23
35	P DUNN	3:48:22	D ANDERTON	3:48:55	B WATTS	3:49:19	H TAZI	3:49:54	R STOLZLECHNER	3:50:23
36	N YOUNG	3:48:23	J PERKS	3:48:55	A TANNER	3:49:20	L MICCOLL	3:49:55	G ROBERTS	3:50:23
37	F SANZ	3:48:24	D SCOREBY	3:48:55	G BAKER	3:49:20	I MCDONALD	3:49:55	J GREENLEES	3:50:23
38	S AMBLARD	3:48:25	R CAGE	3:48:56	C CRAVEN-SMITH-MILNES	3:49:20	M BURKE	3:49:55	D VISSER	3:50:23
39	P MOREAU	3:48:25	S HEARN	3:48:56	R DOUGLAS	3:49:22	P HODGKINSON	3:49:55	M CRISPO	3:50:23
40	J ORGAN	3:48:26	S JENKINS	3:48:56	C KINSCH	3:49:22	F HARRISON	3:49:55	Y KUBO	3:50:24
41	A HINCE	3:48:26	D GLOCK	3:48:56	C BATHGATE	3:49:23	Y KOURSAROS	3:49:55	T SPITERI	3:50:24
42	A FOSBEARY	3:48:26	P EDINGTON	3:48:56	B POELMAN	3:49:24	C ALVAREZ	3:49:55	M LECI	3:50:24
43	T PORTER	3:48:26	G SMITH	3:48:56	M LEE	3:49:24	C SLATTER	3:49:55	I BUCHANAN	3:50:24
44	W KERR	3:48:26	D BARROWLOUGH	3:48:56	T GARRITTY	3:49:24	C SMALLMAN	3:49:55	P WILLIAMS	3:50:24
45	A CLARKE	3:48:27	T MATHER	3:48:57	I WATSON	3:49:25	D DAVENPORT	3:49:55	D KELLY	3:50:24
46	H ALLEN	3:48:27	E JENSEN	3:48:57	R REYNOLDS	3:49:25	M VIVES	3:49:55	S EVANS	3:50:24
47	C BLACKMORE	3:48:27	H WINTER	3:48:57	J SMITH	3:49:26	P BROWN	3:49:56	T SPICER	3:50:25
48	A MARTINS	3:48:27	L BLUMBERG	3:48:57	S HOLT	3:49:26	B NORTON	3:49:56	J WRENCH	3:50:25
49	R KILBY	3:48:27	T JENSEN	3:48:57	P WEATHERALL	3:49:26	T MCCLUSKEY	3:49:56	A MILLS	3:50:25
50	C KERSHAW	3:48:27	F FERNANDEZ DE YBARRA	3:48:58	C RODEN-DAVIES	3:49:27	A WALSH	3:49:56	R CONAN	3:50:25
51	S LITTLE	3:48:27	P WHITTICK	3:48:58	A TAYLOR	3:49:27	J KNIGHT	3:49:56	B ELLIOTT	3:50:26
52	H MACDONALD	3:48:27	D WOODLEY	3:48:59	M CDONALD	3:49:27	P WEST	3:49:57	D SINGLETON	3:50:26
53	A COLLINS	3:48:27	E GARAY	3:48:59	N ALLCARD	3:49:27	I MAYHAW	3:49:58	R CLARKE	3:50:26
54	T WATTLEY	3:48:28	S LLOYD	3:48:59	C HILL	3:49:28	P HARRISON	3:49:59	N SHIMADA	3:50:26
55	A JARVIS	3:48:28	S TANNER	3:48:59	D BENNETT	3:49:28	J THOMPSON	3:49:59	P SHAWLEY	3:50:26
56	U DUCKWORTH	3:48:29	J CORFIELD	3:48:59	K CORRIGAN	3:49:28	T WINCHESTER	3:50:00	J TOWNSEND	3:50:26
57	I GARDNER	3:48:30	B MOTT	3:49:00	R DEE	3:49:28	L BOON	3:50:00	G CABELL	3:50:27
58	M PUGH	3:48:30	D DOWBEKIN	3:49:00	J KERREC	3:49:29	H LAFFINEUR	3:50:00	P KEAN	3:50:27
59	J BUTROID	3:48:31	G O'REILLY	3:49:01	P DAINES	3:49:29	A RIDLEY	3:50:00	B ALLEN	3:50:27
60	S TOMES	3:48:31	J DOWNES	3:49:02	G KENDRICK	3:49:29	K GARNETT	3:50:01	D MACLAREN	3:50:27
61	W DALE	3:48:32	J WEBSTER	3:49:02	N COOK	3:49:29	T SCOTT	3:50:01	P HARRIS	3:50:27
62	P DUNNING	3:48:32	F VAN DEN BOSCH	3:49:02	C THUNDERCLIFFE	3:49:30	S SCANLON	3:50:02	S PANTER	3:50:27
63	M GOODALL	3:48:32	K MEASURES	3:49:02	T ASHTON	3:49:30	R SELLS	3:50:02	W STEELE	3:50:28
64	R GREEN	3:48:33	J ALDRIDGE	3:49:02	J MCINTYRE	3:49:30	C TOY	3:50:02	O KORSEN	3:50:28
65	S CASTELL	3:48:33	S LEATHES	3:49:02	P CONROY	3:49:31	S SMITH	3:50:02	G COSTANTINI	3:50:28
66	J MOORE	3:48:33	J MARSHALL	3:49:02	J HERTLING	3:49:32	A JACOBSON	3:50:03	J PALMER	3:50:28
67	D MC DONAGH	3:48:34	J WALLER	3:49:02	P VENNING	3:49:33	V CROUSLE	3:50:03	J JOHNSON	3:50:29
68	I KAINTH	3:48:34	M SOUTHGATE	3:49:02	W BEHRENDS	3:49:34	W NELSON	3:50:03	M STORRAR	3:50:31
69	L DAVIES	3:48:34	M DAY	3:49:02	D ROBERTSON	3:49:34	D WIGHT	3:50:04	C REVELLI	3:50:31
70	S HARRY	3:48:34	D PEMBROKE	3:49:02	G BRANDON	3:49:35	A GIDDINGS	3:50:05	T JONES	3:50:31
71	S KHAN	3:48:35	J WILD	3:49:02	C BACON	3:49:35	K WILLIAMSON	3:50:05	M LOVE	3:50:32
72	M HANNINGTON	3:48:35	A HIGGINS	3:49:02	N ADAMS	3:49:35	A WAKE	3:50:05	H ROBINSON	3:50:32
73	S CHERRY	3:48:36	M ANDERSON	3:49:03	B WILLIAMS	3:49:36	T PEDERSEN	3:50:05	D GOODEY	3:50:32
74	I GRIFFITHS	3:48:36	D HEPPENSTALL	3:49:03	F EMMELHAINZ	3:49:36	G DOBSON	3:50:05	L BROOMFIELD	3:50:33
75	P ATKINS	3:48:36	A JENKINS	3:49:04	J LOHNINGER	3:49:36	M POTTER	3:50:05	D COCKER	3:50:33
76	I FULLER	3:48:37	P WEAVER	3:49:05	A PILLINGER	3:49:38	M MCCONNELL	3:50:06	D BAILEY	3:50:33
77	G WOOLLEY	3:48:37	E CHAUVET	3:49:06	L TAMBURINI	3:49:38	P MILES	3:50:06	P OWEN	3:50:33
78	G RICHARDSON	3:48:37	J LOVELL	3:49:06	G BATCHELOR	3:49:38	S WILLINGTON	3:50:06	S MILLS	3:50:33
79	A VINCENT	3:48:37	J WILLIAMS	3:49:06	K BASSETT	3:49:39	J BURR	3:50:06	C OLEARY	3:50:33
80	D WILLIAMSON	3:48:37	P WEST	3:49:06	A ADOLPHUS	3:49:40	J HERMANS	3:50:07	P DAVEY	3:50:34
81	R BISHOP	3:48:38	L GOAD	3:49:06	K WILLO	3:49:40	D BADGER	3:50:08	L CLARKE	3:50:34
82	P GREENHALGH	3:48:38	K COOKE	3:49:06	I BARTON	3:49:40	J WATSON	3:50:08	A BARNES	3:50:35
83	M HURST	3:48:38	C LIDDLE	3:49:06	S SWINNEY	3:49:40	S RAYNER	3:50:08	B MCKEEVER	3:50:35
84	C COLLETT	3:48:38	B BROWN	3:49:06	R BRADSHAW	3:49:40	G TERRY	3:50:09	P BARNES	3:50:35
85	D HATTON	3:48:39	D BRIGDEN	3:49:07	M VAN DEN AARDWEG	3:49:41	A GILLEN	3:50:10	L BUMFORD	3:50:35
86	N DAVIES	3:48:39	D JEWELL	3:49:07	G GORDON-WILKIN	3:49:41	A ANTHONY	3:50:10	J WIGZELL	3:50:35
87	J BOWLEY	3:48:40	S JACKSON	3:49:08	A MCCLEAN	3:49:41	K SCHAEPPI	3:50:11	D CHIVERS	3:50:35
88	J PICKERING	3:48:40	M JONES	3:49:08	T CLISBY	3:49:41	I SNEDDON	3:50:11	K PARRY	3:50:36
89	J PURNELL	3:48:40	R SCOTT	3:49:09	J CAVE	3:49:42	K PHIPPS	3:50:11	S HEARSON	3:50:36
90	S DIGHTON	3:48:40	D NORTON	3:49:09	M HUNT	3:49:42	R INGRAM	3:50:11	M GEISSLER	3:50:36
91	P GAY	3:48:40	M COOPER	3:49:09	J WIGGINS	3:49:42	D WALKLING	3:50:12	C BEASLEY	3:50:36
92	S VENENCIA	3:48:40	J THOMPSON	3:49:09	T DOHAN	3:49:42	M STUART	3:50:12	W ARCHER	3:50:37
93	J GREEN	3:48:41	I GRIFFIN	3:49:10	G HORDER	3:49:43	S JONES	3:50:12	H LOVKVIST	3:50:37
94	F SMITH	3:48:41	E MORRISSEY	3:49:10	A GAULT	3:49:43	J WHEATCROFT	3:50:12	P LISTER	3:50:37
95	H OWEN	3:48:41	G WENTWORTH	3:49:10	M BRENNAN	3:49:43	C KIRK	3:50:13	W MUNSON	3:50:37
96	P MALYON	3:48:41	D LAY	3:49:10	R NORTON	3:49:43	F SMITH	3:50:13	T KING	3:50:38
97	P CANU	3:48:41	S SZITTARIE	3:49:11	K WOTTON	3:49:44	K THOMAS	3:50:13	A HALL	3:50:39
98	H GEBHARDT	3:48:41	P DAVIDSON-HOUSTON	3:49:11	E JENKINS	3:49:44	T GALL	3:50:13	K HORDER	3:50:39
99	E PAGE	3:48:41	T MICHELIS	3:49:11	I MIKKELSEN	3:49:45	G THOMSON	3:50:13	J BENNETT	3:50:39
100	R BLACKWELL	3:48:42	R PARKER	3:49:12	I BANDINI	3:49:46	P NORTH	3:50:13	M BROOKS	3:50:40

	10001-10100		10101-10200		10201-10300		10301-10400		10401-10500	
1	A MILLS	3:50:40	M CONCANNON	3:51:01	L HUGHES	3:51:29	J BORLAND	3:51:51	K BELL	3:52:24
2	Z MAREK	3:50:40	N DAVEY	3:51:01	N DAVEY	3:51:29	I HINES	3:51:51	H ALDRED	3:52:24
3	J MCGETTRICK	3:50:41	I SUTCLIFFE	3:51:01	J BROADHEAD	3:51:29	A BATEMAN	3:51:52	D BATH	3:52:24
4	A TANT	3:50:41	G WALLIS	3:51:01	S MILLHOFT	3:51:29	D LUCKMAN	3:51:52	M SCHLAEFLI	3:52:24
5	R MESHBERG	3:50:41	S BERRY	3:51:02	A EGAN	3:51:30	G EVANS	3:51:53	L NOTTAGE	3:52:24
6	G MOODY	3:50:41	M LEE	3:51:02	C GRANGER	3:51:30	M EALES	3:51:53	A STAMMERS	3:52:24
7	S FITZPATRICK	3:50:41	S BARBIERI	3:51:02	K MATTHEWSON	3:51:31	T WHEELDON	3:51:53	K BINGHAM	3:52:24
8	S CARTWRIGHT	3:50:41	V MARTIN	3:51:02	F DAVIES	3:51:31	M BEVERIDGE	3:51:53	H BURGESS	3:52:24
9	J HIGHWOOD	3:50:42	J MEGENS	3:51:03	C DE ROHAN	3:51:31	B BUDGE	3:51:53	G BROWNING	3:52:24
10	S WELBURN	3:50:42	G WELLINGS	3:51:03	W DENT	3:51:31	U GEORGSON	3:51:53	R STURESSON	3:52:25
11	J HAYES	3:50:42	D ELWIN	3:51:03	P WATERS	3:51:31	M DREW	3:51:53	E ANSLOW	3:52:25
12	C HILL	3:50:42	S YEELES	3:51:04	M TUCKER	3:51:31	K LENNARD	3:51:53	G MARTIN	3:52:25
13	E BARKER	3:50:42	R JONES	3:51:04	A TUCKER	3:51:32	I TELFER	3:51:53	B GARMAN	3:52:26
14	L HOYT	3:50:42	G PARKER	3:51:04	T SCRIPPS	3:51:32	R ROBINSON	3:51:53	B WILLEY	3:52:26
15	T STORIE	3:50:42	R DOUGLAS	3:51:04	P EVANS	3:51:32	P SHAW	3:51:53	W LIPYEAT	3:52:26
16	G SMITH	3:50:43	S ROWLAND	3:51:05	E KIRKLAND	3:51:32	J MAGEE	3:51:53	G JENKINS	3:52:26
17	H BIDMEAD	3:50:43	V OVERTON	3:51:05	J HAMMOND	3:51:32	S LACEY	3:51:53	P SULSKI	3:52:27
18	M O HAGAN	3:50:43	W HENDY	3:51:05	T LONGHURST	3:51:32	R GORDON	3:51:53	A STEVENS	3:52:27
19	K LYTHGOE	3:50:43	N COOPER	3:51:05	P HARVEY	3:51:32	J PERRY	3:51:53	M TURNER	3:52:27
20	C TEMBY	3:50:44	S HUME	3:51:06	A REYNOLDS	3:51:32	R SAMWAYS	3:51:54	S MICALLEF	3:52:27
21	J LLOYD	3:50:44	C WILLIS	3:51:06	C ASHE	3:51:32	R MOORE	3:51:54	I GOODWIN	3:52:27
22	E GOODREID	3:50:44	T JEFFERISS	3:51:08	G COOKE	3:51:32	G JACKSON	3:51:54	P WILKES	3:52:28
23	G JONES	3:50:44	D COLLINS	3:51:08	E JONES	3:51:32	B BROWN	3:51:54	G PINTO	3:52:28
24	N STANSFIELD	3:50:44	A FINN	3:51:08	M COHEN	3:51:33	K GITTOS	3:51:54	N OAKLEY	3:52:28
25	F GAMBLE	3:50:44	T FAIRMAN	3:51:08	P GAITELY	3:51:33	D JUBIN	3:51:54	H SEABORN	3:52:28
26	D WRIGHT	3:50:44	A OLIVIER	3:51:09	W AGG	3:51:33	M WILLIAMS	3:51:54	G SAMUELSEN	3:52:28
27	A BOND	3:50:44	B ORMROD	3:51:09	A RUSHTON	3:51:34	D SMITH	3:51:54	D EDWARDS	3:52:29
28	O JACQUES	3:50:44	B WATSON	3:51:09	B CHALLACOMBE	3:51:34	P LACOMBE	3:51:55	C BENNETT	3:52:29
29	W BAYLISS	3:50:44	E CHMARA	3:51:09	U PIRONI	3:51:34	P GURNEY	3:51:55	A READDIE	3:52:29
30	F AEBI	3:50:45	M SUETT	3:51:09	G DEAN	3:51:34	M SCORER	3:51:55	J LUTOMSKI	3:52:29
31	T JACKSON	3:50:45	P PRINCE	3:51:10	P ROBERTS	3:51:34	M HOOPER	3:51:55	D ROGERS	3:52:29
32	P FORSTER	3:50:45	R WALKER	3:51:10	G WELLS	3:51:35	K MCCORMICK	3:51:56	C HAYDON	3:52:30
33	G FREI	3:50:45	P ROGERS	3:51:10	A HENLEY	3:51:36	R PATTERSON	3:51:57	B ARIGHO	3:52:30
34	R MITCHELL	3:50:45	M RICHARDSON	3:51:10	B FRAMPTON	3:51:36	P DENNY	3:51:57	M TAYLOR	3:52:30
35	M POWELL	3:50:46	V FARRELLY	3:51:11	C SCAMPUCCI	3:51:36	T DUIVENVOORDEN	3:51:57	G CROWTHER	3:52:30
36	J WILKINS	3:50:46	S NICOLL	3:51:11	P O'BRIEN	3:51:37	C WHITE	3:51:58	J WOODROW	3:52:30
37	T VALENTINE	3:50:46	G NASH	3:51:11	C BROBYN	3:51:37	J CAIRNS	3:51:58	P NAUGHTON	3:52:31
38	G SHAKED	3:50:46	S DERBYSHIRE	3:51:12	J ANDERSON	3:51:37	D HEWITT	3:51:59	C ADAMS	3:52:31
39	K LAZARUS	3:50:47	J NEILLIS	3:51:12	J SOWERBY	3:51:38	D THOMAS	3:51:59	B MORAN	3:52:31
40	D MANSFIELD	3:50:47	P GOLDFINCH	3:51:13	B HAMILTON	3:51:38	K FULCHER	3:52:01	M MC CAFFERTY	3:52:31
41	E ROSE	3:50:47	H DABBS	3:51:13	A TUBB	3:51:38	M ABBOTT	3:52:01	L SIMPSON	3:52:31
42	M SMITH	3:50:47	A COSTIFF	3:51:13	G SEVENO	3:51:38	K SMART	3:52:02	C DONNELLY	3:52:31
43	B PRATT	3:50:47	E FRASER	3:51:14	P QUINN	3:51:40	S BARTON	3:52:02	N METH	3:52:32
44	G HULL	3:50:47	J O'REILLY	3:51:14	C MAHER	3:51:41	G SPILLER	3:52:04	A MURRAY	3:52:32
45	P HARDING	3:50:47	L SANTOS	3:51:14	T HARRIS	3:51:41	E SMALLEY	3:52:04	A GALLOWAY	3:52:32
46	Y WOOLSEY	3:50:47	S HILL	3:51:14	T BEESTON	3:51:42	S DALY	3:52:04	A HOLMES	3:52:32
47	W DAVIDSON	3:50:47	R FRASER	3:51:14	N FOX	3:51:42	J THORNHILL	3:52:04	A GOULD	3:52:32
48	D BISSCHOP	3:50:48	J THOMPSON	3:51:15	R LOUTH	3:51:43	B CARLSSON	3:52:04	G MATTHEWS	3:52:32
49	R YEATS	3:50:48	R HELEY	3:51:15	M CHAMBERLAIN	3:51:43	P KING	3:52:04	G RICHENS	3:52:34
50	R DONNER	3:50:48	C KINGHAM	3:51:16	T YOKOI	3:51:43	M VENESS	3:52:05	R FROSCH	3:52:34
51	R SUSSKIND	3:50:48	W HEITSCHNEIDER	3:51:16	G MORGAN	3:51:43	C LEMOINE	3:52:05	R EVELEIGH	3:52:34
52	S SMITH	3:50:48	D AITKEN	3:51:16	S HENRY	3:51:44	G DAVIES	3:52:05	A HARTLEY	3:52:35
53	C BOYES	3:50:48	C SMYTH	3:51:16	T YOUNG	3:51:45	D NUTTALL	3:52:06	D WITCOMB	3:52:35
54	P WARREN	3:50:49	P SKIDMORE	3:51:17	D BANKS	3:51:45	W VOIGT	3:52:06	R NAVARRO	3:52:35
55	D KELLY	3:50:49	P GILMOUR	3:51:19	C MACINNES	3:51:45	M BARWOOD	3:52:06	I CRUMMACK	3:52:36
56	L COLE	3:50:49	N BARKER	3:51:19	M UDD	3:51:45	D WESTON	3:52:07	G WILLIAMS	3:52:36
57	P TEUBER	3:50:49	R SAYLES	3:51:20	K FJELLSTROM	3:51:45	T LINES	3:52:07	P MAUND	3:52:36
58	L SGARZI	3:50:50	N COUPAR	3:51:20	J SHORTER	3:51:45	M MOSELEY	3:52:07	J HOLLISTER	3:52:36
59	K MCCAUGHEY	3:50:50	N MERIDEW	3:51:20	C LEGGATT	3:51:45	L CASTELLANE	3:52:07	A CATESBY	3:52:36
60	A SENET	3:50:50	P QUINN	3:51:20	J STEAD	3:51:45	P WESTON	3:52:08	M HUMPHREYS	3:52:37
61	B GRANT	3:50:51	R THOMPSON	3:51:21	I PATTISON	3:51:45	J WHITE	3:52:08	P BOWKER	3:52:37
62	A DENNIS	3:50:52	A PRICE	3:51:21	M FENNEY	3:51:45	T PAYNE	3:52:08	M PIKE	3:52:37
63	G DAVIS	3:50:52	I WINFIELD	3:51:21	J CHARLTON	3:51:45	P MCCULLAGH	3:52:08	B HARPER	3:52:37
64	B SIGGERS	3:50:53	A PARNWELL	3:51:21	R DAVIES	3:51:45	J MABWAI	3:52:09	M WILSON	3:52:37
65	C AXFORD	3:50:53	N BURDETT	3:51:21	R BERIAIN	3:51:45	S ALLEN	3:52:09	T WHITE	3:52:37
66	G WHINCUP	3:50:53	E MORASSI	3:51:21	J SMITH	3:51:45	S FOLDNES	3:52:09	S BARNES	3:52:38
67	R DULING	3:50:53	D LING	3:51:21	R CAMPBELL	3:51:45	M PARRY-JONES	3:52:09	J FUSTER	3:52:38
68	I WOOLLEY	3:50:53	I THOMAS	3:51:21	M MANWARING	3:51:45	T TIMMERMAN	3:52:09	P ADLER	3:52:38
69	M SMITH	3:50:53	S YOUNG	3:51:22	I THOMAS	3:51:45	M RAMSEY	3:52:10	E AUSTIN	3:52:39
70	G GIBBONS	3:50:53	J SOLOMON	3:51:22	J KEOHANE	3:51:45	W FELLOWS	3:52:11	R HUTCHINSON	3:52:39
71	M HUTTON	3:50:53	S WILSON-BACON	3:51:22	R COOPER	3:51:45	R WITHERS	3:52:14	E MARKWARDT	3:52:39
72	F TOLAND	3:50:53	M EHRENBERG	3:51:22	M WILLIAMSON	3:51:45	T LAVY	3:52:14	D GORDON	3:52:39
73	C EWINGS	3:50:53	C VAN DEN ABEELE	3:51:22	J SMITH	3:51:45	J KOSTELYK	3:52:14	P BULLEN	3:52:40
74	R HILTON	3:50:53	P KAISER	3:51:22	A CRAWLEY	3:51:45	F SHENTON	3:52:14	D WYKES	3:52:40
75	A FARNELL	3:50:53	A MASSIMI	3:51:23	G FORSLUND	3:51:45	J BYRNE	3:52:15	J CROSKERRY	3:52:40
76	G EDWARDS	3:50:53	M WATERS	3:51:23	D HEDGES	3:51:45	C MAY	3:52:15	B BATES	3:52:41
77	P MCINNES	3:50:54	M STRINGER	3:51:23	P DOYLE	3:51:45	S MADIGAN	3:52:15	A GOODWIN	3:52:41
78	H KRIER	3:50:54	A DOUAY	3:51:23	M WARD	3:51:45	P HALL	3:52:16	F CEDROLA	3:52:41
79	T BERGSTEN	3:50:54	J PETERS	3:51:24	A ETHERINGTON	3:51:45	P PIERCE	3:52:16	M RATCHFORD	3:52:41
80	C TUCKER	3:50:54	K HAWKSWORTH	3:51:24	R KIRKBY	3:51:46	R CHAPLIN	3:52:16	N PFEIFFER	3:52:41
81	L HOOYMANS	3:50:54	J BARKER	3:51:24	A GALLEY	3:51:46	A SHIRLEY	3:52:17	I DIBBLE	3:52:42
82	J HILL	3:50:54	L TREBILCOCK	3:51:24	J SUMMERHAYES	3:51:46	S THREADER	3:52:17	J ROSS	3:52:42
83	W GRIFFITHS	3:50:55	R WARNE	3:51:24	H TAYLOR	3:51:47	J LITTLEFAIR	3:52:17	M SOTO	3:52:42
84	M DAY	3:50:55	O VIGDENES	3:51:24	M MAROCCO	3:51:47	C PRICE	3:52:17	B JENNER	3:52:42
85	J PINHORNE	3:50:56	C MOUNTFORD	3:51:24	S RIDOUT	3:51:47	C LYNN	3:52:17	A MOLLOY	3:52:43
86	A PALMER	3:50:57	M PAYNE	3:51:24	J FEENEY	3:51:47	C CAZES	3:52:17	A CRAWFORD	3:52:43
87	P DICKINSON	3:50:57	J KING	3:51:25	I CONQUEST	3:51:47	P FREER	3:52:19	R HOSKING	3:52:43
88	R GRAHAM	3:50:57	A HENSMAN	3:51:25	R FINCH	3:51:47	J TIMMINS	3:52:19	S FRAZER	3:52:43
89	A BOTTON	3:50:57	D WHYTE	3:51:25	B HICKS	3:51:48	T PRICE	3:52:20	P WEST	3:52:43
90	J CHESSMAN	3:50:57	A WOODS	3:51:25	P CHAPPELL	3:51:48	E SMITH	3:52:21	K MASEFIELD	3:52:43
91	J DAWE	3:50:57	J SMITH	3:51:26	J MADDEN	3:51:48	J MADDEN	3:52:21	K CONSTABLE	3:52:44
92	J CLIFTON	3:50:57	B DURANT	3:51:26	P CACI	3:51:48	T BIGGS	3:52:21	A PORTER	3:52:44
93	J HUNT-DAVIS	3:50:57	L HEDIN	3:51:26	O THOMAS	3:51:48	R OLIVER	3:52:21	R MAYES	3:52:44
94	C REY	3:50:58	R SHEPHERD	3:51:27	S COLE	3:51:50	K SORENSEN	3:52:22	S ADAMS	3:52:44
95	I ALTON	3:50:58	R PERRY	3:51:27	R HAYDOCK	3:51:50	R BROWN	3:52:22	D BAINBRIDGE	3:52:44
96	R JEFFRIES	3:50:59	A SAUNDERS	3:51:27	J TAYLOR	3:51:51	M REYNARD	3:52:23	T RAJA	3:52:44
97	D WHITLAM	3:50:59	M FINCH	3:51:27	P BONNER	3:51:51	A HOLMES	3:52:23	J NUGENT	3:52:44
98	J TOBIN	3:51:00	A HOODLESS	3:51:28	J RASMUSSEN	3:51:51	D ALLEN	3:52:23	M MIDDLETON	3:52:44
99	V MILLER	3:51:00	J HUMM	3:51:28	S GARDINER	3:51:51	T BOWLER	3:52:23	L POWLING	3:52:44
100	M GILHOOLY	3:51:00	M JOHNSON	3:51:28	C SYDENHAM	3:51:51	N STEWART	3:52:24	C MARVELL	3:52:44

	10501-10600		10601-10700		10701-10800		10801-10900		10901-11000	
1	T STEWART	3:52:44	J SAYNER	3:53:05	S TAYLOR	3:53:34	G FURLAN	3:53:58	P DAVIES	3:54:20
2	S TOTOLA	3:52:44	P GREENWOOD	3:53:05	A HUDSON	3:53:35	R SMITHERAM	3:53:58	C PFEUTER	3:54:20
3	S PUNTON	3:52:44	R ROWLES	3:53:05	M COLLINS	3:53:35	G LOGUE	3:53:58	M SAUNDERS	3:54:20
4	D BARTLETT	3:52:44	D DAY	3:53:06	S BULBACZYNSKYJ	3:53:35	J DYER	3:53:58	P RAMSWELL	3:54:20
5	S NELSON	3:52:44	G MORGAN	3:53:06	S BIEDUL	3:53:35	C JOYCE	3:53:58	R CREMIN	3:54:20
6	A BEER	3:52:45	C GOURSAUD	3:53:07	S HODGES	3:53:35	D SMITH	3:53:58	C LOUGHLIN	3:54:21
7	R LUNN	3:52:45	N MCIVER	3:53:07	A BAGWELL	3:53:35	S TEWS	3:53:58	R LOVELL	3:54:21
8	B PASS	3:52:45	A RATEAU	3:53:07	L ALLEN	3:53:36	D BROWN	3:53:58	R CHAPMAN	3:54:22
9	J REEVES	3:52:46	A TATTERSALL	3:53:08	F GORDON	3:53:37	A BARBER	3:53:59	A BAM	3:54:22
10	D DE CROOS	3:52:46	M JOY	3:53:08	E OKURA	3:53:37	A MCLEAN	3:53:59	D BISH	3:54:23
11	H MACPHERSON	3:52:46	R RATEAU	3:53:08	N RICHMOND	3:53:37	T ROBINSON	3:53:59	E BEVAN	3:54:23
12	M MANNALL	3:52:46	J CLARKE	3:53:08	J DAVIES	3:53:38	S BRACKENBURY	3:53:59	B TAYLOR	3:54:23
13	A SCOTT	3:52:47	R JACKSON	3:53:09	B SMITH	3:53:38	G DOBIE	3:53:59	P HOEHNO	3:54:24
14	I SCOTT	3:52:47	K BACON	3:53:09	R VALINS	3:53:38	P LEONG	3:53:59	J ARNAU	3:54:24
15	A GRANT	3:52:47	H APPEL	3:53:10	T BARNES	3:53:40	K PARDOE	3:54:00	D LANGLEY-HOBBS	3:54:24
16	S HUTCHISON	3:52:47	M LAMBERT	3:53:10	T HARPER	3:53:40	M TWOGOOD	3:54:00	A SMITH	3:54:24
17	K BATEY	3:52:48	M CANNADINE	3:53:11	S LOEFFLER	3:53:40	J VAN DIJK	3:54:00	I PEAR	3:54:26
18	P BONDS	3:52:48	A OSBORNE	3:53:11	J DOLAN	3:53:40	A FORD	3:54:01	B HAUGLUM	3:54:26
19	S DAVIS	3:52:49	C HOLMES	3:53:11	D BOWLES	3:53:41	I HARRISON	3:54:01	P HAUGLUM	3:54:26
20	D HALE	3:52:49	R BRIGHT	3:53:11	B WILLIAMS	3:53:41	K HUNTER	3:54:01	D NEWLAND	3:54:27
21	G MOODY	3:52:49	F ITCHENER	3:53:12	P BLACKWELL	3:53:41	A NEWMAN	3:54:02	A NEWLAND	3:54:27
22	P CRONK	3:52:49	T CAULTON	3:53:13	S CUNNINGTON	3:53:41	E GRIFFITHS	3:54:02	D BENNETT	3:54:28
23	D WEBB	3:52:49	S ROBERTS	3:53:14	A KINDON	3:53:41	L BROOKS	3:54:03	H ALBRECHT	3:54:28
24	D ECCLES	3:52:49	A HIRONS	3:53:14	J WELLS	3:53:41	W BILLINGTON	3:54:03	H CRIPPS	3:54:28
25	W KAY	3:52:49	P LOWRIE	3:53:15	P WASSELL	3:53:42	J MARSDEN	3:54:03	M COLVILLE	3:54:29
26	C COURANT	3:52:50	E PAUL	3:53:15	N WHARTON	3:53:42	S PARKER	3:54:03	W CASSON	3:54:30
27	R BENNINGTON	3:52:50	R KERR	3:53:15	T KITE	3:53:42	G MCCABE	3:54:03	V TOWNSEND	3:54:30
28	P ETHERIDGE	3:52:50	R BAXENDALE	3:53:15	F WIBBERLEY	3:53:42	B ASTRAND	3:54:03	W OWENS	3:54:30
29	N SHORT	3:52:50	J WARREN	3:53:16	P HARRISON	3:53:42	T ANDREWS	3:54:04	J RANGER	3:54:30
30	H SINGH	3:52:50	P DAVITT	3:53:16	J BOWYER	3:53:42	K BURROWS	3:54:04	D MCMILLAN	3:54:32
31	S DUFF	3:52:52	F VAN NIJLEM	3:53:17	G BELL	3:53:42	M PARPERLS	3:54:04	G SKINNER	3:54:32
32	A RODWAY	3:52:52	W BOERMA	3:53:17	R BALLANTINE	3:53:43	A WATKINS	3:54:04	M YOUNGSON	3:54:33
33	T HOLLOWAY	3:52:52	G BURSTON	3:53:17	D VIZCHINO	3:53:43	R PATTENDEN	3:54:06	D NEWTON	3:54:33
34	M MORAN	3:52:52	S BARLOW	3:53:17	A SMITH	3:53:43	R SCHMID	3:54:06	J JACQUES	3:54:33
35	B CLARINVAL	3:52:52	C MILLSON	3:53:18	S BYRNE	3:53:43	J TYSON	3:54:06	A ROCKEY	3:54:34
36	P GREY	3:52:52	G STREET	3:53:18	P PURDUE	3:53:43	A LEVER	3:54:06	C ZACHARA	3:54:34
37	D OWEN	3:52:53	M ORMROD	3:53:18	P HOLMAN	3:53:44	E GOSNEY	3:54:07	M LEWIS	3:54:34
38	S JOHANSSON	3:52:53	T WEBSTER	3:53:18	D MAYLOTTE	3:53:44	A BROWN	3:54:07	D BOWDEN	3:54:35
39	H GISHOLT	3:52:54	G THOMPSON	3:53:18	N PRICE	3:53:45	S MELLING	3:54:07	D BARTLETT	3:54:35
40	J SMITH	3:52:54	P STIMSON	3:53:19	V YOUNG	3:53:45	P CANNELL	3:54:08	T TER HEERDT	3:54:36
41	V GREEN	3:52:54	N TAYLOR	3:53:19	E HEGARTY	3:53:45	D PATERSON	3:54:08	P DURRANS	3:54:36
42	D GILL	3:52:54	R HOWELLS	3:53:19	L BARWICK	3:53:45	B TRACEY	3:54:08	S RHEINWALD	3:54:36
43	E BURKE	3:52:55	P GREEN	3:53:19	D BENNETT	3:53:45	S MINETT	3:54:08	D BANCROFT	3:54:36
44	H LONSE	3:52:55	R AUST	3:53:19	A DAVIES	3:53:45	M DARLINGTON	3:54:09	L SMITH	3:54:36
45	S HUNT	3:52:55	K STANLEY	3:53:19	L BEVAN	3:53:45	M TALLAND	3:54:09	W MACLEOD	3:54:37
46	J BROWNSWORD	3:52:56	M PYE	3:53:19	P LEWIS	3:53:45	T WATSON	3:54:10	S MANNION	3:54:37
47	G DUMLER	3:52:56	J TWOMEY	3:53:19	N COLE	3:53:45	G EDMUNDS	3:54:10	A BAKER	3:54:37
48	D QUIBELL	3:52:56	S BURKE	3:53:19	R RELTON	3:53:46	C LEMOR	3:54:10	B SHEARD	3:54:37
49	S HYNES	3:52:56	F BURNS	3:53:19	G DUESTER	3:53:46	V YOUNG	3:54:10	S MOORE	3:54:38
50	B THOMPSON	3:52:56	M STONEY	3:53:19	C SWALLOW	3:53:46	L BLONDEAU	3:54:11	M ROGERS	3:54:38
51	E JONES	3:52:56	R STONEY	3:53:19	R SIMPKINS	3:53:47	M SEBILLE	3:54:11	G SOUTHWELL	3:54:38
52	G SNAPE	3:52:57	P MARTIN	3:53:20	A MAPLETHORPE	3:53:47	E SAVAGE	3:54:11	R LUYTEN	3:54:38
53	J MERIAUX	3:52:57	P JONES	3:53:20	P CREE	3:53:48	J COLEMAN	3:54:11	A KIRK	3:54:38
54	G BEEVERS	3:52:57	P CLARKE	3:53:20	P SIMPSON	3:53:48	M ROLLINGS	3:54:12	D HOGG	3:54:39
55	G CASATI	3:52:57	A POWELL	3:53:20	I MCCANDLISH	3:53:48	S RICH	3:54:12	R BAILEY	3:54:39
56	M HALL	3:52:57	G CAPELLI	3:53:20	R PAGE	3:53:48	E LANG	3:54:12	C PATTISON	3:54:39
57	D HORDON	3:52:58	D STEWARD	3:53:21	S BUNDY	3:53:48	J BISHOP	3:54:12	M PATTISON	3:54:39
58	I PEGGS	3:52:58	S SIN	3:53:21	B JEFFERIES	3:53:49	A BOLTON	3:54:13	J NICHOLLS	3:54:40
59	D STEVENS	3:52:58	D SHUCKSMITH	3:53:21	M MASSEE	3:53:49	S WALLACE	3:54:14	R HAYWOOD	3:54:40
60	V WILLIAMS	3:52:58	P CLIFTON	3:53:22	D EADES	3:53:49	J NEWBY	3:54:14	H JACKSON	3:54:40
61	A ROBERTS	3:52:58	R WHITEBREAD	3:53:22	C MILLER	3:53:49	J EDDY	3:54:14	S BORGIEL	3:54:41
62	D BROWNE	3:52:58	M THOMAS	3:53:22	K COLE	3:53:49	C RICHER	3:54:14	D CARLISLE	3:54:41
63	R BENNETT	3:52:58	S GUNN	3:53:22	J BOLTON	3:53:49	J SARGENT	3:54:15	D GUILFOYLE	3:54:41
64	B LAWLOR	3:52:59	G GELDARD	3:53:23	K MCMANUS	3:53:49	V SCHWANOT	3:54:15	S KRAMER	3:54:41
65	M CHAFFEY	3:52:59	J LEE	3:53:23	M WILLEY	3:53:50	L ISAAC	3:54:15	J FROST	3:54:42
66	D STEAD	3:52:59	S APPLETON	3:53:23	J HINDLE	3:53:51	D DICKSON	3:54:15	C OHARA	3:54:42
67	D GERMAN	3:52:59	B CZAKO	3:53:23	R MINNS	3:53:51	S ALLEN	3:54:15	R VIRTANEN	3:54:43
68	M COOK	3:52:59	B HOLM	3:53:24	R BELL	3:53:51	C WHITE	3:54:15	H RUNCIMAN	3:54:43
69	D KIRKHAM	3:53:00	M MILLICHIP	3:53:25	S HIGGINS	3:53:51	M DAVIES	3:54:15	C DABROWSKI	3:54:43
70	B PETTERSSON	3:53:00	R CROOKS	3:53:25	S PILE	3:53:51	M DALTON	3:54:15	C BARKER	3:54:43
71	P COLLIN	3:53:00	F ROBINSON	3:53:25	R MCLUCKIE	3:53:53	G CONNER	3:54:15	D GAIT	3:54:43
72	G CATON	3:53:00	C YEADON	3:53:25	D BARTRAM	3:53:53	D DAVIS	3:54:15	D HOLMES	3:54:44
73	S RYE	3:53:00	A PLUMB	3:53:25	J ELLIS	3:53:53	G PRIESTLEY	3:54:15	P BIRNIE	3:54:44
74	W HOLDEN	3:53:00	E HUHN	3:53:25	R COSTA	3:53:53	L BROTHERDALE	3:54:15	D ROLLINSON	3:54:44
75	R LEIMER	3:53:00	S FLETCHER	3:53:26	M WOOD	3:53:53	P TOZER	3:54:15	K FORBES	3:54:44
76	Y GATWARD	3:53:00	A WIDGER	3:53:26	D WILKINSON	3:53:53	D O'KEEFE	3:54:15	A STREET	3:54:45
77	A MARRS	3:53:00	N WHITE	3:53:26	A BLAKE	3:53:54	G MAY	3:54:15	R PATRICK	3:54:45
78	M LAURSEN	3:53:00	I WILSON	3:53:26	J OATES	3:53:54	I STEARN	3:54:15	P GAITELY	3:54:46
79	R KENNEDY	3:53:00	R THOMAS	3:53:26	D PLAYFORD	3:53:54	C LAW	3:54:15	L CLEALL	3:54:46
80	N MACKENZIE	3:53:00	S ARCHER	3:53:27	K HOSHEMI	3:53:54	J TAYLOR	3:54:16	J FITZGERALD	3:54:46
81	P SANDALL	3:53:00	N ANSTEE	3:53:27	W CRONE	3:53:54	L ROELLEKE	3:54:16	D WALSH	3:54:46
82	R BROWN	3:53:00	R RIGDEN	3:53:28	P TRELFA	3:53:55	R HORTON	3:54:16	R POTTER	3:54:47
83	J NORLEY	3:53:00	K MILLS	3:53:28	R SPEERS	3:53:55	R WOLSTENHOLME	3:54:16	M MC CLOY	3:54:47
84	J HAZELL	3:53:00	D NEIL	3:53:29	R MOSES	3:53:55	A TUBB	3:54:16	P MCGURK	3:54:47
85	M PITT	3:53:00	T MC NULTY	3:53:29	R BOWDEN	3:53:55	W SCULLY	3:54:16	L BARNETT	3:54:47
86	M CLAYTON	3:53:01	D SNOWBALL	3:53:29	P ARNOLD	3:53:56	M JONAS	3:54:16	J THOMPSON	3:54:47
87	K YOUNG	3:53:01	L KROMAN	3:53:29	T TURNER	3:53:56	J FORD	3:54:16	A CLAYTON	3:54:47
88	G KLOSTERMAIER	3:53:02	T CORNELIS	3:53:30	A DOWDLE	3:53:56	T GALLACHER	3:54:18	J LEGROVE	3:54:48
89	N COCKRAN	3:53:02	R BARWICK	3:53:30	D BRADLEY	3:53:56	P ROBERTS	3:54:18	R COCHRANE	3:54:48
90	A BOUGHTON	3:53:02	P RENWICK	3:53:30	G PARRY	3:53:56	S SYRON	3:54:18	B ATTWOOD	3:54:48
91	S YAMADA	3:53:02	A PHILBRICK	3:53:30	P ROSTERN	3:53:57	D BOYCE	3:54:18	J FLETCHER	3:54:48
92	F D'SA	3:53:03	K BELL	3:53:30	C FRASER	3:53:57	E CIANCARELLA	3:54:18	G HARKUS	3:54:48
93	M MOORE	3:53:03	D MALLABY	3:53:31	C GOCHER	3:53:58	P PETRI	3:54:18	T FORSTER	3:54:48
94	R RICHARDS	3:53:03	J BASS	3:53:31	D COLVIN	3:53:58	A STENHOUSE	3:54:19	P GAMBLING	3:54:48
95	C DAVIES	3:53:03	J ALFORD	3:53:32	S LIMBRICK	3:53:58	J RANDALL	3:54:19	S MERFORT	3:54:48
96	K HARVEY	3:53:03	P FRENCH	3:53:32	T SHAKES	3:53:58	F WARD	3:54:19	K KENNEDY	3:54:48
97	B CONWAY	3:53:04	S DAVIES	3:53:32	R ROOME	3:53:58	S KELLY	3:54:19	C HANNAH	3:54:50
98	D VICTORIN	3:53:04	M MCGEE	3:53:33	L GREEN	3:53:58	S WALTERS	3:54:19	R BROOKS	3:54:50
99	G WINTLE	3:53:04	G LINGLEY	3:53:33	C HAMMOND	3:53:58	G LAURENCE	3:54:19	D HRNCIR	3:54:50
100	M BREWER	3:53:05	J CONQUEST	3:53:34	P MANNING-PRESS	3:54:19				

	11001-11100		11101-11200		11201-11300		11301-11400		11401-11500	
1	A OVERY	3:54:50	P BENNETT	3:55:20	W SCHUMANN	3:55:46	G MALKIN	3:56:14	P NEWSHOLME	3:56:47
2	P RETIMANU	3:54:51	P SEVENO	3:55:20	B ROWE	3:55:46	J CROSS	3:56:14	J VILLASENOR	3:56:47
3	B CLAYDON	3:54:51	C FREW	3:55:21	C WALKER	3:55:46	E EASTERBY	3:56:14	G FLRMYNG	3:56:47
4	M FORTH	3:54:51	M TEULON	3:55:21	J OBERDA	3:55:47	J OLDING	3:56:14	C CANGELOSI	3:56:48
5	M MAYALL	3:54:52	G SMITH	3:55:22	B DARNBROOK	3:55:48	T ENGLAND	3:56:14	H JONES	3:56:48
6	C BLOODWORTH	3:54:52	P MARANGON	3:55:22	C WELLS	3:55:48	L BAKKEN	3:56:14	W HOLL	3:56:49
7	L ZAKOVA	3:54:52	H HARR	3:55:22	D OBERTHUER	3:55:48	L SANDS	3:56:14	M NORTH	3:56:49
8	D PEMBERTON	3:54:53	R SHAMBLER	3:55:23	D PENNEY	3:55:48	M EZURE	3:56:14	P BAYLISS	3:56:49
9	P ROGERSON	3:54:54	P KIRKTON	3:55:23	J ALBINUS	3:55:49	J FRAMPTON	3:56:14	R TOBIN	3:56:49
10	J STARK	3:54:54	M TOOTH	3:55:23	M STACEY	3:55:49	T THORNEYCROFT	3:56:15	E ALDERTON	3:56:49
11	M TAYLOR	3:54:54	D MORTON	3:55:24	S SHELDON	3:55:49	F KIELSTRA	3:56:15	M ALDERTON	3:56:49
12	J HILL	3:54:54	S FENNER	3:55:24	A SHELDON	3:55:50	R KEELING	3:56:15	P BENSON	3:56:50
13	W CONNOLLY	3:54:55	R ANNETTS	3:55:24	S BUCKLEY MELLOR	3:55:50	T REDDICK	3:56:15	R EDGINGS	3:56:50
14	A SHIELDS	3:54:55	G KEANE	3:55:24	J TUOHY	3:55:51	T THURSTON	3:56:15	N DAVIS	3:56:51
15	D MCKANNA	3:54:55	J CANNON	3:55:25	M MCCLELLAND	3:55:51	K RUNDEREIM	3:56:15	G FICAIO	3:56:51
16	A SPENCER	3:54:55	G VAN GOSSUM	3:55:25	R BOSANQUET	3:55:51	L ROBBINS	3:56:16	G PHILLIPS	3:56:51
17	G ROEBUCK	3:54:55	S HART	3:55:25	M RULE	3:55:53	A BUCKETT	3:56:16	N BURNS	3:56:52
18	D OVERTON	3:54:55	K BOND	3:55:25	G PIZZATO	3:55:53	G CURTIN	3:56:17	D MACGREGOR	3:56:53
19	I EVANS	3:54:55	J HUMPHRIES	3:55:25	R SOMMERVILLE	3:55:54	C PEARCE	3:56:17	A BULL	3:56:54
20	S RUTTER	3:54:55	A MILLER	3:55:25	J WILCOX	3:55:54	A MORALEE	3:56:17	J BRAUVALLET	3:56:55
21	J TIPPING	3:54:56	P TILLER	3:55:26	A BAKER	3:55:54	J BRITTO	3:56:17	G BLACKBURN	3:56:55
22	A WEEKES	3:54:56	K FORDER	3:55:26	S BUCKINGHAM	3:55:54	S BUNKER	3:56:18	J SPICKERNELL	3:56:56
23	S CASHIN	3:54:57	P RUDER	3:55:26	J CZECH	3:55:55	D SEAMAN	3:56:18	M RICHARDSON	3:56:57
24	P PARTINGTON	3:54:57	N MCDONAUGH	3:55:27	K WEBER	3:55:55	G WILMER	3:56:18	I STAFFORD	3:56:57
25	J LOW	3:54:57	C STEWART	3:55:27	D OCONNOR	3:55:55	G BROWN	3:56:18	L MCKENNA	3:56:57
26	P TAYLOR	3:54:57	R JONES	3:55:27	L GAIMSTER	3:55:56	G VEEKMANS	3:56:18	K WINSTANLEY	3:56:57
27	G NEASHAM	3:54:58	D EPPS	3:55:27	M TSUKUDA	3:55:56	D WILLIAMSON	3:56:19	C KENNY	3:56:57
28	L JONES	3:54:58	M CARSLAKE	3:55:27	S SADDLER	3:55:57	H KREJCI	3:56:19	P MEADURES	3:56:57
29	R FOSTER	3:54:58	L PAYN	3:55:27	B SVEEN	3:55:57	P SEAMAN	3:56:19	P STONE	3:56:57
30	A BENNETT	3:54:58	J RAGGETT	3:55:27	D EDEN	3:55:58	P PANNETT	3:56:20	S FORSTER	3:56:57
31	A SPEED	3:54:59	A EDGE	3:55:28	R WILLIAMS	3:55:58	L MASON	3:56:20	J VANNI	3:56:57
32	R WATTERS	3:54:59	D WEBB	3:55:28	R KNIGHT	3:55:58	T MATHEWS	3:56:20	A GUMMOW	3:56:57
33	H HOBDAY	3:55:00	A FARMER	3:55:29	S JUOZAITIS	3:55:59	C LANE	3:56:21	L WHARTON	3:56:57
34	M OSTER	3:55:01	H TANAKA	3:55:29	M PENDLEBURY	3:55:59	L GAUGHAN	3:56:21	R COX	3:56:57
35	P SIMPSON	3:55:01	G LICHFIELD	3:55:29	I MACKENZIE	3:55:59	J NEWCOMBE	3:56:21	A WATKINS	3:56:57
36	K WOOD	3:55:01	D SKINNER	3:55:30	C SNEATH	3:55:59	D ROCK	3:56:21	S HARVEY	3:56:57
37	P CALLAN	3:55:01	N FINLEY	3:55:30	G STANLEY	3:56:00	C BRYAN	3:56:21	A LEWIS	3:56:57
38	J OOSTENBRUG	3:55:02	G BARRON	3:55:31	R WHEELER	3:56:00	P WHITEHEAD	3:56:22	A LYNCH	3:56:57
39	J TROTTER	3:55:02	C STIRRATT	3:55:31	G GILMARTIN	3:56:00	P HYDE	3:56:22	A MARKWARDT	3:56:57
40	T UDVARDI	3:55:02	F SANTUCCI	3:55:31	R MERCER	3:56:00	M WELLS	3:56:22	J PULLING	3:56:57
41	A MASON	3:55:02	F GOODWIN	3:55:32	R BUTLER	3:56:00	A MANTHY	3:56:22	V JACKSON	3:56:57
42	A WATERMAN	3:55:02	D KNIGHT	3:55:32	P DEE	3:56:00	J CHEESMAN	3:56:22	N SCREEN	3:56:57
43	A MASON	3:55:03	S PEARSON	3:55:32	K SCHAUFELBERGER	3:56:01	K BISHOP	3:56:22	D MANNING	3:56:57
44	K BRIGHT	3:55:03	B PEARSON	3:55:32	D MITCHELL	3:56:01	R MARTIN	3:56:22	I LANCASTER	3:56:57
45	H DHANJI	3:55:04	P JONES	3:55:32	L BARDEN	3:56:01	K THOMAS	3:56:22	A BRITTON	3:56:57
46	B BRETT	3:55:04	P DEBLING	3:55:32	J LOTT	3:56:01	E GOLDENHEIM	3:56:22	T PARKER	3:56:57
47	S HONEY	3:55:04	A CADU	3:55:32	B JEFFERIES	3:56:02	A ORTALI	3:56:22	C PHILIP	3:56:57
48	T ANDERSON	3:55:04	L FRADIN	3:55:32	S O'KEEFE	3:56:02	J RUSH	3:56:22	C PARRY	3:56:57
49	J TROSSMO	3:55:04	P WOODGATE	3:55:33	C BOWES	3:56:02	J BISSET	3:56:23	R ASHTON	3:56:57
50	N WHITE	3:55:04	W BOWDEN	3:55:33	J DOYNE	3:56:02	P HAYWARD	3:56:23	J CROSKERRY	3:56:57
51	R POWNALL	3:55:04	S JOHNSON	3:55:33	R AGNEW	3:56:04	K OWEN	3:56:23	C SMITH	3:56:57
52	C EASTON	3:55:04	D KETTLEWELL	3:55:34	W PRIEST	3:56:04	K SUTTON	3:56:23	M CURCHER	3:56:57
53	J MERRIMAN	3:55:04	I EVERSLEY	3:55:34	G STOKES	3:56:04	J MCSHERRY	3:56:23	M GOOD	3:56:57
54	J HAYNES	3:55:04	T TURTON	3:55:34	A MORRIS	3:56:04	I CRAINE	3:56:23	M CRISPI	3:56:57
55	P WILKINSON	3:55:05	F MAWSON	3:55:34	R KITSON	3:56:04	N NOTLEY	3:56:23	C DEDMAN	3:56:57
56	C PAYNE	3:55:05	W CROFTS	3:55:34	P VAN DER MEER	3:56:04	G WOOD	3:56:24	A HAMILTON	3:56:57
57	P TRICKETT	3:55:05	K ROWE	3:55:34	P GRUSON	3:56:05	A WHITMORE	3:56:24	J MARSHALL	3:56:57
58	R NICHOLLS	3:55:05	C WESTON	3:55:34	S COOK	3:56:05	R BARRY	3:56:24	M FORD	3:56:57
59	D ROUPRICH	3:55:06	A HOARE	3:55:35	B COLCLOUGH	3:56:05	R ELLIOTT	3:56:24	M THIEL	3:56:57
60	T EVANS	3:55:07	J HAIGH	3:55:36	A CHALMERS	3:56:06	S PIATT	3:56:24	J JAMESON	3:56:57
61	K HULME	3:55:07	S LAMB	3:55:36	D LEWIS	3:56:06	A LEWIS	3:56:25	P STOTT	3:56:57
62	R CHRISTOPHER	3:55:07	K GREGORY	3:55:36	M ANDRADE	3:56:06	E CARRERO	3:56:25	D BRENCHLEY	3:56:57
63	J WILLIAMS	3:55:07	C ALLEN	3:55:36	P FRANCIS	3:56:06	J DRUETT	3:56:25	S COOK	3:56:58
64	D GREGORY	3:55:07	D BISHOP	3:55:37	V WILLGREN	3:56:06	B FORD	3:56:25	J GREER	3:56:58
65	A SCANE	3:55:07	P FORKINS	3:55:37	B BARRETT	3:56:07	E MCDONALD	3:56:25	J CHEZEAUD	3:56:58
66	H ALT	3:55:08	R CAWKWELL	3:55:37	P MUMBY	3:56:07	A SUNDSTROM	3:56:25	J FARRELL	3:56:58
67	J PADILLA	3:55:08	K MINNE	3:55:38	M GRIFFIN	3:56:07	D CORLEY	3:56:25	J MATTHEWS	3:56:58
68	J TRUEBA	3:55:09	P HARRIS	3:55:38	E VAN DEN BOSCH	3:56:08	R WHITTET	3:56:26	M HERENCIA	3:56:58
69	M BOWYER	3:55:10	R PANTER	3:55:38	G BLACKWELL	3:56:08	A SCONTUS	3:56:28	J WHITE	3:56:59
70	A RIPLEY	3:55:11	J GODRON	3:55:38	D EVANS	3:56:08	R ABBATE	3:56:28	J O'DALY	3:56:59
71	R REINGAARD	3:55:11	J BIRCH	3:55:38	A BLYTH	3:56:09	R CLARKSON	3:56:31	C VANSTONE	3:56:59
72	G WALLACE	3:55:11	C LEAK	3:55:38	J TOWERS	3:56:09	A PARTRIDGE	3:56:33	E DE SMET	3:56:59
73	D MCLAY	3:55:12	D ROBERTS	3:55:38	W WEBB	3:56:09	R CLARK	3:56:33	K RANKIN	3:57:00
74	P ZAKIERSKI	3:55:12	Z DHANJI	3:55:38	R CHAMBERS	3:56:09	S LANDER	3:56:33	V ANDERSON	3:57:00
75	J BISHOP	3:55:12	P BELLENOUE	3:55:38	B MCCARTHY	3:56:09	J DEVALL	3:56:33	D STURGEON	3:57:00
76	G DAVIES	3:55:13	L ALLEN	3:55:38	D WILLIAMSON	3:56:09	J MCCABE	3:56:34	J TINKER	3:57:01
77	J FINLAY	3:55:13	J OLIVER	3:55:38	D MOLE	3:56:09	G LEYLAND	3:56:34	H PAETSCH	3:57:01
78	J CRESSWELL	3:55:13	R SUAREZ	3:55:38	R DYER	3:56:10	V CLINTON	3:56:34	R PEARSON	3:57:01
79	R HOLMES	3:55:13	D BUCKINGHAM	3:55:39	W NEWMAN	3:56:10	A KENDRICK	3:56:36	D WRAY	3:57:02
80	S BYRNE	3:55:13	F GOLDIE	3:55:40	G THOMPSON	3:56:10	B GELLARD	3:56:36	M BECNHEKROUN	3:57:03
81	P BROWN	3:55:13	J TURTON	3:55:40	A WOOLLEN	3:56:10	P MILLS	3:56:37	A CALVERT	3:57:03
82	C PITKIN	3:55:13	J FLORIOT	3:55:41	S SINCLAIR	3:56:10	S LEDWARD	3:56:37	A CONNELL	3:57:03
83	J BRENNAN	3:55:13	K GILLOTT	3:55:41	A CAHILL	3:56:10	I NEWMAN	3:56:37	N SERGEANT	3:57:04
84	I CONROY	3:55:13	J WILCE	3:55:41	A RICHARDSON	3:56:10	J SANDS	3:56:37	T SILLETT	3:57:04
85	J BEACOCK	3:55:13	C ITAMI	3:55:41	A THOMAS	3:56:10	P CUMINE	3:56:38	B MUSTOE	3:57:04
86	L WIIG	3:55:13	A THOMAS	3:55:42	A CHRISTENSEN	3:56:11	G WEST	3:56:40	R GORDON	3:57:05
87	D HAMILL	3:55:13	A PUGH	3:55:42	R SQUIRRELL	3:56:11	R DUNN	3:56:40	J DUPRAT	3:57:05
88	A BARTLEY	3:55:13	S FIELD	3:55:42	J POWER	3:56:11	P THOMPSON	3:56:40	D BROWN	3:57:05
89	B SAYERS	3:55:14	D BROWN	3:55:42	C CREGG	3:56:11	N WATINE	3:56:42	M HUGHES	3:57:05
90	M BAKER	3:55:14	N PERRY	3:55:42	G FOULDS	3:56:11	S BARNES	3:56:43	V MENDES	3:57:06
91	S COLLINS	3:55:15	C NAUS	3:55:42	S RISLEY	3:56:11	P FREEDMAN	3:56:43	G HORTON	3:57:06
92	I WALTER	3:55:15	S WRIGHT	3:55:42	P GRACE	3:56:11	B LEE	3:56:43	B HARRISON	3:57:06
93	R THOMPSON	3:55:16	J CARAGIORGIS	3:55:43	D WILD	3:56:12	C LENEHAN	3:56:44	F SANDHAM	3:57:06
94	K FRANZ	3:55:16	J HEEKIN	3:55:43	S UZZELL	3:56:12	J CLAVEY	3:56:44	P COUSINS	3:57:07
95	E HARGREAVE	3:55:16	S JONES	3:55:44	M COLQUHOUN	3:56:12	D BALE	3:56:44	L WARD	3:57:07
96	J DAVISON	3:55:17	M KILMINSTER	3:55:44	G POLLARD	3:56:12	A EDWARD	3:56:45	J BRICOUT	3:57:07
97	T CHAPMAN	3:55:18	P WATERMAN	3:55:44	G GLEESON	3:56:13	K BIBBY	3:56:45	G PARSONS	3:57:07
98	J WALKER	3:55:20	A DUSSES	3:55:45	N JONES	3:56:13	D SMITH	3:56:45	M DUDLEY	3:57:07
99	N ANDERSON	3:55:20	M DOBSON	3:55:45	E THURSTON	3:56:14	D NEALE	3:56:46	W MUEHLHUBER	3:57:07
100	G HOLDEN	3:55:20	A HASELDEN	3:55:45	N WOOLHOUSE	3:56:14	A MCCULLOCH	3:56:47	G GREEN	3:57:07

#	11501-11600		11601-11700		11701-11800		11801-11900		11901-12000	
1	M TOWLER	3:57:08	P MAKIN	3:57:30	E JEWELL	3:57:52	P CLARK	3:58:14	R HUGHES	3:58:32
2	J BROWN	3:57:08	G WOOD	3:57:30	C STOKES	3:57:52	J DONOGHUE	3:58:14	J FLYNN	3:58:32
3	R HARRISON	3:57:08	J STEED	3:57:30	K BASTIAN	3:57:52	A BARRETT	3:58:15	M WILLIAMS	3:58:32
4	M NUNN	3:57:08	N FOREMAN	3:57:30	L GUNN	3:57:53	N COSTER	3:58:15	J DRENNAN	3:58:32
5	J LEADBEATER	3:57:08	D BROOKS	3:57:30	J PELLS	3:57:53	A SIMON	3:58:15	R WALTERS	3:58:32
6	K HILLS	3:57:08	W DIXON	3:57:30	G CROWE	3:57:53	E CHILVERS	3:58:16	J MCDOWELL	3:58:33
7	P MINION	3:57:09	R ANDERSON	3:57:31	D WRIGHT	3:57:53	B LOCKE	3:58:16	J BIRD	3:58:33
8	M JACKSON	3:57:10	G ROSSL	3:57:31	T HUTCHINSON	3:57:53	T WHITE	3:58:16	K KAMMERER	3:58:33
9	J HILL	3:57:10	C FAGAN	3:57:31	W KIDD	3:57:54	M FOREN	3:58:16	B GLEDHILL	3:58:34
10	P PARSONS	3:57:10	G PRICE	3:57:31	R HAWKSLEY	3:57:54	J WARBY	3:58:16	A WRIGHT	3:58:34
11	A LONG	3:57:10	M LUSTY	3:57:31	D WILKINS	3:57:55	C STEPHENS	3:58:16	M AGNEW	3:58:34
12	J MAY	3:57:10	B THOMAS	3:57:32	C BELLWOOD	3:57:55	P JONES	3:58:17	J FLACK	3:58:34
13	J FURY	3:57:10	J EVANS	3:57:32	S ST JOHN PARKER	3:57:56	M BURTON	3:58:17	J DOURS	3:58:34
14	D HASLAM	3:57:10	K HARDING	3:57:32	M DRANE	3:57:56	A BATES	3:58:17	P HANVEY	3:58:34
15	C WESTMAAS	3:57:11	J POWER	3:57:32	R PLATTEN	3:57:56	D LYNCH	3:58:17	R FORD	3:58:34
16	K HAWKINS	3:57:11	P NANJI	3:57:32	D CORTI	3:57:56	P REDHEAD	3:58:17	G NORRIS	3:58:35
17	T COOPER	3:57:12	E CIANCHI	3:57:32	S REMBELLOW	3:57:57	R TALFMAN	3:58:17	C WHITEFOORD	3:58:35
18	S DAVIES	3:57:12	D WHITE	3:57:33	C BOALER	3:57:57	B GARTH	3:58:18	G DITTRICH	3:58:35
19	G CRAMPTON	3:57:12	P WALKER	3:57:33	G PLATTEN	3:57:57	N HULSE	3:58:18	T RAWCLIFFE	3:58:35
20	M PERRY	3:57:12	J GREEN	3:57:33	P HAYNES	3:57:58	I HALL	3:58:18	P RADFORD	3:58:35
21	B REID	3:57:13	J ROYER	3:57:33	C JONES	3:57:58	M TURNER	3:58:19	S PROSSER	3:58:35
22	J SANGHERA	3:57:13	G HEDGES	3:57:33	Y AUBREE	3:57:58	P HERON	3:58:19	D JONES	3:58:35
23	A PEDERSEN	3:57:13	E MARTIN	3:57:34	T NUTT	3:57:58	S LAWS	3:58:19	D GILE	3:58:36
24	F KARL	3:57:13	S KEE	3:57:34	D TAYLOR	3:57:58	P SMITH	3:58:19	A OSTROWSKI	3:58:36
25	P GORANSSON	3:57:15	S NEWELL	3:57:34	I TRUFFET	3:57:59	R YOUNG	3:58:19	J JOANIQUET	3:58:36
26	D HUMPHRIES	3:57:15	J LOCKLEY	3:57:34	B RIXEN	3:58:00	I ISAACSON	3:58:19	S COLLIER	3:58:36
27	B WILLSHER	3:57:16	T SMITH	3:57:34	J CASTELAIN	3:58:00	R JUNG	3:58:19	A PRESCOT	3:58:36
28	R GILMOUR	3:57:16	T LEWIS	3:57:34	R LLOYD	3:58:00	A HAYMES	3:58:19	G DARBY	3:58:37
29	M HNYDA	3:57:16	D SMITH	3:57:35	A DAVIES	3:58:00	B SINAR	3:58:20	G WILLIAMS	3:58:37
30	M NORMAN	3:57:16	D MILWAIN	3:57:35	D RUNDLE	3:58:00	P O'NEILL	3:58:20	F MOURIAUX	3:58:37
31	J SAUNDERS	3:57:16	M HASLEY	3:57:36	K WEBB	3:58:00	J SLUKA	3:58:20	B BEARMAN	3:58:38
32	V LINDSEY	3:57:16	H RICHARDSON	3:57:36	D BROWN	3:58:00	J GLOCK	3:58:20	J BONNEFOY	3:58:38
33	J HEREDITH	3:57:17	M GARRATT	3:57:36	K WAIGHT	3:58:00	M SEARLE	3:58:20	M MACKAY	3:58:38
34	J JARVIS	3:57:17	R HYLAND	3:57:36	G PICKUP	3:58:00	D ANSELL	3:58:20	V SAVILLE	3:58:39
35	S DALY	3:57:17	A NIVEN	3:57:37	J DAVIES	3:58:01	J KENNEDY	3:58:21	T JOHNSTONE	3:58:39
36	A RANGER	3:57:17	A HOKSVOLD	3:57:37	G HILLS	3:58:01	L LEVERTON	3:58:21	R HARRISON	3:58:40
37	W WYKES	3:57:17	P WELLS	3:57:37	A DI ROMA	3:58:02	I CLARK	3:58:21	A BAKER	3:58:40
38	A COLLINGBOURNE	3:57:17	P BUTCHER	3:57:38	R BOXER	3:58:02	D NEWMAN	3:58:22	B HUNTER	3:58:40
39	J AMORY	3:57:17	A WARHAFTIG	3:57:38	C LIGNIERES	3:58:02	N FRANKLIN	3:58:22	W LORD	3:58:40
40	D HOLTBY	3:57:18	I COTTIS	3:57:38	A WOOD	3:58:02	P CUMINGS	3:58:22	A CHORA	3:58:40
41	U DEUMANN	3:57:18	D OWEN	3:57:39	G MAUROUDIS	3:58:02	S REYNOLDS	3:58:22	K HELKE	3:58:40
42	D THOMPSON	3:57:18	H VYSE	3:57:39	T MICKLETHWAITE	3:58:02	J MOTTRAM	3:58:23	B GARRETY	3:58:40
43	J EASTER	3:57:18	J ST CLAIR ROBERTS	3:57:39	M BOTT	3:58:03	D FROUD	3:58:23	G WEST	3:58:41
44	B DUGGAN	3:57:19	M CRISTILLI	3:57:40	R CRAGGS	3:58:03	P MAISEL	3:58:23	O SAMSON	3:58:41
45	P HARVEY	3:57:19	E LIU	3:57:40	J VARTAN	3:58:03	D TURNER	3:58:23	K GALLAGHER	3:58:41
46	E BJERKE	3:57:19	D CARDY	3:57:41	J CLARKE	3:58:03	O STROEMOE	3:58:24	E HUGHES	3:58:41
47	P BYATT	3:57:19	T CASEY	3:57:41	J CLARKE	3:58:03	S TAYLOR	3:58:24	P LEONARD	3:58:41
48	N HEAP	3:57:19	K ROBERTS	3:57:41	R DEKOCK	3:58:04	S JONES	3:58:24	C HAYWARD	3:58:42
49	S MORTON	3:57:19	B WENHAM	3:57:41	K ASHWOOD	3:58:04	D MCMILLAN	3:58:24	M LUDLOW	3:58:42
50	R BOURNE	3:57:20	D BISHOP	3:57:41	O LHOTELLIER	3:58:04	V BOWES	3:58:25	L PARKER	3:58:43
51	C WITHAM	3:57:20	P DAVIDSON	3:57:41	D HEWITT	3:58:04	C WALSH	3:58:25	N MOUNTFORD	3:58:43
52	S HOWARD	3:57:20	P GATELY	3:57:41	P LYNE	3:58:04	J HOLE	3:58:25	S THORRINGTON	3:58:43
53	P CHAUVEAU	3:57:20	C LITTLE	3:57:42	J MCAULIFFE	3:58:04	C BIRCH	3:58:25	S HOPE	3:58:44
54	W CANSICK	3:57:21	J SESIL	3:57:42	S WOODHAM	3:58:04	T POTTS	3:58:25	D BEVAN	3:58:44
55	C CARR	3:57:21	J LEE	3:57:43	K LOENG	3:58:04	S BROADWAY	3:58:25	D SHORE	3:58:44
56	G PRIOR	3:57:21	P BELSHAW	3:57:43	S WANG	3:58:04	I CHANT	3:58:26	J RHODES	3:58:44
57	G TUNLEY	3:57:21	D WILCOX	3:57:44	M HANLON	3:58:05	C HALL	3:58:26	M MILLINGS	3:58:44
58	G GASSER	3:57:21	S WINDMILL	3:57:44	G HOLLINGSHEAD	3:58:05	M HOBAN	3:58:26	A SMALLWOOD	3:58:45
59	G PURNELL	3:57:22	J CROAD	3:57:44	M EGGENSCHWILER	3:58:05	S FARRER	3:58:26	A MCGHIE	3:58:45
60	F BAINVEL	3:57:22	R KEESON	3:57:44	T EDDY	3:58:05	P FRASER	3:58:26	A OLIVEIRA	3:58:45
61	R HEATH	3:57:22	F PERCHAT	3:57:44	D CHIRGWIN	3:58:05	A HONOUR	3:58:27	G MACNAMARA	3:58:46
62	S FOSTER	3:57:22	L LARKINS	3:57:44	D ELLIS	3:58:05	C DRAKE	3:58:27	C EVANS	3:58:46
63	D KIDD	3:57:22	D LEACH	3:57:44	G MARTENSSON	3:58:06	M JONES	3:58:27	L VALERIO	3:58:46
64	J LANGHAM	3:57:22	B GOULD	3:57:45	K BARTH	3:58:06	R DANIEL	3:58:27	J NEWELL	3:58:46
65	K DAWSON	3:57:22	I GOODALL	3:57:45	D EAST	3:58:06	M SILMON	3:58:27	R DOYLE	3:58:47
66	K BLAKEY	3:57:23	P HARRIS	3:57:45	H SAHOTA	3:58:06	J BOOKER	3:58:27	C JOHNSON	3:58:47
67	B READING	3:57:23	S JAHANS	3:57:45	P JOOSEP	3:58:06	J CHARPANTIER	3:58:27	M DEXTER-STEELE	3:58:47
68	P BOBIA	3:57:23	J ALLAM	3:57:46	P CHANEL	3:58:06	J HOWORTH	3:58:27	J CUFFE	3:58:47
69	M ARNOLD	3:57:23	G JONES	3:57:47	M THURLBY	3:58:07	G JORDAN	3:58:27	J HUMPHREYS	3:58:48
70	R PLUMB	3:57:23	T WEBSTER	3:57:47	A HIGGINS	3:58:07	S LEDAMOISEL	3:58:27	D LLEWELLYN	3:58:48
71	S PLUMB	3:57:23	M MALONEY	3:57:47	R JENKINS	3:58:07	J SEARLE	3:58:27	M LUFF	3:58:48
72	T SARSON	3:57:23	P MOORE	3:57:47	G AITKEN	3:58:07	D ENGLISH	3:58:27	S DOOLEY	3:58:48
73	G NORRIS	3:57:23	D CANAVAN	3:57:47	G GRANT	3:58:07	A POOLE	3:58:27	V AF ROSENBORG	3:58:48
74	A COOKE	3:57:24	J CLISBY	3:57:47	A VERNOUM	3:58:08	D GRISTOCK	3:58:27	K SWAIL	3:58:48
75	V EARLEY	3:57:24	L STONE	3:57:48	V JAMIESON	3:58:08	K PAYNE	3:58:27	G WILLIAMS	3:58:49
76	J GLOVER	3:57:24	E BLACKBURN	3:57:48	J MCGOWAN	3:58:08	D MCGUINNESS	3:58:27	J SHORT	3:58:49
77	M BOL	3:57:24	K SUMMERS	3:57:48	G DAWES	3:58:08	D LEUTY	3:58:27	P BAKER	3:58:49
78	E FIELDS	3:57:24	D QUILTER	3:57:48	K MORRIS	3:58:08	A QUILLEY	3:58:27	P CLIFFORD	3:58:49
79	M TAYLOR	3:57:24	L HOSHEMI	3:57:48	I COLLINS	3:58:08	C HALL	3:58:27	P CARDIFF	3:58:49
80	T SINCLAIR	3:57:24	J SCOTT	3:57:48	B GRINHAM	3:58:08	S WILD	3:58:27	J LIPCZYNSKI	3:58:49
81	B KELLY	3:57:24	G BROWN	3:57:48	J MARQUIS	3:58:08	H MANOE	3:58:27	K MITCHELL	3:58:49
82	A ROBE	3:57:25	K MORDEN	3:57:49	G LAUNDON	3:58:08	P GALLAGHER	3:58:28	D LISTON	3:58:50
83	C SOLANKI	3:57:25	I CHIPPERFIELD	3:57:49	T CLARKE	3:58:08	R PROBETS	3:58:28	S DAVIS	3:58:50
84	P NORTHWOOD	3:57:25	D ARRAN	3:57:49	I SEILZ	3:58:08	R MEROLA	3:58:28	K HUDSON	3:58:50
85	G HALPERN	3:57:26	P BROMILOW	3:57:49	J PHALIPOU	3:58:08	J RIGBY	3:58:28	M DUDLEY	3:58:51
86	G SMITH	3:57:26	K BATTEN	3:57:49	B ELLISON	3:58:09	R JAMES	3:58:28	M MILLS	3:58:51
87	A HARPER	3:57:26	D WILSON	3:57:49	V WATKINS	3:58:09	S SUMMERS	3:58:29	R RATCLIFFE	3:58:51
88	J MENDUM	3:57:26	F WEBER	3:57:49	A HARMAN	3:58:09	T LEONARD	3:58:29	C YOUNG	3:58:51
89	A WILLIAMS	3:57:26	J TURNER	3:57:49	I SMITH	3:58:09	D MILLER	3:58:29	S BARCLAY	3:58:51
90	M PULLEN	3:57:26	P MACKIE	3:57:49	P BRADY	3:58:09	H BAHMANN	3:58:30	J ANDREWS	3:58:52
91	P RAWSON	3:57:26	J BUCK	3:57:50	E JOHNSON	3:58:10	K LISSENDEN	3:58:30	W WHITTELL	3:58:52
92	P RONAYNE	3:57:27	G WRETHAM	3:57:50	J FISHER	3:58:10	C LI	3:58:30	B HUMPHREYS	3:58:52
93	L FROST	3:57:27	S HAYLEY	3:57:50	A SPENCER	3:58:11	A MAVIN	3:58:30	A BISS	3:58:53
94	W LENZEN	3:57:28	F PITT	3:57:50	P MCCARTHY	3:58:11	C ROBSON	3:58:30	R NELL	3:58:53
95	J CAPPS	3:57:29	A SPRINGER	3:57:51	P DEATH	3:58:11	G SAWYER	3:58:30	B GRIFFITHS	3:58:54
96	H BONE	3:57:29	J BLACKBURN	3:57:51	S CUNNINGHAM	3:58:11	J CLARKE	3:58:31	P THIBURCE	3:58:54
97	A MATHER	3:57:30	M STACEY	3:57:51	J BEYNON	3:58:12	F LEGENDRE	3:58:31	T BAKER	3:58:54
98	S CHOWN-DUNNE	3:57:30	A BLIZARD	3:57:51	D REYMOND	3:58:13	D KOFKIN	3:58:31	T JOHN	3:58:55
99	A GIBSON	3:57:30	D BILKEY	3:57:52	W SHIPTON	3:58:14	C LEGG	3:58:32	E DAVIS	3:58:56
100	S TEMPEST	3:57:30	A QUINN	3:57:52	J WOOKEY	3:58:14	S PARSONS	3:58:32	K TURNER	3:58:57

#	12001-12100		12101-12200		12201-12300		12301-12400		12401-12500	
1	I COOPER	3:58:57	A DODD	3:59:22	A SNELSON	3:59:46	M BRODERICK	4:00:20	M HALL	4:00:50
2	J MOORE	3:58:58	E ROSS	3:59:22	R ELEANOR	3:59:46	R PERING	4:00:21	A RODNEY	4:00:50
3	S HILLS	3:58:58	R DRAKEFORD	3:59:22	R CLARKE	3:59:46	M MCSHANE	4:00:21	F VALLER	4:00:50
4	P HOLT	3:58:58	M HARDING	3:59:22	A LEEDS	3:59:47	E NAISMITH	4:00:21	N CARTER	4:00:51
5	G MOUNSEY	3:58:59	J HALL	3:59:22	G PETTENGELL	3:59:47	A PICKUP	4:00:22	J KEGERREIS	4:00:51
6	M YEOMANS	3:58:59	P HEALY	3:59:23	K DALE	3:59:47	R WATSON	4:00:22	M TOULCHER	4:00:51
7	J LINDH	3:58:59	D DENHAM	3:59:23	P YOUNGMAN	3:59:47	Q WATSON	4:00:22	D CAVE	4:00:51
8	R PORTER	3:59:00	J ANDERSON	3:59:23	D BLAND	3:59:47	R JARDIN	4:00:22	J CANNELL	4:00:51
9	J HOPKINSON	3:59:00	D ROOKE	3:59:23	D CULLERN	3:59:48	J BRAND	4:00:22	T SONNTAG	4:00:51
10	K EVANS	3:59:00	P WILLIAMS	3:59:23	F DOSSIN	3:59:48	J HOLMAN	4:00:22	A MCGARRY	4:00:52
11	P FORRESTER	3:59:00	E PARIS	3:59:23	P DAVISON	3:59:48	P KUH	4:00:23	M EDMONDSON	4:00:52
12	V GEMMELL	3:59:00	M SIMON JUNIOR	3:59:24	L WRIGHT	3:59:49	C DAVIES	4:00:23	M LETLEY	4:00:52
13	A BAHON	3:59:00	R LOWE	3:59:24	F HUSJORD	3:59:49	M MASKELL	4:00:23	R GILES	4:00:53
14	P HORAN	3:59:00	R SHORE	3:59:25	A BRULE	3:59:50	S MAJOR	4:00:23	D WHEELER	4:00:53
15	P STRETTEN	3:59:01	P PACKER	3:59:25	L SMITH	3:59:51	A AUGE DE RANCOURT	4:00:23	M CALVERT	4:00:53
16	L WILLIAMS	3:59:01	J SPIGHT	3:59:25	P JAUSSELY	3:59:51	R CROSBY	4:00:23	I FELLINGHAM	4:00:53
17	S IIYAMA	3:59:01	I FORD	3:59:26	J MORGAN	3:59:51	V ROBINSON	4:00:23	D FLETCHER	4:00:53
18	L BLOMSTEN	3:59:01	G JONES	3:59:26	J HAWORTH	3:59:51	G CALOW	4:00:23	C LUDLOW	4:00:53
19	I NEALE	3:59:02	B DEWIS	3:59:26	E JOERCHEL	3:59:51	G BURROUGH	4:00:23	J LOOSEMORE	4:00:54
20	D MCLEAN	3:59:02	P BOWELL	3:59:26	A SINGH	3:59:51	R HODSON	4:00:23	C GIL	4:00:54
21	G PEACOCK	3:59:02	L GRUNDY	3:59:26	M SPRASON	3:59:52	A GOODMAN	4:00:23	G HANCOCK	4:00:55
22	G MEECH	3:59:02	R PUTTOCK	3:59:27	D VALLER	3:59:52	M DONOGHUE	4:00:23	S MCGRORY	4:00:55
23	I COX	3:59:02	J WILKINSON	3:59:27	P BIRKINSHAW	3:59:52	J WILDMAN	4:00:24	E TORNABONI	4:00:55
24	C CLARK	3:59:03	M WHITE	3:59:27	J ANCILL	3:59:52	D MCKEOWN	4:00:24	K GOULD	4:00:56
25	J CLACK	3:59:03	E JOHNSON	3:59:27	G LOCK	3:59:52	M CHATTENTON	4:00:24	S NICHOLS	4:00:57
26	B GRINDLEY	3:59:03	E MACMILLAN	3:59:27	P SKINNER	3:59:53	D FAIRLEY	4:00:25	G WATSON	4:00:58
27	J BOWER	3:59:03	P BURLINSON	3:59:27	M JONES	3:59:53	R HOLLAND	4:00:25	M COURT	4:00:59
28	R CRAMER	3:59:04	R MOULDING	3:59:27	L COLLETT	3:59:54	P FALVEY	4:00:25	J DOLAN	4:01:00
29	J MOLONEY	3:59:04	J GIBBARD	3:59:27	S LORD	3:59:55	M MCGINTY	4:00:25	J BREEN	4:01:00
30	S CROWLEY	3:59:04	M WRAGG	3:59:27	A GIDLEY	3:59:55	J WEBBON	4:00:25	M POTTAGE	4:01:01
31	P JENNINGS	3:59:04	J HALE	3:59:27	S WINTER	3:59:55	G TYSON	4:00:25	J GRIFFITHS	4:01:01
32	I COLLIER	3:59:04	C WEBB	3:59:27	B HARMER	3:59:55	D BISSET	4:00:26	A LUNDIE	4:01:02
33	G BIGG	3:59:04	T MCGILL	3:59:28	D HUTTON	3:59:56	M LYONS	4:00:26	T HOWE	4:01:03
34	B O'BRIEN	3:59:05	S GIBSON	3:59:29	P CASHMAN	3:59:56	G WALLACE	4:00:26	H WESTGAARD	4:01:03
35	S KETTLES	3:59:05	D HANNAH	3:59:29	D COOPER	3:59:57	R DALLEY	4:00:27	B RAND	4:01:03
36	K REYNOLDS	3:59:05	A HUGHES	3:59:29	P COOPER	3:59:57	G GRIFFITHS	4:00:27	T CLARK	4:01:04
37	R SCHAU	3:59:05	P FITZGERALD	3:59:30	B ROBERTS	3:59:57	S WINGFIELD	4:00:28	P RICHARDS	4:01:04
38	M ATKINSON	3:59:05	Y NAKAMURA	3:59:30	R WILLOUGHBY	3:59:57	B JOHNSON	4:00:29	S EDGLEY	4:01:05
39	J WEELER	3:59:05	J BRIDGES	3:59:31	C EDWARDS	3:59:59	S WARD	4:00:29	T MEDD	4:01:05
40	B WILKINS	3:59:06	G BENNETT	3:59:31	J WITHERALL	3:59:59	T FROST	4:00:29	B BAYLISS	4:01:05
41	C HARVEY	3:59:06	J GREEN	3:59:31	K DAVIES	3:59:59	D ROBERTSON	4:00:29	K EMMISON	4:01:05
42	E SIMPSON	3:59:06	E GATTI	3:59:31	S LEESE	3:59:59	C CAMPBELL	4:00:30	S PRICE	4:01:05
43	A BLACKLEY	3:59:06	P WORTHINGTON	3:59:31	K MARSHALLSAY	3:59:59	N WATTS	4:00:30	S LUCAS	4:01:06
44	A STANDAGE	3:59:06	J WHITAKER	3:59:31	P RICHARDS	3:59:59	J O'BRIEN	4:00:30	G GLEW	4:01:06
45	E HALES	3:59:07	A GLADMAN	3:59:32	G BUDINGER	4:00:00	P ABNETT	4:00:30	C SMITH	4:01:07
46	M MANSON	3:59:07	M OFFER	3:59:32	M WILLIAMS	4:00:00	R JOHNSON	4:00:30	M RUSSELL	4:01:07
47	D DOMONEY	3:59:07	J BOUWER	3:59:32	J LALANNE	4:00:00	E MILLER	4:00:30	D PALMER	4:01:07
48	R FRANKCOM	3:59:08	K WESTON	3:59:33	R HARRIS	4:00:00	C LETCHFORD	4:00:30	M THOMAS	4:01:07
49	S LEWIS	3:59:08	S KEMP	3:59:34	M TAYLOR	4:00:00	P FRIEDLI	4:00:30	S HALEWOOD	4:01:08
50	G BLANEY	3:59:08	S TILLBROOK	3:59:34	S CAPELING	4:00:00	C TAYLOR	4:00:30	G JONES	4:01:08
51	A GIBSON	3:59:08	G WORTS	3:59:34	K SHUFFLEBOTTOM	4:00:01	S GUYATT	4:00:30	R WARD	4:01:08
52	N OROSZ	3:59:08	A CHEUNG	3:59:34	S BARRETT	4:00:02	C POTTS	4:00:30	J SANZ	4:01:08
53	P HAWES	3:59:08	J COLDWELL	3:59:34	L GAZZANI	4:00:02	S AMBRIDGE	4:00:31	M BLACK	4:01:10
54	C FRYER	3:59:08	K NUTTER	3:59:34	L SIMPSON	4:00:02	F MALLETT	4:00:32	N KRUK	4:01:11
55	T OAKES	3:59:08	M PUPIUS	3:59:35	J RIDD	4:00:02	N PRENTICE	4:00:32	J EGEA	4:01:12
56	M SKIPP	3:59:09	J HAYCOCK	3:59:36	S MEACHAM	4:00:02	F OHANLON	4:00:33	D DAINTY	4:01:13
57	J ENESCOTT	3:59:09	J MCKENZIE	3:59:36	I KING	4:00:03	C ELLIOTT	4:00:33	S MCGUGAN	4:01:14
58	C WILKIE	3:59:09	L ROOKE	3:59:36	D STOCKLEY	4:00:03	M FAHY	4:00:33	M WARD	4:01:15
59	J CLARK	3:59:10	M JAMES	3:59:36	G WOOLDRIDGE	4:00:04	D LOBLEY	4:00:34	R FRASER	4:01:15
60	E KNAPPER	3:59:10	J JACKSON	3:59:37	R BAKER	4:00:05	M FLECKNOE	4:00:34	D SCOTT	4:01:15
61	H BERTRAM	3:59:10	P DAVIES	3:59:37	J HAWKINS	4:00:05	J BROWN	4:00:34	P AIREY	4:01:15
62	W LOEBLING	3:59:10	C ABRAHAMS	3:59:38	P KNIGHT	4:00:05	D BORTON	4:00:35	M SIEKMANN	4:01:15
63	J LE PIOULLE	3:59:10	T HOWE	3:59:38	P GOVIER	4:00:05	K VERNON	4:00:36	N ISLAM	4:01:15
64	R GUINNESS	3:59:10	A FISHER	3:59:38	M SCHULTE	4:00:05	G SANKEY	4:00:37	K FOKER	4:01:15
65	M ARCHER	3:59:10	J PETERSEN	3:59:38	C GIBBONS	4:00:05	A WOOLVEN	4:00:37	M FEARN	4:01:16
66	S BURNS	3:59:11	N DUPAIN	3:59:38	R GIBBONS	4:00:05	S MOULDING	4:00:38	T RAYMER	4:01:16
67	M LUEBLING	3:59:11	F ANDREUSSI	3:59:39	C MILTON	4:00:06	A CABLE	4:00:38	B SHEPHERD	4:01:17
68	J MEADS	3:59:11	A MASON	3:59:39	M STOREY	4:00:06	D KELLETT	4:00:39	R THOMAS	4:01:18
69	J HEARNE	3:59:12	M ORTON	3:59:39	D LANGE	4:00:06	V CAGNES	4:00:39	D PILKINGTON	4:01:18
70	T WARD	3:59:12	M GANNON	3:59:39	A DARKES	4:00:06	C BEALBY	4:00:40	R GRAHAM	4:01:18
71	M CHAMBERS	3:59:13	N BELL	3:59:39	J MARTIN	4:00:07	T DENCH-LAYTON	4:00:41	J MCVICAR	4:01:18
72	P FENECH	3:59:13	S RUGMAN	3:59:39	M NEATE	4:00:07	A PRICE	4:00:42	R ABBOTT	4:01:18
73	R MACE	3:59:14	D HEDGES	3:59:39	A COULSON	4:00:07	T PETTERSEN	4:00:43	A MARGUERAT	4:01:18
74	A BUTTER	3:59:15	A SANDERS	3:59:39	J LIVSEY	4:00:07	S SMITH	4:00:43	N STEWART	4:01:19
75	D CHAPMAN	3:59:15	H VICKERS	3:59:40	D BAILLIE	4:00:08	B WILLIAMS	4:00:43	R BURLEY	4:01:19
76	C BYTHELL	3:59:16	B ALLARD	3:59:40	C WERNHULT	4:00:08	D SIDHU	4:00:44	T NILSSON	4:01:20
77	T GOUGH	3:59:16	D BRIERLEY	3:59:41	N SKILDHEIM	4:00:08	U GUMMELT	4:00:44	J PRESTON	4:01:20
78	G MACDONALD	3:59:17	J DONNELLY	3:59:41	B FORREST	4:00:09	D LANCASTER	4:00:44	J O'HARA	4:01:21
79	R MOORE	3:59:17	R DYSON	3:59:41	C SAINTY	4:00:09	P ANDRIOLA	4:00:44	P TIMMINS	4:01:21
80	B GLOVER	3:59:17	G SWIFT	3:59:42	A BROWN	4:00:10	S MCGEOWN	4:00:44	A EATON	4:01:21
81	R FULLER	3:59:18	P RUDD	3:59:42	K WILLIAMS	4:00:10	D LANG	4:00:44	T MITCHELL	4:01:21
82	N GREEN	3:59:18	S BROOKS	3:59:42	T CLARK	4:00:11	N MESSARRA	4:00:44	S HAGUE	4:01:22
83	J DAVIS	3:59:18	T GRIER	3:59:42	T YOUNG	4:00:11	P PRICE	4:00:45	P TAYLOR	4:01:23
84	S REILLY	3:59:18	G JONES	3:59:43	G CHAPMAN	4:00:12	M MARSHALL	4:00:46	H GILL	4:01:23
85	D CARTER	3:59:19	R KEELER	3:59:43	D PAGE	4:00:13	M STRIMER	4:00:46	D HARGREAVES	4:01:23
86	A HOUSE	3:59:19	E NYE	3:59:43	F OCONNOR	4:00:14	J MOORE	4:00:46	D MORGAN	4:01:24
87	S HOLDING	3:59:19	D SEPHTON	3:59:43	C ROSS	4:00:14	J HART	4:00:46	K SELLICK	4:01:24
88	I THIERSTEIN	3:59:19	N WALSH	3:59:44	P STEVENSON	4:00:15	S WHITE	4:00:46	C FLOOD	4:01:24
89	C VOUTAZ	3:59:19	K HUMPHRIES	3:59:44	K BECKER	4:00:16	F SMITH	4:00:46	H PLAYER	4:01:24
90	M RENSHAW	3:59:19	M MAW	3:59:45	M BOLTON	4:00:16	T FOGARTHY	4:00:47	D PLEASS	4:01:25
91	K FRESLE	3:59:20	D ANDREWS	3:59:45	R HOLNESS	4:00:16	C MALTBY	4:00:47	T VICKERS	4:01:25
92	C ENGLAND	3:59:20	R MELIA	3:59:45	P HUNTER	4:00:17	M PHILLIPS	4:00:47	D LEWIS	4:01:25
93	J CHAMBERS	3:59:20	D NICHOLLS	3:59:45	W HARRIES-JONES	4:00:17	J STOWELL	4:00:47	L THOMPSON	4:01:25
94	D HAWORTH	3:59:20	B SAYER	3:59:45	L MANSON	4:00:18	J DAVIDSON	4:00:48	D CASSORET	4:01:25
95	J BYRD	3:59:21	T SCRIVEN	3:59:45	L KELLY	4:00:18	T CLARK	4:00:48	M PENNAL	4:01:26
96	D KENT	3:59:21	M FRASER	3:59:45	M VON HELDEN	4:00:18	T PEACOCK	4:00:48	J BUTTERWORTH	4:01:27
97	S OMIYA	3:59:21	P DALE	3:59:45	L TRUEMAN	4:00:18	M BOTTING	4:00:48	D LAW	4:01:27
98	A BROWN	3:59:21	B INGVARDSEN	3:59:45	D BROWN	4:00:18	F STALLARD	4:00:49	S GWALTER	4:01:28
99	K FRYER	3:59:21	A KEITH	3:59:46	D WESTON	4:00:19	N FULLER	4:00:49	J MCCORRY	4:01:28
100	S BOTTRILL	3:59:22	A RISEBOROUGH	3:59:46	R BROUGHTON	4:00:19	N CARLSEN	4:00:50	I CHAFFEY	4:01:28

#	12501-12600		12601-12700		12701-12800		12801-12900		12901-13000	
1	D CAFFYN	4:01:28	A WEST	4:01:54	C GERRAD	4:02:21	P CONLAN	4:02:53	J NUGENT	4:03:17
2	N DE BROUWER	4:01:28	I HICKS	4:01:55	D GASH	4:02:21	H VITT	4:02:53	J COX	4:03:17
3	R HOLDEN	4:01:28	B ELLIOTT	4:01:55	M HUMPHRIES	4:02:21	B DOLLIN	4:02:53	C BRINTON	4:03:17
4	D HARDING	4:01:28	M BONORAND	4:01:55	P MANNION	4:02:21	P WADDINGTON	4:02:53	T SWAIN	4:03:18
5	K WINNERY	4:01:29	T PASSAM	4:01:55	L BUTCHER	4:02:22	D SAWTELL	4:02:53	R COSSON	4:03:18
6	R BROOKS	4:01:30	R JACKSON	4:01:56	R ROWLATT	4:02:22	E LOVERING	4:02:53	C JONES	4:03:18
7	G GARCIA	4:01:30	J MITCHELL	4:01:56	T MCGORTY	4:02:23	A SINGH	4:02:53	D PARKER	4:03:18
8	G MAPP	4:01:30	L BRUNET	4:01:57	C CARSCADDEN	4:02:24	C SHAW	4:02:53	R RICKARD	4:03:19
9	R BURCOMBE	4:01:30	M BROOKS	4:01:58	R HANSEN	4:02:24	S SMITH	4:02:53	R CARBY	4:03:19
10	K BROCKMAN	4:01:31	D WALKER	4:01:58	H COENEN	4:02:24	C JESSUP	4:02:53	C WOMERSLEY	4:03:19
11	C COLMAN	4:01:31	D STUBBS	4:01:58	M WHITE	4:02:24	G WILKINSON	4:02:53	A CHINERY	4:03:19
12	H EDWARDS	4:01:32	W MCCRACKEN	4:01:58	A HUTCHINSON	4:02:24	D GORDON	4:02:53	G BAILEY	4:03:20
13	J CONSTANTINE	4:01:32	M WHITE	4:01:59	M ASHWELL	4:02:24	W BARRETT	4:02:53	I SAGE	4:03:20
14	R LANE	4:01:32	S WYATT	4:01:59	J MERCADER	4:02:24	S JOEL	4:02:54	M OPHIELD	4:03:20
15	T SHEA	4:01:32	N DAVID	4:01:59	N PAGE	4:02:25	L CHADDERTON	4:02:54	J MASSINGHAM	4:03:21
16	D MILES	4:01:32	C WOODMAN	4:01:59	A GERAUER	4:02:25	S SALTER	4:02:54	P NEWTON	4:03:21
17	A PENAZZI	4:01:33	B THORNTON	4:02:00	M HARGREAVES	4:02:26	G JONES	4:02:54	E BAILEY	4:03:21
18	T PUMPREY	4:01:33	J POTTER	4:02:00	J BACON	4:02:26	R DRUCKES	4:02:55	A SYSON	4:03:22
19	M CUNNINGHAM	4:01:33	L NILSSON	4:02:00	A BAZZONI	4:02:26	C SHARP	4:02:55	I YORKE	4:03:22
20	P WEBB	4:01:33	D ANDRUCH	4:02:00	N FARRANT	4:02:27	I OWERS	4:02:55	J DUDLEY	4:03:22
21	J LAVY	4:01:33	R SOUTHWELL	4:02:00	J HALSALL	4:02:27	K KNAUER	4:02:55	S HAIG	4:03:22
22	S GROVES	4:01:34	D LANGE	4:02:00	N TABERNER	4:02:28	K PRESTON	4:02:56	R LEWIS	4:03:22
23	J BRUCE	4:01:35	A WALKER	4:02:00	G HOLLINS	4:02:28	D HARRISON	4:02:56	K KNOTT	4:03:22
24	R VANN	4:01:36	P HARMON	4:02:00	V LANDERYOU	4:02:28	D TOSELAND	4:02:56	C EADES	4:03:23
25	D MARSHALL	4:01:36	R DOBBIE	4:02:00	D GOODALL	4:02:29	W MILEWSKI	4:02:56	A DUDLEY	4:03:23
26	R BAKER	4:01:36	G WRIGHT	4:02:00	P TAYLOR	4:02:29	R BUTTON	4:02:57	A FRANCIS	4:03:24
27	J KORFF	4:01:36	J JARROLD	4:02:01	C MOORE	4:02:30	H RALPH	4:02:57	G BAYLEY	4:03:24
28	P MILLER	4:01:37	G PHILLIPS	4:02:02	C SMITH	4:02:30	B SADGROVE	4:02:57	K ROSENBERG	4:03:24
29	P BURGE	4:01:37	S MCNUFF	4:02:02	B NEWPORT	4:02:30	P MINNIS	4:02:58	A HIZETTE	4:03:25
30	M ADAMS	4:01:38	D BIRKIN	4:02:03	M JOYCE	4:02:30	M ELLING	4:02:58	G YOUNG	4:03:25
31	A PASSMORE	4:01:38	V DERWENT	4:02:03	A GUILD	4:02:31	R GIBSON	4:02:58	S LANGSTROM	4:03:25
32	A FISHER	4:01:38	T CROALL	4:02:03	R BRASSINGTON	4:02:31	J MEUBLAT	4:02:59	J SHARP	4:03:26
33	N WHITTAKER	4:01:39	M WILLIAMSON	4:02:04	M DELPY	4:02:33	A MAHONEY	4:03:00	T HEALY	4:03:26
34	A PETTIFER	4:01:39	D BUMBY	4:02:04	P NEWTON	4:02:33	M GARCIA	4:03:00	G SPENCE	4:03:27
35	M DILALLO	4:01:39	I TROEGER	4:02:04	H GARROD	4:02:33	P SHAW	4:03:00	W BONNER-DAVIES	4:03:27
36	I BALL	4:01:39	J MIDDLEMAS	4:02:04	P GIBSON	4:02:33	P ANDREW	4:03:01	G READING	4:03:27
37	A FAIRWEATHER	4:01:40	A WILD	4:02:04	L STAPLETON	4:02:33	D MCARTHUR	4:03:01	T JENNINGS	4:03:27
38	A LETO	4:01:40	J WILLIAMS	4:02:04	J DUNCAN	4:02:33	M BROKENSHAW	4:03:01	D DARBY	4:03:28
39	N RIDGERS	4:01:40	R BRAMLEY	4:02:04	C MURPHY	4:02:34	N PECK	4:03:01	D POUGET	4:03:28
40	S ELLIOTT	4:01:40	R PRINCE	4:02:04	G DE CARVALHO	4:02:34	A HARRIS	4:03:01	R WILLER	4:03:28
41	L MATTARUCCO	4:01:40	A MACKAY	4:02:04	C BEATTIE	4:02:35	J MCLEMAN	4:03:01	S GOODWIN	4:03:28
42	D JORDAN	4:01:41	D WANDERKA	4:02:05	I WADE	4:02:36	R MEDLOCK	4:03:02	D JACKSON	4:03:28
43	R PAGE	4:01:41	M JONES	4:02:05	T DIXON	4:02:36	M HUSTWAIT	4:03:02	P VOWLES	4:03:29
44	R DREW	4:01:41	H SAITO	4:02:05	M SANGERA	4:02:37	L DE LORENZO	4:03:02	R ATKINSON	4:03:29
45	K HALL	4:01:42	S CRAWFORD	4:02:05	K IVEMY	4:02:38	B LOCKWOOD	4:03:03	M HIRON	4:03:29
46	C STRAW	4:01:42	S WILD	4:02:05	R GILLAN	4:02:38	K WILLIAMS	4:03:03	J NEWMAN	4:03:29
47	M PYNE	4:01:43	G SMITH	4:02:06	C DOANE	4:02:39	D INNES	4:03:03	J JENNINGS	4:03:29
48	G WOOLLEY	4:01:43	R JOHNSON	4:02:06	G LEAVER	4:02:39	R SALMONS	4:03:03	R TAYLOR	4:03:29
49	P SKEVIK	4:01:44	S EARDLEY	4:02:06	D PRICE	4:02:40	D FRASER	4:03:04	P JENKINS	4:03:30
50	B JOHNSON	4:01:44	J DOYLE	4:02:06	V WILLIAMS	4:02:40	N DUFF	4:03:04	J RAPHAELY	4:03:30
51	A CHRISTENSEN	4:01:45	G PENDERGAST	4:02:07	G PIERCE	4:02:40	D HUMBY	4:03:05	A YATES	4:03:30
52	S NEWELL	4:01:45	A EDMEADES	4:02:07	I HUNTER	4:02:40	J HOLDEN	4:03:05	A DEAN	4:03:30
53	M TOMKINSON	4:01:46	E ROBINSON	4:02:07	P HAYWARD	4:02:41	J BRUMWELL	4:03:05	J HARROW	4:03:31
54	L WILSON	4:01:46	J NEWCOMBE	4:02:07	T HANCOCK	4:02:41	G BLAK	4:03:05	N DALE	4:03:31
55	C BRITTON	4:01:47	P CARPENTER	4:02:08	J YOUNGE	4:02:42	S CHATTERLEY	4:03:05	S GURREY	4:03:32
56	G BRIDGES	4:01:47	G DAVIE	4:02:08	K INGARFIELD	4:02:42	L KRUPA	4:03:06	M LINDOP	4:03:32
57	C O'RATHILLE	4:01:47	A JONES	4:02:08	R SCHMUCKI	4:02:44	G WHITE	4:03:06	R MARTIN	4:03:32
58	H STRAPGUTL	4:01:48	R COWLEY	4:02:09	C DICKSON	4:02:44	S FOSTER	4:03:06	K GORE	4:03:32
59	A OTTERWELL	4:01:48	M COWAN	4:02:09	R BONSALL	4:02:45	R HATCHMAN	4:03:06	A FENTON	4:03:32
60	J MCCULLIE	4:01:48	D WOODS	4:02:09	D THOMAS	4:02:45	S BONNINGTON	4:03:06	S KERR	4:03:32
61	J IVERS	4:01:48	J LAMBERT	4:02:10	I BAILEY	4:02:45	C FINCH	4:03:06	D CROMBIE	4:03:32
62	P CANHAM	4:01:49	A MERRY	4:02:10	R BATCHELOR	4:02:45	J CHEESMAN	4:03:07	S THOM	4:03:32
63	B JEYES	4:01:49	V FORBES	4:02:10	C BUCKNALL	4:02:46	M WILKINSON	4:03:07	G DAVIES	4:03:32
64	D VIVIEN	4:01:49	B COPE	4:02:10	P THOMAS	4:02:46	R VEIASCO	4:03:07	S MORRIS	4:03:32
65	T HADFIELD	4:01:49	L HARTLEY	4:02:10	D HISTEAD	4:02:46	C PRIOR	4:03:07	M SAMETT	4:03:32
66	R HUGHES	4:01:49	J PORTUS	4:02:11	D MCGEACHIE	4:02:46	B BEAVEN	4:03:07	M BURNS	4:03:32
67	B MURRAY	4:01:50	B STURE	4:02:11	B JENKINS	4:02:46	J BRYAN	4:03:08	F FONTANGE	4:03:33
68	D WILLIAMS	4:01:50	T DAVIS	4:02:12	N BULLOCK	4:02:47	G ELCOCK	4:03:08	A SMITH	4:03:33
69	A HOWARD	4:01:50	E THORNES	4:02:12	K SPRATLEY	4:02:47	R ENGLISH	4:03:08	E HARVEY	4:03:33
70	R TOOZE	4:01:50	J WHELAN	4:02:13	S WHITE	4:02:47	R RATCLIFFE	4:03:08	D CHIDDICKS	4:03:33
71	P BROWN	4:01:51	V SCHWARZ	4:02:13	T EDWARDS	4:02:48	G EVANS	4:03:08	E BATES	4:03:34
72	J BUTCHER	4:01:51	C NELSON	4:02:13	G HILL	4:02:48	C FARR	4:03:08	F AMOS	4:03:34
73	M STRANG	4:01:52	P SEAMAN	4:02:13	J COCKLIN	4:02:49	J ASHTON	4:03:09	G STEED	4:03:34
74	C DREWERY	4:01:52	S DART	4:02:13	E STACEY	4:02:49	T DEAN	4:03:09	A BRIND	4:03:35
75	S PATERSON	4:01:52	M SUTTON	4:02:13	S LUCY	4:02:49	L SAVAGE	4:03:10	M MILTON	4:03:35
76	S BODDY	4:01:52	A FUSARO	4:02:14	M SLACK	4:02:50	W GREEN	4:03:10	R NORTON	4:03:35
77	G FLETCHER	4:01:52	K GREGSON	4:02:14	D DEWDNEY	4:02:51	G COONEY	4:03:10	L JACKSON	4:03:35
78	R SHEPHERD	4:01:53	M HUNTLEY	4:02:14	G THOMAS	4:02:51	R MUNDAY	4:03:11	J HOLLOWAY	4:03:35
79	G BUELL	4:01:53	P STERN	4:02:14	M FIANDER	4:02:51	R DUNGEY	4:03:11	J SEGGIE	4:03:35
80	J BLACKISTON	4:01:53	G WILLSHER	4:02:15	A FRITH	4:02:51	K WAGER	4:03:11	B MCHUGH	4:03:35
81	J DORE	4:01:53	M ASPINALL	4:02:16	J CONNAGHTON	4:02:52	C RICHARDSON	4:03:11	N HALE	4:03:36
82	J PRESSLEY	4:01:53	M TINDLE	4:02:16	D BARRASS	4:02:52	P CAHILL	4:03:11	R GARRARD	4:03:38
83	P BARNES	4:01:53	S PRESTON	4:02:16	M GALE	4:02:53	D BROGDEN	4:03:11	M KARLSSON	4:03:38
84	A WILKES	4:01:53	H FERRIDGE	4:02:16	M COLEMAN	4:02:53	C CANCEL	4:03:11	A RUTHERFORD	4:03:38
85	S KERRIGAN	4:01:53	O SHEA	4:02:16	R STANDERWICK	4:02:53	P CHENERY	4:03:11	D ASHLEY	4:03:38
86	D SCOTT	4:01:53	B ENGEL	4:02:17	P DEGUTIS	4:02:53	D PRESTON	4:03:11	T FERRUZZI	4:03:38
87	A MAHONEY	4:01:53	M ALCORN	4:02:17	S SHERIDAN	4:02:53	A MABERT	4:03:11	A JONES	4:03:39
88	T ROBERTS	4:01:53	G HILL	4:02:17	C WALKER	4:02:53	P DUNCAN	4:03:13	A BENMOSSA	4:03:39
89	D WILKINS	4:01:53	J STARRS	4:02:18	S FRYER	4:02:53	J MCKECHNIE	4:03:14	R QUINTON	4:03:40
90	C CHALMERS	4:01:53	D BATH	4:02:18	P JENKINS	4:02:53	D BURKE	4:03:14	A MALCHERCZYK	4:03:40
91	A GOUDIE	4:01:53	B BISSET	4:02:18	S ROBSON	4:02:53	M LLOYD	4:03:14	R HALE	4:03:40
92	J MUNNS	4:01:53	F LAVENDER	4:02:18	J MATTHIEWS	4:02:53	A HARRIS	4:03:14	M COHEN	4:03:40
93	L HEARLE	4:01:53	R GUTHRIE	4:02:18	M SCHUELEIN	4:02:53	A CAPORALI	4:03:15	R DOWLE	4:03:40
94	A SIMMONS	4:01:53	P SMITH	4:02:18	E PETERMANN	4:02:53	A HALLIDAY	4:03:15	K BUNDE	4:03:40
95	A OLIVER	4:01:53	P DAY	4:02:19	O KARABARDAK	4:02:53	J BACH	4:03:15	H COLLINS	4:03:42
96	J SIMPSON	4:01:53	D BARCLAY	4:02:19	F LATHAM	4:02:53	J BILLINGS	4:03:15	C SIMMONS	4:03:43
97	R BLOXHAM	4:01:53	G JOUBIN	4:02:20	I DUNCAN	4:02:53	E TROTTER	4:03:15	A FRANKE	4:03:43
98	R GOVIER	4:01:54	C HUNT	4:02:20	E BUTLER	4:02:53	E PERRY	4:03:15	S FOSTER	4:03:43
99	K FERRIS	4:01:54	K MURRAY	4:02:20	T LLOYD	4:02:53	D FLETCHER	4:03:16	G PROOT	4:03:45
100	J LIPSON	4:01:54	T O'KELLY	4:02:21	O VANDEVELDE	4:02:53	M KELLY	4:03:16	A GELLWITZ	4:03:45

#	13001-13100		13101-13200		13201-13300		13301-13400		13401-13500	
1	G RODERICKS	4:03:45	T COLLINS	4:04:19	F PETIT	4:04:59	D GODWIN	4:05:33	J COOPER	4:06:04
2	A SOANES	4:03:46	J HAMBLING	4:04:19	C ALLEN	4:04:59	C VASSUER	4:05:33	J ASQUITH	4:06:05
3	T O'DONNELL	4:03:46	P JOHNSON	4:04:20	M BERGEAULT	4:04:59	P RIDDLE	4:05:33	P MULDER	4:06:05
4	A MACLEOD	4:03:46	E BROWN	4:04:21	J TILLETT	4:05:00	D SALTER	4:05:33	B GARRATT	4:06:05
5	S BELLENOUE	4:03:47	A COLE	4:04:21	T OLDING	4:05:00	S KLEIN	4:05:34	P TAYLOR	4:06:05
6	P JUNG	4:03:47	A LAWTON	4:04:21	B GRAINGER	4:05:00	A LAW	4:05:34	T CALLADINE	4:06:05
7	H GUNTRIP	4:03:48	E MCNALLY	4:04:22	B HOLBROOK	4:05:00	J LUMSDEN	4:05:35	R GOODWIN	4:06:05
8	D THOMPSON	4:03:48	N BURDELL	4:04:22	C MCKEOWN	4:05:00	J MEREDITH	4:05:35	R ANDERSON	4:06:06
9	B BLACK	4:03:48	R BARTLETT	4:04:23	L MATTHEWS	4:05:00	J RAINEY	4:05:35	P STENSON	4:06:06
10	R MICHAEL	4:03:48	S FALKNER	4:04:23	M MOLYNEUX	4:05:00	D CORNWALL	4:05:35	J BIRD	4:06:06
11	S DOKSAETER	4:03:49	T PARKINSON	4:04:23	S JONES	4:05:00	R FOSTER	4:05:36	S GUIGUES	4:06:06
12	S KING	4:03:49	W HUGHES	4:04:23	M HAMMOND	4:05:00	T GRINSELL	4:05:36	M DODSON	4:06:06
13	B ADDY	4:03:49	G MISCIALI	4:04:23	M BOTTOM	4:05:00	C COLLINS	4:05:36	L BRIGHT	4:06:06
14	M MCINTOSH	4:03:50	F PHILLIPS	4:04:24	A PHILLIPS	4:05:00	P STANDEN	4:05:37	D USHER	4:06:06
15	K HOPTON	4:03:50	A CRESSWELL	4:04:24	D ADAMSON	4:05:01	J KEARNS	4:05:37	J MCGUINESS	4:06:06
16	A MORTON	4:03:50	M CUNNINGHAM	4:04:25	D CLEMSON	4:05:03	S ROUGHLEY	4:05:37	H KOCH	4:06:06
17	L KYD	4:03:50	R MILLER	4:04:25	R WATKINS	4:05:04	J MANSFIELD	4:05:37	J FAIRHURST	4:06:07
18	A BIRD	4:03:50	D ROBSON	4:04:25	B DORROFIELD	4:05:04	N BAILY	4:05:37	J FORSTER	4:06:07
19	D BARTON	4:03:50	J BUGLER	4:04:25	M CLARK	4:05:04	I STRAUGHAN	4:05:37	C ROBINSON	4:06:08
20	N SHIPLEY	4:03:50	D CHEESEMAN	4:04:26	P WHITEFIELD	4:05:06	T FILSTRUP	4:05:38	D BELLOT	4:06:08
21	S FLETCHER	4:03:50	R KIRKHAM	4:04:27	J PINNOCK	4:05:06	J MC INTOSH	4:05:38	B NICHOLSON	4:06:08
22	T BIRD	4:03:50	M SCALES	4:04:27	G PACIFERO	4:05:06	A HANSEN	4:05:38	M WHILES	4:06:09
23	V BARNETT	4:03:51	P KIRKHAM	4:04:27	J JONES	4:05:07	L HEDDON	4:05:38	P WILLIS	4:06:09
24	V LOVEDAY	4:03:52	M WESTACOTT	4:04:28	G WEST	4:05:07	J MAUXION	4:05:38	R HOBMAN	4:06:10
25	J DESCAMPS	4:03:52	R FELICI	4:04:28	N SANDS	4:05:07	D HOWELLS	4:05:39	K FAULKNER	4:06:13
26	L OLIPHANT	4:03:52	P MASON	4:04:29	A HOWARD	4:05:07	M THOMSON	4:05:39	T MELVIN	4:06:13
27	R BROOM	4:03:52	Y HOLLAND	4:04:29	P BEASLEY	4:05:07	P WORRALL	4:05:39	A HAWTHORNE	4:06:14
28	T KAWAKAMI	4:03:53	K CRANE	4:04:30	D BLADES	4:05:07	N LATHAM	4:05:39	J GILLESPIE	4:06:14
29	M PRYNNE	4:03:53	A RADLEY	4:04:30	T KERWIN	4:05:07	D CORBETT	4:05:39	A FENN	4:06:15
30	G BENNETT	4:03:53	M DALTON	4:04:30	D COOK	4:05:07	A WORRALL	4:05:39	A HARPER	4:06:15
31	J LEROY	4:03:53	T HARDING	4:04:30	P EXON	4:05:08	A EVANS	4:05:39	N ADAMSON	4:06:16
32	A MURRAY	4:03:54	J MONTAGNE	4:04:30	M JOTCHAM	4:05:08	B WILKINSON	4:05:40	D ROBERTS	4:06:16
33	A MEATON	4:03:54	D MARECHAL	4:04:31	A DEAN	4:05:08	R HADDON	4:05:40	R BROAD	4:06:17
34	L BLUNT	4:03:55	D BELL	4:04:31	K BURGESS	4:05:08	M BROWN	4:05:40	M PRICE	4:06:17
35	B HAZELTINE	4:03:55	C MELLOR	4:04:32	J THOMPSON	4:05:09	A SMALLWOOD	4:05:40	D REYNOLDS	4:06:18
36	J SCOTT	4:03:56	M BROWN	4:04:32	M KNIGHT	4:05:09	A STANDFAST	4:05:41	B COOKE	4:06:18
37	J LARKIN	4:03:56	L WESSON	4:04:33	R CARPANO	4:05:10	D DOBSON	4:05:41	R LAWSON	4:06:18
38	K CORRIE	4:03:56	M WILSON	4:04:33	A BADENHURST	4:05:10	K SCHMIDT	4:05:41	A STONE	4:06:18
39	C BLOXHAM	4:03:57	P HOLLICK	4:04:33	K WOLTON	4:05:10	M BRETHERTON	4:05:41	C HIPWELL	4:06:18
40	W DAWBER	4:03:58	K BARKER	4:04:34	N RAMSDEN	4:05:10	M KERSTEN	4:05:42	M TEXIER	4:06:19
41	D FLETCHER	4:03:58	P BLAKE	4:04:34	K BUTLER	4:05:10	J BAYFIELD	4:05:42	J MONCAUT	4:06:19
42	G WARD	4:03:58	T BYRNE	4:04:34	J JAMESON	4:05:11	J DAVIES	4:05:43	C WOODWARD	4:06:19
43	B LYNCH	4:03:58	P JEFFREY	4:04:35	S RIDDLE	4:05:11	M BENSON	4:05:43	K THYNNE	4:06:19
44	P BARRIE	4:03:58	J WELCH	4:04:35	S KIRBY	4:05:12	A GUNN	4:05:44	V SIMMONDS	4:06:19
45	K STEVENSON	4:03:58	K BAXTER	4:04:35	T NATALE	4:05:12	P BOWERS	4:05:44	J SMITH	4:06:19
46	L LLOYD	4:03:59	S BOWEN	4:04:37	G RIVAT	4:05:13	M BOLSHAW	4:05:45	P FLAMANK	4:06:19
47	H DAVIES	4:03:59	A HOLDEN	4:04:37	M GREEN	4:05:14	P LIGHTFOOT	4:05:46	A BISHOP	4:06:20
48	S TURNER	4:04:00	T HAGGETT	4:04:37	W HARTEN	4:05:14	C HYLAND	4:05:46	S CAINE	4:06:20
49	R ANNAN	4:04:01	D ASKER	4:04:37	P COLLINS	4:05:14	B FISHER	4:05:48	D PATEY	4:06:20
50	J SLATER	4:04:01	S BOSTOCK	4:04:37	L IVES	4:05:14	A CAMPBELL	4:05:50	A KOFFMAN	4:06:21
51	D LAWS	4:04:01	J CAMPBELL	4:04:38	M BURNHOPE	4:05:15	A GOULD	4:05:50	A RAUWERDA	4:06:21
52	R SINGLETON	4:04:01	J WORTS	4:04:38	G CINQUE	4:05:15	A MORGAN	4:05:50	R BATES	4:06:21
53	D SMITH	4:04:02	C DE COCK	4:04:39	P GARNER	4:05:15	L FOOTE	4:05:50	S PORTER	4:06:21
54	C MESSENT	4:04:02	C TRAVIS	4:04:39	S COX	4:05:16	E PARRY	4:05:50	S BURKE	4:06:22
55	I LITTLE	4:04:02	B THOMPSON	4:04:39	A TOVAGLIERI	4:05:16	K OKTABEC	4:05:51	C SAMPSON	4:06:22
56	V FOULSHAM	4:04:03	G JOHNSON	4:04:40	A ROSS	4:05:16	M LOFTUS	4:05:51	S TIGHE	4:06:23
57	U ERDMANN	4:04:03	J BLUNDELL	4:04:41	S BIERIS	4:05:16	G FOOTE	4:05:51	C VIOL	4:06:23
58	T DIXON	4:04:03	W STEVENS	4:04:41	P GARBUTT	4:05:17	J SHARP	4:05:51	J SELL	4:06:23
59	A DEVERELL	4:04:03	N FENNEL	4:04:41	A DAWSON	4:05:17	A OWENS	4:05:52	D HAWLEY	4:06:24
60	S MANSBRIDGE	4:04:04	N HARRISON	4:04:41	K SERVATJOO	4:05:19	M JEFFREY	4:05:52	R THOMPSON	4:06:24
61	Y MORREY	4:04:04	T BECKER	4:04:42	C GILL	4:05:19	C GILL	4:05:52	N CARTER	4:06:24
62	S WILLIAMS	4:04:04	J BERTHE	4:04:42	T VAN DER KROON	4:05:21	M LITTLE	4:05:52	A PRICHARD	4:06:24
63	N IVEY	4:04:04	A COURT	4:04:42	D MOLLE	4:05:22	E HOGG	4:05:52	P DENENBERG	4:06:25
64	A MORRIS	4:04:04	S HOLLOWAY	4:04:42	B VEIDEN	4:05:22	N STARR	4:05:53	J CARSAC	4:06:25
65	S LEWIS	4:04:05	J BLAIR	4:04:43	N HEMMANT	4:05:22	G DACEY	4:05:53	P COOK	4:06:26
66	D EYERS	4:04:05	B CHESHIRE	4:04:43	M FOSTER	4:05:23	S DOYLE	4:05:54	W MORGAN	4:06:26
67	K PINCHEN	4:04:05	B BATER	4:04:44	S AERI	4:05:23	C CARROLL	4:05:54	J MARKHAM	4:06:26
68	J BEE	4:04:05	A KARLSEN	4:04:45	D BRINT	4:05:23	D WHALL	4:05:54	B TIMS	4:06:27
69	R BURNS	4:04:06	A CAILLOL	4:04:45	P SHALDERS	4:05:23	B FURNISH	4:05:54	J TEIXEIRA RIBEIRO	4:06:27
70	L HICKMAN	4:04:06	D JEFFRIES	4:04:46	R SAUNDERS	4:05:24	J PERKINS	4:05:54	L PENNEY	4:06:28
71	M ALDRIDGE	4:04:07	S ILLINGWORTH	4:04:47	J CLARK	4:05:24	A MC INTOSH	4:05:54	G CHINELLATO	4:06:29
72	A GORDON	4:04:08	J MOUROUX	4:04:48	A LANGTON	4:05:24	V NICOLL	4:05:54	P GUIGUES	4:06:29
73	D WILLIS	4:04:08	T DERRINGTON	4:04:48	R FARRELL	4:05:25	D WALLIS	4:05:55	N CANHAM	4:06:31
74	G WARD	4:04:08	T HUGHES	4:04:48	J ROBERTS	4:05:25	R ENGLISH	4:05:55	A CLARKE	4:06:33
75	E KNOLL	4:04:09	R MAY	4:04:48	E KAYUM	4:05:25	J WAITE	4:05:55	J THORN	4:06:34
76	J PEMBERTON	4:04:09	C HAMBLETON	4:04:49	C WREN	4:05:25	G FOULKES	4:05:55	P HACKER	4:06:34
77	G WORTHINGTON	4:04:10	N TAYLOR	4:04:49	R STEVENSON	4:05:25	R NIXON	4:05:55	G LEAITY	4:06:34
78	N PEMBERTON	4:04:10	T FEIL	4:04:49	P TURNER	4:05:25	D WYNNE	4:05:55	C FLETCHER	4:06:34
79	M RYAN	4:04:10	T WARWICK	4:04:49	C BRYAN	4:05:26	S EVANS	4:05:55	C TURNER	4:06:34
80	G WHITE	4:04:10	C ELLIS	4:04:50	G BORGO	4:05:26	G CLEMENTS	4:05:56	S COLLINSON	4:06:34
81	J CHILDS	4:04:11	R CARR	4:04:50	J OWEN	4:05:26	J LATHWELL	4:05:56	J WELLS	4:06:35
82	D HOCKLEY	4:04:11	R WALLACE	4:04:50	C RAPLEY	4:05:26	C TAYLOR	4:05:57	O LLERHEAD	4:06:35
83	R EMERY	4:04:13	P SAUNDERS	4:04:51	T POIKOLAINEN	4:05:27	B SUTTON	4:05:58	J NASH	4:06:35
84	J KARTZ	4:04:13	W MOORE	4:04:52	D GAVAGHAN	4:05:27	M BOYLE	4:05:58	D TAYLOR	4:06:35
85	R OSBORNE	4:04:14	S BAKER	4:04:53	R JONES	4:05:28	P RICKETTS	4:05:58	T TAYLOR	4:06:35
86	J HARVEY	4:04:14	G LUCAS	4:04:53	M BENBOUGH	4:05:29	M STURGESS	4:05:59	J AUSTIN	4:06:36
87	R BEECHENER	4:04:15	E KEEFE	4:04:53	G KIRK	4:05:29	A HINES	4:06:00	G WANSTALL	4:06:36
88	R KERFOOT	4:04:15	F KING	4:04:54	S DESBOROUGH	4:05:30	P CORTELLINI	4:06:00	M BRECHEC	4:06:36
89	S RUDELOFF	4:04:15	M JONES	4:04:54	G KENT	4:05:30	A SBORO	4:06:00	G MANGAN	4:06:37
90	G WALTON	4:04:15	N COURSE	4:04:55	M PARFETT	4:05:30	S JAMES	4:06:00	M BENNETT	4:06:38
91	J O'DONNELL	4:04:15	S CROFT	4:04:55	N CLEMSON	4:05:31	C REES	4:06:01	S COTTLE	4:06:38
92	C REASON	4:04:15	D BENNET	4:04:55	J WHITING	4:05:31	A POSTLETHWAITE	4:06:02	K FULLER	4:06:39
93	M DUGELAY	4:04:16	F MC KENNA	4:04:55	B WUYAM	4:05:31	J MCDONNELL	4:06:02	M MASON	4:06:39
94	M LUYT	4:04:16	J CRAWFORD	4:04:56	N TOMLINSON	4:05:31	P RICHARDSON	4:06:02	M WOMBWELL	4:06:39
95	W MCCORMACK	4:04:17	M COLLINSON	4:04:56	P SINCLAIR	4:05:31	J BOWKER	4:06:02	C BOND	4:06:39
96	C MCGHEE	4:04:18	B UNWIN	4:04:56	D BAKER	4:05:31	B BROOKSBY	4:06:03	C BASHAM	4:06:40
97	D HOCKEY	4:04:18	M CLOKE	4:04:57	G WALKER	4:05:32	D HUTCHINSON	4:06:03	T MILLAR	4:06:40
98	H MAWER	4:04:18	I WORMALD	4:04:57	S DEAN	4:05:32	P WHITEHEAD	4:06:04	D WILLINGHAM	4:06:40
99	G SECKER	4:04:18	A FODOR	4:04:58	L WEBB	4:05:32	R BROWN	4:06:04	S IRELAND	4:06:41
100	M MAITLAND	4:04:19	A BIGGAR	4:04:59	A PARSONS	4:05:32	A CHIARALUCE	4:06:04	N HOWARD	4:06:41

#	13501-13600		13601-13700		13701-13800		13801-13900		13901-14000	
1	B BENNETT	4:06:41	A JONES	4:07:10	S CROSSCOMBE	4:07:43	A CHATFIELD	4:08:21	E BULLOWS	4:08:55
2	M WALES	4:06:41	A BELL	4:07:11	N MARKHAM	4:07:43	G HARRIS	4:08:21	B WITCOMB	4:08:55
3	R NORTHWOOD	4:06:41	C SPRIGG	4:07:12	I WARD	4:07:44	A MACKINTOSH	4:08:22	P GIBSON	4:08:55
4	S DARLINGTON	4:06:41	C SCOTT	4:07:12	A JOYCE	4:07:45	N GLYNN-DAVIES	4:08:23	L JUDD	4:08:55
5	A APPLETON	4:06:41	G RIGOGLIOSO	4:07:12	G DAVAUX	4:07:45	M PRATT	4:08:24	D LAWERENCE	4:08:55
6	P SIEPERMANN	4:06:41	A VICCARI	4:07:12	A BELL	4:07:46	W FOSDICK	4:08:24	S CLARKSON	4:08:55
7	R TABELING	4:06:41	W ROBINSON	4:07:12	B PAVITT	4:07:46	G ADAMS	4:08:24	T HARLAND	4:08:55
8	S TAYLOR	4:06:41	S THOMAS	4:07:12	M WALTON	4:07:46	P BAUMANN	4:08:24	D ROBBINS	4:08:55
9	J DELLER	4:06:41	I FERGUSON	4:07:13	A MOWATT	4:07:47	G SIMPSON	4:08:25	M MCKAY	4:08:55
10	A MARIANI	4:06:41	B DAVIES	4:07:14	R HARVEY	4:07:47	J WILLIAMS	4:08:25	C NEAL	4:08:56
11	S JAMIESON	4:06:42	J HILL	4:07:14	F SMART	4:07:47	J OWEN	4:08:27	F WILLCOCKS	4:08:56
12	G NASH	4:06:42	D BEAUVOISIN	4:07:15	N ROBINSON	4:07:48	P CRANFIELD	4:08:27	J BARRETT	4:08:57
13	F ARDLEY	4:06:43	P DANIELS	4:07:16	B ROBERTSHAW	4:07:49	J FUCHS	4:08:27	M LONGLEY	4:08:57
14	P FROOME	4:06:44	R COOK	4:07:17	I MURRAY	4:07:50	T JOHNSON	4:08:27	N DAWSON	4:08:57
15	M ROUTLEDGE	4:06:44	S JONES	4:07:18	S KLEPKA	4:07:50	J LEWIS	4:08:27	H BAUER	4:08:57
16	J WELLS	4:06:44	P ANDREWS	4:07:18	R WALKER	4:07:50	G DEA	4:08:28	K ANDREWS	4:08:57
17	M NOTTAGE	4:06:45	R HAYLER	4:07:18	A FIGIEL	4:07:50	P FLETCHER	4:08:28	R RONAN	4:08:58
18	J PETERS	4:06:46	M FARMAN	4:07:18	J PAUL	4:07:51	D FOX	4:08:28	S ASHTON	4:08:58
19	J GREEN	4:06:46	A CONNER	4:07:19	A ICETON	4:07:51	L ELKINS	4:08:28	J SAUNDERS	4:08:58
20	C PAGET	4:06:46	M NEWMAN	4:07:19	M DUMAS	4:07:51	G GAUTIER	4:08:28	R DIETZE	4:08:58
21	R KNOWLES	4:06:47	S KLEPPE	4:07:19	M RAPALI	4:07:52	A MURRIE	4:08:28	M SARRAZIN	4:08:58
22	D DOMENICO	4:06:47	D KOEP	4:07:19	J COCKBURN	4:07:52	E BERK	4:08:29	A BARTLETT	4:08:59
23	P JOHNSON	4:06:47	M JACKSON	4:07:19	K GUNN	4:07:53	I WOOLCOTT	4:08:29	G EGLIN	4:08:59
24	P DI SALVO	4:06:48	I TAYLOR	4:07:19	D SIMMANS	4:07:53	M WELCH	4:08:29	J MATTHEWS	4:09:00
25	A JOHNSON	4:06:48	J SPINK	4:07:20	D BOWLES	4:07:53	G HILL	4:08:29	R INGLIS	4:09:01
26	M ONODA	4:06:48	G HUTCHINSON	4:07:20	M OWEN	4:07:53	M MORFEY	4:08:29	D EDWARD	4:09:01
27	E HALL	4:06:49	L BARROW	4:07:20	P BARRELL	4:07:54	M MCCULLOCH	4:08:29	R JEFFREYS	4:09:01
28	F PEARSON	4:06:49	B MEYER	4:07:20	A ST JOHN OF BLETSO	4:07:54	G AUDRA	4:08:30	M JONES	4:09:01
29	B JOHN	4:06:49	O PISANI	4:07:20	J WELSH	4:07:54	J TOWNSEND	4:08:30	A BURNETT	4:09:02
30	M SHIELDS	4:06:50	N MATSUURA	4:07:20	D CHILDRESS	4:07:55	T HICKS	4:08:31	C TRICE	4:09:03
31	S WATKINS	4:06:50	D BARTLETT	4:07:20	P NOON	4:07:55	N RAYCRAFT	4:08:31	M LEASK	4:09:03
32	J BRANNIGAN	4:06:50	I MILLER	4:07:21	T CRYSELL	4:07:56	P HUGHES	4:08:32	D WILLIAMS	4:09:04
33	P JAT	4:06:50	D KING	4:07:21	K FOX	4:07:56	A COUGARD	4:08:32	G GREEN	4:09:04
34	G FISCHER	4:06:50	D MANUEL	4:07:22	B STEVENTON	4:07:56	A MARRS	4:08:32	B HOBDAY	4:09:05
35	D BARTON	4:06:51	R APPLEBY	4:07:23	M BAYLISS	4:07:56	T GRIMM	4:08:33	C TOWNSEND	4:09:05
36	G BRIVIO	4:06:51	S REID	4:07:24	P BUCKLEY	4:07:57	A BROOKS	4:08:33	P SNOAD	4:09:05
37	J HOLDER	4:06:51	A MADURA	4:07:24	D RANDALL	4:07:57	P MORTIER	4:08:33	S GLADWELL	4:09:06
38	J ENGRAND	4:06:52	E BROWN	4:07:24	F CAFFINI	4:07:57	T GLANVILL	4:08:34	S FAWTHROP	4:09:06
39	K HENDY	4:06:53	A REES	4:07:24	D BELCHER	4:07:58	M MORALES	4:08:34	V EVANS	4:09:06
40	K HARRISON	4:06:53	D STEDMAN	4:07:24	D BARNARD	4:07:58	R DIAZ	4:08:34	J MCNICHOLAS	4:09:06
41	P SUMONDS	4:06:53	J JONES	4:07:24	M TODD	4:07:58	C WILLIAMS	4:08:35	D FISHER	4:09:06
42	A WHITE	4:06:53	G HELM	4:07:24	G HARVISON	4:07:58	J PIOTROWSKI	4:08:35	R CALDWELL	4:09:07
43	J CZAUDERNA	4:06:53	D HELM	4:07:24	D HOLT	4:07:59	R HARRIS	4:08:35	M PULLING	4:09:07
44	J VERMEIREN	4:06:54	J MORGAN	4:07:24	M HUNT	4:07:59	K OSCROFT	4:08:36	J SCHOLZ	4:09:07
45	C VALLEJO	4:06:54	C PATTERSON	4:07:25	P TAYLOR	4:07:59	C ARCHIBOLD	4:08:36	T CATCHPOLE	4:09:07
46	P MACKLEY	4:06:54	C TAYLOR	4:07:25	R CHURCH	4:07:59	J GREEN	4:08:36	T EDEN	4:09:08
47	R WATKINS	4:06:54	N SCOTT	4:07:26	K MAGGS	4:08:00	W TRAVERS	4:08:37	G TAMBURINI	4:09:08
48	A RENNISON	4:06:54	I BURNS	4:07:26	P HALLEWELL	4:08:00	P COATES	4:08:38	J JORDAN	4:09:08
49	S MCCAUSLAND	4:06:55	G SOUTAR	4:07:26	J WILLIAMS	4:08:01	A WHEELER	4:08:38	P COLEMAN	4:09:08
50	P JOHNSTONE	4:06:55	J BUNN	4:07:27	I SAARINEN	4:08:01	B O'NEILL	4:08:39	P BAYLISS	4:09:08
51	R LOWRIE	4:06:56	H WEAVER	4:07:28	J HALL	4:08:01	G DUCKWORTH	4:08:39	R LAWRENCE	4:09:09
52	D BEESON	4:06:56	B FOSTON	4:07:28	M WEBSTER	4:08:02	R EDDY	4:08:39	D TAYLOR	4:09:10
53	G AUSTEN	4:06:56	J POLLARD	4:07:28	M THIES	4:08:02	L HALL	4:08:39	P GILMARTIN	4:09:10
54	A SCOTT	4:06:57	M CONNAGHTON	4:07:28	P JENNINGS	4:08:02	P PURSER	4:08:39	B WHITMORE	4:09:10
55	F CACI	4:06:57	J TERCHI	4:07:29	D TALBOT	4:08:03	J HALL	4:08:39	M GREAVE	4:09:10
56	N MCDAVID	4:06:57	T REYNOLDS	4:07:29	B GOODAYLE	4:08:03	R TAYLOR	4:08:40	A HIGHAM	4:09:10
57	J STACEY	4:06:57	I CAMPBELL	4:07:29	K RUSSELL	4:08:03	R SMITH	4:08:40	C BRADLEY	4:09:10
58	G HARTWELL	4:06:57	R HAGAR	4:07:30	I WITHAM	4:08:03	D SEARLE	4:08:40	M DAVIES	4:09:10
59	S WISE	4:06:58	P DIFFEY	4:07:31	D PRICE	4:08:03	L THORNTON	4:08:40	P VANNEAU	4:09:10
60	J WRIGHT	4:06:58	M BAILEY	4:07:31	H MACGREGOR	4:08:03	A SPENCE	4:08:40	M SCOTT	4:09:10
61	J SWENY	4:06:59	J BOYLE	4:07:31	M SMITH	4:08:03	P KITCHENER	4:08:42	L JACK	4:09:11
62	B CONWAY	4:06:59	W DINEEN	4:07:32	A DEIGNAN	4:08:04	G RAND	4:08:42	E DUNN	4:09:11
63	H LONG	4:07:00	P BULL	4:07:32	R JAMES	4:08:04	A SUTCH	4:08:42	S O'NEILL	4:09:11
64	K SACHTLEBEN	4:07:00	P LAWSON	4:07:32	A WILSON	4:08:05	R NICHOLLS	4:08:43	J CARTER	4:09:11
65	H SOUTHGATE	4:07:00	V PUDDICOME	4:07:32	A MEARON	4:08:05	F EVANS	4:08:43	D KELLY	4:09:11
66	I KNIGHT	4:07:01	J CHAPLIN	4:07:32	S MADDISON	4:08:05	T VAN LENNEP	4:08:43	M COLES	4:09:12
67	M PALMER	4:07:01	C LODIEL	4:07:33	W RULF	4:08:05	P WICKS	4:08:43	C ORWIN	4:09:12
68	R SACHTLEBEN	4:07:01	D HOARE	4:07:33	T FELTON	4:08:06	D WHITBY	4:08:44	R DORAM	4:09:13
69	M DEACY	4:07:02	R HANDSCOMBE	4:07:33	K COOK	4:08:06	C GOSLING	4:08:44	A JONES	4:09:13
70	D THORPE	4:07:02	A MORGADO	4:07:34	S TUCKER	4:08:06	S FOX	4:08:45	J BROUGH	4:09:13
71	C SPENCER	4:07:02	S FLEMING	4:07:35	J UZZELL	4:08:07	B DAVIES	4:08:45	W BEDWELL	4:09:14
72	M HOPKINS	4:07:02	C HOARE	4:07:35	M BATTEN	4:08:07	R PETHERS	4:08:45	M HEATH	4:09:14
73	G CLARK	4:07:02	R RATTI	4:07:35	M HARVEY	4:08:07	M REDSELL	4:08:46	G CLARKE	4:09:14
74	S JEWSBURY	4:07:03	K ALLEN	4:07:35	B BIRTWISTLE	4:08:08	D BROWN	4:08:46	T BACON	4:09:14
75	D HALL	4:07:03	S BURRELL	4:07:35	A BEALES	4:08:08	M ORGAER	4:08:46	P SOLOMONS	4:09:14
76	D WILKINSON	4:07:03	T WARREN	4:07:35	M EASON	4:08:09	A JONES	4:08:47	A HOLDEN	4:09:14
77	K TOTTENHAM	4:07:04	B SMITH	4:07:35	K GARNER	4:08:10	C HIBBERD	4:08:47	L GOLD	4:09:15
78	C STUBBS	4:07:04	K POLLEY	4:07:35	D PRICE	4:08:10	P GOLD	4:08:47	K CONNOLLY	4:09:15
79	L GREGORY	4:07:04	M HILLARY	4:07:35	U GUMMELT	4:08:10	R WATTON	4:08:47	M WILLETT	4:09:16
80	J RODIE	4:07:04	A TYSON	4:07:35	L SMITH	4:08:11	B BELL	4:08:47	J ROSSI	4:09:16
81	D SIMONS	4:07:04	J HALLIDAY	4:07:35	J GOULDING	4:08:12	S FENTON	4:08:48	M REES	4:09:17
82	M MAQUET	4:07:04	T DRAPER	4:07:35	B TAYLOR	4:08:12	J FORD	4:08:48	C SMITH	4:09:17
83	G BLIX	4:07:04	D DAVOLL	4:07:35	R MASON	4:08:13	J TROWBRIDGE	4:08:49	R BARTHOLOMEW	4:09:17
84	D BARROW	4:07:04	M HFFER	4:07:36	S ADAMSDALE	4:08:13	A POTTER	4:08:49	J JOSSA	4:09:18
85	M WILLIAMS	4:07:04	G BLACK	4:07:36	E VAUGHAN	4:08:13	G SINGH	4:08:50	J JENNER	4:09:18
86	C MINTERN	4:07:05	C KIRKWOOD	4:07:36	P DICKINSON	4:08:14	P SHARPE	4:08:50	L GILFILLAN	4:09:18
87	N TAYLOR	4:07:05	L PERRIN	4:07:36	D SCHLOSSER	4:08:14	P MOULTON	4:08:51	E MOUNTFORD	4:09:19
88	E BRANNIGAN	4:07:05	J BIRRI	4:07:37	J WILLIAMS	4:08:14	S RUSSELL	4:08:51	S WILSON	4:09:19
89	S KIRKWOOD	4:07:06	R WELLS	4:07:38	C HOMES	4:08:14	A FLOOK	4:08:51	M MCCARTHY	4:09:20
90	A CAIE	4:07:07	L BURGESS	4:07:38	J CHANTLER	4:08:15	T TANAKA	4:08:52	J CAIGER	4:09:20
91	S WHITE	4:07:07	C WALTERS	4:07:39	Y AZIZ	4:08:16	M PENFOLD	4:08:52	J WILLIAMS	4:09:20
92	D WILSON	4:07:07	K BRACKETT	4:07:40	S BORFECCHIA	4:08:16	H SULLIVAN	4:08:52	S SHREEVE	4:09:20
93	R JAMIESON-CALEY	4:07:07	M DE WINTER	4:07:41	M MIKHAEL	4:08:16	I ROBINSON	4:08:52	I RHODES	4:09:20
94	J BROWN	4:07:07	J MORAN	4:07:41	M BURKE	4:08:16	P DARLINGTON	4:08:52	J HARRINGTON	4:09:20
95	L SHARMAN	4:07:08	P WILLIAMS	4:07:41	A MORTON	4:08:16	E MCNAMEE	4:08:53	C COULSON	4:09:21
96	P BAIRD	4:07:08	A BROSCOMBE	4:07:41	S KEOGH	4:08:17	R HARDING	4:08:53	J REID	4:09:21
97	G VAN TONDER	4:07:08	J RASCH	4:07:42	J BULLEN	4:08:18	F DULING	4:08:54	J JOHNSON	4:09:21
98	B DUNNE	4:07:08	B KVIKVIK	4:07:42	P GILLEN	4:08:19	S HOLLOWAY	4:08:54	G HALL	4:09:22
99	N FREEMAN	4:07:09	P PARADISE	4:07:42	C HALLIDAY	4:08:19	C JONES	4:08:55	T O'KEEFFE	4:09:22
100	J BIRCH	4:07:10	P NCNALLY	4:07:43	C SPENCER	4:08:20	I BAKER	4:08:55	J LAVERY	4:09:22

	14001-14100		14101-14200		14201-14300		14301-14400		14401-14500	
1	G AUSTIN	4:09:22	K TIMMS	4:09:57	O DYER	4:10:28	K STONE	4:10:53	G CHAPRON	4:11:28
2	G HARRIS	4:09:22	R KELLY	4:09:57	C LLEWELLYN	4:10:28	G CHARLTON	4:10:53	S COFFEY	4:11:28
3	J SETFORD	4:09:22	K THOMAS	4:09:57	R GARLAND	4:10:29	M BEGUIN	4:10:54	B VANDERSPEKCANDERKODY	4:11:28
4	M SMITH	4:09:23	I SMITH	4:09:57	C BILLE	4:10:29	A HINEY	4:10:54	K SCOTT	4:11:28
5	K BERRY	4:09:23	V LONGLEY	4:09:57	P ELLINGTON	4:10:29	N POWELL	4:10:54	P COX	4:11:28
6	R JONES	4:09:23	I JONASSON	4:09:57	A GRIECO	4:10:29	T ATKINSON	4:10:54	G SAUL	4:11:28
7	N LOW	4:09:23	C GIBSON	4:09:58	P MALTAS	4:10:30	J SPENCER	4:10:54	J MORGAN	4:11:29
8	S SELVIN	4:09:23	I DAVIDSON	4:09:59	D HAMILTON	4:10:30	A LEONARD	4:10:56	R TRODD	4:11:29
9	A MOSS	4:09:24	A JAMES	4:09:59	P ANDREWS	4:10:30	L CARPENTER	4:10:57	I MORRIS	4:11:29
10	M PARKER	4:09:24	P RICE	4:09:59	E WILLIAMS	4:10:30	M DAMMS	4:10:58	A KEEN	4:11:29
11	J WALLER	4:09:24	D EVANS	4:09:59	L BARNES	4:10:30	O SANDNES	4:10:58	A VANCE	4:11:29
12	J TERVIT	4:09:24	S WALLER	4:09:59	S CAWTE	4:10:30	P HIGGINS	4:10:58	B CLIFTON	4:11:29
13	M WAKLEY	4:09:24	G GOODMAN	4:10:00	G MERCHANT	4:10:30	M SKINDERHAUG	4:10:58	P HEADLAND	4:11:30
14	J NEEDS	4:09:24	M HOBBS	4:10:00	A KIDD	4:10:30	G NORDIN	4:10:59	P BOURASSA	4:11:30
15	V STONE	4:09:24	T REDDISH	4:10:01	V BRUCE	4:10:31	J GOUVEIA	4:10:59	A CLYNE	4:11:31
16	D WATERHOUSE	4:09:24	R NOAKES	4:10:01	S TREACY	4:10:31	A VATANEN-NIKKINEN	4:10:59	M PANNET	4:11:31
17	W BRODRICK	4:09:24	L REDDISH	4:10:01	M GUY	4:10:31	D NASH	4:11:01	K ROBINSON	4:11:31
18	I SIMPSON	4:09:25	J MOSS	4:10:02	F MASON	4:10:32	D SWADLING	4:11:01	C ENDACOTT	4:11:31
19	M HAWTREE	4:09:25	J MCKENZIE	4:10:02	J DALE	4:10:32	M BELSHAM	4:11:02	V SMITH	4:11:31
20	C JARVIS	4:09:26	A MOORE	4:10:03	D TINBERGEN	4:10:32	D SMITH	4:11:02	V FURBANK	4:11:32
21	T NEWING	4:09:26	I VIDAL	4:10:03	J ROBERTSON	4:10:33	S COX	4:11:03	D TOBIN	4:11:32
22	J HALL	4:09:28	D WRIGHT	4:10:03	J ROGERSON	4:10:34	F BAJWA	4:11:03	F WICKENS	4:11:32
23	R DANIEL	4:09:28	K SQUIRES	4:10:03	H SAVOURNIN	4:10:34	K LAPPALAINEN	4:11:03	K BELCHER	4:11:32
24	S WHITMARSH-KNIGHT	4:09:29	I GARTH	4:10:04	A MATTHEWS	4:10:34	T WHITE	4:11:03	J STEADMAN	4:11:32
25	J WOODS	4:09:29	R KERSBERGEN	4:10:04	R SIMMONDS	4:10:34	B WHEELDON	4:11:03	B BRIERS	4:11:32
26	A FRAPPELL	4:09:30	L SIGNORELLY	4:10:04	C DUGGAN	4:10:34	M KLINCKE	4:11:04	B JAMES	4:11:32
27	D FARIES	4:09:30	A JARVIS	4:10:04	D CAMPBELL	4:10:35	V FAIRCLOUGH	4:11:04	K BURDEN	4:11:33
28	P JEFFREY	4:09:31	K ALLANSON	4:10:05	P GUYOT	4:10:35	I BAKER	4:11:05	A GILL	4:11:33
29	S THACKER	4:09:31	J DICKINSON	4:10:06	K SANDISON	4:10:35	I TOMLINSON	4:11:05	D BROADWELL	4:11:33
30	A SHERLOCK	4:09:32	C GARDINER	4:10:06	D FARRIER	4:10:35	R HARDEN	4:11:05	C BRYAN	4:11:33
31	M TOUDIC	4:09:33	I WAKEFIELD	4:10:09	P FLYNN	4:10:35	R HOYLE	4:11:05	R EVANS	4:11:33
32	M COLE	4:09:33	J BURNAN	4:10:09	B SMITHERS	4:10:36	P THORN	4:11:05	S DIXON	4:11:34
33	A COLOE	4:09:33	L STAGG	4:10:09	N VALLANCE	4:10:36	M ROBSON	4:11:07	D KEMBER	4:11:34
34	P HIGGS	4:09:34	A CHEESMAN	4:10:09	K ILLINGWORTH	4:10:36	G CROSSLEY	4:11:07	S FOERDE	4:11:34
35	M SUTCLIFFE	4:09:34	J TUHEY	4:10:09	A HEWITT	4:10:36	A TRUDGILL	4:11:07	S MOUND	4:11:35
36	S COBBALD	4:09:34	A BARRON	4:10:09	G DALE	4:10:36	M WILLIS	4:11:07	G THOMPSON	4:11:35
37	B KELLINGTON	4:09:35	R SYRETT	4:10:09	D BRUNK	4:10:37	G TRUDGILL	4:11:07	I CORDINGLEY	4:11:35
38	W CURRIE	4:09:35	D BYRNE	4:10:09	A BLAKE	4:10:37	P LEE	4:11:08	P ROUTH	4:11:35
39	A CHAMPION	4:09:36	L MILLER	4:10:10	K WHARNSBY	4:10:37	A INWOOD	4:11:08	C MORRIS	4:11:35
40	D TITUS	4:09:36	I THOMSON	4:10:10	K BRINDLE	4:10:37	P GRANT-MILLS	4:11:09	Y FAGE	4:11:35
41	R INGLES	4:09:37	K WILKINSON	4:10:10	J MCINNES	4:10:38	I MARSHALL	4:11:10	T HOWARD	4:11:37
42	I DOWSON	4:09:37	D ALLEN	4:10:10	A ELLIS	4:10:38	G WHITTAKER	4:11:10	M BARNWELL	4:11:37
43	J BUNK	4:09:39	P BELTON	4:10:11	E SMITH	4:10:38	C SWINDELLS	4:11:10	C GIBSON	4:11:38
44	S NIELD	4:09:39	T PHILIPS	4:10:11	G BARNETT	4:10:38	C GRUE	4:11:11	N EDESON	4:11:38
45	A NEWNHAM	4:09:40	A BROWNE	4:10:12	P GROOM	4:10:39	D LEWIS	4:11:11	J REES	4:11:38
46	Y MERCIER	4:09:40	W HENNESSY	4:10:12	J RYAN	4:10:39	M CONSIDERA	4:11:12	S GWILLIAM	4:11:39
47	S HUTCHINS	4:09:41	J WOODHOUSE	4:10:12	D FORD	4:10:39	G TEE	4:11:12	P KERRINS	4:11:40
48	P BURCHELL	4:09:41	I SKIVINGTON	4:10:12	A LANGNER	4:10:39	J HAMMOND	4:11:12	I BURDON	4:11:42
49	P MILL	4:09:42	W BOYD	4:10:12	S O'CONNOR	4:10:39	G RICHARDS	4:11:12	R BARNES	4:11:43
50	R ONEILL	4:09:42	L BOYD	4:10:12	K SCHEFFLER	4:10:39	C MCKAY	4:11:12	P BUSH	4:11:43
51	W MULLINEAUX	4:09:42	R PARSON	4:10:12	S PEARCE	4:10:39	D LAUGHTON	4:11:12	N PITCH	4:11:43
52	A GREENHALGH	4:09:42	D HUGHES	4:10:12	S PERKINS	4:10:39	D BOURDIER	4:11:12	R BROWN	4:11:43
53	J HARPER	4:09:42	R KEYS	4:10:12	E ORECCHIA	4:10:40	R DORNEY	4:11:12	R SHARMAN	4:11:43
54	P HERN	4:09:42	J HAZELL	4:10:13	A GALBRAITH	4:10:40	P ROBERTSON	4:11:12	V STUTTARD	4:11:44
55	J SHAW	4:09:42	M DUFFY	4:10:13	G ANDERSON	4:10:40	D BAUCHOP	4:11:12	S CARTWRIGHT	4:11:45
56	R LEECH	4:09:42	M BASTICK	4:10:14	A COLLINS	4:10:40	T RICHARDS	4:11:12	D GREAVES	4:11:46
57	M CONNELLY	4:09:42	M COYNE	4:10:14	I MEADE	4:10:40	T MCCABE	4:11:12	S COLLINS	4:11:46
58	T DALEN	4:09:43	C PESCOD	4:10:14	R MOWAT	4:10:40	S PRATT	4:11:12	J HEMPEL	4:11:47
59	I KOS	4:09:43	L HAM	4:10:14	C FIELDING	4:10:41	L ROBINS	4:11:13	E EJDERFALL	4:11:47
60	M SOUTHERTON	4:09:43	B DUNLEA	4:10:15	N CONGDON	4:10:41	D PRATT	4:11:13	M SMOLEK	4:11:47
61	E BROWNE	4:09:43	K GRIFFIN	4:10:15	S NEEDHAM	4:10:41	T QUIRK	4:11:13	S HALL	4:11:48
62	G SPOONER	4:09:43	J PARE	4:10:15	B OSBORNE	4:10:41	J LOWNDS	4:11:13	E CROSSINGHAM	4:11:49
63	A ROSTRON	4:09:43	T HINTON	4:10:15	S WRIGHT	4:10:41	D LEWIS	4:11:13	R EVANS	4:11:49
64	V SMITH	4:09:43	R HOWARD	4:10:16	G BARWELL	4:10:41	M FRANSESE	4:11:13	P MENZIES	4:11:50
65	A BLAMIRE	4:09:43	J GODON	4:10:16	H MARTIN	4:10:42	M MCSHANE	4:11:13	B WALKER	4:11:50
66	D WRIGHT	4:09:43	A PETFORD	4:10:16	W OP DE BEECK	4:10:42	A DANIELSSON	4:11:13	M REED	4:11:50
67	B SMITH	4:09:43	P DAVISON	4:10:16	J HALL	4:10:42	M MOUNTAIN	4:11:13	H YOSHIDA	4:11:50
68	J PEDERSEN	4:09:43	M HUTCHIN	4:10:17	R ARNELL	4:10:43	R NAY	4:11:14	T HUXLEY	4:11:51
69	G HALL	4:09:43	B TARRANT	4:10:17	E BENSON	4:10:43	R HAYLER	4:11:14	C BETTERIDGE	4:11:52
70	K HAMILTON	4:09:45	S JACKSON	4:10:17	J CLARKE	4:10:43	W ALTENAU	4:11:14	D WESTON	4:11:52
71	F CARRADUS	4:09:45	L COETZEE	4:10:17	B WATERS	4:10:43	C HIGGINSON	4:11:14	P CROCKER	4:11:52
72	D BAKER	4:09:46	T GILJE	4:10:17	A HOWARD	4:10:44	M DOWNHAM	4:11:14	L FREESTONE	4:11:52
73	J PARKER	4:09:46	K ROE	4:10:18	K ALLEN	4:10:44	J VAN DER WOUDE	4:11:14	C ELLISON	4:11:52
74	L HAMILTON	4:09:47	H SCHLEINZER	4:10:18	R PIPE	4:10:44	A TURNHAM	4:11:14	K GREEN	4:11:52
75	A ROWTON	4:09:47	A JACK	4:10:18	D SANDELL	4:10:45	L CHAPMAN	4:11:14	K GRANT	4:11:52
76	C WILLIS	4:09:47	C BARKE	4:10:18	B SOLLY	4:10:45	A PERRETT	4:11:15	A BARTLETT	4:11:52
77	S ATKIN	4:09:48	M LAZES	4:10:18	R DALLAWAY	4:10:45	L RANKIN	4:11:16	G BORLEY	4:11:52
78	G WRAY	4:09:49	R SADLER	4:10:18	S NORRIS	4:10:45	P DAVISON	4:11:17	G TREDRAY	4:11:53
79	G MORGAN	4:09:50	A YOUNG	4:10:18	P FELDMAN	4:10:45	M HOPKINS	4:11:18	G SUTTON	4:11:54
80	M TURTON	4:09:50	G ROSS	4:10:18	M MULDER	4:10:46	D CANNON	4:11:18	D JAMES	4:11:56
81	A SOERENSEN	4:09:50	B EDWARDS	4:10:19	P KNIGHTLEY	4:10:46	H LEES	4:11:19	D OWERS	4:11:56
82	M REMUSZ	4:09:51	A JONES	4:10:19	J HACKETT	4:10:46	A FRENCH	4:11:19	T HURST	4:11:56
83	T METCALFE	4:09:51	A CHALMERS	4:10:22	M KENT	4:10:46	J RAGGERTY	4:11:19	M BAHACHILLE	4:11:56
84	N HALSALL	4:09:52	D BOYD	4:10:23	A CUNNELL	4:10:46	K KAWASHIMA	4:11:20	G HOGG	4:11:57
85	D SALTER	4:09:52	G CAPE	4:10:24	M MORRISH	4:10:47	C MITCHELL	4:11:21	P STEINER	4:11:57
86	E CHILDERHOUSE	4:09:52	P BROWN	4:10:24	H CORNELIS	4:10:47	K HOUGHTON	4:11:21	P HALLIDAY	4:11:58
87	L ALESSANDRINI	4:09:52	B JACOBSON	4:10:24	I JONES	4:10:47	K BUSHELL	4:11:22	E BOND	4:11:58
88	A BELL	4:09:53	R FULLER	4:10:24	G BARRIELLE	4:10:48	A BROUGHTON	4:11:22	A PLACE	4:11:58
89	F DE MAEYER	4:09:53	J FISHER	4:10:25	E LEE	4:10:48	S STOREY	4:11:23	S SLATER	4:11:59
90	S WHITTAKER	4:09:53	A HENDERSON	4:10:25	M JENKINS	4:10:48	A WADSWORTH	4:11:23	S OGORMAN	4:11:59
91	J JOHANSEN	4:09:54	C COPLEY	4:10:25	S LAHLOU	4:10:50	P COBBETT	4:11:25	M BREENE	4:11:59
92	M HOGAN	4:09:54	D NUNN	4:10:25	D LAVERTY	4:10:50	G PERIGO	4:11:25	P SMITH	4:12:00
93	J WAGHORN	4:09:54	T SAYWELL	4:10:26	M LANGSTROM	4:10:50	C PELLETIER	4:11:26	K AYTON	4:12:00
94	C TOMKINS	4:09:54	C COURAGIER	4:10:26	A PACK	4:10:51	G SWANSON	4:11:26	M ORR	4:12:01
95	M BULL	4:09:54	I ZEMLJARIC	4:10:26	S HEWETT	4:10:51	P BYFLEET	4:11:26	B HOLMES	4:12:01
96	M POBJOY	4:09:54	N BENNETT	4:10:27	P DEADMAN	4:10:51	R WINDSOR	4:11:26	G TURNER	4:12:01
97	I STUTTARD	4:09:55	C BROWN	4:10:27	C WILLIS	4:10:52	M YOUNG	4:11:27	S ADAMSON	4:12:02
98	S BAKER	4:09:55	E BOWERS	4:10:27	P NAVARRO	4:10:52	D KILGALLON	4:11:27	P SMITH	4:12:02
99	P WISE	4:09:55	J ASPOAS	4:10:27	R DZIALDOW	4:10:52	J FOOT	4:11:27	G WOODS	4:12:02
100	D WOOD	4:09:56	A JAMES	4:10:28	J BUTTERWORTH	4:10:52	A SQUIBB	4:11:28	J HALL	4:12:03

#	14501-14600		14601-14700		14701-14800		14801-14900		14901-15000	
1	A HOPKINS	4:12:03	W GRANT	4:12:36	D COLE	4:13:06	H TRICKER	4:13:41	I SIMPSON	4:14:06
2	H HERZIG	4:12:04	L BAVERSTOCK	4:12:37	F TAYLOR	4:13:06	P HARDY	4:13:41	A WOOLGAR	4:14:07
3	R ONEILL	4:12:04	M STAPLETON	4:12:37	L BAYLES	4:13:06	G HARRISON	4:13:41	A ELEY	4:14:08
4	C HOPKINS	4:12:04	W BILSLAND	4:12:38	P NEWELL	4:13:06	J CULLINGHAM	4:13:41	J SCHLUTER	4:14:08
5	S PARKER	4:12:04	T HARVEY	4:12:38	D LISTER	4:13:06	R KEAY	4:13:42	D HEARLE	4:14:09
6	J MAGUIRE	4:12:04	R CROPPER	4:12:38	S SYMONDS	4:13:07	S KEAY	4:13:43	R COLLISTER	4:14:09
7	J MOULSON	4:12:05	I LIDDLE	4:12:39	A HENDY	4:13:07	C STAGG	4:13:43	K WATANABE	4:14:09
8	A KELLY	4:12:06	B WILLIAMS	4:12:40	N HUNT	4:13:07	A BOWLES	4:13:43	M COOKE	4:14:09
9	A BROOK	4:12:07	D WILLIAMS	4:12:40	E BARNES	4:13:07	D DRAKELEY	4:13:43	M MOUIT	4:14:10
10	K KAVANAGH	4:12:08	M WHEELDON	4:12:40	S WESTPHAL	4:13:07	J SMITH	4:13:43	K BAYFIELD	4:14:10
11	B KAINTH	4:12:08	R APPLEBY	4:12:40	C ROMUALD	4:13:07	J GREGORY	4:13:43	R CHALASANI	4:14:10
12	A LEEK	4:12:08	P RICKETT	4:12:40	J DIGHTON	4:13:07	J FAIRCLOUGH	4:13:43	R MACKINLAY	4:14:11
13	D ANDERSON	4:12:08	J CLIFF	4:12:40	J WOOD	4:13:07	D LANE	4:13:43	L COCHARD	4:14:11
14	L VORALIA	4:12:09	J GALLACHER	4:12:40	C HARRISON	4:13:07	A HUGHES	4:13:44	G PAYAN	4:14:12
15	D THOMAS	4:12:09	J THOLE	4:12:40	C FISHER	4:13:07	S BUSH	4:13:44	B JOHNSON	4:14:12
16	D PALMER	4:12:09	S PLATTS	4:12:40	M KIBBLE	4:13:08	S HUDSON	4:13:44	J SNELL	4:14:12
17	A PRICE	4:12:09	J FOSTER	4:12:40	E GORDON	4:13:08	P STOCKWELL	4:13:44	R KENDALL	4:14:12
18	L SIMMONS	4:12:09	G DAVIDSON	4:12:40	P BROAD	4:13:08	J BLOGG	4:13:44	P REVELL	4:14:13
19	I VENTERS	4:12:09	B PARKIN	4:12:40	R PERRIMENT	4:13:08	N GRACE	4:13:44	E PRESTON	4:14:13
20	A DARK	4:12:09	W WIEDICKE	4:12:41	S BINNS	4:13:08	W BAKER	4:13:45	W WIRSCHING	4:14:14
21	J GIBBS	4:12:10	D DARBY	4:12:41	P CORFIELD	4:13:08	D KEY	4:13:45	J CLAXTON	4:14:14
22	L MONTENOVO	4:12:10	P LONGMAN	4:12:41	B PELLETIER	4:13:08	P HILL	4:13:45	A DACHE	4:14:14
23	G SEMPLE	4:12:11	M BUCKINGHAM	4:12:41	S HUNT	4:13:08	T THOMPSON	4:13:45	A PROSSER	4:14:15
24	D BARLOW	4:12:11	T HARDING	4:12:42	N BUTLER	4:13:08	A TAYLOR	4:13:45	R DORNAN	4:14:15
25	S ALLERTON	4:12:11	M JANDS	4:12:42	S FOSTER	4:13:09	L RADFORD	4:13:46	G SKINNER	4:14:16
26	C GRENCOCK	4:12:11	C SAUNDERS	4:12:42	T VINING	4:13:09	R HUGHES	4:13:46	M LEWIS	4:14:16
27	J FOWLER	4:12:11	D WHY	4:12:42	D MEECH	4:13:09	G AVIS	4:13:47	S CLAYTON	4:14:16
28	D VERZOTTI	4:12:11	M HILLIER	4:12:43	J TAYLOR	4:13:10	S GOODWIN	4:13:48	M WOODHAMS	4:14:16
29	P GRUNDY	4:12:12	R EGGAR	4:12:43	K HURST	4:13:10	S WALKER	4:13:48	S SHARDLOW	4:14:16
30	M SCHOFIELD	4:12:12	D WATKINSON	4:12:43	D MCNEILL	4:13:11	M WALTERS	4:13:48	R JANSEN	4:14:17
31	M LONDON	4:12:13	J NODDER	4:12:43	V VILAR	4:13:11	D PHILLIPS	4:13:48	D CONNELLY	4:14:17
32	P GRIFFIN TEALL	4:12:14	T ELLEER	4:12:44	P HANNAH	4:13:11	P DAHLE	4:13:49	D JACKSON	4:14:18
33	M MATTHEWS	4:12:14	B COURTNEY	4:12:44	K DURHAM	4:13:11	R HYLAND	4:13:50	H ROESELER	4:14:18
34	C RICHARDS	4:12:15	C HOPKINS	4:12:45	A HINDLET	4:13:11	V DAVIES	4:13:50	C TOBITT	4:14:19
35	M BARKER	4:12:15	E EDDES	4:12:45	K STEVENS	4:13:12	A CLISSOLD	4:13:50	K BUTTLE	4:14:19
36	R WATKINS	4:12:15	J LOCKLEY	4:12:45	D CROSBY	4:13:12	K RICHARDS	4:13:51	V SGARZI	4:14:19
37	K CUNNINGTON	4:12:15	M BEUAN	4:12:46	D DRAPPER	4:13:13	M KUCZKIEWICZ	4:13:51	N GARNER	4:14:19
38	T CALLAGHAN	4:12:16	M MILLER	4:12:46	H ABRAHAMSSON	4:13:13	S REDFEARN	4:13:51	C BRADE	4:14:20
39	D HARGREAVES	4:12:16	C PAUL	4:12:46	R CHELL	4:13:13	A CUMMING	4:13:52	B HAMPSON	4:14:20
40	G MCEWAN	4:12:17	B BRENNAN	4:12:46	M LEWIS	4:13:14	R GREGORY	4:13:52	D SCOTT-BEDDARD	4:14:20
41	C BARKER	4:12:17	M PRICE	4:12:46	J BLUETT	4:13:14	P LEVENE	4:13:52	V BURKE	4:14:20
42	O DAVIES	4:12:17	F WILLDAY	4:12:47	M GOMME	4:13:15	M DIACK	4:13:52	D KEENE	4:14:20
43	P DAVENPORT	4:12:17	M MURPHY	4:12:47	J ROBSON	4:13:15	N CROFT	4:13:53	L DHAINE	4:14:20
44	J DUNCAN	4:12:18	M CABLE	4:12:47	A SOHR	4:13:15	C BAALAM	4:13:53	C ALTOFT	4:14:21
45	S MARTIN	4:12:18	D SCHOFIELD	4:12:48	A ELSOME	4:13:15	R VAN DER LINDEN	4:13:53	I ROSS	4:14:21
46	R CALDWELL	4:12:18	W THOMAS	4:12:48	I REBELLO	4:13:16	S CHAMPION	4:13:53	R SELFE	4:14:22
47	C BLYTH	4:12:18	A OAKES	4:12:49	T HOLMAN	4:13:16	P GERKEN	4:13:54	A WALSH	4:14:23
48	F WALSH	4:12:18	P PENTNEY	4:12:49	E GIBON	4:13:16	P FITZSIMMONS	4:13:54	D HARNETT	4:14:23
49	F MELLING	4:12:18	C KIELY	4:12:49	J CLARK	4:13:16	A FARLEY	4:13:54	P BODNARSKY	4:14:23
50	M DUFFY	4:12:18	D BITHELL	4:12:51	F SALIBA	4:13:16	P BOLKE	4:13:55	J MCKIBBIN	4:14:24
51	B CAPENER	4:12:19	B BUCKLE	4:12:51	J BICKLEY	4:13:16	A SMITH	4:13:55	J HANCOCK	4:14:24
52	D KU	4:12:19	M LABOYRIE	4:12:52	D PRESTON	4:13:16	J BARRETT	4:13:55	J DEVINE	4:14:25
53	M BENSON	4:12:20	J PERKINS	4:12:52	A TILBROOK	4:13:16	M EVANS	4:13:55	L COUSINS	4:14:25
54	S WEBB	4:12:20	D SUTTON	4:12:52	G LLOYD-JONES	4:13:17	R PAUL	4:13:55	A WHITE	4:14:27
55	S STRINGER	4:12:20	E DUFF	4:12:53	R BOURNE	4:13:17	F SORNETTE	4:13:55	C FURNESS	4:14:27
56	M SMITH	4:12:20	J FOX	4:12:53	D HARDY	4:13:18	M MARTIN	4:13:56	M DIN	4:14:27
57	H GUNER	4:12:20	V VERHOEVEN	4:12:53	A FIDGE	4:13:19	H CAMPBELL	4:13:56	J BALL	4:14:27
58	I JOHNSON	4:12:20	D GEORGE	4:12:54	P PATTISON	4:13:19	L REEKIE	4:13:56	G HARDING	4:14:28
59	F CONNOR	4:12:20	R WHITEHEAD	4:12:54	P THOMAS	4:13:19	G OSGUTHORPE	4:13:58	R WALKER	4:14:28
60	A PAYNE	4:12:20	R ADAMS	4:12:55	B ELLIOTT	4:13:20	K CRELLIN	4:13:59	B HALE	4:14:28
61	I PATTERSON	4:12:20	B MEREDITH	4:12:55	R PHILLIPS	4:13:20	M SOUTH	4:13:59	M LINDLEY	4:14:29
62	D KANE	4:12:20	S COOPER	4:12:55	M GOREHAM	4:13:20	P COLLINS	4:14:00	S GARNER	4:14:29
63	M CAVANAGH	4:12:20	J SZCEPUREK	4:12:55	B ETZOLD	4:13:20	Z SEXTON	4:14:00	J ALLSOPP	4:14:30
64	S KING	4:12:20	C SPUIJBROEK	4:12:56	G FULLWOOD	4:13:20	M ATKINS	4:14:00	M HIGGINS	4:14:31
65	R HOLYOAKE	4:12:20	G PENDRY	4:12:56	J ROBERTS	4:13:21	M LOWSON	4:14:00	V WOODGATE	4:14:31
66	J COTTAM	4:12:21	A COMETTE	4:12:56	C HADGRAFT	4:13:22	C DAVIES	4:14:01	T COOLE	4:14:32
67	M RIDDING	4:12:21	A DYETT	4:12:57	K WATSON	4:13:23	J BARRETT	4:14:01	J AVEY	4:14:32
68	M BRADLEY	4:12:21	D HIGGS	4:12:57	B THOMAS	4:13:24	I JONES	4:14:01	S COOK	4:14:33
69	C WILLIS	4:12:21	N WILKS	4:12:57	C BOYLES	4:13:24	D JONES	4:14:01	N COLMAN	4:14:33
70	J ROBBINS	4:12:21	S JEREMY	4:12:57	G STACK	4:13:24	D KELTIE	4:14:01	K LAMBURN	4:14:33
71	P WILSON	4:12:21	P GILDERDALE	4:12:58	B GRIMWOOD	4:13:26	G HIGHMOOR	4:14:02	A MALLPRESS	4:14:33
72	C BARDIAU	4:12:21	G RUMARY	4:12:58	C LEACH	4:13:26	S HAY	4:14:02	T RIVERS	4:14:33
73	T MCCABE	4:12:21	M HEDDERLY	4:12:58	N HEDDERLY	4:13:28	K PHIPPS	4:14:02	A JANSEN	4:14:33
74	P SCRAFTON	4:12:23	J HARRIES	4:12:58	A BROWN	4:13:28	J SCHAEFER	4:14:02	J O'DONOVAN	4:14:34
75	I ROBSON	4:12:24	W MOORE	4:12:58	D HOWARD	4:13:29	J WILLIAMS	4:14:02	M FARRAGE	4:14:34
76	L BAKER	4:12:24	I MARTIN	4:12:59	J FRANCIS	4:13:29	G SMITH	4:14:02	D NOTARIO	4:14:34
77	S TURNER	4:12:25	D FIELD	4:12:59	J WATKINS	4:13:30	V MARSHALL	4:14:02	S DRACUP	4:14:34
78	P BURSNALL	4:12:25	R CHILDRESS	4:12:59	A DAVISON	4:13:30	G TAIT	4:14:02	R PARKER	4:14:35
79	L SMITH	4:12:25	J WALKER	4:12:59	S FRUCH	4:13:31	M MORGAN	4:14:02	E LOMBROSO	4:14:37
80	N PADHIAR	4:12:25	P WRIGHT	4:13:00	W HEYBURN	4:13:31	I LAM	4:14:03	K CARLTON	4:14:40
81	P WILLIAMSON	4:12:25	S BROWN	4:13:00	W COVEY	4:13:31	D MCNEELANCE	4:14:03	W SCOTT	4:14:41
82	G JONES	4:12:25	S SHARPE	4:13:01	K URWIN	4:13:32	A CLARK	4:14:03	J TULLY	4:14:42
83	H PRITCHARD	4:12:26	A BRIDGES	4:13:01	J MCBRIDE	4:13:33	R BRADSHAW	4:14:03	J ELMS	4:14:44
84	C INGRAM	4:12:26	F WAGSTAFF	4:13:02	J HARDY	4:13:34	J BYDE	4:14:03	M PIGOTT	4:14:45
85	R ERDIN-SIEBER	4:12:26	P FULTON	4:13:02	P BRANN	4:13:35	L BATTERSBY	4:14:04	S BIANCHINI	4:14:45
86	G MITCHINSON	4:12:28	J MEARS	4:13:02	P CASSON	4:13:36	R PORTULAS	4:14:04	B ROBERTS	4:14:45
87	P BURNS	4:12:28	P HOUGHTON	4:13:03	S STENHOUSE	4:13:37	I MAHONEY	4:14:04	A FISK	4:14:46
88	S EDELSTON	4:12:28	E CROOKE	4:13:03	F FEHILY	4:13:37	R JENNER	4:14:04	V FLORES	4:14:46
89	C WINTLE	4:12:30	P OGDEN	4:13:03	M CATLING	4:13:38	P CROSSFIELD	4:14:04	K TAYLOR	4:14:46
90	J LUCAS	4:12:30	M MCGARVEY	4:13:03	T MOORE	4:13:38	A HALLAM	4:14:05	T INGLETON	4:14:46
91	D SPENCE	4:12:31	R CURTIS	4:13:03	R WILLIAMS	4:13:39	R AGGALEY	4:14:05	S BROKENSHAW	4:14:46
92	A BARNES	4:12:31	D GLADWELL	4:13:04	M WILLIAMS	4:13:39	G CAMPBELL	4:14:05	B WHYBROW	4:14:46
93	R PEEBLES	4:12:31	J JONES	4:13:04	A BARNES	4:13:39	C NICKSON	4:14:05	J SOULIER	4:14:46
94	C FARRANT	4:12:33	K HICKS	4:13:04	A FLORACK	4:13:39	N KYRITSIS	4:14:05	S MEADOWS	4:14:47
95	D EVANS	4:12:34	S HART	4:13:04	A DURRANT	4:13:39	W GIFFARD	4:14:06	A PEREIRA	4:14:47
96	J FLAVELL	4:12:35	R DAWBER	4:13:04	A TURNER	4:13:40	P KLEIN	4:14:06	R DREW	4:14:47
97	D SLADE	4:12:35	M MARSHALL	4:13:04	A MCFARLANE	4:13:40	J CLARKE	4:14:06	G DONOHOE	4:14:47
98	T SMITH	4:12:35	C LAVY	4:13:05	J GORDON	4:13:40	M NEMETH	4:14:06	P SMITH	4:14:48
99	T SOLAN	4:12:35	S SPENCER	4:13:05	S PROFFITT	4:13:40	C DAVENPORT	4:14:06	J SMITH	4:14:49
100	G GILLETT	4:12:35	R VIAN	4:13:06	A JUDGE	4:13:41	A PAYNE	4:14:06	P HOLLINGSWORTH	4:14:50

	15001-15100		15101-15200		15201-15300		15301-15400		15401-15500	
1	M RASMUSSEN	4:14:50	P STUART	4:15:28	L MACCALLUM STEWART	4:15:58	D BOLES	4:16:33	G WILLCOX	4:17:10
2	J DEMMON	4:14:50	A SALE	4:15:28	D WILCOX	4:15:59	S BENJAMIN	4:16:33	R JONES	4:17:10
3	M ALLEN	4:14:50	R MILLS	4:15:28	P BARRON	4:15:59	G HUGHES	4:16:34	J HARLEN	4:17:11
4	R CARR	4:14:50	P HYNES	4:15:28	E TAWSE	4:15:59	C ALTY	4:16:34	J HARRIS	4:17:11
5	D BURNS	4:14:50	M HOWARD-DAWSON	4:15:29	F MASSON	4:16:00	J BOLTON	4:16:34	I PIKE	4:17:12
6	R WOOD	4:14:50	K DAVISON	4:15:29	M ARLOW	4:16:00	S BRETT	4:16:35	T JENSEN	4:17:12
7	P WHIFFEN	4:14:50	T HUMPHREYS	4:15:30	J CARTWRIGHT	4:16:00	D MEANEY	4:16:36	C WARDALE	4:17:12
8	L TRIGGS	4:14:50	D DALBY	4:15:30	D NEWRICK	4:16:01	G HOSKING	4:16:36	C DOLBY	4:17:13
9	S HERBERT	4:14:50	M PAGE	4:15:30	H PALMER	4:16:01	B KINGHORN	4:16:37	G SQUIRE	4:17:13
10	J BOLAM	4:14:50	J SNARE	4:15:31	J FLINT	4:16:01	W SHEPPARD	4:16:37	E ABBOTT	4:17:14
11	G NICHOLSON	4:14:50	S FAGG	4:15:31	J BALDWIN	4:16:02	T HALL	4:16:38	P RIORDAN-EVA	4:17:14
12	E GRIFFITHS	4:14:50	R CHALKE	4:15:31	B RUSSELL	4:16:02	M CRONIN	4:16:38	K EVANS	4:17:15
13	R CROOKS	4:14:50	K KEEGAN	4:15:31	B DAVIES	4:16:02	V FREEMAN	4:16:39	C WALSH	4:17:15
14	S MITCHELL	4:14:50	S ELLISTON	4:15:32	G MILLS	4:16:02	P MCERLAIN	4:16:39	A RAYMOND	4:17:15
15	S MACE	4:14:50	J WHALE	4:15:32	A JONES	4:16:02	M MACDONALD	4:16:39	G GREEN	4:17:16
16	N FOORD	4:14:51	A LESCH	4:15:32	J COX	4:16:02	J PICKARD	4:16:39	I HUTCHISON	4:17:16
17	G PANSERI	4:14:51	E BYWATER	4:15:32	G KEMP	4:16:02	A JACKMAN	4:16:40	D BAMFORTH	4:17:16
18	M MOLNEY	4:14:52	M BAILEY	4:15:32	A WATTERS	4:16:02	U BUMBACHER	4:16:40	A TALBOT	4:17:16
19	R HEATHER	4:14:53	E BLIZZARD	4:15:33	P WOODS	4:16:02	D TROTT	4:16:40	P HOLT	4:17:16
20	H LONNE	4:14:53	T FISHER	4:15:33	D ROWE	4:16:02	M FUSSELL	4:16:40	A PEACOCK	4:17:17
21	M MCINALLY	4:14:53	A MATTOCK	4:15:33	D SCOTT	4:16:02	J LEPELTIER	4:16:40	F CONROY	4:17:17
22	C TRAVERS	4:14:54	P HARPER	4:15:34	T COCKS	4:16:02	P EMERY	4:16:40	M HILLS	4:17:17
23	S WATKINS	4:14:56	M THOMPSON	4:15:34	B GUILLOUD	4:16:02	P LAW	4:16:40	A JOSLIN	4:17:17
24	R SOHR	4:14:57	G MILLAR	4:15:34	P DYER	4:16:02	P DAVIDSON	4:16:40	D THOMPSON	4:17:17
25	S HUILLET	4:14:57	E DAVIES	4:15:35	B DAVIES	4:16:02	H MCMILLAN	4:16:40	J STONE	4:17:18
26	K BLACKSHAW	4:14:57	B WEBB	4:15:35	L REASON	4:16:02	P MCCULLOCH	4:16:40	G PHILLIPS	4:17:18
27	J WOODRUFF	4:14:58	E SMITH	4:15:35	C LAWTON	4:16:02	D KENNERSON	4:16:41	K NELSON	4:17:18
28	H KRAUSE	4:14:59	P TOUX	4:15:36	K HENDRY	4:16:02	Y KOSAKA	4:16:41	P MOSLEY	4:17:18
29	D MC CORMACK	4:14:59	M ASHCROFT	4:15:36	B GREEN	4:16:02	A FOREMAN	4:16:41	M DENIS	4:17:19
30	O HENRIKSEN	4:14:59	T HEASMAN	4:15:36	A GRAHAM	4:16:03	K MCKINNEY	4:16:42	M FREEMAN	4:17:19
31	R GIRLING	4:15:00	M ADAMS	4:15:36	M HENNESSY	4:16:03	P MITCHELL	4:16:43	E LOHOU	4:17:19
32	H FERSCHMANN	4:15:00	R QUEST	4:15:37	S PARKER	4:16:03	D YOUNGER	4:16:43	C BUCKLEY	4:17:19
33	W RAIN	4:15:01	R BINGHAM	4:15:37	G GUALLINO	4:16:03	E BAKER	4:16:43	C PAGE	4:17:19
34	H SALISBURY	4:15:01	S BHADHA	4:15:38	R NEE	4:16:04	B WOOD	4:16:44	D LAWRENCE	4:17:20
35	P DAWSON	4:15:01	B BRETT	4:15:39	C HILL	4:16:05	M GARRETT	4:16:44	P ROE	4:17:20
36	P DAVID	4:15:02	B NEARY	4:15:39	M TRUNDLEY	4:16:05	K BROWNING	4:16:45	R WALLER	4:17:20
37	R SHEFFIELD	4:15:03	D EDMONDS	4:15:39	P HUGHES	4:16:05	M STURGES	4:16:45	L O'CONNOR	4:17:21
38	P GARSIDE	4:15:03	J WILLIAMS	4:15:40	J FITTER	4:16:06	D LEE	4:16:45	R WRIGHT	4:17:21
39	D BUNYAN	4:15:03	K SEARS	4:15:40	J PRITCHARD	4:16:06	C LAWTON	4:16:45	J WHITEAKER	4:17:22
40	S SKINNARD	4:15:03	M LILLEY	4:15:40	S MARTIN	4:16:06	S PHILLIPS	4:16:46	S WINNE	4:17:25
41	J HARTSHORN	4:15:05	T FOERS	4:15:40	A COLES	4:16:07	D GREEN	4:16:46	R PEDERSEN	4:17:26
42	P BUTTERWORTH	4:15:05	A SNAPE	4:15:41	G BIGGS	4:16:07	H RIDGWELL	4:16:46	P NIELSEN	4:17:27
43	B STANIER	4:15:06	D BIRDNO	4:15:41	P BUCK	4:16:07	R JENKINS	4:16:47	D DAVIES	4:17:28
44	G PARKER	4:15:06	L GEBAUER	4:15:41	R PAISLEY	4:16:07	P HOLLIS	4:16:47	P DEAN	4:17:28
45	M BAKER	4:15:06	R ALLEN	4:15:42	M GRIFFITHS	4:16:08	N LAVY	4:16:49	D WILLIAMS	4:17:28
46	T COMFORT	4:15:07	K VAN DER ZWET	4:15:42	J BURKE	4:16:10	L MILLER	4:16:50	M WILKS	4:17:29
47	M MANT	4:15:07	I HURRY	4:15:42	N SUMMERS	4:16:11	I PAUL	4:16:50	A REAY	4:17:29
48	J PICHARDO	4:15:08	A RAINE	4:15:42	P DANIELS	4:16:11	D EDWARDS	4:16:50	B ROWLES	4:17:29
49	K PAGE	4:15:09	P HUGHES	4:15:42	M PATTERSON	4:16:12	C ANGOVE	4:16:51	S BEELEY	4:17:30
50	A BIZEUL	4:15:09	H WILSON	4:15:42	A HOWE	4:16:13	J BARNARD	4:16:51	M PARSONS	4:17:30
51	D KIRK	4:15:10	S THOMPSON	4:15:43	T MCQUEEN	4:16:13	D VAN DEN BERG	4:16:51	R TAYLOR	4:17:31
52	A BOTHEREL	4:15:10	D BISHOP	4:15:43	S MOTT	4:16:15	N PETERS	4:16:51	K TENNANT	4:17:31
53	K MOUNTER	4:15:10	P WILLIAMS	4:15:43	J MILLYARD	4:16:16	S JOHNSON	4:16:51	P BARDEN DE LACROIX	4:17:32
54	N WILLIAMSON	4:15:10	M CHRISTENSEN	4:15:44	A STEWART	4:16:16	A GARDNER	4:16:51	H AYLWARD	4:17:32
55	R TURNER	4:15:11	R GELDARD	4:15:44	C GIL-TIENDA	4:16:17	R STIDWELL	4:16:51	M SMITH	4:17:33
56	A ORTON	4:15:11	R BLACKMORE	4:15:44	S COLLINS	4:16:19	P EDGE	4:16:51	A BETTANY	4:17:33
57	D VALLANCE	4:15:13	G JORDAN	4:15:44	C DENNIS	4:16:19	T ATKINSON	4:16:51	P COPEMAN	4:17:33
58	E SANDALL-BALL	4:15:13	N DAVIES	4:15:44	J FLETCHER	4:16:19	D ASHWORTH	4:16:52	R AXTON	4:17:33
59	A PERKINS	4:15:13	A NELSON	4:15:44	K STAIN	4:16:19	R JOHNSON	4:16:52	L WALKER	4:17:33
60	J HAYNES	4:15:13	B BRIER	4:15:44	N BROWN	4:16:20	G TUCKWELL	4:16:52	P HANNON	4:17:33
61	J WAGNER	4:15:14	J BOS	4:15:44	C ALDEN	4:16:21	D PERKINS	4:16:53	M GATTI	4:17:33
62	M BOLTON	4:15:14	W STEELE	4:15:44	B ALDEN	4:16:21	S WADE	4:16:54	T HODGKINSON	4:17:33
63	D BINNER	4:15:15	G GERARDTS	4:15:45	H WATANABE	4:16:21	B SINGH	4:16:54	C BROWN	4:17:34
64	K NORDAL	4:15:15	P ASKEW	4:15:45	S FOREMAN	4:16:23	R ETHERINGTON-SMITH	4:16:54	J GRAY	4:17:34
65	D LEE	4:15:16	P O'DONNELL	4:15:45	A JONES	4:16:23	S BREAKWELL	4:16:54	M ROBERTS	4:17:34
66	M BULL	4:15:16	N BAIRNER	4:15:45	A HUTCHINSON	4:16:23	T GRASS	4:16:54	R HOGARTH	4:17:34
67	D EVANS	4:15:17	J HUGHES	4:15:46	K COTTIS	4:16:24	J CUNDICK	4:16:55	D TURNER	4:17:34
68	G MATHIAS	4:15:17	S HEFFERNAN	4:15:46	C SERUGO	4:16:24	N SMITH	4:16:55	R STUBBINGS	4:17:34
69	S WARD	4:15:18	M HALL	4:15:47	M COSTIN	4:16:24	G COLBOW	4:16:56	R LYE	4:17:35
70	A LEE	4:15:18	M COPE	4:15:47	P PANAYIOTOU	4:16:24	P CLIFFORD	4:16:57	J HOGG	4:17:35
71	P MORTIMER	4:15:18	M ZNETYNIAK	4:15:47	R ELLIS	4:16:24	B LOVEGROVE	4:16:57	C DRING	4:17:35
72	S MITCHELL	4:15:18	R SEAGER	4:15:48	T WILLIAMS	4:16:24	R MENERY	4:16:57	K KENDALL	4:17:36
73	P WOODS	4:15:18	B NIELSEN	4:15:48	J CONLON	4:16:24	Y HIRAI	4:16:57	W KIRTLEY	4:17:37
74	A BROOKS	4:15:19	B JONES	4:15:48	S PARTRIDGE	4:16:24	P SPINNEY	4:16:58	R DEVEY	4:17:37
75	H GARNETT	4:15:19	D SEAGER	4:15:48	A LARKIN	4:16:25	A GACHES	4:16:58	B BROUGHTON	4:17:38
76	J CHESSHER	4:15:19	D FULHAM	4:15:49	A CROFT	4:16:25	J HEMPSTEAD	4:16:58	W DEMPSEY	4:17:38
77	P EVANS	4:15:19	H HEROUARD	4:15:49	L TOYLEMONDE	4:16:25	S HYDE	4:16:59	C NADEN	4:17:39
78	A FILER	4:15:22	N LITTLE	4:15:49	K FAIRS	4:16:26	P EVANS	4:16:59	I MILBURN	4:17:39
79	P DANIELS	4:15:23	M SWALLOW	4:15:50	B SKOPALIK	4:16:26	P LONG	4:17:00	S MANSELL	4:17:39
80	A SUTTON	4:15:23	Y GODON	4:15:50	A SMITH	4:16:27	T DUCK	4:17:00	K RISBY	4:17:40
81	C PRICE	4:15:23	J FARLEY	4:15:50	C SHARP	4:16:27	J FLAHERTY	4:17:00	D WARD	4:17:40
82	J HEATH	4:15:23	A HAYCOCK	4:15:50	A PANTALL	4:16:27	R WILSON	4:17:01	J NIEMI	4:17:40
83	P ROOTS	4:15:24	S TEW	4:15:51	A CROFT	4:16:27	S STEVENSON	4:17:02	D CHRYSTIE	4:17:40
84	N BURTON	4:15:25	N CLARK	4:15:52	A ELLIS	4:16:27	S DIXON	4:17:03	S GALLOP	4:17:40
85	J LESQUEREUX	4:15:25	L VAUCELLE	4:15:52	J SPEAKMAN-BROWN	4:16:27	N BILSON	4:17:04	S WILDMAN	4:17:40
86	J BATHAM	4:15:25	J BRADBURY	4:15:52	G GORMAN	4:16:28	P HAM	4:17:05	L TAYLOR	4:17:41
87	J BUTCHARD	4:15:26	G LEAHAIR	4:15:52	J MARHAM	4:16:28	A LOFTUS	4:17:05	M ANDREWS	4:17:41
88	G QUIRK	4:15:26	R CLARK	4:15:53	W GLUMPF	4:16:28	D SAWYER	4:17:05	B HATTRY	4:17:41
89	V KERNICK	4:15:26	J WALLIS	4:15:53	C SERGEANT	4:16:28	D NUNN	4:17:05	R KING	4:17:41
90	F WERNER	4:15:26	K HOWE	4:15:53	J CUNLIFFE	4:16:28	G ABRAHAM	4:17:06	O WALLIS	4:17:42
91	M CONROY	4:15:26	N ROSENGREN	4:15:54	J MITCHELL	4:16:29	P HARTINGTON	4:17:07	T LYNCH	4:17:42
92	S HOLLAND	4:15:26	B ROOK	4:15:54	C HESLIP	4:16:29	S JANDRON	4:17:07	L SHORT	4:17:42
93	G HEATLEY	4:15:27	S SEHMI	4:15:55	A BEALBY	4:16:30	B MONCRIEFFE	4:17:07	A FRENCH	4:17:42
94	G BRINDLEY	4:15:27	P ROGERS	4:15:55	R BOILEAU	4:16:30	V BALFOUR	4:17:07	R ANGELL	4:17:42
95	B CROPPER	4:15:27	K WHYTE	4:15:56	J BURBURY	4:16:30	A TEAL	4:17:07	K BAGGLEY	4:17:43
96	B HURFORD	4:15:27	K SHERIDAN	4:15:56	K RHODES	4:16:31	K NIEDER	4:17:08	D GRAHAM	4:17:43
97	J HOPE	4:15:28	G JONES	4:15:56	B PAVEY	4:16:31	D GALLAGHER	4:17:09	L DIFFORD	4:17:43
98	K AUSTIN	4:15:28	D BENNETT	4:15:56	P GAUTHIER	4:16:31	A OSBORN	4:17:09	W BELL	4:17:43
99	C MARLOW	4:15:28	N BULLOCK	4:15:58	S ROLES	4:16:32	N HOLLAND	4:17:09	R SCOTT	4:17:43
100	M KELLY	4:15:28	D SMITH	4:15:58	K RENDELL	4:16:32	M GOTTS	4:17:09	M PAINE	4:17:43

#	15501-15600		15601-15700		15701-15800		15801-15900		15901-16000	
1	T BURTON	4:17:43	S LYONS	4:18:20	A MILLER	4:18:59	L GRIGSBY	4:19:34	R WILLIAMS	4:20:10
2	R MCFADYEN	4:17:44	U MALIK	4:18:20	P MARTIN	4:18:59	J STAPLEY	4:19:34	F LEAHY	4:20:10
3	J HERAS	4:17:44	M HICKS	4:18:20	N RICHARDSON	4:19:01	P CHAMBERLAIN	4:19:34	S PROUDLOVE	4:20:11
4	R FULFORD	4:17:46	M FRYER	4:18:21	B HARRIS	4:19:01	G HICKEY	4:19:34	B COULSON	4:20:11
5	J FARTHING	4:17:46	A REUTER	4:18:22	S OERTEFORS	4:19:01	M CHAMPKINS	4:19:35	E HILLE	4:20:11
6	N MAHER	4:17:47	K JUPP	4:18:22	W TALBOT	4:19:01	J NICHOLL	4:19:36	S TAYLOR	4:20:11
7	T LOVELL	4:17:47	A TIBBETT	4:18:22	F LEE	4:19:02	C DABIN	4:19:36	A REID	4:20:13
8	A CHRISTODOULOU	4:17:47	T TROFINCZUK	4:18:22	T LOVERIDGE	4:19:02	J COSOLETO	4:19:36	J GYBEN	4:20:13
9	D HADFIELD	4:17:47	N SWINDEN	4:18:22	D MASINI	4:19:03	D BULL	4:19:36	M BUTCHER	4:20:14
10	C SMITH	4:17:48	A SHEPHERD	4:18:23	N BAGSHAW	4:19:03	A ENGELS	4:19:36	S MAYNARD	4:20:15
11	J HILL	4:17:48	L TOVEY	4:18:23	D FREEMAN	4:19:04	P SEARES	4:19:36	C ROBERTS	4:20:15
12	T CLEMENT-JONES	4:17:48	T RAPSON	4:18:23	J PACO	4:19:04	I WILSON	4:19:36	G DAVIDSON	4:20:16
13	M BERRYMAN	4:17:48	C JONES	4:18:24	N GRIEVESON	4:19:04	K MCBRIDE	4:19:36	S BATTERLEY	4:20:17
14	N GARDINER	4:17:48	T PETCH	4:18:24	G BOSWELL	4:19:06	P O BRIEN	4:19:39	D BAILEY	4:20:17
15	P CHAPMAN	4:17:48	M KENNY	4:18:24	J ROONEY	4:19:06	M MURZELL	4:19:39	J GALE	4:20:18
16	R COUCHMAN	4:17:49	J HARSAGYI	4:18:26	D MUDDIMER	4:19:07	S EVERETT	4:19:40	J WHITAKER	4:20:18
17	J WRIGLESWORTH	4:17:49	R BYRNE	4:18:27	H NEILL	4:19:07	M RICHARDSON	4:19:40	S PYZER	4:20:18
18	D STRAIN	4:17:49	S BRAMLEY	4:18:28	D JOHNSON-NEWELL	4:19:07	A LEISTER	4:19:41	H WHITEHEAD	4:20:19
19	W STRAIN	4:17:49	J GREEFE	4:18:28	N MIYAMOTO	4:19:07	A KNIGHT	4:19:41	J PAILLARD	4:20:19
20	S PEREIRA	4:17:50	D TEASDALE	4:18:29	L MOHAMMED	4:19:08	P WYATT	4:19:41	S BARRETT	4:20:19
21	C FUGE	4:17:50	R POOLEY	4:18:29	J POLLANEN	4:19:08	D PATTON	4:19:41	J KING	4:20:19
22	B PEREIRA	4:17:51	R MCMASTER	4:18:29	K LEIMO	4:19:08	T JAMIESON	4:19:42	D COULL	4:20:19
23	A ATHANI	4:17:51	S PARKER	4:18:29	R MONEY	4:19:09	J FARMER	4:19:42	A CAMPBELL	4:20:19
24	R GRUNDY	4:17:52	D MCCARTHY	4:18:29	A WILLIS	4:19:10	C HOWE	4:19:42	A SELLERS	4:20:19
25	D PEREIRA	4:17:52	R BROSCH	4:18:29	B CAMPBELL	4:19:10	D BITTAN	4:19:42	D CHAPMAN	4:20:19
26	D WOOFF	4:17:53	C O'NEILL	4:18:30	J NOLAN	4:19:11	S FARMER	4:19:43	M JONES	4:20:19
27	W MILMAN	4:17:53	X DELAGE	4:18:30	D WILLIAMSON	4:19:12	G CHAPPELL	4:19:43	B LONG	4:20:21
28	R STEELE	4:17:53	H CAZALET	4:18:30	J TAYLOR	4:19:12	A SCULLION	4:19:43	L NORTON	4:20:21
29	M GILLESPIE	4:17:53	P SMITH	4:18:31	R GREENWELL	4:19:12	J PRICE	4:19:43	G ALBON	4:20:22
30	W ALLEN	4:17:55	D MATTHEW	4:18:31	R HILLMAN	4:19:13	P PURCELL	4:19:44	Z SALEEM	4:20:22
31	S BRAITHWAITE	4:17:55	R HINSHAW	4:18:31	P JONES	4:19:13	P ATKINSON	4:19:45	P SMITH	4:20:22
32	K FIELDING	4:17:55	N MATTHEWS	4:18:32	S TAYLOR	4:19:13	R ATKINSON	4:19:45	P HINDE	4:20:23
33	S BUTTERWORTH	4:17:56	B ASHFORD	4:18:33	S PAIN	4:19:13	M REILLY	4:19:45	F ROUSSEL	4:20:23
34	K YOUNG	4:17:56	M GEORGE	4:18:33	J UPTON	4:19:13	R HALE	4:19:45	D MITCHELL	4:20:25
35	K LINGARD	4:17:56	D EDE	4:18:33	D HALL	4:19:15	E JACKSON	4:19:46	J NOTON	4:20:26
36	C SMITH	4:17:56	D EVANS	4:18:34	L ARNETT	4:19:15	J LOMAS	4:19:46	G DAVIS	4:20:26
37	C CHOWN	4:17:57	M POWER	4:18:35	S DIXON	4:19:15	J WARD	4:19:46	R DUNCAN	4:20:26
38	M PERCOX	4:17:57	K SONES	4:18:35	G YOUNG	4:19:15	S ROWE	4:19:46	A KEELING	4:20:26
39	T HARRISON	4:17:57	G HALL	4:18:36	C ALDOUS	4:19:17	P STEBBING	4:19:46	M SHEEHAN	4:20:27
40	E O'KEEFFE	4:17:57	A MILLS	4:18:37	J CONNOLLY	4:19:17	T WATZLING	4:19:46	G CALLINICOS	4:20:28
41	A STANLEY	4:17:58	C WELLMANN	4:18:37	C HAYES	4:19:17	B HARFORD	4:19:46	G DALE	4:20:29
42	G MORT	4:17:58	I WILD	4:18:37	J BAKER	4:19:17	A VILJOEN	4:19:46	R GROSSHANS	4:20:29
43	P WILLIS	4:17:59	S HOPE	4:18:37	S ATKIN	4:19:18	B DRAYCOTT	4:19:47	P CASHMAN	4:20:30
44	B PARROTT	4:17:59	W CLIFFORD	4:18:38	T SOUTH	4:19:18	J WEBSTER	4:19:47	S ISMAIL	4:20:30
45	D WILKES	4:17:59	D WATTS	4:18:38	D HAZLETON	4:19:18	D BOWMAN	4:19:47	C STATON	4:20:30
46	B KANE	4:17:59	J SOPER	4:18:39	D BLANCHET	4:19:18	J EDWARDS	4:19:50	R EGGLETON	4:20:30
47	D WHITTAKER	4:17:59	J SIMPSON	4:18:39	P CROUCHLEY	4:19:19	L JUNGBAUER	4:19:50	S SAUNDERS	4:20:30
48	K WILSON	4:17:59	W ODLING	4:18:39	J MAUNDER	4:19:19	L HAIGH	4:19:51	D HEWITT	4:20:31
49	S BOSWELL	4:17:59	C AVERY	4:18:40	B SHEPHERD	4:19:19	G MILLS	4:19:52	M WAITE	4:20:31
50	G SMITH	4:17:59	G WAITE	4:18:40	N TEARE	4:19:19	M BUTCHER	4:19:52	R WILSON	4:20:32
51	S CARLISLE	4:17:59	E SALWAY	4:18:40	J DICKIE	4:19:19	B TURNER	4:19:52	D IVEMY	4:20:32
52	J JONES	4:17:59	P NISBET	4:18:41	E NEWTON	4:19:21	J TAYLOR	4:19:52	A DRING	4:20:32
53	A HARGREAVES	4:18:00	F PORTER	4:18:42	P HOOIJMAIJERS	4:19:21	M GLENTWORTH	4:19:52	M ELYSEE	4:20:33
54	E PALMER	4:18:00	C LANG	4:18:42	C WILLEY	4:19:21	P WILMSHURST	4:19:53	J RICHARDSON	4:20:34
55	S BURRELL	4:18:01	R LEE	4:18:43	P BURTON	4:19:21	P MOORE	4:19:53	G MASON	4:20:34
56	R HAMMERTON	4:18:01	M RADFORD	4:18:43	N WOOD	4:19:21	M JEFFERIES	4:19:53	J WAKEFIELD	4:20:34
57	S SLATER	4:18:01	B RULTEN	4:18:43	B WINDER	4:19:21	S FOLWELL	4:19:54	T PELLISSIER	4:20:34
58	D WILKES	4:18:02	M CARTER	4:18:44	K BORER	4:19:21	J QUINN	4:19:54	C BOYLAN	4:20:34
59	D MOSS	4:18:03	A BEOCHAT	4:18:44	D WRIGHT	4:19:22	B GRIFFITHS	4:19:54	M WILLOUGHBY	4:20:34
60	J BARRETT	4:18:03	A WILLIS	4:18:44	A TREVORROW	4:19:22	P REES	4:19:54	M COLEBROOK	4:20:35
61	H ALCOCK	4:18:04	R COOMBE	4:18:44	M HARTLEY	4:19:22	P MICHALSKI	4:19:55	S WOODHEAD	4:20:35
62	B WIESMANN	4:18:04	I GILLARD	4:18:44	S HARVEY	4:19:23	E OWSLEY	4:19:55	R MUSSARD	4:20:35
63	M JOHNSON	4:18:05	J CONDRON	4:18:44	P BREEN	4:19:23	D WHITMORE	4:19:55	J GRAY	4:20:35
64	R RYDER	4:18:05	D PARSONS	4:18:45	R TINNYUNT	4:19:23	M STOCKWELL	4:19:55	D DONALDSON	4:20:36
65	G MOSS	4:18:06	G KENT	4:18:45	R KOEN	4:19:23	A BENDON	4:19:56	S CARLSSON	4:20:36
66	P THOROUGHGOOD	4:18:07	G SIBLEY	4:18:45	J PURKISS	4:19:23	P MCGILLOWAY	4:19:56	T DODD	4:20:36
67	R CLARKE	4:18:07	J CORCORAN	4:18:45	W STEVENS	4:19:23	P CLARK	4:19:57	F FLOOD	4:20:37
68	A MOON	4:18:08	E JAMES	4:18:46	A DAINES	4:19:23	J LORD	4:19:57	E CHONG	4:20:37
69	K COTTER	4:18:08	B MURPHY	4:18:47	G SHAW	4:19:23	P RANSON	4:19:57	B HAY	4:20:37
70	C PARSONS	4:18:08	E GIULIANI	4:18:47	P SMITH	4:19:23	W MOORE	4:19:58	N GORRILL	4:20:38
71	C BHAGWANJI	4:18:08	S WILSHAW	4:18:47	S BERNAU	4:19:24	F HOLMES	4:19:58	G DITCHBURN	4:20:38
72	G ESSEN	4:18:09	L GUEST	4:18:48	K GIFFORD	4:19:24	P EDWARDS	4:19:58	J WILD	4:20:38
73	A BELL	4:18:10	D BENSON	4:18:48	S EDDY	4:19:24	G REYNOLDS	4:19:59	R BARFOOT	4:20:39
74	K HEFFER	4:18:10	D MAUNDER	4:18:48	J PAYNE	4:19:24	D WYNN	4:20:00	J SWIFT	4:20:40
75	J HILTON	4:18:10	D DURKIN	4:18:49	M COOK	4:19:24	D PICCHIONE	4:20:01	C PAPA	4:20:41
76	L ATKINSON	4:18:11	S BANNISTER	4:18:49	J RANKIN	4:19:24	B WALTON	4:20:02	S WINGROVE	4:20:41
77	M AUSTIN	4:18:11	M SHIPTON	4:18:49	N ARMSTRONG	4:19:25	G CLARKE	4:20:02	G UGOLINI	4:20:41
78	M FOOTE	4:18:11	M WHITLOCK	4:18:50	J BOURGEAULT	4:19:25	G PHILLIPS	4:20:02	R HUMPHRIES	4:20:41
79	C DUNCAN	4:18:11	L HOPKINS	4:18:50	D HORROBIN	4:19:25	H HAYDON	4:20:03	D TRABUCCHI	4:20:42
80	J TAYLOR	4:18:11	R YOUPA	4:18:50	K SCHOENHOLTZ	4:19:25	R IRWIN	4:20:03	G CREESE	4:20:42
81	C RUSS	4:18:12	P PITT	4:18:50	N HORROBIN	4:19:25	C THOMAS	4:20:03	T PEARSON	4:20:42
82	S CHADWICK	4:18:12	J EDWARDS	4:18:50	A YOST	4:19:26	J POTTER	4:20:03	M SAVORE	4:20:42
83	M GONZALEZ	4:18:13	A VILLARI	4:18:50	K HACK	4:19:26	K HINKS	4:20:04	D FREEZE	4:20:43
84	B KING	4:18:14	J GIROD	4:18:52	H MITCHELL	4:19:28	M TOOZE	4:20:04	J JOBLING	4:20:43
85	P DUFFY	4:18:15	D LANG	4:18:52	D JOHNSON	4:19:28	A CONROY	4:20:04	P WINTER	4:20:43
86	C TAYLOR	4:18:15	R HARRIS	4:18:53	T WEBB	4:19:28	J MUNN	4:20:04	M JONES	4:20:43
87	D HAZELL	4:18:15	R SPEER	4:18:53	N GOSNELL	4:19:28	F BOUCHER	4:20:04	M CAPELL	4:20:43
88	E CORRAN	4:18:16	A DUNMORE	4:18:53	M JONES	4:19:28	E WIDDICOMBE	4:20:04	T WALKER	4:20:43
89	P MCLAUGHLIN	4:18:16	O WOLF	4:18:54	M COCKCROFT	4:19:28	K HUDSON	4:20:05	S MCCLUREY	4:20:43
90	P WHITEHEAD	4:18:16	P JACKSON	4:18:54	G MARTIN	4:19:29	D PATTEN	4:20:05	H WISCHKONY	4:20:44
91	G MACHRAY	4:18:17	P NUTLEY	4:18:55	J CARROLL	4:19:30	P MONAGHAN	4:20:05	J BURDEN	4:20:44
92	J PERRETT	4:18:17	K EDWARDS	4:18:55	P BARRINGTON	4:19:30	D JONES	4:20:05	P BAGNALL	4:20:44
93	J OAKES	4:18:17	P BLAKE	4:18:56	S STEVENS	4:19:31	G STUYVEN	4:20:05	H WALTERS	4:20:44
94	D COX	4:18:17	A MCQUATER	4:18:56	R CLARK	4:19:31	J USHER	4:20:06	D GILBERT	4:20:46
95	R FARMER	4:18:18	D SCOTT	4:18:57	M MALT	4:19:31	F ADAMS	4:20:08	I BESWICK	4:20:47
96	M ROUSELL	4:18:18	A RANDALL	4:18:57	D GUNTHER	4:19:32	T MITCHELL	4:20:08	A RADELHOF	4:20:47
97	A O'SULLIVAN	4:18:18	K SHEPPARD	4:18:58	D COLEY	4:19:32	M SLOAN	4:20:09	J KERR	4:20:48
98	M QUINLIVAN	4:18:19	R CONNOR	4:18:58	D STIMSON	4:19:32	G HICKINSON	4:20:09	M LING	4:20:48
99	H HOWARD	4:18:19	D HOWES	4:18:58	D CARDEN	4:19:32	T KOTANI	4:20:10	D LITTLE	4:20:48
100	M FIELDER	4:18:20	C OWEN	4:18:58	L HAINING	4:19:33	L WALPOLE	4:20:10	S WARD	4:20:49

#	16001-16100		16101-16200		16201-16300		16301-16400		16401-16500	
1	J HEDGES	4:20:49	K SHARIF	4:21:18	A VAN ZUILEN	4:21:54	P HESLING	4:22:29	K HILL	4:23:13
2	D TILLEY	4:20:49	G HARRIS	4:21:18	V GIESELER	4:21:55	P CHILCOTT	4:22:29	R HOLCOMBE	4:23:13
3	L CALLAN	4:20:50	A HATTON	4:21:18	P KIRBY	4:21:55	P GOODWIN	4:22:30	C POTTER	4:23:14
4	W COBB	4:20:52	J WILLIAMSON	4:21:18	J FARRY	4:21:55	I HARPER	4:22:31	D NAJAC	4:23:14
5	P SEAR	4:20:52	S JEFFORD	4:21:19	M KENNEDY	4:21:55	C MORGAN	4:22:31	R BARTLETT	4:23:15
6	L CLAY	4:20:53	T BANKS	4:21:19	M SCHMIPF	4:21:57	M SALKELD	4:22:31	S LOIZOU	4:23:15
7	D POWELL	4:20:53	J KING	4:21:19	G DAYUS	4:21:57	R KLOPPER	4:22:31	S MCQUEEN	4:23:15
8	P BRADY	4:20:54	J EVELEIGH	4:21:20	W JENKIN	4:21:58	L BOYES	4:22:31	C GREEN	4:23:16
9	I FOSKEW	4:20:54	P TOWNSEND	4:21:20	L MURDEY	4:21:59	G PERROTT	4:22:31	R ALLSOP	4:23:16
10	D READ	4:20:54	P SICKLING	4:21:21	K WATTS	4:21:59	M HUGHES	4:22:32	M GUY	4:23:16
11	K SWAINE	4:20:55	J JELLEY	4:21:22	R TRACEY	4:21:59	N SUMMERS	4:22:32	T WINSOR	4:23:16
12	C LEON	4:20:55	G DAVIS	4:21:22	N CROFT	4:22:00	J DONNELLON	4:22:33	D SPENCER	4:23:16
13	B SAUNDERS	4:20:55	D JONES	4:21:22	C PHILLIPS	4:22:00	P YATES	4:22:33	P LEWIS	4:23:16
14	P TURNER	4:20:55	S HERVIEW	4:21:22	R HILLIER	4:22:00	V GROSSI	4:22:35	K BULLERS	4:23:17
15	J GARDINER	4:20:55	I CAMPBELL	4:21:23	R KEMP	4:22:00	J JAMISON	4:22:35	G STAFF	4:23:17
16	M SURRY	4:20:56	F PAYNTER	4:21:23	J BERRYMAN	4:22:00	J HUGHES	4:22:35	D CALDWELL	4:23:17
17	S WILLETT	4:20:57	N HOWE	4:21:23	I BRUCE	4:22:00	A DAVIES	4:22:36	C WOODWARD	4:23:17
18	M LANGFORD	4:20:57	N MEDLOCK	4:21:24	A WARKUSS	4:22:00	G FRITH	4:22:37	M OTTER	4:23:18
19	D ROBERTS	4:20:57	S FELTHAM	4:21:24	P WYLIE	4:22:01	T WRIGHT	4:22:37	P HELPS	4:23:18
20	P BOSSON	4:20:57	A IVESON	4:21:24	R SABZEVARI	4:22:01	V HICKS	4:22:37	N PIPER SMITH	4:23:18
21	R CIEREBIEJ	4:20:57	J LEWIS	4:21:24	A WRIGGLESWORTH	4:22:01	M ANDERSON	4:22:37	J LAVIN	4:23:18
22	J PRITCHARD	4:20:57	N HODGKINS	4:21:24	A GREEN	4:22:01	M SMITH	4:22:37	I RUSSELL	4:23:19
23	P LINNEY	4:20:57	M BLAKELEY	4:21:24	A FISHLOCK	4:22:02	J HURREN	4:22:38	W LOBB	4:23:19
24	C NOLAN	4:20:57	J EAGLETON	4:21:25	R CHARLESWORTH	4:22:03	W MILNE	4:22:39	S NAYLOR	4:23:21
25	M EDGE	4:20:57	A DOUGLAS-PENNANT	4:21:26	M TROTH	4:22:03	N THOMAS	4:22:39	C HURT	4:23:21
26	P SLATER	4:20:58	A STRINGER	4:21:26	D HERON	4:22:03	A GREENWOOD	4:22:39	S HUGHES	4:23:21
27	J MCKELLAR	4:20:58	M NORRIS	4:21:26	G CALDWELL	4:22:03	U FRANCK	4:22:39	J FARRELL	4:23:21
28	J MCKEOWN	4:20:59	S GORMER	4:21:27	A TERZOLI	4:22:03	D GRINHAM	4:22:39	D EDWARDS	4:23:21
29	K PARK	4:20:59	R WHENRAY	4:21:27	J BIGGINS	4:22:03	S FRETE	4:22:41	R SMYTH	4:23:22
30	J GALLEYMORE	4:20:59	J TOTTEY	4:21:28	R DANIELS	4:22:04	P KEANE	4:22:41	N COOK	4:23:22
31	D BERGER	4:20:59	J SHAW	4:21:29	L DANIEL	4:22:04	D HUNTER	4:22:42	H LENZEN	4:23:22
32	A CRISPIN	4:20:59	R CROSBIE	4:21:30	A PALMER	4:22:04	C DAYMAN	4:22:43	P WARDELL	4:23:22
33	O ZAMBRANO	4:20:59	B PEAKE	4:21:30	C EMPTAGE	4:22:05	L HUNT	4:22:43	T DOBSON	4:23:23
34	I WEBBER	4:21:01	R ALLEN	4:21:30	P WHITE	4:22:06	M BRANNON	4:22:44	S DOEHR	4:23:23
35	M CAMERON	4:21:01	P TAYLER	4:21:30	N DUMBLEBY	4:22:07	H WERKER	4:22:44	H KEYTE	4:23:23
36	J PURDY	4:21:01	J COWLEY	4:21:30	R FOSTER	4:22:07	A CARSLAW	4:22:44	E BALDONI	4:23:24
37	R SARRAFF	4:21:01	R PLATT	4:21:31	P BOWES	4:22:07	T JOHNSON	4:22:44	T BLOWER	4:23:24
38	P SMART	4:21:01	J HOLDEN	4:21:32	J LEWIS	4:22:07	C JARVIS	4:22:44	H FRUTIGER	4:23:24
39	I EVANS	4:21:01	L DAVIS	4:21:32	P SMITH	4:22:08	T JOHNSON	4:22:44	R BURGESS	4:23:25
40	M HALL	4:21:01	A BARNWELL	4:21:32	M KNIGHT	4:22:08	R POWELL	4:22:45	T NEAL	4:23:25
41	M WAREHAM	4:21:01	P WILLIAMSON	4:21:32	M MOUNTJOY	4:22:08	S MELTON	4:22:45	A SALENGRO	4:23:25
42	L ADLER	4:21:02	B TEMPLE	4:21:32	N HINE	4:22:09	N HINE	4:22:45	Y COSTE	4:23:25
43	D RHYS	4:21:03	L HOANG	4:21:33	D GUYONNET	4:22:09	P BROOK	4:22:45	E HAMILTON	4:23:25
44	S WHITBY	4:21:04	J MARCHANT	4:21:33	I HARGREAVES	4:22:09	S PATTERSON	4:22:46	A WENZEL	4:23:25
45	C TROMAN	4:21:04	A DARSLEY	4:21:34	M SPENCE	4:22:09	K HILL	4:22:46	M EASTBURN	4:23:25
46	M HUTCHINGS	4:21:05	M SULLIVAN	4:21:34	S SEAGAR	4:22:09	S LAING	4:22:46	M BROWN	4:23:26
47	R MORRIS	4:21:05	L MYERS	4:21:35	A MCCOY	4:22:09	R BERRY	4:22:46	D HILL	4:23:26
48	P OLLIF	4:21:05	R QUINN	4:21:36	A WARD	4:22:09	I THOMPSON	4:22:46	L HUMBERT	4:23:26
49	A COOPER	4:21:05	L DEIGHTON	4:21:36	R HANNAFORD	4:22:09	J BURFORD	4:22:46	A MUGFORD	4:23:27
50	R PERKINS	4:21:05	C HEWITT	4:21:37	Y GOODWIN	4:22:10	J COLLETT	4:22:46	M NEWCOMBE	4:23:27
51	J DELONNETTE	4:21:06	G WALKER	4:21:37	T WALLER	4:22:10	P MERRIKIN	4:22:48	S SMITH	4:23:28
52	R HOLMES	4:21:06	S BARRETT	4:21:37	C SCHERMER	4:22:11	J GAYLOR	4:22:48	M MCCANN	4:23:28
53	G WHIPP	4:21:06	A THOMAS	4:21:37	G COTTERILL	4:22:11	F TEROL	4:22:48	W DOYLE	4:23:28
54	R GREEN	4:21:06	P HEBBLETHWAITE	4:21:38	S MOLONEY	4:22:11	G HARRISON	4:22:48	J LODGE	4:23:28
55	E HOLDEN	4:21:06	S BASOGLU	4:21:38	P NEWSOME	4:22:11	J TILBY	4:22:48	J KELLETT	4:23:28
56	P CHANING-PEARCE	4:21:06	S BOXALL-HUNT	4:21:38	C PURVES	4:22:12	D LITTLETON	4:22:51	D MATTHEWS	4:23:28
57	Y EDWARDS	4:21:06	M WOLFMAN	4:21:40	P SMITH	4:22:12	P SMITH	4:22:51	T SIBBETT	4:23:28
58	S GREEN	4:21:06	D PAPWORTH	4:21:40	L STRATFORD	4:22:12	J PETERS	4:22:51	R FRENCH	4:23:29
59	P ABBOTT	4:21:06	C DUGGAN	4:21:40	R BUCKBY	4:22:12	A CLARK	4:22:51	M HOHOL	4:23:29
60	K STEPHENS	4:21:06	G PENN	4:21:42	S HARRISON	4:22:12	R MILTON	4:22:51	A RAE	4:23:29
61	M DIXON	4:21:06	S NAREAHO	4:21:42	D KEITH	4:22:12	C GRAINDORGE	4:22:51	M BARRETT	4:23:29
62	R HARRISON	4:21:06	R EDDY	4:21:42	A WATSON	4:22:12	O SONESSON	4:22:52	M SHEARER	4:23:30
63	R KNEEN	4:21:07	D LANE	4:21:43	C CUNLIFFE	4:22:13	E LOVSIN	4:22:52	J DUNN	4:23:30
64	J MILES	4:21:07	G YOUNGSON	4:21:43	R WYNNE	4:22:14	P CARRUTHERS	4:22:53	M PERRY	4:23:30
65	C GRITZMAKER	4:21:07	T LAMBARD	4:21:43	A CHURMS	4:22:14	J BLAKELOCK	4:22:53	D HAMMERTON	4:23:31
66	B HILL	4:21:08	F MOGGAN	4:21:43	A BUCKLAND	4:22:15	J MCDONALD	4:22:54	M HULME	4:23:31
67	R HOLMES	4:21:09	J POUILLOI	4:21:43	T KING	4:22:15	M KING	4:22:54	B SIRETT	4:23:31
68	S GODDARD	4:21:09	N STEEPLES	4:21:44	J GREGGAIN	4:22:15	T BRIGGS	4:22:54	R HODDER	4:23:32
69	R ELVINS	4:21:10	R KING	4:21:44	P GUNDRY	4:22:16	A TAYLOR	4:22:54	J MORRIS	4:23:32
70	P DODDS	4:21:10	A BRYAN	4:21:45	S PAGE	4:22:17	S PATERSON	4:22:55	D KINGSTON	4:23:32
71	B CLINTON	4:21:10	T SATO	4:21:45	M BRADLEY	4:22:17	K PATERSON-JONES	4:22:55	T WELSH	4:23:33
72	C VOSLOO	4:21:10	A VENALAINEN	4:21:45	J MUSSETT	4:22:17	A EDIS	4:22:55	K COOPER	4:23:33
73	D COPLEY	4:21:10	R BROWN	4:21:45	R HARDY	4:22:17	C RAWSON	4:22:57	E TREANOR	4:23:33
74	C KELLY	4:21:10	A TIVEY	4:21:45	E HUYKE	4:22:19	S SYMONDS	4:22:58	N POTTER	4:23:33
75	J STOKES	4:21:11	P CHAUFFOUR	4:21:45	E BURNS	4:22:19	R VINCENT	4:22:58	B CHANA	4:23:34
76	M WALLACE	4:21:11	F BATES	4:21:45	F PASSARELLA	4:22:19	G WILLSMORE	4:22:58	T FREEMAN	4:23:34
77	J ONDRASIK	4:21:11	J DA COSTA	4:21:45	T WILSON	4:22:21	D HIBBINS	4:22:58	R WRIGHT	4:23:34
78	D ROWE	4:21:11	J LONCKE	4:21:45	K SUTHERLAND	4:22:21	B HOWELL	4:22:58	J SMITH	4:23:34
79	I PATTERSON	4:21:11	V KEILTY	4:21:46	A MILBURN	4:22:22	A SPONG	4:22:58	W FRAZER	4:23:35
80	D YOUNG	4:21:11	B BOON	4:21:46	P BLACKBURN	4:22:22	M MCGUIRE	4:22:59	J DAVIES	4:23:36
81	M ROYCROFT	4:21:12	T WHEELDON	4:21:46	B BLACKMAN	4:22:23	W COLLINS	4:22:59	J BINGLEY	4:23:37
82	G RUSSELL	4:21:12	R BOLZIUS	4:21:46	B WENNSTROM	4:22:23	T WILSON	4:23:01	P VECCHIA	4:23:37
83	R PETTS	4:21:12	J PAIN	4:21:46	S THACKER	4:22:23	M ANGEAR	4:23:03	D NOVICK	4:23:39
84	C ROPER MEDHURST	4:21:12	G HISCOCK	4:21:47	R PORTER	4:22:24	A PENFOLD	4:23:03	L SMITH	4:23:39
85	H FRANKLIN	4:21:12	J HART	4:21:47	W KLEIN	4:22:24	M QUIRICONI	4:23:03	M MARUGLIANO	4:23:40
86	A JOHNSON	4:21:12	H MCELENEY	4:21:47	G BRUCE	4:22:25	Y FARLEY	4:23:04	N MAY	4:23:40
87	D STUBBLES	4:21:13	M WISE	4:21:47	M OLIVER	4:22:25	M LISTER	4:23:04	B GALE	4:23:41
88	D GRETTON	4:21:14	S MILES	4:21:47	C COWLEY	4:22:26	T HAMMOND	4:23:05	N HEIGHWAY	4:23:41
89	J COOK	4:21:14	W PINK	4:21:47	P SWAIN	4:22:26	J HIND	4:23:06	D PAYNE	4:23:42
90	S MCTIERNAN	4:21:14	G WILLIAMS	4:21:47	T KING	4:22:26	M ST CYR	4:23:07	A PEGDEN	4:23:42
91	R MORLEY	4:21:14	E BOTTOMLEY	4:21:48	A HEAD	4:22:26	S JAY	4:23:08	R FLETCHER	4:23:42
92	D EVANS	4:21:15	A FINN	4:21:49	N BUTLER	4:22:26	H WHITMORE	4:23:09	G PROIETTI	4:23:42
93	A KIURU	4:21:16	D ATTREE	4:21:49	A RICHARDSON	4:22:27	D HEAP	4:23:09	P VAN HOVEN	4:23:42
94	F HANRAHAN	4:21:17	W SMITH	4:21:50	H BARNABY	4:22:27	K MOSLEY	4:23:10	T EASON	4:23:42
95	J GREENLEES	4:21:17	C BURGESS	4:21:50	J LEDDY	4:22:27	M PETROVIC	4:23:10	R DE LA RUE BROWNE	4:23:42
96	T SCOTT	4:21:17	P TIDD	4:21:50	D HARTSHORN	4:22:27	R GRIPTON	4:23:10	C FILBY	4:23:42
97	M ROBERTS	4:21:17	P SMITH	4:21:50	S THAKOR	4:22:28	D MADDEN	4:23:11	M GINGER	4:23:42
98	T POOLE	4:21:17	R BALLANTYNE	4:21:51	E HENSMAN	4:22:28	P SAUNDERS	4:23:12	G SNAZLE	4:23:42
99	B WOODYATT	4:21:17	S FITZPATRICK	4:21:52	A MIGGIANO	4:22:28	M VANJARA	4:23:13	S FERULLO	4:23:43
100	S HARRIS	4:21:18	T CUNNINGHAM	4:21:53	H ABLITT	4:22:28	S EVANS	4:23:13	J KEHOE	4:23:43

#	16501-16600		16601-16700		16701-16800		16801-16900		16901-17000	
1	J TUCK	4:23:43	P MCBARRON	4:24:16	B PARKINSON	4:24:53	A WILLIAMSON	4:25:33	R ANDERSON	4:26:08
2	H WALKDEN	4:23:43	E CRIPPA	4:24:16	T JONES	4:24:54	A ARCHER	4:25:33	M BROMLEY	4:26:08
3	B CALLAWAY	4:23:44	B EGGLESTON	4:24:17	D BETHELL	4:24:54	C BANKS	4:25:33	H WONG	4:26:08
4	K GOULDING	4:23:44	C RICHARDS	4:24:17	H PARKER	4:24:54	J SUTTON	4:25:34	A HILL	4:26:09
5	R GOODWIN	4:23:44	L RICHARDS	4:24:18	H BRAUN	4:24:55	S BENN	4:25:35	T HOWCHEN	4:26:09
6	P HARBAUGH JR	4:23:45	D CHITTENDEN	4:24:18	P GODDARD	4:24:57	P GREEN	4:25:35	M LERIBAUX-RODEN	4:26:09
7	H STEAD	4:23:45	R EMERY	4:24:18	A PARKER	4:24:57	G MITCHELL	4:25:35	W RODEN	4:26:09
8	K HUTCHINSON	4:23:45	J LONGMAN	4:24:18	C CAMPBELL	4:25:00	J DRISCOLL	4:25:36	S PORT	4:26:10
9	M WESSON	4:23:45	D BONNER	4:24:20	I WHITEHEAD	4:25:01	C SCRIVEN	4:25:36	T BURNS	4:26:11
10	H WAGNER	4:23:46	P NAYEE	4:24:20	J HEATH	4:25:03	L STRANGE	4:25:36	M EAST	4:26:11
11	N BASSETT	4:23:46	T SNUKIS	4:24:20	R MELVILLE TAYLOR	4:25:03	G WHITE	4:25:36	D PORTER	4:26:12
12	V HINDE	4:23:47	Z JONES	4:24:20	J FAIRHEAD	4:25:04	J DEWEY	4:25:37	I BULPETT	4:26:12
13	R MORRIS	4:23:48	S MADDEN	4:24:20	M SCOTT	4:25:04	D KNIGHT	4:25:38	M ATTWOOD	4:26:13
14	R SAWYER	4:23:48	N SACKETT	4:24:21	M HOLDEN	4:25:04	M SPRING	4:25:38	C MICHAEL	4:26:13
15	S RUGGINS	4:23:49	P AMOS	4:24:21	B BRADLEY	4:25:04	R NOON	4:25:38	A COZENS	4:26:14
16	J POTTER	4:23:50	D MCROY	4:24:23	M CLARE	4:25:05	P CRIBB	4:25:38	W STEPHENSON	4:26:14
17	A SMITH	4:23:51	D SQUIRES	4:24:23	N DALEY	4:25:06	A UGOLINI	4:25:39	P WELLS	4:26:15
18	W MOODY	4:23:51	K PORTER	4:24:24	R PATTISON	4:25:06	R ROBINSON	4:25:40	B RANKINE	4:26:15
19	S RAINE	4:23:51	P DEAN	4:24:24	L LEEVES	4:25:06	M BACHINI	4:25:40	R MACKMURDIE	4:26:15
20	R LAWSON-CRUTTENDEN	4:23:52	S MOSS	4:24:24	L GNOLI	4:25:06	R DIX	4:25:40	A BRADBURY	4:26:15
21	N PITCHELL	4:23:52	F HERBERT	4:24:24	P FLETCHER	4:25:06	J GREENWOOD	4:25:41	D HAYES	4:26:15
22	A WILLIAMSON	4:23:52	J APPLETON	4:24:25	G MOORE	4:25:07	W MURRAY	4:25:41	K HOLBROOK	4:26:15
23	M WHITE	4:23:52	G REDGE	4:24:25	T LETHBRIDGE	4:25:07	F QUAYLE	4:25:42	M HARGREAVES	4:26:15
24	J WHARTON	4:23:53	D ROBINSON	4:24:25	P SMITH	4:25:07	H HEMETSBERGER	4:25:42	E MUSTO	4:26:15
25	A WARREN	4:23:53	R EVANS	4:24:25	M KENDALL	4:25:08	A GOOD	4:25:42	D STOUT	4:26:15
26	D AVERY	4:23:53	M JARVIS	4:24:25	T MUIRHEAD	4:25:08	J HEMETSBERGER	4:25:42	M HOLMES	4:26:15
27	T DANIEL	4:23:53	C BROWN	4:24:26	M WEISINGER	4:25:09	K MAIN	4:25:43	G HAMMOND	4:26:16
28	J HARLIN	4:23:54	M BRAYNE	4:24:27	P ADDY	4:25:09	F RAINS	4:25:43	C EVANS	4:26:16
29	G HAGUE-HOLMES	4:23:54	P JOHNSON	4:24:28	P BUNNETT	4:25:09	A DANIEL	4:25:43	L CHOFFIN	4:26:16
30	D TUITE	4:23:54	P SANDFORD	4:24:28	H FISHER	4:25:09	B CHEETHAM	4:25:43	A LYONS	4:26:16
31	A MILLS	4:23:54	M NASH	4:24:28	A RYAN	4:25:09	R RITTENOUR	4:25:43	D WOOD	4:26:16
32	R SUTTON	4:23:54	J BATTERSBY	4:24:28	A HUTTON	4:25:09	T MCDONALD	4:25:43	G CLOUD	4:26:17
33	S SMITH	4:23:54	E COLES	4:24:28	J RILEY	4:25:09	R GARCIA	4:25:43	D GRAHAM	4:26:17
34	R ELLIS	4:23:55	D RUSSELL	4:24:29	L LEA	4:25:09	D GOTTSCHALT	4:25:43	G RAE	4:26:17
35	A JONES	4:23:55	A TAYLOR	4:24:29	C LEA	4:25:09	A RADCLIFFE	4:25:43	R WALKER	4:26:17
36	B INMAN	4:23:55	J MALONE	4:24:30	D SCOTT-SAWYER	4:25:10	R FAIRCHILD	4:25:44	K WILLIAMS	4:26:17
37	M DUBLIN	4:23:56	M CARGILL	4:24:30	P COLES	4:25:11	C MILLER	4:25:44	G CHARVERIAT	4:26:17
38	D BARRY	4:23:56	P KELLY	4:24:30	M GEDYE	4:25:11	G SMITH	4:25:44	J FRIZZELL	4:26:18
39	K BARKER	4:23:56	P BELLI	4:24:31	P HENLEY	4:25:11	M JOHNSON	4:25:44	M WOODS	4:26:18
40	T QUINN	4:23:56	G BLAKE	4:24:31	K WOODWARD	4:25:11	D WHITEMAN	4:25:44	J NEAL	4:26:22
41	P DUCIE	4:23:56	D POLLET	4:24:32	C DIXON	4:25:12	M THOMPSON	4:25:44	P FROST	4:26:22
42	R RAMSAY WILLIS	4:23:56	S ELSEY	4:24:32	L FORBES	4:25:12	K PAPE	4:25:45	D WRAGG	4:26:22
43	S COOK	4:23:56	C ELSEY	4:24:32	A ARMSTRONG	4:25:13	M LEFEVRE	4:25:45	K JOKIPII	4:26:23
44	A BIRKENHEAD-ROBERTS	4:23:56	A WHITEFIELD	4:24:32	R MANLY	4:25:13	D BUTCHER	4:25:45	G HEANEY	4:26:23
45	S SWINNERTON	4:23:56	P CHEUNG	4:24:32	S MAHOMO	4:25:14	C HYDE	4:25:46	M LAWSON	4:26:24
46	D BALABANOFF	4:23:56	P WHITFORD	4:24:33	R GOODLET	4:25:14	P CUFFE	4:25:46	M BODART	4:26:24
47	K ELDRED	4:23:56	D CLARKE	4:24:33	D SUMRAY	4:25:14	S LAMB	4:25:47	F SHARPE	4:26:24
48	P RAMAGE	4:23:57	J THYNE	4:24:33	M TITMUSS	4:25:15	A ATKINS	4:25:47	B IVARSSON	4:26:25
49	E HARVEY	4:23:57	J SAPIRE	4:24:33	J WILSON	4:25:15	S PETO	4:25:48	N QUINN	4:26:26
50	R WHITE	4:23:57	J WILLIAMS	4:24:33	G INGLIS-JONES	4:25:15	A PICKETT	4:25:48	M FOY	4:26:26
51	C PRINCE	4:23:57	P SEAL	4:24:34	A COYSTON	4:25:15	B MARSHALL	4:25:48	P DEMPSEY	4:26:26
52	K MACAULAY	4:23:58	P RYAN	4:24:35	G MARSHALL	4:25:15	R BROWN	4:25:49	J LANGFORD	4:26:29
53	B TAYLOR	4:23:58	A MILES	4:24:35	J ESKRIETT	4:25:15	M MORAGHAN	4:25:49	E COYLE	4:26:29
54	P GODDARD	4:23:59	G ATKINS	4:24:35	R REYNOLDS	4:25:15	B HARDING	4:25:50	L UJVARI	4:26:29
55	C MENLOVE-PLATT	4:23:59	P DUNNING	4:24:35	A PEARCE	4:25:15	S HELLIWELL	4:25:51	C THOMPSON	4:26:29
56	S STARBROOK	4:23:59	D HANNAH	4:24:35	P RIGBY	4:25:16	Y GIORDA	4:25:52	A HILL	4:26:30
57	P BERRY	4:23:59	T KEENE	4:24:36	M BRADY	4:25:16	R BINGHAM	4:25:53	R WILLIAMS	4:26:30
58	L BORIA	4:24:00	H DAVIS	4:24:37	C ROSE	4:25:16	P JELLEYMAN	4:25:53	J BALLANTYNE	4:26:31
59	W COLLINS	4:24:00	G CARDY	4:24:37	E POZZI	4:25:16	G CLARKE	4:25:54	P PETERS	4:26:31
60	P MCLEAN	4:24:00	A KELLY	4:24:37	S MCKAY	4:25:16	R MONTGOMERY	4:25:54	P VEAZEY	4:26:32
61	P LOOS	4:24:01	M QUAZAR TIGHE	4:24:38	C RANSOM	4:25:17	S SLIGHT	4:25:55	J HOFFMANN	4:26:32
62	D MUNN	4:24:01	C DREWRY	4:24:38	C LEWIS	4:25:17	B BENNION	4:25:55	A CRAIG	4:26:32
63	D KENNEDY	4:24:01	D THOMAS	4:24:38	K GARFORTH	4:25:17	W COURTNEY	4:25:56	E BINDSLEV	4:26:33
64	R BAILEY	4:24:01	C HEXLEY	4:24:38	J SMITH	4:25:18	A HOWELL	4:25:57	T FEWELL	4:26:33
65	H NAGATA	4:24:01	J HEXLEY	4:24:38	M HELPS	4:25:19	K SIMPSON	4:25:57	A KELLY	4:26:34
66	J THOMPSON	4:24:02	D ALFORD	4:24:38	E EVANS	4:25:19	M O'DONNELL	4:25:57	S BRAMLEY	4:26:34
67	R VIVLANO	4:24:02	R SANDERS	4:24:39	J WATTS	4:25:20	I MCLEAN	4:25:57	M WIGGINS	4:26:34
68	A GRAHAM	4:24:02	F BANKS	4:24:39	N BUNT	4:25:20	P CHARNLEY	4:25:57	D BOSWELL	4:26:34
69	M HORSMAN	4:24:02	S CLAYS	4:24:40	D WHEELWRIGHT	4:25:20	P DIXON	4:25:57	P BORNS	4:26:35
70	R JOHNSTON	4:24:02	J ALVAREZ	4:24:40	S MONAGHAN	4:25:21	J LUKER	4:25:58	C PALMER	4:26:35
71	G TAYLOR	4:24:03	A CELADA	4:24:40	R ODRISCOLL	4:25:22	R LUKES	4:25:58	D KENNY	4:26:35
72	J DAVIES	4:24:03	B BRADY	4:24:40	I MACHAN	4:25:22	R PARKER	4:25:59	M HEWETT	4:26:36
73	E PAYNE	4:24:05	T SPERLING	4:24:41	A PATRICK	4:25:22	R GIBBONS	4:25:59	G HARCUP	4:26:36
74	R SPRUNGLI	4:24:07	T LIDDERTH	4:24:41	J BEGGS	4:25:22	A GOODALL	4:25:59	M LONG	4:26:36
75	G FITZGERALD	4:24:07	M VALENTINE	4:24:41	J FLAYE	4:25:22	D ADAMS	4:25:59	R WESTWOOD	4:26:36
76	J KILSBY	4:24:08	N BARTLETT	4:24:41	M SCANLON	4:25:22	D DRAKEFORD	4:26:00	J WINZAR	4:26:36
77	G SINICAUT	4:24:09	J THOMAS	4:24:42	A FRITH	4:25:23	S BOTTOMLEY	4:26:01	L RISBY	4:26:36
78	J JONES	4:24:10	K JANISZEWSKI	4:24:43	D JOHNSON	4:25:23	K VINE	4:26:01	J BRODRICK	4:26:37
79	A BARTON	4:24:11	J JACKSON	4:24:43	B MANGAN	4:25:24	M WRIGHT	4:26:01	W MALLOY	4:26:38
80	J KIRWAN-TAYLOR	4:24:12	R LAWSON	4:24:44	D PAYNE	4:25:24	A EATON	4:26:01	M BELLAMY	4:26:38
81	G PRIOR	4:24:12	M LORD	4:24:44	K DALE	4:25:24	M POWELL	4:26:02	M FOOKES	4:26:38
82	F PICARD	4:24:12	K DAVIES WALTERS	4:24:45	T NEARY	4:25:25	E BARRINGTON	4:26:03	K KELLY	4:26:38
83	M CLANET	4:24:13	J EVANS	4:24:45	F FIRMANI	4:25:25	D ATKINSON	4:26:03	B RUSERT	4:26:38
84	A WATERFIELD	4:24:13	D FLINT	4:24:45	P WESSELS	4:25:25	M VIBE	4:26:04	J WILKINSON	4:26:39
85	S RIDER	4:24:13	A MUSKETT	4:24:47	M NOVELLINI	4:25:25	N HORTON	4:26:05	T HUGHES	4:26:39
86	P ROBERTS	4:24:13	J EASON	4:24:48	M MCANENEY	4:25:26	D HIGGS	4:26:05	M EVANS	4:26:39
87	A LEGGOTT	4:24:13	P RALPH	4:24:48	R LEDINGHAM	4:25:26	J STOCK	4:26:05	J HOLLAND	4:26:39
88	N LILLICO	4:24:13	G RUTTER	4:24:48	P MCNALLY	4:25:26	M PRAGER	4:26:05	C JOLLIFFE	4:26:39
89	A SPOONER	4:24:13	J STARK	4:24:49	R CLARKE	4:25:29	P HODGSON	4:26:06	P BISHOP	4:26:39
90	K BOGSTRAND	4:24:14	P BROWN	4:24:50	A CLOUGH	4:25:30	P SMITH	4:26:06	A TANNER	4:26:39
91	D WORT	4:24:14	M HOPES	4:24:51	S SMITH	4:25:31	A MCFARLAND	4:26:06	P FOSTER	4:26:39
92	C FRYER	4:24:14	K ADAMS	4:24:52	B MCBRIDE	4:25:31	E WALLACE	4:26:06	T KAMINSKI	4:26:40
93	P FLANNIGAN	4:24:14	M HIGDON	4:24:52	P PRINGLE	4:25:32	T FUENTES	4:26:06	D TRACEY	4:26:40
94	R TURNER	4:24:14	E DOCHERTY	4:24:52	J BRIGGS	4:25:32	G O'CONNOR	4:26:06	R STURGIS	4:26:40
95	P TIDSWELL	4:24:14	D TAYLOR	4:24:52	T CHEETHAM	4:25:32	M COOK	4:26:06	F GARCIA	4:26:40
96	K HOYLE	4:24:15	R DAVIES	4:24:52	D MOREL	4:25:32	A JOHNSON	4:26:06	S BUGEJA	4:26:40
97	S MORGAN	4:24:15	G AYLEN	4:24:52	Y PEERS	4:25:33	A COLLINSON	4:26:07	S SUTTON	4:26:41
98	G THIJSSEN	4:24:15	A HORSLEY	4:24:52	J ROME	4:25:33	P COOK	4:26:07	N SYMEOU	4:26:42
99	J CLAXTON	4:24:15	P MURRAY	4:24:52	J ROME	4:25:33	P SMITH	4:26:07	R MASSAGRAND	4:26:42
100	C STRONG	4:24:16	M KENNEDY	4:24:52	N SEAL	4:25:33	S MAURICE	4:26:08	C BACON	4:26:43

	17001-17100		17101-17200		17201-17300		17301-17400		17401-17500	
1	N MORNINGTON-WEST	4:26:44	M MCGREGOR	4:27:18	A JACKSON	4:27:53	M THREDGLE	4:28:33	P FREEMAN	4:29:10
2	N COX	4:26:45	S MANN	4:27:19	R ASHMOLE	4:27:53	A POOLE	4:28:33	S DARRACOTT	4:29:12
3	P MACGREGOR	4:26:45	H NORDMANN	4:27:19	F GODFREY	4:27:53	I GRAETZ-KESWANI	4:28:34	R BOWMAN	4:29:12
4	A REEVES	4:26:45	R BEADLE	4:27:19	G THOMAS	4:27:53	M PRYER	4:28:35	M COUTTS	4:29:12
5	R PHILLIPS	4:26:46	G BASER	4:27:19	A WISEMAN	4:27:53	S BRUTON	4:28:35	C ASHCROFT	4:29:13
6	S ARORA	4:26:46	F SAVARY	4:27:22	L MACASKILL	4:27:53	I MACFARLANE	4:28:36	A ASHCROFT	4:29:13
7	E BRADFORD	4:26:46	E WHYMAN	4:27:23	D CALVERT	4:27:55	R MATCHAM	4:28:39	A TAYLOR	4:29:13
8	M WILKINS	4:26:46	T BRODIE	4:27:23	A HARRIS	4:27:55	H OSTERMAN	4:28:39	B WARD	4:29:14
9	J KINGSTON	4:26:47	F DOLAN	4:27:23	J COX	4:27:56	L MARR	4:28:39	M SIMPSON	4:29:14
10	T ROGERS	4:26:47	B MAVAHEBI	4:27:23	R GILBERT	4:27:56	R COLLINS	4:28:40	D DREW	4:29:14
11	K CAUDWELL	4:26:47	M JONES	4:27:24	W HASLER	4:27:56	H HACKEL	4:28:40	J HARLEY	4:29:15
12	P GALLANT	4:26:47	T MCBEATH	4:27:24	D PLANT	4:27:57	P AYLOTT	4:28:40	M CARLBALK	4:29:16
13	P BOOTH	4:26:48	C ADAMS	4:27:24	R HODGSON	4:27:57	M SMITH	4:28:40	S MURRAY	4:29:16
14	A ROBERTS	4:26:48	G PEARSON	4:27:25	T STUBBS	4:27:58	C WEST	4:28:40	L BRADFIELD	4:29:16
15	J MCKENNA	4:26:48	T HURLEY	4:27:25	A SMITH	4:27:58	J KING	4:28:41	L LEWENDON	4:29:16
16	K RUSTON	4:26:50	D SHIPLEY	4:27:25	M DUNCAN	4:27:58	G WARNER	4:28:41	R HARDING	4:29:16
17	S EDWARDS	4:26:50	T KUMLIN	4:27:27	B WIGHTMAN	4:27:58	S HORRY	4:28:41	R CLAIRICI	4:29:17
18	M HARRIS	4:26:50	J CONWAY	4:27:27	G JEFFS	4:27:59	A MILLS	4:28:41	J DIAMOND	4:29:18
19	M COLEMAN	4:26:51	A JENNINGS	4:27:27	P BURTON	4:27:59	K BURGESS	4:28:42	P DOWNES	4:29:18
20	J COLEMAN	4:26:51	A MATTEI	4:27:27	N JORDAN	4:28:00	C MCHENRY	4:28:42	A PARKIN	4:29:19
21	R CRABTREE	4:26:52	J MCCLUSKEY	4:27:27	L ALIKER	4:28:00	N STAY	4:28:42	G BALLIN	4:29:19
22	A ANTONIOU	4:26:52	R NEUSCHULER	4:27:28	Y NYGARD	4:28:00	C LEICESTER	4:28:42	M CUBITT	4:29:19
23	A SOWERBUTTS	4:26:53	K FARRELL	4:27:28	E MYRIE	4:28:02	W JENNISON	4:28:42	R EDWARDS	4:29:20
24	P FAHY	4:26:53	J DIZER	4:27:28	S BROLLY	4:28:02	A BENKHARMAZ	4:28:42	K KHOSA	4:29:20
25	J KEW	4:26:54	A MURPHY	4:27:29	J REARDON	4:28:03	B CROWE	4:28:42	C JONES	4:29:20
26	I HUDSON	4:26:56	B JOHNSON	4:27:29	D MOSBY	4:28:03	J CLEMENT	4:28:42	R SMITH	4:29:20
27	FENNER	4:26:56	S HEWITT	4:27:31	J O'CONNOR	4:28:04	D NICHOLSON	4:28:43	B GOODALL	4:29:20
28	R LANGRISH	4:26:56	J WASHFORD	4:27:32	A HICKINBOTHAM	4:28:04	S SHACKLEFORD	4:28:43	P ANDREWS	4:29:20
29	E REES	4:26:57	M RIMELL	4:27:32	C POOLE	4:28:04	R FERRARONI	4:28:43	V WOOD	4:29:20
30	J STEIN	4:26:57	D BARTON	4:27:33	J POTTER	4:28:05	A HAMMOND	4:28:43	C WATTON	4:29:20
31	A STEVENS	4:26:57	R SCARRATT	4:27:33	I VELTMAN	4:28:06	I TALASSI	4:28:44	P WELHAM	4:29:20
32	N MARSHALL	4:26:58	S HAMPTON	4:27:33	G STREVENS	4:28:06	P CARROLL	4:28:44	P MURRAY	4:29:20
33	S BARKER	4:26:58	A MAYES	4:27:34	G WITTLINGER	4:28:06	G DAWSON	4:28:44	D WALTERS	4:29:20
34	R COURTIER	4:26:58	J SUTTON	4:27:34	A CHARRIER	4:28:08	S MICHAELS	4:28:44	J MCDONALD	4:29:20
35	C MOORE	4:26:58	D MAYES	4:27:34	E KING	4:28:08	C GORDON	4:28:45	R WEST	4:29:21
36	M RAISS	4:26:58	A MARTIN	4:27:34	W MITCHELL	4:28:10	N JOHANSSON	4:28:45	B MOORE	4:29:21
37	D MCELLIGOTT	4:26:59	G RILEY	4:27:34	J LEWIS	4:28:11	R JAMES	4:28:46	I JAMIESON	4:29:21
38	P YOUNG	4:26:59	S TAKAHASHI	4:27:35	J COOPER	4:28:11	N LEWIS	4:28:47	M SWAN	4:29:21
39	D STARR	4:26:59	B ELDER	4:27:35	K SCOTT	4:28:11	M ROWLAY	4:28:49	J TWAMLEY	4:29:21
40	B SHOULTS	4:27:00	P COWDRY	4:27:35	R BRAGG	4:28:13	W WORTS	4:28:49	R REDFORD	4:29:22
41	C SPRAGGINS	4:27:00	T NEWMAN	4:27:35	P PRISLEY	4:28:13	J PETERSEN	4:28:50	C HOWE	4:29:22
42	W FORDHAM	4:27:00	D LIVERMORE	4:27:36	G MCMANUS	4:28:14	W GILLETT	4:28:50	L VANMAERCKE	4:29:23
43	I JOHNSTON	4:27:00	A MCBRIDE	4:27:36	D EVANS	4:28:15	R ADAMS	4:28:50	C WHEELWRIGHT	4:29:24
44	W LAMB	4:27:00	M VARNEY	4:27:36	F DUNLOP	4:28:15	D WALKER	4:28:50	K PALMER	4:29:24
45	C HUNT	4:27:00	J ELKINS	4:27:37	J OREGAN	4:28:16	R BELL	4:28:50	R BARKER	4:29:24
46	C TAYLOR	4:27:00	A ROSIN	4:27:37	A POLIDORI	4:28:16	M MCADAM	4:28:50	J PICKETT	4:29:25
47	G NORMAN	4:27:00	A WESTLAKE	4:27:37	D TATE	4:28:16	G SMITH	4:28:50	C BLAKELEY	4:29:25
48	B BELEI	4:27:00	A COLE	4:27:38	P WATSON	4:28:17	R WOODHOUSE	4:28:50	J GARRETT-PEGGE	4:29:25
49	J BRUCE	4:27:00	W GOODALL	4:27:38	G HARDING	4:28:17	M SIROT	4:28:50	A ROSS	4:29:25
50	R LLOYD	4:27:01	D ROTHMAN	4:27:40	A TRAINOR	4:28:17	R SHERWIN	4:28:50	L ARNOLD	4:29:26
51	N COUCH	4:27:02	D DART	4:27:40	T JOHNSON	4:28:17	I WILLARD	4:28:51	S TAYLOR	4:29:26
52	P WARD	4:27:02	P BAILIE	4:27:41	C OTOOLE	4:28:17	J HANSFORD	4:28:51	C HARRIS	4:29:26
53	I SNOWDEN	4:27:02	C KEENAN	4:27:41	G WILLIAMS	4:28:17	L RUSSELL	4:28:51	M LEFEVRE	4:29:26
54	P MOSTON	4:27:02	F DANIEL	4:27:42	J TAMPLIN	4:28:17	C RUZICH	4:28:52	J ROSS	4:29:27
55	I TANNER	4:27:02	B REDMAN	4:27:42	J TULLY	4:28:17	S TINDLE	4:28:52	D RIDGWAY	4:29:29
56	T BIRD	4:27:03	C ROBERTS	4:27:42	M RAYFIELD	4:28:18	A DUNHAM	4:28:52	J MURPHY	4:29:29
57	F ELLIS	4:27:04	B DURY	4:27:42	C FIELD	4:28:18	M DALLAS	4:28:52	C DOWLING	4:29:29
58	S TASKER	4:27:04	P WEST	4:27:43	P KNIGHTLY	4:28:18	J CHRISTIANSEN	4:28:52	J PINNINGTON	4:29:30
59	F MORRIS	4:27:04	P CUFFE	4:27:43	R GILL	4:28:18	S CANTELLOW	4:28:52	R BREEN	4:29:31
60	I SCOREY	4:27:05	J BRUCE	4:27:43	V GRAY	4:28:19	H HILL	4:28:55	M BATEMAN	4:29:31
61	J GRIFFIN	4:27:05	J MCCANDLESS	4:27:44	R GILL	4:28:19	E SULLIVAN	4:28:55	D YOUNG	4:29:32
62	P WOJCIK	4:27:05	A DUKE	4:27:44	R DEARSLEY	4:28:19	S HIBBERT	4:28:55	J AGUILAR	4:29:32
63	L THOMAS	4:27:05	R LLOYD	4:27:44	I MOWBRAY	4:28:19	J SWABY	4:28:55	E HARRIS	4:29:32
64	D LEECH	4:27:05	M JOHNSON	4:27:44	S SCOTT	4:28:20	R LYMAN	4:28:56	D FOLEY	4:29:32
65	D SWAFFIELD	4:27:05	D PROSSER DAVIES	4:27:44	S CARTER	4:28:20	F HASLETT	4:28:58	T MURPHY	4:29:33
66	J KEELEY	4:27:05	G AUJLA	4:27:44	R BUCKANAN	4:28:20	J CARLTON	4:28:59	A PIERCE	4:29:33
67	W HONEYMAN	4:27:05	E BROWN	4:27:44	A EDBROOKE	4:28:21	W MCMURTRY	4:28:59	H JEFFERIES	4:29:33
68	P KAUFMAN	4:27:05	B TWITE	4:27:44	D HAYES	4:28:22	R WINNING	4:28:59	J BRYANT	4:29:33
69	W PAIN	4:27:05	D LOCK	4:27:44	P DIMELOE	4:28:22	J CRAVEN	4:28:59	P BRYANT	4:29:33
70	A KERSTING	4:27:06	R LEVINE	4:27:45	M HUGHES	4:28:22	J FOGDEN	4:28:59	S CLOWES	4:29:33
71	A WEEKS	4:27:06	J STEINSON	4:27:45	C HEARN	4:28:22	D LINN	4:28:59	P BREEN	4:29:33
72	B BEECH	4:27:06	J THORNALLEY	4:27:46	P HOWES	4:28:22	N JAMES	4:28:59	R CARMICHAEL	4:29:33
73	C RIGG	4:27:07	P WALTON	4:27:47	J WHATLEY	4:28:22	F SCHMID	4:29:00	D EASTHOPE	4:29:33
74	D CANNAN	4:27:07	S MUSGRAVE	4:27:47	A CAMPBELL	4:28:23	R BAINBRIDGE	4:29:00	J MORDECAI	4:29:33
75	D SCOTT	4:27:07	P DIXON	4:27:47	D NIGHTINGILL	4:28:23	N SPOONER	4:29:00	A WOODS	4:29:33
76	H WILLIAMS	4:27:07	W NEILL	4:27:47	R BURBIDGE	4:28:24	M GODFREY	4:29:00	J GREEN	4:29:34
77	S EWIN	4:27:08	B TENNYSON	4:27:47	D SHEPHERD	4:28:25	P RICHARDSON	4:29:01	E MORLEY	4:29:34
78	M NICHOLLS	4:27:08	S MATTERSON	4:27:47	S SPRAGUE	4:28:25	C FRENCH	4:29:01	G BOLDORI	4:29:34
79	N HOWE	4:27:09	W STANLEY	4:27:47	B DELAPERRELLE	4:28:25	R SLOMAN	4:29:02	D WICKHAM	4:29:35
80	P WRIGHT	4:27:09	D SUMMERS	4:27:47	M BIGGS	4:28:25	A CARTER	4:29:02	S DAFFEY	4:29:35
81	M MAYSON	4:27:10	A HUNT	4:27:47	G MORGAN	4:28:25	A RATCLIFFE	4:29:02	N CAMPBELL	4:29:35
82	D COFFEY	4:27:10	K PERSSON	4:27:47	P BARKER	4:28:25	R KRAUT	4:29:02	A LEE	4:29:36
83	R MURRAY	4:27:10	A HARRIS	4:27:47	S SHARPE	4:28:25	S MARSHALL	4:29:02	M MCCOY	4:29:37
84	D FORD	4:27:10	R TODD	4:27:47	R DENISON	4:28:27	I ASCROFT	4:29:03	J TINKER	4:29:37
85	J WATES	4:27:11	T MILLAR	4:27:47	J TURNER	4:28:28	M THEOPHILUS	4:29:04	F ITOH	4:29:38
86	L BOWEN	4:27:12	D DIPLOCK	4:27:49	M HUGILL	4:28:28	K THEOPHILYS	4:29:04	C LAWRENCE	4:29:38
87	W LEITH	4:27:13	S MOLLOY	4:27:49	M ENGLAND	4:28:29	N BASSETT	4:29:05	H MOSS	4:29:38
88	K WOOD	4:27:13	P THORNALLEY	4:27:49	J NUNN	4:28:29	D COPPOCK	4:29:06	M TAYLOR	4:29:39
89	D HARRIS	4:27:13	C TRINCA	4:27:50	R COOK	4:28:30	P LAW	4:29:06	S LISI	4:29:41
90	I SUTHERLAND	4:27:16	I CAMERON	4:27:50	R ROWE	4:28:30	D JEFFERIES	4:29:06	M CROSSLAND	4:29:41
91	A PANTON	4:27:16	E DEED	4:27:50	S PATEL	4:28:31	A MACKAY	4:29:06	B SMITH	4:29:42
92	E ROGERS	4:27:17	J HILDEBRAND	4:27:50	R COOK	4:28:31	R KENWORTHY	4:29:07	J MILLS	4:29:43
93	M RIVALDI	4:27:17	H DAMM	4:27:51	D SEIFERT	4:28:31	I MURRAY JOHN	4:29:08	J OCHIN	4:29:43
94	K BUTCHER	4:27:17	D BECK	4:27:51	S WHITEHEAD	4:28:31	S WAITE	4:29:08	R SARRADE	4:29:43
95	D DAVIES	4:27:17	C LARBY	4:27:51	P COGLE	4:28:31	M JONES	4:29:08	I MACKIE	4:29:43
96	H SEACOMBE	4:27:17	E SKINNER	4:27:51	D GIBNEY	4:28:31	V CAMPBELL	4:29:08	N FROHLICK	4:29:43
97	W MORETON	4:27:18	P CUSHINGS	4:27:51	R WATERS	4:28:31	S MELLEY	4:29:08	T GOUGH	4:29:44
98	A WILLIAMS	4:27:18	R HEALD	4:27:52	G RINGROSE	4:28:32	L CLARK	4:29:08	R PERRY	4:29:44
99	D MOUTRIE	4:27:18	B BABB	4:27:52	G MAYES	4:28:32	K HORAN	4:29:09	C ABERCROMBIE	4:29:44
100	G JONES	4:27:18	S DOBINSON	4:27:53	D PRENTIS	4:28:33	J ARCHER-THOMSON	4:29:10	W TERRY	4:29:44

#	17501-17600		17601-17700		17701-17800		17801-17900		17901-18000	
1	S DOPSON	4:29:45	G DAVIES	4:30:16	S SMITH	4:30:48	T NIKKILA	4:31:20	M FORREST	4:32:03
2	S CHANDLER	4:29:45	J NOSWORTHY	4:30:16	M WORSLEY	4:30:48	R KNIGHTON	4:31:20	F MACAULAY	4:32:03
3	D BOLLER	4:29:45	P PAWLEY	4:30:16	C ADCOCK	4:30:48	I BROWN	4:31:20	A CLARK	4:32:05
4	C SLESSOR	4:29:45	P KILLEEN	4:30:16	C SCOTT	4:30:49	H HAIDE	4:31:20	A POWERS	4:32:06
5	T BROOKES	4:29:45	J ELIE	4:30:17	J COUSINS	4:30:49	T HINKLEY	4:31:20	C OWEN	4:32:06
6	M STACK	4:29:46	E NEGRINI	4:30:17	S BARROW	4:30:49	K JACKSON	4:31:21	S ACHER	4:32:06
7	W PONTIN	4:29:46	M BARRATT	4:30:17	S ANDERSON	4:30:49	J BANNER	4:31:21	J PACKMAN	4:32:06
8	B SPECK	4:29:47	G BERDUGO	4:30:17	P WEST	4:30:49	M JONES	4:31:21	M ABBOTT	4:32:06
9	B BARRANCE	4:29:47	A COLLENETTE	4:30:17	N BIRD	4:30:49	W MILLER	4:31:21	I WALTERS	4:32:06
10	S CLOUGH	4:29:47	L MAKIN	4:30:18	P COULSON	4:30:49	D RAFFO	4:31:22	H SJOEGREN	4:32:07
11	J LITTLER	4:29:47	S RANDALL	4:30:18	T LATTANZIO	4:30:50	M CARVETH	4:31:23	M ELLERTON	4:32:08
12	G DANIELS	4:29:47	E LACCHINI	4:30:18	L TAYLOR	4:30:50	P KNIGHT	4:31:23	A CROSS	4:32:08
13	M BROWNING	4:29:47	T WORN	4:30:18	F SCHMIDT	4:30:51	K JONES	4:31:23	M WILKINSON	4:32:10
14	D DORDEVIC	4:29:48	G MANN	4:30:19	S YOUNG	4:30:51	C HOOD	4:31:23	M BLASEBALK	4:32:11
15	K DORDEVIC	4:29:48	J FELDHAUS	4:30:20	A BALDOCK	4:30:51	G ROGERS	4:31:24	A BOZARTH	4:32:11
16	M ELSHAW	4:29:48	A CARTWRIGHT	4:30:20	H FLINDERS	4:30:51	S WOMACK	4:31:25	B BUTLER	4:32:11
17	J HANCOCK	4:29:49	R ROADKNIGHT	4:30:21	M DAVIES	4:30:52	J MILLER	4:31:25	M EMERY	4:32:12
18	L SMITH	4:29:49	M RIMELL	4:30:22	L FRIIS	4:30:52	L MITCHELL	4:31:25	R HORDER	4:32:12
19	P HOWELL	4:29:49	L ASTRUC	4:30:22	C CRAVEN-BARTLE	4:30:53	M ZAPICO	4:31:26	M EDWARDS	4:32:14
20	R WRIGHT	4:29:49	T GRIFFITHS	4:30:25	A BEADLE	4:30:54	H SWANEPOEL	4:31:26	R WILKINS	4:32:15
21	M PREEDY	4:29:49	K VISSER	4:30:26	P HOLTON	4:30:54	R BARING	4:31:26	R POND	4:32:17
22	G MCNEILL	4:29:49	R YARDE	4:30:26	E RUDD	4:30:54	J GOOSE	4:31:26	U KALLENBACH	4:32:17
23	B ROBERTS	4:29:50	R MEARES-DAVIES	4:30:26	D TOWNSEND	4:30:55	A HAY	4:31:27	M ALLAN	4:32:17
24	D SWIDENBANK	4:29:50	L REISMAN	4:30:26	C BAMFORD	4:30:55	C HOWELL	4:31:27	D DASHWOOD	4:32:17
25	M WILKINSON	4:29:50	E READER	4:30:27	M SKIPPER	4:30:55	I JONES	4:31:28	B EVANS	4:32:17
26	D CRAIG	4:29:51	V MOORCROFT	4:30:27	P MORRISON	4:30:55	S HARRIS	4:31:28	J OAKE	4:32:17
27	N TARBATH	4:29:51	H KAIJANEN	4:30:27	C MARKWICK	4:30:56	G HARRORD	4:31:29	T ANDREW	4:32:17
28	J MORTASSAGNE	4:29:52	D BRETT	4:30:28	A JOYCE	4:30:56	L BARBER	4:31:29	J MILLER	4:32:17
29	H VALLANCE	4:29:52	N POPE	4:30:28	P BRENNAN	4:30:56	D HEALY	4:31:29	A CASTLE	4:32:20
30	J LEA	4:29:53	J DALEY	4:30:28	W STUDMAN	4:30:56	I BODDY	4:31:29	G BROWN	4:32:21
31	D COLLISON	4:29:53	R BABE	4:30:28	D SMITH	4:30:59	V CUNNINGHAM	4:31:30	J BROOKS	4:32:21
32	S SOUTHCOTT	4:29:53	S RIOT	4:30:28	R BRIDE	4:31:00	H ROBINSON	4:31:30	P STROUD	4:32:23
33	N HOSKINS	4:29:54	D O'NEILL	4:30:28	J RAWCLIFFE	4:31:00	W HARRIS	4:31:31	D KEEN	4:32:23
34	I RICHTER	4:29:54	J CLARKE	4:30:28	T FULTON	4:31:00	J TRUPIN	4:31:31	D WELDING	4:32:23
35	G WIGHT	4:29:55	C RUSSELL	4:30:28	M FULTON	4:31:01	J SCANTLEBURY	4:31:31	M CROOK	4:32:23
36	J WALKER	4:29:55	L ANDERSSON	4:30:28	M MILLER	4:31:01	R SMITH	4:31:32	C EASTEAL	4:32:24
37	C HOWARD	4:29:55	C CARTHY	4:30:28	G EVERTON	4:31:01	G CURRIN	4:31:33	J ELSON	4:32:24
38	P VAN DER HULST	4:29:55	S TARBUCK	4:30:29	D MOLES	4:31:02	W GARDNER	4:31:35	C CURPHEY	4:32:24
39	N SMITH	4:29:55	Y ANDREOTTI	4:30:30	A DACHE	4:31:02	T BROCK	4:31:35	C BARKER	4:32:25
40	F RANCE	4:29:55	J ANDREOTTI	4:30:30	O SONDERGAARD	4:31:02	C CAMERON	4:31:35	H DURNERIN	4:32:26
41	R FORDREE	4:29:55	B TULLOCH	4:30:31	H PESENDORFER	4:31:03	C HERD	4:31:35	M MORRIS	4:32:26
42	C WATT	4:29:55	J PORAJ-WILCZYNSKI	4:30:31	W DURBAND	4:31:03	M BOINON	4:31:35	J MARSHALL	4:32:27
43	G POVEY	4:29:55	L PARKER	4:30:31	I STURZAKER	4:31:03	J WILLIS	4:31:36	J THOMAS	4:32:27
44	R ITEN	4:29:55	J STANCOMBE	4:30:31	P SAYER	4:31:04	R MACKIE	4:31:37	P MASTERS	4:32:28
45	J PEARSON	4:29:55	T EVANS	4:30:32	G HOYLAND	4:31:04	E BONNER	4:31:38	D WILLIAMSON	4:32:28
46	M MUFFITT	4:29:55	M BARTLETT	4:30:32	C SMITH	4:31:04	P FULLER	4:31:38	M CROCKER	4:32:28
47	C PEARSON	4:29:55	S O'BRIEN	4:30:32	P SCARROTT	4:31:05	G SINGER	4:31:39	P HARMAN	4:32:28
48	S PENGELLY	4:29:55	M WILLIS	4:30:32	C SHERMAN	4:31:05	W GASSON	4:31:39	R COPPING-EATON	4:32:29
49	J KINGSTON	4:29:55	S WAVING	4:30:32	J MOREL	4:31:05	D MARTIN	4:31:39	D PORTHOUSE	4:32:29
50	N DAVIES	4:29:56	V LEONG	4:30:32	D CORKER	4:31:05	G TAYLOR	4:31:39	B BALDE	4:32:30
51	T CARY	4:29:56	B SEAMARK	4:30:32	G WARD	4:31:05	G HORSLER	4:31:40	M DODD	4:32:30
52	D WEST	4:29:56	M RUSSELL	4:30:33	F MCKIERNAN	4:31:05	V MALLEN	4:31:40	T MCKENNA	4:32:32
53	B JOEL	4:29:56	E MORRISON	4:30:33	R PAWSEY	4:31:08	H JAMES	4:31:40	D O'CONNOR	4:32:32
54	B LINGWOOD	4:29:56	E PYWELL	4:30:33	P SMITH	4:31:08	K CRANSWICK	4:31:40	C TEDMAN	4:32:32
55	P LAY	4:29:56	R BURNS	4:30:33	P HORDERN	4:31:08	G REES	4:31:41	O MORGENBORD	4:32:32
56	D ADELSBERG	4:29:57	J FUTCHER	4:30:33	J FIDO	4:31:08	J ROUND	4:31:41	I JALKANEN	4:32:32
57	A PAUL	4:29:57	R DALLEY	4:30:33	J HOPWOOD	4:31:09	W ELLIS	4:31:42	D ALLAN	4:32:33
58	W LEWIS	4:29:58	J DIPPLE	4:30:34	J TAYLOR	4:31:09	P ELVIDGE	4:31:42	S JOHN	4:32:33
59	A WILSON	4:29:58	C JOHNSON	4:30:34	D WESSON	4:31:10	J YARDLEY	4:31:42	K SECCOMBE	4:32:34
60	R ELLWOOD	4:29:59	W HODDER	4:30:34	V ELKINGTON	4:31:10	M ZANDI	4:31:42	R VINCENT	4:32:35
61	K SIBBERING	4:30:00	C STACE	4:30:34	L HALL	4:31:10	M VINES	4:31:42	H RINGLAND	4:32:35
62	P HAYWARD	4:30:00	R LOCKWOOD	4:30:34	C COOPER	4:31:11	S WINES	4:31:42	R COGGIN	4:32:35
63	P WILSON	4:30:01	C WHITE	4:30:34	J LOCKLEY	4:31:11	P PRESCOTT	4:31:42	G JACKSON	4:32:37
64	D COWAN	4:30:01	T WRIGLEY	4:30:34	G WATKIN	4:31:11	R ELVIDGE	4:31:42	A KING	4:32:37
65	S PULGIES	4:30:01	M SENLECQ	4:30:34	K GRANT	4:31:11	P TOWNSLEY	4:31:44	J STENSLAND	4:32:38
66	A HICKSON	4:30:02	G BURROWS	4:30:34	G EWEN	4:31:11	W ADAMS	4:31:45	N LABROW	4:32:39
67	B BAILEY	4:30:04	D RUNDLE	4:30:34	M JAMES	4:31:11	E O'MAHONY	4:31:45	M AUSUSTINE-COX	4:32:39
68	D KENT	4:30:04	P SNELL	4:30:34	E EDDES	4:31:11	M RABAIOTTI	4:31:45	D HARRIS	4:32:39
69	L WHARRAD	4:30:05	M BUSBY	4:30:34	C HARRIS	4:31:11	P DOWSON	4:31:45	V SAYERS	4:32:40
70	M GRIFFITHS	4:30:05	N APPLETON	4:30:35	R MCKEE	4:31:11	V BRAYBROOKS	4:31:46	E BULLIMORE	4:32:40
71	R GRIFFITH-BIRD	4:30:05	M EVANS	4:30:35	R STRACHAN	4:31:11	P DAVIES	4:31:47	P GOUGH	4:32:40
72	M MAYNARD	4:30:05	P RICE	4:30:35	B HALL	4:31:11	D BROWN	4:31:48	W THOMAS	4:32:40
73	R EVANS	4:30:06	S WALLER	4:30:35	E BOYCE	4:31:11	Y CULLEN	4:31:49	R KYBERT	4:32:41
74	F SHANNON	4:30:07	I BAYLEY	4:30:36	P WATTS	4:31:11	J HARBORD	4:31:51	M POWELL	4:32:41
75	P HEATH	4:30:07	C CRIDLAND	4:30:36	D MCGUIRE	4:31:11	R KEITHLEY	4:31:52	S DENNY	4:32:42
76	R MUNDY	4:30:08	T EXALL	4:30:37	J BAILEY	4:31:11	B JOHNSON	4:31:55	J BISHOP	4:32:43
77	M BULL	4:30:08	G BAINGER	4:30:38	M BARRATT	4:31:11	B POGORZELSKI	4:31:55	J SMITH	4:32:43
78	S VIGAR	4:30:09	A COOPER	4:30:38	D BLOW	4:31:11	M WATT	4:31:56	P ADAMS	4:32:44
79	J TARR	4:30:09	R WIGGS	4:30:39	R GALANTE	4:31:11	S WHAWELL	4:31:57	A WILKINSON	4:32:45
80	P WOOD	4:30:09	S JACKSON	4:30:39	R WEBB	4:31:11	M WHAWELL	4:31:58	K PREECE	4:32:45
81	P BROOKE-ANDERSON	4:30:09	R RAMPA	4:30:39	D HEIZ	4:31:11	G KANE	4:31:58	T DOCHERTY	4:32:46
82	G COXON	4:30:09	A WARREN	4:30:40	G GILCHRIST	4:31:11	D MOTHERSDALE	4:31:58	M SIMMONS	4:32:47
83	P MONTROSE	4:30:10	K MORRIS	4:30:40	S THORNTON	4:31:11	S WAKEMAN	4:31:58	H MILROSE	4:32:48
84	S RILEY	4:30:10	R REAY	4:30:40	S LEA	4:31:11	R SLOAN	4:31:58	D LLOYD	4:32:48
85	H KLEPPA	4:30:10	D LEWIS	4:30:40	C WILLSHAW	4:31:11	C BONNING	4:31:58	J WALTERS	4:32:48
86	M LAW	4:30:11	A WEBSTER	4:30:40	J MACHENS	4:31:11	K ROBERTS	4:31:58	A GORE	4:32:48
87	B SOLLER	4:30:11	R ROSE	4:30:42	S BOLTON	4:31:11	T MURPHY	4:31:58	D TOLLEY	4:32:49
88	M CHILTON	4:30:11	J MARTIN	4:30:42	G CREASY	4:31:12	M JAKEMAN	4:31:59	W ARCHER	4:32:49
89	N CRAIG-HARVEY	4:30:11	G FISHER	4:30:43	R JONES	4:31:12	C HENSON	4:31:59	C THOMAS	4:32:49
90	E NIERMANN	4:30:13	J WILKINSON	4:30:43	M ELLIOTT	4:31:12	J BISHOP	4:31:59	K BIRCH	4:32:49
91	G ANDERSON	4:30:13	B ANTHONY	4:30:43	K JAMES	4:31:13	S JOHNSON	4:32:00	A ROLLO	4:32:50
92	M CONNELLY	4:30:13	G STUART	4:30:44	J SKAN	4:31:15	K TAYLOR	4:32:00	J WALLBANK	4:32:50
93	J BATEMAN	4:30:14	W BUTCHER	4:30:44	M HARRIS	4:31:15	I DAVIES	4:32:00	M SMITH	4:32:50
94	P BEWERS	4:30:14	A PEASE	4:30:44	A LIPSCOMBE	4:31:16	P HAYMAN	4:32:01	J WRIGHT	4:32:50
95	N NUCKLEY	4:30:14	E COOK	4:30:44	S WHITEHURST	4:31:17	J GERIN	4:32:01	P PATTON	4:32:50
96	R COHEN	4:30:15	P HARRY	4:30:45	P PULLEN	4:31:17	J DAVIES	4:32:01	M HILL	4:32:52
97	J BLAKE	4:30:15	G BULTER	4:30:46	A HARRISON	4:31:17	I TURNER	4:32:02	A THOMPSON	4:32:53
98	K ROBINSON	4:30:15	D MATTHEWS	4:30:47	R HARRISON	4:31:18	R JOHNSON	4:32:02	S WESSON	4:32:53
99	S PARRY	4:30:16	A KIRK	4:30:47	P GILLARD	4:31:18	A BANKS	4:32:03	M DICKENS	4:32:54
100	J BATEMAN	4:30:16	A DOBSON	4:30:48	M JUKES	4:31:19			J EIKELENBOOM	4:32:55

#	18001-18100		18101-18200		18201-18300		18301-18400		18401-18500	
1	A CLARK	4:32:55	M FREEMAN	4:33:44	H KIMURA	4:34:32	I BENSTED	4:35:19	R EVANS	4:35:52
2	S HILLS	4:32:56	B STEFFENS	4:33:48	M CAVE	4:34:33	J BAGNALL	4:35:19	A WILLIAMS	4:35:52
3	T GRAY	4:32:57	J GERSEN	4:33:48	T DUCK	4:34:33	P WILLIAMS	4:35:19	A DAWSON	4:35:52
4	S SMITH	4:32:58	G ADAMS	4:33:49	R MEACHIN	4:34:34	T HUGHES	4:35:20	P GOULD	4:35:52
5	M STONES	4:32:58	P CHUNN	4:33:49	P MAGILL	4:34:34	P FLATLEY	4:35:21	A FITZGERALD	4:35:52
6	G ROBINSON	4:32:58	R CHUNN	4:33:49	G FORD	4:34:34	C DODMAN	4:35:21	M READ	4:35:52
7	P WIEGAND	4:32:59	O NIJJAR	4:33:49	J PETRIDES	4:34:35	S KLEIN	4:35:21	H EDGAR	4:35:52
8	P JEULAND	4:32:59	D OWEN	4:33:49	M MAYOR	4:34:35	M ROLFF	4:35:22	J SHARPE	4:35:53
9	J BROOKES	4:33:00	J BAYLISS	4:33:49	S KITTERIDGE	4:34:36	P GRAHAM	4:35:22	S WRANGHAM	4:35:53
10	C RUDGE	4:33:00	B BURGESS	4:33:50	P HINES	4:34:36	D MARDEN	4:35:22	N PAUL	4:35:54
11	K CHANDLER	4:33:00	N COOPER	4:33:51	J REDDEN	4:34:37	A TALBOT	4:35:22	A LESLIE	4:35:54
12	R LLEWELLYN	4:33:01	P VAN OOSTERWIJCK	4:33:51	D COOP	4:34:37	D GOODWIN	4:35:22	L SHELTON	4:35:55
13	M BOYLES	4:33:02	M WILD	4:33:52	D CAMPBELL	4:34:37	G LANNIGAN	4:35:22	J COLAS	4:35:55
14	J WHITTAKER	4:33:04	N ATKINS	4:33:53	R PLAISTER	4:34:38	M BARTER	4:35:23	S BENNETT	4:35:55
15	A SUMNALL	4:33:04	J BAKE	4:33:53	S BERRY	4:34:39	R HAKKIM	4:35:24	J MALLARD	4:35:56
16	D COLEMAN	4:33:05	R MOUNTAIN	4:33:54	R COLVILLE	4:34:39	K DYBDAHL	4:35:24	E PARIS	4:35:56
17	A HUMPHREYS	4:33:05	M ALLAN	4:33:54	D GILL	4:34:40	R CLACK	4:35:25	P ASHDOWN	4:35:57
18	K SEARLE	4:33:06	I BAILEY	4:33:54	J COLLEY	4:34:40	C GASPARDI	4:35:26	C BAITUP	4:35:57
19	R PRENDERGAST	4:33:06	P TREMERE	4:33:54	P MOSS	4:34:43	H WALKER	4:35:26	R BAITUP	4:35:58
20	M MANSELL	4:33:06	P BEVAN	4:33:55	I HULBERT	4:34:45	D REARDON	4:35:26	M DUNN	4:35:58
21	C WARNER	4:33:06	A CALLAWAY	4:33:55	S WICKS	4:34:45	S PAYNE	4:35:26	R POSKITT	4:35:58
22	L BENNETT	4:33:06	K LAWSON	4:33:55	D QUARENDON	4:34:46	A LITTLEFORD	4:35:27	D PRICE	4:35:59
23	S BRADLEY	4:33:06	G BONSEY	4:33:55	D WATTS	4:34:47	A CORNISH	4:35:27	P HEDDON	4:35:59
24	A VAN STRAALEN	4:33:07	L DUFFY	4:33:55	J DENNETT	4:34:47	P HALL	4:35:28	N ELLEMAN	4:35:59
25	K WILLIAMS	4:33:07	G VINCENT	4:33:55	A GRACE	4:34:47	J GRACE	4:35:28	E CLAYSON	4:35:59
26	A GROVER	4:33:08	C SMITH	4:33:55	C ROWE	4:34:48	E LEE	4:35:28	R GRAZIOLI	4:35:59
27	M HUNTER	4:33:08	H DOI	4:33:56	V BRAMWELL	4:34:48	M DOWNER	4:35:29	B BRADSHAW	4:35:59
28	P PARSONS	4:33:10	D BATTY	4:33:56	M JENKINS	4:34:48	C FOY	4:35:29	D LEACH	4:36:01
29	S SKILTON	4:33:10	P FRANKLIN	4:33:56	G RIDDING	4:34:49	C BACON	4:35:30	S NEILD	4:36:01
30	D GILMAN	4:33:10	A WHITE	4:33:57	J BUDGETT	4:34:49	J IBISON	4:35:30	H WENZEL	4:36:02
31	A NEALE	4:33:11	C DIMMOCK	4:33:58	P JAMIESON	4:34:50	H HOOPER	4:35:31	G JAMES	4:36:04
32	D MOORE	4:33:11	P MIDGEN	4:33:59	D BINNS	4:34:50	F RICKUS	4:35:31	S COLE	4:36:06
33	G FORREST	4:33:12	R CORBETT	4:34:00	J PENDLETON	4:34:50	P CARTER	4:35:32	A THOMPSON	4:36:06
34	C REEKIE	4:33:12	A BAILEY	4:34:00	D LAWRENCE	4:34:51	J DOUGLAS	4:35:33	R FORDE	4:36:07
35	D PALMER	4:33:13	D ASHTON	4:34:01	T HARTSHORN	4:34:52	L BRIGHT	4:35:33	S SMART	4:36:08
36	D COX	4:33:13	S VARNEY	4:34:02	R MUNN	4:34:52	R BERRY	4:35:33	R CHAMBERS	4:36:08
37	C POLLMER	4:33:13	P BARBER	4:34:04	C PARTON	4:34:52	B ERNEST	4:35:34	O SODERLUND	4:36:08
38	J HOLDEN	4:33:13	L CONNERTON	4:34:05	M GIBSON	4:34:52	N POLLOCK	4:35:34	K WHITE	4:36:09
39	S NIBLETT	4:33:13	W HIDGE	4:34:05	C CLOT-GODARD	4:34:53	R COATES	4:35:34	S PATERSON	4:36:09
40	C COOPER	4:33:14	S RICHARDS	4:34:06	R LANSLEY	4:34:53	D WALTERS	4:35:35	G WEBB	4:36:09
41	P DENT	4:33:15	K HUNT	4:34:07	T RUECK	4:34:53	S OXBORROW	4:35:35	C HOGUE	4:36:10
42	C POTTS	4:33:16	D BRIGGS	4:34:07	B DRUMM-SHALE	4:34:54	R CLARKSON	4:35:35	H NAPPER	4:36:10
43	A SMITH	4:33:17	P LONGLEY	4:34:08	M GAUTHAM	4:34:54	K WOOFF	4:35:36	N BRENNER	4:36:11
44	P SUA	4:33:18	D WOODROOFE	4:34:09	J MICHAELIS	4:34:55	J LANCASTER	4:35:36	N JACOBSEN	4:36:11
45	F SAWYER	4:33:18	D MCKAY	4:34:10	P COLE	4:34:55	M MASTERS	4:35:36	S EDWARDS	4:36:11
46	P HODGE	4:33:18	S TAYLOR	4:34:10	P REIJERSE	4:34:56	R STANDFAST	4:35:36	R BUSST	4:36:12
47	P CROWLEY	4:33:19	P ALDER	4:34:11	B HANS	4:34:56	D SMITH	4:35:36	D PARKER	4:36:12
48	P BROWN	4:33:19	W SIGGERS	4:34:11	T HARRINGTON	4:34:56	P BOULTBEE	4:35:37	G AHERNE	4:36:13
49	S JULIAN	4:33:21	G BELCHER	4:34:11	C FOX	4:34:56	D CHILDS	4:35:37	T MURPHY	4:36:13
50	P LEWIS	4:33:21	L GORDON	4:34:11	J HARVEY	4:34:56	S MALME	4:35:37	S UNDERWOOD	4:36:13
51	R MURRAY	4:33:21	J REEK	4:34:11	L CUMMINGS	4:34:56	M WAKEFIELD	4:35:37	A RIMINGTON	4:36:14
52	R ANDREWS	4:33:22	A ROBERTSON	4:34:11	R CREW	4:34:57	J PEARSON	4:35:37	C VINE	4:36:15
53	D CURRAN	4:33:22	S PEARCE	4:34:11	J HALL	4:34:57	G HILDERLY	4:35:37	M CHARLTON	4:36:15
54	P ALDOUS	4:33:23	P JOSLIN	4:34:13	P CASEY	4:34:57	J FARMER	4:35:38	R BEECH	4:36:15
55	I BARNARD	4:33:24	J FIELDER	4:34:13	R HORNE	4:34:57	R GRAY	4:35:38	A GRIFFIN	4:36:15
56	T AHIR	4:33:24	O MAYFIELD	4:34:13	T RULE	4:34:58	T MOSS	4:35:38	D DOBLE	4:36:15
57	S WILKINSON	4:33:24	K ANDERSON	4:34:14	L HUDSON	4:34:59	W EDWARDS	4:35:39	S MANSFIELD	4:36:16
58	T GAUVAIN	4:33:26	A FARREN	4:34:16	M DOWNES	4:34:59	R WORSLEY	4:35:40	D TEAGUE	4:36:16
59	R WALTON	4:33:26	R ATKINS	4:34:16	S BALDY	4:34:59	B SADLER	4:35:40	J BROWNE	4:36:17
60	W MCKENZIE	4:33:26	M FARREN	4:34:16	P JOHNSON	4:35:00	D KNIGHT	4:35:40	C HEALEY	4:36:17
61	A CRAZE	4:33:26	J FIELDER	4:34:17	M CONNOLLY	4:35:00	M CRAIG	4:35:41	L WALTON	4:36:17
62	J REES	4:33:27	J WILLS	4:34:17	G HALEY	4:35:00	J DAVIS	4:35:41	I SPAXMAN	4:36:17
63	M TESTER	4:33:27	P FRIEND	4:34:17	M PRATT	4:35:01	D MACDONALD	4:35:41	A MACKAY	4:36:18
64	T FALLON	4:33:27	R BROOKE	4:34:18	N MATON	4:35:01	R WILLIAMS	4:35:41	M FURLONG	4:36:19
65	J DOBSON	4:33:28	R WHITCOMB	4:34:18	E MUTZ	4:35:01	F CUVELETTE	4:35:42	D WELLS	4:36:20
66	M TOWLER	4:33:28	J WHITE	4:34:19	I NEVILLE	4:35:01	M BONNER	4:35:43	M GRIFFITHS	4:36:21
67	M STREETER	4:33:30	R EGLEN	4:34:19	C DAVIS	4:35:01	W PAYNE	4:35:43	D JENKINS	4:36:22
68	M LAWLEY	4:33:30	H MOYSER	4:34:19	P MARGERUM	4:35:02	I MURAKAMI	4:35:43	A CATTERALL	4:36:23
69	T BOOTH	4:33:30	R BAVERSTOCK	4:34:19	J LEE	4:35:02	M HENAUGHAN	4:35:43	D WEBB	4:36:23
70	S WILLIAMS	4:33:30	N BAILEY	4:34:19	A WILTSHIRE	4:35:02	P NICOLLET	4:35:43	D RYAN	4:36:23
71	D GOSLING	4:33:31	J JACKSON	4:34:19	N CRESWELL	4:35:02	A SAVOLAINEN	4:35:44	C MULLIGAN	4:36:24
72	D BOWEN	4:33:31	P GAHAGAN	4:34:20	A THOMPSON	4:35:03	A LIVETT	4:35:44	J PAGE	4:36:24
73	P FARMER	4:33:31	A FLETCHER	4:34:20	K WEIGHT	4:35:03	C PILLEY	4:35:45	D TAYLOR	4:36:24
74	F BOWEN	4:33:31	D WOFFINDIN	4:34:20	M COX	4:35:03	M BURGESS	4:35:45	P MOONEY	4:36:25
75	M BEDNALL	4:33:31	M HILL	4:34:20	T VON MEREY	4:35:03	J WRANGLES	4:35:45	B COLE	4:36:25
76	A MOORE	4:33:32	D SIMPSON	4:34:20	L WILKINSON	4:35:03	P SLANE	4:35:45	W HADFIELD	4:36:25
77	R STUNT	4:33:33	K PEARCE	4:34:20	K WENZEL	4:35:04	I ROEBUCK	4:35:45	M POOLE	4:36:25
78	J BAKER	4:33:33	T ROSE	4:34:21	C HAYN	4:35:04	G NOVAK	4:35:45	C BARNES	4:36:27
79	C SCANLAN	4:33:33	G HAWKINS	4:34:22	A BRADMAN	4:35:05	C RAYMOND	4:35:45	C BLAKEY	4:36:27
80	A CARTWRIGHT	4:33:34	I WHITE	4:34:23	M JACKSON	4:35:06	C TILSON	4:35:45	K BERRY	4:36:28
81	T LLEWELLYN	4:33:34	S LLOYD	4:34:25	J POWELL	4:35:07	B WRANGLES	4:35:46	R MATTHEWS	4:36:29
82	D HERRING	4:33:34	P DREW	4:34:26	B BILINGHAM	4:35:08	S BALLS	4:35:46	G CUNNING	4:36:29
83	R STARBUCK	4:33:34	S ILES	4:34:27	T BURGESS	4:35:08	P TREADGOLD	4:35:46	K KUEN	4:36:30
84	W BLACKMORE	4:33:34	J GLEDHILL	4:34:28	R BAKER	4:35:09	R COATES	4:35:47	J DUFF	4:36:30
85	C THURSTON	4:33:35	M TIMMINS	4:34:30	P BATTIMELLI	4:35:10	L HOPE	4:35:47	P NEWMAN	4:36:30
86	M DOWNING	4:33:35	M POULTON	4:34:30	C MILLS	4:35:10	P BARDEN	4:35:47	B SULLIVAN	4:36:30
87	R HAIGH	4:33:36	J SCOTT	4:34:30	M WHITTELL	4:35:10	S HARDMAN	4:35:48	G WATERS	4:36:31
88	J FLANDERS	4:33:37	M GEE	4:34:30	G ADAMS	4:35:11	D SAYERS	4:35:48	B VALLELY	4:36:31
89	R SYKES	4:33:37	D ROONEY	4:34:31	C DARDEL	4:35:11	M ROSSI	4:35:48	N ROTH	4:36:32
90	G BRYANT	4:33:37	G WILLIAMS	4:34:31	C GREEN	4:35:13	M KENNEDY	4:35:49	P JACKSON	4:36:32
91	D WILCOX	4:33:37	C DAVISON	4:34:31	M READER	4:35:13	S TYLER	4:35:50	D SCRIMGEOUR	4:36:32
92	M SHARPE	4:33:38	D WIBBERLEY	4:34:31	A HOPKINS	4:35:14	J O'BRIEN	4:35:50	J FINCH	4:36:32
93	J BURKINSHAW	4:33:39	S RADFORD	4:34:32	J WILKINSON	4:35:14	D DAVEY	4:35:50	L WILKINS	4:36:32
94	M PIKE	4:33:40	D RIMMER	4:34:32	T BROCKINGTON	4:35:14	T SHEPHERD	4:35:50	C LANDER	4:36:33
95	P KEEN	4:33:40	K MCDONALD	4:34:32	J STOCK	4:35:16	A IRVIN	4:35:50	H MASON	4:36:33
96	G BAXTER	4:33:41	A O'BOYLE	4:34:32	F MURRAY	4:35:16	R EPPEY	4:35:50	E PHILPOTT	4:36:33
97	N MCPHEAT	4:33:41	I RAPP	4:34:32	J DUMOULIE	4:35:16	G BUXTON	4:35:51	C CLARK	4:36:33
98	H ANSTEE	4:33:43	S OAKLEY	4:34:32	S BARBER	4:35:17	M HUTTON	4:35:51	J TROTTER	4:36:33
99	J FILMER	4:33:43	J WOJCIECHOWICZ	4:34:32	D WISEMAN	4:35:17	O SCOULAR	4:35:51	K STANGER	4:36:34
100	D GREEN	4:33:43	A EVANS	4:34:32	M SANTOS	4:35:17	S EVANS	4:35:52	P ROBICHON	4:36:34

#	18501-18600		18601-18700		18701-18800		18801-18900		18901-19000	
1	I THOMSON	4:36:35	L WATMORE	4:37:06	A ESSE	4:37:46	B NEUBAUER	4:38:22	J DALEY	4:39:04
2	C GILLIES	4:36:35	M SIBLEY	4:37:06	G DAWSON	4:37:47	D SMITH	4:38:23	J SECKINGTON	4:39:05
3	M FENLON	4:36:35	S SWAIN	4:37:06	J ENGLISH	4:37:47	E BOYD	4:38:23	S LOVEMORE	4:39:05
4	M ROUSE	4:36:36	R SOTOURI-ZANJANI	4:37:06	R HAMILTON-BROWN	4:37:48	E ROUGHTON	4:38:24	N TOMKIN	4:39:07
5	W CROSBY	4:36:37	M MCDONALD	4:37:06	A HILTUNEN	4:37:49	I TAYLOR	4:38:24	J DONOHOE	4:39:08
6	K STAFFORD	4:36:37	M BOBLIN	4:37:06	D SMITH	4:37:49	I HOAD	4:38:25	C THOMAS	4:39:08
7	A TWAMLEY	4:36:37	I DUFFIELD	4:37:06	C BENNETT	4:37:49	W MORSE	4:38:25	F WEBB	4:39:08
8	M O'SULLIVAN	4:36:37	C GALVIN	4:37:06	G MYCOCK	4:37:50	R FOSTER	4:38:25	J NEWTON	4:39:08
9	D MCCROSSAN	4:36:38	E PUGH	4:37:07	C BENNETT	4:37:50	P TEMPLE	4:38:26	P UNITE	4:39:08
10	M SOPHOCLIDES	4:36:38	A WATERS	4:37:07	P JONES	4:37:50	J SHOCHOT	4:38:26	J DOWNEY	4:39:08
11	B HOLLIDAY	4:36:39	P BROWN	4:37:08	L PARK	4:37:51	D LEITH	4:38:28	K GREEN	4:39:08
12	J FAUX	4:36:40	J MIRMBAL	4:37:08	J FAREY	4:37:51	W FITZGERALD	4:38:29	D LANCASHIRE	4:39:08
13	S STEER	4:36:40	R COOMBS	4:37:08	J HARRISON	4:37:51	S GHOSLEY-SMITH	4:38:29	M JACKSON	4:39:08
14	C HAYES	4:36:41	P COOMBS	4:37:09	G ALDRIDGE	4:37:51	L BRYANT	4:38:30	M CONNOLLY	4:39:08
15	P SHORT	4:36:41	M HIBBETT	4:37:09	D KENT	4:37:52	W KAISER	4:38:31	K AYLMER	4:39:08
16	K WOOD	4:36:42	C HARVEY	4:37:09	P BAKER	4:37:52	J BAKER	4:38:31	H MILLER	4:39:08
17	D NORMAN	4:36:42	D BAYLISS	4:37:10	D NICOL	4:37:52	D DAVIES	4:38:32	G YOUNG	4:39:09
18	R WOOD	4:36:42	J PARR	4:37:11	A DAVIDSON	4:37:54	J SHERWIN	4:38:32	B FELTHAM	4:39:09
19	M MOORE	4:36:42	C MCPARTLAND	4:37:11	A CRUMPTON	4:37:54	P LAUWERS	4:38:32	S WEBER	4:39:09
20	A SCOTT	4:36:43	M STRIKE	4:37:11	B LEVY	4:37:54	G WOOD	4:38:32	I DAVIES	4:39:09
21	A ABBOTT	4:36:43	J GAMBLE	4:37:11	J PARK	4:37:55	K BOWKER	4:38:32	J GUY	4:39:10
22	P HULL	4:36:43	S WHITTINGTON	4:37:11	A SLOUGH	4:37:55	M YAMAGUCHI	4:38:32	B ANSELL	4:39:10
23	G COMERFORD	4:36:43	D BROWN	4:37:12	T MINTER	4:37:55	D WILLIAMS	4:38:33	J NEWBERRY	4:39:10
24	J LARSEN	4:36:43	K BAKER	4:37:12	K TAYLOR	4:37:55	N RYAN	4:38:33	L WILLIAMS	4:39:10
25	D JOHNSTON	4:36:44	J BAKER	4:37:12	B STAFFORD	4:37:56	K GRAHAM	4:38:34	C OLDFIELD	4:39:10
26	J FELINE	4:36:44	C PURVIS	4:37:12	A TARRANT	4:37:56	J JONES	4:38:34	J HENDERSON	4:39:10
27	J WARNER	4:36:44	G HAWLEY	4:37:12	E BAKER	4:37:57	M WOOD	4:38:34	S WYNN	4:39:10
28	M COHEN	4:36:44	E MORT	4:37:13	L WYNTER	4:37:57	P SHALLIS	4:38:35	A WICKENS	4:39:10
29	J JONES	4:36:44	A HUNT	4:37:13	C FAIRHEAD	4:37:57	J NOMURA	4:38:35	M SEIF	4:39:12
30	Q REGER	4:36:44	J POLLOCK	4:37:13	S MUNCASTER	4:37:58	R BAIOCCO	4:38:36	L BROOK	4:39:12
31	W COTTON	4:36:44	H HUTCHINGS	4:37:14	C ALLEN	4:37:58	K FAIRBANK	4:38:36	M HARDY	4:39:12
32	K GILDER	4:36:44	S UPTON	4:37:14	L SLUMAN	4:37:58	R PALMER	4:38:38	W WHITNEY	4:39:13
33	A NEW	4:36:45	I RILEY	4:37:15	D HATCH	4:37:58	J SAYER	4:38:38	A POLLITT	4:39:14
34	K ALAIN	4:36:46	M REDGRAVE	4:37:16	A BOWEN	4:37:58	P DRISCOLL	4:38:38	A RUSSELL	4:39:16
35	J HAMMOND	4:36:47	R SPOONER	4:37:16	C HUGHES	4:37:58	S COOMBES	4:38:38	J DA ROSA	4:39:16
36	J UNSWORTH	4:36:47	B TREGONNING	4:37:17	J GREEN	4:37:59	G SHANNON	4:38:38	J MOGRIDGE	4:39:16
37	D UPTON	4:36:47	B OLSEN	4:37:18	D DOW	4:37:59	J BAGWELL	4:38:39	D BURROWS	4:39:17
38	R STUTTARD	4:36:48	P STEVENS	4:37:18	J BALL	4:37:59	T DYER	4:38:40	J GOLD	4:39:17
39	D KLETT	4:36:48	D PARROTT	4:37:19	C BOOTS	4:38:00	C PAWSON	4:38:40	R LAWLESS	4:39:18
40	S HIGHAM	4:36:48	C BROOKS	4:37:19	J TOYNBEE	4:38:00	P CATTON	4:38:41	R PHILLIPSON	4:39:18
41	M CLIFFORD	4:36:49	R CROUCH	4:37:20	M SLACK	4:38:01	S AMIN	4:38:41	A HIGGINS	4:39:18
42	J HERBERT	4:36:49	D ELSE	4:37:20	D BEDFORD	4:38:01	J ROBINSON	4:38:41	D COX	4:39:19
43	J PYE	4:36:49	P FARRANT	4:37:21	R WALKER	4:38:02	M PORTUS	4:38:41	L SCOTT	4:39:20
44	R DRANE	4:36:49	T TEHRANIAN	4:37:21	J CARDY	4:38:03	D LANDEG	4:38:42	J MCGRATH	4:39:20
45	D ROBINSON	4:36:50	R BETTINGER	4:37:21	A ROSS	4:38:03	P JOHNS	4:38:42	M GODFREY	4:39:20
46	R LESTER	4:36:51	J BETTINGER	4:37:22	A WATT	4:38:05	A HYDE	4:38:43	A FYFE	4:39:20
47	J SEARS	4:36:51	A COPE	4:37:23	R FITTER	4:38:06	L HALL	4:38:43	W FURSMAN	4:39:20
48	P PERKINS	4:36:51	T JONES	4:37:25	A WATKINS	4:38:07	J GREEN	4:38:44	G ANDREW	4:39:20
49	S PIPPIN	4:36:52	C CANNON	4:37:25	M CAMSEY	4:38:07	L ELMS	4:38:45	A HUSBAND	4:39:21
50	I PAGE	4:36:52	A WILLIAMS	4:37:25	K CATES	4:38:08	N HALL	4:38:45	P JONES	4:39:21
51	F MYERS	4:36:53	G LETT	4:37:25	S GLENDINNING	4:38:09	K JOHNSON	4:38:45	M TEMPLEMAN	4:39:22
52	A CARVER	4:36:54	R FOSTER	4:37:26	D RANDALL	4:38:09	J DARK	4:38:45	C TSCHOEGL	4:39:23
53	G COLLIER	4:36:54	B MNYAMA	4:37:26	M KEIGHER	4:38:09	V WILLIAMS	4:38:45	A KARANDIKAR	4:39:23
54	T HARGITAI	4:36:54	D BOARDMAN	4:37:26	J WATTS	4:38:09	K ROUSE	4:38:46	J LANE	4:39:23
55	A RAVESSOUD	4:36:54	M BEGIN	4:37:27	M EDINGTON	4:38:12	R ALLSOPP	4:38:46	H MILLIGAN	4:39:24
56	M BEREZICKI	4:36:55	J BAILIE	4:37:27	J WELCH	4:38:12	L MONK	4:38:46	D LODGE	4:39:24
57	D HORNADY	4:36:55	J MENZIES	4:37:27	R BURNS	4:38:12	H DOWER	4:38:46	K PAYNE	4:39:24
58	P DOREE	4:36:55	S LAMBURTH	4:37:28	A WELLING	4:38:12	N WALKER	4:38:46	A HILDREW	4:39:24
59	M THOMPSON	4:36:55	R YEOMANS	4:37:29	G OWEN	4:38:12	J BUNYARD	4:38:46	G WRIGHT	4:39:25
60	C BORGGREN	4:36:56	M JOLLY	4:37:30	M WATTS	4:38:12	C DOWLING	4:38:47	M ARNOLD	4:39:26
61	T ONEILL	4:36:56	A RAMSDEN	4:37:30	R LAWRENCE	4:38:12	R MELLOY	4:38:47	J SUTCLIFFE	4:39:28
62	A BARNES	4:36:56	B GOLDSMITH	4:37:32	R WILLIAMS	4:38:12	G WALLACE	4:38:47	B CHANDLER	4:39:29
63	B PATERSON	4:36:57	J DUNMORE	4:37:32	D CULLEN	4:38:12	M WOLFSON	4:38:47	N EDWARDS	4:39:30
64	G EVANS	4:36:57	Y OKADA	4:37:33	K BORWELL	4:38:12	A DICKINSON	4:38:47	L FOX	4:39:31
65	J MAJOR	4:36:58	A GREENWOOD	4:37:33	J HOWARD	4:38:12	A MANSFIELD	4:38:47	L CRACK	4:39:31
66	P MILLAR	4:36:58	D GOODCHILD	4:37:33	G COLLINS	4:38:12	P PAGE	4:38:48	D JOY	4:39:31
67	T JONES	4:36:58	J WOLF	4:37:36	S MCWILLIAM	4:38:12	D ROBINSON	4:38:48	V BENNETT	4:39:32
68	S MUDDLE	4:36:59	J ELLIOTT	4:37:38	M MONAGHAN	4:38:12	I THOMPSON	4:38:49	S ASHFORD	4:39:32
69	S RAMAGE	4:36:59	D LESTER	4:37:38	K IMAI	4:38:12	C HOOK	4:38:49	J GARFOOT	4:39:33
70	G SALE	4:36:59	P OWEN	4:37:38	L ROBINSON	4:38:13	R O'CONNOR	4:38:49	M NOTT	4:39:34
71	J NASH	4:36:59	P KEATING	4:37:38	R HALL	4:38:13	A RICHARDS	4:38:50	K SNAPE	4:39:34
72	C COOPER	4:37:00	A SMITH	4:37:38	L HYLAND	4:38:14	C CHEESMAN	4:38:51	M COHEN	4:39:34
73	A COLES	4:37:00	S UTTERIDGE	4:37:38	D VERE	4:38:14	J DALE	4:38:51	A BROCCANELLO	4:39:35
74	C TARRANT	4:37:00	L CARPENTER	4:37:38	D MUNDY	4:38:14	J ANDERSON	4:38:51	B MCGEORGE	4:39:35
75	V BATTY	4:37:00	J BEIRNE	4:37:38	R BESZANT	4:38:15	D LEACH	4:38:51	T MILLS	4:39:36
76	M WILLS	4:37:01	R KING	4:37:38	S BLOT	4:38:15	P STANTON	4:38:51	M HODGINS	4:39:37
77	S JOWSEY	4:37:01	M HARDY	4:37:38	D EDWARDS	4:38:15	L WATERS	4:38:52	L MASTRODDI	4:39:37
78	V GULLIVER	4:37:01	S MORLEY	4:37:38	J CHAMPION	4:38:15	L DAWE	4:38:52	P DESECK	4:39:37
79	W SNAITH	4:37:01	G TREMERE	4:37:39	M ALLEN	4:38:15	D CRANKSHAW	4:38:52	K BARNES	4:39:37
80	T ITOH	4:37:02	J MILLER	4:37:41	K JOHNS	4:38:16	N SMIT	4:38:52	C FERNANDEZ	4:39:38
81	G BICKLEY	4:37:02	S HAMMARSTEDT	4:37:41	D COLEMAN	4:38:16	S OWENS	4:38:52	J STORER	4:39:38
82	A CADDICK	4:37:02	W FRECH	4:37:42	R REID	4:38:16	H HOPKINS	4:38:53	A PLATTEN	4:39:39
83	M KECEK	4:37:03	M HEAVEY	4:37:42	M TAYLOR	4:38:16	D OWENS	4:38:54	W BRUNO	4:39:39
84	P BATTY	4:37:03	K USHER	4:37:43	J CARTER	4:38:17	C LANE	4:38:54	N MAYNE	4:39:39
85	A MORROW	4:37:03	M BAGGOTT	4:37:43	L DURBIN	4:38:18	W TOTTERDELL	4:38:54	B SCHNOOR	4:39:39
86	A GOUGH	4:37:03	C RAINE	4:37:43	M CALDECOURT	4:38:18	A BOLLAND	4:38:54	D DAY	4:39:39
87	T HALL	4:37:03	A HYMAN	4:37:43	C PEDERSEN	4:38:18	J PLUMB	4:38:55	B BELL	4:39:39
88	P DAWKINS	4:37:04	A BROWN	4:37:43	T BAKER	4:38:18	J EDWARDS	4:38:55	M HAMPSHIRE	4:39:39
89	B GODDARD	4:37:04	A PERKINS	4:37:43	G MURPHY	4:38:19	R DOVEY	4:38:56	A MARTIN	4:39:39
90	D BARTLETT	4:37:04	J MAY	4:37:43	M FOULGER	4:38:19	M GREEN	4:38:59	K MUELLER	4:39:39
91	S DAVIES	4:37:04	P HAGERSTAD	4:37:44	S JACOB	4:38:19	J ALLARD	4:38:59	I HOPPER	4:39:41
92	F PHELAN	4:37:04	G BARWICK	4:37:44	M LEIBRICK	4:38:19	R HOLLINESHEAD	4:38:59	J BEAUMONT	4:39:42
93	H THORMAN	4:37:04	J LITTLE	4:37:44	A SEWERNIAK	4:38:20	S CARRIGAN	4:39:00	S PHILLIPS	4:39:43
94	P SILVESTER	4:37:04	A WENMAN	4:37:44	M HANKS	4:38:20	M BARKER	4:39:01	N WRIGHT	4:39:44
95	T WEST	4:37:04	P TAKKINEN	4:37:44	G SMITH	4:38:20	R BISSET	4:39:02	Y SOLOMON	4:39:46
96	J ROTH	4:37:05	A STANT	4:37:44	H PACK	4:38:21	I FLOWERS	4:39:02	A COOPER	4:39:47
97	M SHIMMEN	4:37:05	J WHELAN	4:37:44	J SELLORS	4:38:22	M CASPER	4:39:03	G MILLMAN	4:39:49
98	M GILES	4:37:05	D RABOZZI	4:37:45	J SPARROW	4:38:22	M BRAZIER	4:39:04	J BAYBUTT	4:39:49
99	D WILLIS	4:37:06	T WILLMOTT	4:37:45	C THOMPSON	4:38:22	L RAMPLING	4:39:04	K JEFFERIES	4:39:50
100	B BECK	4:37:06	M AIMABLE	4:37:45	C MACHIN	4:38:22	B HILL	4:39:04	A HAGGAR	4:39:50

#	19001-19100		19101-19200		19201-19300		19301-19400		19401-19500	
1	M ANTELL	4:39:51	M DOWLING	4:40:35	K MAY	4:41:13	C GOBBY	4:42:11	W FINNERMORE	4:42:54
2	G MANN	4:39:52	C SAMS	4:40:35	M KRUIS	4:41:13	R LIMBRICK	4:42:11	T DOWDS	4:42:54
3	A LEVIT	4:39:53	S MEREDITH	4:40:35	B FURNESS	4:41:13	M FRAMPTON	4:42:11	J WILLIAMSON	4:42:54
4	B FOSTER	4:39:53	P SCARRY	4:40:36	G BRIGGS	4:41:15	N THOMAS	4:42:12	J BECK	4:42:54
5	P BAYLEY	4:39:53	R BLYTH	4:40:36	R PIERCY	4:41:15	K WADHAMS	4:42:12	W BURROWS	4:42:54
6	R NEWELL	4:39:53	S BERRY	4:40:37	D STEBLER	4:41:15	G MAGGS	4:42:12	P TURNER	4:42:56
7	M BROCK	4:39:53	B COLE	4:40:37	D CHALONER	4:41:15	B TALLING	4:42:12	D SPECTOR	4:42:57
8	D ALLEN	4:39:54	C STANBRIDGE	4:40:38	M EVANS	4:41:16	L OUTTERIDGE	4:42:12	S ERIKSSON	4:42:57
9	G DAVIES	4:39:55	E SCOTT	4:40:38	T WILLIAMSON	4:41:17	P SEVIOUR	4:42:12	A BROWN	4:42:58
10	P PARKES	4:39:55	T O'CONNOR	4:40:39	D PAYN	4:41:17	C CHAPMAN	4:42:12	I BUNCE	4:42:58
11	M BUNTING	4:39:56	S ROSS	4:40:39	L LANE	4:41:17	M BANKS	4:42:12	A MOONEY	4:42:58
12	N DIXON	4:39:56	H MARRIOTT	4:40:40	M HOLTON	4:41:17	M PARISH	4:42:13	P BRIGNELL	4:43:01
13	J DEACON	4:39:56	A HUNTER	4:40:41	D ELLIOTT	4:41:18	K MCLEOD	4:42:13	K KRAIL	4:43:02
14	A SWALES	4:39:56	J PRECUZZI	4:40:42	R PARKER	4:41:19	M GOODBODY	4:42:14	A NUNN	4:43:02
15	J HIPKISS	4:39:57	H LOTWICK	4:40:42	I MOULTRIE	4:41:20	J DENT	4:42:14	H HARRISON	4:43:02
16	S POLLARD	4:39:57	H WHITTAKER	4:40:42	R RICHARDSON	4:41:20	R COLLING	4:42:16	P KNOWLEY	4:43:02
17	J DOBSON	4:39:58	D BEWLEY	4:40:43	F PIERRO	4:41:20	S ROWLANDS	4:42:16	R ALLARDYCE	4:43:02
18	G MONTALDI	4:40:00	K SHIMURA	4:40:43	D HETHERINGTON	4:41:21	D SOULSBY	4:42:17	N ENGLISH	4:43:03
19	I MARSHALL	4:40:02	S AVES	4:40:44	T HUNNINGS	4:41:21	P DRUMMOND	4:42:17	J PEARSON	4:43:03
20	T PUGH	4:40:02	A MUNRO	4:40:44	P ENGLER	4:41:21	S WARNES	4:42:17	M BENNING	4:43:05
21	M MUDSON	4:40:02	V MANDEL	4:40:44	A JONES	4:41:22	C JARDINE	4:42:17	B BARNETT	4:43:05
22	J MEREDITH	4:40:02	U SCHUTZ	4:40:45	J NUNN	4:41:22	J JOYCE-NELSON	4:42:17	D RYAN	4:43:05
23	R CAMBRE	4:40:02	K HAWKEY	4:40:45	R ARTHERS	4:41:23	H THOMSON	4:42:17	A BARNETT	4:43:06
24	H HILL	4:40:02	G FROSCHAUER	4:40:45	A MORRISON	4:41:23	P THOMASON	4:42:17	A KAVANAGH	4:43:06
25	H GARDINER	4:40:02	T GARLICK	4:40:46	E GIBSON	4:41:24	G HASTINGS	4:42:18	L WOOTTEN	4:43:07
26	P SCARR	4:40:02	N HAWKEY	4:40:46	M TREGENT	4:41:24	D BROWN	4:42:18	B HARPER	4:43:08
27	D WILLIS	4:40:02	J MCALEAR	4:40:47	D GAUNT	4:41:24	T KEFFORD	4:42:18	A ZBOROWSKI	4:43:08
28	A REA	4:40:02	C WHITE	4:40:47	R PEPPIATT	4:41:24	R DOUGHTY	4:42:19	R PHILPOT	4:43:08
29	G LONGHURST	4:40:02	E NUNN	4:40:47	M JOHNSON	4:41:24	D HIRST	4:42:19	G SHEPHERD	4:43:09
30	E BROUGHER	4:40:02	K ADAMS	4:40:47	J HOGAN	4:41:25	P WILLGOOSE	4:42:21	R TAYLOR	4:43:09
31	J SIMPSON	4:40:02	M MCMAHON	4:40:47	M HANLON	4:41:25	T WYER	4:42:21	P NAYLOR	4:43:10
32	C HOLLIDAY	4:40:02	G DAWSON	4:40:49	P RYDER	4:41:25	A LEIGH	4:42:22	P HUGH-JONES	4:43:11
33	F COLLINS	4:40:02	N CHAPMAN	4:40:51	M DUNNING	4:41:25	J BARTON	4:42:22	K KERSHAW	4:43:11
34	C WRIGHT	4:40:02	S DEBOOS	4:40:51	R WHITE	4:41:26	G TAYLOR	4:42:24	I COLEMAN	4:43:12
35	M CREWE	4:40:02	J NAPIER	4:40:52	R ANDREWS	4:41:27	N BALL	4:42:24	S ISNARD	4:43:12
36	E PAUL	4:40:02	M GULLIFORD	4:40:52	P WEBBER	4:41:27	B WRIGHT	4:42:25	J MILHARADAS	4:43:12
37	L RYAN	4:40:02	S BISHOP	4:40:53	H VAN BIJLERT	4:41:28	M URMSTON	4:42:25	B LAUER	4:43:12
38	G HUDSON	4:40:03	A POVEY	4:40:53	A DAVIS	4:41:29	J AGER	4:42:25	R CLEGG	4:43:13
39	S RYAN	4:40:03	J KEARNEY	4:40:53	J BLAMIRE	4:41:30	D HARRISON	4:42:25	A MCCABE	4:43:13
40	T CASBOLT	4:40:03	R DIPROSE	4:40:53	A BONICH	4:41:31	K WHITMORE	4:42:26	S COOPER	4:43:13
41	D WICKS	4:40:03	T GOLIASCH	4:40:53	G TRAILOR	4:41:36	R GARRETT	4:42:27	D NICHOLS	4:43:14
42	C BRETHERTON	4:40:04	T SCHIFTER	4:40:53	I WILKINSON	4:41:37	M GRADY	4:42:27	M WORSFOLD	4:43:14
43	S HADGRAFT	4:40:04	J SINCLAIR	4:40:53	A CARTER	4:41:37	M PROWTON	4:42:27	A MITCHELL	4:43:14
44	G ATTER	4:40:05	B COLLINGBOURNE	4:40:53	B HARDY	4:41:37	K TYTLER	4:42:28	T BROPHY	4:43:15
45	N MALKIN	4:40:06	P WEBSTER	4:40:53	M GUARD	4:41:38	L FULLER	4:42:28	P WOODWARD	4:43:15
46	I POTTS	4:40:06	E TVEIT	4:40:53	J DAVIS	4:41:39	R ROBERTS	4:42:31	M HOUGHTON	4:43:16
47	H PIHLAJAMA	4:40:08	G MURRAY	4:40:53	D HODGES	4:41:41	T FOALE	4:42:31	R CLARKE	4:43:16
48	R DRUMMOND	4:40:09	M SACRE	4:40:53	D KERR	4:41:41	D WILKS	4:42:32	R GRIGGS	4:43:16
49	J BALL	4:40:11	P MIDDLETON	4:40:54	E LEE	4:41:41	H HARADA	4:42:32	H BUDDEN	4:43:17
50	A MORRIS	4:40:11	J ASKEW	4:40:54	J IRWIN-SINGER	4:41:41	M PERRY	4:42:33	I LARGE	4:43:18
51	M LLOYD	4:40:12	E ALIU	4:40:54	J KENNETT	4:41:41	J KEEBLE	4:42:33	B GOODMAN	4:43:18
52	R MORGAN	4:40:14	V BALDWIN	4:40:55	S PERRY	4:41:42	J YORK	4:42:34	G SPINK	4:43:18
53	J ALDRIDGE	4:40:15	C WATERS	4:40:55	P KENNETT	4:41:42	M CHRISTOV	4:42:34	T THIRUVENGADAM	4:43:18
54	W WEBSTER	4:40:15	P WALKER	4:40:55	S WOODWARD	4:41:43	B GODQUIN	4:42:34	G CARR	4:43:18
55	M PARISH	4:40:16	C HOVEN	4:40:55	A STACEY	4:41:43	J ADAMS	4:42:34	C BARRETT	4:43:18
56	S WOON	4:40:16	L REEVE	4:40:55	M PARR	4:41:43	S WEIN	4:42:35	R OTTER	4:43:18
57	S GREGORY	4:40:17	J HILLS	4:40:55	C SULLIVAN	4:41:43	I THOMPSON	4:42:35	H O'BRIEN	4:43:18
58	P CHADWICK	4:40:18	D LANHAM	4:40:55	C BAGSHAW	4:41:43	P KNOWLES	4:42:35	L DOBBY	4:43:18
59	P BREWER	4:40:18	U DAHLQVIST	4:40:55	G LUCKING	4:41:44	P CLARKE	4:42:36	C QUINN	4:43:19
60	B ROBERTS	4:40:19	S WOOD	4:40:55	B ELLISTON	4:41:44	J ALLEN	4:42:36	J SEXTONE	4:43:20
61	N JOHNSON	4:40:19	S SYMINGTON	4:40:55	P PATRICK	4:41:45	M KELSEY	4:42:36	C MURCH	4:43:20
62	P NEAL	4:40:19	T SHIELDS	4:40:55	C ELLIGOTT	4:41:46	J BRINKLOW	4:42:37	G BUNTING	4:43:20
63	D HARRIS	4:40:19	J ASHTON	4:40:57	C HUGHES	4:41:47	M HUGHES	4:42:37	D WASHINGTON	4:43:20
64	T EASTMAN	4:40:19	G WATTS	4:40:58	R OSBORNE	4:41:47	J DOBIE	4:42:38	C HUMPHRIES	4:43:22
65	A SPARROW	4:40:20	D PLEWS	4:40:58	N BAKER	4:41:47	P COLEMAN	4:42:39	V HIND	4:43:22
66	P COLLIER	4:40:20	J HAYES	4:40:59	J VAN DER VELDEN	4:41:48	J SADLER	4:42:39	P SCADDAN	4:43:24
67	K HUSSAIN	4:40:20	R SHERLOCK	4:40:59	P BRANSON	4:41:48	E BISHOP	4:42:40	D BLUNDELL	4:43:24
68	D WALLACE	4:40:20	S GIN	4:40:59	A TAYLOR	4:41:48	L TURNER	4:42:40	M GREEN	4:43:25
69	M CURTIS	4:40:21	A GILFILLAN	4:41:00	G STUART-COLE	4:41:49	P SHELBOURNE	4:42:40	M HUNT	4:43:25
70	L WILSON	4:40:21	M HALL	4:41:01	A PITTAWAY	4:41:50	G BROOKS	4:42:40	L LESLIE	4:43:26
71	S PALLETT	4:40:21	S BROUGH	4:41:01	D LIMBERT	4:41:51	K SCOTT	4:42:40	J FAFOURNOUX	4:43:26
72	B PALLETT	4:40:22	P SHERWOOD	4:41:01	D SMITH	4:41:51	C JOY	4:42:40	S JONES	4:43:27
73	D PREECE	4:40:24	A HAMER	4:41:01	J COLLINSON	4:41:51	A ROGERSON	4:42:40	Y TAKADA	4:43:28
74	P GRIFFITHS	4:40:25	P BEALE	4:41:02	K ROWNTREE	4:41:52	M HAYES	4:42:41	R MILLS	4:43:29
75	S LEVY	4:40:25	D RAYMENT	4:41:02	J TAYLOR	4:41:52	L MCFARLANE	4:42:43	H BROWNLIE	4:43:29
76	M OAKLEY	4:40:25	P MACK	4:41:02	L MARWOOD	4:41:52	P SYMONDS	4:42:45	P HAMMOND	4:43:30
77	A OAKLEY	4:40:26	J LEANDER	4:41:02	N SHIMMINS	4:41:52	N SMITH	4:42:45	S LAWRENCE	4:43:30
78	F ARCHER	4:40:26	P NAPPER	4:41:02	A CAPDEVILA	4:41:52	J FAULKNER	4:42:46	M WRIGHT	4:43:31
79	G POTTON	4:40:26	J BRIGHT	4:41:03	T KERSHAW	4:41:52	J GAMMAN	4:42:46	R JENNER	4:43:31
80	A MESSITT	4:40:27	D GOODWIN	4:41:03	G MATIJASIC	4:41:53	G DUNCAN	4:42:47	M OSBORN	4:43:31
81	J BOULTON	4:40:28	R HOEIEM	4:41:03	S VITTORI	4:41:55	K MOUSLEY	4:42:47	S BELL	4:43:31
82	N BONNER	4:40:28	B STUBBS	4:41:03	C ARAM	4:41:56	J DOBSON	4:42:47	C DAVIES	4:43:31
83	T FINNIS	4:40:28	A STEPHENSON	4:41:04	L WINKWORTH	4:41:57	M DEPAILLAT	4:42:47	K HOLMES	4:43:32
84	L HEARNE	4:40:29	G WILLIAMSON	4:41:04	S SMITH	4:41:57	S BAILEY	4:42:48	R TAIT	4:43:32
85	P CUMBER	4:40:29	I PARISH	4:41:05	D WILKINSON	4:41:58	A PREMCHAND	4:42:49	C BRADLEY	4:43:32
86	G GIDDINS	4:40:29	A THOMAS	4:41:06	D MAGEE	4:41:58	A SLATER	4:42:49	U HULTQVIST	4:43:32
87	A SKNNER	4:40:29	P GREATOREX	4:41:06	R HADFIELD	4:41:58	R MELLER	4:42:50	O GORMLEY	4:43:33
88	J HARVEY	4:40:30	D CREIGHTON	4:41:06	I PARRY	4:42:01	T SLATER	4:42:50	A MURARI	4:43:33
89	M ROSS	4:40:31	T BRUNTON	4:41:06	A COLLIER	4:42:01	A ANDRONIKOU	4:42:50	S HEPPELL	4:43:34
90	S BUXTON	4:40:31	K TOWSE	4:41:07	J HUNTER	4:42:01	C BUTTER	4:42:50	J MACKAY	4:43:35
91	S BLYTH	4:40:31	L HARDY	4:41:08	M TODD	4:42:02	A WOODS	4:42:50	T BARBARY	4:43:35
92	F COSTELLA	4:40:32	D DOWSETT	4:41:08	D SIMPSON	4:42:04	F DEACON	4:42:51	A LAHHAM	4:43:36
93	J LAKE	4:40:32	J NEWTON	4:41:09	H CLOSE	4:42:04	R STOREY	4:42:51	J BROWN	4:43:36
94	A JACKSON	4:40:32	M DINAN	4:41:10	N WOODS	4:42:05	R WILSON	4:42:51	G JONES	4:43:36
95	R TOTTEM	4:40:33	M LUNN	4:41:10	S SAWYERS	4:42:05	M TAKAYANAGI	4:42:51	S HARADA	4:43:36
96	T ROBERTS	4:40:33	J MABON	4:41:11	J BIRD	4:42:05	N TATTERSALL	4:42:52	W TUNNICLIFFE	4:43:36
97	A QUINLAN	4:40:34	C LUNN	4:41:11	K HUFFEY	4:42:05	C HOUSEMAN	4:42:52	P DIBLEY	4:43:37
98	J LEAR	4:40:34	B SOHR	4:41:12	A BELCHAMBERS	4:42:06	W READ	4:42:53	S WIERZBICKI	4:43:39
99	R VAIDYANATHAN	4:40:34	P GREGAN	4:41:12	R LONG	4:42:09	K ANDERSSEN	4:42:53	E AUSTIN	4:43:39
100	A FARRELL	4:40:35	J BARTON	4:41:12	I DORWARD	4:42:11	P GRATTAN	4:42:54	G TIMMS	4:43:39

	19501-19600		19601-19700		19701-19800		19801-19900		19901-20000	
1	J HARRIS	4:43:40	M MORRIS	4:44:36	A SPINK	4:45:33	G CORDERY	4:46:32	N SOMERVILLE	4:47:18
2	M BECK	4:43:40	W GREEN	4:44:36	C MILLAR	4:45:33	D KAY	4:46:32	P ROBINSON	4:47:18
3	P GODSIFF	4:43:41	M GAMBLE	4:44:37	D RAIMBACH	4:45:34	R FINNIE	4:46:32	K WESTWOOD	4:47:19
4	J MONAGHAN	4:43:41	R STOKES	4:44:38	R READ	4:45:35	M MCHALE	4:46:32	M THORPE	4:47:19
5	G BORRI	4:43:44	R BETTS	4:44:38	C MANSELL	4:45:36	T LAFFERTY	4:46:32	J TURNER	4:47:19
6	A HUMPHREY	4:43:44	A VAN DER PANT	4:44:38	L WISE	4:45:36	M VISZKED	4:46:33	P SEYMOUR	4:47:20
7	M FORREST	4:43:45	S MULLANEY	4:44:38	T RUSSELL	4:45:38	L WESTWOOD	4:46:33	S KEENE	4:47:20
8	T TALBOT	4:43:45	R YOUNG	4:44:38	D EDWARDS	4:45:38	C WAITE	4:46:33	M BARTON	4:47:21
9	A TAYLOR	4:43:45	S LEWIS	4:44:38	E ADAMSON	4:45:38	B WOODBRIDGE	4:46:33	H RANA	4:47:21
10	J NICHOLSON	4:43:46	J OUSTRIC	4:44:39	C MASON	4:45:38	A FOX	4:46:33	I WALL	4:47:21
11	J BAINBRIDGE	4:43:46	A BECK	4:44:39	S JAKUBOWSKI	4:45:41	R PEAD	4:46:34	D PRITCHARD	4:47:22
12	P DRAYTON	4:43:46	P AUSTIN-WALKER	4:44:40	C MCALLISTER	4:45:41	S CONSTABLE	4:46:35	P KOSCIEN	4:47:22
13	R JULIAN	4:43:47	P LAMB	4:44:41	C STUART	4:45:41	E KITNEY	4:46:35	A WHEELER	4:47:23
14	J RANN	4:43:48	G PHILLIPS	4:44:41	R HARRISON	4:45:41	H THOMAS	4:46:35	G HALL	4:47:23
15	S MCKIE	4:43:48	A HUCKLE	4:44:41	G DYER	4:45:41	G RAMSAY	4:46:35	G HOWARTH	4:47:23
16	S WILSON	4:43:48	P HOLMES	4:44:42	A MEADOWS	4:45:41	J LYNCH	4:46:36	C HAYDEN	4:47:24
17	J RUSSELL	4:43:48	J MARTIN	4:44:42	G CHEVILLON	4:45:42	M MACKAY	4:46:37	M SAGGS	4:47:26
18	G WAGNER	4:43:49	J GRUNDY	4:44:43	T RIDEOUT	4:45:43	J CRICK	4:46:37	M SYKES	4:47:28
19	J WRIGHT	4:43:49	M BLANCH	4:44:44	D RYDER	4:45:43	C PARKIN	4:46:38	R MOBSBY	4:47:29
20	C TINDALL	4:43:50	J JONES	4:44:44	R WARRILOW	4:45:44	G COOPER	4:46:38	B BARNETT	4:47:29
21	D RATTUE	4:43:51	J SELINGE	4:44:44	E GAMBLE	4:45:45	C MCNIELL	4:46:38	D DONOHOE	4:47:30
22	R SHARMAN	4:43:51	P VEYSSET	4:44:44	M CAMPBELL	4:45:46	M BRUCE	4:46:39	R OTTAWAY	4:47:31
23	L GUBBINS	4:43:51	V TAYLOR	4:44:45	J ALLEN	4:45:46	M ADDISON	4:46:39	P KING	4:47:32
24	A WAYNE	4:43:53	M SAYER	4:44:45	G DAVIES	4:45:47	M POWER	4:46:40	J PARISH	4:47:35
25	B DEAKIN	4:43:54	L HALPIN	4:44:45	J DUPREE	4:45:47	D CADBY	4:46:42	R GROVE	4:47:35
26	I BARNES	4:43:55	C HALPIN	4:44:46	C PURSER	4:45:48	K ALLARD	4:46:42	A BAKER	4:47:36
27	P TOWNSLEY	4:43:55	B GARNER	4:44:46	K BARNES	4:45:50	D MACKRILL	4:46:43	D MACE	4:47:36
28	B CAMPION	4:43:56	G EDWARDS	4:44:46	G MARTIN	4:45:50	I FERMOR	4:46:43	S DAVIES	4:47:36
29	S LOGUE	4:43:58	C PEARTON	4:44:46	J BALLIN	4:45:50	D COAKLEY	4:46:44	J PENKIN	4:47:36
30	B BLAKE	4:43:58	G SYME	4:44:48	G SUTCLIFFE	4:45:52	L FERMOR	4:46:44	J PENKIN	4:47:37
31	R DALLISON	4:44:00	K YAMADA	4:44:51	C MEACHIN	4:45:52	M GREENE	4:46:45	S BRETT	4:47:37
32	R JENKINS	4:44:00	T LAWRANCE	4:44:52	R FRAKE	4:45:52	P DAY	4:46:48	G RIZZO	4:47:37
33	D LAVAN	4:44:01	M BERRY	4:44:53	R MCGRATH	4:45:53	W FROST	4:46:48	M CRAWFORD	4:47:38
34	R BURNHAM	4:44:02	J KARNIEWICZ	4:44:54	J COWAN	4:45:53	B CHANDLER	4:46:49	D SHUCKSMITH	4:47:38
35	R DE SILVA	4:44:02	O BROWNE	4:44:54	A BRYANT	4:45:53	T NAGOSHI	4:46:49	D PARKER	4:47:38
36	D PATON	4:44:02	J SANCHIS	4:44:54	P JACKSON	4:45:53	G LITTLER	4:46:49	C BRASSINGTON	4:47:38
37	L CORDELL	4:44:03	B JORDI	4:44:54	D JACKSON	4:45:54	P ANTONIONI	4:46:49	V TARR	4:47:38
38	D SHARP	4:44:03	A BARTON	4:44:55	N BRAGGINS	4:45:55	D FANTUZZI	4:46:50	T DANIELS	4:47:38
39	T ALFORD	4:44:03	T HANSCOMB	4:44:56	E BROOKS	4:45:55	M BLACKMAN	4:46:50	S LATHAM	4:47:39
40	D BABU	4:44:03	G BRIERLEY	4:44:56	D BIRKS	4:45:55	R TAYLOR	4:46:51	T NICHOLSON	4:47:39
41	D KING	4:44:04	L DORAN	4:44:56	P THORN	4:45:55	A BLAKE	4:46:51	C GORDON	4:47:40
42	R SEGAAR	4:44:04	S MCCURDIE	4:44:57	R HARLE	4:45:56	S SHEARDEN	4:46:51	E KAYNE	4:47:40
43	P DRIES	4:44:04	D BANIN	4:44:57	P PARKIN	4:45:57	P CHAPMAN	4:46:51	C MATTHEWS	4:47:40
44	M HOLBERSON	4:44:05	P TACEY	4:44:57	M DUFFIN	4:45:57	G GARDINER	4:46:52	L NICHOLS	4:47:40
45	R DIMENT	4:44:05	I WILLIS	4:44:58	E HARLE	4:45:58	M WILLIAMS	4:46:52	R VERRALL	4:47:40
46	J BRYAN	4:44:05	V BETTS	4:44:58	M BROWN	4:45:59	G GOODALL	4:46:52	E PFEIFFER-REUTELER	4:47:40
47	C LLOYD	4:44:05	D CHURCHILL	4:44:58	D WHITE	4:45:59	D TOWNEND	4:46:52	D BANNER	4:47:41
48	M GARDINER	4:44:06	R PECH DE LACLAUSE	4:44:58	J CREED	4:45:59	D GAY	4:46:52	S COOPER	4:47:42
49	K SMITH	4:44:06	J DIVISIA	4:44:58	P WALKER	4:45:59	F ROBIN	4:46:52	G JONES	4:47:43
50	M TEELING	4:44:07	A GOURLAY	4:44:59	P LOVETT	4:45:59	R STANLEY	4:46:53	D O BRIEN	4:47:44
51	N RAZEY	4:44:07	A SANDERSON	4:45:00	M OUTHWAITE	4:45:59	C ABURN	4:46:54	J HANDS	4:47:44
52	E GUTTERIDGE	4:44:07	S WILLIAMS	4:45:00	C BOSWELL	4:45:59	D BAKER	4:46:55	I BROOK	4:47:44
53	M MARTIN	4:44:07	D GAIONI	4:45:00	G BONE	4:46:00	P FORSANS	4:46:56	U KATTAN	4:47:44
54	I SHARP	4:44:07	R PICKERING	4:45:01	R LAWRENCE	4:46:00	E HARPER	4:46:56	A GALER	4:47:44
55	C BUNCE	4:44:07	R EPSTEIN	4:45:01	J LUYA	4:46:00	P BROUGH	4:46:57	S RYAN	4:47:44
56	C BAILEY	4:44:07	S BROWN	4:45:04	J GREENWOOD	4:46:01	R CULLUM	4:46:58	A MOORE	4:47:44
57	R GUTTERIDGE	4:44:07	S WOODS	4:45:04	A TOVEY	4:46:01	P SUMMONS	4:46:59	S BUTLIN	4:47:44
58	K MILLER	4:44:07	J BARRASS	4:45:04	D JOHNSON	4:46:01	N BATCHELOR	4:47:00	W ANDREWS	4:47:44
59	N WILSON	4:44:07	A HEPPELL	4:45:04	R GAWLER	4:46:01	K LOMAS	4:47:00	A KHAN	4:47:44
60	C ANDERSON	4:44:08	A LUMB	4:45:04	K NEWBOULT	4:46:02	R LEE	4:47:01	A JAY	4:47:44
61	T HURRELL	4:44:09	K MORRIS	4:45:04	P NEARNEY	4:46:02	J MORGAN	4:47:02	M JAY	4:47:44
62	J BENTZEN	4:44:10	L NORDLUND	4:45:06	A EVANS	4:46:03	R HARPER	4:47:02	K ADLEM	4:47:44
63	A ALLEN	4:44:11	B NORDLUND	4:45:06	J RICHARDS	4:46:03	A DZIK-JURASZ	4:47:02	D STANDING	4:47:44
64	H BENJAMIN	4:44:13	J BROADBENT	4:45:07	N CROZIER	4:46:03	A EEK	4:47:03	M BURGES	4:47:44
65	P SNOOK	4:44:13	R VAN HOOF	4:45:07	R SAMBRIDGE	4:46:03	L HENSMAN	4:47:03	J MATTHEWS-STROUD	4:47:44
66	C DUNNE	4:44:15	J HUNTINGDON	4:45:09	P BROOME	4:46:03	R BARESCH	4:47:04	P KELLY	4:47:44
67	S ASHFORD	4:44:16	J HUGHES	4:45:10	K CAREY	4:46:06	M HALL	4:47:04	P BYRNE	4:47:44
68	M COULSON	4:44:18	W ARCHIBALD	4:45:10	H TALERMAN	4:46:08	D GILDER	4:47:05	D BURKE	4:47:44
69	M STEWART	4:44:18	B COSHALL	4:45:12	A PIPE	4:46:08	V BROWNETT	4:47:05	J WARING	4:47:44
70	D MALSAIT	4:44:20	J WILDMAN	4:45:14	P BUSH	4:46:08	D BRICKWOOD	4:47:05	T BROUT	4:47:44
71	S COLLINSON	4:44:20	A KING	4:45:14	I WATSON	4:46:09	G CLARK	4:47:06	J COUPE	4:47:44
72	S ROBINSON	4:44:22	L SHAW	4:45:15	D SHOEBRIDGE	4:46:10	J DOBSON	4:47:07	Y RAYNAL	4:47:45
73	G PHILLIPS	4:44:22	J PETERS	4:45:15	J RAISEN	4:46:10	M FISHER	4:47:08	J ROUGHLEY	4:47:45
74	B TAYLOR	4:44:22	A STANTON-PRECIOUS	4:45:15	R PHILLIPS	4:46:14	K WHITE	4:47:08	S HILL	4:47:48
75	S BENNETT	4:44:22	D KELLY	4:45:15	S HARRIS	4:46:15	J WEST	4:47:09	G HEWITT	4:47:49
76	S STEADMAN	4:44:23	W SLEIGHT	4:45:15	R OPIE	4:46:15	I MCELLIGOTT	4:47:10	J BAYLISS	4:47:50
77	L FALCONE	4:44:25	J SCOTCHER	4:45:15	S DONOVAN	4:46:15	G DALTON	4:47:10	M FREEMAN	4:47:52
78	A GOOD	4:44:25	D COSTER	4:45:15	A MEACHAM	4:46:16	D SWAIN	4:47:10	M WEBB	4:47:52
79	R BROWNE	4:44:25	G JEPSON	4:45:16	M WOODS	4:46:17	C TODD	4:47:10	S HARRIS	4:47:53
80	M PARKINS	4:44:25	M ROSE	4:45:16	Y ISHIGE	4:46:17	R CHURCHILL-COLEMAN	4:47:10	A RAYNER	4:47:55
81	H GRAHAM	4:44:25	N COSTER	4:45:17	K BENTLEY	4:46:17	I RANDHAWA	4:47:10	P DEACON	4:47:56
82	B PETTIFER	4:44:26	P SHREEVES	4:45:17	J CHANNON	4:46:21	J WILSON	4:47:10	J BECKETT	4:47:58
83	S JONES	4:44:27	P LAWRENCE	4:45:17	Y KAMINO	4:46:22	K SMART	4:47:10	D LAMBERT	4:47:58
84	P RYAN	4:44:28	A SPENCE	4:45:18	H WHITEMORE	4:46:22	A POTOCKI	4:47:12	S BHOLA	4:48:00
85	S ALLEN	4:44:28	B HOLLAND	4:45:19	D FRASER	4:46:22	A GAROLFI	4:47:13	K GERMAN	4:48:00
86	H VINE	4:44:28	M KYTE	4:45:19	S BARTLETT	4:46:22	R MATTHEWS	4:47:13	B LEGGETT	4:48:01
87	M MILLER	4:44:28	M GODSLAND	4:45:20	R OSBORNE	4:46:22	K DOWLEY	4:47:14	G STARKEY	4:48:02
88	B SMITH	4:44:30	J ASKEW	4:45:21	I STANTON	4:46:22	M FUTTIT	4:47:14	J SEEDS	4:48:02
89	D PETERS	4:44:32	K BENEST	4:45:23	E WILDMAN	4:46:22	N HOLLOWAY	4:47:14	S YULE	4:48:02
90	M EDWARDS	4:44:33	A SIMONS	4:45:24	P DAVIS	4:46:24	M TULLY	4:47:14	M MCCLELLAND	4:48:03
91	H LEWIS	4:44:33	L CORNO	4:45:24	A SLOMAN	4:46:26	C LAWS	4:47:15	N BEARD	4:48:03
92	D LIGHTFOOT	4:44:34	J ROLL	4:45:27	D ARMSTRONG	4:46:27	J GARNER	4:47:15	P TALBOT	4:48:04
93	M BOOCOCK	4:44:34	L BAKER	4:45:28	W STREVENS	4:46:27	F SIMMONS	4:47:16	G YULE	4:48:04
94	R NELSON	4:44:35	G MERLIN	4:45:28	M BARNETT	4:46:27	B CAHILL	4:47:17	K THEAKER	4:48:04
95	P BELL	4:44:35	P MATTHEWS	4:45:29	A SHEARER	4:46:28	J BAIN	4:47:17	N YOUNG	4:48:04
96	L HAWKSWORTH	4:44:35	SPENCER JONES	4:45:29	L TURNBULL	4:46:29	M DANIELS	4:47:17	B SMITH	4:48:05
97	J NICHOLLS	4:44:35	P DOYLE	4:45:29	J BLACKMAN	4:46:29	L KEIGHLEY	4:47:17	C BEUKES	4:48:05
98	I WILSON	4:44:36	R MARTIN	4:45:29	F COETZEE	4:46:30	J DAVEY	4:47:18	T ISHII	4:48:05
99	J HAIRE	4:44:36	B GODFREE	4:45:30	D BUTLER	4:46:30	J CROSBY	4:47:18	A FRANKS	4:48:05
100	C BURGER	4:44:36	D CLUNE	4:45:31	R KEMLO	4:46:30	S NEWTON	4:47:18	D GADD	4:48:05

#	20001-20100		20101-20200		20201-20300		20301-20400		20401-20500	
1	K SEKYERE	4:48:05	D JENKINS	4:49:04	R DOUGLAS	4:50:00	D TUCKEY	4:50:49	W MAIRS	4:51:47
2	I BOSLEY	4:48:05	R HINDE	4:49:05	J ROBERTS	4:50:00	S LAWRENCE	4:50:49	J CUDDY	4:51:47
3	P SPILLER	4:48:05	R GIBLEN	4:49:07	M RASMUSSEN	4:50:01	D LAWRENCE	4:50:49	C ADMAS	4:51:47
4	A POWELL-CHATFIELD	4:48:05	P KANE	4:49:08	M SHEPPARD	4:50:02	G FREEZER	4:50:49	N SLATER	4:51:48
5	S KRISTENSEN	4:48:06	M GALE	4:49:09	G DAWSON	4:50:03	N GILMER	4:50:49	D CLIFTON	4:51:49
6	D HUBBLE	4:48:06	I CROXFORD	4:49:09	B DASCOMBE	4:50:03	J TREMAYNE	4:50:51	L BALFOUR	4:51:49
7	J CATEL	4:48:07	D HACK	4:49:11	S MORRISSEY	4:50:03	N THORP	4:50:51	H ROBERTS	4:51:50
8	C HOLLINGSWORTH	4:48:13	R DAVIS	4:49:11	H BLADT	4:50:03	J GOODCHILD	4:50:51	B ANEX	4:51:51
9	N BROWN	4:48:14	M EVANS	4:49:11	L MCLOUGHLIN	4:50:04	M FIELD	4:50:52	S QURESHI	4:51:52
10	B WEBB	4:48:16	L FOX	4:49:13	E MARTIN	4:50:04	A O'RAWE	4:50:53	P MURPHY	4:51:52
11	L LINNETT	4:48:16	F PHILO	4:49:13	G WATT	4:50:04	G HOLDEN	4:50:54	S JENNINGS	4:51:52
12	M KATZ	4:48:16	B WILLIAMS	4:49:14	J LINK	4:50:05	J MORRIS	4:50:54	R DEAN	4:51:52
13	J HADDON	4:48:19	M TODD	4:49:14	J REARDON	4:50:05	A MAY	4:50:56	W SYER	4:51:53
14	D COATES	4:48:19	V BARRETT	4:49:14	S CLEMENTS	4:50:05	J JACKSON	4:50:56	S MCCARTY	4:51:53
15	G CARRATT	4:48:19	G BENNETT	4:49:14	Y HISADA	4:50:06	J SPALL	4:50:56	T BIGGS	4:51:54
16	T WINSHIP	4:48:21	E KEAN	4:49:15	P WHITE	4:50:07	R BUTCHER	4:50:57	J ROGERS	4:51:54
17	R WILKINSON	4:48:22	A HESTER	4:49:16	M ARENDS	4:50:07	M PARDOE	4:50:57	M GILBERT	4:51:54
18	P PEARCE	4:48:23	D HESTER	4:49:16	M WILLIAMS	4:50:08	A WORMAN	4:50:57	B WATMORE	4:51:54
19	D SURRIDGE	4:48:24	D ROBERTS	4:49:16	A REES	4:50:08	G BLAKE	4:50:57	C BAILEY	4:51:55
20	B WOLFSON	4:48:24	R MAYO	4:49:16	T COLCOMBE	4:50:08	M BURCHETT	4:50:58	O SAFA	4:51:55
21	S GARDENER	4:48:25	B MARABELLE	4:49:17	S PARKINSON	4:50:08	C TOWNLEY-RIVETT	4:50:59	A FARRINGTON	4:51:56
22	B JONES	4:48:25	D PENMAN	4:49:18	I SUNTER	4:50:09	P BUDDEN	4:50:59	F HAVERTY	4:51:56
23	J CHURCH	4:48:25	S DEAR	4:49:18	A BURN	4:50:09	D CRAWFORD	4:51:03	N MORGAN	4:51:56
24	M DECASTRO	4:48:26	T GADENNE	4:49:18	N ELLINOR	4:50:10	I MASON	4:51:03	K PARKER	4:51:56
25	E LEE	4:48:26	A HUBBARD	4:49:19	W DEVINE	4:50:10	R RYAN	4:51:04	K POOKE	4:51:56
26	C DENNY	4:48:26	R FAWTHROP	4:49:20	P FLAHERTY	4:50:11	P ZABINSKI	4:51:05	J TAYLOR	4:51:56
27	H KAHRS	4:48:26	J BALLINGER	4:49:20	A FLAHERTY	4:50:11	M SMALL	4:51:05	M RYAN	4:51:56
28	J WELLS	4:48:27	N COCKCROFT	4:49:21	R GRIFFITHS	4:50:11	L WELSFORD	4:51:05	D SMITH	4:51:58
29	S DAWETT	4:48:27	R BRINKLOW	4:49:21	B ONEILL	4:50:11	A GILLESPIE	4:51:05	C STYLES	4:52:00
30	N LEE	4:48:27	S LAWRIE	4:49:22	G BROWN	4:50:12	A STAVELY	4:51:08	B BOEKBINDER	4:52:01
31	S WILLIAMS-GARDNER	4:48:28	M WOOD	4:49:22	K REVILL	4:50:15	S OXLEY	4:51:08	G ROADKNIGHT	4:52:02
32	J DEW	4:48:28	B MOSS	4:49:22	T JONES	4:50:16	A RYLE	4:51:08	C TUCKER	4:52:05
33	R OMAHONEY	4:48:28	D KERRY	4:49:26	G BENSON	4:50:16	M HALL	4:51:09	G THEOCHAROUS	4:52:06
34	S PEARCE	4:48:28	A WELLS	4:49:26	M MCCAFFREY	4:50:16	J NEWDICK	4:51:10	A PRITCHARD	4:52:06
35	K ARTHUR	4:48:29	T GEORGE	4:49:27	I THOMSON	4:50:17	D OXENHAM	4:51:11	A OAKES	4:52:07
36	P HARGREAVES	4:48:29	J DONALDSON	4:49:27	M COLLINS	4:50:17	A MCDONALD-LIGGINS	4:51:12	R OATES	4:52:07
37	D OWEN	4:48:30	B HARRISON-JENNINGS	4:49:28	A CARRINGTON	4:50:18	M RICHARDS	4:51:13	S THORNTON	4:52:08
38	P WOOD	4:48:30	R SWINNEY	4:49:28	R DAVISON	4:50:19	K COWELL	4:51:15	J MURPHY	4:52:08
39	C WEBSTER	4:48:30	M SANFORD	4:49:28	R LOADER	4:50:21	M TAYLOR	4:51:16	P LITHERLAND	4:52:08
40	G MARTIN	4:48:30	R SMITH	4:49:29	N BUSSA	4:50:21	J ROBERTS	4:51:16	R DIMMICK	4:52:08
41	D TALBOT	4:48:30	C MCDONALD	4:49:29	A QUY	4:50:21	H GRAYSTON	4:51:17	G MCKENZIE-BELL	4:52:09
42	P ZOLFAGHARI	4:48:30	A DAVIES	4:49:29	T TUOMINEN	4:50:21	C LEE	4:51:18	J CERDO	4:52:09
43	M HADLEY	4:48:30	J ASTLEY	4:49:31	G LOCKE	4:50:21	A LIGHT	4:51:18	M QYIRK	4:52:09
44	C NEWELL	4:48:31	J HANLON	4:49:32	F MUSIELLO	4:50:23	M WARE	4:51:18	J MCGUIRE	4:52:10
45	A MCDONALD	4:48:31	A KIDBY	4:49:32	J BARKER	4:50:23	D FIELD	4:51:18	A MARSH	4:52:10
46	J DANTON-REES	4:48:31	A THOMPSON	4:49:33	K BUCHAN	4:50:23	R CLOUGH	4:51:18	M THOMAS	4:52:10
47	P LEYLAND	4:48:31	K LUMSDEN	4:49:33	R PAVITT	4:50:23	B TURNER	4:51:18	K MANN	4:52:11
48	M BYROM	4:48:31	P BAKER	4:49:33	T STEPHENS	4:50:24	K O'BRIEN	4:51:18	O NYSTROM	4:52:12
49	M ARMITAGE	4:48:31	S CUSHING	4:49:33	G NORCOTT	4:50:24	A FORD	4:51:19	J TORDO	4:52:12
50	D TURNER	4:48:31	P HIGGS	4:49:33	J STEWART	4:50:24	R BURFORD	4:51:19	A JOHNSON	4:52:12
51	G COLEMAN	4:48:33	P HOLDER	4:49:33	L POND	4:50:24	A HUTCHINSON	4:51:21	E THILLIER	4:52:16
52	G TALLENTS	4:48:33	R NELSON	4:49:33	P EVANS	4:50:25	R DENHAM	4:51:21	S WILLIAMS	4:52:18
53	J BALCHIN	4:48:33	M RATTLEY	4:49:33	L TRAILOR	4:50:25	J MANSFIELD	4:51:21	R TURNER	4:52:18
54	P PREMA	4:48:35	K SMITH	4:49:33	J DYER	4:50:25	J CLARKSON	4:51:23	R BERWICK	4:52:18
55	C GRAINGER	4:48:35	B WATSON	4:49:35	R SHADWELL	4:50:26	S LABRUM	4:51:23	G LEWIS	4:52:22
56	T PAPE	4:48:35	C SMITH	4:49:35	B LAMBERT	4:50:26	N WATTS	4:51:23	S COLEMAN	4:52:22
57	S HEINIGER	4:48:35	M KINGETT	4:49:37	M SPARGO	4:50:26	M BATES	4:51:24	K CRAGG	4:52:22
58	L GREEN	4:48:35	T BRADFIELD	4:49:37	S EVANS	4:50:26	T FREEMAN	4:51:25	R TUFFNELL	4:52:22
59	P WOOLSTON	4:48:35	A ROWDEN	4:49:38	G PAOLUCCI	4:50:26	G MAHER	4:51:25	K FLETCHER	4:52:22
60	T IKOLI	4:48:35	P MC WEENEY	4:49:39	P DE ROSA	4:50:26	A HACHIYA	4:51:26	T WAIN	4:52:22
61	J SMALL	4:48:36	T DUNOUCHEL	4:49:40	P GRUNDY	4:50:28	S GRYLLS	4:51:27	P ASHBOURNE	4:52:22
62	A KLINGESPOR	4:48:36	J GILSON	4:49:40	B ROSSET	4:50:28	S RANDALL	4:51:28	S KNIGHTS	4:52:22
63	F WRIGHT	4:48:37	H DYSON	4:49:40	L MCNEEL	4:50:29	P CARTER	4:51:28	I MARCOUL	4:52:23
64	R VALOPPI	4:48:38	C CHAPELL	4:49:40	A FLATLEY	4:50:29	S YEUNG	4:51:28	J EASTER	4:52:25
65	L WRIGHT	4:48:39	P SMITH	4:49:40	J VAN VLIET	4:50:30	J KAUFMAN	4:51:28	M PEDDER	4:52:26
66	N SIMPSON	4:48:43	J BUTCHER	4:49:40	H OWEN	4:50:31	D BAILEY	4:51:29	I MCDOUGALL	4:52:27
67	L ORBIN	4:48:48	D MACDERMOT	4:49:40	G SCOTT	4:50:33	T LAWLESS	4:51:30	D CROWTHER	4:52:27
68	V DERUSSY	4:48:48	J HALL	4:49:41	J BREAKS	4:50:34	P JONES	4:51:30	B BLUNDELL	4:52:28
69	M CLARE	4:48:48	S ASPINALL	4:49:43	A SNOAD	4:50:34	R STOKER	4:51:30	P BRAZIER	4:52:30
70	B WALKER	4:48:48	R GRIFFITH	4:49:43	S SCOTT	4:50:36	S THOMAS	4:51:30	D LYDON	4:52:32
71	T BUTLER	4:48:48	J BAERISWYL	4:49:44	D WHIPP	4:50:36	R KNOWLES	4:51:31	P CROSKERRY	4:52:32
72	H DHILLON	4:48:50	M BRAUND	4:49:45	M OSBORNE	4:50:36	S THOMPSON	4:51:32	J WILLCOX	4:52:33
73	B BOND	4:48:50	D ROBERTS	4:49:45	J CROMPTON	4:50:37	H STEINER	4:51:32	R WALL	4:52:35
74	A MCCLELLAND	4:48:51	J HARRIS	4:49:46	K BROOM	4:50:37	L TEMPEST	4:51:34	M BROMAGE	4:52:36
75	O GRAHAM	4:48:51	R BOREHAM	4:49:47	B ONEILL	4:50:37	P WILLIAMSON	4:51:34	J MORRISON	4:52:36
76	M SMITH	4:48:51	A DEARSON	4:49:47	N ENTWISTLE	4:50:37	M STATTERS	4:51:34	A FOX	4:52:37
77	N BENNETT	4:48:52	E CLARKE	4:49:47	E SKIDMORE	4:50:37	G GILBERT	4:51:35	P GANGE	4:52:37
78	S SAMPSON	4:48:52	M DODDS	4:49:51	P HEWETT	4:50:37	N PENNY	4:51:36	A REGAN	4:52:39
79	J POWLES	4:48:52	M PIPER	4:49:51	T COLLINS	4:50:37	P THOMSON	4:51:36	J BOX	4:52:41
80	A NICOL	4:48:53	B SMITH	4:49:52	U ST JOHN	4:50:38	J ARNOLD	4:51:36	S DAVISON	4:52:42
81	R HAMILTON	4:48:53	T KERR	4:49:53	K MATTHEWS	4:50:38	P GOURDON	4:51:37	J PRUVOT	4:52:44
82	A BOWLES	4:48:53	D BOULTER	4:49:53	D BURGESS	4:50:39	P BURGESS	4:51:38	I MATCHAM	4:52:45
83	A FENOGLIO	4:48:53	M BROOKER	4:49:55	W PECK	4:50:39	J MARGOLIN	4:51:39	L MALKIN	4:52:45
84	B GOOSSENS	4:48:53	A MAVROMOUSTAKIS	4:49:55	K KRZEMINSKI	4:50:40	C FISHER	4:51:40	D GOULD	4:52:47
85	E BLAKIE	4:48:54	P GRAY	4:49:55	J SUMMERS	4:50:41	B IDDLES	4:51:40	P WAKEFORD	4:52:47
86	F HADERER	4:48:54	M FOAT	4:49:55	A DORMAN	4:50:45	P VAN UCHELEN	4:51:41	B BALDWIN	4:52:49
87	T BLISSETT	4:48:55	J WOODS	4:49:56	G THOMAS	4:50:45	R WANDS	4:51:43	S CLOWRY	4:52:49
88	A RIGG	4:48:55	R HUGHES	4:49:56	T SINCLAIR	4:50:45	M WHEATON	4:51:43	J KIRKWOOD	4:52:49
89	R FELLOWS	4:48:55	M CARVER	4:49:56	A NIX	4:50:45	M DI MICCO	4:51:43	J STANYON	4:52:51
90	S HERCOCK	4:48:56	G DANIELS	4:49:56	L EZZIDIO	4:50:45	D LEDLIE	4:51:43	E NOKES	4:52:51
91	P BRAID	4:48:57	B EDWARDS	4:49:56	J HOHENBERG	4:50:45	P RILEY	4:51:43	A HIRST	4:52:52
92	H BRAITHWAITE	4:48:58	B POWELL	4:49:57	J SMITHERS	4:50:45	M KITCHER	4:51:44	J CLOUSTON	4:52:53
93	R LEONARD	4:48:58	R HOUSE	4:49:58	G BAILEY	4:50:45	S DAWSON	4:51:44	S PERRAULT	4:52:55
94	G WIMBLETON	4:48:59	M CALVERT	4:49:58	P HIGGINS	4:50:46	A RILEY	4:51:44	B UTTRIDGE	4:52:56
95	P LANE	4:49:00	H BOS	4:49:58	I HOMER	4:50:46	J CRYAN	4:51:45	C MCWATT-GREEN	4:52:56
96	A JENKINS	4:49:00	S BUSH	4:49:58	M SINTON	4:50:47	N HUGHES	4:51:45	A STANDISH	4:52:56
97	M CAPS	4:49:00	T STANDING	4:49:59	E HERSCHENFELD	4:50:48	N EMERY	4:51:45	W COTSFORD	4:52:56
98	C WHITE	4:49:01	J HERVE	4:49:59	P MCGRORY	4:50:48	T MAULE	4:51:46	J PICKARD	4:52:56
99	J FLYNN	4:49:03	R PIROUX	4:49:59	C DRAKE	4:50:48	S MURRAY	4:51:46	J MCKEAG	4:52:56
100	N RUTHERFORD	4:49:03	L O'TOOLE	4:50:00	R HARDING	4:50:48	S CUDDY	4:51:47	A LEAK	4:52:56

	20501-20600		20601-20700		20701-20800		20801-20900		20901-21000	
1	R CLARKE	4:52:57	W POOLE	4:54:03	V SZEKERES	4:54:53	M JOHNSON	4:55:52	W OAKES	4:56:51
2	C LEWIN	4:52:57	J SHAW	4:54:04	B DAVEY	4:54:55	P SMITH	4:55:52	E PARI	4:56:51
3	M KENEALY	4:52:58	J ASHTON	4:54:05	E HOPKINS	4:54:56	T HAWE	4:55:54	G BISOGNANI	4:56:52
4	G LOCK	4:52:59	M TRACZYK	4:54:05	E GALLIMORE	4:54:56	J WILKINSON	4:55:54	G PORTER	4:56:52
5	D VINCENT	4:52:59	J PATIS	4:54:08	H FARROW	4:54:56	A SUTTON	4:55:55	D HOLMES	4:56:52
6	R STRINGER	4:53:00	A HOWLETT	4:54:08	M RAYNER	4:54:56	A PARKER	4:55:56	K PORTLAND	4:56:52
7	P COCKLIN	4:53:00	R BUNN	4:54:08	J BEAUMONT	4:54:57	C UNWIN	4:55:58	B CHATTERTON	4:56:52
8	M BELL	4:53:00	F MACINTOSH	4:54:08	G HEELER	4:54:58	V SMITH	4:55:58	A HARRIS	4:56:52
9	T ATKINSON	4:53:00	A SAMMONS	4:54:09	R GOUGH	4:54:58	D CONGREVE	4:55:58	G WALL	4:56:52
10	D JONES	4:53:00	T LEE	4:54:09	S OBRIEN	4:54:58	M O'SULLIVAN	4:55:59	D HORN	4:56:53
11	A PEARCE	4:53:00	E CORMICAN	4:54:11	M HOLWILL	4:54:59	D BUTLER	4:55:59	P LONG	4:56:53
12	S PORTWOOD	4:53:00	A JAMES	4:54:11	A FURNIVAL	4:55:01	M STEVENSON	4:55:59	A BOND	4:56:53
13	S WINDLE	4:53:01	S COTTAGE	4:54:12	B JOHNSON	4:55:01	K FLETCHER	4:56:00	A SECKINGTON	4:56:53
14	S COCKSHULL	4:53:01	A RIORDAN	4:54:12	L BROOKE	4:55:02	R DREW	4:56:00	J SECKINGTON	4:56:53
15	T BURDIN	4:53:05	R IREDALE	4:54:12	J BAKER	4:55:02	G BEALES	4:56:01	J CLARKE	4:56:53
16	K FISHER	4:53:05	J SAUNDERS	4:54:12	M FIRMIN	4:55:03	P WILMORE	4:56:02	W GRACE	4:56:53
17	R RICHARDS	4:53:06	R BEASLEY	4:54:13	J HILLABY	4:55:04	P ROSS	4:56:03	U THURM	4:56:53
18	R CLYDESDALE	4:53:06	M LEWIN	4:54:13	P MILES	4:55:04	D LEGGETT	4:56:03	R JONES	4:56:54
19	N KARONIAS	4:53:07	D FORBES	4:54:15	A HOOKER	4:55:04	F CASTRO	4:56:03	R ADAMS	4:56:55
20	N CLARKE	4:53:08	H KLEIN	4:54:15	P EDWARDS	4:55:06	S CASTRO	4:56:03	H BENNETT	4:56:56
21	T MIDDLETON	4:53:09	D NICHOLS	4:54:15	N KUMAR	4:55:06	A WILKINSON	4:56:04	D JONES	4:56:57
22	R NICHOLLS	4:53:12	A ALATI	4:54:16	P KENNY	4:55:06	S BERTONI	4:56:04	K SMITH	4:56:57
23	J TIPPING	4:53:14	W ROFFEY	4:54:16	B WILLS	4:55:06	L MORTLOCK	4:56:04	J WARDLAW	4:56:58
24	D ELLAM	4:53:14	T ROFFEY	4:54:16	S HUTCHISON	4:55:06	J STANTON	4:56:05	C MARTIN	4:56:59
25	J TEELUCK	4:53:15	K MOONEY	4:54:16	A MAIDEN	4:55:06	R ATKINSON	4:56:06	K ONIONS	4:57:00
26	S DROWLEY	4:53:15	G RUSSELL	4:54:17	M THOMSON	4:55:07	A PARSONS	4:56:06	J BARBOUR	4:57:02
27	A HOLTON	4:53:16	S THURLEY	4:54:17	A YEUNG	4:55:08	D FRANCIS	4:56:06	R STAMP	4:57:03
28	P TRACEY	4:53:17	J MCKENZIE	4:54:18	O TJELDFLAAT	4:55:10	A BROOKER	4:56:07	M SNOW	4:57:04
29	R MARK	4:53:17	M CHAMPNESS	4:54:20	G O'LEARY	4:55:10	W KENDALL	4:56:10	M VENUS	4:57:04
30	A BLAGG	4:53:17	G ALMOND	4:54:21	C HOPKINS	4:55:10	K HEWITT	4:56:10	I ROSE	4:57:04
31	W MARTIN	4:53:18	C HALE	4:54:22	F LEVINSON	4:55:11	I LA VALETTE	4:56:11	A BUNBURY	4:57:05
32	S MORSE	4:53:18	F BONTOFT	4:54:22	A ALFORD	4:55:12	K MORTON	4:56:12	N OLIVER	4:57:05
33	D TURTLE	4:53:19	M COOPER	4:54:22	R STRACHAN	4:55:13	R JOHNSON	4:56:13	A COOK	4:57:05
34	M OLSSON	4:53:20	M EVERISS	4:54:22	J REBBECK	4:55:14	A MOY	4:56:13	D SMITH	4:57:06
35	J HATELEY	4:53:21	B HERRICK	4:54:23	D PIERCE	4:55:14	D CORNHILL	4:56:14	J VAN DEN BERGH	4:57:06
36	P MORLEY	4:53:24	D COWLEY	4:54:24	C PRATTY	4:55:14	D PITT	4:56:16	K GRIFFTIHS	4:57:06
37	D PRICE	4:53:24	J HOLLAND	4:54:24	S PRATTY	4:55:14	F UOPI	4:56:16	T TYRIDAL	4:57:06
38	K DOLBY	4:53:26	P VOLA	4:54:25	L BAYFIELD	4:55:14	G HADLEY	4:56:17	D RICHARDS	4:57:06
39	S FINNEY	4:53:26	M DAWKINS	4:54:26	J HOLT	4:55:14	R SCANES	4:56:18	B DARLEY	4:57:07
40	A ERIKSON	4:53:26	J BROADWAY	4:54:26	P FAGER	4:55:15	M CRAWLEY	4:56:18	A TINKLER	4:57:07
41	K PEACOCK	4:53:26	V MULLETT	4:54:26	T MORGAN	4:55:17	A BARLEY	4:56:18	W MACDONALD	4:57:07
42	M SYMONS	4:53:27	A DALE	4:54:27	G HIMS	4:55:19	F WESTERHOLM	4:56:19	R MOULDING	4:57:07
43	P EDWARDS	4:53:27	C ALLEN	4:54:27	A CLIFT	4:55:19	J CONLEY	4:56:19	R LAWS	4:57:08
44	J KETT	4:53:27	A COOTES	4:54:30	K BASSETT	4:55:19	S HARDIE	4:56:20	R SHEPHERD	4:57:08
45	R DITCHFIELD	4:53:28	D BANCROFT	4:54:30	K LIDLOW	4:55:20	R HOGENDOORN	4:56:22	J MOUNTFORD	4:57:08
46	D FISHER	4:53:28	C BLACK	4:54:30	M NORTH	4:55:20	J WATTS	4:56:22	J JOHN	4:57:08
47	R STATON	4:53:29	I BOYD	4:54:31	M WHITWORTH	4:55:21	W FLEMING	4:56:23	J TRINCKAUF	4:57:08
48	D COX	4:53:29	A MITCHELL	4:54:31	T BARRINGTON	4:55:21	M BENNETT	4:56:23	D MATTHEW	4:57:09
49	J COLLINGS	4:53:30	F GRIFFITHS	4:54:31	S FOXCROFT	4:55:21	N COOTE	4:56:24	G DONOVAN	4:57:09
50	M CRUMP	4:53:32	J SMITH	4:54:31	G DOOLEY	4:55:22	R GRAY	4:56:24	N CHRISTIE	4:57:09
51	M SCANLON	4:53:33	M STARKEY	4:54:32	J FARR	4:55:23	J DAGUES	4:56:25	J EVERETT	4:57:09
52	L BANCHETTI	4:53:34	B FLETCHER	4:54:33	A CAPPLEN	4:55:23	A NANNERY	4:56:25	J DENNESS	4:57:09
53	S CLIFFORD	4:53:35	A MOGG	4:54:34	P OLSON	4:55:23	M AU-YEUNG	4:56:26	J WAREHAM	4:57:10
54	J MOWBRAY	4:53:35	P BALDWIN	4:54:35	L FAZACKERLEY	4:55:25	J GASCOIGNE	4:56:26	T PAGE	4:57:11
55	S WRIGHT	4:53:38	K BROOKS	4:54:35	K LING	4:55:26	J ROBERTSON	4:56:27	P EVANS	4:57:11
56	S SABATING	4:53:38	D JONES	4:54:35	W SCHINDLER	4:55:27	P TOUHEY	4:56:27	A BROOKER	4:57:11
57	D COTTON	4:53:39	A PAWSON	4:54:35	D HEYS	4:55:27	P KEARS	4:56:28	M WALSH	4:57:12
58	R LE-BIHAN	4:53:39	A PRIDELL	4:54:37	A WILSON	4:55:28	C GRADWELL	4:56:28	P HOLMES	4:57:12
59	D CHAPPLE	4:53:39	A BUTLER	4:54:37	R TREWHELLA	4:55:28	J CLARKE	4:56:28	N LEFEBVRE	4:57:13
60	N VAN DER BORGH	4:53:40	C HOCKING	4:54:37	S SPINKS	4:55:28	P WHITE	4:56:28	C OREGAN	4:57:15
61	T PRIOR	4:53:40	W COWLEY	4:54:38	R FLINTHAM	4:55:28	M HARWOOD	4:56:29	J SMITH	4:57:15
62	M JACKSON	4:53:40	B NYHOLT	4:54:39	V LONG	4:55:28	N HODGES	4:56:30	G SVENPELT	4:57:15
63	A CAMINADA	4:53:42	A CLARK	4:54:39	J DRUMMOND	4:55:29	I GRIMES	4:56:30	H HORGAN	4:57:15
64	C MILES	4:53:43	T IRISH	4:54:39	J HEALES	4:55:29	C PLAICE	4:56:30	M BRITTON	4:57:16
65	M MCLEMAN	4:53:43	S RUTHERFORD	4:54:40	A STOTT	4:55:29	R LAMBERT	4:56:30	D FARR	4:57:17
66	R LAMB	4:53:43	M WELCH	4:54:40	M MOON	4:55:30	T SHEPHARD	4:56:30	G BULGER	4:57:18
67	J ASHTON	4:53:44	H LYNCH	4:54:40	M HUNT	4:55:31	H EDWARDS	4:56:30	A SMITH	4:57:18
68	D HADDEN	4:53:45	J FOURIE	4:54:40	R DUENGEN	4:55:31	J MCCORMICK	4:56:30	M BRAZIER	4:57:19
69	L WRAY	4:53:45	G WELCH	4:54:41	E LUMMIS	4:55:31	M ADOFACI	4:56:30	J BENNETT	4:57:19
70	P BRIEN	4:53:45	D HALL	4:54:41	S KAMICHI	4:55:33	A GREEN	4:56:31	J TUNNICLIFFE	4:57:20
71	G HAYWARD	4:53:46	W BLONDEEL	4:54:42	J LEOST	4:55:33	C HOWLE	4:56:31	W HOLDERNESS	4:57:21
72	D BODEY	4:53:48	M CHARLES	4:54:42	J OWEN-BROWNE	4:55:34	P GEANEY	4:56:31	G MILLS	4:57:23
73	Y SHAYLER	4:53:48	J HART	4:54:42	C COOPER	4:55:34	J MELLON	4:56:32	M PFEIFFER	4:57:23
74	K RATTLE	4:53:48	J OGLIVIE	4:54:42	G EYLES	4:55:34	S QUEST	4:56:34	D PATEL	4:57:23
75	A HEMS	4:53:49	K BELL	4:54:42	C HUGHES	4:55:35	E NOBLE	4:56:34	J BENSON	4:57:23
76	D SMITH	4:53:49	E SANDERSON	4:54:43	P OUVRARD	4:55:35	S BUDD	4:56:35	C ALLARD	4:57:23
77	J MANSFIELD	4:53:50	A PIGRAM	4:54:43	D HILTON	4:55:38	M MCLAUGHLIN	4:56:36	P BUTLER	4:57:24
78	G SLADE	4:53:50	C DICKINSON	4:54:44	M HATCH	4:55:38	E SAUNDERS	4:56:37	P MUNRO	4:57:25
79	C WILLIAMS	4:53:50	M BROWN	4:54:44	S BAYFORD	4:55:39	J COUNSELL	4:56:37	R TOPHAM	4:57:27
80	Y WATERHOUSE	4:53:52	J MESTON	4:54:44	M READING	4:55:40	R TAYLOR	4:56:39	L DIMALINE	4:57:30
81	R JOYCE	4:53:52	J ABBOTT	4:54:44	G KNIGHTS	4:55:42	L HILL	4:56:40	S DODDINGTON	4:57:30
82	W BATCHELOR	4:53:53	M BAILEY	4:54:44	V PAINE	4:55:43	N SPILLER	4:56:40	A CASCIELLO	4:57:30
83	D MASON	4:53:54	J TAYLOR	4:54:44	S HILL	4:55:44	T ROBERTS	4:56:40	S QUINLIUAN	4:57:33
84	L WRIGHT	4:53:54	J BANKS	4:54:45	S GRANT	4:55:44	J TAYLOR	4:56:41	R ANDERSON	4:57:35
85	J SHARRATT	4:53:54	M BLACKBURN	4:54:45	J PORT	4:55:44	M CLARK	4:56:42	R PALMER	4:57:35
86	M HEWSON	4:53:54	R SKOYLES	4:54:45	K GREEN	4:55:44	S TAYLOR	4:56:42	S LITTLE	4:57:36
87	M POWER	4:53:55	T ONO	4:54:46	L HELGESSON	4:55:44	A ASTINGTON	4:56:42	T MCBRIEN	4:57:36
88	K QUINN	4:53:55	A LINDMAN	4:54:48	S TIMOTHY	4:55:44	M SINCLAIR	4:56:42	A NEWMAN	4:57:37
89	D WHITEHEAD	4:53:56	A WEBB	4:54:48	L THARP	4:55:44	M WADDINGTON	4:56:43	N SEAWARD	4:57:38
90	S RICHARDSON	4:53:56	D LYONS	4:54:49	S MOE	4:55:45	D SARGEANT	4:56:43	S WYNNE	4:57:38
91	P NIXSON	4:53:57	J EDGELLER	4:54:49	A PEGLEY	4:55:45	B HUNTER	4:56:44	D SMITH	4:57:40
92	J MOFFAT	4:53:58	J SELLARS	4:54:49	M MORGAN	4:55:45	M ROSSER	4:56:44	V LEWIS	4:57:41
93	D MERRETT	4:53:59	J HOLMES	4:54:49	T BUCKLEY	4:55:46	T HILL	4:56:45	R REES	4:57:41
94	M BEER	4:53:59	S COULT	4:54:49	A STANLEY	4:55:46	K SALVIDGE	4:56:45	B GOUGH	4:57:43
95	R GOLDUP	4:54:01	S BUSHILL	4:54:49	M MAXWELL	4:55:48	P EISENHARDT	4:56:47	N GIESELER	4:57:43
96	S KEYTE	4:54:01	C WEST	4:54:50	G MORRIS	4:55:48	P HOLLAND	4:56:49	C BUSHELL	4:57:43
97	A MOSS	4:54:02	J SIMON	4:54:51	G SCANLON	4:55:49	S KNOTT	4:56:49	M SANSOM	4:57:43
98	N DAVIES	4:54:02	S SLINN	4:54:52	G GREEN	4:55:51	V BARLEY	4:56:49	P BRIDGEWATER	4:57:45
99	S LEVENE	4:54:03	R ARMSTRONG	4:54:52	B MIRAMS	4:55:51	V ASHTON	4:56:49	P GODDARD	4:57:45
100	K ALLEN	4:54:03	S HODGSON	4:54:52	A FRANK	4:55:51	A OLIVER	4:56:50	J PENNELL	4:57:45

#	21001-21100		21101-21200		21201-21300		21301-21400		21401-21500	
1	A DAVIS	4:57:46	A HOLLAND	4:58:42	E KAYE	4:59:36	J UNSWORTH	5:00:22	S HYLAND	5:01:22
2	D DALTREY	4:57:46	R BERREEN	4:58:42	R FOOT	4:59:36	N FLINT	5:00:22	D JOHNSON	5:01:24
3	M LOFTING	4:57:47	K JONES	4:58:42	P DUTSON	4:59:36	S BROWNER	5:00:23	S ENEVER	5:01:24
4	A MANN	4:57:47	N HEISSAT	4:58:42	T LEDGER	4:59:36	K GREGORY	5:00:23	B SYLVESTER	5:01:25
5	D HILL	4:57:48	R DAVEY	4:58:42	F SUSSEX	4:59:36	D EXALL	5:00:23	S GIBSON	5:01:26
6	M BURRELL	4:57:48	H WILLIAMS	4:58:43	P COLEMAN	4:59:38	J HOWE	5:00:25	D MCCARTHY	5:01:26
7	I WARD	4:57:48	D HODGE	4:58:44	M DICKER	4:59:38	J BAGLEY	5:00:25	M WILKINSON	5:01:27
8	D MELESSACCIO	4:57:49	J BILL	4:58:45	C MATHER	4:59:38	R BLAND	5:00:26	A WILLIS	5:01:27
9	E HANSEN	4:57:50	P COLLISON	4:58:46	P BISHOP	4:59:38	M MARSH	5:00:27	D CLARK	5:01:27
10	J DRENNAN	4:57:50	J CROOK	4:58:46	C LLOYD	4:59:38	H JONES	5:00:27	J BRYANT	5:01:28
11	N ASQUITH	4:57:50	J HARVEY	4:58:48	A COX	4:59:38	J WHITE	5:00:28	G SMITH	5:01:28
12	A PRITCHETT	4:57:51	K BOOTH	4:58:48	A WELDON	4:59:38	D TILLEY	5:00:28	K CHORLEY	5:01:28
13	G FIRTH	4:57:52	B TEASDALE	4:58:48	D GIBSON	4:59:38	S HYDE	5:00:29	J MONCUR	5:01:28
14	R BROWNE	4:57:52	W HOWARD	4:58:48	A VAUGHAN	4:59:39	R BLOGG	5:00:29	L PARTRIDGE	5:01:29
15	G REGALIA	4:57:52	S OLDRIDGE	4:58:48	G JOHNSON	4:59:41	B STEWART	5:00:30	M WILLIAMS	5:01:29
16	G BRAYBROOK	4:57:52	K BELL	4:58:49	R LYNCH	4:59:41	M ELLIOTT	5:00:30	J REAH	5:01:29
17	J WEBSTER	4:57:52	J WHITE	4:58:49	J GARVEY	4:59:42	A KNIGHT	5:00:30	A KINGSTON	5:01:29
18	D WALTON	4:57:52	S WAGSTAFF	4:58:49	M PARK	4:59:42	J PFISTER	5:00:30	M LINDSAY	5:01:30
19	D WHEATON	4:57:52	M COURTMAN	4:58:49	P BARBER	4:59:42	P HYLAND	5:00:30	A GREALISH	5:01:30
20	C STEVENSON	4:57:53	M PEREIRA	4:58:50	G PETTIT	4:59:43	A WILLIS	5:00:30	J THOMSON	5:01:30
21	D LIGGETT	4:57:53	S POOLE	4:58:50	C SMITH	4:59:44	J CHAPPELL	5:00:30	D STUBBINGS	5:01:30
22	K HARDING	4:57:53	E JENKINS	4:58:52	P DALE	4:59:44	K MCQUEEN	5:00:31	H JONES	5:01:31
23	L LAWES	4:57:54	R MILLETT	4:58:53	N HARRIES	4:59:44	P THOMAS	5:00:31	P ADAMS	5:01:31
24	J REVILL	4:57:55	A FRASER	4:58:54	D BRASIER	4:59:44	G CLARE	5:00:31	D LOWE	5:01:35
25	D OWEN	4:57:55	B FOX	4:58:56	C WHERRY	4:59:46	D ROWLANES	5:00:32	C HOLMES	5:01:35
26	J DAPLYN	4:57:56	P JONES	4:58:56	J MCCONNELL	4:59:46	S KERSHAW	5:00:32	D BULMER	5:01:36
27	R PHILP	4:57:56	C MONKS	4:58:58	S SCARF	4:59:47	J WRIGHT	5:00:32	S BILLIN	5:01:36
28	J MOGER	4:57:57	G FIELD	4:59:00	P DAVIES	4:59:47	P TCHAIKOVSKY	5:00:33	N DAVIDSON	5:01:37
29	R MCCANN	4:57:59	A PINE	4:59:01	D LAY	4:59:47	G WHITE	5:00:33	C MATTHEWS	5:01:41
30	Y SANCHIS	4:57:59	C COTMORE	4:59:01	J TIMONEY	4:59:47	R WALKER	5:00:33	D MACLEOD	5:01:41
31	T MACCANN	4:57:59	K JOWETT	4:59:02	J CANNAN	4:59:48	S STEPHENS	5:00:35	R SMITH	5:01:41
32	P GAZE	4:57:59	E ELLIOT	4:59:03	A PAGET	4:59:48	A JACOBS	5:00:35	N BUXCEY	5:01:42
33	G DONALD	4:58:00	D TRANTER	4:59:03	D BALL	4:59:48	W SMITH	5:00:36	J WAITE	5:01:42
34	L COPLAND	4:58:01	S EDWARDS	4:59:04	C LAKEY	4:59:48	R VAN HEERDEN	5:00:36	A HIETIKKO	5:01:43
35	D COMISSAR	4:58:01	T WHEELDON	4:59:05	P NEWMAN	4:59:49	D MOREY	5:00:36	L STEWART	5:01:43
36	D TIDSWELL	4:58:01	J GIBSON	4:59:05	P NEWMAN	4:59:49	D WADDELL	5:00:36	A PEART	5:01:43
37	A STJERNQVIST	4:58:01	G HARDY	4:59:05	G DAVIES	4:59:49	P MAYNARD	5:00:37	G DRIVER	5:01:45
38	A RICHARDSON	4:58:01	D WITHERS	4:59:05	B SEAL	4:59:49	R CHARLTON	5:00:38	A BALDING	5:01:45
39	P PELLANT	4:58:04	R SPALL	4:59:06	A ASHTON	4:59:50	G WADDELL	5:00:38	W ROSEWELL	5:01:45
40	S OMBUDSTVEDT	4:58:04	J JAMES	4:59:07	T SHILSON	4:59:50	V LEVAK	5:00:38	G WRIGHT	5:01:46
41	H COUCHERON-AAMOT	4:58:04	J WILKINSON	4:59:07	F VELIA	4:59:50	W HUMPHRIES	5:00:39	J MAXWELL	5:01:47
42	P BESWICK	4:58:04	S RAWLINSON	4:59:08	A JESSUP	4:59:50	J EDWARDS	5:00:40	W HETHERINGTON	5:01:48
43	P MARSHALL	4:58:06	B WATSON	4:59:08	K ROSE	4:59:51	P READ	5:00:41	P SCHOOLING	5:01:48
44	B LI	4:58:06	T WHALEN	4:59:08	D COLEMAN	4:59:53	M EADY	5:00:41	A THOMPSON	5:01:50
45	J BRIOZZO	4:58:08	W BARRETT	4:59:08	J KING	4:59:54	P COCKCROFT	5:00:42	M COLE	5:01:51
46	P EVERETT	4:58:08	R ASHDOWN	4:59:08	B LAMBERT	4:59:55	J BOWKER	5:00:43	P MCDERMOTT	5:01:52
47	V BREWSTER	4:58:09	G TAYLOR	4:59:09	S HOLMES	4:59:55	C BONNETTE	5:00:45	W KACZMARCZYK	5:01:53
48	R COATES	4:58:10	A SAVAGE	4:59:09	B JONES	4:59:57	M WINZER	5:00:46	M COHEN	5:01:54
49	J BIRD	4:58:10	P SIMPSON	4:59:10	M GILL	4:59:57	J WOOD	5:00:46	G MABBETT	5:01:56
50	D GIBSON	4:58:10	I CAMPBELL	4:59:10	J FOLEY	4:59:58	J WALSH	5:00:47	P HALLMAN	5:01:57
51	A BASSI	4:58:11	R POVEY	4:59:10	C FISHER	4:59:59	C MARCHMONT	5:00:47	A HERRING	5:01:59
52	A NOAKES	4:58:12	P TAYLOR	4:59:10	H IRWIN	4:59:59	J DUBOIS	5:00:49	S SKINNER	5:01:59
53	S WAUGH	4:58:13	N DAVEY	4:59:10	J MARTIN	4:59:59	K ASHMORE	5:00:49	D FILLER	5:01:59
54	B SAYERS	4:58:13	A BREARLEY	4:59:11	P SELL	4:59:59	N MEMMOTT	5:00:49	P FRETTER	5:01:59
55	C SIMON	4:58:13	T BLINKHORN	4:59:11	A YIALONITES	4:59:59	T WILLIAMS	5:00:49	J EVESON	5:02:01
56	K MILLS	4:58:13	N WHITTET	4:59:12	W HARDY	5:00:00	S BROOKE	5:00:49	A SWANNELL	5:02:02
57	M PAGE	4:58:14	K HUNT	4:59:13	P WAITE	5:00:00	R ZAFFARONI	5:00:49	R LAMBLE	5:02:04
58	J PAYNE	4:58:14	J HOFFMAN	4:59:13	L BOLTON	5:00:01	M KING	5:00:51	M COLLETT	5:02:07
59	G PAPADOPOULLOS	4:58:14	B HILL	4:59:14	P KIPENAKIS	5:00:01	C COLLETT	5:00:52	C CRAWLEY	5:02:07
60	G EDE	4:58:14	P CREAK	4:59:14	M TAYLOR	5:00:01	R MOONEY	5:00:54	T BEVAN	5:02:07
61	J BELLAMY	4:58:16	J MASON	4:59:14	A JACKSON	5:00:02	R BARNETT	5:00:56	T RUDD	5:02:08
62	J COLLING	4:58:16	S JOHANNESSEN	4:59:14	V KNELL	5:00:02	S AYEN	5:00:58	R FRAMPTON	5:02:09
63	D MORRIS	4:58:16	J KIMBERLEY	4:59:15	H FARR	5:00:05	I SHERWOOD	5:00:58	K HALLIWELL	5:02:09
64	D BREWIS	4:58:16	B JOHANNESSEN	4:59:15	D MCKEOWN	5:00:06	G COIA	5:00:59	J BOOGAARD	5:02:12
65	P LAWRENCE	4:58:16	P BROOK	4:59:15	A SMITH	5:00:06	M BUSH	5:01:01	A MOWER	5:02:13
66	M WAYLAND	4:58:16	G LESTER	4:59:16	M BERGER	5:00:08	F COOPER	5:01:02	K WALTERS	5:02:13
67	G UDALL	4:58:18	J HOLMES	4:59:17	H BALDWIN	5:00:09	A HARVEY	5:01:02	S HAMILTON	5:02:15
68	R HEARSON	4:58:18	D TETT	4:59:17	P GULLIVER	5:00:10	J CARBURY	5:01:02	G KENNARD	5:02:15
69	J ALLUM	4:58:19	I BATES	4:59:17	P SPIEGEL	5:00:11	A REX	5:01:02	R STONE	5:02:16
70	J CLARK	4:58:20	R GRAHAM	4:59:18	R CORNELIUS	5:00:11	M TOWNSEND	5:01:03	R ALLEN	5:02:17
71	P HARRISON	4:58:20	J DACOSTA MACHADO	4:59:19	F HOUCHIDAR	5:00:12	B LUNDSTROM	5:01:03	M CHAPMAN	5:02:19
72	M CLARKE	4:58:20	S FITZPATRICK	4:59:19	A BRINDLE	5:00:14	M DONNELLY	5:01:03	M DAVID	5:02:20
73	A PATCHETT	4:58:21	A BIGGAR	4:59:20	A WORKMAN	5:00:15	T HASKINS	5:01:05	R KINGDON	5:02:20
74	D HOTTMAN	4:58:22	G KIRKPATRICK	4:59:21	A OGILVY-STUART	5:00:16	S PATERSON	5:01:05	M WELCH	5:02:20
75	R BOWIE	4:58:22	P SAVILL	4:59:22	N BULLEN	5:00:16	M HUGHES	5:01:09	L SALMON	5:02:21
76	A TUITT	4:58:24	M HARRIS	4:59:22	G MORGAN	5:00:17	M LIVROZET	5:01:09	A BAXTER	5:02:21
77	R DU PARCQ	4:58:24	I DOWLING	4:59:23	D DRAYTON	5:00:17	R LIVROZET	5:01:10	A BRAND	5:02:22
78	S CLUTTERBUCK	4:58:24	D KING	4:59:23	S GIBBS	5:00:17	L DOUGLAS	5:01:12	T WARD	5:02:22
79	R PENNEY	4:58:25	J SINGER	4:59:24	K IVERSEN	5:00:17	H CARLSSON	5:01:12	R PRICE	5:02:23
80	P SKELTON	4:58:25	A BURGESS	4:59:24	G CROWE	5:00:17	A BULLOCK	5:01:13	E DAGUES	5:02:23
81	P DUGGAN	4:58:26	B JONES	4:59:26	M HUMBER	5:00:18	J ROWELL	5:01:13	A TERHORST	5:02:24
82	A BASHFORD	4:58:26	P TOMLIN	4:59:28	M SIMMONDS	5:00:19	C STONE	5:01:14	R JONES	5:02:24
83	G JACKSON	4:58:28	K PAULING	4:59:28	E SCOTT	5:00:19	M LORGERE	5:01:14	S HUGHES	5:02:25
84	E ALLINGHAM	4:58:28	M MARCH	4:59:28	D MCCARTHY	5:00:19	W SIMMS	5:01:14	J RUSSELL	5:02:25
85	N HANNINGTON	4:58:28	A GRICE	4:59:29	B HUSK	5:00:20	A HOLDEN	5:01:14	B RICHARDS	5:02:27
86	A SEBERRY	4:58:29	J MC GUINNESS	4:59:29	J SCOTT	5:00:20	T KAVANAGH	5:01:14	C JUDGE	5:02:28
87	A BULLER	4:58:30	C BENSLEY	4:59:29	B MCHALE	5:00:20	S GRIFFITHS	5:01:14	O METHAM	5:02:28
88	A STONHAM	4:58:31	P WILSON	4:59:29	B TOOTH	5:00:21	J HOUGH	5:01:14	P GIBBINS	5:02:29
89	S BARNETT	4:58:31	T CLARKE	4:59:29	K GOULD	5:00:21	T DUKE	5:01:14	S COLLING	5:02:30
90	M BELL	4:58:32	G CUTHBERT	4:59:29	L SHEEDY	5:00:21	N DUDMAN	5:01:15	M DAVENPORT	5:02:30
91	L SAUNDERS	4:58:36	D CROOK	4:59:31	K TOMIZU	5:00:21	W ROLSTONE	5:01:15	C JOHN	5:02:31
92	M HOWSON	4:58:37	V BHUNDIA	4:59:32	L SWINBURNE	5:00:21	D PRESCOTT	5:01:15	N MOORE	5:02:32
93	C WAITE	4:58:38	P STOTT	4:59:32	J HILL	5:00:21	N HERODOTOU	5:01:19	J CLARE	5:02:33
94	W SHIPTON	4:58:39	P MURPHY	4:59:34	A CURNOW	5:00:22	Y GLEN	5:01:20	A FISHER	5:02:33
95	L BREWIS	4:58:40	G CONROY	4:59:36	R PILLAR	5:00:22	L THOMPSON	5:01:20	M GAMBLE	5:02:34
96	J ROBINSON	4:58:40	S JEGGO	4:59:36	M APPELQUIST	5:00:22	J LUNNEY	5:01:21	W COPP	5:02:34
97	J MACKIN	4:58:40	A PAPWORTH	4:59:36	J WELLS	5:00:22	C DALTON	5:01:21	V WHITE	5:02:34
98	L ALLEN	4:58:40	N BAMBER	4:59:36	S GARDNER	5:00:22	B MYLAM	5:01:22	A BOTTOMLEY	5:02:34
99	I ASHWORTH	4:58:41	S MACLEAN	4:59:36	S DHILLON	5:00:22	A LONGSTAFF	5:01:22	B WILES	5:02:35
100	K WINTER	4:58:41	L BAILEY	4:59:36	G COLES	5:00:22	A WINKWORTH	5:01:22	A EMPSON	5:02:36

	21501-21600		21601-21700		21701-21800		21801-21900		21901-22000	
1	A CARR	5:02:37	I HATAI	5:03:55	J FRICKER	5:05:15	I CLARKE	5:06:40	W CHENG	5:08:11
2	J ROWLAND	5:02:37	J HENDRY	5:03:55	P WALTERS	5:05:16	W MARSDEN	5:06:41	C NORTHWAY	5:08:12
3	D BRAZIER	5:02:37	A LORD	5:03:55	A BRIDGEMAN	5:05:16	K PEEL	5:06:44	N ALLISON	5:08:13
4	A MCQUEEN	5:02:38	T LOWE	5:03:57	T LWIN	5:05:16	C WARBURTON	5:06:44	W CHUBB	5:08:14
5	D WRIGHT	5:02:38	M MCGARRY	5:03:57	P BARRATT	5:05:18	J JONES	5:06:45	B REEVES	5:08:14
6	G LAKE	5:02:38	N DAVIS	5:03:58	T GOULDS	5:05:20	M DEVERELL	5:06:46	S PORTUPHY	5:08:15
7	S BARNES	5:02:39	W PHILLIPS	5:04:01	M DOHERTY	5:05:20	J FOLEY	5:06:46	F THOMAS	5:08:18
8	J PAUL	5:02:40	P FLEISCHER	5:04:01	H RODWELL	5:05:20	J HODGKINS	5:06:50	L HOGAN	5:08:19
9	E FRATTON	5:02:40	J MORGAN	5:04:02	B KILFORD	5:05:20	J THACKER	5:06:50	R WEATHERBY	5:08:19
10	B KIRK	5:02:40	V GAIGER	5:04:03	P WALKER	5:05:20	K WEST	5:06:51	D WALKER	5:08:20
11	P HICKS	5:02:41	P STEELE	5:04:03	I DAVOLL	5:05:21	M PICKIN	5:06:52	C GREEN	5:08:20
12	G PHILIPPON	5:02:42	P BEALES	5:04:04	P NUTTING	5:05:23	J SHEEDY	5:06:52	S LOCK	5:08:23
13	A BOFFIN	5:02:42	D CHILTON	5:04:05	T BAILEY	5:05:23	D BIRD	5:06:53	B MCDONNELL	5:08:23
14	R KING	5:02:43	A FOULKES	5:04:06	T MORBY	5:05:25	D LAMB	5:06:54	A RIVERA	5:08:26
15	M CASCARINA	5:02:43	B OAKLEY	5:04:07	D REID-SIMMS	5:05:26	S MARSHALL	5:06:55	S AHMED	5:08:29
16	I NAREAHO	5:02:44	A SPARSHOTT	5:04:08	P GREEN	5:05:26	A TOWLER	5:06:55	L THORPE	5:08:30
17	J BIRCH	5:02:44	P GRAY	5:04:08	R IRVING	5:05:28	M STRETTON	5:06:56	A CROFTS	5:08:31
18	Y SHIGIHARA	5:02:44	J HOWARD	5:04:10	D WISE	5:05:29	B ASKEW	5:06:58	D COOPER	5:08:32
19	A TAPLIN	5:02:45	F EL-KHALIL	5:04:13	D HEARTFIELD	5:05:29	J BOTT	5:06:58	J THOMPSON	5:08:33
20	Y TANAKA	5:02:45	D MAUREL	5:04:13	T LUNDESTAD	5:05:29	A BOOTH	5:06:59	C DAWSON	5:08:33
21	T ROUGLEY	5:02:45	D LEE	5:04:14	R KONRADSEN	5:05:29	A PURCHASE	5:07:00	R CLARKE	5:08:39
22	G HUDSON	5:02:46	P DENNIS	5:04:16	G JOLLIFFE	5:05:31	R LEWIS	5:07:02	N CARTWRIGHT	5:08:39
23	L MEWBURN-CROOK	5:02:46	B GARDINER	5:04:16	E UPSON	5:05:31	P WILTSHIRE	5:07:02	L DAVIES	5:08:39
24	A DAVIES	5:02:46	D TRANTER	5:04:17	B HUNT	5:05:33	M JENKINS	5:07:03	K DEWHURST	5:08:39
25	M DEVENEY	5:02:46	P DUNKLEY	5:04:17	T WEIGHT	5:05:34	P HEALY	5:07:03	L BURNS	5:08:39
26	P NEWTON-SMITH	5:02:47	C RATA	5:04:18	S GEE	5:05:34	K WENBORN	5:07:03	B BEDBOROUGH	5:08:40
27	D WARMAN	5:02:48	J TOMLINSON	5:04:19	P ANDERSEN	5:05:34	M KERR	5:07:04	R BEDBOROUGH	5:08:40
28	J MARTINSSON	5:02:48	P DAVIES	5:04:20	C MOBSBY	5:05:34	D BROOKE	5:07:05	W MERFIELD	5:08:41
29	M STEWART	5:02:48	L WILLETTS	5:04:21	P BULL	5:05:35	S DOVEDI	5:07:05	D CLAYTON	5:08:45
30	J DAVIES	5:02:48	D JOHNSON	5:04:21	B STEER	5:05:36	C OSBORN	5:07:05	J HUNTER	5:08:45
31	J HERBERT	5:02:49	K WIGNALL	5:04:22	K MCGEEVER	5:05:38	C KIMBER	5:07:05	R WALLEN	5:08:46
32	T LANGER	5:02:49	A HOWARD	5:04:23	P HASLAM	5:05:40	G HAMMERSLEY	5:07:06	M WALLEN	5:08:47
33	R SHERIDAN	5:02:50	M MANWARING	5:04:23	W JONES	5:05:40	J SKINGSLEY	5:07:07	W WEISE	5:08:49
34	R GOSDEN	5:02:52	A WINTON	5:04:25	L ANDERSSON	5:05:41	R CAMPOS	5:07:11	A PARK	5:08:49
35	S CAWTHERAY	5:02:52	M LEWTAS	5:04:25	K JOHNSON	5:05:44	T EMMOTT	5:07:12	L DELATTRE	5:08:49
36	C MERRITT	5:02:53	W KENNEDY	5:04:27	H GIBSON	5:05:44	C OAKMAN	5:07:12	D HEWITT	5:08:52
37	J ELLIS	5:02:55	K TWEEDIE	5:04:27	K HOWE	5:05:45	D BROADHURST	5:07:13	S PAINTER	5:08:53
38	W CANFIELD	5:02:55	B WILSON	5:04:28	C MILES	5:05:45	J TURNER	5:07:14	J BAILES	5:08:57
39	H SELZAM	5:02:56	C SHEEHY	5:04:29	S STONEMAN	5:05:46	G DAVISON	5:07:14	K GLEDHILL	5:08:58
40	J ADAM	5:02:57	M NASH	5:04:29	T SPATE	5:05:46	A SCHECHTER	5:07:15	R FOSTER	5:08:59
41	S FARLEY	5:02:57	K JACOBS	5:04:29	H GORNALL	5:05:46	P AARON	5:07:17	B HIRST	5:09:00
42	G ASHBY	5:02:57	F LESLIE	5:04:30	S DIBBS	5:05:48	J BRADFIELD	5:07:18	S HOLMES	5:09:00
43	S PAXTON	5:02:58	K BURTON	5:04:30	S DENNIS	5:05:49	M CUMMINS	5:07:19	H EVANS	5:09:05
44	D STOTT	5:02:59	D WHITEHOUSE	5:04:30	S ROBERTSON	5:05:50	D ASHWORTH	5:07:19	J SCHILLIGER	5:09:05
45	J BASHAM	5:02:59	C HENDRY	5:04:30	R DOBBS	5:05:51	P SHARP	5:07:19	H KOEP	5:09:05
46	R CLEEVES	5:03:00	U COLELLA	5:04:30	S BONINI	5:05:51	A BROOM	5:07:19	S BROWN	5:09:05
47	R ELLIOTT	5:03:02	L TORNIERI	5:04:30	K HOMEWOOD	5:05:52	J ROBINSON	5:07:19	R LEDER	5:09:05
48	J HUGHES	5:03:04	N FRATTON	5:04:30	A CRYAN	5:05:52	M WRIGHT	5:07:20	R VAN DER WAALS	5:09:06
49	N EMBLETON	5:03:08	P WHITEHOUSE	5:04:32	D CALDWELL	5:05:53	M COX	5:07:24	G GALLOWAY	5:09:09
50	C COOPER	5:03:08	L MALDOY	5:04:33	H WRIGHT	5:05:55	N ROBBINS	5:07:26	M SHEEHAN	5:09:10
51	A WILLS	5:03:10	J FOSTER	5:04:33	A FORD	5:05:55	F CHIVERS	5:07:26	T LYNCH	5:09:11
52	B MAYO	5:03:10	G GRANT	5:04:35	M PARSONS	5:05:57	N HOMEWOOD	5:07:26	S WARRINER	5:09:12
53	M TOLEMAN	5:03:11	R LESLIE	5:04:36	B BROUGH	5:05:57	K WARREN	5:07:27	I BROWN	5:09:13
54	M COTTERALL	5:03:12	D SMILEY	5:04:36	P GOODE	5:05:57	A BILLINGHURST	5:07:29	H CLARK	5:09:13
55	C WESTON-BAKER	5:03:12	C BERRIDGE	5:04:36	W HURLEY	5:05:59	R WAITE	5:07:30	E DONOHOE	5:09:14
56	W WOODS	5:03:13	P CHALLIS	5:04:40	P ELLING	5:05:59	P DURDEN	5:07:31	S ELLIS	5:09:16
57	A WATERSON	5:03:13	A BHANGOO	5:04:40	P EVERARD	5:06:00	C PRYCE	5:07:33	S WRIGHT	5:09:16
58	H PURKARTHOFER	5:03:14	I BENSUSAN	5:04:41	R GOODWIN	5:06:01	M BROOKS	5:07:33	M ESTABA	5:09:17
59	C STRIDE	5:03:14	T HOLLAND	5:04:42	D CARTMAN	5:06:01	J AMBELEZ	5:07:34	M GREENE	5:09:17
60	A TOOGOOD	5:03:15	F BENSUSAN	5:04:44	K GREEN	5:06:01	A HENCHLEY	5:07:34	S PRICE	5:09:18
61	L WOOD	5:03:15	R TIVNANN	5:04:45	P HASLETT	5:06:01	T CHUMP	5:07:34	H SHOTTER	5:09:20
62	L MASON	5:03:16	G BRADBURY	5:04:46	L RYMES	5:06:01	N WILSON	5:07:36	P ANDREWS	5:09:21
63	M MORRIS	5:03:16	P FISH	5:04:46	J SCOTT	5:06:02	R BROADHEAD	5:07:39	R CAMPBELL	5:09:21
64	R SHAW	5:03:17	S BALL	5:04:48	P HARTERY	5:06:02	M GARRIDO	5:07:43	N GRIFFIN	5:09:21
65	D CLANCHY	5:03:19	P HOFFMANN	5:04:50	I PERRY	5:06:03	A SCORER	5:07:43	A PERCIVAL	5:09:25
66	R ABBOTT	5:03:23	C ARMSTRONG	5:04:51	P HAAS	5:06:03	D FOARD	5:07:44	M SALTER	5:09:25
67	D GOLLICKER	5:03:25	K DANBY	5:04:51	J CHADWICK	5:06:05	S CHILD	5:07:44	M PALMER	5:09:26
68	S LOVELOCK	5:03:26	D BECK	5:04:51	A GRIFFITHS	5:06:06	D WILSON	5:07:44	S BHAMRA	5:09:26
69	M GALE	5:03:27	I ROBINSON	5:04:51	J PEDLEY	5:06:07	M MULLETT	5:07:45	A WELBURN	5:09:27
70	R NOBLE	5:03:27	S HARTWELL	5:04:52	T MANNING	5:06:11	K CHAMPION	5:07:45	B CASS	5:09:28
71	G PENMAN	5:03:27	T BEASOR	5:04:53	C JEAL	5:06:11	A JACKSON	5:07:45	P ROE	5:09:29
72	I MCDOWALL	5:03:28	Y ROBINARD	5:04:53	D STEWART	5:06:12	A MORRIS	5:07:45	A PARKES	5:09:29
73	A MANCKTELOW	5:03:28	C PASETTI	5:04:53	M KIRKMAN	5:06:12	R RAUCH	5:07:46	L PURSER	5:09:29
74	I MATTHEWS	5:03:28	N HONEYMAN	5:04:53	N HEYWOOD	5:06:14	A SIMMONS	5:07:47	M PURSER	5:09:30
75	R TRUETT	5:03:29	S SURRIDGE	5:04:56	I MACDONALD	5:06:16	M SILVA	5:07:47	D BOWLES	5:09:31
76	F FOULDS	5:03:33	A SOLE	5:04:58	D COLMAN	5:06:19	B EDWARDS	5:07:48	D BROWN	5:09:31
77	C ROSSI	5:03:33	S LAUDER	5:04:59	G NUTTER	5:06:19	A TROUT	5:07:48	F HODGE	5:09:31
78	A BIDGOOD	5:03:34	C STRICKLAND	5:05:00	L GEAKE	5:06:19	V REYNOLDS	5:07:48	K HUGHES	5:09:33
79	B PECK	5:03:34	J SCOTT	5:05:01	C WILLIAMS	5:06:19	G LANDS	5:07:48	C CORNELL	5:09:35
80	J BELL	5:03:34	J PRYER	5:05:02	A FREEMAN	5:06:19	P MARLOW	5:07:49	J SHIPMAN	5:09:36
81	E MACKINTOSH	5:03:35	P MARSHALL	5:05:02	K BOLTON	5:06:19	I DENHAM	5:07:54	G DI CARMINE	5:09:36
82	G TORDO	5:03:35	J MARSHALL-JENKINSON	5:05:02	M HIGASHI	5:06:20	P CLARKE	5:07:55	S KNOWLES	5:09:36
83	M BRANWHITE	5:03:37	G KELLER	5:05:02	J HAUGHTON	5:06:20	B ROBERTS	5:07:55	E MASEFIELD	5:09:37
84	E GRANT	5:03:38	A SVE	5:05:04	A VOLLER	5:06:21	T BROWN	5:07:58	C TIPPER	5:09:37
85	P COVENEY	5:03:38	A BERTOLI	5:05:04	S CHAUDHURI	5:06:21	A BARBER	5:07:58	J HARBRON	5:09:37
86	W FAIRWEATHER	5:03:38	J RIDDLE	5:05:05	A BARLOW	5:06:22	I ALLSUCH	5:08:00	C MACKENZIE	5:09:38
87	S POPE	5:03:40	T FOX	5:05:05	M ELLIOTT	5:06:25	C KELLY	5:08:00	J HUGILL	5:09:38
88	P HALL	5:03:40	A DENT	5:05:05	M CANHAM	5:06:26	J SMITH	5:08:00	G WHITCOMB	5:09:39
89	R SOAR	5:03:41	A FRESHWATER	5:05:07	J LAYBURN	5:06:27	B BEAVAN	5:08:00	W SALKELD	5:09:40
90	G HODGSON	5:03:41	N DIGIAMBERARDINO	5:05:09	P PROSSER	5:06:27	M MUNISE	5:08:01	T SHOTTON	5:09:41
91	J HAYTON	5:03:46	S WYNN	5:05:09	R ANGELES	5:06:30	M WATSON	5:08:02	R VIDLER	5:09:42
92	B TAYLOR	5:03:48	R BAKER	5:05:09	D BURBIDGE	5:06:30	W TODD	5:08:03	B SMITH	5:09:44
93	H DARBY	5:03:48	N WHITEHEAD	5:05:09	F ILLINGWORTH	5:06:33	J PURCELL	5:08:04	A GELLATLY	5:09:45
94	S BARLOW	5:03:50	G TURNBULL	5:05:10	C HARRIS	5:06:34	B GREEN	5:08:05	S WESBTER	5:09:45
95	T SWINNEY	5:03:51	A RICKELL	5:05:10	W KESBY	5:06:35	J DEVLIN	5:08:05	S BOULTON	5:09:45
96	J JONES	5:03:53	A GARVEY	5:05:11	R SAPIANO	5:06:37	J SHERRARD	5:08:05	P BURR	5:09:46
97	A CLARK	5:03:54	S SMITH	5:05:12	C BAKER	5:06:37	S JENKINS	5:08:08	G HARRINGTON	5:09:48
98	K BROWN	5:03:55	G PERKIS	5:05:12	R SCOFIELD	5:06:37	R HOLTON	5:08:08	R ROSSI	5:09:48
99	A BROOKS	5:03:55	E FIELDING	5:05:13	A PICK	5:06:40	B GORMAN	5:08:09	D CROMBIE	5:09:48
100	P WILLIAMS	5:03:55	R CHARLES	5:05:14			B HEWITT	5:08:10	R LONG	5:09:49

#	22001-22100		22101-22200		22201-22300		22301-22400		22401-22500	
1	M VULPINARI	5:09:49	A WHITING-HALL	5:11:08	S ROSENBERG	5:12:51	K KOIDE	5:14:48	S BAKER	5:16:42
2	A CONNOR	5:09:50	M HACON	5:11:08	M DALTON	5:12:54	C ROBERTS	5:14:48	N CLARK	5:16:43
3	S MAI	5:09:50	S HALL	5:11:08	K HART	5:13:00	R DELANEY	5:14:48	A MACLENNAN	5:16:43
4	G HOWE	5:09:50	D SMITH	5:11:08	D CARTER	5:13:03	A NEAL	5:14:50	G COMER	5:16:44
5	H SINGH	5:09:50	O COHEN	5:11:10	R GELL	5:13:04	H MORRIS	5:14:50	C WEBSTER	5:16:46
6	D ODDY	5:09:51	P HILL	5:11:11	J MCCORMICK	5:13:04	D HONEY	5:14:50	P BOWERMAN	5:16:47
7	I FAGG	5:09:51	B RICKERS	5:11:11	M MCGOUGH	5:13:08	D DIAK	5:14:51	S BRODIE	5:16:54
8	B COLTHUP	5:09:52	E RICHARDSON	5:11:12	I MCKINNELL	5:13:09	N ROBINSON	5:14:52	A WILKINSON	5:16:55
9	P BENNETT	5:09:52	I SILCOCK	5:11:13	K MYNETT	5:13:10	P HALPIN	5:14:52	R BROWN	5:16:55
10	M SOHR	5:09:52	D UMBERS	5:11:13	A LENTILLAC	5:13:10	T JULNES	5:14:52	P POOLE	5:16:57
11	P SLATER	5:09:52	M JOINER	5:11:15	D JENNINGS	5:13:12	A LIVINGSTONE	5:14:53	P ROBERTS	5:16:57
12	F ABBOTT	5:09:53	D GOLFIERA	5:11:15	G HONEYBUN	5:13:12	J BERRIDGE	5:14:53	E CADDICK	5:16:59
13	M SANDERSON	5:09:53	C STRANGE	5:11:16	L YOUNGHUSBAND	5:13:16	N BROYD	5:14:53	M SMALL	5:16:59
14	D MILNER	5:09:53	D SIME	5:11:17	J DOCWRA	5:13:16	G PINTO	5:14:54	A SMALL	5:17:00
15	H GOULD	5:09:53	R TAYLOR	5:11:18	R STANDAERT	5:13:17	D CHIPPINDALE	5:14:55	P NICOLAS	5:17:04
16	J BULMAN	5:09:54	F GIWA	5:11:18	I WHITE	5:13:17	M PREW	5:14:56	P GHIRARDI	5:17:10
17	D ILOTT	5:09:54	G CABLE	5:11:19	D MCTAVY	5:13:17	A WILLIAMSON	5:15:00	P SMITH	5:17:10
18	P BUCHAN	5:09:54	P HEATON	5:11:21	R TAYLOR	5:13:18	F HALLIDAY	5:15:01	C HACKETT	5:17:12
19	J WOODCOCK	5:09:54	P AGUADO	5:11:22	C KEENAN	5:13:19	D LETTERBOROUGH	5:15:02	J BREMNER	5:17:13
20	C BRYSON	5:09:56	S FOULDS	5:11:22	K OSBORNE	5:13:19	S HUNT	5:15:03	G RAPOPORT	5:17:13
21	B STOBO	5:09:57	K BAYLISS	5:11:22	E PEXTON	5:13:19	S DILLAWAY	5:15:04	P COGIN	5:17:13
22	C DEXTER	5:09:58	C ALMOND	5:11:22	P FORD	5:13:19	M STROUD	5:15:06	J SPALDING	5:17:16
23	T BRAZIER	5:09:59	P MALHAN	5:11:24	M LUHAR	5:13:21	V DEAN	5:15:08	A PRESTON	5:17:25
24	N MASON	5:09:59	C WILLIAMSON	5:11:25	J ALCON	5:13:22	A GUTHRIE	5:15:08	J NABHOLTZ	5:17:25
25	D PAULINE	5:09:59	R LE-MOIGANAN	5:11:26	S JENNINGS	5:13:22	D THOMSON	5:15:08	C SMITH	5:17:26
26	O RENNIE	5:10:00	P WINCHCOMBE	5:11:31	S HILL	5:13:23	R VAIL	5:15:09	J KIRKHAM	5:17:27
27	J FLINT	5:10:01	I CROW	5:11:32	D DAVIS	5:13:23	P KING	5:15:10	W HINMAN	5:17:28
28	M CHADWICK	5:10:02	O THOMPSON	5:11:32	P ANDREASSON	5:13:24	E HACKER	5:15:11	F LANE	5:17:28
29	J STARGATT	5:10:03	C EDWARDS	5:11:33	D INGRAM	5:13:24	A LANE	5:15:11	S WALMSLEY	5:17:29
30	K BEVAN	5:10:03	V PEARCE	5:11:33	J KEMP	5:13:25	K SULLIVAN	5:15:12	J MCMAHON	5:17:29
31	T GUNDERSEN	5:10:03	G HOWE	5:11:34	S FROW	5:13:26	V HUNT	5:15:13	G BLOOMFIELD	5:17:29
32	M PARTINGTON	5:10:06	J FARRIER	5:11:34	P GRIFFIN	5:13:26	M PEARSE	5:15:14	R PRICE	5:17:29
33	K ROUSSEL	5:10:07	G PLOWMAN	5:11:35	P EDWARDS	5:13:29	L BESZANT	5:15:14	N STYLES	5:17:29
34	D O SULLIVAN	5:10:08	P GIDDINGS	5:11:35	J GRIFFIN	5:13:31	M LEWIS	5:15:15	W MORROW	5:17:31
35	K SHEA	5:10:08	A JENNISON	5:11:36	D PEEL	5:13:31	A HAWKINS	5:15:16	F WRAGG	5:17:31
36	G DAYMAN	5:10:10	R RENWICK	5:11:36	A SALMINEN	5:13:32	J SCHNEIDER	5:15:17	A CLUTTERBUCK	5:17:32
37	D FULLER	5:10:11	A HARRISON	5:11:36	N YSTEHEDE	5:13:35	D WOOD	5:15:17	T O'KORO	5:17:32
38	A CURTIN	5:10:11	M HARRISON	5:11:38	R ALEXANDER	5:13:35	K LEE	5:15:18	R KNOX	5:17:33
39	J DURRANT	5:10:13	B HISCOCK	5:11:38	R KELLY	5:13:36	J GRUNWELL	5:15:18	L OSTOLAZA	5:17:35
40	A LIDSTONE	5:10:15	M HOLLAND	5:11:39	P SLATER	5:13:36	D BEATTIE	5:15:18	L RAZZELL	5:17:39
41	A NICHOLLS	5:10:16	C RIGBY	5:11:39	J HUCKER	5:13:37	M FILOCAMO	5:15:18	R DIXON	5:17:40
42	J GAME	5:10:16	G PORLCHESTER	5:11:40	R WOOD	5:13:41	A BROWNING	5:15:19	T POTOCKA-HUNT	5:17:42
43	J BUSH	5:10:17	P GILLOOLY	5:11:41	R EBURN	5:13:42	S KREITEM	5:15:21	D WIGGIN	5:17:42
44	S BOWKER	5:10:17	S WESTHEAD	5:11:44	J KNEVETT	5:13:43	W ROBINSON	5:15:21	K RUSS	5:17:42
45	S MORGAN	5:10:18	E MORGAN	5:11:45	R KEEFE	5:13:43	B LEE	5:15:24	A EDWARDS	5:17:43
46	D BATTISON	5:10:19	D HENDY	5:11:46	C CARTER	5:13:43	C MILLARD	5:15:27	M GOBEL	5:17:46
47	P MELLOR	5:10:20	D EASTHAM	5:11:47	C BELL	5:13:44	G FROSDICK	5:15:28	N BAGE	5:17:48
48	R DERRICK	5:10:20	M GUMBRELL	5:11:49	D POON	5:13:44	A KEEBLE	5:15:33	M BAGE	5:17:48
49	E HENDERSON	5:10:20	G WOODING	5:11:49	J BOND	5:13:44	J MARSH-HOBBS	5:15:35	D OBRIEN	5:17:49
50	J WALPOLE	5:10:20	G GARDINER	5:11:49	M EVANS	5:13:44	I DOWNIE	5:15:35	D BURRELL	5:17:50
51	A KNIBBS	5:10:20	D SMITH	5:11:49	H SULLIVAN	5:13:44	J PETERSEN	5:15:37	J TURNBULL	5:17:53
52	J OATES	5:10:20	M SMITH	5:11:52	M THOMPSON	5:13:44	P MCNIEL	5:15:38	R JOWETT	5:17:55
53	E BERTHIER	5:10:23	A LUCKHURST	5:11:53	R MAUND	5:13:44	K ANDERSON	5:15:39	P DE WESSELOW	5:17:55
54	G OUTTERSIDE	5:10:23	J SOMERVILLE	5:11:56	P MARTIN	5:13:47	R MILNE	5:15:39	D BLAKIE	5:17:55
55	C HOWARD	5:10:24	J WILLIAMS	5:11:57	C SMITH-SOLBAKKEN	5:13:49	A GUY	5:15:39	S SEARES	5:17:56
56	R SMITH	5:10:30	A PAYNE	5:11:57	S FLETCHER	5:13:51	P JONES	5:15:40	J SAWYER	5:17:56
57	O NILSEN	5:10:31	R SPEIGHT	5:11:57	C RICHARDS	5:13:52	J PLENT	5:15:41	R TEASDALE	5:17:57
58	H VIK	5:10:33	N SMITH	5:11:57	G KENNEDY	5:13:53	B AZURDIA	5:15:42	N FERNANDO	5:17:57
59	W MARTIN	5:10:34	M ROWLAND	5:12:01	J BRISCOE	5:13:54	T BEST	5:15:43	J HOPKINSON	5:17:57
60	G WILLIAMS	5:10:34	S RYAN	5:12:03	K COMPER	5:13:54	J BATH	5:15:43	J ATTENBOROUGH	5:18:02
61	J PAYTON	5:10:35	A DAVIES	5:12:03	J RICHES	5:13:57	R LELE	5:15:47	P WYATT	5:18:05
62	C LAERENCE	5:10:35	E REID	5:12:03	F MCLEOD	5:13:58	H FORD	5:15:49	M MURPHY	5:18:05
63	P CHITTENDEN	5:10:35	J SHARPLEY	5:12:03	P WILKES	5:13:59	M KILBURN	5:15:49	S JOHNSON	5:18:07
64	S BEST	5:10:37	T MCNALLY	5:12:04	H WILKES	5:13:59	K RUTTY	5:15:49	W RHODES	5:18:07
65	C CROUCH	5:10:37	S FERGUSON	5:12:05	N CHIELENS	5:14:00	T WELCH	5:15:50	L HAMP	5:18:07
66	P TILBROOK	5:10:38	A THOMAS	5:12:06	M FILLERY	5:14:01	L THYNNE	5:15:51	J GASSON	5:18:07
67	J RAISER	5:10:38	M DUNK	5:12:06	J GOODSON	5:14:01	J HUGHES	5:15:51	K MCVANEY	5:18:08
68	R ISAAC	5:10:39	D BURRELL	5:12:08	G GOODSON	5:14:03	N EASTMEAD	5:15:54	N TAYLOR	5:18:09
69	A GORDON LENNOX	5:10:39	W PEARSON	5:12:08	M BAKER	5:14:08	D ROLFE	5:15:57	S NOVAK	5:18:10
70	G ENGLAND	5:10:39	B MCCUSKER	5:12:09	N PAYNE	5:14:10	P JONES	5:15:58	T DAY	5:18:13
71	S CANAVAN	5:10:39	A MOHAMED	5:12:09	D ALLAWAY	5:14:10	D KING	5:15:58	S MUNISI	5:18:13
72	J SOWERBY	5:10:40	B TOUCHOT	5:12:09	B DICKERSON	5:14:12	D NEWTON	5:15:58	J PFEIFFER	5:18:13
73	C WILLIAMS	5:10:41	D SIMPSON	5:12:10	R PENNEY	5:14:12	R DAVISON	5:15:58	L ROAN	5:18:17
74	M FOYSTER	5:10:44	C EMES	5:12:10	S EDWARDS	5:14:12	P SHERRELL	5:15:58	S DUNNE	5:18:17
75	F MCAULAY	5:10:44	J DAVIES	5:12:10	R CARTER	5:14:15	P MONTAGUE	5:15:59	I SMOUT	5:18:18
76	B TERRY	5:10:44	T STENSON	5:12:15	M HAWORTH	5:14:15	K MAXWELL	5:15:59	G DYER	5:18:19
77	N ASHER	5:10:45	M BLOOR	5:12:15	A WILKINSON	5:14:17	S BAILEY	5:16:00	L ARNOLD	5:18:19
78	S MASON	5:10:45	R WHITE	5:12:16	P BURTON	5:14:17	N THOMSON	5:16:00	A COUCH	5:18:19
79	R MASON	5:10:46	D COHEN-ALLORO	5:12:16	R ARNOLD	5:14:17	N BROOKS	5:16:01	S BEADLE	5:18:21
80	M WALTERS	5:10:46	S ROGERS	5:12:16	K O DONOGHUE	5:14:17	A JARRETT	5:16:09	G SAUNDERS	5:18:22
81	G PETTITT	5:10:47	B HALL	5:12:16	J THAIN	5:14:20	L DUDLEY	5:16:11	A KENCH	5:18:22
82	S LEVETT	5:10:47	R JEWELL	5:12:17	C WALKER	5:14:20	C FRANCIS	5:16:12	T TURNER	5:18:28
83	A MOL	5:10:48	B WOMACK	5:12:18	B O'BRIEN	5:14:20	S TATTAM	5:16:13	M INGEBRIGTSEN	5:18:28
84	O BAIRD	5:10:50	K WOODHAMS	5:12:23	C REID	5:14:22	N BYRNE	5:16:13	G PASNE	5:18:28
85	M DILKS	5:10:50	M COCKKERELL	5:12:26	J KEITH	5:14:25	C JEFFERY	5:16:15	D STEELE	5:18:28
86	D MADDAMS	5:10:50	C SHREEVE	5:12:26	G EXTENCE	5:14:25	A SMITH	5:16:15	B ADAMS	5:18:28
87	D HOUSE	5:10:55	J EGGEBERT	5:12:27	P HUBBARD	5:14:31	P MARSHALL	5:16:15	E ROBERTSON	5:18:28
88	P DANIELS	5:10:56	F PIZZOLON	5:12:27	P BOSWELL	5:14:33	G BLOOD	5:16:15	M OLBERTZ	5:18:28
89	S NESBIT-BELL	5:10:57	B HARBY	5:12:27	S STEWART-HADDOW	5:14:33	A TRINDER	5:16:27	A HATHAWAY	5:18:28
90	P NAYLOR	5:10:57	P O'CALLAGHAN	5:12:27	N O'BRIEN	5:14:34	T WORBOYS	5:16:28	P GIBSON	5:18:29
91	F O'CALLAGHAN	5:10:58	B KENNY	5:12:27	E SMITH	5:14:37	A WESSON	5:16:30	S LEVIANI	5:18:30
92	R BOUY	5:11:00	B WILSON	5:12:38	A KENNETT	5:14:38	D RIGBY	5:16:34	E DALY	5:18:31
93	J GINTY	5:11:00	D DENHAM	5:12:40	I FRASER	5:14:39	S MILLEN	5:16:35	W HANCOCK	5:18:34
94	K BOUTCHER	5:11:00	R PIGDON	5:12:48	R WELCH	5:14:44	E MURPHY	5:16:37	M CREAGH	5:18:35
95	E GRASSO	5:11:00	P GRAY	5:12:48	I OVERTON	5:14:45	H OCONNELL	5:16:38	J ODONOVAN	5:18:36
96	J DENING	5:11:01	A FATHULLA	5:12:49	A WOOD	5:14:47	D GUILLAUME	5:16:39	A HENRY	5:18:40
97	P BEAUSIRE	5:11:02	R HAGGERTY	5:12:50	D WORRALL	5:14:48	J CLARKE	5:16:40	K CURRY	5:18:41
98	J JOHNSON	5:11:04	S MCLAREN	5:12:50	R WINT	5:14:48	G GREEN	5:16:40	C TURNER	5:18:42
99	P EDWARDS	5:11:04	R LOWE	5:12:51	G BREEDS	5:14:48	N KEE	5:16:42	G URVOY	5:18:42
100	C HACON	5:11:07	M BARNES	5:12:51	W YOUNG	5:14:48	J TEBBS	5:16:42	C TOWNSLEY	5:18:49

	22501-22600		22601-22700		22701-22800		22801-22900		22901-23000	
1	J COURT	5:18:53	B BOYLE	5:20:49	E WILCOCK	5:22:42	I BLAYNEY	5:24:44	M BULL	5:27:11
2	C MAYNARD	5:19:01	E LATTER	5:20:49	S HALL	5:22:42	J REDHEAD	5:24:46	H DETER	5:27:14
3	G WILLIAMS	5:19:01	S CRUTTENDEN	5:20:49	L PASCALL	5:22:43	T SPAANSEN	5:24:47	A WEBB	5:27:15
4	P EASY	5:19:02	J WATERS	5:20:50	F HASSALL	5:22:43	B CHURCHILL	5:24:47	H WILSON	5:27:17
5	A GAGEN	5:19:04	W SAUNDERS	5:20:52	C DOMMERSNES	5:22:46	J DAVIS	5:24:48	Q ABBAS SYED	5:27:17
6	B TIMS	5:19:07	S CLARK	5:20:52	A HUSSAIN	5:22:46	J JOHNSON	5:24:49	M HARRIS	5:27:17
7	P HANRATTY	5:19:10	C CARTLIDGE	5:20:53	K BARNES	5:22:49	M DOUGHTY	5:24:49	M CHAMBERLAIN	5:27:18
8	N YANDLE	5:19:11	A MAYHEW	5:20:53	G LUXFORD	5:22:49	R DOYLE	5:24:49	G BARTON	5:27:18
9	I TRANTER	5:19:11	K THOMPSON	5:20:55	S LANDER	5:22:50	J HALL	5:24:50	S KUROZUMI	5:27:23
10	H DUFFY	5:19:11	A READ	5:20:57	J WALTON	5:22:52	S ELDRED	5:24:50	P DONCASTER	5:27:26
11	D CODURI	5:19:11	C BELFIORI	5:20:59	M CEFFERTY	5:22:53	S MILLARD	5:24:53	P WADE	5:27:32
12	P DYE	5:19:12	J BRISTOW	5:21:00	F MICCOLL	5:22:53	S BURNHAM	5:24:53	K WEST	5:27:35
13	J HUFF	5:19:12	E CLOUGH	5:21:00	R OGUNJIMI	5:22:56	G ASHWORTH	5:24:54	G MASHFORD	5:27:37
14	J FITZGERALD	5:19:12	D SHEPPARD	5:21:01	J KENNEDY	5:22:57	L CARVILL	5:24:55	A HORVATH	5:27:37
15	P HEWES	5:19:12	W PARBAIOLA	5:21:01	P CAINE	5:22:58	J PAUL	5:24:55	P NIGHTINGALE	5:27:37
16	R BURTON	5:19:12	A MICHAEL	5:21:02	K MISTRY	5:23:01	P MCCARTHY	5:24:57	J BURKE	5:27:39
17	P HANNETT	5:19:12	R PAYNE	5:21:02	A COLLIER	5:23:01	F MEWES	5:24:58	R BUTCHER	5:27:40
18	P MACDONALD	5:19:12	C RICHARDSON	5:21:02	M LEWIS	5:23:03	A SMITH	5:24:59	I BAMBER	5:27:42
19	D WALSH	5:19:12	V MASCOLL	5:21:03	C FENECH	5:23:05	P SMITH	5:24:59	S BARROWMAN	5:27:43
20	R BENNETT	5:19:12	I HARBER	5:21:03	M HEYER	5:23:08	J TODD	5:25:02	D SAUNDERS	5:27:49
21	D FALLOON	5:19:14	R PATEL	5:21:06	S DEACON	5:23:09	S SLADE	5:25:02	J COLEMAN	5:27:49
22	S KETTELL	5:19:15	S SMITH	5:21:07	M REBELLATO	5:23:09	A O'DONNELL	5:25:03	I SHAW	5:27:50
23	A FRASER	5:19:17	D PARRY	5:21:08	G COLHOUN	5:23:09	C CHAPMAN	5:25:04	J AVERY	5:27:54
24	C LOCKLEY	5:19:22	J ZIMMER	5:21:09	J STRANG	5:23:09	P NOBLE	5:25:06	S WATTS-CHERRY	5:27:54
25	M PRICE	5:19:23	C COURTNEY	5:21:09	P FORD	5:23:09	R ZOTTINO	5:25:06	M DENNISON	5:27:55
26	B NIELSEN	5:19:23	J COURTNEY	5:21:09	D FRANCE	5:23:10	P MEACOCK	5:25:07	S CHEESE	5:27:55
27	B CASTELL	5:19:26	J HUGHES	5:21:09	G SMITH	5:23:11	P MURPHY	5:25:10	C SHURROCK	5:27:59
28	R DORRILL	5:19:26	G DANIELS	5:21:13	A THOMAS	5:23:11	P KEARNEY	5:25:12	B PATE	5:28:01
29	U AEBI	5:19:27	P ALMAZ	5:21:13	K OMAGARI	5:23:12	M PETTINGER	5:25:13	G LOVEWELL	5:28:01
30	C STONE	5:19:27	D FARRIN	5:21:13	D CHAPMAN	5:23:14	J HITCHCOCK	5:25:15	R BOX	5:28:02
31	I JACKSON	5:19:28	E SPIKINGS	5:21:14	A TAYLOR	5:23:15	G JAYARAM	5:25:17	J CUTHBERT	5:28:05
32	P MORTON	5:19:28	G SPICER	5:21:14	P TULLY	5:23:19	S LITCHFIELD	5:25:18	T SMITH	5:28:06
33	R STOREY	5:19:31	F BOURNE	5:21:14	E WOODHAMS	5:23:19	J PODZORSKA	5:25:18	T HOUGHTON	5:28:07
34	S ZERA	5:19:31	J DAVIS	5:21:16	R HALL	5:23:19	M WINTLE	5:25:18	D FELLOWS	5:28:08
35	J SLATER	5:19:33	S BROWN	5:21:16	J SNEAD	5:23:20	M RAWLINSON	5:25:20	B HARGIS	5:28:08
36	J BOYLE	5:19:35	L MILES	5:21:19	R SMITH	5:23:20	K TUFFEN	5:25:20	M RANSOME	5:28:09
37	J SIMMONS	5:19:36	E PORRAS	5:21:19	N CROOK	5:23:30	K HOWARD	5:25:20	M PILLINGER	5:28:11
38	D KEMP	5:19:38	P STINSON	5:21:21	D THORPE	5:23:31	S CULLEY	5:25:21	G DODDS	5:28:11
39	B WILLIAMS	5:19:38	D HYNAM	5:21:21	G HORSFALL	5:23:32	B BRIERS	5:25:23	I COOK	5:28:12
40	H FRADLEY	5:19:41	K SUTTON	5:21:22	G RAINBOW	5:23:35	J TAYLOR	5:25:24	B MOTT	5:28:12
41	P HARTLEY	5:19:43	E HICKS	5:21:22	R MORRIS	5:23:37	N GUITTON	5:25:25	D TATTERSALL	5:28:13
42	J ANSELL	5:19:43	D COUCH	5:21:23	G COLOGNESI	5:23:41	L BUCKINGHAM	5:25:26	B MORGAN	5:28:18
43	K FRADLEY	5:19:44	R ELLIOT	5:21:24	E COCOZZA	5:23:43	D STEWART	5:25:27	C RUTHERFORD	5:28:19
44	J FARRER	5:19:45	C NEALE	5:21:26	P BARNHAM	5:23:44	S WREN	5:25:27	J GRANDFIELD	5:28:19
45	R GIBNEY	5:19:48	A HUGHES	5:21:26	S HARPER	5:23:46	S JARDINE	5:25:27	C REED	5:28:19
46	E ASQUITA	5:19:49	M RICHARDS	5:21:26	R DOUGAL	5:23:49	C MCKENNA	5:25:28	L SMITH	5:28:21
47	P TURNER	5:19:49	M OSBORNE	5:21:30	A BEALE	5:23:49	L DOVE	5:25:29	R SMITH	5:28:22
48	R TIGH	5:19:50	M DAWSON	5:21:30	I WINTERBORN	5:23:49	M SALMON	5:25:30	A COOPER	5:28:25
49	K BREWSTER	5:19:51	A ROWLAND	5:21:32	C LAIT	5:23:49	L SALMON	5:25:30	R STARLING	5:28:28
50	T HOKI	5:19:51	G READER	5:21:32	V HARDING	5:23:50	B DRAPER	5:25:30	G HUGHES	5:28:28
51	R EDWARDS	5:19:52	P SEAGO	5:21:33	N LEWIS	5:23:51	D COVE	5:25:31	B BENNEYWORTH	5:28:29
52	F YOSHIMITSU	5:19:54	M MILLAN	5:21:33	M KELLY	5:23:51	I UDDIN	5:25:32	A BASS	5:28:30
53	T PRICE	5:19:57	C GEDDES	5:21:34	T ROWBOTHAM	5:23:52	J BROAD	5:25:36	T CUFF	5:28:31
54	M BADVIE	5:19:57	J BRITTON	5:21:36	P RAMSEY	5:23:55	S WEBSTER	5:25:36	C PANTING	5:28:32
55	M WINGROVE	5:19:57	I KAYE	5:21:36	R WEAVER	5:23:55	S TREHIOU	5:25:37	K MERCER	5:28:35
56	J ALEXANDER	5:19:59	C RICE	5:21:36	J CAHILL	5:23:56	K SEAR	5:25:37	A KNIGHTS	5:28:35
57	C ADAMS	5:19:59	M JEFFERY	5:21:39	M LANDER	5:23:56	L GOETRIK	5:25:39	T SHINOHARA	5:28:35
58	L DOWSEY	5:20:00	D MANNERS	5:21:40	G WILLIAMS	5:23:57	L THOMAS	5:25:39	G TUTTLE	5:28:35
59	K BAKER	5:20:01	A BUCHER	5:21:41	S MCINTYRE	5:23:57	T ROY	5:25:41	T LANGLEY	5:28:35
60	L SMITH	5:20:04	R BRETT	5:21:47	C RUNKEE	5:23:58	D MACINNES	5:25:43	T MEGNIN	5:28:35
61	C TYLER	5:20:05	L STURT	5:21:47	A LAING	5:23:58	S MCGLYNN	5:25:44	C LONGSTREET	5:28:35
62	S GRAVES	5:20:06	C ROGERS	5:21:48	M THORNTON	5:24:02	R HAMPSON	5:25:45	M HUNTLEY	5:28:35
63	R WELLS	5:20:07	P SMITH	5:21:49	R GOODMAN	5:24:03	E VAYHINGER-TERSTAPPEN	5:25:49	A MATTHEWS	5:28:35
64	D WALSH	5:20:07	J COLLISON	5:21:49	A ADEBO	5:24:03	L MCNALLY	5:25:51	C SKERRATT	5:28:36
65	J BENNETT	5:20:11	P UMPLEBY	5:21:49	R PEDDER	5:24:03	P WITTS	5:25:51	T ROBERTS	5:28:37
66	J JORDAN	5:20:15	G BARNETT	5:21:51	R FLOWERS	5:24:04	T JOHNSTONE	5:25:54	F TOMLINSON	5:28:38
67	D YARWOOD	5:20:18	S MARCHANT	5:21:52	I WRIGHT	5:24:05	D HEATHER	5:25:55	W FULKER	5:28:42
68	S TILLING	5:20:18	S MOUSTAFA	5:21:53	A YATES	5:24:05	T BREVERTON	5:25:57	C COLEMAN	5:28:44
69	N FORD	5:20:18	G NIXON	5:21:53	M FLANAGAN	5:24:05	J MAREK	5:25:58	C HAND	5:28:46
70	D GOUGH	5:20:20	J NAGLE	5:21:54	J GREEN	5:24:07	K BUCK	5:26:03	R ILLINGWORTH	5:28:46
71	C COOK	5:20:20	C LEKUTIS	5:21:54	R MCLEOD	5:24:07	K LEVERE	5:26:07	M DORR	5:28:48
72	A GOUGH	5:20:21	M MASON	5:21:55	C ELLIS	5:24:07	A MICELI	5:26:15	C LOADER	5:28:52
73	J ELDRIDGE	5:20:21	R WILSON-SMITH	5:21:55	J MC FADDEN	5:24:07	M SPARKS	5:26:18	W PHILLIPS	5:28:58
74	G PARKER	5:20:23	L MOILANEN	5:21:57	M GREENAN	5:24:07	T BUGBY	5:26:22	N TREW	5:28:58
75	V WROE	5:20:24	M PAAJANEN	5:21:58	J PRING	5:24:07	P BAZELEY	5:26:24	C MILLEDGE	5:28:58
76	N CONSTABLE	5:20:24	B DAVIDSON	5:21:58	E HOLLAND	5:24:11	C HOLLINGS	5:26:25	J HILTON	5:28:58
77	R ANDERSON	5:20:24	A QUINN	5:22:01	S MADDOX	5:24:12	G PESKETT	5:26:29	P HILTON	5:28:58
78	N HARVEY	5:20:25	A HUMPHREY	5:22:01	D PADGET	5:24:14	K BOGIE	5:26:30	J HUNTER	5:28:58
79	C STORF	5:20:25	K WINGATE	5:22:07	D GATZIAS	5:24:14	N SIMS	5:26:31	F MERRILL	5:28:58
80	C CUTLER	5:20:25	C ELTON	5:22:09	A MIDDLETON	5:24:19	A LAING	5:26:32	M NOGUCHI	5:29:03
81	C CROSS	5:20:25	P RICHARDSON	5:22:11	A GOODREID	5:24:21	M STYLES	5:26:37	J CANE	5:29:03
82	S LLOYD	5:20:26	B BROWN	5:22:17	A BOWDEN	5:24:22	P COBOULD	5:26:39	A PARTIS	5:29:03
83	M GOLDSMITH	5:20:27	G SMITH	5:22:20	I DUKE	5:24:22	D KNIBBS	5:26:40	J COLLIS	5:29:04
84	L BARON	5:20:27	N BAILLIE	5:22:21	R JESSUP	5:24:24	J BECKETT	5:26:40	D NIGEL	5:29:05
85	K FLANAGAN	5:20:27	M COOPER	5:22:25	G TURNER	5:24:24	K GENT	5:26:42	G WALKER	5:29:05
86	K CLARKE	5:20:29	M ALLEN	5:22:25	V TAYLOR	5:24:25	J WARNER	5:26:47	J CAHILL	5:29:11
87	J BROOKFIELD	5:20:31	A RANKIN	5:22:25	S STEED	5:24:26	B LEWIS	5:26:49	J FRANCIS	5:29:11
88	E HUGHES	5:20:32	J CHAI	5:22:27	A CHRISTIAN	5:24:26	E WATSON	5:26:50	R KIRK	5:29:12
89	S CHERNACK	5:20:33	H WILLIAMS	5:22:27	D KEYANI	5:24:27	J ROWLAND	5:26:51	R OSTLE	5:29:13
90	H COOPER	5:20:34	P HANDS	5:22:28	K PARKER	5:24:27	V GATEHOUSE	5:26:55	C WARBURTON	5:29:13
91	J HALPIN	5:20:35	J DUFFAY	5:22:29	D LEVENE-SAYER	5:24:27	K MATON	5:26:55	M MULLAN	5:29:15
92	J PHILLIPS	5:20:37	H PATEL	5:22:31	R WOOD	5:24:29	M JONES	5:26:56	R MARTIN	5:29:18
93	C SAWYER	5:20:38	D OWENS	5:22:32	D ADKINS	5:24:35	R RAWLINSON	5:26:59	D STEHMEYER	5:29:19
94	D PORTLOCK	5:20:38	J WELCH	5:22:33	B MALONE	5:24:35	R YAMAZAKI	5:27:05	B CREWE	5:29:23
95	S BROWNE	5:20:38	L GRICE-ROBERTS	5:22:34	S WINYARD	5:24:38	M SIMPSON	5:27:05	K KITCHENER	5:29:23
96	D SULLIVAN	5:20:44	D BRADFORD	5:22:34	J WHITEHOUSE	5:24:38	N SCHENUS	5:27:05	J SKELDON	5:29:23
97	D CARBERRY	5:20:44	S BORASO	5:22:36	D BARTON	5:24:38	R HAM	5:27:05	B BYRNE	5:29:26
98	D TURPIN	5:20:45	S HAMILTON	5:22:37	S SKINNER	5:24:41	E HEALEY	5:27:06	J HEWKIN	5:29:26
99	E KJAER	5:20:45	S BARKER	5:22:38	S HEBDON	5:24:42	G BARDILL	5:27:09	R BARR	5:29:26
100	S MCCABE	5:20:49	J CLARKE	5:22:39	M BENDING	5:24:44	J JESSEN	5:27:09	A RAMSDEN	5:29:27

	23001-23100		23101-23200		23201-23300		23301-23400		23401-23500	
1	Y SMITH	5:29:29	S SKINNER	5:31:54	N SINGH	5:34:13	V HUMPHRIES	5:37:25	M PANANCEAU	5:40:22
2	A FAULKNER	5:29:29	P SLATER	5:31:54	C JOHN	5:34:13	F ELLIS	5:37:26	J SMITH	5:40:25
3	V COOK	5:29:30	P KAVANAGH	5:31:55	D DEAN	5:34:14	D EARL	5:37:28	C MELAUGH	5:40:26
4	D FLYNN	5:29:30	M THISTLETHWAYTE	5:31:55	J MADIN	5:34:17	M BAXTER	5:37:31	D WRAY	5:40:27
5	B PALMER	5:29:31	H WILSON	5:31:55	P REILLY	5:34:19	D BAXTER	5:37:31	S ROCCIA	5:40:30
6	L NOVAK	5:29:33	E SEXTON	5:31:56	S MCNAMEE	5:34:23	B ROBINSON	5:37:32	M WARBURTON	5:40:32
7	G THOMAS	5:29:34	J MARSH	5:31:58	J SILVEY	5:34:25	S BOND	5:37:38	J FLANAGAN	5:40:35
8	A BAZZONI	5:29:34	S HICKS	5:31:59	E MCMAHON	5:34:28	G GIBERTONI	5:37:40	F MURTAGH	5:40:35
9	J MORAN	5:29:35	I CROUCH	5:31:59	J JOHNSON	5:34:28	G MORTON	5:37:44	T KITSON	5:40:35
10	M ADLER	5:29:35	J PRESTON	5:31:59	M UOPI	5:34:29	K EL GANA	5:37:50	F WHITE	5:40:35
11	A DOSSETTER	5:29:41	G CULLEN	5:31:59	P WILLIAMS	5:34:29	L WALTON	5:37:53	G WILLETTS	5:40:43
12	A PAYNE	5:29:42	S FLETCHER	5:31:59	S WILLIAMS	5:34:29	R CAILE	5:37:53	S BEVITT	5:40:44
13	N TOBITT-YATES	5:29:44	R PENN	5:32:01	G UOPI	5:34:30	G POPE	5:37:55	D BOWEN	5:40:44
14	P YATES	5:29:44	J ALLEN	5:32:01	G ROTOLI	5:34:34	M CLAPPERTON	5:37:56	B SILVER	5:40:45
15	I GASCOYNE	5:29:46	M LONGMAN	5:32:01	P PEROTTA	5:34:39	J COULSON	5:37:59	R SUTTON	5:40:46
16	M PLATO	5:29:52	E TURNER	5:32:02	M RAIMOND	5:34:39	D EYERS	5:38:01	J ASTLEY	5:40:50
17	A FRANCIS	5:29:55	T COKE	5:32:03	M FERNANDO	5:34:47	D COWEN	5:38:03	A MARCHI	5:40:51
18	I JENKINS	5:29:59	S PANGBORN	5:32:04	J WINSTANLEY	5:34:51	T FOLEY	5:38:04	C WALLWORK	5:40:51
19	S GOTHAM	5:30:04	A WALKER	5:32:04	M WINSTANLEY	5:34:51	R FERRIN	5:38:04	D WALLWORK	5:40:51
20	E PHIPPS	5:30:05	S CLARKE	5:32:08	L GOLDSTEIN	5:34:55	B PEARCE	5:38:05	A FRIEND	5:40:51
21	R MILBURN	5:30:07	M SWAN	5:32:10	L TUFFEN	5:34:59	D CLOTHIER	5:38:06	R SNOEK	5:40:52
22	L GRAVINA	5:30:08	W WATERS	5:32:14	K WATSON	5:35:00	M HAWES	5:38:10	J DAILLY	5:40:54
23	P JACKSON	5:30:09	A BROWN	5:32:15	J DEVLIN	5:35:05	R LYON	5:38:10	N DOFFMAN	5:40:55
24	R THRIPPLETON	5:30:09	G WOODS	5:32:16	P MCGEACHIN	5:35:09	F VILLALOBOS	5:38:11	B SMITH	5:40:57
25	V HOLDING	5:30:09	L ENGLAND	5:32:16	E DEVINE	5:35:10	S HEWISON	5:38:12	D ANDERSON	5:41:00
26	N ISAAC	5:30:10	C GILLILAND	5:32:17	D SPILSBURY	5:35:10	J GALLAGHER	5:38:14	W CASENGHI	5:41:03
27	M HUWEL	5:30:15	C MICHAEL	5:32:21	N STURMEY	5:35:11	A THORPE	5:38:15	B VALOPPI	5:41:03
28	B HURDITCH	5:30:16	M MOUNT	5:32:24	A RABY	5:35:11	J DAVYS	5:38:15	J CULLEN-O'CONNOR	5:41:04
29	J PEWTRESS	5:30:17	B BIGGS	5:32:24	D KELLY	5:35:12	J DAMMARELL	5:38:17	F MORRIS	5:41:04
30	M ROWDEN	5:30:19	P DIX	5:32:25	H JAMES	5:35:15	N CURTIS	5:38:19	M WHITMARSH	5:41:06
31	P VANDERHEYDEN	5:30:19	M TRUSSLER	5:32:29	N SYDENHAM	5:35:15	A TURNER	5:38:22	P CHEAL	5:41:06
32	A TWIGG	5:30:22	B COONEY	5:32:30	M TAYLOR	5:35:15	B BAKER	5:38:23	A BULL	5:41:10
33	E PARLOUR	5:30:23	K SPARROW	5:32:30	T CAMERON	5:35:17	J COSTA	5:38:24	E PRESTON	5:41:11
34	K FORD	5:30:23	J LONG	5:32:30	J VILLEGAS	5:35:17	P BURKE	5:38:25	E DOWLING	5:41:11
35	B ANDERSON	5:30:23	G KEELING	5:32:31	L MCCALLUM	5:35:19	R FARRELL	5:38:26	J CRESSWELL	5:41:15
36	D BARKER	5:30:24	J HYNES	5:32:32	J ADCOCK	5:35:20	S RUNECKLES	5:38:26	F RAWNSLEY	5:41:15
37	J JACKSON	5:30:24	A FROST	5:32:36	M YOUPA	5:35:20	J HODDY	5:38:26	C HILL	5:41:21
38	C STARK	5:30:28	G MAY	5:32:36	L PEACOCK	5:35:23	G COOK	5:38:29	A MACDONALD	5:41:23
39	B WARD	5:30:29	P CRONIN	5:32:42	J CREWES	5:35:26	D HOOKER	5:38:29	C COWLIN	5:41:26
40	G WIGGIN	5:30:29	G GRAHAM	5:32:44	B SCOTT	5:35:28	C FARR	5:38:36	A JONES	5:41:26
41	W MANKIN	5:30:29	P MURPHY	5:32:44	L HEAD	5:35:28	B THILLIER	5:38:36	L FERRIER	5:41:31
42	W GEHRKE	5:30:31	J ALKINS	5:32:45	A BAILEY	5:35:29	H JOSEPH	5:38:36	J FERRIER	5:41:31
43	P BROWNBILL	5:30:36	M HAY	5:32:49	T CARROLL	5:35:29	M FISHPOOL	5:38:37	C PALMER	5:41:34
44	H HOPKINS	5:30:36	M WELLS	5:32:51	J NEWMAN	5:35:33	A FISHPOOL	5:38:38	A KING	5:41:39
45	W SIM	5:30:38	D DOLAN	5:32:54	T SOLLIS	5:35:33	C BRENNAN	5:38:44	B EMLEY	5:41:40
46	W MOULTON	5:30:38	M MERRELL	5:32:54	S MADDRELL	5:35:33	T GIBBS	5:38:45	G GIFFIN	5:41:41
47	D HYETT	5:30:38	M SHIMURA	5:32:54	B GOLLOP	5:35:35	S ADDY	5:38:50	E BROWN	5:41:41
48	S BAKER	5:30:39	I FRITH	5:32:56	S ATKINSON	5:35:35	D DRAPER	5:38:51	P BROWN	5:41:41
49	C BENCH	5:30:40	T WILKIE	5:32:59	J MCINTOSH	5:35:36	M THOMPSON	5:38:51	M HANNIGAN	5:41:42
50	G MEIKLE	5:30:44	P BULLEN	5:33:02	G FOX	5:35:36	P THOMPSON	5:38:51	J O'NEILL	5:41:42
51	K GRANT	5:30:48	K HOPKINS	5:33:03	P DUDLEY	5:35:37	J BLOW	5:38:52	G TAYLOR	5:41:43
52	L MONK	5:30:52	M ACKROYD	5:33:03	T HIORNS	5:35:40	E SNOW	5:38:55	R BALUKIEWICZ	5:41:45
53	P KEERIE	5:30:57	K NEILSON	5:33:04	M ROBINSON	5:35:41	A ANWAR	5:38:56	S JONES	5:41:50
54	G WARREN	5:30:57	P COMPER	5:33:06	J SPENCER	5:35:43	G WARD	5:38:56	J FRIGGENS	5:41:50
55	M DOBDON	5:30:59	A PULLING	5:33:08	B TOMPKINS	5:35:44	P FALLON	5:38:58	M KILVERT	5:41:52
56	K MARSHALL	5:30:59	N TUNNICLIFFE	5:33:09	R JONES	5:35:48	C INGLIS	5:38:59	I ROBINSON	5:41:52
57	J REAVILL	5:31:01	D FENSOM	5:33:10	J LACK	5:35:52	D DUNNING	5:38:59	D BARLOW	5:41:52
58	N DALTON	5:31:02	A BRILLI	5:33:11	B LACK	5:35:53	E THOMAS	5:39:00	M HARTLEY	5:41:53
59	Z KARIM	5:31:03	K SMITH	5:33:12	R DELSINI	5:35:53	F MASSON	5:39:00	T DOSS	5:41:54
60	M TYRRELL	5:31:05	R STRAWBRIDGE	5:33:12	B COLES	5:36:01	M THOMAS	5:39:01	T PATEL	5:41:54
61	R HOGG	5:31:05	J RICHARDS	5:33:14	B HARWOOD	5:36:04	D WILLOTT	5:39:02	A WALLER	5:41:55
62	A MOON	5:31:06	C SIMMONS	5:33:17	A HALFYARD	5:36:06	W RONCA	5:39:02	A SLOCUMBE	5:41:55
63	E ANNONI	5:31:07	J MACKAY	5:33:17	J MILLER	5:36:06	S FRANCIS	5:39:03	O BIGGS	5:41:56
64	A HAMPTON	5:31:08	A RENNY	5:33:18	A CORNELIUS	5:36:09	M BEDETTI	5:39:03	G BAKER	5:41:56
65	P HANCOCK	5:31:10	A ALLITT	5:33:21	M DEARSON	5:36:14	R D'ATH	5:39:05	P LINDEGAARD	5:41:57
66	T BRACKLEY	5:31:13	R TALBOT	5:33:21	L BRADLEY	5:36:14	H JACKSON	5:39:06	W TODD-JAMES	5:41:57
67	T CROSS	5:31:19	A RICE	5:33:21	D HOGGETT	5:36:19	A BERNSTEIN	5:39:07	J ECCLESTON	5:41:57
68	G THAKERAR	5:31:19	B OSULLIVAN	5:33:22	S BROOKS	5:36:19	I RATNAIKE	5:39:09	C HERRINGTON	5:42:01
69	R SHAH	5:31:20	R MCGUIRE	5:33:23	M COFFILL	5:36:19	T LENNIE	5:39:10	D ATTER	5:42:01
70	J BEAMISH	5:31:20	S BATCHELOR	5:33:23	T SIMONS	5:36:21	A KING	5:39:11	M HODGES	5:42:03
71	J WEATHERALL	5:31:21	J GILMARTIN	5:33:24	C ALLEN	5:36:31	D LLOYD	5:39:11	R JONES	5:42:03
72	M REED	5:31:25	D DAVIES	5:33:25	R GODDARD	5:36:32	D MARTIN	5:39:11	P RAWLINSON	5:42:08
73	Y YUSUF	5:31:27	J FRENCH	5:33:25	I ABBAS	5:36:33	S BARTHOLOMEW	5:39:11	S SAUNDERS	5:42:09
74	T BLACK	5:31:28	S MADDOCKS	5:33:26	K ANGELL	5:36:39	S LLOYD	5:39:11	E TURNBULL	5:42:09
75	N HOUGHTON	5:31:28	C COTTER	5:33:26	T CARSBERG	5:36:42	L WINNING	5:39:11	E TIMSON	5:42:10
76	J SPRECKLEY	5:31:28	J MOLLANE	5:33:26	D SLADE	5:36:47	J GREENFIELD	5:39:11	B SAMPSON	5:42:16
77	J JAMES	5:31:29	K CHIVERS	5:33:28	R EATON	5:36:47	M DIXON	5:39:11	S ZAMBONI	5:42:18
78	D TURNER	5:31:29	J HARRISON	5:33:32	G FORD	5:36:47	J THOMPSON	5:39:11	W HOBBS	5:42:21
79	K FRENCH	5:31:35	J DEMAIN-GRIFFITHS	5:33:32	N BROOM	5:36:49	L BOOTLAND	5:39:11	N CLARK	5:42:24
80	B BELLAMY	5:31:35	P MOORE	5:33:36	T WILLIAMS	5:36:51	G PETERS	5:39:11	P GIBSON	5:42:24
81	S REYNOLDS	5:31:35	T ROBERTS	5:33:41	B SMITH	5:36:52	M ARAKI	5:39:11	D BYRNE	5:42:24
82	T REYNOLDS	5:31:35	P GOSLING	5:33:47	K LYNN	5:36:53	J HARTJE	5:39:16	R BROWN	5:42:27
83	R MICHAUD	5:31:35	L COLLIER	5:33:48	A CHERNACK	5:36:54	R PETRUZZI	5:39:20	E PILLINGER	5:42:28
84	S KNIGHT	5:31:38	B COLLIER	5:33:48	C PLENT	5:36:55	T ATKINSON	5:39:21	A JONES	5:42:30
85	J WRENCH	5:31:38	P MILLER	5:33:54	T JONES	5:36:56	H SCHUTTE	5:39:24	G GRANT	5:42:40
86	M GRAGE	5:31:40	G TAURISANO	5:33:55	N VANSON	5:36:57	A RANSOME	5:39:25	P SCOTT	5:42:46
87	H AIRHART	5:31:41	D EDWARDS	5:33:57	R PENSON	5:36:58	M CROCKER	5:39:25	E SCOTT	5:42:46
88	P RAY	5:31:44	S TAYLOR	5:33:57	D SHEPHERD	5:36:59	A BURGESS	5:39:26	A DUFF	5:42:46
89	E FERNEE	5:31:44	W JOHNSTONE	5:33:57	R ARROWSMITH	5:37:00	E CURRAN	5:39:26	G HINCHCLIFFE	5:42:48
90	R WHEATON	5:31:44	R LAXMAN	5:33:58	K DOVE	5:37:00	D GILL	5:39:31	D WALKER	5:42:49
91	R MILLER	5:31:45	J ALLBONES	5:34:01	M WILSON	5:37:00	C MENDE	5:39:31	T COWLING	5:42:54
92	C SWAYNE	5:31:48	J ALLEN	5:34:01	B WHYMARK	5:37:03	T NOBLE	5:39:45	D PLUMB	5:42:54
93	A SWAYNE	5:31:49	M HESP	5:34:02	M MANNION	5:37:03	V BAALHAM	5:39:55	P REEVE	5:42:58
94	E DA PAIXAO	5:31:50	P TAYLOR	5:34:03	J ARNOLD	5:37:03	G ROBERTS	5:39:59	K REEVE	5:42:58
95	N WILKINSON	5:31:50	M BROOKS	5:34:07	V BRIGGS	5:37:04	R SOUTHAM	5:40:10	W WILKINS	5:42:59
96	P THOMAS	5:31:51	D YOUNG	5:34:07	M BRIGGS	5:37:04	M DORRINGTON	5:40:10	K ANDERSON	5:43:02
97	E CASE	5:31:51	W ROGERS	5:34:10	J STACKHOUSE	5:37:13	S SMEDLEY	5:40:14	D SIMMONS	5:43:02
98	J EDWARDS	5:31:51	R RAJAKRISHNGN	5:34:12	M CLACK	5:37:18	B CHAPMAN	5:40:17	N SWAFFER	5:43:02
99	D PORTZENEM	5:31:52	E MATTHEWS	5:34:13	G COOPER	5:37:22	A SIMMONS	5:40:18	R SOUTHWELL	5:43:05
100	S GRATTON	5:31:53	K WATSON	5:34:13	D ROE	5:37:22	I PAGE	5:40:20	R ELDER	5:43:07

#	23501-23600		23601-23700		23701-23800		23801-23900		23901-24000	
1	C CAMILETTI	5:43:10	I WALDMEYER	5:46:33	L ROBERTS	5:49:48	L BUTLER	5:54:40	M BERGIN	5:59:28
2	A HAWES	5:43:10	P CARTER	5:46:33	S ADAMS	5:49:48	Y TURNER	5:54:42	A MORRISON	5:59:31
3	S GODWIN	5:43:12	J HACKER	5:46:39	P BLAKE	5:49:48	C CLARKE	5:54:42	P BAINES	5:59:36
4	B MILLS	5:43:14	R PARSONS	5:46:43	P WATSON	5:49:50	R JENNINGS	5:54:42	S PITMAN	5:59:44
5	E EDMONDS	5:43:15	E PERKS	5:46:47	B HILARY	5:49:52	N JENNINGS	5:54:42	J JACKSON	5:59:44
6	C FASSOMS	5:43:21	R BRISTOW	5:46:48	F BAILLIE	5:49:52	R JENNINGS	5:54:42	P FRIEL	5:59:47
7	A BASS	5:43:23	J TERHORST	5:46:50	C FRANCOME	5:49:55	P WALLER	5:54:42	D CURTIS	5:59:52
8	J ARNOLD	5:43:27	S BROWN	5:46:53	L THOMAS	5:50:01	M LUCY	5:54:49	D CRACKWELL	5:59:53
9	M BLUETT	5:43:33	R BROOMHEAD	5:46:53	I FOWLER	5:50:03	C PIGRAM	5:54:49	A FIGGETT	5:59:55
10	D RIDEOUT	5:43:34	S MCANULTY	5:47:00	W AYLOTT	5:50:03	K JONES	5:54:50	I DAVIES	5:59:56
11	A MUNDY	5:43:34	C HYNES	5:47:02	A BAGGOTT	5:50:05	S BOLLAND	5:54:58	J GRAHAM	5:59:57
12	G KEMP	5:43:44	N MONTAROUP	5:47:12	B GROVES	5:50:19	J HALLAS	5:54:59	R BRIND	5:59:58
13	P MULCAHY	5:43:44	M SUEUR	5:47:14	S PORTMAN	5:50:20	L BREAR	5:54:59	P COVENEY	5:59:58
14	V DENNIS	5:43:44	J GARDINER	5:47:14	M GAMMON	5:50:20	D REDDICK	5:55:02	V CROSS	5:59:59
15	C DENNIS	5:43:44	J GARDINER	5:47:14	N LAIRD	5:50:20	K RATCLIFFE	5:55:02	E HIRST	5:59:59
16	M MCFADYEN	5:43:46	J VAN DEN BEGIN	5:47:14	R JENKINS	5:50:20	A MORRISON	5:55:02	J GILL	6:00:04
17	N A'HEARN-KEHOE	5:43:47	L FOWLER	5:47:14	P NEILSON	5:50:24	T STANTON	5:55:02	B HALL	6:00:04
18	P HARDY	5:43:50	M BEESE	5:47:14	R MILLER	5:50:26	S KENWARD	5:55:04	J MCCAVISH	6:00:09
19	D BROWNE	5:43:50	G BALT	5:47:14	M JUMAA	5:50:26	R HENDERSON	5:55:05	S MAGUIRE	6:00:10
20	R MUNTZ	5:43:51	B DUENGEN	5:47:14	S COLE	5:50:27	I HEFFRON	5:55:06	E COWLEY	6:00:10
21	T SHERIDAN	5:43:53	K SILFANG	5:47:17	L AUSTIN	5:50:29	N PERRY	5:55:15	D GRIFFITHS	6:00:10
22	T MAXWELL	5:43:53	G TRIMM	5:47:19	S JOHNSON	5:50:29	F JONES	5:55:15	V SAUNDERS	6:00:10
23	J OVENDEN	5:43:55	R ETHERIDGE	5:47:21	K CROOK	5:50:30	C HAWKINS	5:55:15	D BROCKWELL	6:00:10
24	K COX	5:44:02	M IRELAND	5:47:21	R LEE	5:50:31	I YOUNG	5:55:24	R STEARN	6:00:10
25	B LORD	5:44:05	M THOMPSON	5:47:21	C MARSH	5:50:31	J HAYDEN	5:55:25	J FULTON	6:00:10
26	C WILLIAMS	5:44:05	W PLUCKROSE	5:47:21	G CLOUGH	5:50:32	B FOSTER	5:55:26	W FERRIDAY	6:00:10
27	L GRACE	5:44:05	G GOREY	5:47:26	H PATON	5:50:38	T REID	5:55:29	M SERGENT	6:00:10
28	G BENNETT	5:44:10	P BRENNAN	5:47:28	J GRIFFITHS	5:50:43	C STREETER	5:55:56	C WALLIS	6:00:10
29	H FIRTH	5:44:14	N NEW	5:47:29	J DELANEY	5:50:48	S WARRICK	5:55:58	H BARRETT	6:00:10
30	R MASON	5:44:14	P THOMAS	5:47:34	P TAPP	5:51:11	S KARSTENS	5:55:58	C HOODLESS	6:00:10
31	E CARPENTER	5:44:17	D GASSER	5:47:34	D MARTIN	5:51:15	G LILLIEROTH	5:56:07	T HOODLESS	6:00:10
32	K PASCOE	5:44:17	S WHITE	5:47:35	D SPECK	5:51:20	M SWANN	5:56:08	S WOODALL	6:00:10
33	A REID	5:44:22	S WHITE	5:47:35	J JARRETT	5:51:23	M BOLTON	5:56:08	B BALDWIN	6:00:10
34	E DONOVAN	5:44:29	J HOLMES	5:47:36	D BATES	5:51:23	G SPAULL	5:56:09	G MAKAROWICZ	6:00:10
35	D LEWIS	5:44:29	W BELLARIS	5:47:36	S HARDY	5:51:27	E KLAVER	5:56:14	S HENDERSON	6:00:11
36	D CORRADINE	5:44:31	C TAPPER	5:47:37	D JOYCE	5:51:27	D NOBLE	5:56:18	R CLEMENTS	6:00:53
37	W CRYER	5:44:33	D HICKIE	5:47:37	C HARPER	5:51:28	N DRAGE	5:56:21	D SMITH	6:00:54
38	P HODGES	5:44:35	D O'BRIEN	5:47:41	R HARPER	5:51:28	J DUKE	5:56:29	A JONES	6:00:56
39	J KAMINSKI	5:44:35	A GWINNELL	5:47:44	A JAMES	5:51:28	L BURTON	5:56:30	B ANKERS	6:01:02
40	E DEVLIN	5:44:43	M AMY	5:47:46	D BENNETT	5:51:30	J ROBERTSHAW	5:56:34	J HOWARD	6:01:02
41	J FORD	5:44:43	T TOWN	5:47:47	M CHAN	5:51:33	S BROWN	5:56:34	M WEBB	6:01:02
42	D MARKS	5:44:48	M SHIELDS	5:47:47	G BRANSON	5:51:35	T BARRY	5:56:34	M HOWES	6:01:02
43	K CHAPMAN	5:44:50	D TANN	5:47:47	F PIZZICHEMI	5:51:44	M EVANS	5:56:47	P IVES	6:01:13
44	I CLUBB	5:44:52	M FARADAY	5:47:47	P JACOBS	5:51:47	B JOHNSTON	5:56:58	M PERRY	6:01:19
45	Y STEWART	5:44:53	J WILLER	5:47:47	D JACOBS	5:51:48	R JOHNSTON	5:56:58	J CLEMENT	6:01:23
46	S CROSS	5:44:55	J WALLACE	5:47:47	V DIBLEY	5:51:57	N PEARSON	5:56:59	G POTE	6:01:24
47	D CONSTABLE	5:44:55	J AVERY	5:47:47	I ORTON	5:51:59	A DOWNS	5:56:59	G RUSSELL-HOLMES	6:01:37
48	S FOSTER	5:45:00	B DOHERTY	5:47:48	M COX	5:52:01	A MCLELLAN	5:56:59	R HALVORSEN	6:01:39
49	G WHITTLE	5:45:00	C EVERETT	5:47:49	I WESSON	5:52:03	S BENSTEAD	5:57:00	C WEATHERLEY	6:01:39
50	S CHAPPELL	5:45:00	T MELLETT	5:47:50	B DOBSON	5:52:12	A CAMP	5:57:01	P WEATHERLEY	6:01:39
51	P PALMER	5:45:00	J ORIORDAN	5:47:51	M SIMMONDS	5:52:16	J KHOO	5:57:01	C RYALL	6:01:40
52	I WALLIS	5:45:00	N MAYLOR	5:47:51	P CADOGAN	5:52:16	D BARKER	5:57:07	L MAPP	6:01:40
53	J HANNAN	5:45:01	A SURGENOR	5:47:51	S STUART	5:52:19	I PERRY	5:57:12	R STONE	6:01:41
54	A GENT	5:45:01	S CHALLANS	5:47:53	T SCARF	5:52:26	S GOODYEAR	5:57:13	R SNGH BASSAN	6:01:48
55	D EDWARDS	5:45:07	G MACLEOD	5:47:53	A COSTAR	5:52:30	M MORGAN-JONES	5:57:13	J TOLLEY	6:02:03
56	M BARKER	5:45:07	J SHERWOOD	5:47:58	R HALFYARD	5:52:35	H BISKOP	5:57:21	C HEMMINGS	6:02:07
57	P SARGEANT	5:45:07	Q COCHRAN	5:48:02	M RAYNER	5:52:35	A BUNTING	5:57:21	G TYE	6:02:08
58	W FOLEY	5:45:08	A QUICK	5:48:02	R HOWLETT	5:52:36	H COHEN	5:57:25	J DAKERS	6:02:10
59	A MILLIGAN	5:45:08	C SHAW	5:48:06	M AYLING	5:52:36	D ADAMSON	5:57:40	T JAMES	6:02:10
60	T HERON	5:45:09	N WOODALL	5:48:07	A HODGE	5:52:38	M GLOVER	5:57:47	R GOODFELLOW	6:02:12
61	L SHIRLEY	5:45:11	P SHERRINGTON	5:48:09	J HASTINGS	5:52:38	C DAVIES	5:57:47	M PROCTOR	6:02:14
62	K GARNHAM	5:45:11	S LANGMAN	5:48:09	B HASTINGS	5:52:38	K BOSELEY	5:57:47	L WILKINS	6:02:14
63	J TILTON	5:45:16	C PHILLIPS	5:48:09	R CREWE	5:52:40	P BRIGHTMAN	5:57:56	A CONKIE	6:02:17
64	G GRAVES	5:45:24	A GIBSON	5:48:09	R MORGAN	5:52:40	C LIVESEY	5:57:57	D SULLIVAN	6:02:28
65	R GRAVES	5:45:24	R PYBURN	5:48:09	J CLINK	5:52:40	J PEACOCK	5:57:59	H BELCHER	6:02:28
66	H ARIK	5:45:25	J PORT	5:48:09	G CASADEI	5:52:46	J RAVEN	5:58:00	J SEAMAN	6:02:29
67	P WEST	5:45:25	H MORSHEAD	5:48:09	A CARTER	5:52:46	M RAVEN	5:58:00	S JOHNSON	6:02:29
68	M TINEY	5:45:34	A PAGE	5:48:11	A HENDERSON	5:52:46	S HAMILTON	5:58:03	I ROTHWELL	6:02:29
69	D WARNER	5:45:37	P CROSSAN	5:48:17	G EVANS	5:52:49	P BOWMAN	5:58:03	S OWEN-WILLIAMS	6:02:29
70	B GREENSMITH	5:45:38	D WHITEHEAD	5:48:28	M COSTELLO	5:52:54	R CROUCH	5:58:10	B KIRK	6:02:44
71	M DAVIS	5:45:38	D EVANS	5:48:32	S EGGAR	5:52:54	S BARKLEY	5:58:10	D TYE	6:02:47
72	G BRACKSTONE	5:45:40	H FORD	5:48:32	C SPINK	5:52:59	S BARKLEY	5:58:18	M WROE	6:02:51
73	M DAVIS	5:45:42	P GARDINER	5:48:33	F GAFFNEY	5:53:00	J BENFIELD	5:58:18	K JANIS	6:02:54
74	S LOVICK	5:45:42	E MAEDA	5:48:35	A TINDALL	5:53:04	P BLAKESLEY	5:58:20	S WEBB	6:02:55
75	H HUMPAGE	5:45:44	A WHITEFORD	5:48:35	T HULETT	5:53:04	H JONES	5:58:20	J GRAHAM	6:03:04
76	S FITZPATRICK	5:45:45	P PALMER	5:48:37	M JACOBS	5:53:07	T ASHBURNER	5:58:24	P MENSAM	6:03:04
77	K HARDING	5:45:48	P HAWKES	5:48:42	R DOMMETT	5:53:11	J DURRANT	5:58:28	M WEGERLE	6:03:04
78	D NUGENT	5:45:50	J HAZEL	5:48:43	M BUNCH	5:53:16	D SMITH	5:58:32	M HUGHES	6:03:16
79	D MANSON	5:45:54	J HOWE	5:48:44	P JOHNSON	5:53:33	P MCGILLIVRAY	5:58:32	N ALLISON	6:03:24
80	K ARNOLD	5:45:55	K GRIEVE	5:48:44	J CORNWALL-TOMBS	5:53:38	P BLUNT	5:58:37	B LEWIS	6:03:32
81	J WASTELL	5:45:55	G WRIGHT	5:48:44	S JONES	5:53:44	R GRIFFITHS	5:58:40	E GOOD	6:03:33
82	P SMITH	5:45:57	W WARREN	5:48:45	M KOSAK	5:53:49	V HUNT	5:58:43	L PARKER	6:03:37
83	A WASE	5:45:57	B DAVIES	5:48:55	L WAINMAN	5:53:52	D MCCARRICK	5:58:43	P CLACK	6:03:41
84	B SMITH	5:45:58	M BRAMHAM	5:48:58	W WAINMAN	5:53:52	G LEWIS	5:58:43	J HOULDERSHAW	6:03:49
85	A BENNETT	5:45:58	L SCOTT	5:48:58	P IVERS	5:53:54	A GILBERT	5:58:43	A TURNER	6:04:06
86	C WILDERSPIN	5:45:59	T NOBLE	5:48:59	W SEAGER	5:53:54	D ANDERSON	5:58:44	M FOUQUE	6:04:07
87	K EARLE	5:46:05	A WREN	5:49:00	N NALDEN	5:53:54	K HARRISON	5:58:44	M REID	6:04:13
88	D HARBORD	5:46:05	J KERCHER	5:49:12	I NORGAARD	5:53:54	A HICKEY	5:59:02	J KELLY	6:04:20
89	M TILLEY	5:46:05	A ROWLEY	5:49:14	K THOMAS	5:53:54	J WALKER	5:59:03	O WAYE	6:04:27
90	J WALTERS	5:46:05	G FRIEDMAN	5:49:14	E VALT	5:53:55	C STEWART	5:59:10	D GRAINGE	6:04:39
91	J WOLSTENCROFT	5:46:08	C LEVERIDGE	5:49:15	J EAST	5:53:56	R IVERSEN	5:59:16	S HOWELLS	6:04:47
92	M KING	5:46:08	R HORSLER	5:49:15	A EPTON	5:54:02	G IVERSEN	5:59:17	N JODE	6:05:01
93	G HAMER	5:46:16	A SHARPE	5:49:16	N NEIGHBOUR	5:54:12	D MCCORMACK	5:59:17	K BRUCE	6:05:01
94	T MILLIGAN	5:46:25	T HAMILTON	5:49:20	S LEWIS	5:54:14	M DUVAL	5:59:17	P FRENCH	6:05:11
95	R HENN	5:46:25	J MILLE	5:49:24	J DENNIS	5:54:26	R FAINT	5:59:18	G LEBRETT	6:05:11
96	B SAUNDERS	5:46:27	S CLEAVER	5:49:24	K HEMANTHA KUMAR	5:54:27	L GRINBERGS	5:59:23	D GEE	6:05:11
97	M TEMPLEMAN	5:46:27	J HAZELWOOD	5:49:36	O RODRIGUEZ	5:54:35	L ARTHURELL	5:59:25	G WATTS	6:05:22
98	C LAUGA	5:46:27	C HAMILTON-BATE	5:49:41	S BALANDRAN	5:54:36	A SMITH	5:59:25	D RIDLEY	6:06:02
99	A BARNARD	5:46:30	R MCKENNA	5:49:45	G SIMON	5:54:37	D GILBERT	5:59:27	J MURPHY	6:06:09
100	K TEWKESBURY	5:46:32	A THOMPSON	5:49:48	F BLACK	5:54:37	J KERR	5:59:28	A CHELTON	6:06:13

	24001-24100		24101-24200		24201-24300		24301-24400		24401-24450	
1	K LEUNG	6:06:13	P KELLY	6:14:55	R EXON	6:27:10	K HALL	6:46:02	A STRACEY	7:13:54
2	J TAYLOR	6:06:24	S MERRITT	6:14:56	M BATES	6:27:30	S FAIRNINGTON	6:46:14	P FURZEY	7:14:18
3	R SHACKELL	6:06:31	P JACKSON	6:15:00	D NEALE	6:27:30	P MORRIS	6:46:58	S ESCRITT	7:16:17
4	R LODGE	6:06:36	M WHITTAKER	6:15:01	P DENT	6:27:57	J GORRIE	6:47:09	J COURTMAN	7:16:18
5	S FERGUSON	6:06:40	R START	6:15:01	P SQUIRRELL	6:28:09	A BROWN	6:47:29	P TUFFIN	7:16:26
6	C BURNS	6:06:45	W ALLPRESS	6:15:01	R WHITTLETON	6:28:09	B CURTIS	6:47:50	L MULLAN	7:17:00
7	S DAVIES	6:06:48	D VALE	6:15:01	M DEJOURNETTE	6:28:10	D FERRIS	6:47:57	E THOMAS	7:17:00
8	K GRANT	6:06:48	M YARROW	6:15:04	B MORIARTY	6:28:45	M THOMAS	6:47:57	L BORSHEIM	7:17:10
9	J GOODALL	6:06:56	D OXBORROW	6:15:17	G CLAYTON	6:28:45	S MEADOWS	6:47:57	T NAERLAND	7:17:11
10	M SALTER	6:07:05	A STONARD	6:15:20	J WEBSTER	6:28:47	C WISE	6:47:58	E WRIGHT	7:17:11
11	K KOBAYASHI	6:07:08	M MC GUINNESS	6:15:21	C SADDLER	6:28:48	R CARDER	6:47:58	J ALLEN	7:17:34
12	B BHOJANI	6:07:21	K COLLINS	6:15:30	J SADDLER	6:28:48	S WILLIAMS	6:48:12	P ENVILLE	7:18:01
13	V LAVIN	6:07:25	S SARDI	6:15:31	J WORF	6:28:52	J CAMERON	6:48:25	B ROGERS	7:18:02
14	T COOKSEY	6:07:30	M TREACY	6:15:34	R BUSHNELL	6:28:58	V MOORE	6:48:32	U HOLT	7:18:02
15	R KIRK	6:07:54	J URQUHART	6:15:47	W MARSH	6:29:01	S PACEY	6:48:39	A BILLSON	7:19:40
16	T THOMPSON	6:08:02	P RAINBIRD	6:15:59	F BROWN	6:29:17	D THOMAS	6:48:46	K DRAKE	7:19:41
17	F WITTS	6:08:03	I BAILEY	6:16:09	M CLARKE	6:29:54	T MCGEOGHAN	6:48:47	J SOLEY	7:21:28
18	M MOSCHELLA	6:08:08	K GILBERT	6:16:30	L DOSS	6:29:56	F FERRETT	6:49:25	M ROGERS	7:21:40
19	A NUNEZ	6:08:10	P STREET	6:16:31	H MCGEORGE	6:29:56	M JARVIS	6:49:46	L CAIN	7:21:40
20	S HOGARTH	6:08:10	M THOMAS	6:16:38	K HUNT	6:30:22	D GREGORY	6:49:46	A WILLIAMS	7:22:00
21	N BARBER	6:08:10	V LE CUIROT	6:16:38	K BUNNISS	6:30:29	J DELL	6:50:10	A SUTCLIFFE	7:24:28
22	L RUNKEE	6:08:27	J WATTS	6:16:38	W GREENWOOD	6:30:30	N PARAGREEN	6:50:10	M EYRE	7:24:36
23	B NOBLE	6:08:42	D BLACKWELL	6:16:38	L CORBELL	6:31:46	P WILLIS	6:50:12	R STYLES	7:24:36
24	N THOMSON	6:08:44	J GOLDSMITH	6:16:38	D EATON	6:31:59	D MCGUIRE	6:50:48	J GREENWOOD	7:25:32
25	J ATKINS	6:08:45	M PEREZ BADELL	6:16:43	R REHAL	6:32:01	P MITCHELL	6:51:29	S WOODRUFF	7:26:13
26	G CARNES	6:08:45	J LOWE	6:16:46	W GIBNEY	6:32:01	V HUNT	6:51:33	H WATSON	7:29:10
27	E ARETZ	6:08:50	R SAUNDERS	6:16:47	P SADRA	6:32:06	B HUNT	6:52:11	M BORGEN	7:30:16
28	Y CETINKAYA	6:08:55	L WEST	6:17:13	A SAWOJKA	6:32:48	M LEE	6:52:16	B ROBINSON	7:31:22
29	R HOOPER	6:09:01	E COPPINS	6:17:22	C BAXTER	6:33:01	C ODERBOLZ	6:52:16	R CLARK	7:32:19
30	T BONSON	6:09:04	M DUNN	6:17:29	P BROWN	6:33:01	H TIDSWELL	6:52:22	M HOLLINGDALE	7:33:43
31	P CORROON	6:09:09	G LAWLOR	6:17:29	T RUNCINAN	6:33:03	D GOOD	6:52:23	E SELKIRK	7:34:37
32	S PAYNE	6:09:09	R WAINWRIGHT	6:17:38	B HOLDICH	6:33:04	M GOOD	6:52:23	D WHEATON	7:35:12
33	J SIMCOX	6:09:09	L SMITH	6:17:45	J IRELAND	6:33:04	T SEAGER	6:52:25	D FORSTER	7:36:56
34	S KENNY	6:09:16	M GAMMON	6:17:48	F CALLAGHAN	6:33:04	H REEVE	6:52:29	M TAYLOR	7:37:22
35	D ROY	6:09:16	M ROWE	6:17:49	D PIZZEY	6:33:04	R MULDOON	6:52:52	P BARNES	7:41:59
36	P WILLIAMS	6:09:16	A TALLIS	6:17:51	L PLUMB	6:33:06	M JONES	6:52:54	R KNIGHT	7:42:27
37	P SINNOS	6:09:17	S WHITBY	6:17:57	L KNIGHTON	6:33:07	K PINYOUN	6:52:55	D HURST	7:53:31
38	M PATEL	6:09:18	A TAYLOR	6:18:17	D CRITCHLEY	6:33:14	J HEATH	6:53:08	W CAYLESS	7:55:27
39	E HAGGARTY	6:09:46	M PENNEY	6:18:21	P MURPHY	6:33:14	S POPE	6:53:08	K POULSON	8:04:41
40	K NOONAN	6:09:56	E BOWD	6:18:24	V TAGGART	6:33:18	M HINCHLIFFE	6:53:22	Y WILLIAMS	8:04:41
41	G COOK	6:10:19	C NICHOLS	6:18:26	S STRAWBRIDGE	6:33:39	C BURTON	6:53:23	R ALEXANDER	8:08:24
42	C MALENEY	6:10:19	J BHAGWANJI	6:18:26	R RYAN	6:33:39	J KING	6:53:29	V CONNERTON	8:08:24
43	J O'HALLORAN	6:10:19	A BIRKWOOD	6:18:34	B RYAN	6:34:33	S MELSICK	6:53:42	E BANKS	8:14:49
44	B HANNAFORD	6:10:20	R ARTHURS	6:18:37	G BEAN	6:34:34	J O'REILLY	6:54:07	L FLOREY	8:15:03
45	K HEAD	6:10:32	D LATIMER	6:18:46	S CORVETTI	6:34:34	L TURNER	6:54:09	S STEAD	8:15:10
46	A ROTHWELL	6:10:32	M WALDEN	6:18:54	E BONI	6:34:57	S MOORE	6:54:16	J AINSWORTH	8:15:19
47	N SIFLEET	6:10:34	S GREEN	6:19:01	R HARWOOD	6:34:59	L NEALE	6:54:35	A O'DONOVAN	8:33:25
48	P MEATHER	6:10:34	S HIRANO	6:19:05	J MCINTOSH	6:35:14	I CUNNINGHAM	6:54:40	P SADLER	8:38:25
49	V ZOTTINO	6:10:41	C TRETHEWEY	6:19:06	C BRADSHAW	6:35:31	R BONE	6:54:43	S DAVIES	8:49:26
50	D WICKENS	6:10:42	P COLLETT	6:19:15	J CLARK	6:35:48	B JENKINS	6:54:43	T DORRELL	8:54:56
51	B SCAMANS	6:10:46	R WOODFORD	6:19:35	S FOX	6:36:56	H WATSON	6:54:54		
52	K WHITE	6:10:46	S PARKER	6:19:35	M PERCIVAL	6:37:24	G SMITH	6:54:55		
53	G DAVIES	6:10:49	D LONG	6:19:40	A JOHNSTON	6:37:24	G FUNNELL	6:55:05		
54	C COCKSHULL	6:10:50	K IKEDA	6:19:55	R LINCOLN	6:37:32	B MCINTYRE	6:55:24		
55	E HOWARD	6:10:50	C WRIGHT	6:20:14	J MCKNIGHT	6:37:33	S HAM	6:55:54		
56	P SYRETT	6:10:50	C FULLER	6:20:24	S HAINES-CROFT	6:37:34	O LALAUZE	6:56:00		
57	M THORLEY	6:10:50	J MORRIS	6:20:25	J OTHEN	6:37:42	R KEYWORTH	6:56:00		
58	S EALEY	6:10:50	N BHATT	6:20:31	G WILLIAMS	6:37:44	S POTTS	6:56:53		
59	P MOTTE	6:10:50	L WEISS	6:20:33	L MACRAE	6:38:00	M HIRST	6:56:54		
60	S RANGER	6:10:56	C STEEL	6:20:36	M HOGG	6:38:00	E CARLAW	6:57:27		
61	D RUSSELL	6:11:28	R ALLEN	6:20:41	D ANDREWS	6:38:01	I KOTECHA	6:57:27		
62	L FOSKER	6:11:28	M MCRORY-WILSON	6:20:54	K JONES	6:38:03	S HAKIMI	6:57:48		
63	J COTTAM	6:11:33	D BUTLER	6:21:36	L FANTIN	6:39:41	J VICKERS	6:58:14		
64	R WARD	6:11:33	J REEVES	6:22:18	N JACKSON	6:40:02	R COUVERTURE	6:58:50		
65	M UPJOHN	6:12:03	M HOOD	6:23:06	J HOWELL	6:40:02	H NOTA	6:58:50		
66	D HARDINGHAM	6:12:04	J TAYLOR	6:23:06	D PRICE	6:40:12	A LALL	6:59:12		
67	T BRYANT	6:12:05	B KIERAN	6:23:07	A KEDZIORA	6:40:47	P MILLS	6:59:24		
68	R VINE	6:12:14	A SMITH	6:23:10	B BALDRIDGE	6:40:54	L JOBSZ	6:59:37		
69	N GOLDS	6:12:22	G SAN MIGUEL	6:23:13	C BALDRIDGE	6:40:55	H LENIHAM	7:00:07		
70	M LUCAS	6:12:22	L CALVERT	6:23:19	A PEEL	6:41:29	J COX	7:00:25		
71	K WEBSTER	6:12:30	S BARKER	6:23:19	T MOORE	6:41:53	J HENOCQ	7:00:48		
72	R PATEL	6:12:44	C RICHARDSON	6:23:28	T SHAMMON	6:42:05	M TITCOMBE	7:01:16		
73	P KING	6:12:51	P BARKER	6:23:35	G SCOTT	6:42:19	J BLANCHARD	7:01:16		
74	W HUGHES	6:12:53	A GREEN	6:23:36	J PAGE	6:42:19	A BARTON	7:01:52		
75	P MILNER	6:12:59	M KEIGHLEY	6:23:40	S ARKLE	6:42:26	C GREENE	7:02:02		
76	J CALOW	6:12:59	B MCGOUGH	6:24:03	A AUSTIN	6:42:27	A MORRIS	7:02:11		
77	E BRODRICK	6:13:04	R CAHILL	6:24:09	S WILSON	6:42:44	A CLACK	7:03:44		
78	C SANDERS	6:13:19	J HAY	6:24:10	J CHESTER	6:42:56	M FINCH	7:03:55		
79	E POWELL	6:13:19	B BUTLER	6:24:15	A SHADBOLT	6:42:57	D BLAKE	7:04:39		
80	J POWELL	6:13:27	P CARROLL	6:24:21	J LYONS	6:42:59	Z CURRY	7:05:07		
81	R IRLAM	6:13:27	M COULTER	6:24:37	M AMBROSE	6:43:00	Y PATTERSON	7:05:28		
82	P BEACH	6:13:31	A NE'EMAN	6:24:37	T MCINULTY	6:43:03	I SMITH	7:05:52		
83	D REED	6:13:34	N ANYAGGBUNAM	6:24:41	S KELCHER	6:43:36	P RUSSELL	7:05:53		
84	W JACKSON	6:13:34	J SMEATON	6:24:41	J HARRISON	6:43:36	C MACRENZIE	7:06:10		
85	G REGAN	6:13:45	R LANGFORD	6:24:48	K STANTON	6:43:44	H WILKINS	7:06:13		
86	L SCHLACKMAN	6:13:46	R CARPENTER	6:24:48	J POOLE	6:43:45	A PATEL	7:07:44		
87	S HICKLIN	6:13:55	D HANNEY	6:24:52	A BILL	6:43:56	M LEVEN	7:08:15		
88	M TAPPER	6:13:56	M PERRY	6:25:04	G DAVIES	6:44:26	S CONLAN	7:08:15		
89	D LANG	6:13:59	F GAUTIER	6:25:18	D KENNY	6:44:32	B DOVE-EDWIN	7:08:31		
90	P CARTER	6:14:01	P FELLOWS	6:25:22	J LEONARD	6:44:32	M ESTAUGH	7:08:57		
91	A PEASE	6:14:03	T BOWERS	6:25:36	S BHOGAL	6:44:43	M COTTON	7:09:12		
92	R YOUNG	6:14:23	J ETHERINGTON	6:25:51	A CLEWLEY	6:44:43	R WOODFORD	7:09:16		
93	D HARRISS	6:14:35	M HAMILTON	6:25:58	M CHILDS	6:45:47	A MORAN	7:09:19		
94	J TAYLOR	6:14:42	R IBBOTSON	6:25:58	D FEARN	6:45:57	V SAVILL	7:09:20		
95	M HARRIS	6:14:44	C BRETT	6:26:16	C ANDREWS	6:45:57	G PARTINGTON	7:09:24		
96	P HARRIS	6:14:44	H NAGAI	6:26:40	A FEARN	6:45:57	V RODDY	7:09:24		
97	S DOWNS	6:14:44	T DAVIES	6:26:48	T KYTE	6:45:58	M PATTENDEN	7:09:44		
98	G COLEMAN	6:14:44	J WOOD	6:26:48	N WATT	6:45:59	G BATHGATE	7:09:45		
99	S CATANZARO	6:14:54	A KOTAK	6:26:54	E POLLARD	6:46:00	J VAUGHAN	7:09:48		
100	A WARD	6:14:55	A BUTLER	6:27:10	A TOPLISS	6:46:01	S METCALFE	7:10:19		

The 1993 NutraSweet/BSAD Wheelchair London Marathon

MEN

								WOMEN			
1	G	VANDAMMO	1:44:10	26	C	SADLER	2:26:12	1	R	HILL	2:03:05
2	I	NEWMAN	1:46:15	27	M	SANDBERG	2:27:54	2	L	ANGGRENY	2:09:16
3	D	HOLDING	1:51:22	28	J-O	MATTSSON	2:30:16	3	T	GREY	2:12:25
4	H	ERIKSSON	1:55:24	29	B	NORMAN	2:30:21				
5	H	NELISSE	1:55:34	30	P	GUEST	2:30:24				
6	D	VAN DIJK	1:56:15	31	P	CARRUTHERS	2:34:11				
7	I	THOMPSON	1:57:24	32	C	OOTIERS	2:34:27				
8	D	WESLEY	1:59:10	33	M	KEAT	2:39:44				
9	D	TODD	1:59:14	34	M	AGAR	2:39:59				
10	I	DA SILVA	1:59:30	35	F	ALBERS	2:43:07				
11	J	VAN DE HOEK	1:59:32	36	M	WILDIG	2:43:46				
12	J	VAN BUREN	2:02:03	37	P	V/A FEEST	2:46:15				
13	A	VANDENBROEK	2:02:10	38	P	SCAYSBROOK	2:51:39				
14	D	GRAY	2:06:49	39	D	DURAND	2:59:32				
15	E	GRAZIER	2:11:37	40	P	DOWNING	3:03:52				
16	T	GEEVE	2:12:12	41	J	BOUTWOOD	3:06:06				
17	K	BREEN	2:12:17	42	D	BREVITT	3:08:01				
18	C	MADDEN	2:13:20	43	G	OXFORD	3:08:57				
19	R	POWELL	2:14:39	44	S	ANDERSON	3:13:13				
20	A	CHEEK	2:14:45	45	R	CASSELL	3:13:22				
21	B	COOPER	2:15:01	46	J	McKENNA	3:13:22				
22	J	GOESSENS	2:18:28	47	W	VAN HATTEN	3:21:04				
23	M	KETTRICK	2:20:27								
24	C	BAGLEY	2:22:46								
25	I	LEA	2:23:09								

The 1993
NutraSweet
Mini Marathon

BOYS 11-13

	1-100		101-200		201-300		301-346	
1	SAMUEL HAUGHIAN	13.09	SIMON HUNT		HUGO JANERING		CHRISTOPHER TERRY	
2	JOHN BALDWIN	13.45	JAMES LOUGHLIN		ALAN WEBB		CHRISTOPHER TWIN	19.00
3	MARCUS HARDING	13.52	DAVID GRIDLEY		WILLIAM THORLING		SEAN CAIRNS	
4	BEN CHAPMAN		MICHAEL PATTERSON		JOESPH ADEMOSU		STEWART CHILVERS	
5	LEE SABATINO		PAUL AYRES		REMMOND JOHNSON		TOM HINES	
6	JOSEPH WILSON		ROSS BRAITHWAITE		EDWARD SIMMONS		JAMES HOLMES	
7	TSEGAY BEREH	14.00	YGNACIO SANTANA	15.40	SAM HAYNES		LEO BABSKY	
8	DANNY SMITH		REZA GHODSE		MARK RIORDAN		JAMES KEOTHARANG	19.10
9	BEN GOLDIE		EDWARD MULLANE		ANDREW PRESCOTT	17.00	ADAM CHANDLER	
10	BARRY HEAPY		STUART BENNETT		ANTHONY EGBAH		LEWIS RHODES	19.20
11	GARETH NOBLE		ROBERT PICKFORD		PETER SCRIPPS		CHRISTOPHER BURRIDGE	
12	JAMIE SPENCER		MORGAN JONES		NICK WILCOX		DAVID ALLEN	
13	STEPHEN HOLMES		LOGAN COUTTS		LOUIS PARKER		TERRY WESTON	
14	DANNY HART		NEILL COLLINS		MARC ROLLINGS		KOFI DEBRAH	
15	CHRIS NICOL	14.10	DAN MESSER		ADAM TWOHEY		STEWART SMITH	
16	JAMIE SINCLAIR		JAMES GRANT		ADAM TAYLOR		GAVIN YOUNG	
17	MARTIN WILKINSON		RICHARD WILLIAMS		STUART KIRK		MARK JACKSON	
18	JOHN HARRIS		JAMIE MCCULLAGH		ADAM WRIGHT		TIMOTHY BARRETTO	19.50
19	MICHAEL GYLES		TIM FAGG		JOHN KEANE		BRADLEY CAUCHI	
20	GLENN ANTINORI		JODY RICE		WESLEY MANNING		CHRISTOPHER MOFFAT	
21	CHRIS HODGES		DEAN BUTCHER		JAMES WRIGHT		JOHN LOWTHER	20.00
22	JOHN LOUGHLIN		NEIL CARPENTER		LUKE CATHORNE		MICHAEL MULLANE	
23	DANIEL HAMMOND		MICHAEL TYE		LEE WHELAN	17.10	LLOYD MALCOLM	
24	GREGORY PALMER	14.20	ANDREW FREEMAN		STUART TAYLOR		MICHAEL EHRHARDT	20.10
25	JAMES WRIGHT		ROGER GOLDIE		DAVID RATCLIFFE		STEVEN FOLEY	
26	DOUGLAS MCCLEAN		GEORGE DICKENS		HENRY WRIGHT		LUKE CANHAM	
27	NATHAN JAMES		DEJI DAVIES	15.50	HARRY BOND		STEPHEN TAYLOR	
28	MICHAEL ALLISON		KRISTIAN EMBERTON		ROGER CHALLINOR		JACK PASCOE	
29	ALEC SALMON		OWEN WALKER		DAVID BENNETT		JODY CONNOLLY	
30	KEVIN QUINN		EDWARD RENSHAW		STEPHEN DAY		TOM REED	
31	NICHOLAS HIGGS		FAWAD KHAN		JUSTIN STEELE		OMAR ALI	20.40
32	PAUL GIBSON		MATTHEW TAYLOR		TOMMY HAYES	17.20	AUSTEN CONN	20.50
33	LIAM HOPKIN	14.30	LUKE TEVERINI		LANRE OLAIYA		EWAN MANNINGTON	
34	DANIEL DYER		PHILIP WESTCOTT		IAN SHAPIRO		CRAIG GRAVIS	
35	LUKE MARTIN		MICHAEL WEBSTER		STEVEN CLARK		SAMED HUNASSER	
36	CARL LAYTON		ROBERT LOOKER		JOE SHEASGREEN		BRIAN HATSIMELETTOU	21.00
37	RICHARD OSBORNE		JAMES HAWKINS		JASON LEWIS		CHRISTOPHER MATTIN	
38	MARTIN CASSAR		TIMOTHY RAWLINGS		GARETH COLLINS		JAMIE MCNALLY	
39	JASON MILLER	14.40	DANNY GIBNEY		JAMES SAMS		ENOCH SHOWUNMI	
40	DEAN REIDY		THOMAS GAUNT		TOM HASLER		SIMON DAINTY	
41	DARREN HERBERT		PAUL BARKER		LEE JOHNSON		HASIAN SAGKOL	
42	WILLIAM MUIRHEAD		MARK SANDELL	16.00	NEIL GORDGE		MARK MCDOUGALL	
43	MARK SMALLWOOD		STUART THOMPSON		TOM BLYTH		EUGENE MINOGUE	
44	CARL DALY		ANDREW CORNICK		TIMOTHY HALE		SHAUN O'CONNELL	
45	MATTHEW WIGG		PETER SELL		JONATHAN BRUNT		LEON SERAPHIN	
46	MARK LEMON		GARETH INGHAM		ALEXANDER COLCHESTER		MUSTAPHA EGAN	
47	MARTIN WOOLITT		JOHN SANKEY		ADRIAN GREENWOOD			
48	ADAM BERRY		DANIEL LITTLE		THOMAS WINSTONE			
49	KEVIN HUNT		NEIL HEALEY		JOHN SMILEY			
50	RICHARD HUNT		DERRICK GORDON	16.10	SIMON FINCH	17.30		
51	ADRIAN LLOYD		LEWIS LAWS		PRAVIN MEPANI			
52	DAVID SQUIRES		JOHN BOLEY		SEAN NAMMOCK			
53	IAN MITCHELL	14.50	DANIEL BLUNDELL		DAVID KELLY			
54	PETER EVANS		ADAM WARD		CHRISTOPHER SHARP			
55	NEIL ROGERS		ANDREW MUTTON		MOMEN HELEM			
56	TOM SOLOMON		JUNIOR NARTEY		ALBERT AOV-BOAKYE			
57	RICKY ALEXANDER		ROBERT BAIN		CHRIS CODY			
58	NICHOLAS EVANS		DEAN MCCARTHY		LEE HACK			
59	ROBERT STOCKMAN		SEAN GREENHALGH		ADRIAN GOLBOURN			
60	NEIL LOVEMORE		PAUL TANTER		JONATHON COTTLE			
61	ANTHONY PIKE		MATTHEW HENDRY		MICHAEL GINTUCH			
62	JAMIE WEATHERHEAD		MARK HUCKSTEPP		JOHN SCRIPPS	17.40		
63	RICHARD COLE		IAN STEVENS		DANIEL DICKSON			
64	GAVIN SMITH		LEE CLARK		MARK CHAMBERLAIN			
65	STEPHEN MARRINER		DANIEL MOCOCK		PHILIP HARDY			
66	KEVIN IVES		ROY ABI-ELIAS		PETER FERGUSON			
67	MATTHEW NICHOLLS	15.00	STEVEN PAYNE		MARK BEERLING			
68	RYAN BARRY		GARY PRATT	16.20	RICHARD SELLAR	17.50		
69	CHRISTOPHER PURSER		PATRICK SISUPALAN		CHRISTOPHER ATHERASI			
70	JAMES SHIPLEY		STEEVEN SHARPE		PAUL READ			
71	GARY WALSHAM		STEPHEN BRITTAN		ARTHUR LEWIS-NUNES			
72	THOMAS PONDS		DAVID REEVES		TERRY FRANCIS			
73	STEVEN WHITE		MARK SLINEY		KEVIN EARL			
74	ARTHUR O'DONNELL		MICHAEL JONES		CHRISTOPHER VAN	18.00		
75	BEN NUTLEY		STEVEN KLEIN	16.30	MARTIN BASSETT			
76	SAM BALE		EDWARD COX		ANTONY MAY			
77	LIAM YIANNI		MARK LAMBOURNE		LEFKOS HAJITTOFS			
78	SHAUN LYDON		SEAN ROGERS		PETER BUSH	18.10		
79	MICHAEL SMITH	15.10	DARREN LAMBERT		PAUL WILMOT			
80	JACK MORRIS		DANIEL HAYNES		ANDREW SUTHERLAND			
81	MARC GUEVARA		ANDREW FISK		DALE RAVEN	18.20		
82	CHRISTOPHER ROWE		JUSTIN HORNE		BARRY HOLLIS			
83	ANTHONY DOUGHTY		BODE OGUNLEYE		KIERAN SAVJAN			
84	CHRIS DAVIES		PETER GAUNTLET		CHRISTOPHER HEATON			
85	KEVIN BENTON		DANNY YOUNG		MAWLID ABDI			
86	CHRISTOPHER HOGG		JAMES MONAHAN	16.40	KEVIN TUFTON			
87	STUART HAYDAY		TOM MORGAN		ROBERT DAVIES	18.30		
88	SIMON SPEAR		STUART COLNAN		SEAN MCHUGH			
89	GEORGE SLOSS	15.20	PETER ADEMRELE		ALEX COX			
90	JAMES TINKER		DAVID EVERITT		JONATHAN HYLTON			
91	ANDREW TIERNAN		RICHARD GAYLE		ALASTAIR CUNNINGHAM	18.40		
92	RICHARD HUNTER		NICHOLAS HENDRY		PAUL WICKERSON			
93	MARK DELAHOYDE		COLIN GRIFFIN	16.50	JAMES CHEESEMAN			
94	ALEC JONES		SUNDAY OLAIYA		RICHARD CARTER			
95	GAVIN PECK		STEPHEN MORGAN		MARTIN ROBERTSON			
96	MICHAEL SHARKEY		MANUEL DE		CHRISTOPHER REYNOLDS			
97	COLIN CALVERT	15.30	KEVIN OAKES		MATTHEW SUTTON			
98	CRAIG POTTER		JANOS TOTH		LAURENCE MATTHEWS			
99	IAN GALVIN		STEVEN SHIPPEY		AZEEM WARD			
100	PHILIP KNIGHT		MARK TYRRELL		DANIEL WILBRAHAM			

BOYS 14-15

#	1-100		101-200		201-300		301-332
1	SCOTT TOMPSETT	12.32	GRAHAM JONES		MARK COUGHLAN		CHRISTOPHER KERR
2	STEPHEN BRIFFETT	12.48	ROBERT WILMER		STEPHEN ARCHIBALD		DANIELLE MARTELLE
3	PAUL HAGAN	12.57	MATHEW BOOTHBY		RICHARD CAREY		ROBERT ABREY
4	TOM EVANS		JAY RAWAL		SIFUR RAHMAN		BEN LAWS
5	JOE DANIELS		LEIGH DENAGHY		KETANI RAOUF		BRETT MARTIN
6	JAMES BADERMAN		GRAHAM WILLIS		IAN HAYWOOD		KALEB RODNEY
7	ANDREW ROPER		PAUL SNOOK		THOMAS RICH		DANIEL KESSIE
8	GAVIN MALEY	13.00	KEITH ALLEN		DANIEL SLATER		ANMOL BANGAR
9	JOHN DIFFEY		GERALD OXFORD		MICHAEL DORIS		EDMUND SUTTON
10	JASON MAGUIRE		GREG SMITH		CHRISTOPHER DOWIE		TERRY BALL
11	JULIAN BAKER		RICHIE SAVAGE		MATTHEW O'CONNOR		AJAYRAL KHERA
12	DARREN WALSHAM		JARVED SARDAR		STEPHEN PRICE	16.20	JASON TROFIMCZUK
13	MARK BAYLISS		SEAN JEREMIAH	14.40	JOHN HAMILTON		SAUD ADEN
14	REYNALDO GUEVARA	13.10	ALAN HEARNE		RICHARD ALEXANDER		NICHOLAS WESTRAY
15	STEPHEN BAYLISS		DOUGLAS HUNTER		KINGSLEY HAMILTON		MICHAEL CLIFFORD
16	KEVIN CRESSY		DANIEL HELBO-DAWES		TAIWO OGUNLEYE		JEREMY JOHNFINN
17	RONNIE JONES		ADAM LANE		ROSS FLEMING		RAZAH CHOONKA
18	KWABENA MENSAM		ALFRED LAWALE		AWOYOMI HARRISON		PETER ALLIBONE
19	TIM DALTON		BEN AVERBACK		MARK WORSFOLD		LEE SMITH
20	WILLIAM KIRKLAND		DERMOT TWOMEY		PHILLIP MCDOUGALL	16.30	GRAHAM FURNEYO
21	MILTON HERNANDEZ		GARETH EVANS	14.50	JAMES SMITH		OMAR FAHMY
22	MATTHEW HOUGHTON	13.20	RICHARD CHURCH		ANDREW KEMPTON		OZGUR CEREN
23	EDDIE SMITH		KEVIN LUI		JASON MCELROY		SHERWAN HUSSAIN
24	RICHARD DAGGER		EDWARD HIME		JOHN CRIMMINS		TUMDE ADEWPO
25	RICKY COOMBES		DANIEL MCLENNY		JAN WALKER		STEFAN HOMER
26	STUART AUSTIN	13.30	ALAN CARENTER		JAMES LETCHFORD	16.40	ROCKY D'JELAL
27	CONOR BASQUIL		TIMOTHY LAY		ROBIN WILLIAMSON		SIMON COOKE
28	HUGO DIAS		AYEN UDDIN		LIAM DOHERTY		GAVIN AVIS
29	CARL SHORTER		BILLY WILSON		NEIL REYNOLDS		JAMIE BARRETT
30	SIMON ASHLEY		RICHARD FREEMAN		DAVID MOSS		JAMES DEACON
31	DAVID SHARPSTONE		ROSS PARRY		WAYNE BROWN		FOROKE SHOWUNMI
32	DANNY DODDS		CHRIS NEOPHYTOU	15.00	PAUL GLINWOOD		MICHAEL TURNBULL
33	IAN MARKS		MICHAEL ADEMRELE		TONY COLLINS		
34	BEN SULAMAN		BEN FORD		ELKEPHIET ETTENEFI		
35	KIRK WATTS		MATTHEW SHARP		JAMIE HAZEL		
36	NEIL CAHILLANE	13.40	DAMION TEAGUE		SAM WILSON		
37	DANIEL STEVENS		JOHN MARTIN		JASON JACKSON		
38	DENNIS SMITH		LUKE HUTCHESON		STEPHEN FELLOWS	17.00	
39	NIKKI BOXALL		SEAN LARRIER		MICHAEL WILSON		
40	SEMPRAB TESFAMARIAM		SCOTT WELLS		GARY MASON		
41	ADAM BLADES		JOSEPH SUNDAY		JAMES AUSTIN		
42	JOHN JEFFREY		BEN COTTLE		JAMIE REEVES		
43	DAREN LOW		PAUL BYRNE		KRIS MCREYNOLDS		
44	ANDREW WILKINSON		MATTEW READ		SCOTT JARRED		
45	GREG NEWMAN		DANNY TUCKER	15.10	WESTLEY LAWS		
46	RICKY REEVES		YOHANNES MICHAEL		DARREN ROBINSON		
47	CHRISTIAN ELLIOTT	13.50	NEIL WATKINS		VICTOR RODRIGUES	17.10	
48	MARCUS WILCOX		MARTIN SMITH		NASIR UDDIN		
49	NICKY HARRIS		MARK PADFIELD		VI CHU		
50	JAMES CLARKE		STEPHEN BRANSON		CHRISTOPHER WHITELEY		
51	STUART HAYES		GARY HULKES		DARRAN O'GRADY		
52	ANDREW GOUDIE		ALAISTAIR YULE		MICHAEL CHANDLER		
53	HAYDEN RUSHTON		GEORGE CURRY		AUGUSTINE APPIAH-DANKWAH		
54	CHARLES COX		BEN MURTAGH	15.20	ANTHONY BRIGGS	17.20	
55	CHRISTOPHER WAITE		RICHARD DIXON		DAMIEN MALLOY		
56	SAM ADU		JONATHON SETTY		MARK THOMAS		
57	MICHAEL GALVIN	14.00	TOM LOWTHER		MICHAEL MAKER		
58	NICHOLAS THOROGOOD		BARRY WALSH		ANTHONY WHITE		
59	CRAIG LARKIN		PAUL MUSKETT		DOUGLAS BARLTROP		
60	ALEX TANNER		ALLAN MUNDAY		DANIEL OLIVERA		
61	MARK ROGERS		SAM THOMSON		GREIG AVERY		
62	ANDREW WARD		MATTHEW SMITH		GAVIN CLARKE	17.30	
63	JOEL HAMMOND		DEAN CRANSTON	15.30	NASMON COHEN		
64	MATTHEW BOUCHER		DANNY HAYWARD		GARY CLARK		
65	DAVID TURNER		ANDREW ARGENT		ADAM KNIGHT-MARKEGI		
66	ROBIN MILLER		IAN CUNNINGAHM		JAMES HYLTON		
67	NEIL BENJAMIN		ROBERT POWER		TONY PRENDERGAST		
68	ALEX HUNTE		MARK WOODS		BENN ASHFORD		
69	SEBASTIAN PAPINI		BEN SHADBOLT	15.40	BEN SADLER		
70	WILLIAM HUNTER		DARYL WEST		MICHAEL CHAPPELL		
71	CHRISTOPHER LAGDEN	14.10	DEAN JOHNSON		EDDIE CAIRNS		
72	TOM HAYES		KEVIN CADMAN		STEPHEN SCANNELL		
73	STEPHEN MILLER		TIMOTHY DELAHOY		DARREN ORANGE		
74	ABRAHAM TEWELDEBRHAM		DANNY LOWING		PAUL NICHOL		
75	DAVID THOMAS		CHARLIE OSBORN		DARREN CARPENTER	17.40	
76	ALEX HANKS		BARRY LUSCOMBE		BABS ODENEYE		
77	GUISEPPE SANTANGELO	14.20	DANIEL BURFORD		PAUL MOUTARDE		
78	JOHN WILSON		STEVEN ROBERTSON		ANDREW LUSCOMBE		
79	GRAEME JOHNS		NOLAN HOWARD		STEPHEN ADAMS		
80	MATTHEW DAY		MATTHEW SIMPSON		GARY POLLITT		
81	ADAM DEAN		WARREN SCHENK		CHRIS GOODISON		
82	JON COLACO		DOUGLAS HOLLAND	15.50	JAWEED SHAH		
83	JODY HESLING		GRAHAM ARCHER		MARC ELGAR	17.50	
84	RUPERT TAYLOR		QIASS ISSA		JAIME MOYA		
85	BEN VALLINS		ASWAD SAUNDERS		NIGEL BARCLAY		
86	PAUL MODLOCK		EWAN ALLDEN		SIMON BARNARD		
87	IAN POUNCETT		MARK DINSDALE		DONAL MCHUGH		
88	PETER LLOYD		JOHN BENBOW		BEN BOND		
89	RICHARD PATTERSON		OGHALE EFUE		DAVID POWELL		
90	NICHOLAS HURROCKS		JOHN DISSON		ANDREW ARTEMIS		
91	RAMESH SINHA		DANNY WHITTER	16.00	AHMED MOHAMMED		
92	ROBERT GRAHAM		VISIIAL AIRY		IAN TILLEY		
93	LUKE STANTON	14.30	KEVIN HUGHES		DAVID POWER		
94	MATTHEW WILMOTT		SHANE WAREHAM		NEIL TILLEY	18.10	
95	ANDREW WORWOOD		SIMON BYNG		SERYOZHA CROSBY		
96	LAWRENCE MCGEE		BRADLEY BROWN		ROBERT HAWKINS		
97	JEROME PHELPS		DAVID MCQUEEN		SIMON BODDY	18.30	
98	PAUL STOCKER		STEVEN MICHAEL		DAMIEN AHMED		
99	ROBERT PRATT		GWILYM OWEN		RICHARD BUTCHER		
100	DARREN VERGA		STEVEN SANFORD	16.10	IAIN DOWDESWELL		

BOYS 16-17

	1-100		101-200		201-273	
1	EDDIE GRACE	11.42	GLEN STEVENS		MARTIN SPENCER	
2	MATTHEW WALDRAM	11.49	ROELS MUNUKU		AMIT RAWAT	16.00
3	STEPHEN SHARP	11.54	DANIEL MILLS		DAVID TOMPKINS	
4	RAYMOND WARD	12.00	JASBIR GILL		PHILLIP TAMPLIN	
5	ANDREW TAPPIN	12.10	PAUL CAWALAN		DANIEL HAYCRAFT	
6	JAMOS LOVELL		MARK WESTON		RUDY ROBINSON	
7	KEVIN CARVOSSO		ROBERT FINNIS		JOHN COLE	
8	GAVIN MASON	12.20	JON LOBO		BOZLUR RAHMAN	
9	GREGORY ASHE		MICHAEL PARRY	14.20	RICHARD GRAY	
10	CHRISTOPHER HALL		ADAM WALZER		ARRON BONNING	16.10
11	KEITH MURPHY		SIMON SEIGAR		ROSS DAVIS	
12	LIAM O'FLAHERTY		SHAUKAT NIWAZ		RISHI SHARMA	
13	BENJAMIN WOODD		RAJESH SINHA		MARK QUINN	
14	STEPHEN JONES		IAN PEASE		NICOLAS QUIN	16.20
15	SIMON HENTY		RICHARD HURT		SIMON LANG	
16	DAX GALLOWAY	12.30	GEOFF DEANE		GARY ORANGE	
17	DOUG WARNER		DANIEL PEARCE		TREVOR CARPENTER	16.30
18	MARTIN COOPER		DANIEL EWENS		RENO JONES	
19	BEN HAMILL		BEN SAYERS		PAUL ALLAN	
20	JOHN MARKS		BRETT HUTCHINSON		SOCRATES IOANNIDES	
21	ABDI WARSAME		SIMON COOTE	14.30	THOMAS DIBBLE	
22	JAMES BATESON		EDWARD WHITEMAN		MICHAEL OLADIPO	16.40
23	JOHN MCCALLUM		BOE WALTON		SIMON SPROSTON	
24	SIMON GATT		TERRY GOLDSMITH		MICHAEL MCEVOY	
25	NATHAN BANCE		DAVID PIPE		MATHEW WILLIAMSON	
26	ABDELBACK AMED		ROBERT PATTISON		DALBIR GILL	
27	JEREMY BRADLEY	12.40	DAVID QUICKENDEN		NADER ABRAHIM	16.50
28	STUART TAYLOR		KIRK MARSHALL		STUART TUCKER	
29	GREGORY MAYNE		ABBEY DAWAN		ALAN CHEUNG	
30	JUSTIN BAMFORD		BENJAMIN BONNER		ALAN MCQUEEN	
31	BEN WHITBY		MARK BAKER	14.40	SIMON FAYOYIN	17.00
32	ROBERT GOULD		SANTJAY LOBO		BRIAN MASON	
33	PAUL CAVALLO		GRAEME JONES		CHRISTOPHER CHRISTODOULOU	
34	DAVID KING		MATTHEW HOBBS		RAYMOND DELSOL	
35	ALPEN ENVER	12.50	TERRY SIMMONS		DANIEL ROSSEK	
36	BOSCO OCHANA		KIERAN NOTT		DAVID KENNINGTON	
37	MARTIN READHEAD		KARL MILLS		ROBERT MOTT	17.10
38	MARLON ANDERSON		RICKY GOLDSWAIN		ALLAN MEEK	
39	GORDON TYLER		BRADLEY RUDDOCK		PHILLIP DORAN	
40	ANDREW NEOPHYTOU		CHRIS WAINWRIGHT		RICHARD CHAPMAN	
41	ALEX GIBBINS	13.00	TYRONE BROWNE		GEORGE KWAMI	
42	DAN MARKS		PETER HAMILTON		HUEKLIN HYLTON	17.20
43	RICARDO LANCA		PHILIP DODDS		MARC DOUGLAS	17.30
44	JODY SAVAGE		LEE MARTIN	14.50	ROBERT HALL	
45	MARTIN DOBSON		DANIEL JENNER		KRIMO RIZKI	
46	JASON BEERAJE		JONATHAN WILDER		PETER JONES	
47	SID LOWE	13.10	ROBERT MINOR		AMIN NAROEE	
48	ANDREW HOMER		JOHN TUNBRIDGE		THOMAS DEAL	17.40
49	DOUG PONCIA		SIMON COLTON		DAMIAN PATERSON	
50	JASON WALSH		JAMES CASSIDY		BEN WILKES	
51	DARREN TONER		NIGEL LEIGH	15.00	LUKE TOWNSEND	
52	JASON COOPER		EDDIE VASON		PAUL NICHOLAS	
53	JASON OWENS		ROBERT HAYWARD		ADIL RANA	
54	RYAN TURNER	13.20	MARK GALES		ROY NICHOLL	
55	BEN WELLER		COLIN ALDERMAN		STEWART CARROLL	17.50
56	STEFAN GIBBERD		IAN PAWSEY		JACK HODD	
57	PETER YATES		ANTHONY HAYNES		SAM PASCOE	18.30
58	STEPHEN JENNINGS	13.30	STEVEN MICHAEL		RICHARD MORGAN	
59	LEE GREATOREX		MARK PADFIELD		DARREN GREEN	
60	PAUL COHEN		KHAI-VAN HUYNH		DANIEL BETHEL	18.40
61	GAVIN CROOK		RICHARD ALLSFORD		DANIEL CAFFERY	18.50
62	JOSHUA WESTBURY		LEON GIDDINGS		PAVLOS CONSTANTINOU	
63	TOM SOUTH		JAMES NORTH		DARREN TROFIMCZUK	19.00
64	DINO DICESARE		NICOLAS BLACK		CHARLES ASHOK	
65	MANFRED RUIZ		DERRICK VERNAL		RICHARD DOMENECH	19.20
66	ANDREW NOBLE		STEVEN PARCHMENT	15.10	JAMES CONNELLY	
67	GRAHAM GRIMWOOD		HAYDEN HARBUD		DAVID CORREIA	19.50
68	SIMON MINIHANE		JASON COKER		JETHRO MEYDANCI	
69	ROBERT PAGNAMENTA	13.40	WAYNE ROBBENS		GEORGE HAMMELL	
70	PAUL CHILVERS		PAUL KELLY	15.20	SCOTT MORRELL	
71	MARK LYNCH		DUNCAN SMITH		JASON BROWN	
72	MARK REGAN		SAPURAN GILL		RICHARD DAVIS	
73	ALEX FENN		NICKY GARDNER		CHRISTOPHER COAKLEY	
74	ANDREW OGG		GEORGE HARVEY			
75	DANIEL BRASSINGTON		JAMIE MCELROY			
76	CHRIS HATCH		ADAM GREEN			
77	JOHN DOMINEY		BEN MARSHALL			
78	TOM SMITH		THOMAS BANNISTER	15.30		
79	HAKEEM OSHIYEMI		AKBAR SHAH			
80	JAMES GORDON	13.50	IAN ALSTON			
81	JEREMY COLLIS		SHAUN PLUCKROSE			
82	PATRICK DAVIS		GEOFERY SHARP			
83	PAUL FELBY		ZEAN FOLEY			
84	SCOTT BELLAS		IRFAN MUKADAM			
85	IAN AARONS		JOHN CHANDLER	15.40		
86	MARK EVELEIGH		STEVE GOLDSMITH			
87	ANTHONY GORMAN		ANDREW PRICE			
88	JOEL MCLAGAN	14.00	SAMU MHANGO			
89	RUSSELL SEGAL		LUCAS BYNG			
90	ROBERT WHITE		NABIL EKLAI			
91	TERRY MUSKETT		BARRY FRITH			
92	STUART CRESSY		RALPH FRITH			
93	PETER WATKINS		AKBAL AHMED	15.50		
94	JASON VANDER		TONY DELEKAT			
95	STUART HENNELLY		MARK KENT			
96	KEVIN CHARSLEY	14.10	ALI ABUL			
97	BILLY HOWARD		TOM HOLLAND			
98	MARK MOUTARDE		TERRY POTTICARY			
99	TIM BROWN		JOHN DALY			
100	OWEN WHITBREAD		JAMES O'DRISCOLL			

GIRLS 11-13

	1-100		101-200		201-300		301-344	
1	KELLY POWER	14.46	KRISTIE WALLER		DIONNE GREENE		LAUREN GREEN	
2	ALLA OUVAROVA	14.55	ANNA MARSHALL		KATE HALLAM		KATE VICKERY	
3	CAROLINE WALSH	15.02	KELLY HARPER		SACHA HATFIELD		STELLA PILOYA	
4	BETH WILSON		LISA SPARROWHAWK		JESSICA ROBINSON		ELAINE MCCULLOCH	
5	GEMMA GLADDEN	15.10	SARAH MANLEY		KATIE MCGUINESS		VANESSA HALIPI	
6	ROWENA GRUNDY		CLARE SHARKEY		KATE SELLARS		PEPPA ROBINSON	22.00
7	KATE HAYES		JOANNE STACE	17.30	DANIELLE BOUCHER		CAROLINE DOBSON	
8	ZOE MORRELL		KATIE HALL		REBECCA HAYNES		SARAH CAHILL	
9	CAREAN VERNON		VICTORIA JOHNSON		ANGELA FROST		AMY SMITH	
10	KEMILA BRAITHWAITE	15.20	SIOBHAN LENNON		CHAMADE HARTLEY		ZARA WARSHALL	
11	ABIGAIL BROWN		NATALIE TRAINI		DIANE GEORGE	19.20	MICHELLE MCKENNY	
12	KATRINA MCDONALD		RONNIE GIBBONS	17.40	EMMA WEST		KATY ASHFORD	
13	HELEN MATTHEW		LUCY ATUNUMUO		JOANNA WEBB		LAURA TARR	22.30
14	CLARE GUTCH	15.30	SARAH LINDSAY		CAROLINE IBBS		ALANNA SMITH	
15	CLAIRE COLMER		RACHELL YANKEY		DEBRA CANTON		ANITA LONGMAN	
16	DONNA MUSKETT		LISA SHELFER		SACHA SPRAGG		LUCY THOMAS	
17	ELEANOR PLATT	15.40	THERESA UNSELD		ALISON WESTWOOD		SERENA HAMILTON	
18	KIRSTY JENNINGS		CHIARA EDWARDS		KATE SMITH		ANTOINETTE HAYWOOD	
19	KATY RICHARDSON		JOANNA TROTMAN		ALISON KIRKHAM		MAXINE MARSHAL	
20	LOUISE FAIR	15.50	LISA MCLEAN	17.50	EMMA FAULKENER		KATY DOWDESWELL	23.00
21	JOANNE TOMES		KATRINA LOGAN		LEIGH HENTY	19.30	SARA ELGHALY	
22	KAY GALVIN		REBECCA ROSE		CHRISTINA KARATSKOS		HELEN DEAN	
23	JULIE MARTIN		LUCIE KNIGHT		JOANNE LOARING		SHERRY SAMUELS	23.20
24	SALLY OSBOURNE		LAUREN TEMPLETON		CELESTINE JONES		NICOLA MOLLOY	
25	JANE SAWKINS	16.00	SARAH LEWSLEY		BUSOLA SANNI		EMMA HAYWARD	
26	JANE OLIVER		LORRAINE LEE		ANITA BROWN		NATALIE COMPTON	24.20
27	LOUISE NEVILLE	16.10	NATALIE LEAL		EMMA-JANE PETROU		ANISHIA HURRELL	
28	VICKY MORTIMER		TRACY COATES		AMANDA FAIRCLOTH		PENELOPE STENHOUSE	
29	NICOLA MUSKETT		LINDSEY SMITH		OLYREMU OMISHORE	19.40	DAISY HUNT	
30	FUNMI JEGEDE		SARAH HOGARTH		LAURA SNOOK		SARAH LOUISE	25.10
31	MICHELLE ROSS		SHAFEEKA FAKHOURY		DEANNE REYNOLDS		GABBI JONES	
32	MICHELLE MORGAN		CLAIRE STRUTHERS		KELLY FEENEY		ANN QUINN	
33	TARA HIBBERT		SARAH BENNETT		CORENA HERNANDEZ		TRACEY SMITH	
34	MICHELE RENWICK		LOUISE RODGER		VICTORIA MORSE		MIRIAM ALLEN	
35	DANIELLE MURPHY	16.20	JESSICA MELLER	18.00	AMANDA HIPPLE		NATALIE BROOMS	
36	JULIE BLEASDALE		SARA DANEVE		CARLY ENGLAND		LEANDRA POLIUS	
37	LINDSAY HUGHES		STACY LEACHMAN		ANNA DALY	19.50	LUCY BRACE	
38	KATIE FEENEY		LOUISE WALKER		VICKY MCLEAN		TERESA WILKS	
39	MANDY O'SHEA		KATIE HOPKINS		PAULA MAGUIRE		TERRIE GOODEY	
40	FAYE RICHARDS		MAXINE EASY		YEVONNE ASHEN		SARINA EVELYN	
41	KATE FOGARTY		LOUISE OVENS		LISA WHITE		BIRGIT CROSS	
42	SUZANNE SCRACE	16.30	JOANNA FAWKES		JOANNE MCALPINE		OPHELIA FRANCIS	
43	STEPHANIE BURNS		RUTH BALE		KELLY MANSBRIDGE		KAMNA PATEL	
44	CARALEA WHITTERS		TIFFANY ROSENBERG	18.10	CHARLOTTE HAYES		SARAH MARKS	
45	KELLY ROGERS		DANIELLE COULBERT		RACHEL AYRES	20.00		
46	ANNA TROAKES		LORAINE CAMFIELD		LEANNE CURREN			
47	NATALIE LOVELL		RINA PATEL		LEANE PROSSER			
48	NWANGO NWANGUMO		CLAIRE LEADBETTER		SHARLEEN JUSTIN			
49	SARA DAREVE		GABRIELLE BRIFFETT		IRIS DA			
50	NATOYAH HORSFORD	16.40	CLARE TURNER		CARLIE HOOKER			
51	KATIE RODGERS		JUDITH ELLIMAN		JENNI PIPER			
52	NATALIE ANDREWS		CAHRIN EVANS		DAWNE STOCKS			
53	RACHEL O'DEA		VICTORIA TAYLOR		EMMA RAYNER			
54	LOUISE HOUGHTON		DENISE GAYLE		CELIA ENYIOKO			
55	ROBIN HALE		KERRY ASKEW	18.20	KERRY-ANN TILLEY			
56	ANGELA MURPHY		KARINA BERNARD		VICTORIA MANNING			
57	VALENTINE PAPINI		KATE MCLENNAN		GERALDINE STAINES			
58	LAURA CAREY		CARLY STOCK		ANGELA EDWARDS			
59	ZOE KOURTIS		GEMMA BLACK		NINA D'CRUZ 20.10			
60	SARAH BIRKENSTEINS		LOUISE GROVER		JOANNE KENNY			
61	LOUISE EDWARDS	16.50	NATASHA BOWEN		HANNAH MONTAIGUE			
62	ROSE-ANNE SKELTON		INGRID EISEL		GEMMA TAYLOR			
63	REBECCA THISTLETHWAITE		KATIE HALL		MARTINA FUREY	20.20		
64	TANYA LAYTON		ERICA WELSH		DENISE FUREY			
65	JOANNE HAVILL		LAURA TOMKINS		MONICA TURNES			
66	DONNA CONWAY		LAURA ENGLAND	18.30	KATE PORTER			
67	KAREN CROSSLEY		VICTORIA LONG		EMILY LIPMAN			
68	HAYLEY DAWS		TRACEY ALLARDICE		LAURA HANSFORD			
69	BRENDA MAGUIRE		SIOBHAM MAGUIRE		SARAH WOOLLARD			
70	LAURA CLEARY		SARAH HUBBARD		CAROLINE TAYLOR			
71	VICKI FERGUSON		NICOLE TRAINI		AOIFFE LYNCH	20.30		
72	REBECCA DICKER	17.00	GERALDINE LEAL		BRENDA LANYERO			
73	CAROLINE QUINN		KATHERINE WALDRAB		KRISTINA THOMAS			
74	ALEXANDRA GOODWIN		MELISSA DONNELLY		ALEXANDRE GERRARD			
75	SARAH MASH		CLARE MATHESON	18.40	NIOMI MACLEAN-DALEY			
76	MARISA MARSTON		ULEMU MHANGO		CHANTELLE MILLER			
77	KATIE ROLSTONE		NAOMI CORDING		NATALIE PLESNER			
78	HAYLEY COX		ANNA MELVIN		ELEANOR SIMPSON	20.40		
79	CLAIRE LEWIS		LAURA STEVENS		RACHEL BIRCH			
80	REBECCA GIBSON		CLAIRE ANGELL		CHERYL ROBERTS			
81	GIULA DICESARE		GEMMA ANDERSON	18.50	LOUISE BORLAND			
82	LYNSEY HIGGS		KATY JONES		JENNA GRAY			
83	SARAH HAYWOOD		PATRICIA O'DONNELL		STACY SNOOKS	20.50		
84	JOANNE GILLETT		LOUISE GRIFFITHS		CARMEL CLINTON			
85	SARAH HAZELL	17.10	JORDIE FOURNILLIER		SARAH CUTTS			
86	HOLLY LOMAX		JOANNE TOMES		RACHAEL NEAL			
87	MELANIE ECCLES		KATRINA COFFEY	19.00	CELIA ENDERBY			
88	JESSY ZEND		LEONA SEPHAPHIN		JENNY TILLEY	21.00		
89	LISSA SEMERDAK		RHIANNON JOHNS		ABIGAIL MURRAY			
90	DONNA ARNOLD		HIND NACIRI		CAROLINE MONTIER			
91	KATY COX		GENEVIEVE NOBLE		ALIX PUNTER			
92	SARAH LOVEGROVE	17.20	JULIA LANGE		LUCY ALSTON			
93	AMY LEWIS		PAULA MONAGHAN		JESSICA HILBERY			
94	MARCIA FLETCHER		CLAIRE TOMPSETT		EMMA WOODCOCK			
95	LOUISE ALLEN		AMY JACKSON		SARAH MAXWELL			
96	LAURA ANDERSON		BETHAN EVANS		JENNIFER BLACKEBY	21.20		
97	EVELYN AKINTOLA		EMMA SHEPHERD	19.10	CLAIRE HILLIARD			
98	JOANNE BAKER		VICTORIA HARRIOTT		KATIE ALLISON	21.40		
99	KATIE LAWLER		EMMA KENNING		SUSANNAH HALE			
100	ANTONIA REDHILL		REBECCA WOMAN		ALICE WATSON			

GIRLS 14-15

	1-100		101-200		201-300		301-319	
1	SANDIE BADHAM	14.46	EMMA HAYWOOD		MADELEINE REED		TANYA DECASTRO	25.00
2	VICKY PRENDERGAST	14.59	HELEN ADAMS		YUE-ZHEN HO	20.40	MARIA BELL	
3	SIOBHAN O'SHEA	15.02	ANGI GRENESKI	18.00	FIONA SCOTT		KAREN ALLARDICE	
4	CARRIE-ANNE HAGUE		GRACE IMPEY		MARTINA GRIFFIN		NICOLE MOHAMMED	
5	JOANNA PARKE	15.10	LYNDSEY BROWN		BRYONI BEVITT		SALLY O'SULLIVAN	25.10
6	NICOLA ANDERSON		TRUDI ELSE		SHARON JUSTIN		KELLY ANDERSON	25.20
7	KATHERINE LEE		LENA MCMANUS	18.10	REBECCA JOLLY		CATHERINE BELL	
8	KATHERINE DULLEY		ANNA-LEIGH BANCROFT		SUSAN BRAND	20.50	SHAMA YOUNAS	
9	KIRSTY MACAULAY	15.20	ERICA FOGG		RACHEL PORTE		EMMA FINNIS	
10	CATHERINE MURRAY		NATASHA RENWICK		ANGIE DONNELLY		FIDAN YENGIL	
11	DAVINA MCFARLANE	15.30	NAOMI GODFREY		ZOE TURNER		KELLY DRAKE	
12	CLAIRE MASTERSON		LISSA PRITCHARD	18.20	KAREN THOMAS		NICOLA CARTWRIGHT	
13	KELLY CRICKMORE		KATIE SCOTT		CLAIRE GARLINGE		DENISE SPENCER	
14	KIRSTY MARTIN	15.40	CLAIRE GALBRAITH		NATASHA LOVELL		KELLY O'BRIEN	
15	TERESA WEBSTER		KAREN KENDALL		LAYLA GUEST		KELLY ROGERS	
16	LOUISE DULLEY		CLAIR RUGGLES		CAROLYN BIRT		KATRINA CHANDLER	
17	GILLIAN BASSETT		NATASHA CATES		SALLY WOOD	21.00	ANGELA LYNN	
18	CLAIRE MCKENNA	15.50	ELIZABETH KIRKHAM		PENNY STEVENS		DAYLEA WELLINGTON	
19	HAYLEY BELLAS		HELEN VICKERY		FAYE WARD	21.10	LAURA MARTIN	
20	JULIA CHAPMAN	16.00	JENNIFER KELLY		CATHERINE O'CONNOR			
21	AMANDA COULBERT		VICKI WHEELER		NICOLA DAWKINS	21.20		
22	FIONA COX		SARAH BAYLIS		JOANNA GOULD			
23	ESME CLARK		NATALIE SLOSS		MARIA TYLER			
24	ABI BALFOUR		MICHELLE BIGGS	18.30	JOANNE WESTRAY			
25	EMMA LASHMAR	16.10	NIKKI LEATHERS		NICOLA LEOW			
26	LAURA CARDY		GAYVALYN LIM		ZOE POLYDOROU			
27	CHIDI NWANGUMO		KERRY JONES		GRACE O'DONNELL			
28	ABIJAH BALFOUR		PETA ADDERLEY		NICOLE WATTS			
29	ANDREA BARTLETT		NATALIE BRIDGES		MICHELLE DIXON	21.30		
30	ALEX DAVIES		CARRIE JOHNSON	18.40	EMMA QUEALLY			
31	KATIE WARING		MASUMA BEGUM		KELLY-ANN VICTOR			
32	CATHERINE DAVIS	16.20	NATALIE DIAMOND		HAMEDA KHANUM	21.40		
33	LOUISE FALZON		KERRY ELLINGFORD		FIONA TAMPLIN			
34	EMILY DE		LUCY BATTEN		CANDY DUNNE	21.50		
35	LAURA SHELTON		CLARE NECK		GEMMA ROBINSON			
36	LUCY LAKER		LUCINDA JOHNSON		LOUISE QUINELL			
37	LISA GOODSELL		LARAINE DANIELEWICZ		ZELICA MENSA			
38	LEEANN HONOUR		EMMA HOSKINS	18.50	BUKI COKER			
39	ROSALINE DEARDON	16.30	LUCIA MANCUSO		VICTORIA NUBI			
40	ELEANOR SIMMONS		CLAUDIA GINSBURG		SIOBHAN MCCANN	22.00		
41	RACHEL JONES	16.40	CHERYL FENN		CLAIRE MOORE			
42	KATIE OGG		REBECCA BAKER		ALICE RUSSELL			
43	JACLYN PECK		JACKIE LANGLEY		LEE EDWARDS			
44	HANNAH BARTRAM		GILLIAN COOKE		GEMMAI COPELAND			
45	JOANNE DOUGLAS		ROSALINDA BENNETT		LISA CORFIELD	22.10		
46	HATTIE BERTENSHAW		KATIE HAZELL		HELEN BARRETT			
47	AMANDA CROUCH		JOANNE CHILDS		KATHERINE LYALL			
48	LARISSA BESTONSO	16.50	JESSICA BAILEY		SUZANNE MCKENNER			
49	POLLY SHOEBRIDGE		FAYE CHOWN		NICOLA HAZEL			
50	HELEN WEBB		RUTH KELLY	19.00	EMMA SAWERS	22.20		
51	LUCY GODDEN		CATHERINE BROOM		VICKI SEMERDAK			
52	LOUISE COX		VICKY WEBBER		KIM DARBY			
53	KEELEY HOLLIS		JESSICA GARROGAN	19.10	NICOLA MILLER-DIXON			
54	LYNSEY MOORE		EMMA NUTLEY		LAURA LOVE			
55	AMANDA DALY		DONNA KNIGHT		JOANNE CAPPER			
56	TRINA DIPACE		GEMMA FORD		DONNA BYRNES			
57	GOWRY SISUPALAN		ADELLE BRUCE		PEACE ORU	22.30		
58	IRENE STYNES	17.00	UZUMMA ERUME		JADE DEWING			
59	MAXINE MAUNDERS		DONNA FIELDS	19.20	PEARL DEWING			
60	NICHOLA NORMAN		KARLA WALTER		LAURA PORTER			
61	JOANNE RACKSTRAW		SAMANTHA SOLLAS		RACHEL EDWARDS			
62	ANNA MORGAN		VANIA SWABY		ALEXANDRIA LAWRENCE			
63	ELEANOR HANSFORD		CHANTELLE HURRELL		THANYA MANOHARAN			
64	EMILY CUMMING		KAREN BAILEY		SALLY EDWARDS			
65	HANNAH GREEN		KEMI ABASS		HARMINDER PANESAR			
66	ANNETTE HAQUE		ALISON HAYES		JOANNE HAYES	23.00		
67	VICKY GOODWIN		DONNA PHILLIPS		TIZZY MCKENZIE	23.10		
68	PHILLIPA SYME		LEIGH HAYWARD		SAPHINE BLAKE			
69	KAREN THURSTON		CLAIRE SHEEHY	19.30	HEIDI BRANDAN			
70	JOLENE HURT	17.10	NICOLA DARE		ANITA RUGGERI	23.20		
71	KATE BALCHIN		EVETTE TALBERT		JULIE MOYS			
72	JANE CRAWLEY		KIRSTY PRINGLE		CLAUDIA NETTLEFORD			
73	NICOLA SMITH		LINDSEY MCKINNIE		LORNA ORANGE			
74	TASHFEEN KHOLASI		KELLY CONSTANTINE		CHRISTINA BORG			
75	SARAH-JAYNE WESTON	17.20	TONI BRIDGES		ANNETHA MILLS			
76	XAVIERA SKELTON		EMMA ANTHONY	19.40	SAIRA RAZA	23.30		
77	LISA SAVAGE	17.30	FLEUR RAGGATT	19.50	TRACY FOLEY			
78	TINA MILLER		NATALIE WHITE		MARIA DALY			
79	CARLA FRANCOME		ALISON YOUNG		JULIE SUTTON			
80	SARAH DOWIE		ANNA YOUNG		KATIE ADAMS	23.40		
81	LAURA WARBECK		LISA CARPENTER		JEMMA BUCKLE			
82	SARAH JONES		AIDEEN MCKENNA		LAUREN RAPOCIOLI	23.50		
83	TANYA WARD		ELAINE MCCORMACK		SARAH MCDONALD			
84	SHIREEN MOOSAFUR		DAVINIA PETCH		ERNESTINE SMITH			
85	KERRY JONES		MARIA SARMIENTO	20.00	SIBEL TANER			
86	PHILLIPA CROWLEY	17.40	MONICA SAMUEL		RACHEL BARTLETT			
87	JULIE COOPER		TRACY PALMER		CORINNE ABELA			
88	LISA MIDDLETON		KAREN BARKE		SANDRA COVE	24.00		
89	TRACEY DOLIN		KAREN BROUGHTON		AMARDEEP PANESAR	24.20		
90	HAYLEY BURNS		KATY WATKINS		GERALDINE GIRARDI			
91	CLAIRE BIRD		ELEANOR APPLEBY		ELIZABETH YIANGOU	24.30		
92	SHARON SCLATER		TAMMY GALBALLY		SUNITA JASWAL			
93	CATHERINE HESELTINE		AMY RHODES	20.10	SARAH DUFF			
94	BISI IKUOMOLA		KATIE DONOVAN	20.20	WEBI ANYIA			
95	LEONIE DIXON		ELIZABETH OGUNDE		JOANNE MOORE	24.40		
96	CLAIRE LASHMAR	17.50	DENICE MCHUGH		EGGIE EADIE			
97	KATIE CASEY		EMILY PASCHOUD		DONNA HECTOR			
98	EMILY WHITEMAN		HELEN ROBERTSON		DEIDRE CANAII	24.50		
99	EMMA GRAHAM-HARRISON		LISA CARRUTHERS		MARGARET THOMSON			
100	JOANNE MORGAN		SUSAN POTTEN	20.30	JANICE MOSS			

GIRLS 16-17

#	1-100		101-200		201-242	
1	SHARON MURPHY	13.44	NATASHA PLUCKROSE		MARSHA FREDERICK	
2	CLAIRE MOORE	14.05	JOANNE SAWYER		TERESA EVANS	
3	CRISTINA HODGSON	14.24	KIRSTY FERGIE		SARAH MIDDLETON	
4	HEIDI SEAL		ELEANOR MILS		NAJLAT FOX	22.50
5	LISA DURGE	14.50	KELLEE BURRAGE		CATHERINE ARCHER	
6	ISABELLA MANN		MARIANNE GARVEY		JOANNE NELSON	
7	BECKY O'CARROLL		EMILY LEWIS	19.30	FIONA SHAW	
8	RACHEL PORTE	15.30	SHEILA SHERIDAN		LINDSAY POUNDS	23.10
9	CAROLINE BROWN		STACY JONES	19.40	LOUISE BUTCHER	23.30
10	NICOLA HENSON		MICHELLE KEILY		CELINA EMSDEN	23.40
11	RACHEL SMITH	15.50	EMMA SALTMARSH		CATHERINE BUCK	
12	KERRY MARTIN		ANGELA HEARN		FIONA EMSDEN	24.00
13	GEORGINA SPIER		KERRY MITCHELL		KARLEEN HARTWELL	
14	SHARON THORN		VICTORIA JENKINS		CHERYL QUINN	
15	ELAINE MULHERE		DONNA MARKS		NICOLA MUNDAY	
16	SHANTI CONN		NAOMI GLEN		JOANNE JAMES	
17	KEELIE BROOKS	16.20	NIAMH DILWORTH		CAROLINE JELLY	
18	CARLY BOWEN		SARAH JORDAN	19.50	SARAH KHAN	
19	REBECCA BEAVER		HELEN TEKIE	20.00	MICHELLE FRANEY	
20	ALLISON PHILLIPS		LAURA OWEN		ZUITA GRUNBERG	
21	DIANE WOODMAN	16.30	LORRAINE DUBLIN		JAMILA WANI	24.20
22	ELIZABETH BOWERS		SARAH VERLANDER		ALISON KINNETT	24.30
23	PAULA COOPER		ANNA EVANS		CAROLINE BATH	
24	SALLY SEARLE		ELIZABETH TURNER		JULIE SLATER	
25	EMMA HERON		KATIE TEBBEY		YINKA ODENEYE	
26	ELINOR DAVIES	16.40	MARY HUSSEY		PENNY MURPHY	
27	MARY WILSON		SYLVIA HARE	20.10	MUNA ALI	
28	KIRSTIN SHARP		LAURECE MORTIMER		RITA RUGGERI	
29	AMANDA WILMER		ELOISE CHRISTEN		ELIF GUR	
30	JANICE O'TOOLE		CAROL BROWN	20.20	SARAH PRICE	
31	LUCY CASH		TRACEY FORDHAM		NICHOLA SMALL	
32	AMANDA BAILEY		KATHERINE CARDONES		VICKIE AJAYI	
33	ROCHELLE WITHEY	16.50	VICKY WIGMORE		CARLA TAYLOR	
34	SAMANTHA HADDAD		YVONNE HAWKIN		GAILE HUDSON	
35	CLAIRE WHITAKER		JANE NG		EMMA MUNNELLY	
36	KRISTY HAGUE		SARAH BODDY	20.30	HELEN WESTWOOD	
37	KATE SIMPSON	17.00	JO OLIVER		LUCINDA TIBBOTT	
38	LAUREN MCFIE		MICHELLE KERR		ANDREA DURNELL	
39	RASHPOL SAHOTA		SARAH MARSH		GENEVIEVE BROWN	
40	CLAIRE WILLIAMS		KAREN DOHERTY		JIGNA PATEL	
41	SUSAN EDWARDS		LOUISE KNIGHT	20.40	ACHEIRA PERERA	
42	ALANA DEARDON		NYBEN JOSEPH		KIRI HOUGH	
43	JOANNE PECK		DELPHINA THOMAS			
44	DEBBIE CARTER		RACHEL FISHER			
45	HEIDI CLOHERTY	17.10	CLAIRE POTTER			
46	HAYLEY MARTIN		LEANNE BOND	21.00		
47	KATE ATKINS		JOANNE BRUNT			
48	SHAYNE BELLAS		KATIE DAVIES			
49	JASMIN ARMSTRONG	17.20	HELEN MCQUEEN			
50	ELSPETH LUMBY		VICKI NELSON			
51	VERONICA MEEHAN		STELLA HAMILTON			
52	MARIE GRATTON-KANE		ZVAI NANGATI	21.10		
53	ELIZABETH MARTINELLI	17.30	PENNY CLARKE			
54	VIKKI BALCHIN		SARAH ALLEN			
55	SALLY GODDEN		ALISON CRONIN			
56	KATE CRAWFORD	17.40	OLWIN SISUPALAN			
57	LAURA HURLEY		ZARA GUERMALLOU			
58	LEILA TRUBRIDGE		MICHELLE O'BRIEN			
59	HELEN ROOKE		CHRISTINE ADELMAN			
60	KAREN EDWARDS	17.50	KAREN SPIKINS	21.20		
61	EMMA JANE		DONNA MCNAMARA			
62	VICKY GRAY		TARA KING			
63	SARAH DEAKEN		AMBERINE GILLANDI			
64	MAEVE TOMLINSON		JUSTINE PENN			
65	LINDA WORGER		REBECCA CULLUM			
66	HELEN MAILLARD		CAROLINE GREASBY			
67	LAURA POWELL	18.00	JILLIAN CONN	21.30		
68	ELEANOR DICK		SIOBHAN LINEHAN			
69	TINA QUINLIVAN		ARTI VASHIAHT			
70	SARAH BECKLEY	18.10	NANCY BENNETT			
71	TARYN MAHER		LISA BOARDMAN			
72	YVONNE RENTON		CLAIRE MILLOY			
73	CLAIRE BEARD		WENDY TILLEY			
74	TARA MAGUIRE		CLARISSA BOWLEY			
75	TRACEY PROBERT		CAMILLA SCOTLAND	21.40		
76	LEE LANDAU		NATALIE JONES			
77	FIONA STENSON		MICHELLE TALBOT			
78	CELESTE THOMAS		JODIE WADMORE			
79	REBECCA LANGE		KAREN BELL			
80	ALENA REDWOOD		ELOISE HAIR			
81	FRANCES ROONEY	18.30	PATRICIA DAVIS	21.50		
82	NICOLA CONSTANT		JASMIN MONTEIRO-BROWN			
83	TRACY JOHNSTONE		CHERIE PORTER			
84	JODIE THOMAS	18.40	NICOELA HURRELL	22.00		
85	MICHELLE WEBSTER		RASWINDER BHAMRA			
86	MARYSIA ZAPASNIK		SALLY CRIMMINS			
87	LOUISE PEARCE		SAHARA WILLIAMS			
88	CHLOE FISHER		LYNN DANIEL	22.20		
89	CATHERINE NEVILLE	18.50	ANASTASIA TSOULKAS			
90	ZARINA CAMAL		MARIA WILSON			
91	CHLOE GEORGE		ANNE SHEPHERD	22.10		
92	SHERREE BALLARD		ELIZABETH BRIGGS			
93	NATALIE RENNIE	19.00	ROSEMARY IFILL			
94	JENNY NICHOLSON		MICHELLE WAITIMAS			
95	CHLOE ALLAN		KAREN GRAVIS	22.30		
96	SARAH FOX		CLAIRE SCANLON			
97	NAOMI KOTEN		JADE SE-THO			
98	CLAIRE TURNER	19.10	KATRINA ALADE			
99	ANNE SULLIVAN		EMMA MEHEGAN	22.40		
100	LIZ MCKENNER		MEGAN ROWLANDS			

The 1993
NutraSweet/BSAD
Wheelchair
Mini Marathon

1	GRAHAM BURNS	11.47
2	DOUGLAS GRAHAM	13.01
3	CHRIS HAWKINS	13.02
4	MELODY WARREN	13.12
5	TUSHAR PATEL	14.39
6	DARREN FORD	16.25
7	MARK HOLMES	17.26
8	CRAIG BEAZLEY	20.51
9	LIZZIE ROWSEL	26.37
10	ABDI SAAD	30.05

Picture Acknowledgements

The publishers would like to thank the photographers of Allsport UK and all those who entered the Olympus Cameras 'Essence of the Marathon' photographic competition, many of whose photographs have been included in this book.

The publishers and Olympus Cameras would also like to take this opportunity to thank those who assisted Lord Snowdon as members of the judging panel –
Andrew Cowan of the Hamilton Gallery;
Sue Davies, OBE,
Eamonn McCabe, picture editor of *The Guardian*;
Amanda Nevill of the Royal Photographic Society;
Raymonde Watkins, art director of the *Telegraph Weekend Magazine*.

Where there is more than one picture on the page the pictures are numbered a, b, c, etc, clockwise from the top left of the page

David Ahmed 40a; Allsport 14, 22, 28, 30, 33b, 34b, 34c, 106b; (Tony Andrews) 54; (Chris Barry) 55, 59a, 59b, 59c, 66; (Shaun Botterill) 26, 104b, 106a; (Simon Bruty) 23; (Phil Cole) 70b, 80, 82b, 82f, 83, 86, 87a, 91; (Mike Cooper) 68b, 70a, 71b; (Andreas Doring) 90b; (Tony Duffy) 24; (Tom Hevezi) 76a; (Mike Hewitt) 35c; (John Hoffman) 49, 116b; (Trevor Jones) 32; (Mike King) 77, 78c, 79, 90a, 92b, 93, 94, 95, 103, 104a; (Bob Martin) 16, 45, 71a, 98; (Simon Miles) 31; (Gray Mortimore) 35a, 38, 102a, 102b, 107, 112-113, 114b; (Steve Morton) 29, 44; (Andrew Murray) 42-43a, 42-43b, 114a; (Adrian Murrell) 21; (Jon Nicholson) 25a, 25b, 27; (Tertius Pickard) 63a, 69, 120; (Steve Powell) 34a; (Chris Raphael) 20; (Dan Smith) 35b; (Oli Tennant) 33a; (Peter Terry) 82a, 82c, 82d, 82e, 85, 87b; (Anton Want) 36; Louise Arimatsu 74a; Simon Ashmore-Fish 108a; Paul Atherton 116a; Alan Bloomfield 67a; Clive Brunskill 117; D. Burrows 47b; Colorsport, 9, 10, 15, 17; David Constantine 100-101, 105; Philip Coomes 50-51, 63e; Richard Crooks 108b; P.J. Eady 53a; Marcella Griso 63b, 78b; Mark Hakansson 110b, 115; Norman Harris 99a, 99b, 99c; Philippe Haÿs 48, 62, 75; Lionel Hithersay 63f; Hulton-Deutsch Collection, 11, 12, 13; Ian Jennings 60, 64; Augustine John 73, 76b; Peter Jordan 96, 97, 119; David Joyner 89; Tony Kau 58, 65; Andrew Lovell 56-57; Natali Marjanovic 88a, 111; D. Martin 67b; Graham McDermott 76c, 84, 110a; Hayley Metz 52b; André Needham 61, 109; Nick O'Brien 41; Bryan O'Hara 52a; Peter O'Toole 74c; Mike Peters 68a; Graham L. Piggott 7, 39; S.E. Rowse 78a; J.E. Smith 92a; Alan Stone 118; Andrew Sole 53b; Saffron Summerfield 40b; Cecile Tait 63c, 74b, 81; Andrew Walters 46; A.C. Wicker 72; D. Wills, 47a, 63d